AMERICAN COLLOQUY

American Colloquy

Edited by
LEONARD LIEF
*Hunter College of the
City University of
New York*
and
DAVID HAWKE
Pace College

THE **BOBBS-MERRILL** COMPANY, INC.
A SUBSIDIARY OF HOWARD W. SAMS & CO., INC.
Publishers · INDIANAPOLIS · NEW YORK

Cover design by Andrew Kner

COPYRIGHT © 1963 BY THE BOBBS-MERRILL COMPANY, INC.
PRINTED IN THE UNITED STATES OF AMERICA
LIBRARY OF CONGRESS CATALOG CARD NO. 63-12191

First Printing

Contents

PREFACE   xi

Part One. ". . . One People . . ."

1. THE AMERICAN CHARACTER

We, the People, In Quest of Ourselves
    DANIEL J. BOORSTIN   5
Analysis of the American Character
    HENRY S. COMMAGER   14
The American Family
    MARGARET MEAD   24
A Holiday Ramble
    JAMES THURBER   34

2. TIME AND PLACE

A Small Western Town
    ERIC SEVAREID   45

TWO VIEWS OF SALEM
Salem Village
    EDWARD EGGLESTON   54
A Visit to Salem
    ARTHUR MILLER   59
The Kitchen
    ALFRED KAZIN   64
The Suburban Way of Life
    LEWIS MUMFORD   76
Saratoga
    HENRY JAMES   82
Camping
    BERNARD DE VOTO   93

3. CITIZENS AND LEADERS

"You French?"
    T. S. MATTHEWS   99

George Washington
      WILLIAM CARLOS WILLIAMS   106
Notes and Comment (on the Death of Grandma Moses)
      THE NEW YORKER   113
Abraham Lincoln
      FRANCIS GRIERSON   115
The Last Full Measure
      KEVIN CORRIGAN   122
Off Limits for Conscience
      ALAN LEVY   129

Part Two.
"... The Forms to Which They Are Accustomed..."

1. FREE ENTERPRISE

Horatio Alger
      FREDERICK LEWIS ALLEN   139
FORD AND MASS PRODUCTION
My Philosophy of Industry
      HENRY FORD   143
Henry Ford
      ROGER BURLINGAME   152
The Personification of Corporation
      THURMAN ARNOLD   162
Corporate Capitalism and "The City of God"
      ADOLF A. BERLE, JR.   170
The Workingman Looks at the Boss
      ERIC HOFFER   175
Labor, Leisure, and the New Class
      JOHN KENNETH GALBRAITH   180

2. EDUCATION

Education
      JAMES AGEE   191
Bringing Up Children—French Way, Our Way
      LAWRENCE WYLIE   204
The Catcher in the Rye Complex
      HENRY EBEL   213
Education and Some American Temptations
      WILLIAM LEE MILLER   225

Training for Statesmanship
  GEORGE F. KENNAN   233

3. SCIENCE

Understanding Science
  JAMES B. CONANT   247
A Scientific Experiment
  BENJAMIN FRANKLIN   257
Science
  E. B. WHITE   262
The Encouragement of Science
  J. ROBERT OPPENHEIMER   264
A Vapor Moving North-Northwest
  DANIEL LANG   275
Science and Social Change
  BRUCE STEWART   287
How Human Is Man?
  LOREN EISELEY   299

Part Three. "... These Truths"

1. LIBERTY AND EQUALITY

The Declaration of Independence   309
Contributions of the West to American Democracy
  FREDERICK JACKSON TURNER   315
The Aristocratic Origin of American Freedom
  PETER VIERECK   324
Abundance, Mobility, and Status
  DAVID POTTER   328
Equal or Better in America
  SEYMOUR MARTIN LIPSET   348
Lincoln and the Declaration
  HARRY V. JAFFA   360
The American Immigrant and Ideologies
  OSCAR HANDLIN   368

2. THE POLITICAL BANDS

The Democratic Malady
  WALTER LIPPMANN   381

Democracy: Its Presumptions and Realities
    LEARNED HAND   388
On the Publick
    JAMES FENIMORE COOPER   399
The Price of Union
    HERBERT AGAR   405
How I Became President
    HARRY S. TRUMAN   417
The Art of the Primary
    THEODORE H. WHITE   428

3. THE WIDE WORLD

The National Purpose
    ARCHIBALD MACLEISH   439
The Shape of the U.N.
    E. B. WHITE   449
Our National Talent for Offending People
    D. H. RADLER   462
America Under Pressure
    ADLAI E. STEVENSON   478
The Search for Challenge
    DAVID RIESMAN   488
Remarks at the Peace Banquet
    WILLIAM JAMES   502
Inaugural Address
    JOHN F. KENNEDY   508

Part Four. "... The Pursuit of Happiness..."

1. POPULAR TASTES

Proof That We Are Not Barbarians
    RUSSELL LYNES   519
High, Low, and Modern
    IRVING KRISTOL   529
Billy the Kid: Faust in America
    MARSHALL FISHWICK   548
Abuse of the Past—Norman Rockwell
    WRIGHT MORRIS   560
The American Sense of Humor
    LOUIS KRONENBERGER   573

2. THE ARTS

Art in America
    JOHN A. KOUWENHOVEN   585
Beat Literature and the American Teen Cult
    JAMES F. SCOTT   598
Nobility and the United States
    OSCAR MANDEL   614
The American Finds His Country
    HILTON KRAMER   627
The Cultural Importance of Art
    SUSANNE K. LANGER   634

3. RELIGION

Roger Williams
    MOSES COIT TYLER   647
Religion in Virginia
    THOMAS JEFFERSON   653
The Contemporary Upswing in Religion
    WILL HERBERG   657
The New Piety
    HENRY C. MESERVE   669
My Father Enters the Church
    CLARENCE DAY   680
God in the Colleges
    MICHAEL NOVAK   690
Happiness, Prosperity and Virtue
    REINHOLD NIEBUHR   705

INDEX OF AUTHORS AND TITLES   727

Preface

This book is based on a simple idea: students in composition courses might well profit from a collection of readings centering about one major theme. These essays by Americans about America have been chosen to afford students of composition a body of readings broad enough to permit choice and limited enough to provide a coherent intellectual experience. We propose no provincial or chauvinistic emphasis on America but merely an emphasis upon some of the problems and issues that confront the student as an American, presented in the idiom most familiar to him: American English.

Although the essays are grouped topically to facilitate the observation of relationships, it should be possible to consider them individually or in a variety of combinations. The questions that follow each selection, however, are designed to bring into focus increasingly complex considerations that grow out of a cumulative progress through the book. Many raise points of comparison and contrast requiring cross-reference among the essays, the kind of study that for most students is at once the most difficult and the most stimulating. The problems for writing and discussion are, therefore, an integral part of our intention: to give the student a coherent unit of reading and study from which his own writing may grow.

Rhetorical problems are left to the province of the individual instructors—where, perhaps, they properly belong. Nevertheless, the standard forms of exposition—definition, illustration, comparison and contrast, argumentation, and the use of personal narrative—are represented. The questions, however, deal with thematic rather than rhetorical matters.

We believe that these essays will afford a balance to the traditional emphasis on British literature and later survey courses;

they will be useful, too, for courses in American civilization. But it is in composition courses that the thematic coherence of the essays built around a familiar theme will be most useful.

For their help in collecting material, we wish to thank the following: Professors Raymond Carol, St. John's University; Raymond Raimondi, Orange County Community College; and Norman Silverstein, Queens College of the City University of New York. We are further indebted to Dean James R. Kreuzer of Queens College for having faith in this book when it was merely an idea and for giving us invaluable suggestions during its preparation. We wish to acknowledge also the help of Pace College and, in particular, the office of Dean Joseph F. Sinzer, for courtesies extended during the preparation of this book.

A special word of thanks must go to Ruth Ann Lief, Brooklyn College of the City University of New York. It was she who wrote many of the questions that follow each essay; her suggestions on organization and style are reflected on every page. To her, this book is gratefully dedicated.

L.L.
D.H.

AMERICAN COLLOQUY

Part One. One People

1. THE AMERICAN CHARACTER
2. TIME AND PLACE
3. CITIZENS AND LEADERS

1. *The American Character*

We, the People, In Quest of Ourselves
DANIEL J. BOORSTIN

> *Daniel Boorstin (1914-   ), Professor of American History at the University of Chicago, has written extensively on the American character. A theme implicit in all his work is that "American democracy is unique" and possesses "a 'genius' all its own" that prevents it from being judged by European standards. Concern for "our uniqueness" has not led to soft judgments. In his most recent work, two collections of essays entitled* America and the Image of Europe *(1960) and* The Image: Or What Happened to the American Dream *(1962), Mr. Boorstin remarks that American culture is characterized "by two qualities—braggadocio and petulance."*

We Americans are a people in quest of ourselves. Ever since our birth as a nation we have been trying to find a mirror in which to see our true image. And this anxious uncertainty about the kind of people we are still distinguishes us among the nations of the world.

Thus, our concern today over what peoples abroad think of us comes not only from our desire to win the international popularity contest with Soviet Russia. Of course, we want to assess the results of the millions that we pour into foreign aid and propaganda. But we are usually less interested in what others think of our form of government or our foreign policy than in what they think of us as people. We are a little like the adolescent who waits for those around him to help him discover who he really is.

Unlike us, the people of Western Europe, and of many other parts of the world, have had for centuries a pretty clear image of themselves—of how to behave like Englishmen, for example, or Japanese.

From The New York Times Magazine, *April 26, 1959. Reprinted by permission of the author.*

Of course, they have been helped by longer histories and richer national literature. While they have had only to live up to a role assigned by their past, Americans have been trying to guess the role demanded by their future.

Our history, far from showing us what we are really like, helps account for our self-conscious search for identity. As a nation of immigrants, all of us have had to suffer cultural amnesia—to forget ancient images and break old molds. Our nation was born without nationalism. It was created by reluctant rebels, often more eager to be authentically English than to be ambiguously American. The government they established was less the product of anybody's grand vision than a by-product of the struggle of colonials to preserve their rights as Englishmen and as citizens of their separate colonies. Americans thus acquired their "Americanness" less from a desire to be American than from an inability to be as English as they wished.

Although the new nation took the name of the United States, there never came into our language an unequivocal adjective to designate our nationals. (The word "United-Statesian" would have been disconcertingly precise, though the equivalent *estadounidense*, despite its awkwardness, came into Spanish.) The people of the United States called themselves "Americans"—expressing both an expansiveness and a vagueness in the national character. Those who share the hemisphere with us have long since come to call themselves by more precise names—"Canadians" or "Mexicans."

In the early decades of national life, Americans wrote and talked endlessly about American opportunities and the American future, but when we look to their writings for a description of the national character we find a boast, an apology, or a prophecy. Thomas Jefferson, for example, foresaw an "Empire for Liberty," populated by unborn millions, with unconfined boundaries—possibly including Cuba and Canada.

The classic self-definition of the American intellectual character was Ralph Waldo Emerson's "American Scholar." Emerson's conclusion was that every American should strive "to be a unit . . . to yield that peculiar fruit which each man was created to bear." Instead of a clarion call for a new American character (as it has usually been considered), this should more accurately be described as a foghorn, bleating the American's uncertainty about where he was, who he was and who he might become.

Some of those—like Daniel Webster—who talked at greatest length about what it meant to be an American said the least that was concrete. Their self-descriptions, echoing abstractions like "Empire," "Equality" and "Destiny," had the hollow ring of a Fourth-of-July oration.

The more we study these early American efforts to describe the American character, the easier it is to understand why Americans turned with relief to what foreigners had to say about them. While the variety of American life led New Englanders or Virginians to take flight in cloudy national ideals and pompous metaphors, European travelers characterized us in vivid detail: they called us rude, friendly, materialistic, generous, outspoken, superficial, religious, irreverent. Their portraits were full of contradictions, but at least they reassured Americans that a national character existed.

Among the most acute of the nineteenth-century observers were the English—great social novelists like Charles Dickens, popular adventure novelists like Capt. Frederick Marryat, novelists of manners like Anthony Trollope (and his less famous mother, Frances Trollope), social critics like William Cobbett and Harriet Martineau, and scientists like Sir Charles Lyell. The books these returning travelers wrote became best sellers here. Charles Dickens' "American Notes," despite the harsh words it had to say about some American institutions, sold over fifty thousand copies within a week. Many others did almost as well.

Of course, Americans were irritated at the frequently unflattering portraits of themselves. They insisted that Dickens was an ungrateful guest; that the others, too, were prejudiced, dishonest, sensational and willfully misleading in their use of every dramatic episode—the cruel flogging of a Negro, the aggressive inquisitiveness of a rude shipmate, or an eye-gouging fight between backwoodsmen—as if it were an epitome of the national character. But they pored over these accounts with rapt curiosity.

It is hard to imagine the English or the French of that day (or of ours) caring so much what foreign travelers said about them or seriously using the observations of tourists to form estimates of themselves. But we have always been poor at self-portraiture. And from the beginning foreigners have been so helpful to us that we have come to lean heavily on them for descriptions of ourselves.

In our own century, however, particularly in recent years, Americans themselves have been working hard to draw sharper lines around the national image. As American history and literature have become academically respectable subjects, all the tools of scholarship —and of pedantry—have been used to anatomize the American character.

A few books resulting from this study—like V. L. Parrington's "Main Currents in American Thought"—have a scope and grandeur and concreteness that actually help in American self-definition. The Civil War has become a cult, and its most popular interpreters, Carl Sandburg and Bruce Catton, find clues to the national character in this great trauma of national life. The numerous American history book clubs and the popularity of historical novels on American subjects, like Margaret Mitchell's "Gone With the Wind," express not merely an upsurging patriotism, but an acute self-consciousness, a determination to use every scrap of information to learn the mode we should live up to. Influential works of sociology —David Riesman's "The Lonely Crowd," William H. Whyte Jr.'s "The Organization Man," Max Lerner's "America as a Civilization" and J. Kenneth Galbraith's "The Affluent Society"—appeal because they tell us what it's like to be an American.

But the more concretely we describe ourselves, the more diffuse, complicated and contradictory the image becomes. For our history— despite its brevity—is a story of diverse regions and conflicting traditions. The more we learn of New England Puritanism, the sharper appears the contrast with the ways of other regions. The more we learn of the South, the clearer it becomes that there have been many Souths, with many different traditions.

We have only lately begun to discover in detail the distinctiveness of our different immigrant groups—English, Irish, German, French, Polish, Italian, Jewish and Japanese—and the variety of American religions, the peculiarities of the suburb, the metropolis, the farm, of the white-collar classes and the junior executives. The shrewdest prophets of American politics today are those who look closely at the differences between groups of varying racial, religious and national origin and at the differences even between individual counties.

Events of the past twenty years have only increased our confusion. Take, for example, our notion that we are a brave new world offering escape from tradition-ridden Europe. This was one of the longest, strongest threads in our thinking. But the course of history since World War II has snapped that thread. Through NATO and the Marshall Plan we have become defenders of Western Europe's religious and political traditions. Today we bulwark an older, liberal-Christian Europe against newer atheistic totalitarian forces.

At the same time, our peculiar history as an ex-colonial people somehow still gives us sympathy for all peoples who try to start afresh. In technology, education, social customs and even in politics —we remain among the most experimental, fluid, forward-looking nations. Yet, in our attitude to religion, our reverence for law and our anti-utopianism, we champion the past.

European critics call us a "materialist" nation. But if we are a people obsessed by things it is in a very different sense from that in which any other people has ever been. Waste is part of the American way of life. Just as the superabundant population of China has set the stage for the Chinese waste of human life, so our superabundant natural resources have allowed us to waste everything else. "Know-how," modernity, efficiency, progress—this year's model, not last— these, and not reverence for things, are the keynotes of American life.

Not least bewildering is the fact that the citizens of those very countries into which we have poured our resources without clearly calculating the cause or the effect are loudest in calling us "materialist," in accusing us of "calculating" the cost of everything. They say we trade on the poverty, disease, starvation and backwardness of mankind. Other critics, however, reproach us for our fuzzy idealism, for taking the burdens of the world on our shoulders, for trying to subsidize the human race. Seldom has a nation been so bitterly reproached for possessing at the same time the deviousness of a Machiavelli and the innocence of the Good Samaritan.

But there have been, and still are, advantages in this vagueness about our national character. Because we have not been fenced in by rigid expectations, we have been free to be ourselves in a thousand different ways. The American representative abroad who is unclear about his role is at least not condemned to a stiff and "proper" role, like that which the British civil servant long played in India. We have been free to let our national image change with new opportunities, free to forget obsolete notions of ourselves.

There are also dangers. The greatest danger lies not in our uncertainty about the American character and American ideals, but rather in our feeling that we must act as if we were certain.

We judge American foreign policy not by whether it serves our national interest, but by whether it can be made to seem a noble expression of American ideals and the American character. We find it too easy to believe that because our definition of ourselves is imprecise, our character and our ideals can be universal. We confuse our foreign policy by supposing that it is not enough to get other people on our side, but that we must try to make them more like us.

Refusing to stand for anything so precise as our national interest, we are bewildered over what we do stand for. No wonder we are relieved to find a single enemy and to agree on what we are against. A foreign observer of American politics might call us a nation of "antis."

Our two-party system, different from that of any other country, is congenial to this way of thinking. Each party need only be against the other; neither need clearly define its own program. The anti-communism which now unites the American people is only the most recent example of our readiness to agree on what we are against.

In this sense, the anti-communist crusade of Senator Joseph McCarthy—like the anti-slavery crusade in the North and the anti-abolition crusade in the South before the Civil War, the anti-trust movement in the late nineteenth century, and the anti-munitions-makers and anti-war movement of the Nineteen Twenties—was in an old American vein. The "liberal" critics of Senator McCarthy (who were relieved to find anti-McCarthyism as their uniting slogan) wrote him off as an ambitious and ruthless politician.

Too few noted that the Senator's passionate anti-communism also expressed a pathetic and bewildered effort to protect what was "truly American," without knowing quite what it was that had to be protected. He was one of many Americans who have felt obliged to make up in passion what they have lacked in clarity.

Anxious search for a national character can make us tools for such American chauvinists, for men-on-horseback and empire-builders. It can kill the spontaneity, drift and unpredictability that have been the promise of American life. The insistence on defining our purposes breeds the nervous insecurity that leads to persecution and the frantic search for heretics and traitors. It makes us haunt ourselves with a specter of "un-Americanism" at home while it leads us abroad into futile crusades against universal evils.

Most of our politicians and our professors dare not admit that it is enough for us to go about our business, that we can improve our way of life without being able to describe our national character or our ideals. They must seem to have the grand view, to be taking thought and talking "principles." Probably the most difficult thing in the world is to make a powerful people renounce crusading and go about their own business. The most fruitless venture on which any people has ever engaged is the effort to sell an "American way of life" to people from the Himalayas to Timbuktu.

The openness, the imprecision, of our definition of ourselves is one of our great national resources. It can remain so only if we do not plague ourselves and confine ourselves by an imaginary image with which we hope to charm the world.

PROBLEMS FOR WRITING AND DISCUSSION

1. Would you agree with Boorstin that we are a nation of "antis"? As you progress through this book, hold Boorstin's judgment as well as your own in mind. Keep asking yourself whether this generalization along with others made in this essay—both those that irritate and those that please you, those that seem true from your own experience and those that seem false—are belied or verified by the other essays.

2. Boorstin asserts that Americans, unlike other peoples, have sought their identity in the opinions of non-Americans about them. Does he offer any evidence that non-Americans have found a mirror which reflects the "true images" of national character? Do you think it likely that a Frenchman or a Canadian could define his national character with more accuracy than that with which an American could define his? Why?

3. The analogy often is drawn today between the new nations of Asia and Africa and the birth of the United States. Drawing on material from this essay, discuss the implications of the analogy to see where it holds and where it breaks down.

4. What does Boorstin mean when he writes: "The greatest danger lies not in our uncertainty about the American character and American ideals, but rather in our feeling that we must act as if we were certain" (p. 10)?

5. Boorstin cites the popularity of *Gone With The Wind* as an illustration of Americans' "acute self-consciousness." Discuss a book that you have read recently which seems to you to illustrate the same self-consciousness.

6. Why, in Boorstin's view, does the clue to national character seem constantly to elude Americans?

7. Whether or not such a thing as "national character" can be fixed, what virtues and what dangers does Boorstin see in the Americans' eager quest for identity?

8. Boorstin hints that it might be wise for Americans to tend to their own business. Does he define what their business is? Do you think it possible or advisable today for Americans to narrow the scope of their "business"? Justify your answer.

9. Boorstin is critical of the political behavior of Americans. Describe one specific tendency of American life that you find disconcerting and

point out the implications of this tendency for America nationally or internationally.

10. Boorstin describes Emerson's definition of American character as a "fog-horn"; yet he himself extols the "spontaneity, drift and unpredictability that have been the promise of American life." What relation do you see between this "promise" and Emerson's plea that every American "yield that peculiar fruit which each man was created to bear"?

11. As an American, do you identify yourself with a "national" character or with the character of a particular group *(e.g.,* middle-class, working-class, leisure-class, intelligentsia, Protestant, Jewish, Polish, Italian, etc.)? Describe concretely your identification. If you feel none, explain why.

Analysis of the American Character

HENRY S. COMMAGER

Henry Steele Commager (1902-   ) has spent his life teaching and writing American history. Currently Professor of American History and American Studies at Amherst College and Adjunct Professor of History at Columbia University, he is well known for The Growth of the American Republic, *a two-volume textbook written with Samuel Eliot Morison and now in its fifth edition, and* The American Mind *(1950), which is concerned with "ideas that illuminate the American mind" as it has evolved since the "watershed of the '90's." All his work is marked by an informal style that has helped to make him one of the most widely read contemporary historians.*

The American is optimistic, takes for granted that his is the best of all countries, the happiest and most virtuous of all societies, and that the best is yet to be. He lives, therefore, much in the future, makes ambitious plans, thinks nothing beyond his powers, has boundless faith in each new generation. It is commonly said that America is a young country. That is only partially true, but it is certainly true that it is, above all others, a country made for young people, a paradise for children—at least for children who have the good fortune to be Nordic.

The American has always known good fortune—material and spiritual; he has been victorious over nature, and over all enemies. He takes good fortune for granted, and regards any interference

From Nineteenth Century and After, *Vol. 145, April 1949. Reprinted by permission of* The Twentieth Century, *London, and the author.*

the largest numbers and the best equipment, and those who lament American materialism will do well to remember the tens of thousands of planes and tanks, the millions of tons of shipping, that turned the tide in the last war. Faith in numbers has something to do, too, with the cheerfulness with which Americans accept political defeat, for most Americans believe that the majority cannot be wrong.

The American is ingenious and experimental. This is in part an inheritance from the frontier, in part a consequence of democracy. He likes to do old things in a new way, and the fact that something has never been done before seems to him a challenge rather than an obstacle. Wonderfully inventive in all merely mechanical matters, he is almost equally inventive in the realm of politics, social relationships, and war. There were antecedents, of course, but he largely invented the federal system, the written constitution, the constitutional convention, and the modern colonial system, and there are some who would insist that he took out the original patent on democracy. His willingness to experiment augurs well for international relations. No one person or people can claim authorship of international organization, but none will deny that Woodrow Wilson was chiefly responsible for the League of Nations and Franklin Roosevelt for the United Nations.

The American is, too, intensely practical. He is the born enemy of all abstractions, all theories and doctrines. Benjamin Franklin is his favorite philosopher and, after him, William James, who asserted that it was only minds debauched by learning that ever suspected common sense of not being true. He requires that everything serve a practical purpose—religion, education, culture, science, philosophy. He has produced great speculative sciences, but he admires Edison rather than Willard Gibbs; he has produced speculative philosophers, but he cherishes William James above Santayana or Royce. His education is practical, and only in America do you find graduate schools of journalism, of business administration, of architecture and of law.

This trait, also, is regarded by many Europeans as deplorable, but it has its points. It means that philosophy has been used for

with it—any setback, depression, defeat—as an outra
nature. He is, in many ways, singularly innocent. He is
with evil, as the Germans, for example, or the Rus
known it, and of all his philosophers only Josiah Roy
neglected—has attempted to solve the problem of evil.
world wars, even Dachau and Buchenwald, have not bro
to him a sense of evil, and he is therefore, in some degree,
of understanding the fear and despair that affect so larg
the world.

This optimism, and what we must call innocence, ha
backs. The corollary of the feeling that America is supe
assumption that other nations and peoples are inferior
sumption goes back to the early days of the Republic, w
almost an article of faith among Jeffersonians. In our o
has found support in the high standard of material prospe
Americans enjoy and in our fortunate freedom from wh
"power politics." We tend to ascribe to our own genius
is in fact ascribable to the bounty of nature and the a
geography. Lowell's famous complaint that the nineteen
English displayed a "certain condescension toward foreign
be echoed now by most European people when thinking
cans. It cannot be denied that there is a tendency among
to equate plumbing and kitchen fixtures with civilization.

This is natural enough, for American culture is pred
material, its thinking quantitative, its genius inventiv
mental and practical. The American tends to compu
everything in numbers—even qualitative things. He takes
statistics of population growth, of college enrollment, of
circulation. He wants the highest office buildings, the larges
of telephones, the most books in his libraries.

This faith in numbers is often looked upon as naïve, s
as vulgar, by Europeans. It has its advantages. For the
wants the highest standard of living; he rejoices when an
lion children are at school. He can fight when outnum
the history of the Confederacy testifies—but prefers to fi

practical purposes. Pragmatism, the most characteristic of American philosophies, is the obvious example. Even more interesting, however, is the Americanization of Idealism or Transcendentalism. That philosophy, which in Germany, and even in England, lent itself to the cultivation of individual salvation and to conservatism and even reaction, became in America a powerful instrument for social reform. It means that education has broken away from its classical mold and been required to serve the needs of society. It means that religious leaders have abandoned theology for humanitarianism. It means that in the realm of politics the American will not waste his vote on third parties; will not follow the will-o'-the-wisp of speculative theories.

Every foreigner laments that there are no discernible differences between the Democratic and the Republican Parties, but Americans know instinctively that parties are organizations to run the government, not to advance theoretical principles, and the American party system is, along with the British, the most efficient in the world. American practicality extends into the fields of international relations. Americans want an international organization that can function efficiently, regardless of abstract questions of sovereignty. They are interested in its practical activities—in relief, in science and education, in the suppression of civil war and disorder—and they judge any organization by its immediate effectiveness.

Yet the American record here is not wholly encouraging, and some of the difficulties of present-day international relations—to say nothing of the fiasco of the League of Nations—are traceable to qualities in the American character. The American is accustomed not only to success, but to speedy success. He is something of a perfectionist, and he is not patient. As he has solved his own problems of Federal relation, he is inclined to think that the problems of international relations are equally simple, and to ascribe the failure of international organizations, whether imperial or world, to a natural depravity in foreigners.

He is always ready with advice to other nations—ready to tell the British how to manage India, for example, or to advise the French what to do about their Far Eastern Empire. He thinks a federation of Europe should be as easy as a federation of American states. He has little patience with that long agony of trial and error that makes up so much of European history, and if he cannot have some assurance of speedy success he is likely to lose interest.

The American is politically mature—a statement which will seem palpably mistaken to outsiders who are accustomed to regard American politics as childish. Superficially—and sometimes more than superficially—American politics are childish: the conventions, the campaigns, the antics of Congressmen, of State Legislatures and Governors. Yet it is simply a historical fact that the American people have had longer experience in self-government than any other people. The American is the oldest Constitution, the oldest federal system and the oldest democracy in the world. While people like the French, the Germans, the Italians, who pride themselves on their political wisdom, have gone through revolution after revolution, the Americans have never known a revolution, unless the Civil War be regarded as one, and American political history has been singularly peaceful and even placid.

In America, as in Britain, change has come through evolution, rather than through revolution, and on the whole it has kept pace with the will of the people. The American Congresses can hold their own with any other legislative body in the world; American Presidents have been as able, on the average, as the Presidents or Prime Ministers of any other nation. In every crisis Americans have chosen courageous and bold leaders. There is no reason to suppose that this capacity for political maturity is on the wane.

American political maturity is something to be read from the long term rather than the short term of history. There was nothing politically mature about the Congress that defeated the League of Nations, or about the Congress that enacted the Smoot-Hawley tariff of 1929, or about the Congress that took refuge in the neutrality legislation of the mid-Thirties. Foreigners may be forgiven if they are bewildered by American vacillation on the Palestine issue, or the recent curious reservations on expenditures under the Marshall Plan. They may be forgiven too, if they find themselves bewildered by the political immaturity that finds short-term dividends in appeal to racial and national prejudices—by the appeals to the Irish vote, the Jewish vote, the Italian vote.

Americans customarily regard politics as a game, and bring to it some of the standards of sportsmanship that they bring to their games. These standards are not as high as they were a generation ago, but they are still high. The American has tried to conduct his wars, too, in accordance with the rules of the game, and has never been able to understand opponents who disregarded the rules. He has made peace in a spirit of sportsmanship and fairness, and Churchill's famous phrase, "magnanimous in victory," applies to the United States as well as to Britain. Historians were long inclined to regard Reconstruction as a ruthless affair, but by comparison with what happened after civil wars in France, in Spain and in Russia, American Reconstruction was a love-feast. Spain was overwhelmingly defeated in 1898, but the treaty was a fair one, and to the astonishment of most Europeans the United States actually gave up Cuba—though not the Monroe Doctrine which seemed to justify hegemony over the Caribbean. Nor did the United States ask—or expect—anything of a material character for herself after either World War I or World War II. There is no reason to suppose that the American character has changed in this respect. Many Europeans are inclined to regard the Marshall Plan as a sinister device to get control of the European economy for American profit, but to the average American it is simply a new form of lend-lease.

For the American—it seems almost immodest to say it—is goodnatured and generous. That generosity springs, to be sure, from abundance, and therefore comes easy. In no other country has philanthropy been so extravagant. The individual American is kindly, amiable, gregarious and friendly, and these qualities characterize Americans in the mass, as well. As the G.I., overseas, was ready to make friends—even with the enemy—so the nation has been ready to make friends, perhaps a bit too ready—witness our Latin-American policy. This generosity has been casual rather than calculated, and it has not always extended to things of the mind and spirit. Yet, on its purely material side, it is something that can be counted on, confidently enough, in the future.

The American is democratic and equalitarian, by conviction, if not in practice. He takes for granted the superiority of democracy to any other form of government or society, and he proclaims, with utmost sincerity, his faith in equality. The sense of equality—as Tocqueville pointed out over a century ago—permeates his conduct, his language and literature, and religion. Democracy has deep philosophical foundations, but it is not so much the conclusion of philosophy as the common sense of the matter, and so, too, with equality. Southerners, who defiantly "keep the Negro in his place," repeat the phrases of the great Declaration with no consciousness of insincerity; Northerners, who tremble at the prospect of being inundated by southern Europeans and Jews, regard themselves, without conscious hypocrisy, as real democrats. What seems to outsiders palpable insincerity is to most Americans merely embarrassing exception to the rule. The exceptions are outrageous, but it is significant that no one suggests changing the rule.

Yet here, too, there are important qualifications to be made. As the American tends to take both democracy and equality for granted, he does not inquire too closely into palpable violations of both. He assumes, for example, that his political system is the most democratic in the world, whereas in fact it is less democratic than that of several other nations—Britain, for example, or Norway. He is less prepared to correct economic inequalities than are most other peoples, and excuses the most extreme variations in wealth and poverty on the easy theory of rugged individualism. Thus he tolerates conditions of poverty, slums, ill-health and inadequate educational facilities that would not be tolerated in any other democratic nation of comparable wealth and are not in fact tolerated in Scandinavia or in Australia or New Zealand or Switzerland.

Long convinced that there are no "classes" in America in the Old World sense, he seems unaware of the rapid growth of class-consciousness and the potential danger of class conflict in the twentieth century. He is ready to preach to all other peoples the gospel of democracy and equality, but deeply resents the suggestion that he set his own house in order first. He exposes himself to suspicion and resentment by the extent to which he indulges in anti-Semitism, condemns Negroes to the status of second-class citizens, and accepts the Nazi doctrines of racism.

The American as an individualist is inclined to distrust any public or official bodies. He is, by nature, anti-authoritarian. His own experience has given him little reason to fear or distrust government, but that distrust is deeply ingrained. On the whole he prefers private charity to public, prefers even private international organizations to official ones. He believes that almost anything can be achieved if people will only sit down and talk things over, and Franklin Roosevelt's tendency to circumvent the State Department and rely upon personal relations was entirely characteristic.

This individualism, so sharp in the nineteenth century, is on the wane. Americans who were, in the past, fierce nonconformists, are coming increasingly to demand conformity. In a hundred ways—in speech, dress, manners, food, furnishing—America is becoming more and more uniform and standardized. The demand for conformity is extending even to things of the mind—witness the interest in loyalty oaths, in patriotic clichés, in agreement on political and even economic fundamentals. All this is in part the result of recent pressures, which always tend to squeeze out the eccentric, and in part, the result of growing stability in society and economy.

Along with individualism, and related to it, goes carelessness and lawlessness. The American is careless about speech, dress and manners, about tradition, precedent and law, about the rights of others. He is careless, too, about larger things—about natural resources, for example, or about honesty in politics or in business. This carelessness is, doubtless, a trait of youth; it may be doubted whether a United States that has achieved world leadership can continue to indulge itself in it.

Can the American, who is too careless even to vote in Presidential elections, be trusted with democracy? Can the Congress, which cannot even reform its own procedure, which yields so readily to lobbies and pressure groups, which shows so little appreciation of its dignity and responsibility, be trusted to conduct foreign affairs? Can a people who pay so little attention to the history, traditions and character of other nations be trusted with world leadership? These are awkward questions.

Most of the traits which we have distinguished as American are positive; most of them, too, might be called favorable. There are, of course, traits that are less flattering. On the whole Europeans can be relied upon to call these to our attention.

There is an undeniable strain of vulgarity in the American character—vulgarity which can be seen at its worst in advertisements, in the movies, and on the radio and television. There is a strain of lawlessness which can be traced in the statistics of police courts or can be noted by anyone who cares to check on traffic violations. With the passing of orthodox religion and of puritanism, and with growing urbanization, moral standards have grown lax. Divorces and juvenile delinquency are on the increase; the soldier of World War II was far laxer in morals than the soldier of World War I, and neither compared favorably with the soldiers of the Union and Confederate Armies. There has been a gradual decline in the standards of sportsmanship; there has been a gradual growth in class-consciousness and snobbery; there has been an alarming increase in intolerance.

What does all this add up to, so far as the role of America in world affairs is concerned? What emerges most impressively are the positive traits. The American is optimistic, experimental, practical, intelligent, mature, generous, democratic and individualistic. He has heretofore fulfilled his responsibilities and can be expected to do so in the future. He has, in the last analysis, little confidence in other countries—except Britain—little confidence in their ability, their intelligence, or their good will. He is therefore inclined to think that the rest of the world will have to follow American leadership—not primarily because America is so rich and powerful, but because the American way is the sensible, practical and right way.

PROBLEMS FOR WRITING AND DISCUSSION

1. In what respects does Commager's picture of the American character differ from Boorstin's? In what respects does it agree? Which view of the American character fits better with your own? Which view does more to alter judgments you have held about America? Specify the judgments.

2. Draw up a list of the various characteristics of Americans that Commager cites. Are they arranged arbitrarily in the essay, or do you see a pattern or connection among them?

3. Authors in this book will use the word *materialist* again and again to refer to an American characteristic. Do Commager and Boorstin define the word, and if so do they define it differently? How does your understanding of the word differ from theirs?

4. Commager writes that in politics "Americans believe that the majority cannot be wrong." Do you believe he is right? What dangers are implicit in this American belief? See, for example, "The Democratic Malady" (p. 381).

5. Using some fairly recent event, discuss Commager's observation that Americans "customarily regard politics as a game."

6. Commager also asserts that Americans are intensely practical—in, for example, education. What are some of the results of this practicality? See, for example, "Training for Statesmanship" (p. 233).

7. Discuss Commager's idea that the American is "incapable of understanding the fear and desire that affect so large a part of the world."

8. Does Commager explain the motivation of what Boorstin calls the "futile crusades against universal evil" Americans conduct abroad?

9. Boorstin contends that Americans, because they do not know what they are *for*, attack what they are *against*, what they see as "evils." Commager claims Americans have no conception of "evil," yet he too points to their efforts at reforming the world. How do you explain this seeming contradiction in the interpretation of American character?

10. What light do Boorstin and Commager throw on contemporary problems confronting America (*e.g.*, universal disarmament, aid to underdeveloped nations, the United Nations, federal aid to education, the political extremists)?

11. Test any one of Commager's generalizations about America against your own experience. Remember, however, that exceptions to Commager's generalizations do not necessarily invalidate them and that your experience need not be one that most Americans share.

12. Is this sketch flattering to Americans, or does it suggest reasons for which such a distinguished American journalist as T. S. Matthews [see "You French?" (p. 99)] would leave America in disgust?

The American Family

MARGARET MEAD

Margaret Mead (1901-) is Associate Curator of Ethnology at the American Museum of Natural History and Adjunct Professor of Anthropology at Columbia University. Although she is perhaps best known for Coming of Age in Samoa *(1928) and other works on Pacific ethnology, she has written three books on America and has recently co-edited* The Golden Age of American Anthropology *(1960). Implicit in all her work on America is a plea for greater elasticity in American mores.*

The American family is at the center of American concern at the present time; its strengths and its weaknesses, its past and its future are being subjected to every kind of scrutiny, pessimistic and optimistic. Americans sometimes make the mistake of thinking that because a subject is being very much discussed, it has somehow suddenly "gotten worse." So there are those who would trace the present emphasis on the family to "an increase in divorce" or more generally to "a breakdown in family life." I do not believe this is accurate. I believe that we are discussing the family because we are overwhelmingly interested in the family, that our ambitions for ourselves and our children have shifted from a concern with individual success on the one hand, and with national security and prestige on the other, to the family.

Parents' major concern in bringing up children today is whether they are bringing up "well adjusted children," and this means quite

Margaret Mead, "The American Family," in The Search for America, *edited by Huston Smith,* © *1959 by Prentice-Hall, Inc., Englewood Cliffs, N.J. Reprinted by permission of the publisher.*

concretely children who will marry and who will be able to get the kind of jobs which go best with family life: steady jobs, jobs with tenure and a pension, jobs with little foreign service or arbitrary moving about from branch to branch, jobs that demand little enough of a man so that he has "something left for his wife and children." For girls, parents hope that they will be attractive enough to find a husband early, and not display any uncomfortable traits —not be too tall, or too intellectual, or too "interested in something peculiar" which might discourage a suitor. They of course want their children to find suitable mates, suitability meaning (much more than it used to) coming from exactly the same "kind of people" stated in religious, economic and ethnic terms, where the two sets of parents-in-law, soon to be co-grandparents, will be congenial and the two mothers-in-law to be can compare notes and adjust their costumes "to complement each other at the wedding." Whereas in the past, American marriage has been extremely open, with young people acting as if they could select their mates independently of their parents' wishes and without need for parental subsidy, they are now narrowing down to fit in with the parents' understandable preference for their children to marry "people just like us."

Several factors are responsible for this shift. Early "going steady" before young people have drivers' licenses or cars of their own or very much money to spend on dates, has meant that courtship is conducted more and more inside the home of one or both of the courting pair. For this, parental consent is necessary. Early marriage, often while one or both of the couples are in school, means that parental financial help is needed and here again parental consent must be had. The kind of behavior which was initiated under the impetus of World War II—when parents, fearful that their children might have no future, let them "have their happiness now"— and that was perpetuated by the GI bill of rights which gave young husbands a kind of nuclear independence while they attended college, has carried over after the Korean War to a steadily growing pattern of parental subsidy of young marriages, while their children are still completing their education. This has often required considerable sacrifice from the middle-aged parents, frequently at just the time when they also have the personal and economic responsibility for *their* parents. In turn there are repercussions, in emphasis on the importance of security and pensions, which represent I believe not so much a premature cautiousness in the twenty-year olds as what they have heard at home. There is a growing objection to retirement at sixty-five which parallels the economic pressures on an increasing number of grandparents who cannot look to their children for help; whose children instead are still looking to them. There is also increasing concern over the earlier death rate of men in the grandparental generation. This death rate may reflect these extended pressures on earning capacities under what is often a triple load, to help support their parents, themselves, and their children's families.

Meanwhile, possibly because of the additional load on parents who a generation ago expected their grown children to be self-supporting and in time possibly to contribute something to them, very little attention has been paid to the increased load on the young people, particularly on the boys whom social pressure is hurrying into the responsibilities of man's estate. Americans have discussed, with varying feelings, the wisdom of taking seventeen- and eighteen-year olds into the armed services, away from home and education into the vicissitudes of foreign service—loneliness, danger, and possibly death. But these vicissitudes are ones which young males have always sought—a period when they could leave domestic ties and be free to adventure and experience dangers that would test their mettle. For those who were to become the intellectual, artistic and political leaders of the next generation, it was a period in which they could test themselves and their abilities among their peers—again away from domestic ties. Universities, armies, merchant marines have been the contexts in which the young males of the past have tested their strength and matured away from the influence of women.

Despite the continued existence of the draft, the present American family system is cutting directly into this age-old style of preparing young men for leadership and responsibility. By the time they reach high school they are expected to have settled career objectives, to work hard to attain them, and to begin to spend enough time with girls so that an early marriage will be assured. They are expected to drive carefully, to abstain from pranks of all kinds, to study hard enough—but not too hard—to make the educational grade. They are expected to marry very young, to have children at once, and to support their wives and children while going to school. Enormous numbers of our future doctors and lawyers, engineers and statesmen, are holding down eight-hour-a-day jobs, trying to do at least passing work in school and college, and giving their wives a hand all night and all weekend in the care of two or three or four small children.

In this steady rush towards domestic responsibility, many valuable things have been sacrificed. Friendship with other boys and other young men on which male minds have fed for all the generations of civilization is pushed aside or indulged in at the expense of the home. Every night that a medical student stays around the hospital to talk, he robs his wife, who is confined all day with a bunch of active irrepressible children, of his company. The image of suitable careers for young men is being broken sharply in half: either absolutely devoted early marriage, fatherhood, and harder work at home than in the office to maintain the family life that is valued so highly, or juvenile delinquency, sexual deviance, alcoholism, mental illness and the "beat bit." Depending upon the socioeconomic class from which he comes, a sixteen-year-old boy's attempt to escape this highly sanctioned road to early responsibility will be called delinquency or instability. The boy himself may choose a "hot rod," a gun, a beard, a kind of hobo existence, or in some cases violence and even murder. The number of intermediate positions, of "youthful mischief," approved college pranks, and wild oats, is steadily being reduced.

With the increasing number of young people who want to go to college, pranks that once would have evoked nothing but smiles and perhaps an uncomfortable half-hour in the Dean's office today mean expulsion. The freedom of young people to experiment with extreme ideas, with ideas of political utopianism, socialism, communism, anarchism, free love, free verse, has been curtailed in the interest of having a faultless security record in case one might want to work for the government at some point in one's life. Appropriately enough, the groups who protest against this increased emphasis on early and complete devotion to family life are also very rigid, very conformist and distressingly humorless. Neither among the hardworking young couples, caught in the treadmill of combining work and education and a batch of babies, nor among the Beatniks, nor among the beat-up members of the city gangs of the slums is there gaiety or humor. Somehow the leeway and the laughter have gone out of things.

It must not of course be thought that this change is all for the bad. It is hard on the young, hard on their parents, and hard on those aspects of our national and international life that call for leadership and innovation. But the homes which the young people are building with so much labor are good homes. In all the known history of civilization, never have fathers taken as much care of their little children as in the United States today. Nor have mothers had as much companionship from their chosen mates, in the kitchen and in the nursery. The children born so close together tumble up together in an atmosphere in which family life is more valuable than the compulsive neatness of the last generation. And fun is obviously one of the things that the family "ought" to have. Fathers are no longer the distant commuters; instead they share with their wives the child care and companionship which was once confined to mothers. A brake is put on divorce by the sheer intensity and weight of this shared domesticity; and there is a temptation to add to it another baby and another, to build ever higher walls against any possibility of escape. Those men who do repudiate these early, enveloping marriages must inevitably be terribly burdened with guilt. But there are approximately two million mother-child households in this country, in which the father is absent, through divorce or death.

The home in which this new kind of young American family lives is both the loved shelter within which they live their lives, and a kind of incubus because none of it is fully paid for. From one point of view it is a nonmaterialistic home; the rooms are designed to make family living pleasant and easy; the kitchen is filled with gadgets to facilitate housework; the pictures on the wall and the books in the bookcases, the pile of records and the record player, the radios and the TV—are all there "for the family." So is the car that stands at the door, chosen first because of the family needs. These are all less symbols of wealth and success, of social striving and social status, than they would have been twenty years ago. They are "necessary" adjuncts of good family life. But the work that goes into making even the initial payments on such a setting for family life is tremendous. It means that the young wife works rather than studies at the beginning of the marriage so that they can get started. It means that the wife will later have to work, not at something she wants to do but so as to support both the continuing payments on the house (now grown a little shabby but far from paid for), the children's education, and the grandchildren that are to come. Our high standard of living is also a high standard of working, working without let up. True there is necessary recreation, but we work at that too, almost as hard.

The price that women pay for this kind of family is harder to assay. Girls are hurried into choice and marriage before they have any sense of themselves as persons or any idea of a relationship that is adult instead of a symbiotic clinging of one adolescent to another, an escape from one home directly into another. If they work to help put their young husband through advanced professional training they run tremendous risks of being lumped with his parents on whom he has been dependent and from whom, in the end, he ran away. In order to keep their family the kind of family that has become the style, to which young people conform almost without challenging it at all, young mothers have one baby after another. No baby in such a home, without help for the mother save from the harried though also delighted young father, gets the kind of care which would fully develop its potentialities. Just as in the past we did not expect the best prepared people to come from homes in which a mother had to care singlehanded for a half dozen children —we used to identify this with the slums—we cannot expect today these children to compare with what the same parents could have made of half as many children. During the period when middle-class families were small, we developed a style of expected activity and autonomy for children which demanded a great deal of parental participation. The modern mother does not have time to give this to each of her children, and there are no grandparents, maiden aunts, servants or much older brothers and sisters to help. For all the warmth and anxious care that the new style of young mother and father expend on their children, the offspring lack the kind of individualized attention which is needed to produce the difference between children who come from homes which give children a headstart towards achievement and ones that are not able to do so.

Finally, the present system of early courtship, early marriage and immediate rapid childbearing, means that women are going to face long years at the end of their lives for which they are making no preparation. Marriages built on undeveloped adolescent interests and child care often provide a very poor background for mature companionship. Both the present style of marriage, and the fear that any association between men and women outside of marriage will threaten the marriage, mean that neither husband nor wife really make friends. The spouse is supposed to be the all purpose companion, for athletics, intellectual life, work, and play. A happily married couple are expected to have no needs except for other couples with children with whom their children can play, who can live next door and keep undesirable neighbors away. These are losses.

Although there are many historical antecedents to our present style of marriage, fear of catastrophe and lack of faith in the future are certainly two important components. These led the parents into promoting this present kind of marriage. They led to the advice to "get your happiness now," "have your children while you can," "don't wait and save until you are too old to enjoy anything." They have led to young peoples' insistence on having a full middle-class standard of living in a "nice suburb" right away, even though they will have to follow the working-class style of buying everything on the installment plan with its casual acceptance of "well, we enjoyed it while we had it, till it was taken away because we couldn't keep up the payments." These fears, of atomic war, of depression, of the pressure of population which has or will "explode," are all pushing people to seize the present moment.

But strangely enough, this cannot be described as "dancing on the Eve of the Battle of Waterloo." People are not, by and large, dancing; only the rebels, the delinquents, the rock'n'roll addicts are dancing. Everybody else is working for sober, middle-aged enjoyments, a home, children, a secure job.

Possibly this may be a kind of unconscious preparation for the rigors of life which lie ahead, for the kinds of decisions which Americans are going to have to make twenty-five and fifty years from now. Possibly the formation of these very tight families, with their lowered premium on the individual, and their high premium on the production and preservation of small biological groups of people tied together by the closest of ties, may be a kind of presage of some unknown type of adventure that awaits the human race, the kind of preparation for trial that the caterpillars make who grow their coats heavier for the especially cold winter that has not yet come but is in the making.

It may be too that the new kind of family which involves the father so closely in the care of his young infants is an experiment in producing a new kind of men and women. Throughout the history of the human race both sexes have been reared primarily by women, and boys had to learn how to be "not women" before they could learn to be men. Now they can learn directly from their fathers, as girls through the ages have learned directly from their mothers. The only problem is, what will they learn? Will the boys learn that fathers, like mothers, are primarily nurturing domestic creatures, concerned only with their homes and their children? If so, who is to learn, where and from whom, what it means to be an explorer, a statesman, an entrepreneur, a scientist, an artist, a prophet?

The die is only partly cast for this kind of family. It is the style, but not yet universal. There are many choices still to be made: by colleges that must build or not build quarters for married students; by parents who, banded together in PTA's, can discourage or promote earlier and earlier dating; by employers who can facilitate or discourage postponement of marriage for further training; by religious groups who can scrutinize anew their attitudes towards family size; by boards and commissions and institutions that must overhaul their retirement ages and their rules for the employment of middle-aged women. There are choices to be made by young people themselves before they tie themselves down for life in decisions made hastily and greedily, often without any pretense of great love, as soon as someone is found who is willing to be the other half of a pair—no more than that, just the other half of a married pair.

Any value in a society—national prestige, wealth, competitiveness, superiority, the pursuit of individual salvation, freedom for the individual, even the family—can be pursued too hard, at the expense of all the other values which make a balanced community life. We say we value the family as the cornerstone of a society devoted to the dignity and importance of the individual human being. Is that the kind of family we are developing today? Or are we perhaps sacrificing too much of the life of the individual human being on the altar of family life?

PROBLEMS FOR WRITING AND DISCUSSION

1. Margaret Mead says, "our ambitions for ourselves and our children have shifted from a concern with individual success on the one hand, and with national security and prestige on the other, to the family." How does this generalization fit your own experience?

2. What basic shifts have occurred in the relationship of parents and children in America, according to Mead, and what are some of the effects?

3. What do young men—and young women too—sacrifice in "this steady rush towards domestic responsibility"? What do they gain?

4. Why, according to Mead, have the "leeway and the laughter . . . gone out of things"?

5. What is the principle point Mead makes about the children of young parents who grow up in this intense family life?

6. Is Mead's concern simply for the children as individuals, or does it extend by implication to the contribution they may make to human affairs? On what evidence do you base your reply?

7. The American home, for all the luxuries and labor-saving devices that fill it, is "a nonmaterialistic home" to Mead. How does her use of *materialism* differ from Boorstin's (p. 5) and Commager's (p. 14)?

8. Do you think the changes in American family life discussed in this essay have brought about any fundamental change in the American character, or are they of superficial importance only? Justify your answer.

9. Although Mead describes changes in American family life, the forces that have brought about these changes are international in scope. How can the intense interest Americans show in the family be explained by what Commager and Boorstin point to as national preoccupations?

10. Mead notes with concern the decreasing emphasis on friendship and on boys' growing to manhood "away from the influence of women." Do these losses seem important to you? What do you foresee as the consequence of the "domestication" of men and the equality of women in carrying economic burdens?

11. Mead suggests what Boorstin and Commager also imply: that the American character is far from fixed. If recent changes in family life have worked changes in the national character, what conceivable "type of adventure" do you suppose "awaits the human race"? Is this concentration on biological preservation prevalent in any society other than the American?

12. Do marriage and the rearing of children appear to you as a refuge from life's uncertainties, as a major challenge and interest, or as a last resort? Discuss and analyze your choice.

A Holiday Ramble

JAMES THURBER

James Thurber (1894-1961), after being graduated from Ohio State, became one of the best-known American humorists of the century with his essays, stories, and cartoons. Working primarily for The New Yorker, *which he joined in 1927, Thurber often drew and wrote about people who move through a world that bewilders and restricts them, as seen in his best-known character, Walter Mitty. His concern for America is clear in many of his short pieces and in* The Male Animal *(1940), a comedy about academic freedom that he wrote with Elliot Nugent. Many of his popular writings and cartoons have been collected in* The Thurber Carnival *(1945), which has been dramatized successfully.*

Now that the reflective years are upon me, I spend considerable time in my study chair, and the avenues and byways of meditation take me into curious but familiar places, inhabited by all kinds of persons, from the immortal to the forgotten. One of the forgotten, except by a few historians and other scholars, and me, is Colonel Thomas Hamilton, of His Britannic Majesty's armed forces. Thomas Hamilton visited the young United States in the early eighteen-thirties and went back to England to write a book about our ancestors, entitled "Men and Manners in America." It seems to me that "Americans Have No Manners" would have been a more apt title for the Colonel's book, which was first published in 1833,

From The New Yorker, *April 2, 1955. Reprinted by permission.* © *1955 The New Yorker Magazine, Inc.*

34

just one year after Mrs. Trollope's famous attack on our flaws and foibles and females. It was, as literary historians know, an era of thrust and parry across the Atlantic, and the English had the best of it until Nathaniel Hawthorne slashed back at them with his "Our Old Home," in the eighteen-sixties. Colonel Hamilton was not only more fastidious than the other social critics on either side, he also had the queasiest stomach, and the year he spent among us could well be described as perfectly dreadful. He was repelled by almost everything he saw and heard, from the way Americans "drink" boiled eggs to the grammar and the personal habits of President Andrew Jackson, a soldier whose fame is likely to outlive the Colonel's by a good ten thousand years, if there is that much planetary time left.

I looked up the Colonel's book in my library the other day and found it buried between "Sybil's Garden of Pleasant Beasts" and Francis Winthrop Palfrey's "The Antietam and Fredericksburg." (I've got to get at that shelf one of these days and separate the blood from the fantasy.) I began rereading some passages I had indignantly marked in the Hamilton book nearly twenty years ago. My copy of "Men and Manners" is a later edition, published in 1843, and in it Hamilton really let himself go. In telling about the first of a couple of informal calls he made at the President's home, the British officer wrote, "He chews tobacco, and kept rolling an enormous quid about in his mouth. He makes sad mistakes, too, in grammar, and asked me about my servitude in the army. The house was dirty, and gave you the impression of a large, ill-furnished, and ill-kept hotel." Of his second visit (I don't know why he kept going back) the Colonel wrote, "The conversation for the first quarter of an hour was about the state of his bowels, the failure of calomel, the success of salts." The Colonel also had ungallant things to say about American ladies and about what he regarded as the slovenly carriage of our West Point cadets, and he took a few stabs at our politicians and statesmen. He was appalled by attacks on their character in the public prints. "The candidate for Congress or the Presidency is broadly asserted to have picked pockets or pocketed silver spoons," the

Colonel wrote. I think it was in 1940 that I encountered a repercussion of this statement in, of all places, one of Ralph Waldo Emerson's essays. The American poet and philosopher in this essay tells about calling on William Wordsworth in the summer of 1833, or just about the time the Colonel's book was being talked about in England. Here is what Wordsworth told his visitor: "My friend Colonel Hamilton, at the foot of the hill, who was a year in America, assures me that the newspapers are atrocious, and accuse members of Congress of stealing spoons." This constitutes the only piece of nineteenth-century literary research I have ever done, and if I have gone considerably out of my way to get it in, I trust that I shall be forgiven.

The great poet's friend and neighbor who lived at the foot of the hill, among the trodden ways, so long ago, happened to be in New York City (I think this is going to be my real topic sentence) during the celebration of Evacuation Day, more than a hundred and twenty years ago. This holiday, now as forgotten as the mocking Colonel's satire, celebrated, "in profuse and patriotic jollification," the departure of the British Army at the end of the Revolutionary War. Evacuation Day was first celebrated in 1783, and the jubilation began with the official raising of the American flag at the Battery, where once the British colors had boldly flown. This ritual was continued every year until 1847. By that time, the tumult and the shouting had long since died down and the significance of the occasion was growing dim. Besides, the chill of late November in the city must have taken the edge off an outdoor show of patriotic fervor as the decades rolled by. Furthermore, the flag that had been raised at the Battery for so many years got burned, I don't know how, and this seems to have formed a good excuse for summer soldiers and sunshine patriots to stay home and drink their rum or Madeira in front of the fireplace. Those two beverages, as you shall see, symbolized for Colonel Hamilton labor and the leisure class. The celebration he witnessed was a kind of double feature, and I'll let the Colonel take it from there. "On the present occasion," he wrote, "it was determined, in addition to the ordinary cause of rejoicing, to get up a pageant of unusual splendour, in honour of the late revolution in France. This revolution, I was informed, originated exclusively in the operative class, or *workies*, as they call themselves, in contradistinction to those who live in better houses, eat better dinners, read novels and poetry, and drink old Madeira instead of Yankee rum. The latter and more enviable class, however, having been taught caution by experience, were generally disposed to consider the present congratulatory celebration as somewhat premature. Finding, however, that it could not be prevented, they prudently gave in, and determined to take part in the pageant." (Karl Marx was about fifteen years old when the Colonel's book came out, and I don't suppose he ever read it; if he had, the term "workies" might have given him a stroke and saved the world most of the hell it is going through now.)

Our dashing Colonel, who was the author of a novel called "Cyril Thornton," fancied himself as a colorist in prose, and he did noisy justice to the Evacuation Day parade, even dropping in a little Greek, which I mercifully omit from his description: "At length the sound of distant music reached the ear; the thunder of the drum, the contralto of the fife, the loud clash of cymbals, and, first and furthest heard, the spirit-stirring notes of the trumpet. . . . On they came, a glorious cavalcade, making heaven vocal with sound of triumph, and earth beautiful with such colouring as nature never scattered from her pictured urn. And first appeared, gorgeously caparisoned, a gallant steed bestrode by a cavalier, whose high and martial bearing bespoke him the hero of a hundred fights. . . ." There is a great deal more of this, but let us turn for a moment to another writer's comments on the long lost holiday. The late George Templeton Strong was one of many old Madeira drinkers, or non-workies, who deplored the passing of Evacuation Day. His diary sorrowfully traces its decline. In 1835, he made this entry: "Glorious Evacuation Day . . . it allows us to kick up our heels all day at our leisure." Clearly, the jugs were still being brought out, more than fifty years after the first flag-raising ceremony. On November 23, 1836, Mr. Strong yelped, "Diabolical outrage! They are not going to give us Evacuation Day—horrible! We shall have to take it!" Six years later, in 1842, he wrote, "It a'nt the Evacuation Day of ten years ago—its glories have departed and nobody thinks about it now."

Many a regional holiday, I have no doubt, has bloomed and gone to seed in America, leaving only a faint trace in the pages of old diaries and almanacs. Repudiation Day, for example, was once a time of riotous carryings-on in Frederick, Maryland, and the surrounding country. On November 23, 1765, about eight years before Barbara Frietchie was born, that proud and valiant county was the first to repudiate the British Stamp Act, levied by England under King George III. I don't know how long this great day was wildly celebrated, but it is probable that the hell-raising, in its heyday, outdid the noise of Evacuation Day farther north, for Maryland is the state of the Battle of the Antietam, of Barbara Frietchie and her flag, and of the heroine who clung perilously to the clapper of a giant swinging bell, to indicate, a little haphazardly, the temper of the state and its toughness.

The Stamp Act the Marylanders couldn't abide placed a tax of one shilling on every pack of playing cards and ten shillings on every pair of dice. No American would long tolerate any such tampering with his games of chance or skill. The Repudiation Act roared that "all proceedings shall be valid and effectual without the use of stamps." After that, a gentleman was on his own, and what he did with cards or dice was no affair of the royal government. I have no roots in Maryland myself, but my great-great-great-grandfather Adam Fischer was born in Virginia, suh, and it may have been a lingering trace of the old blacksmith's blood that brought me to my feet one night some twenty years ago in a large café in southern France; I was quietly playing cards with my wife at a corner table when the proprietor sauntered over and asked to see the ace of clubs, for the purpose of determining whether or not it bore a certain official stamp. Fortunately, I had bought the pack of cards in France, and the required tax stamp was plain to see on the ace. It was touch and go for a moment, but the spirit of old

Adam Fischer, such as it is, or was then, quickly subsided in an exchange of compliments and complaints about taxation, for which the French notoriously have little love.

Here I am, somewhat to my own surprise, in prewar France, after starting from New York in 1783, but this is a casual journey, and we shall now visit Ohio momentarily on our way toward the future. They used to celebrate the birthday of President McKinley out there, on January 29th, and all the gentlemen of the city burst into bloom that day, each one wearing a red carnation, the late President's favorite flower, in his lapel. Oh, I suppose there were a few followers of William Jennings Bryan whose coats were not in blossom. The day had been forgotten before I reached long trousers, and you could no longer tell a Republican from a Democrat on sight.

This brings us to the future, a vast, untrammelled domain, where a man's freedom of thought and action is secure, since nobody has yet devised a method of convicting anyone for what he is probably going to think or do. Several undeclared holidays that might well fit into the American years to come have occurred to me during my contemplations.

Liability Day, for example, could be set aside—say, in January—as the one day of the year during which senators and congressmen would be deprived of immunity and could be sued for libellous remarks made on the floor of the Senate or House. On this day, the kind of senator or congressman that boldly asserts he will be glad to repeat his remarks in private, and practically never does, would be given a chance to prove his courage in full view and hearing of his colleagues, the press, and the visitors' gallery. I doubt whether anything will ever come of this suggestion—unless, of course, it is added to my dossier in the files of the F.B.I.

I don't suppose anything will ever come of Immunity Day, either, but I shall outline my concept of it anyway. On this national holiday, all bars and saloons would be open from 12:01 A.M. until midnight, and our present habit of accusing virtually everybody of practically everything would be not only encouraged but officially condoned. This annual occasion should have a salubrious psychological effect upon the populace by legally releasing inhibitions and repressions. Many persons, in our era of fear and hysteria, are afraid to say what they think about public figures and national affairs, and have become neurotic victims of ingrown reticence, no longer able to tell discretion from timidity, or conviction from guilt. A day of freewheeling criticism would cut down the work of the psychiatrists, thus enabling them to take time out for lunch. On Immunity Day, any citizen could say anything he wanted to about anything or anybody, even Formosa and Chiang Kai-shek, without danger of being hauled to the lockup. This might eliminate—for one day, at least—such incidents as the arrest of a lady and gentleman a year or so ago for discussing the Chinese situation in a public restaurant in Houston, Texas.

Fact Day, to be celebrated on June 21st, a week after Flag Day, should be a day on which only the proved is tolerated, but the truth must, in every instance, be constructive and favorable to those who are criticized. If you know anything good about anybody, it should be generously spoken on Fact Day, without a sniff, leer, wink, or raised eyebrow. Fact Day speakers at rallies or banquets or open-air meetings should attempt to revive in the minds of their listeners the old, abandoned American assumption of innocence, pointing out that guilt is not a matter of guesswork or conjecture, but of proof.

National Misgiving Day, to be held on the last Thursday of October, a month before Thanksgiving Day, could be the occasion for the assembling of American families for the purpose of pooling and enunciating their accumulated doubts, suspicions, and apprehensions, with a view to throwing out, in sober family council, any that may have grown out of mistaken identity, bad telephone connections, hearsay, conclusion jumping, change of life, hyperthyroidism, cussedness, political ambition, malice, animosity, pride, envy, anger, or temporary or permanent loss of mind, grip, or bearings. Misgivings that turn out to be well founded should be carefully examined and appraised by the elder and soberer members of households before they are telephoned to the F.B.I., told to the corner druggist, or passed on to United States senators. Misgiving Day would give the faltering American family a nationally sponsored reason to reassemble and to get to know each other better.

Emergence Day, which could be coincidental with Groundhog Day, would direct nationwide attention to persons who have been falsely accused of undermining or overthrowing, and have holed up in their houses or apartments with the blinds pulled down, the doors locked, and the telephone disconnected. If they have been wrongfully shadowed or tailed and, on emerging, see their shadow or tail, they shall have the right and duty to point out such shadow or tail to the constabulary or other duly constituted authorities, who must then put a shadow on the tail, or a tail on the shadow, and trace it to its lair, or liar. Games for Emergence Day parties instantly suggest themselves, but I shall leave the working out of the rules for such games to persons better qualified for merriment than I am. Nobody would be arrested on Emergence Day for anything he had not done or for anything he had once thought.

It is not my intention, in conclusion, to urge the reinstatement of Evacuation Day as an annual occasion for fun and games or rum and Madeira in New York City, since I believe that New Yorkers can get along on the Fourth of July in their celebration of the defeat of the British. The old, lost holiday has, however, given me an idea for Evaluation Day. J. Edgar Hoover and the F.B.I. properly and soundly object to the evaluation of dossiers on suspected persons by the police or other investigatory organizations, but this has left many of us with what might be called moist qualms. These come from too much worry about who *is* going to do the evaluating, and we who are susceptible to the galloping jumps or the chattering jitters sometimes have nightmares about going through life completely unevaluated. In my own anxiety dream, I am caught with a Russian passport while wearing only the top of my pajamas, usually in the lobby of the Hotel Astor. Just what will take place on Evaluation Day I have not yet worked out in my mind, and I think the arrangements should probably be left to some federal commission, appointed for the purpose. Don't ask me who is going to evaluate the evaluators. I don't know. I am just a writie.

PROBLEMS FOR WRITING AND DISCUSSION

1. Colonel Hamilton's views on America were fairly typical of British opinion. What essentially did he find objectionable?
2. Why does Thurber quote Colonel Hamilton as saying, "The candidate for Congress or the Presidency is broadly asserted to have picked pockets or pocketed silver spoons"?
3. How is Thurber's attitude toward Colonel Hamilton made clear?
4. Explain the connection Thurber makes between "workies" and Karl Marx.
5. Why does Thurber call the future a domain safe for freedom of thought and action?
6. Characterize the holidays Thurber wryly suggests. How do his proposals satirize aspects of contemporary American life and character?
7. How does Thurber's implied criticism reinforce Boorstin's charge (p. 5) that in the absence of knowing what we are *for* we become fanatical in what we are *against*?
8. How do you think Thurber would himself celebrate any one of the holidays he proposes? Support your hypothesis by reference to ideas, techniques, and emphases in the essay that reveal his private and political disposition.
9. Propose in some detail a holiday, in addition to Thurber's, which you think would have a salubrious effect upon the American scene.

2. Time and Place

A Small Western Town

ERIC SEVAREID

> Eric Sevareid (1912-   ) for nearly twenty-five years has been the urbane and literate radio-television journalist for the Columbia Broadcasting System. His first book, Not So Wild a Dream (1946), has been called one of the ablest "autobiographical analyses of an American's education since Henry Adams made his own." It has been followed by two collections of radio essays, In One Ear (1952) and Small Sounds in the Night (1956). Sevareid's deprecating judgment of his writings—he has recommended them for bedtime reading on the assumption that they "can put other people to sleep in the printed form just as effectively as they did when taken by ear"—is one he alone holds.

My father was of the second generation of Norwegian pioneers who came with the Swedes, the Germans, and the Danes to this bleak and barren northwestern country, where the skyline offered nothing to soothe the senses, but where the soil was rich and lumpy in knowing fingers. He was of the second wave. The first which carried in my grandfather, paused, in the fifties and sixties, among the pleasant rolling hills of Iowa and the southern counties of Minnesota, where one was always sure of rain. The land hunger did not die there. The railroads pushed out across the Dakotas, reaching for the fertile and already long-famous Oregon country, and the sons of the first, considering themselves very much Ameri-

---

Reprinted from Eric Sevareid, Not So Wild a Dream by permission of Alfred A. Knopf, Inc. Copyright 1946 by Eric Sevareid. Reprinted by permission of Harold Matson.

can but still easily speaking their European tongues, followed soon after. The westering impulse was still strong in those men when my father went, in the first decade of this century, and those who penetrated North Dakota, sought quick returns as well as permanent homes. For this was bonanza country. The soil was perfect for the crop. There were no hills to circumvent, no forests to clear. It required steadier purpose, harder work, and better men than the finding of gold; but the wheat was their gold. This was the Wheat Rush. So, recklessly they plowed and planted, the same crop year after year. They grew momentarily rich in the years of the First World War, but then the rains ceased. By now the original buffalo grass, which had preserved the soil, was long since plowed away, and without rain the earth lay dried and desolate, the color of old mud, and the hot prairie winds of summer, with nothing to stop them, simply transferred the top soil in the form of fine dust to faraway places. God knows how families survived those years, but they were tough and patient people and they always talked of "next year . . . next year," until even a child could grow sick of hearing it.

(And this, in the very years when the rest of the country flourished in the most extravagant prosperity it had ever known. Before Franklin Roosevelt presented the principle that Americans were one, obliged to care for one another. An idea, I must say, which would have seemed very strange out there in my father's day, when a man still believed that his preservation depended upon himself alone, so that he blamed only himself—and the elements—when he failed.)

Perhaps it was our common dependence upon the wheat that made all men essentially equal, but I do know now, having looked at society in many countries, that we were a true democracy in that huddled community of painted boards. A man might affect pretensions, but he could not pretend for long. We lived too closely together for that. There were, of course, differences in degree of material wealth. There were what was always referred to as the "well-to-do," and we had a few families "on the other side of the tracks." No doubt there was an envy at times and small bitternesses here and there. But no man lived in fear of another. No man had the power to direct another to vote this way or that. No impenetrable combine could foist a candidate upon the people if they did not wish, and it would have been quite impossible to rig an election and get away with it. This was an agrarian democracy, which meant that there was no concentration of capital goods, which meant in turn, since we had no all-powerful landlords, that no class society based upon birth or privilege had a chance to develop. Only a very thick-skinned, insensitive person would dare to "put on airs" in that intimate community. If Mother dressed my brothers and me too prettily for school one day, it was a moral and political necessity that we muddy our clothes as quickly as possible before showing up in the classroom. If this was a Christian democracy, still no virtue was made of poverty; the Scandinavian is too hard-headed for that. But to be poor was no disgrace. If the man of the house in one of the families that lived close to the edge fell ill and could not work, my mother and other mothers carried them baskets of fresh things to eat. It was not charity, not condescension to ease the conscience; it was neighborliness, taken as such, and no one's pride was injured. The Horatio Alger tradition was strong even then, and the village boys really read those insufferable little books. One day when we were out picking wild plums by the river bank, another boy said to me: "Your father is a pretty good man, even if he is the richest man in town." I had no feeling of pride; far from it. I was shocked, and hurried home, close to tears. I demanded the truth of my father, for if this were true, I felt I would be in a highly compromised position; somehow my own worth would be at a discount. Patiently, he demonstrated to me that the charge of possessing great wealth was a false accusation, and I relayed this gratifying information to the proper place without delay.

Later, I read all the exalting literature of the great struggle for a classless society; later, I watched at first hand its manifestations in several countries. It occurred to me then that what men wanted was Velva, on a national, on a world, scale. For the thing was already achieved, in miniature, out there, in a thousand miniatures scattered along the rivers and highways of all the West and Middle West. I was to hear the intelligentsia of eastern America, of England and France, speak often of our Middle West with a certain contempt, with a joke in their minds. They contemned its tightness, its dullness, its bedrock of intolerance. They have much to learn, these gentlemen. For we had, in those severely limited places, an intolerance also of snobbery, of callousness, of crookedness, of men who kicked other men around. The working democracy is boring, most of the time, and dull compared with other systems, but that is a small price to pay for so great a thing.

I must have been very young when *Main Street* was first published. It is a title I remember along with the *Rover Boys*, Horatio Alger, and the Bible. Not that I read it, then, but my mother did and the neighbors up and down our street. I remember the local wrath, and remembering my mother's distress I know it came from being deeply hurt. Of course, in these little places originality was frowned upon, and genius would have been suspect. Of course, the pressure to conform was almost irresistible, and the boundaries of that conformity were appallingly narrow. Of course, art was at a discount and "niceness" the standard of taste. But this terrible indictment bewildered the citizens and made them wonder if all they had tried to do was wrong and had gone for nothing. For they had no other standard by which to measure except the past. And what had the past been? It had been sod huts, a diet of potatoes and gruel. It had been the hot winds in summer that shriveled the crops, and the blizzards of winter that killed the cattle, that brought the pneumonia and influenza that killed their women and children, while the stricken men turned the pages of a home medical guide and waited for the doctor who lived twenty miles away. It had been the gnarled men who sweated beside a kerosene lamp to learn the grammar of their new country's language. It had been the handing on from neighbor to neighbor of a few volumes of the classics, a few eastern newspapers three months old. It had been the one-room schoolhouse in a corner of my grandfather's homestead, where a "bright" aunt could occasionally be prevailed upon to teach the rudiments to tired boys and girls, who had risen before dawn to lug the slops because the family could not afford a hired man. They came together in villages and put paint on the boards of their houses. They planted green trees, made a park as best they could. They put their money together and hired for their children teachers who knew a little more. They sent some sons away to come back with the knowledge of medicine and the law. They built hospitals and colleges. The colleges were not Harvard nor Oxford, but they saw that the right books were there. They thought they had done well. Who, in his present comfort and easy knowledge, is now to sneer? They were of the men who built America; they are now of the men who keep America. They *are* America.

I was to become one of that small swarm of young American journalists who, however deficient in scholarly background, infested foreign capitals, boldly bearded their great men, pugnaciously investigated their political movements, demanded the unornamental truth at a thousand press meetings where our French, British, or Portuguese colleagues approached the great with timid genuflections and regarded us with a mixture of distaste and awe. Instinctively, we looked at men for what they were—as *men*. A title of office, or a "von" or a "de" before their names was no kind of passport to our favor. Partly this was due to the rigorous downrightness of our American journalistic training, but partly to our beginnings in a hundred Velvas.

When "Duff" Aaker died prematurely, why did the whole town mourn his death with such unfeigned sorrow? He was only a country doctor with no wealth, no lineage, no power over them but the power of his personality. I can still feel, when I remember, the tapping of his strong fingers on my chest and the cigar smell of his salt-and-pepper beard. He was one of the first in our town to own an automobile, which he drove with savage speed. He played the piano, the 'cello, and the violin and even *wrote* symphonic music, which would have made anyone else suspect in respectable eyes. He understood my mother's longing for the green and leafy places, and to him alone she could talk. He could denounce the Republican party and vote Nonpartisan League—heresy among the businessmen—and get away with it. He could drink in Prohibition days and get away with that. He could speak so wisely with a dying octogenarian that the old man was happy in dying. In his wrath he could refuse anesthesia to a drunken farmhand, terribly gashed in a pitchfork fight, make him sit upright on a kitchen stool, pour in the iodine overgenerously, and rebuke the man if he grunted.

He drove down one day from the new hospital at Minot to play the organ at the funeral of the local shoemaker, and rushing out of the church tripped, I think, on a croquet arch obscured in the weeds. He was injured internally and died in great pain. My father was a big, stern man, who made stern judgments, and I had never actually heard him speak any praise of the doctor. The night Aaker died my father went up to bed early, without saying goodnight. When we children were going to sleep we could hear his bed shaking. He was sobbing, and we listened in terror all night, for we had never known him to do such a thing. Duff Aaker was the first great man I ever knew about outside of books. No president or premier ever seemed great to me.

Sometimes now it seems to me that my generation lived in preparation for nothing except this war that has ended and which involved my own life so profoundly; but the First World War, which was really the first phase of this one, must have been a very minor interlude for that generation. It surely did not affect our village much. I do remember my father lifting me to the window of a troop train as it halted beside the water tank, in order that we children could shake hands with Uncle Ephraim who was passing through on his way "over there." I remember scolding Arthur Renning, next door, for putting sugar on his bread, knowing that the government in Washington did not want us to put sugar on bread. That's all I remember about that war, except a dream, which is clearest of all. I dreamed the same dream many times. A column of "Huns" was marching down Main Street, past MacKnight's drugstore, and had reached Welo's department store, when I, lying artfully concealed on the roof of the bank, let go with my father's Winchester .22 and mowed them down. They seemed to make no effort to take cover, or to stop me, and they all died instantly. (In the winter when this war was ending in Europe, the British press printed pictures of two German youngsters who had tried to snipe at our men. The captions said: "Examine the faces of these killers, this spawn of the Nazi beasts. Can we treat them as innocent children?")

There were a good many Germans in town, but your parents never talked about them as *Germans,* never pointed them out and set them aside in your mind. Broad women with kindly faces who opened the doors to their clean, good-smelling kitchens and handed you a piece of limp, fragrant coffeecake. They were just the neighbors. You knew they came from Germany, but you did not move them into that side of your mind which contained the Germany of the devilish Kaiser, the spiked helmets, and the savage men who cut the hands from Belgian children. The conception of Germans as a race, with racial (or at least, national) characteristics of their own, was something that did not enter my mind for many years. There were no races with us, except the Negroes, and we saw only one specimen, who worked awhile around Johnson's barber shop, then drifted somewhere else. Undoubtedly, there were Jews among us, a few, but I didn't know what a Jew was until I was almost ready for college. A Jew is still just another person to me. If I do not experience any special reaction in the presence of a Jew, it is not due to broad-mindedness. I cannot. It just isn't there. The toxin was not injected into our bloodstream early enough, for which we give thanks to Velva.

For my father's generation, born in America though they were, the "old country," which they had never seen, still seemed close. He carried a faint Norwegian accent in his speech throughout his life, which came from his early boyhood when few around the farms spoke English. Christmas dinner was never right for him without *lutefisk* and *lefse,* and Pastor Reishus always preached first in Norwegian, then in English. But there came a break with my generation, the third. It happened throughout that northwest country. Talk with visitors in the parlor about the old country bored my brothers and me. I hated the sound of the Norwegian tongue and refused to try to learn it. It meant nothing to me that my grandfather on my mother's side was one of America's most distinguished scholars of Scandinavian literature and life. The books in my classroom dealt only with the United States, and there lay the sole magnet to our imaginations. The thread connecting these northwest people with Europe was thinning out, and with my generation it snapped.

There was another course which changed in that period. We were the first to grow up without the American West shining before the eye of the mind as the vision of the future. Instinctively we knew that the last of the frontiers had disappeared. From the time when the Indian tales lost their spell and we began to think, we wanted to go east. It was the East that was golden. My father did move his family east—a little way, to Minnesota—but not to seek more opportunity, more freedom; years of drought ruined his wheatlands and broke his bank.

PROBLEMS FOR WRITING AND DISCUSSION

1. This essay, dealing with Sevareid's early life in Velva, North Dakota, essentially praises life in a small town. What specific virtues did it have? What were its defects?
2. What passage in the essay best gives the flavor of the life? Why?
3. How are the seemingly disparate topics (the land, ethnic groups, a doctor, the clash of generations) organized into a coherent piece?
4. Discuss the pertinency of the sketch of "Duff" Aaker. What makes Aaker seem particularly American and at the same time a "great man" by any definition of the phrase?
5. In what ways does "the past" shape the people Sevareid speaks of? What sort of men were these "men who built America"?
6. How has the "equality" Sevareid experienced in the Middle West affected him as a journalist? Do you think he exaggerates or honestly clarifies a difference between Americans and Europeans?

7. Sevareid asserts that the Midwesterners of the small town "*are* America." What light does his description of the American journalists' approach to foreigners throw on the question of American character that Boorstin (p. 5) and Commager (p. 14) raise?

8. What in the essay suggests Sevareid would like Americans to revert to the rural simplicity and stern morality of Midwestern America at the beginning of the century?

9. Why does Sevareid relate his dreams of "mowing down" the Huns? How does the account contribute to his picture of the American character?

10. What connection is implied between the closing of the frontiers and the eastward movement of Sevareid's generation and their total involvement in World War II? What had changed in the "business" with which America had to concern itself?

11. Explain Sevareid's comments on the "classless society" and on "conformity" in America.

12. Does your generation, like Sevareid's, reject the dreams and visions of the past for new ones? Specify your own dreams and visions, and point out what seems invalid or inapplicable in those of your elders.

13. What has your own home community taught you that you consider formative of your own character and worth preserving for the future?

TWO VIEWS OF SALEM

Salem Village

EDWARD EGGLESTON

Edward Eggleston (1837-1902) is perhaps best known for The Hoosier Schoolmaster *(1871), a novel widely read in its day and still in print. Several more novels followed, which he saw as "of value as a contribution to the history of civilization in America." Some time in the 1880's he determined to write a history of the United States, but this grand design led to only two volumes—*The Beginners of a Nation *(1896) and* The Transit of Civilization *(1900). The latter, recently reissued as a paperback, was the first attempt at a social history of 17th-century America. The style is lean and tight and yet, as a contemporary put it, "of such beauty and force as to make the book at once a history and a contribution to literature."*

Salem village, an outlying suburb, two or three miles from Salem proper, was almost a frontier town in 1692. Men still wore buckskin breeches and hats with a brim narrow in front and long behind. Wolves, bears, and catamounts were trapped. Some of the settlers had participated in the desperate battle at the Narragansetts' town sixteen years before. The sword and the rapier were still worn at

Reprinted from The Transit of Civilization, *by Edward Eggleston, D. Appleton & Co., 1901.*

the side, the fowling piece six and seven feet in length was in use. Men had been killed by the Indians in the bounds of Salem within three years. Education was generally neglected; even men of substance were sometimes unable to write. The old patriarchs who had made the settlement had just died off; the community had lost its steadfast guides. New clergymen had come in and new magistrates, not with the education of England, but with the scantier training of New England—a training in which the felling axe was more important than the Latin grammar. The new clergy, men of the second and third generations, were, with a few exceptions, profoundly impressed with the necessity of believing anything ghostly or horrible; the supernatural was the basis of their piety. Increase Mather, the bishop by brevet of New England, had published books on the ominous eclipses of 1680 and 1682, and another in 1686 on Illustrious Providences, which was a storehouse of those dragons' teeth that bore such ample fruit in 1692. His abler but less judicious son, Cotton, had issued a book on "Memorable Providences relating to witchcraft and Possessions." It had come to a second edition in the very year before the horrors of Salem.

The village of Salem had the elements needed for a witchcraft mania—a quarrel between minister and people; a circle of young girls from eleven to twenty, including some who worked as helps, who met at the minister's house and practiced together folk-sorcery and that kind of divining that has been the amusement of such for ages. These girls soon began to manifest symptoms of hysteria and hypnotism; one or two married women also had "fits" in sympathy with them. A doctor called to attend them decided that they were afflicted by "an evil hand." There was some heartless and heedless imposture, no doubt, in what followed, but there was also much of self-deception.

The glimpses of the infernal world that we get in Salem are highly incredible. The witches say prayers to a tall black man with a high-crowned hat—always with a high-crowned hat. They ride on sticks and poles, sometimes they are on brooms, and sometimes three are on one pole. One relates that a pole carrying two broke, but, by holding fast to the one in front of her, the witch got safe to her destination. The witches fondle yellow birds, suckling them between their fingers, and one day a girl cries out in meeting that a yellow bird sits on the minister's hat as it hangs on a pin on the pulpit. The witch usually sits on the great crossbeam of the meetinghouse, fondling the yellow bird. One man was seen to nurse two black pigs at his breasts. Sometimes a hog, sometimes a black dog, appears and says, "Serve me." Then the dog or pig "looks like a man," and this man has a yellow bird. Cats naturally abound, white cats and red cats and cats without color. Once a man struck with a rapier at a place designated by one of the girls, and she declared the cat dead and the floor to be all covered with blood. But no one else saw it. This is probably hypnotism, hardly imposture. A great mass of such inconsequent and paltry foolery was believed, not alone by owl-blasted children, but by Stoughton and the other judges, and by pious Samuel Sewall himself, more's the pity! Where is the motive? What prompted the most eminent Christians and leading citizens to prefer so base a life—companions to cats and dogs and devils? Why did this torture of innocent children, this mischief-working witchcraft with endless perdition at the tail of it, give pleasure to rational creatures? The court never once thought to ask.

The trial scenes were perdition. The "afflicted children" screamed, went into spasms, shouted, charged the prisoners with torturing them, and their apparent torments were frightful. They laid to the charge of the accused unheard-of deviltries, such as the killing of wives long dead, attempting to choke aged grandparents, and what not besides. Husbands in some instances turned against wives, in others they adhered to them, were accused themselves, and died with them.

The trials were accompanied by great cruelties. Officers of the law were allowed to plunder the estates of the accused of all movable property. The prisoners had to pay their jail expenses, and many families were utterly impoverished. Prisoners were cast into the dungeon and were "fettered." Goodman Hutchinson complained of certain prisoners for tormenting his wife; additional fetters were put on them, after which Mrs. Hutchinson was "tolerable well." Some were tortured to make them confess; lads were laid neck and heels until the blood gushed from their noses. These were accredited practices at the time. Several died in prison.

The very skill of the accused was against them. One very neat woman walked miles over dirty roads without showing any mud. "I scorn to be drabbled," she said, and she was hanged for her cleanliness. George Burroughs, the minister, was a strong man, much addicted to gymnastics. He carried barrels of cider by inserting his fingers into the bunghole, and held a seven-foot gun at arm's length. He was the devil's man, away with him to the gallows! The first people in the colony became involved. Twenty in all were executed, four or five at a time. Their bodies were ignominiously thrust into holes at the place where they were executed and were scantly covered.

There were brave men and women among them. Giles Corey, an eccentric old man, had at first signed an affidavit of uncertainty about his wife, a woman of piety, and, strange to say, an entire unbeliever in witchcraft. Two of his sons-in-law turned against her, two were for her. But when old Giles was accused he stiffened his neck. He would save his property, which was considerable and might be compromised; he would will it all to his two faithful sons-in-law. He would prove his steadfastness. He made a will, perfect in every part, giving his property to the sons-in-law, and then totally refused to plead and was slowly pressed to death. The constancy of the old man did much to overthrow the partisans of witchcraft. Joseph Putnam, a young man of twenty-two, declared his detestation of the doctrine. He kept some one of his horses bridled and saddled for six months. He armed all his family, and it was understood that he must be taken, if taken at all, pistol in hand. When the mania was at its height he refused to have his child baptized in the village, but carried it to Salem.

The excitement had risen with every arrest. More than fifty badgered souls had confessed that they were witches. Some had fled the country. But the wide extent of the accusations produced a change in the minds of the people. They knew not who would be struck at next. The governor, at length, refused to call the special court together, and after a tedious confinement a hundred and fifty were released by proclamation. The population of Salem had decreased, its business had suffered, and perhaps it never recovered its prosperity. Slowly the people got over the delusion and came to realize the incalculable and irretrievable harm that had been wrought. Judge Sewall, at a general fast, handed up to the minister to be read a humble confession, and stood while it was read. He annually kept a private day of humiliation. Honor to his memory! The twelve jurymen also signed an affecting paper asking to be forgiven. Cotton Mather, who had been very conspicuous and had published a book about it, never acknowledged himself wrong in this or any other matter. From the time it became unpopular he speaks of the witchcraft trials in a far-away manner, as if they were wholly the work of some one else. He was never forgiven, and probably never ought to have been.

The revulsion was complete. No witches were tried or hanged or "swimmed" in America after the Salem trials. In half a lifetime more the ardor of the English people visibly abated, and few witches were thereafter arrested in England.

(For Problems for Writing and Discussion, see the end of the next essay.)

A Visit to Salem

ARTHUR MILLER

Arthur Miller (1915-   ) is one of America's most distinguished playwrights. After graduating from the University of Michigan in 1938, he worked as a manual laborer, in addition to being a writer for the Federal Theatre Workshop, for radio, and for motion pictures. His first play failed, but his next two—All My Sons *(1947) and* Death of a Salesman *(1949)—established his reputation. Four years later, disturbed by domestic political events, Miller wrote* The Crucible *to "show that the sin of public terror is that it divests a man of conscience, of himself." The events of the Salem witch trials, which form the basis of this play, had been for Miller a source of "inexplicable darkness." His plays have been collected in a single volume (1957) for which Miller wrote a critical introduction.*

"The Crucible" is taken from history. No character is in the play who did not take a similar role in Salem, 1692. The basic story is recorded, if briefly, in certain documents of the time. It will be a long time before I shall be able to shake Rebecca Nurse, John Proctor, Giles Corey and the others out of my mind. But there are strange, even weird memories that have connected themselves to this play, and these have to do with the present, and it has all got mixed up together.

I went to Salem for the first time early last spring. I already knew the story, and had thought about it for a long time. I had never

From The New York Times, Feb. 8, 1953. Copyright © by Arthur Miller 1953.

been to Salem before and, driving alone up the brand new superhighway, I felt a shock at seeing the perfectly ordinary, steel sign reading, "Salem 3 mi." I confess it—some part of my mind had expected to see the old wooden village, not the railroad tracks, the factories, the trucks. These things were not real, suddenly, but intruders, as tourists are in the halls of Versailles. Underneath, in the earth, was the reality. I drove into the town.

I asked the courthouse clerk for the town records for 1692. A lawyer-looking man in an overcoat asked for 1941. A lady, who looked like she were planning to sue somebody, asked for 1913. The clerk handed over a volume to each of us and we sat at separate tables, the three of us, turning pages.

The lawyer began copying—possibly from a deed. The woman read perhaps a will—and got angrier. I looked into 1692. Here were wills, too, and deeds, and warrants sworn out, and the usual debris a town leaves behind it for the legal record.

And then . . . dialogue! Prosecutor Hathorne is examining Rebecca Nurse. The court is full of people weeping for the young girls who sit before them strangling because Rebecca's spirit is out tormenting them. And Hathorne says, "It is awful to see your eye dry when so many are wet." And Rebecca replies, "You do not know my heart. I never afflicted no child, never in my life. I am as clear as the child unborn."

They hanged her. She was in her seventies. They had hesitated to go and arrest her because of her high reputation; but they took her from her sickbed, they took her from her lovely house that stands in the countryside yet, and they hanged her by the neck over the long Salem Bay.

The lawyer in the overcoat was copying his deed; the lady was back at the counter, asking the clerk for 1912. Did they know what had happened here?

In the museum all is silent. An old man, looking like a retired professor, is reading a document. Two middle-aged couples come in from their automobile outside and ask to see the pins: The pins the spirits stuck the children with. The pins are in the courthouse, they are told. They look about at the books, the faded fragments of paper that once meant Proctor must hang tomorrow, paper that came through the farmhouse door in the hand of a friend who had a half-determined, half-ashamed look in his eyes.

The tourists pass the books, the exhibits and no hint of danger reaches them from the quaint relics. I have a desire to tell them the significance of those relics. It is the desire to write.

Day after day in the courthouse, until the evenings begin to arrive with forebodings in the night breeze. The locations of the old farmhouses are in my mind, their directions from the spot on which I stand; on Essex Street was a house, perhaps a few yards from here, where Reverend Parris lived and at night discussed with certain others who in the town was acting suspiciously, who might have shown signs of the Devil's touch. Salem was taken from the Hebrew, Sholom, meaning peace, but now in my mind and in the streets it is a dark word.

The stroll down Essex Street I remember, and the empty spaces between the parking meters, the dark storefronts—but further down a lighted store, and noise. I take a look. A candy store. A mob of girls and boys in their teens running in and out, ganging around on the vacant street; a jalopy pulls up with two wet-haired boys, and a whispered consultation with a girl on the running board; she runs into the store, comes out with a friend, and off they go into the night, the proud raccoon tail straightening from the radiator cap. And suddenly, from around a corner, two girls hopping with a broomstick between their legs, and a general laughter going up at the special joke. A broomstick. And riding it. And I remember the girls of Salem, the only Salem there ever was for me—the 1692 Salem—and how they purged their sins by embracing God and pointing out His enemies in the town.

And a feeling of love at seeing Rebecca Nurse's house on its gentle knoll; the house she lay in, ill, when they came, shuffling their feet, ashamed to have to ask her to come to court because the children said she had sent her spirit out.

And the great rock, standing mum over the Bay, the splintered precipice on which the gibbet was built. The highway traffic endlessly, mindlessly humming at its foot, but up here the barrenness, the clinkers of broken stones, and the vast view of the bay; here hung Rebecca, John Proctor, George Jacobs—people more real to me than the living can ever be. The sense of a terrible marvel again; that people could have such a belief in themselves and in the rightness of their consciences as to give their lives rather than say what they thought was false. Or, perhaps, they only feared Hell so much? Yet, Rebecca said, and it is written in the record, "I cannot belie myself." And she knew it would kill her. They knew who they were.

My friends return, the men of my own life—in the hotel taproom a circle of salesmen sitting around, waiting for bedtime. I listen. They are comparing the sizes of their television screens. Which one is the big-earner? Yep, that one. He says less, but they listen more when he says it. They are all wishing they were him. And all a little lost in the eyes, and nice fellas, so damned eager, and men-among-men, and around the eyes ever so faintly lost; laughing a little more than they want to, listening longer than they want to, sorry without sorrow, laughing with less than joy, until up in the hotel room alone there is only one certainty—tomorrow will come. Another day, another chance to find out—who they are. How they got there. Where they're going.

The rock stands forever in Salem. They knew who they were. Nineteen.

PROBLEMS FOR WRITING AND DISCUSSION

1. The two preceding selections remind us of an ugly event that occurred in America, one that Americans have been uneasy about ever since.

Eggleston's interest in the Salem trials is that of a historian, Arthur Miller's that of a playwright. What point of interest do the two men have in common?

2. What conditions prevailed in Salem in 1692, according to Eggleston, that made the ensuing trials likely, if not inevitable?

3. How does the Eggleston essay illuminate the Miller essay?

4. Arthur Miller's description of Salem, Massachusetts, would be effective even had *The Crucible* never been written. Why? What relevance has this description to Miller's main purpose in the essay?

5. Miller's essay was written in 1953. What significance does this fact have for both his essay and *The Crucible*?

6. What quality does Miller admire in the people who were hanged in Salem in 1692, and how does he illustrate it?

7. Why does Miller end his essay with a scene in a hotel taproom? Notice, especially, the diction of the last paragraph.

8. Why does Miller in the early parts of his essay keep referring to the lawyer and the lady as he reads the records for 1692?

9. Miller writes incredulously of people who had "such belief in themselves and a rightness of their consciences" that they died rather than "say what they thought was false." Does this "marvel" characterize Americans generally as Boorstin (p. 5) sees them?

10. Witches belong to a superstition of the past, yet the term "witch-trial" persists to describe contemporary phenomena. With reference to these two essays and those of Boorstin, Commager (p. 14), and Thurber (p. 34), discuss possible explanations for the irrational behavior the term denotes.

The Kitchen

ALFRED KAZIN

Alfred Kazin (1915-) was born and reared in the Brownsville section of Brooklyn that he writes of in the essay that follows. A former literary editor of The New Republic *(1942-43) and contributing editor of* Fortune *(1943-44), he has taught at numerous schools, including Queens College of The City University of New York, the University of Minnesota, and Amherst College. Although* A Walker in the City *(1951), his autobiography, is best known to the general public, Kazin has written or edited many books, including* On Native Grounds *(1942), a study of American literature, and* The Inmost Leaf *(1955), a collection of his own critical essays.*

The last time I saw our kitchen this clearly was one afternoon in London at the end of the war, when I waited out the rain in the entrance to a music store. A radio was playing into the street, and standing there I heard a broadcast of the first Sabbath service from Belsen Concentration Camp. When the liberated Jewish prisoners recited the *Hear O Israel, the Lord Our God, the Lord is One*, I felt myself carried back to the Friday evenings at home, when with the Sabbath at sundown a healing quietness would come over Brownsville.

It was the darkness and emptiness of the streets I liked most about Friday evening, as if in preparation for that day of rest and worship which the Jews greet "as a bride"—that day when the very touch of money is prohibited, all work, all travel, all household duties, even

From A Walker in the City, *copyright, 1951, by Alfred Kazin. Reprinted by permission of Harcourt, Brace & World, Inc.*

64

to the turning on and off of a light—Jewry had found its way past its tormented heart to some ancient still center of itself. I waited for the streets to go dark on Friday evening as other children waited for the Christmas lights. Even Friday morning after the tests were over glowed in anticipation. When I returned home after three, the warm odor of a coffee cake baking in the oven and the sight of my mother on her hands and knees scrubbing the linoleum on the dining room floor filled me with such tenderness that I could feel my senses reaching out to embrace every single object in our household. One Friday, after a morning in school spent on the voyages of Henry Hudson, I returned with the phrase *Among the discoverers of the New World* singing in my mind as the theme of my own new-found freedom on the Sabbath.

My great moment came at six, when my father returned from work, his overalls smelling faintly of turpentine and shellac, white drops of silver paint still gleaming on his chin. Hanging his overcoat in the long dark hall that led into our kitchen, he would leave in one pocket a loosely folded copy of the New York *World*; and then everything that beckoned to me from that other hemisphere of my brain beyond the East River would start up from the smell of fresh newsprint and the sight of the globe on the front page. It was a paper that carried special associations for me with Brooklyn Bridge. They published the *World* under the green dome on Park Row overlooking the bridge; the fresh salt air of New York harbor lingered for me in the smell of paint and damp newsprint in the hall. I felt that my father brought the outside straight into our house with each day's copy of the *World*. The bridge somehow stood for freedom; the *World* for that rangy kindness and fraternalism and ease we found in Heywood Broun. My father would read aloud from "It Seems To Me" with a delighted smile on his face. "A very clear and courageous man!" he would say. "Look how he stands up for our Sacco and Vanzetti! A real social conscience, that man! Practically a Socialist!" Then, taking off his overalls, he would wash up at the kitchen sink, peeling and gnawing the paint off his nails with Gold Dust Washing Powder as I poured it into his hands, smacking his lips and grunting with pleasure as he washed himself clean of the job at last, and making me feel that I was really helping him, that I, too, was contributing to the greatness of the evening and the coming day.

By sundown the streets were empty, the curtains had been drawn, the world put to rights. Even the kitchen walls had been scrubbed and now gleamed in the Sabbath candles. On the long white tablecloth were the "company" dishes, filled for some with *gefillte* fish on lettuce leaves, ringed by red horseradish, sour and half-sour pickles, tomato salad with a light vinegar dressing; for others, with chopped liver in a bed of lettuce leaves and white radishes; the long white *khalleh*, the Sabbath loaf; chicken soup with noodles *and* dumplings; chicken, meat loaf, prunes, and sweet potatoes that had been baked all day into an open pie; compote of prunes and quince, apricots and orange rind; applesauce; a great brown nutcake filled with almonds, the traditional *lekakh*; all surrounded by glasses of port wine, seltzer bottles with their nozzles staring down at us waiting to be pressed; a samovar of Russian tea, *svetouchnee* from the little red box, always served in tall glasses, with lemon slices floating on top. My father and mother sipped it in Russian fashion, through lumps of sugar held between the teeth.

Afterwards we went into the "dining room" and, since we were not particularly orthodox, allowed ourselves little pleasures outside the Sabbath rule—an occasional game of Casino at the dining-room table where we never dined, and listening to the victrola. The evening was particularly good for me whenever the unmarried cousin who boarded with us had her two closest friends in after supper.

They were all dressmakers, like my mother; had worked with my mother in the same East Side sweatshops; were all passionately loyal members of the International Ladies Garment Workers Union; and were all unmarried. We were their only family. Despite my mother's frenzied matchmaking, she had never succeeded in pinning a husband down for any of them. As she said, they were all too *particular* —what a calamity for a Jewish woman to remain unmarried! But my cousin and her friends accepted their fate calmly, and prided themselves on their culture and their strong *progressive* interests. They felt they belonged not to the "kitchen world," like my mother, but to the enlightened tradition of the old Russian intelligentsia. Whenever my mother sighed over them, they would smile out of their greater knowledge of the world, and looking at me with a pointed appeal for recognition, would speak of novels they had read in Yiddish and Russian, of *Winesburg, Ohio,* of some article in the *Nation.*

Our cousin and her two friends were of my parents' generation, but I could never believe it—they seemed to enjoy life with such outspokenness. They were the first grown-up people I had ever met who used the word *love* without embarrassment. *"Libbe! Libbe!"* my mother would explode whenever one of them protested that she could not, after all, marry a man she did not love. "What is this love you make such a stew about? You do not like the way he holds his cigarette? Marry him first and it will all come out right in the end!" It astonished me to realize there was a world in which even unmarried women no longer young were simply individual human beings with lives of their own. *Our* parents, whatever affection might offhandedly be expressed between them, always had the look of being committed to something deeper than *mere* love. Their marriages were neither happy nor unhappy; they were arrangements. However they had met—whether in Russia or in the steerage or, like my parents, in an East Side boarding house—whatever they still thought of each other, *love* was not a word they used easily. Marriage was an institution people entered into—for all I could ever tell—only from immigrant loneliness, a need to be with one's own kind that mechanically resulted in the *family.* The *family* was a whole greater than all the individuals who made it up, yet made sense only in their untiring solidarity. I was perfectly sure that in my parents' minds *libbe* was something exotic and not wholly legitimate, reserved for "educated" people like their children, who were the sole end of their existence. My father and mother worked in a rage to put us above their level; they had married to make *us* possible. We were the only conceivable end to all their striving; we were their America.

So far as I knew, love was not an element admissible in my parents' experience. Any open talk of it between themselves would have seemed ridiculous. It would have suggested a wicked self-indulgence, a preposterous attention to one's own feelings, possible only to those who were free enough to choose. They did not consider themselves free. They were awed by us, as they were awed by their own imagined unworthiness, and looked on themselves only as instruments toward the ideal "American" future that would be lived by their children. As poor immigrants who had remained in Brownsville, painfully conscious of the *alrightniks* on Eastern Parkway—oh, those successes of whom I was always hearing so much, and whom we admired despite all our Socialism!—everything in their lives combined to make them look down on love as something *they* had no time for. Of course there was a deep resentment in this, and when on those Friday evenings our cousin or her two friends openly mentioned the unheard-of collapse of someone's marriage—

"Sórelle and Berke? I don't believe it."
"But it's true."
"You must be joking!"
"No, it's true!"
"You're joking! You're joking!"
"No, it's true!"

—I noticed that my parents' talk had an unnaturally hard edge to it, as if those who gave themselves up to love must inevitably come to grief. Love, they could have said, was not *serious*. Life was a battle to "make sure"; it had no place, as we had no time, for whims.

Love, in fact, was something for the movies, which my parents enjoyed, but a little ashamedly. They were the land of the impossible. On those few occasions when my mother closed her sewing machine in the evening and allowed herself a visit to the Supreme, or the Palace, or the Premier, she would return, her eyes gleaming with wonder and some distrust at the strangeness of it all, to report on erotic fanatics who were, thank God, like no one we knew. What heedlessness! What daring! What riches! To my mother riches alone were the gateway to romance, for only those who had money enough could afford the freedom, and the crazy boldness, to give themselves up to love.

Yet there they were in our own dining room, our cousin and her two friends—women, grown-up women—talking openly of the look on Garbo's face when John Gilbert took her in his arms, serenely disposing of each new *khayimyankel*, poor wretch, my mother had picked for them, and arguing my father down on small points of Socialist doctrine. As they sat around the cut-glass bowl on the table —cracking walnuts, expertly peeling the skin off an apple in long even strips, cozily sipping at a glass of tea—they crossed their legs in comfort and gave off a deliciously musky fragrance of face powder that instantly framed them for me in all their dark coloring, brilliantly white teeth, and the rosy Russian blouses that swelled and rippled in terraces of embroidery over their opulent breasts.

They had a great flavor for me, those three women: they were the positive center of that togetherness that always meant so much to me in our dining room on Friday evenings. It was a quality that seemed to start in the prickly thickness of the cut-glass bowl laden with nuts and fruits; in the light from the long black-shaded lamp hanging over the table as it shimmered against the thick surfaces of the bowl and softened that room where the lace curtains were drawn against the dark and empty streets—and then found its unexpectedly tender voice in the Yiddish folksongs and Socialist hymns they taught me—*"Let's Now Forgive Each Other"; "Tsuzamen, Tsuzamen, All Together, Brothers!"* Those Friday evenings, I suddenly found myself enveloped in some old, primary Socialist idea that men could go beyond every barrier of race and nation and language, even of class! into some potential loving union of the whole human race. I was suddenly glad to be a Jew, as these women were Jews—simply and naturally glad of those Jewish dressmakers who spoke with enthusiastic familiarity of Sholom Aleichem and

Peretz, Gorky and Tolstoy, who glowed at every reminiscence of Nijinsky, of Nazimova in *The Cherry Orchard*, of Pavlova in "The Swan."

Often, those Friday evenings, they spoke of *der heym*, "Home," and then it was hard for me. *Heym* was a terrible word. I saw millions of Jews lying dead under the Polish eagle with knives in their throats. I was afraid with my mother's fears, thought I should weep when she wept, lived again through every pogrom whose terrors she chanted. I associated with that old European life only pain, mud, and hopelessness, but I was of it still, through her. Whenever she would call through the roll of her many brothers and sisters and their children, remembering at each name that this one was dead, that one dead, another starving and sure soon to die—who knew *how* they were living these days in that miserable Poland?—I felt there was some supernatural Polish eagle across the sea whose face I should never see, but which sent out dark electrical rays to hold me fast.

In many ways *der heym* was entirely dim and abstract, nothing to do with me at all, alien as the skullcap and beard and frock coat of my mother's father, whom I never saw, but whose calm orthodox dignity stared up at me from an old cracked photograph at the bottom of the bureau drawer. Yet I lived each of my mother's fears from Dugschitz to Hamburg to London to Hester Street to Brownsville through and through with such fidelity that there were times when I wished I had made that journey too, wished I could have seen Czarist Russia, since I had in any event to suffer it all over again. I often felt odd twinges of jealousy because my parents could talk about that more intense, somehow less *experimental* life than ours with so many private smiles between themselves. It was bewildering, it made me long constantly to get at some past nearer my own New York life, my having to live with all those running wounds of a world I had never seen.

Then, under cover of the talk those Friday evenings, I would take up *The Boy's Life of Theodore Roosevelt* again, and moodily call out to those strangers on the summer veranda in Oyster Bay until my father spoke *his* tale of arriving in America. That was hard, too, painful in another way—yet it always made him curiously lighthearted and left me swimming in space. For he had gone off painting box cars on the Union Pacific, had been as far west as Omaha, had actually seen Sidney Hillman toiling in Hart, Schaffner and Marx's Chicago factory, had heard his beloved Debs making fools of Bryan and Taft in the 1908 campaign, had been offered a homestead in Colorado! *Omaha* was the most beautiful word I had ever heard, *homestead* almost as beautiful; but I could never forgive him for not having accepted that homestead.

"What would I have done there? I'm no farmer."
"You should have taken it! Why do we always live here!"
"It would have been too lonely. Nobody I knew."
"What a chance!"
"Don't be childish. Nobody I knew."
"Why? Why?"
"Alfred, what do you want of us poor Jews?"

So it was: we had always to be together: believers and non-believers, we were a people; I was of that people. Unthinkable to go one's own way, to doubt or to escape the fact that I was a Jew. I had heard of Jews who pretended they were not, but could not understand them. We had all of us lived together so long that we would not have known how to separate even if we had wanted to. The most terrible word was *aleyn*, alone. I always had the same picture of a man desolately walking down a dark street, newspapers and cigarette butts contemptuously flying in his face as he tasted in the dusty grit the full measure of his strangeness. *Aleyn! Aleyn!* My father had been alone here in America as a boy. *His* father, whose name I bore, had died here at twenty-five of pneumonia caught on a garment workers' picket line, and his body flung in with thousands of other Jews who had perished those first years on the East Side. My father had never been able to find his father's grave. *Aleyn! Aleyn!* Did immigrant Jews, then, marry only out of loneliness? Was even Socialism just a happier way of keeping us together?

I trusted it to do that. Socialism would be one long Friday evening around the samovar and the cut-glass bowl laden with nuts and fruits, all of us singing *Tsuzamen, tsuzamen, ale tsuzamen!* Then the heroes of the Russian novel—*our* kind of people—would walk the world, and I—still wearing a circle-necked Russian blouse *"à la Tolstoy"*—would live forever with those I loved in that beautiful Russian country of the mind. Listening to our cousin and her two friends I, who had never seen it, who associated with it nothing but the names of great writers and my father's saying as we went through the Brooklyn Botanic Garden—"Nice! but you should have seen the Czar's summer palace at Tsarskoye-Selo!"—suddenly saw Russia as the grand antithesis to all bourgeois ideals, the spiritual home of all truly free people. I was perfectly sure that there was no literature in the world like the Russian; that the only warm hearts in the world were Russian, like our cousin and her two friends; that other people were always dully materialist, but that the Russian soul, like Nijinsky's dream of pure flight, would always leap outward, past all barriers, to a lyric world in which my ideal Socialism and the fiery moodiness of Tchaikovsky's *Pathétique* would be entirely at home with each other. *Tsuzamen, alle tsuzamen!* How many millions would be with us! China was in our house those Friday evenings, Africa, the Indian masses. And it was those three unmarried dressmakers from the rank and file who fully wrapped me in that spell, with the worldly clang of their agate beads and the musky fragrance of their face powder and their embroidered Russian blouses, with the great names of Russian writers ringing against the cut-glass bowl under the black lamp. Never did the bowl look so laden, never did apples and tea smell so good, never did the samovar pour out with such steaming bounty, as on those Friday evenings when I tasted in the tea and the talk the evangelical heart of our cousin and her two friends, and realized that it was we—we!—who would someday put the world on its noblest course.

"*Kinder, kinder,*" my mother would say. "Enough *discusye.* Maybe now a little music? Alfred, play *Scheherazade!*"

You could melt their hearts with it; the effect of the violin on almost everyone I knew was uncanny. I could watch them softening, easing, already on the brink of tears—yet with their hands at rest in their laps, they stared straight ahead at the wall, breathing hard, an unforeseen smile of rapture on their mouths. Any slow movement, if only it were played lingeringly and sagely enough, seemed to come to them as a reminiscence of a reminiscence. It seemed to have something to do with our being Jews. The depths of Jewish memory the violin could throw open apparently had no limit—for every slow movement was based on something "Russian," every plaintive melody even in Beethoven or Mozart was "Jewish." I could skip from composer to composer, from theme to theme, without any fear, ever, of being detected, for all slow movements fell into a single chant of *der heym* and of the great *Kol Nidre* sung in the first evening hours of the Day of Atonement, in whose long rending cry—of contrition? of grief? of hopeless love for the Creator? —I relived all of the Jews' bitter intimacy with death.

Then I cranked up the old brown Victor, took our favorite records out of the red velvet pleated compartments, and we listened to John McCormack singing *Ave Maria*, Amelita Galli-Curci singing *Caro Nome* ("How ugly she is!" my parents would say wonderingly. "Have you seen her picture? Incredible! But how she sings!"), and Alma Gluck singing *Comin' Thro' the Rye*. The high point was Caruso singing from *La Juive*. He inspired in my father and mother such helpless, intimidated adoration that I came to think of what was always humbly referred to as his *golden voice* as the invocation of a god. The pleasure he gave us was beyond all music. When Mischa Elman played some well-known melody we sighed familiarly at each other—his tone was so *warm*; he bubbled slowly in my ears like the sound of chicken fat crackling in the pan. But Caruso, "that *Italyéner*," seemed to me the echo of some outrageously pagan voice at the roof of the world. While I pushed at the hand-crank and the wheezy sounds of the orchestra in the background came to me as the whispered turnings, sighs and alarms of the crowd around the circus pit, there on high, and rising higher and higher with each note, that voice, that *golden voice*, leaped its way from one trapeze to another. We sat hunched in our wonder, our adoration, our fear. Would he make it? Could any human being find that last impossible rung?

Rachel! Quand du Seigneur la grâce tutélaire. . . .

Then, suddenly bounding back to earth again, there he was before us again, secretly smiling, the tones welling out of him with such brazen strength, such irresistible energy, that he left us gasping. I could see him standing inside the victrola box—a centaur just out of the woods, not quite human, with that enigmatic, almost contemptuous smile on his face. "What a voice!" my father would say over and over, deeply shaken. "What a voice! It's not human! Never was there a voice like it! Only the other day I was reading that when they opened him up after he died they found his vocal chords were ab-solutely unique!" Then, his face white with pleasure, with amazement, with wonder: "Oh that *Italyéner!* Oh that *Italyéner!* What a power he has, that *Italyéner!*"

PROBLEMS FOR WRITING AND DISCUSSION

1. Kazin says that his parents' children were *their* America. What evidence does he give of the discontinuity between the tradition of his parents in the *heym* and the America being prepared in the next generation? What evidence of continuity? Is there evidence that the boy Alfred's identity, as an American Jew, will be more ambiguous than that of his parents? How does this evidence illuminate the difficulty of defining American character?

2. John Gilbert was a silent-film star of the 1920's. Why does Kazin introduce this and other specific details—the foods his family ate on Friday nights, the "Gold Dust Washing Powder" his father used, etc.? How does the essay gain or lose by these details from an era gone by?

3. Why does Kazin use *The Boy's Life of Teddy Roosevelt* to introduce his father's remarks about America?

4. How do the differing attitudes toward love reveal something that affected the lives and destinies of many immigrant families in America, not only Jewish ones?

5. Compare the attitude of Kazin's parents toward romantic love with what you believe to be the prevalent American attitude today. Is your attitude the same as your parents'? If not, what accounts for the difference? What has been most influential in forming your attitude toward love?

6. What did the term *aleyn* (alone) signify for Kazin's family and for Jews in general? Do you think the term would be applicable to other immigrant groups? Would *aloneness* account in part for the frenzied search for national identity described by Boorstin (p. 5)?

7. Both Sevareid (p. 45) and Kazin express deep affection for their parents. Discuss the basic irony in this affection and its effects on the stability of the American character.

8. Sevareid and Kazin, writing of an earlier America than the one of which Mead (p. 24) writes, emphasize the importance of the family in their lives. Kazin speaks more directly and fully of his family, but do his remarks differ essentially from Sevareid's? Is the emphasis on "family" here somewhat different from that which Mead describes?

9. Do Kazin's remarks about his parents bear out Boorstin's view that we have all suffered "cultural amnesia" and been forced "to forget ancient images and break old molds"?

10. Kazin and Sevareid are approximately the same age, yet they write of Americas that seem to share little in time and place. What can men from such divergent backgrounds draw upon that enables them, for all their differences, to share the common experience of being Americans?

The Suburban Way of Life

LEWIS MUMFORD

> Lewis Mumford (1895-   ) is neither an architect nor a city planner, yet he has a world-wide reputation as both. A scholar who writes with the moral fervor of an Old Testament prophet, he has completed twenty books on a variety of subjects, including literature and society. His most recent work is the monumental The City in History (*1961*). "He is," Van Wyck Brooks has said, "too strong meat for minds, accustomed to preciosity, that are inured to the fatalism of our sad time, minds of low vitality that resent this passion of affirmation, this faith in the creative instinct and the world that is emerging."

At the beginning the suburb was the expression of a new way of life, less effortful, less regimented, less sterile, less formalized in every way than that of the production-minded urban centers; and as the emphasis has, with further gains in production, shifted to consumption, this new way of life has tended to become more universal and is no longer purely an expression of discontent with the disordered city; for even tiny historic towns, like Villeneuve-les-Avignon, now have their new suburban fringe.

By the very nature of the retreat, the suburb could be identified by a number of related social characteristics. And first, it was a segregated community, set apart from the city, not merely by space but by class stratification: a sort of green ghetto dedicated to the elite. That smug Victorian phrase, "We keep ourselves to ourselves,"

From The City in History © *1961* by Lewis Mumford. Reprinted by permission of Harcourt, Brace & World, Inc., and Martin Secker & Warburg Limited.

expresses the spirit of the suburb, in contrast to the city; for the city, by its nature, is a multi-form non-segregated environment. Little groups may indeed form social islands within a city, as the various tribes tended to do in the early cities of Islam, or again as people from a Greek or a Polish village might form temporary nests together in the same block in Chicago or New York. But the metropolis was a mixture of people who came from different places, practiced different occupations, encountered other personalities, meeting and mingling, co-operating and clashing, the rich with the poor, the proud with the humble.

Except where the suburb enclosed an original small town core, it tended to remain a one-class community, with just a sufficient fringe of tradesmen and servants to keep it going—the latter often condemned to use the central metropolis as their dormitory. Segregation, in practice, means compulsory association, or at least cohabitation; for if there are any choices, they lie outside the immediate community. Hence the great residual freedom of the suburbanite is that of locomotion. For esthetic and intellectual stimulus, the suburb remains dependent upon the big city: the theater, the opera, the orchestra, the art gallery, the university, the museum are no longer part of the daily environment. The problem of re-establishing connections, on a regional rather than a metropolitan basis, is one of the main problems of city planning in our time.

Not merely did the suburb keep the busier, dirtier, more productive enterprises at a distance, it likewise pushed away the creative activities of the city. Here life ceased to be a drama, full of unexpected challenges and tensions and dilemmas: it became a bland ritual of competitive spending. "Half your trouble," Rudyard Kipling wrote to William James in 1896, "is the curse of America—sheer, hopeless, well-ordered boredom; and that is going some day to be the curse of the world." Kipling put his finger, at that early date, upon the weakness of the suburban way of life.

Thus the genuine biological benefits of the suburb were undermined by its psychological and social defects: above all, the irreality of its retreat. In the town poor men demonstrated: beggars held out their hands in the street: disease spread quickly from poor quarters to the residences of the comfortable, via the delivery boy, the washerwoman, the seamstress, or other necessary menials: the eye, if not carefully averted, would, on a five-minute walk in any direction, behold a slum, or at least a slum child, ragged and grimy.

Even in the heyday of Coketown, sensitive and intelligent souls could not remain long in such an environment without banding together to do something about it: they would exhort and agitate, hold meetings and form parades, draw up petitions and besiege legislators, extract money from the rich and dispense aid to the poor, founding soup kitchens and model tenements, passing housing legislation and acquiring land for parks, establishing hospitals and health centers, libraries and universities, in which the whole community played a part and benefited.

In the suburb one might live and die without marring the image of an innocent world, except when some shadow of its evil fell over a column in the newspaper. Thus the suburb served as an asylum for the preservation of illusion. Here domesticity could flourish, forgetful of the exploitation on which so much of it was based. Here individuality could prosper, oblivious of the pervasive regimentation beyond. This was not merely a child-centered environment: it was based on a childish view of the world, in which reality was sacrificed to the pleasure principle.

As an attempt to recover what was missing in the city, the suburban exodus could be amply justified, for it was concerned with primary human needs. But there was another side: the temptation to retreat from unpleasant realities, to shirk public duties, and to find the whole meaning of life in the most elemental social group, the family, or even in the still more isolated and self-centered individual. What was properly a beginning was treated as an end.

In many places, the change toward playful emptiness and civic irresponsibility can be dated. In private conversation Mr. Justice Brandeis once observed to me that he remembered the time, at the turn of the century, when the wealthy citizens of Boston told their sons, when they reached maturity: "Boston holds nothing for you except heavy taxes and political misrule. When you marry, pick out a suburb to build a house in, join the Country Club, and make your life center about your club, your home, and your children."

That advice was widely followed, not merely by the patricians of Boston and Philadelphia, but by their counterparts in many other big cities in the Western World. Though the result was a wide scattering of upper-class suburbs in the first and second wave of the metropolitan outflow, the exodus also quickened the inner corruption of the city and worked toward its destruction.

Only as a nursery for bringing up children did the suburb prove a more adequate environment, particularly in the early days of the railroad suburb, when each settlement was surrounded by a broad greenbelt of woods and fields. Here children could gambol safely, without supervision; and around the suburban schools was playspace so ample that it became the ideal requirement for all future schools: space for lawn tennis and croquet, for cricket or baseball, football or bowls. Emerson had noted these advantages clearly in his 'Journal,' in 1865: "There is no police so effective as a good hill and wide pasture in the neighborhood of a village, where the boys can run and play and dispose of their superfluous strength and spirits." The suburb established such play space as an essential part of the city: not to be crowded out by high land values. That was a permanent contribution.

But too soon, in breaking away from the city, the part became a substitute for the whole, even as a single phase of life, that of childhood, became the pattern for all the seven ages of man. As leisure generally increased, play became the serious business of life; and the golf course, the country club, the swimming pool, and the cocktail party became the frivolous counterfeits of a more varied and significant life. Thus in reacting against the disadvantages of the crowded city, the suburb itself became an over-specialized community, more and more committed to relaxation and play as ends in themselves. Compulsive play fast became the acceptable alternative to compulsive work: with small gain either in freedom or vital stimulus. Accordingly, the two modes of life blend into each other; for both in suburb and in metropolis, mass production, mass consumption, and mass recreation produce the same kind of standardized and denatured environment.

Even children suffered from this transformation of the whole community into a mere recreation area. For such a segregated community, composed of segregated economic strata, with little visible daily contact with the realities of the workaday world, placed an undue burden of education on the school and family. The smallest village where people still farm and fish and hunt, the drabbest industrial town whose population still engages in essential productive enterprises, has educational possibilities that the suburb lacks. In the end, the operative differences between the contemporary suburb and the big city become increasingly minimal: for in these seemingly different environments reality has been progressively reduced to what filters through the screen of the television set.

But both childhood and the suburb are transitional stages: so a well-planned urban community must have a place for other phases of life and other modes of living. A universal suburb is almost as much of a nightmare, humanly speaking, as a universal megalopolis: yet it is toward this proliferating nonentity that our present random or misdirected urban growth has been steadily tending. A large-scale pattern of expressways and airfields and sprawling car parks and golf-courses envelops a small-scale, increasingly shrunken mode of life.

Yet in its original effort, when the suburb approached nearest the romantic goal, it made a positive contribution to the emerging conception of the city as a mixed environment, interwoven in texture with the country; and many of these contributions need to be appraised and selectively adapted and improved, not discarded.

PROBLEMS FOR WRITING AND DISCUSSION

1. To what does Mumford attribute the universality of the shift to the suburbs?

2. What was the original distinction between suburb and city? Does it still hold?

3. American cities are said to be strangled by suburbs. Does this essay help explain why?

4. What does Mumford see as the greatest weakness in suburban life? Is his appraisal fair?

5. Compare Mumford's view of life in the suburbs with Margaret Mead's picture of the American family (p. 24). May the suburb be simply a larger biological unit dedicated to the propagation and preservation of life? What in the nature of such units makes them inevitably afflicted by "sheer, hopeless, well-ordered boredom"? What possibilities, between the extremes of labor and play, do both Mead and Mumford suggest?

6. Is the increasing demand for adult education understandable in the light of what Mumford calls a "denatured environment"? Do you think education is the answer to the tedium that curses the American suburb? Explain.

7. Mumford says that in both city and suburb "reality has been progressively reduced to what filters through the screen of the television set." To what extent is television educational and to what extent is it a substitute for *living* in a wider human community?

8. How does Mumford's picture of life in the suburb differ from Sevareid's picture of life in the small Midwestern town or Kazin's of life in the city?

9. Does Mumford's critique of the suburb bear out any of Matthews' criticisms of America in "You French?" (p. 99)?

10. Does the essay clarify Van Wyck Brooks's statement (see headnote on p. 76) about Mumford? To what extent do you think city planning can alleviate the problem Mumford presents? To what extent is this "proliferating nonentity" the result not of poor planning but of our "keeping to ourselves" in "an asylum for the preservation of illusion"? Do the problems of the world, the "universal" ills mentioned by Boorstin (p. 5), Commager (p. 14), and Mead as ones Americans have assumed or are affected by, suggest the need for an "asylum"?

11. "A universal suburb is almost as much of a nightmare . . . as a universal megalopolis," writes Mumford. His statement suggests that the emptiness and vastness Henry James (p. 82) comments on have disappeared. Has the loneliness of man under crowded conditions disappeared? How do you account for the lonely crowds?

Saratoga

HENRY JAMES

Henry James (1843-1916) is one of America's most distinguished novelists. Although, after 1866, he was to live most of the time in Europe, he did return to America a few times and recorded his impressions in Portraits of Places *(1883) and* The American Scene *(1911). Possibly because of his European education and residence, he looked at America with the eyes of a foreigner, amused at some things, disturbed by others. In his early novels America appears inimical to cultural and artistic sensibilities, and the American appears as the innocent abroad—ideas that recur with variations in his later fiction. While his travel pieces have never received the attention paid to his novels, they also view America with detachment, sophistication, and insight.*

The sentimental tourist makes images in advance; they grow up in his mind by a logic of their own. He finds himself thinking of an unknown, unseen place, as having such and such a shape and figure rather than such another. It assumes in his mind a certain complexion, a certain colour which frequently turns out to be singularly at variance with reality. For some reason or other, I had supposed Saratoga to be buried in a sort of elegant wilderness. I imagined a region of shady forest drives, with a bright, broad-terraced hotel gleaming here and there against a background of mysterious

Reprinted by permission of Charles Scribner's Sons from The American Scene *by Henry James. Copyright 1907 Charles Scribner's Sons; renewal copyright 1934 Henry James.*

groves and glades. I had made a cruelly small allowance for the stern vulgarities of life—for the shops and sidewalks and loafers, the complex machinery of a city of pleasure. The fault was so wholly my own that it is quite without bitterness that I proceed to affirm that the Saratoga of experience is sadly different from this. I confess, however, that it has always seemed to me that one's visions, on the whole, gain more than they lose by being transmuted into fact. There is an essential indignity in indefiniteness; you cannot allow for accidents and details until you have seen them. They give more to the imagination than they receive from it. I frankly admit, therefore, that the Saratoga of reality is a much more satisfactory place than the all-too-primitive Elysium I had constructed. It is indeed, as I say, immensely different. There is a vast number of brick—nay, of asphalt—sidewalks, a great many shops, and a magnificent array of loafers. But what indeed are you to do at Saratoga—the morning draught having been achieved—unless you loaf? "Que faire en un gîte à moins que l'on ne songe?" Loafers being assumed, of course shops and sidewalks follow. The main avenue of Saratoga does not scruple to call itself Broadway. The untravelled reader may form a very accurate idea of it by recalling as distinctly as possible, not indeed the splendours of that famous thoroughfare, but the secondary charms of the Sixth Avenue. The place has what the French would call the "accent" of the Sixth Avenue. Its two main features are the two monster hotels which stand facing each other along a goodly portion of its course. One, I believe, is considered much better than the other—less of a monster and more of a refuge—but in appearance there is little choice between them. Both are immense brick structures, directly on the crowded, noisy street, with vast covered piazzas running along the façade, supported by great iron posts. The piazza of the Union Hotel, I have been repeatedly informed, is the largest "in the world." There are a number of objects in Saratoga, by the way, which in their respective kinds are the finest in the world. One of these is Mr. John Morrissey's casino. I bowed my head submissively to this statement, but privately I thought of the blue Mediterranean, and the little white promontory of Monaco, and the silver-gray verdure of olives, and the view across the outer sea toward the bosky cliffs of Italy. The Congress waters, too, it is well known, are excellent in the superlative degree; this I am perfectly willing to maintain.

The piazzas of these great hotels may very well be the biggest of all piazzas. They have not architectural beauty; but they doubtless serve their purpose—that of affording sitting-space in the open air to an immense number of persons. They are, of course, quite the best places to observe the Saratoga world. In the evening, when the "boarders" have all come forth and seated themselves in groups, or have begun to stroll in (not always, I regret to say, to the sad detriment of the dramatic interest, bisexual) couples, the big heterogeneous scene affords a great deal of entertainment. Seeing it for the first time, the observer is likely to assure himself that he has neglected an important item in the sum of American manners. The rough brick wall of the house, illumined by a line of flaring gaslights, forms a natural background to the crude, impermanent, discordant tone of the assembly. In the larger of the two hotels, a series of long windows open into an immense parlour—the largest, I suppose, in the world, and the most scantily furnished in proportion to its size. A few dozen rocking-chairs, an equal number of small tables, tripods to the eternal ice-pitcher, serve chiefly to emphasize the vacuous grandeur of the spot. On the piazza, in the outer multitude, ladies largely prevail, both by numbers and (you are not slow to perceive) by distinction of appearance. The good old times of Saratoga, I believe, as of the world in general, are rapidly passing away. The time was when it was the chosen resort of none but "nice people." At the present day, I hear it constantly affirmed, "the company is dreadfully mixed." What society may have been at Saratoga when its elements were thus simple and severe, I can only vaguely and mournfully conjecture. I confine myself to the dense, democratic, vulgar Saratoga of the current year. You are struck, to begin with, at the hotels, by the numerical superiority of the women; then, I think, by their personal superiority.

It is incontestably the case that in appearance, in manner, in grace and completeness of aspect, American women surpass their husbands and brothers; the relation being reversed among some of the nations of Europe. Attached to the main entrance of the Union Hotel, and adjoining the ascent from the street to the piazza, is a "stoop" of mighty area, which, at most hours of the day and evening, is a favoured lounging-place of men. I should add, after the remark I have just made, that even in the appearance of the usual American male there seems to me to be a certain plastic intention. It is true that the lean, sallow, angular Yankee of tradition is dignified mainly by a look of decision, a hint of unimpassioned volition, the air of "smartness." This in some degree redeems him, but it fails to make him handsome. But in the average American of the present time, the typical leanness and sallowness are less than in his fathers, and the individual acuteness is at once equally marked and more frequently united with merit of form. Casting your eye over a group of your fellow-citizens in the portico of the Union Hotel, you will be inclined to admit that, taking the good with the bad, they are worthy sons of the great Republic. I have found, at any rate, a great deal of entertainment in watching them. They suggest to my fancy the swarming vastness—the multifarious possibilities and activities—of our young civilization. They come from the uttermost ends of the Union—from San Francisco, from New Orleans, from Alaska. As they sit with their white hats tilted forward, and their chairs tilted back, and their feet tilted up, and their cigars and toothpicks forming various angles with these various lines, I seem to see in their faces a tacit reference to the affairs of a continent. They are obviously persons of experience—of a somewhat narrow and monotonous experience certainly; an experience of which the diamonds and laces which their wives are exhibiting hard by are, perhaps, the most substantial and beautiful result; but, at any rate, they have *lived*, in every fibre of the will. For the time, they are lounging with the negro waiters, and the boot-blacks, and the news-vendors; but it was not in lounging that they gained their hard wrinkles and the level impartial regard which they direct from beneath their hat-rims. They are not the mellow fruit of a society which has walked hand-in-hand with tradition and culture; they are hard nuts, which have grown and ripened as they could. When they talk among themselves, I seem to hear the cracking of the shells.

If the men are remarkable, the ladies are wonderful. Saratoga is famous, I believe, as the place of all places in America where women adorn themselves most, or as the place, at least, where the greatest amount of dressing may be seen by the greatest number of people. Your first impression is therefore of the—what shall I call it?—of the abundance of petticoats. Every woman you meet, young or old, is attired with a certain amount of richness, and with whatever good taste may be compatible with such a mode of life. You behold an interesting, indeed a quite momentous spectacle; the democratization of elegance. If I am to believe what I hear—in fact, I may say what I overhear—many of these sumptuous persons have enjoyed neither the advantages of a careful education nor the privileges of an introduction to society. She walks more or less of a queen, however, each uninitiated nobody. She often has, in dress, an admirable instinct of elegance and even of what the French call "chic." This instinct occasionally amounts to a sort of passion; the result then is wonderful. You look at the coarse brick walls, the rusty iron posts of the piazza, at the shuffling negro waiters, the great tawdry steamboat-cabin of a drawing-room—you see the tilted ill-dressed loungers on the steps—and you finally regret that a figure so exquisite should have so vulgar a setting. Your resentment, however, is speedily tempered by reflection. You feel the impertinence of your old reminiscences of English and French novels, and of the dreary social order in which privacy was the presiding genius and women arrayed themselves for the appreciation of the few. The crowd, the tavern-loungers, the surrounding ugliness and tumult and license, constitute the social medium of the young lady you are so inconsistent as to admire; she is dressed for publicity. The thought fills you with a kind of awe. The social order of tradition is far away indeed, and as for the transatlantic novels, you begin to doubt whether she is so amiably curious as to read even the silliest of them. To be dressed up to the eyes is obviously to give pledges to idleness. I have been forcibly struck with the apparent absence of any warmth and richness of detail in the lives of these wonderful ladies of the piazzas. We are freely accused of being an eminently wasteful people; and I know of few things which so largely warrant the accusation as the fact that these conspicuous *élégantes* adorn themselves, socially speaking, to so little purpose. To dress for every one is, practically, to dress for no one. There are few prettier sights than a charmingly-dressed woman, gracefully established in some shady spot, with a piece of needle-work or embroidery, or a book. Nothing very serious is accomplished, probably, but an aesthetic principle is recognized. The embroidery and the book are a tribute to culture, and I suppose they really figure somewhere out of the opening scenes of French comedies. But here at Saratoga, at any hour of morning or evening, you may see a hundred rustling beauties whose rustle is their sole occupation. One lady in particular there is, with whom it appears to be an inexorable fate that she shall be nothing more than dressed. Her apparel is tremendously modern, and my remarks would be much illumined if I had the learning necessary for describing it. I can only say that every evening for a fortnight she has revealed herself as a fresh creation. But she especially, as I say, has struck me as a person dressed beyond her life and her opportunities. I resent on her behalf—or on behalf at least of her finery—the extreme severity of her circumstances. What is she, after all, but a "regular boarder"? She ought to sit on the terrace of a stately castle, with a great baronial park shutting out the undressed world, and bandy quiet small-talk with an ambassador or a duke. My imagination is shocked when I behold her seated in gorgeous relief against the dusty clapboards of the hotel, with her beautiful hands folded in her silken lap, her head drooping slightly beneath the weight of her *chignon*, her lips parted in a vague contemplative gaze at Mr. Helmbold's well-known advertisement on the opposite fence, her husband beside her reading the New York *Herald*.

I have indeed observed cases of a sort of splendid social isolation here, which are not without a certain amount of pathos—people who know no one, who have money and finery and possessions, only no friends. Such at least is my inference, from the lonely grandeur with which I see them invested. Women, of course, are the most helpless victims of this cruel situation, although it must be said that they befriend each other with a generosity for which we hardly give them credit. I have seen women, for instance, at various "hops," approach their lonely sisters and invite them to waltz, and I have seen the fair invited surrender themselves eagerly to this humiliating embrace. Gentlemen at Saratoga are at a much higher premium than at European watering-places. It is an old story that in this country we have no "leisure-class"—the class from which the Saratogas of Europe recruit a large number of their male frequenters. A few months ago, I paid a visit to an English "bath," commemorated in various works of fiction, where, among many visible points of difference from American resorts, the most striking was the multitude of young men who had the whole day on their hands. While their sweethearts and sisters are waltzing together, our own young men are rolling up greenbacks in counting-houses and stores. I was recently reminded in another way, one evening, of the unlikeness of Saratoga to Cheltenham. Behind the biggest of the big hotels is a large planted yard, which it is the fashion at Saratoga to talk of as a "park," and which is perhaps believed to be the biggest in the world. At one end of it stands a great ballroom, approached by a range of wooden steps. It was late in the evening; the room, in spite of the intense heat, was blazing with light and the orchestra thundering a mighty waltz. A group of loungers, including myself, were hanging about to watch the ingress of the festally-minded. In the basement of the edifice, sunk beneath the ground, a noisy auctioneer, in his shirt and trousers, black in the face with heat and vociferation, was selling "pools" of the races to a dense group of frowsy betting-men. At the foot of the steps was stationed a man in a linen coat and straw hat, without waistcoat or necktie, to take the tickets of the ball-goers. As the latter failed to arrive in sufficient numbers, a musician came forth to the top of the steps and blew a loud summons on a horn. After this they began to straggle along. On this occasion, certainly, the company promised to be decidedly "mixed." The women, as usual, were much bedizened, though without any constant adhesion to the technicalities of full-dress. The men adhered to it neither in the letter nor the spirit. The possessor of a pair of satin-shod feet, twinkling beneath an uplifted volume of gauze and lace and flowers, tripped up the steps with her gloved hand on the sleeve of a railway "duster." Now and then two ladies arrived alone; generally a group of them approached under convoy of a single man. Children were freely scattered among their elders, and frequently a small boy would deliver his ticket and enter the glittering portal, beautifully unembarrassed. Of the children of Saratoga there would be wondrous things to relate. I believe that, in spite of their valuable aid, the festival of which I speak was rated rather a "fizzle." I see it advertised that they are soon to have, for their own peculiar benefit, a "Masquerade and Promenade Concert, beginning at 9 P.M." I observe that they usually open the "hops," and that it is only after their elders have borrowed confidence from the sight of their unfaltering paces that the latter dare to dance. You meet them far into the evening, roaming over the piazzas and corridors of the hotels—the little girls especially—lean, pale, formidable. Occasionally childhood confesses itself, even when maternity resists, and you see at eleven o'clock at night some poor little bedizened precocity collapsed in slumber in a lonely wayside chair. The part played by children in society here is only an additional instance of the wholesale equalization of the various social atoms which is the distinctive feature of collective Saratoga. A man in a "duster" at a ball is as good as a man in regulation-garments; a young woman dancing with another young woman is as good as a young woman dancing with a young man; a child of ten is as good as a woman of thirty; a double negative in conversation is rather better than a single.

An important feature in many a watering-place is the facility for leaving it a little behind you and tasting of the unmitigated country. You may wander to some shady hillside and sentimentalize upon the vanity of a high civilization. But at Saratoga civilization holds you fast. The most important feature of the place, perhaps, is the impossibility of carrying out any such pastoral dream. The surrounding country is a charming wilderness, but the roads are so abominably bad that walking and driving are alike unprofitable. Of course, however, if you are bent upon a walk, you will take a walk. There is a striking contrast between the concentrated prodigality of life in the immediate neighbourhood of the hotels and the pastoral solitudes into which a walk of half an hour may lead you. You have left the American citizen and his wife, the orchestras, the pools, the precocious infants, the cocktails, the importations from Worth, but a mile or two behind, but already the forest is primeval and the landscape is without figures. Nothing could be less manipulated than the country about Saratoga. The heavy roads are little more than sandy wheel-tracks; by the tangled wayside the blackberries wither unpicked. The horizon undulates with an air of having it all its own way. There are no white villages gleaming in the distance, no spires of churches, no salient details. It is all green, lonely, and vacant. If you wish to enjoy a detail, you must stop beneath a cluster of pines and listen to the murmur of the softly-troubled air, or follow upward the scaly straightness of their trunks to where the afternoon light gives it a colour. Here and there on a slope by the roadside stands a rough unpainted farmhouse, looking as if its dreary blackness were the result of its standing dark and lonely amid so many months—and such a wide expanse—of winter snow. It has turned black by contrast. The principal feature of the grassy unfurnished yard is the great wood-pile, telling grimly of the long reversion of the summer. For the time, however, it looks down contentedly enough over a goodly appanage of grain-fields and orchards, and I can fancy that it may be amusing to be a boy there. But to be a man, it must be quite what the lean, brown, serious farmers physiognomically hint it to be. You have, however, at the present season, for your additional beguilement, on the eastern horizon, the vision of the long bold chain of the Green Mountains, clad in that single coat of simple, candid blue which is the favourite garment of our American hills. As a visitor, too, you have for an afternoon's excursion your choice between a couple of lakes. Saratoga Lake, the larger and more distant of the two, is the goal of the regular afternoon drive. Above the shore is a well-appointed tavern—"Moon's" it is called by the voice of fame—where you may sit upon a broad piazza and partake of fried potatoes and "drinks"; the latter, if you happen to have come from poor dislicensed Boston, a peculiarly gratifying privilege. You enjoy the felicity sighed for by that wanton Italian lady of the anecdote, when, one summer evening, to the sound of music, she wished that to eat an ice were a sin. The other lake is small, and its shores are unadorned by any edifice but a boat-house, where you may hire a skiff and pull yourself out into the minnow-tickled, wood-circled oval. Here, floating in its darkened half, while you watch on the opposite shore the tree-stems, white and sharp in the declining sunlight, and their foliage whitening and whispering in the breeze, and you feel that this little solitude is part of a greater and more portentous solitude, you may recall certain passages of Ruskin, in which he dwells upon the needfulness of some human association, however remote, to make natural scenery fully impressive. You may recall that magnificent page in which he relates having tried with such fatal effect, in a battle-haunted valley of the Jura, to fancy himself in a nameless solitude of our own continent. You feel around you, with irresistible force, the eloquent silence of undedicated nature—the absence of serious associations, the nearness, indeed, of the vulgar and trivial associations of the least complete of all the cities of pleasure—you feel this, and you wonder what it is you so deeply and calmly enjoy. You make up your mind, possibly, that it is a great advantage to be able at once to enjoy Mr. Ruskin and to enjoy Mr. Ruskin's alarms. And hereupon you return to your hotel and read the New York papers on the plan of the French campaign and the Nathan murder.

PROBLEMS FOR WRITING AND DISCUSSION

1. What specific American characteristics emerge from Henry James's description of Saratoga and its frequenters?

2. Why does James admire Saratoga at the same time that he finds it full of the "stern vulgarities of life"?

3. Saratoga is no longer as fashionable as it was in James's time. What American town or resort would you choose as comparable today to Saratoga in 1870? Explain.

4. James says that the ladies of Saratoga "are wonderful," but that their lives lack "any warmth and richness of detail." What does he mean? Compare his estimate with what Margaret Mead has to say about the American woman.

5. What is the function of the description, near the end of the essay, of the surrounding countryside? Does it help you understand the prominence of Saratoga in 1870?

6. James focuses first on the woman dressed to the hilt sitting essentially isolated and then on the isolated farmhouse. How does his allusion to Ruskin unite these two images in a single significance? Is the "aloneness" you sense here comparable to that which Kazin (p. 64) describes?

7. Does his description of Saratoga capture "the swarming vastness—the multifarious activities—of our young civilization" that James speaks of?

8. What does James mean by the phrase "democratization of elegance" (p. 86)? Does he present evidence of other kinds of "democratization"? Would you say that he approves of them?

9. How, as James sees it, does Saratoga differ from a European resort? Are there indications that James regards America as a foreigner would rather than as a native would? Is his alienation from the scenes and people of America an implicit comment on American character—his own included?

10. In what ways does James see American children, as they are displayed at Saratoga, as a breed apart from other children of the world? How are these children different from those of the twentieth century described by Mead (p. 24)?

11. Despite differences in dress and dance music, does James's picture of vacationing Americans contain features with which you are familiar from your own experience?

Camping

BERNARD De VOTO

Bernard De Voto (1897-1955) was teacher, editor, and finally writer, interspersing his sometimes acidulous, always provocative, monthly essay for "The Easy Chair" of Harper's Magazine *with a stream of articles, short stories, and books. The role of the West in shaping the American character was central to much that he wrote, most notably in his famous trilogy—*The Year of Decision: 1846 *(1946),* Across the Wide Missouri *(1948), and* The Course of Empire *(1952). He wrote an undefined kind of history, filled with precise detail, but detail used to create atmosphere rather than to transmit facts. His theme was that the geography of the American continent "conditioned our history." It was men's "response to the continent," he once said, that transformed them from Europeans into Americans.*

Camp is pitched near some watercourse, a small creek or a rushing mountain river, with firewood and grass at hand. If there has been no Indian sign and if there is no reason to apprehend Indians, the fire will be built up when the meal is over. Here is the winesap air of the high places, the clear green sky of evening fading to a dark that brings the stars within arm's length, the cottonwoods along the creek rustling in the wind. The smell of meat has brought the wolves and coyotes almost to the circle of firelight. They skulk just

---

This selection from Bernard De Voto's Across the Wide Missouri *(1947) is reprinted by permission of and arrangement with Houghton Mifflin Company, the authorized publishers.*

beyond it; sometimes a spurt of flame will turn their eyes to gold; they howl and attack one another, and farther out in the dark the howls of their relatives diminish over the plains. In running season there will be the bellowing of the bulls. Horses and mules crop the bunch grass at the end of their lariats or browse on leaves along the creek. The firelight flares and fades in the wind's rhythm on the faces of men in whose minds are the vistas and the annals of the entire West.

It is the time of fulfillment, the fullness of time, the moment lived for itself alone. The mountain men were a tough race, as many selective breeds of Americans have had to be; their courage, skill, and mastery of the conditions of their chosen life were absolute or they would not have been here. Nor would they have been here if they had not responded to the loveliness of the country and found in their way of life something precious beyond safety, gain, comfort, and family life. Besides the specific attributes of that way of life and its country, it is fair to point out an extremity, perhaps the maximum, of American individualism and gusto. Moreover, solitude had given them a surpassing gift of friendship and simple survival proved the sharpness of their wits. There were few books and few trappers were given to reading what there were: talk was everything. In this hour of function there was the talk of friends and equals.

The Americans, and especially the Americans who live in the open, have always been storytellers—one need recall only the rivermen, the lumberjacks, the cowmen, or in fact the loafers round any stove at a rural crossroads—but there have been no stories beyond those told by the map-minded breakers of trails, hunters of beavers, and exterminators of Indians. Most of their yarning has been lost to history, but it was a chronicle of every watercourse, peak, park, and gulch in a million square miles, a chronicle of chance happening suddenly and expectation reversed, of violent action, violent danger, violent mirth, of Indians whose thought was not commensurate with white thinking and therefore inexhaustibly fascinating, a fantasy of mythological beavers or grizzlies, of Welsh Indians or

Munchies or the Fair God, of supernatural beings and spectral visitants and startling medicine and heroes who were cousin to Paul Bunyan. It was a shop talk, trapping, hunting, trailing, fighting and always the lay of the land and old fields revisited and new fields to be found, water and starvation and trickery and feasts. How Long Hatcher had lifted those Apache scalps. How one who was with us last year was eviscerated by a grizzly or gutshot by a Blackfoot. How Old Gave outsmarted a Blackfoot war party, or Tom Fitzpatrick lay in his crevice while the Gros Ventres looked for him, or a Delaware, one of the Ishmaels of the West, had taunted the Arikaras who were killing him piecemeal. How one's partner had wandered into a canyon quite unknown even to these masters of geography, how another had stolen the daughter of a Sioux medicine man or a Taos rancher, how a third had forted up behind his slaughtered horse and held off fifty Comanches. How we came into Taos or the Pueblo of Los Angeles and the willing women there and the brandy we drank and the horses we stole.

Till at last the fire sank. The mountain man rolled up in his robe or blanket on his apishamore, loaded rifle beside him, and knife and pistols within reach, and might lie awhile listening to the wind and water and the coyotes. He might wake a few hours later, kick fuel on the embers, and roast another half-dozen ribs, eating alone while his companions slept and the horses pawed at the end of their pickets. Then sleep again till a grayness ran with the wind across the sky, in the shuddering cold of a mountain dawn someone shouting "Leve! Leve!" and it was time for breakfast on buffalo meat and the day's hazard of hunt or trail. . . . It was a good life.

PROBLEMS FOR WRITING AND DISCUSSION

1. De Voto, Sevareid (p. 45), and James (p. 82) stress individualism as a trait of the Americans about whom they write. Are these three authors using the word *individualism* in the same way? Explain.

2. Do you think De Voto sentimentalizes the mountain man and his way of life? Explain.

3. In what ways does the life of the men De Voto describes meet Mead's specifications (p. 24) for the time-honored way men have become men?

4. Although the minds of these mountain men were filled with the "vistas and the annals of the entire West," De Voto asserts that "the moment lived for itself alone." What truth inheres in this seeming paradox?

5. The mountain men, De Voto believes, "responded to the loveliness of the country and found in their way of life something precious beyond safety, gain, comfort, and family life." Do you think such a response has passed with the closing of the American frontier, or is such a response to "new frontiers" still possible to "map-minded" men? Upon what do you base your answer?

6. The mountain men, according to De Voto, reacted to external threats (wolves, Indians, topographical perils) with "individualism and gusto." Judging from the essays you have read, would you say that Americans today react with "individualism and gusto" to the perils of their condition (overpopulation, ideological defeat, global extermination)? Justify your answer.

7. Is it conceivable that, just as the frontier era now seems to us "the good old days," our era will seem to future generations a time of golden opportunity? Or do you think the challenges of our era surpass the capacity of individual response?

3. *Citizens and Leaders*

"You French?"

T. S. MATTHEWS

T[homas] S[tanley] Matthews (1901-   ) began his career in 1925 as a writer for The New Republic. In 1929 he moved to Time and worked there for twenty-four years as book reviewer, national affairs editor, managing editor, and finally editor. He ended his years as a journalist convinced that the press was "really a part of the entertainment business," and that it "had no power of accomplishment, *though it did have a negative power—to debase taste, harm individuals, etc.*" He retired to London, where he has since written three books, including his autobiography, Name and Address *(1960)*, and O My America! Notes on a Trip *(1962), which ends with these lines: "I hope and try to believe, against an increasing weight of evidence, that our American experiment might yet succeed."*

One unseasonably hot May morning in the forties I landed in New York at a North River pier. With my fellow passengers I lined up to wait my turn for a customs inspector and, when he had passed my three suitcases, queued again to wait my turn for a porter. In spite of the large signs, prominently displayed, proclaiming that there should be no tipping, I knew enough to give my porter a dollar. But I had forgotten that his duties ended at the top of the luggage escalator, and that at the bottom I had to collect my bags and hand them over—with another dollar—to one of the seedy nondescripts hanging about the pier entrance, who would then carry

From Name and Address, *copyright © 1960 by T. S. Matthews. Reprinted by permission of Simon and Schuster, Inc.*

them all of ten feet to a taxi. This last bit of racketeering seemed to me, for some reason, one too many; I seized my suitcases and flung myself and them across the pavement and into the nearest cab.

Momentarily I had upset the system, and the system resented it. As we drove off, hard words followed me. The taxi driver turned his head and said, mildly,

"What seems to be the trouble?"

I told him. I tried to say, as briefly and pungently as I could, what I thought of the welcoming gauntlet an incoming passenger had to run, and of the whole inefficient and damnable system. I paused for breath. The taxi driver said,

"You French?"

Can I really claim to be a good American? I was brought up to believe that Americans can be divided into three classes: good, bad and expatriate. No American citizen who lives out of the country, unless his job demands it, can be considered a good American. Rather to my surprise but not at all against my grain I find myself living in London, but I have no job there, so I haven't that excuse; I simply prefer London to the other cities I know, and I like living in a city.

I know other Americans who feel the same way—though in their case their favorite place to live may be Paris or Rome or Florence —but they have an excuse: their job keeps them there. If it didn't, they would get another job that did. Of the hundreds of thousands of Americans who live abroad, a great many don't regard themselves as exiles but as Americans who are luckier than most. And a few, a very few, like Ernest Hemingway, Jacob Epstein, T. S. Eliot and Bernard Berenson, have made such resounding names for themselves that they are not thought of as expatriates, although Hemingway and Eliot certainly are, and so were Epstein and Berenson.

The government of the United States continues to tax me but will no longer let me vote. If I can live wherever I want to, that seems to me a fair exchange. And as Frank Kent used to say, a contribution to the party war chest is a more effective way of exercising your franchise than marking a ballot. Should I still be allowed to have an opinion about American politics, or to take an interest in U.S. domestic affairs? At any rate, since there's no law against it as yet, I do. And what seems to be the trouble? (There's that taxi driver again.)

First of all, I object to being disqualified as an observer of the American scene. I can't help being an observer of that scene, and an inveterately interested one; and when my friends in the United States tell me, "Ah, you're out of touch," I retort, "But perhaps in focus!" You do get a larger view from a distance, though you lose the details. These are figures of speech, I know, and can only suggest the argument, not define its terms. There is an argument, or at any rate a difference of opinion, between me and my country—or the people who I think have run away with the country.

In the summer of 1956 I spent a day in Libertyville, Illinois, at Adlai Stevenson's farm. He had just been nominated, for the second time, as the Democratic candidate for the presidency, and his campaign was about to get under way. Half a dozen advisers had come to plan the campaign strategy, and the meeting went on almost all day. I was there simply as a friend; but at one point Stevenson asked me, "What do *you* think?"

I said, "I think you should declare war on Ohio."

He laughed; the others stared, and then went on with their serious discussion. And Ohio won again, as expected.

I don't mind being considered a bad Ohioan or a renegade Middlewesterner; and besides, anyone, from Lincoln down, is allowed to change his state with impunity. It's only when you're thought to have cut the umbilical cord that binds you to your native land that your Americanism comes in question. But can you cut the cord?

It seems to me a difficult thing for an American—and for me impossible—to change his nationality, whatever his name and address happen to be. If I never saw the United States again I would never cease to know it as my country; that consciousness goes deeper than loyalty or patriotism—two words that have been dirtied by an ugly kind of American—it is in my blood. I was born and bred there, I hope to return there often, I expect to be buried there. Meantime, as an American who is lucky enough to be able to choose, I think I have a right to travel and live where I like. I shouldn't like to be compelled to live anywhere. I would hate to have to live in Russia, or China, or Hungary, or under any dictatorship. But I shouldn't like to be compelled—by a job or by a law—to live in the United States either. For this is not my day in America. This day belongs to the "100 percenters," the new-rich Texans, the Madison Avenue boys, the professional patriots, the organization men, the hard-eyed herdsmen of political Yahoos, the dogs that eat dogs. If they have really taken over America, and taken it over for keeps, then I think the American experiment has failed. The dinosaur, its tiny brain still dreaming of paradisal forests, is plodding witlessly towards the asphalt lake.

I don't think, however, that the American experiment has utterly failed. Nevertheless, unless I have completely misunderstood its purpose, neither can I see that it has anywhere near succeeded. I should like to think that the majority of Americans are also dissatisfied and disappointed by what we have so far accomplished as a nation. But I don't. Much as I'd like to, I can see little evidence for the hopeful assumption that there are still so many rugged individuals and independent cusses in the United States that they really form a crypto-majority. It looks to me more as if they were a formless, scattered and dominated minority. If it were not so, how could half the country, however shamefacedly, have followed a cynical thug like McCarthy? From fear, yes—fear of Russia? Fear of fear itself. And fear will always find an object. How could an American be proud of his country, how could he help being ashamed, when the voice of McCarthy was heard throughout the world, and was allowed to be heard, as the voice of America? Demagogues, the constant parasites on democracy, come and go, but the rabble whose fears and hatreds they foment are always there to be roused. "McCarthyism" is not dead; it existed long before McCarthy and will long survive him, under different names and other auspices.

Like the hysteria it feeds on, it lies, a quiescent but malignant growth, under the thin American skin.

What has become of the American idea, the hope of raising a standard to which all just men could repair? Has it really petered out into a "dream," or worse, into a nervously advertised and jealously guarded "way of life"? I believe that the American experiment was intended as a conscious revolution in human affairs; that the new nation was to be not only an anthology of the best in Europe, it was to evolve a way of living, for all comers, so superior to Europe's ways that the new republic might some day become unique among the nations—a promised land that would honor its promise to any decent applicant.

What has become of that enormous invitation, and the faith it was based on? From the skeptical or European point of view the invitation and its subsequent withdrawal were alike regulated by economic demand. Once America badly needed cheap labor, and rationalized its need by declaring a limitless capacity for making new American silk purses out of any old European sows' ears. The need fulfilled, the United States will now accept only a strictly limited quantity, grading its quotas by an arbitrary assessment of quality—northern and western Europeans are better stuff than southern Europeans, and Orientals almost unusable. The factory of liberty has stockpiled all the raw material it can handle.

America's faith in its own experiment has been further weakened by a growing preoccupation with self-protection—it used to be called "isolationism" and is now "security": both are fancy synonyms for "the fear of being robbed." It is a preoccupation, most Americans say, that has been forced on them by the threat of Russian aggression. But no Communist threat existed when America began to build up its tariff walls and dam immigration to a trickle: these were protective devices against the whole untrustworthy and envious world. The United States has become an exclusive society. Our demagogues now orate about *preserving* America's liberties, not attaining them. Security is the present goal of the American experiment.

In short, the experiment is over. There are still a few loose ends to be tied up—such as making the economy depression-proof, teaching college boys and girls to read and write, raising the Negroes (and their oppressors, the white trash of both North and South) up from third-class to second-class citizens—but America is a huge success, the greatest success that ever came down the pike. All "good Americans" think so, anyhow, no matter what the rest of the world says. For the result of the American experiment is democracy. As every American schoolboy knows, the United States not only invented democracy but has patented it, and owns the worldwide copyright.

"Democracy" is a word rapidly becoming peculiar to America, and almost meaningless elsewhere. (The Communist "people's democracies" are helping to complete the general confusion.) I think the British, who themselves use the word sparingly though they practice the thing itself more thoroughly than we do, are often puzzled by what Americans mean by democracy. What they mean is American democracy, and that means the American way of life. When Americans get wrought up, as they have been lately, their religious zeal for this central article of faith tends to get out of hand. Then those who do not conform 100 per cent to the tenets of Americanism, "loyalty to the American way of life," and who for any reason are reluctant to "stand up and be counted" on the demand of any rascally patrioteer, are tagged as bad Americans, probably traitors and possibly Communist spies.

A few years ago a retired American general announced to an approving civilian dinner party that any American citizen who refused to jump to his feet, whenever called on, and swear allegiance to the Constitution, should be shot. No one at that particular table, luckily, was packing a shooting iron.

Every morning, in every public school, every American school child recites a Shinto prayer—i.e., pledges allegiance to the flag. The flag is regarded not as a symbol, as in other countries, but as a sacred object in itself; its desecration is blasphemy, and to allow a fold of it to touch the ground is pollution. In like manner, the Constitution has replaced the Bible as an object of veneration. The Constitution too is regarded as a sacred object, a more-than-human document, almost literally inspired.

To make the world safe for American democracy the world will have to be, by one means or another, converted to it. So far, America has drawn back from the implications of this logical extreme. Even Russia seems to have temporarily abandoned its equally logical theory of world-wide revolution. But in each case the logic is there, waiting—and others see it, if we don't. Americans did not like the Germans calling themselves, with blood-curdling sincerity, "the master race." Nor did anybody else. And yet Americans wonder why the United States, with all its generous and well-meaning strength, is so widely disliked and distrusted. The outspoken German claim to be the master race was based on the fancied purity of their bloodlines. The tacit American claim is based on the fancied moral superiority of America.

If you ask the bystanders, you will of course get an un-American (i.e., wrong) view. No responsible American has ever quite said so, but the present aim of America seems to be the moral domination of the world. Americans hate and fear—or say they hate and fear— any sort of world domination, by anybody. It is fear of Communist domination that steers American policy. But suppose that American might could make American right everywhere predominant? Would Americans really hate and fear that world-wide domination? Some Americans, not so long ago, were dreaming of a *Pax Americana,* clamping the volcanic surface of the world together. And such an enforced peace, in that dreamy American view, was to be brought about and maintained by a judicious greasing of palms (tactics) and a show of bombs and intercontinental missiles (strategy).

I do not believe that America is pre-eminent in every respect, or even that it is the real leader of the Western world. It is acknowledged to be the richest and claims to be the most powerful country on earth; but I think the grimly emerging fact is that the West has no real leader. The East has its herdsmen and suffers the brutal discipline of the herd. If Eisenhower and Macmillan and Khrushchev and Mao* are really in charge of our affairs, then God help us all. The world is going to hell, and has been ever since its record began to be kept. Even so, even if the worst happens, as I think it usually does, I believe that some day in the future there will be another America, because the idea behind the American experiment is too tough to die.

The most pathetic fallacy of our barbarous and backward age is that man is in control of his fate. We cling desperately to this sentimental notion, though its true fanatics are mainly to be found among the Communists. Even their fanaticism cannot stand up forever against the evidence. Men once, at certain times and in some places, knew more and better; they knew that "history" is an ambiguous account of man's superficial disasters and recoveries, and that the only fragments of his real record are to be found in the capriciously preserved or capriciously destroyed works of his art. And that human life, whether it be a mystery, tragedy, dream or fungoid disease, is private and personal—in a slave state as in a free republic, in Russia as in America. The only thing I can do about fate is to bow to it as politely as I can, and all I can hope to do about my own life, which has some untraceable connections with others' lives, is to try to find out who I am. One thing I know about myself is that I am an American—whatever that means.

Being born an American may be luckier, much luckier, than being born a Chinese or a Portuguese or a "citizen" of the Dominican Republic, but it cannot free you from the human condition. We're all in that together, separately and alone.

PROBLEMS FOR WRITING AND DISCUSSION

1. How is the meaning of the title clarified by the selection as a whole?
2. Matthews affirms his identity as an American yet does not want to live in America. Why? How, specifically, has America disappointed his expectations?

---

* These names will give place to other names.

3. What would Matthews find objectionable in the people or the resort of Saratoga that James describes (p. 82)? Would Matthews approve of Commager's generalizations (p. 14) about America?

4. Frank Kent, who died in 1958, was one of the most distinguished political reporters of his day. Does his estimate of the ballot sound cynical or sensible to you? Why?

5. Why did Matthews suggest that Adlai Stevenson, presidential candidate in 1952 and 1956, "should declare war on Ohio"?

6. What does Matthews mean when he calls the United States the "factory of liberty"?

7. Matthews, like other writers in this part, is alarmed by the "witch-hunting" in America. To what does he attribute it?

8. Is Matthews justified in charging that America would dominate the world if her "might could make American right everywhere predominant"?

9. "I believe," says Matthews, "that the American experiment was intended as a conscious revolution in human affairs; . . . that . . . it was to evolve a way of living . . . so superior to Europe's ways that the new republic might some day become unique among nations—a promised land. . . ." Yet he equates the American claim to "fancied moral superiority" with the "equally logical theory" of the Communists and with the German theory of racial superiority. Is he logically consistent? Explain.

10. Although Matthews assumes that Americans are responsible for the failure of their experiment, he regards the doctrine "that man is in control of his fate" as a pernicious fallacy. Does he resolve this seeming contradiction?

11. Matthews concludes that since there is no escape from the "human condition" the best he can do with his life is to find out who he is. What one thing does he know for sure about himself? In the light of Boorstin's remarks (p. 5), is Matthews' search for identity typical of the American?

12. Kazin (p. 64) spoke of his dream of world-wide unity. Has his dream anything in common with the aspirations of the American experiment noted by Matthews? In what way does the dream of both men tie in with the sentiments expressed or implied in the Declaration of Independence (p. 309)?

George Washington

WILLIAM CARLOS WILLIAMS

William Carlos Williams (1883-1963), born in Rutherford, New Jersey, for more than half a century simultaneously practiced medicine and wrote poetry "not more than a half mile from where I happen to have been born." As a doctor he specialized in obstetrics; as a writer he concerned himself principally with depicting the American character. In the American Grain *(1925), one of the nearly forty volumes of prose and poetry that he has published, attempts this depiction through a series of sketches of men who helped to shape the nation.*

Washington was, I think, the typically good man: take it as you please. But, of course, a remarkable one. No doubt at all he, personally, was ninety percent of the force which made of the American Revolution a successful issue. Know of what that force consisted, that is, the intimate character of its makeup, that is, Washington himself, and you will know practically all there is to understand about the beginnings of the American Republic. You will know, also, why a crown was offered this great hero at the conclusion of hostilities with Great Britain, and with what a hidden gesture he rejected the idea. Therein you have it: it was unthinkable—or he might have taken it.

Here was a man of tremendous vitality buried in a massive frame and under a rather stolid and untractable exterior which the ladies somewhat feared, I fancy. He must have looked well to them, from a distance, or say on horseback—but later it proved a little too powerful for comfort. And he wanted them too; violently. One can imagine

From In the American Grain, Copyright 1933 by William Carlos Williams. Reprinted by permission of New Directions, Publishers.

him curiously alive to the need of dainty waistcoats, lace and kid gloves, in which to cover that dangerous rudeness which he must have felt about himself. His interest in dress at a certain period of his career is notorious.

The surveying contract which took him to Duquesne and the wilderness thereabouts was, however, the other side of the question. In this he must have breathed a more serious air which cannot but have penetrated to the deepest parts of his nature. The thing is, however, that in his case it did not, as it might have done, win him permanently to that kind of an existence. There was in his nature a profound spirit of resignation before life's rich proposals which disarmed him. As he expressed it, to him it was always his "vine and figtree," home and quiet, for which he longed. Stress he could endure but peace and regularity pleased him better. There must have been within him a great country whose wild paths he alone knew and explored in secret and at his leisure.

Patience, horses or a fine carriage, a widow to wive, a sloping lawn with a river at the bottom, a thriving field, an adopted daughter—that was as far as his desire wandered. All the rest he accepted as put upon him by chance.

Resistance was, I believe, his code. Encitadeled. A protector of the peace, or at least, keeper of the stillness within himself. He was too strong to want to evade anything. That's his reputation for truthtelling. It was a good scratching to him to take it on and see himself through. He knew he would come through.

There was his club life in Alexandria, as a Mason; the ten-mile ride to Church: it warmed him up a little.

As for rebellion, I don't think it entered his mind. I don't see how it could, except from the rear, subconsciously—that fire was too subdued in him. As commander of the troops he resisted, struck and drew back, struck and doubled on his tracks and struck and struck again, then rested.

He couldn't give in. He couldn't give in without such a ruffling within himself that he had no choice but to continue. That's the secret of Valley Forge and the valor and patience of his battle, as great as the other, against an aimless, wavering Congress at Philadelphia. He couldn't give in. I believe he would have gone out and battled it alone if he had felt his army wasted from under him or even left the country. Or else—

Well, there is the night he wandered off alone near Morristown, I think, off toward the British lines on horseback, impatient of warning—to air himself, so to speak, under the stars. Something angry was stirred there.

But seven days in the week it was for him: resist, be prudent, be calm—with a mad hell inside that might rise, might one day do something perhaps brilliant, perhaps joyously abandoned—but not to be thought of.

Such men suffering thus a political conversion of their emotions are, I suppose, always the noteworthy among us. Battle to them must be the expression of that something in themselves which they fear. Washington's calmness of demeanor and characteristics as a military leader were of that cloth.

Some girl at Princeton, was it? had some joke with him about a slipper at a dance. He was full of it. And there was the obscene anecdote he told that night in the boat crossing the Delaware.

But apparently the one man who got it full, who saw him really roused was General Lee—the one who wanted to replace him in command. That was all right. Washington could understand that and forgive it in another. He forgave Lee and restored him to his division with full trust after his return from capture by the British. But when, subsequently, Lee, in direct disobedience of orders, forgetting his position and risking his own whim on an important decision before Monmouth, lost the chance for an important victory—that was different. Immediately after, Washington met him by chance at a country cross road and Lee got it.

It is said no man, before or after, saw Washington in such a rage. This sort of thing Lee had done, he, Washington, knew from top to bottom. It was the firmly held part of himself which had broken loose—in another. Should he, Washington, stop that resistance in himself. What would happen?

No use to ask that now. Here it was: disaster. To Lee then in a fury, he opened the gates of his soul and Lee saw such hell fire that it was the end of him—retired muttering and half silly to his farm in Virginia where he stayed.

The presidency could not have meant anything to Washington. I think he spoke the candid truth about it when he said he neither desired it nor sought it. He merely did his duty. He did it with wisdom since he couldn't do it any other way. He wasn't enough interested to be scheming. Resist and protect: that was the gist of most that he said. Don't go looking for trouble. Stay home. In his very face, even, it was said in Congress he had turned monster under the name of prudence: "a sort of a non-describable chameleon-colored thing called prudence." Alexander Hamilton, a type that needed power, found all this quite to his liking. Washington let him do. He wanted to get back to Mt. Vernon.

America has a special destiny for such men, I suppose, great wench lovers—there is the letter from Jefferson attesting it in the case of Washington, if that were needed—terrible leaders they might make if one could release them. It seems a loss not compensated for by the tawdry stuff bred after them—in place of a splendor, too rare. They are a kind of American swan song, each one.

The whole crawling mass gnaws on them—hates them. He was hated, don't imagine he was not. The minute he had secured their dung heap for them—he had to take their dirt in the face.

From deep within, you may count upon it, came those final words when, his head in his friend's lap, he said with difficulty: "Doctor, I am dying, and have been dying for a long time, . . . " adding to reassure them, "but I am not afraid to die."

He is the typical sacrifice to the mob—in a great many ways thoroughly disappointing.

PROBLEMS FOR WRITING AND DISCUSSION

1. Williams gives Washington credit for 90 per cent of the success of the American Revolution. Yet, at the conclusion of the piece, he says that Washington was "in a great many ways thoroughly disappointing." Why?

2. The secret of Washington, according to Williams, was that "he couldn't give in." Explain.

3. What does the meeting of Washington and Lee reveal about the two men?

4. Why does Williams describe Washington and others like him as, each one, "a kind of American swan song"?

5. The cult of Washington in America is perhaps not so strong or so vocal as the cult of Lincoln. How does this sketch help explain why?

6. Why does Williams call Washington "the typical sacrifice to the mob"? Why should the "crawling mass" hate its outstanding men?

7. Is Williams' treatment of Washington ironical? Is it perhaps a self-conscious search for American identity? Does it exemplify what Henry James might have called the "democratization of heroes"? Explain.

8. Williams is a poet, not a historian—as the absence of conventional biographical detail and discursive continuity indicate. The historian might disagree with much that Williams has written, but Williams seeks the man beyond the facts. How has he used facts to fit his purpose but, at the same time, not been bound by them?

Notes and Comment
(on the Death of Grandma Moses)

THE NEW YORKER

> *"The Talk of the Town"* section of The New Yorker, *which each week opens with* Notes and Comment, *has from its beginning (1925) been a showcase for what can be done with the brief essay. Many well-known writers represented in this book, including E. B. White, have contributed pieces to it. While the tone of "The Talk of the Town" is consistently light and urbane, the intent of individual essays is frequently serious or satiric of contemporary affairs not only in New York City but in the nation.*

The death of a very old person seems no more natural, no less an untoward incursion, than the death of a young one. Perhaps death seems natural only to Nature herself—and even she may have some doubts. Yet we cannot think of the life, now concluded, of Anna Mary Robertson Moses without cheerfulness. To live one allotted span as a farm wife and the mother of ten children, and then, at the age of seventy-six, to begin another, as an artist, as Grandma Moses, and to extend this second life into twenty-five years of unembarrassed productiveness—such a triumph over the normal course of things offers small cause for mourning. If we do mourn, it is for ourselves; she had become by her hundredth year one of those old people who, as old buildings civilize a city or spindly church spires bind up a landscape, make the world seem safer. Shaw and Brancusi were examples; Churchill and Schweitzer still are. They

From The New Yorker, *December 23, 1961. Reprinted by permission* © *1961 The New Yorker Magazine, Inc.*

pay the world the great compliment of being reluctant to leave it, and their reluctance becomes a benediction. Little is said nowadays about the wisdom of age. Perhaps such wisdom is dreaded, for there is melancholy in it. Yet even awkward truths can be gracious and cheering in their expression. Describing her method of painting, Mrs. Moses once said, "I paint from the top down. First the sky, then the mountains, then the hills, then the houses, then the cattle, and then the people."

PROBLEMS FOR WRITING AND DISCUSSION

1. Death is a topic that usually impedes conversation as well as writing. To catch the flavor of a person's life requires great skill. How has the anonymous author of this essay organized his thoughts in order to catch the flavor of Grandma Moses' life?

2. What sentence best sums up the writer's attitude toward the death of a very old person? Explain your choice.

3. "Little is said nowadays about the wisdom of age." Is there anything you have read in this section which makes this remark particularly meaningful for America?

4. The author is obviously interested here in the universal implications of Grandma Moses' life, yet how does her life come through as distinctly American?

Abraham Lincoln

FRANCIS GRIERSON

Francis Grierson (1848-1927) was a boy of ten in Alton, Illinois, when he listened to the last of the Lincoln-Douglas debates. More than forty years later, and after a career as a pianist in Europe, he began to write The Valley of Shadows *(1909), taking two years while "waiting for the proper mood in which to write the portrait of Lincoln as he stood against Douglas at Alton." After that book, he wrote essays steadily. But he passed his last years in poverty, and* The Valley of Shadows, *now considered a classic, remained largely forgotten until Bernard De Voto and Theodore Spencer urged it on the public in a reprint in 1948.*

It was the 15th day of October, 1858. Crowds were pouring into Alton. For some days people had been arriving by the steam-packets from up and down the river, the up-boats from St. Louis bringing visitors with long, black hair, goatees, and stolid, Indian-like faces, slave-owners, and slave-dealers, from the human marts of Missouri and Kentucky; the northern visitors arriving by boat or rail, Abolitionists and Republicans, with a cast of features distinctly different from the types coming from the south.

They came from villages, townships, the prairies, from all the adjoining counties, from across the Mississippi, from far-away cities, from representative societies North and South, from congressional committees in the East, from leading journals of all political parties, and from every religious denomination within

From The Valley of Shadows, *by Francis Grierson, Houghton Mifflin Company, 1909.*

hundreds of miles, filling the broad space in front of the Town Hall, eager to see and hear the now famous debaters—the popular Stephen A. Douglas, United States Senator, nicknamed the "Little Giant," and plain Abraham Lincoln, nicknamed the "Rail-Splitter."

The great debate had begun on the 21st of August at another town, and to-day the long-discussed subject would be brought to a close. Douglas stood for the doctrine that slavery was nationalised by the Constitution, that Congress had no authority to prevent its introduction in the new Territories like Kansas and Nebraska, and that the people of each State could alone decide whether they should be slave States or free. Lincoln opposed the introduction of slavery into the new Territories.

On this memorable day the "irrepressible conflict" predicted by Seward actually began, and it was bruited about that Lincoln would be mobbed or assassinated if he repeated here the words he used in some of his speeches delivered in the northern part of the State. From the surging sea of faces thousands of anxious eyes gazed upward at the group of politicians on the balcony like wrecked mariners scanning the horizon for the smallest sign of a white sail of hope.

This final debate resembled a duel between two men-of-war, the pick of a great fleet, all but these two sunk or abandoned in other waters, facing each other in the open, the Little Giant hurling at his opponent, from his flagship of slavery, the deadliest missiles, Lincoln calmly waiting to sink his antagonist by one simple broadsider. Alton had seen nothing so exciting since the assassination of Lovejoy, the fearless Abolitionist, many years before.

In the earlier discussions Douglas seemed to have the advantage. A past-master in tact and audacity, skilled in the art of rhetorical skirmishing, he had no equal on the "stump," while in the Senate he was feared by the most brilliant debaters for his ready wit and his dashing eloquence.

Regarded in the light of historical experience, reasoned about in the light of spiritual reality, and from the point of view that nothing can happen by chance, it seems as if Lincoln and Douglas were predestined to meet side by side in this discussion, and unless I dwell in detail on the mental and physical contrast the speakers presented it would be impossible to give an adequate idea of the startling difference in the two temperaments; Douglas—short, plump, and petulant; Lincoln—long, gaunt, and self-possessed; the one white-haired and florid, the other black-haired and swarthy; the one educated and polished, the other unlettered and primitive. Douglas had the assurance of a man of authority, Lincoln had moments of deep mental depression, often bordering on melancholy, yet controlled by a fixed, and, I may say, predestined will, for it can no longer be doubted that without the marvellous blend of humour and stolid patience so conspicuous in his character, Lincoln's genius would have turned to madness after the defeat of the Northern Army at Bull-Run, and the world would have had something like a repetition of Napoleon's fate after the burning of Moscow. Lincoln's humour was the balance-pole of his genius that enabled him to cross the most giddy heights without losing his head. Judge Douglas opened the debate in a sonorous voice plainly heard throughout the assembly, and with a look of mingled defiance and confidence he marshalled his facts and deduced his arguments. To the vigour of his attack there was added the prestige of the Senate Chamber, and for some moments it looked as if he would carry the majority with him, a large portion of the crowd being Pro-Slavery men, while many others were "on the fence" waiting to be persuaded.

At last, after a great oratorical effort, he brought his speech to a close amidst the shouts and yells of thousands of admirers.

And now Abraham Lincoln, the man who, in 1830, undertook to split for Mrs. Nancy Miller four hundred rails for every yard of brown jean dyed with walnut bark that would be required to make him a pair of trousers, the flatboatman, local stump-speaker and country lawyer, rose from his seat, stretched his long, bony limbs upward as if to get them into working order, and stood like some solitary pine on a lonely summit, very tall, very dark, very gaunt, and very rugged, his swarthy features stamped with a sad serenity, and the instant he began to speak the ungainly mouth lost its heaviness, the half-listless eyes attained a wondrous power, and the people stood bewildered and breathless under the natural magic of the strangest, most original personality known to the English-speaking world since Robert Burns. There were other very tall and dark men in the heterogeneous assembly, but not one who resembled the speaker. Every movement of his long, muscular frame denoted inflexible earnestness, and a something issued forth, elemental and mystical, that told what the man had been, what he was, and what he would do in the future. There were moments when he seemed all legs and feet, and again he appeared all head and neck; yet every look of the deep-set eyes, every movement of the prominent jaw, every wave of the hard-gripping hand, produced an impression, and before he had spoken twenty minutes the conviction took possession of thousands that here was the prophetic man of the present and the political saviour of the future. Judges of human nature saw at a glance that a man so ungainly, so natural, so earnest, and so forcible, had no place in his mental economy for the thing called vanity.

Douglas had been theatrical and scholarly, but this tall, homely man was creating by his very looks what the brilliant lawyer and experienced Senator had failed to make people see and feel. The Little Giant had assumed striking attitudes, played tricks with his flowing white hair, mimicking the airs of authority, with patronising allusions; but these affectations, usually so effective when he addressed an audience alone, went for nothing when brought face to face with realities. Lincoln had no genius for gesture and no desire to produce a sensation. The failure of Senator Douglas to bring conviction to critical minds was caused by three things: a lack of logical sequence in argument, a lack of intuitional judgment, and a vanity that was caused by too much intellect and too little heart. Douglas had been arrogant and vehement, Lincoln was now logical and penetrating. The Little Giant was a living picture of ostentatious vanity; from every feature of Lincoln's face there radiated the calm, inherent strength that always accompanies power. He relied on no props. With a pride sufficient to protect his mind and a will sufficient to defend his body, he drank water when Douglas, with all his wit and rhetoric, could begin or end nothing without stimulants. Here, then, was one man out of all the millions who believed in himself, who did not consult with others about what to say, who never for a moment respected the opinion of men who preached a lie. My old friend, Don Piatt, in his personal impressions of Lincoln, whom he knew well and greatly esteemed, declares him to be the homeliest man he ever saw; but serene confidence and self-poise can never be ugly. What thrilled the people who stood before Abraham Lincoln on that day was the sight of a being who, in all his actions and habits, resembled themselves, gentle as he was strong, fearless as he was honest, who towered above them all in that psychic radiance that penetrates in some mysterious way every fibre of the hearer's consciousness.

The enthusiasm created by Douglas was wrought out of smart epigram thrusts and a facile, superficial eloquence. He was a match for the politicians born within the confines of his own intellectual circle: witty, brilliant, cunning, and shallow, his weight in the political balance was purely materialistic; his scales of justice tipped to the side of cotton, slavery, and popular passions, while the man who faced him now brought to the assembly cold logic in place of wit, frankness in place of cunning, reasoned will and judgment in place of chicanery and sophistry. Lincoln's presence infused into the mixed and uncertain throng something spiritual and super-normal. His looks, his words, his voice, his attitude, were like a magical essence dropped into the seething cauldron of politics, re-acting against the foam, calming the surface and letting the people see to the bottom. It did not take him long.

"Is it not a false statesmanship," he asked, "that undertakes to build up a system of policy upon the basis of caring nothing about the very thing that everybody does care the most about? Judge Douglas may say he cares not whether slavery is voted up or down, but he must have a choice between a right thing and a wrong thing. He contends that whatever community wants slaves has a right to have them. So they have, if it is not a wrong; but if it is a wrong he cannot say people have a right to do wrong. He says that upon the score of equality slaves should be allowed to go into a new Territory like other property. This is strictly logical if there is no difference between it and other property. If it and other property are equal his argument is entirely logical; but if you insist that one is wrong and the other right there is no use to institute a comparison between right and wrong."

This was the broadsider. The great duel on the high seas of politics was over. The Douglas ship of State Sovereignty was sinking. The debate was a triumph that would send Lincoln to Washington as President in a little more than two years from that date.

People were fascinated by the gaunt figure in long, loose garments, that seemed like a "huge skeleton in clothes," attracted by the homely face, and mystified, yet proud of the fact that a simple denizen of their own soil should wield so much power.

When Lincoln sat down Douglas made one last feeble attempt at an answer; but Lincoln, in reply to a spectator who manifested some apprehension as to the outcome, rose, and spreading out his great arms at full length, like a condor about to take wing, exclaimed, with humorous indifference: "Oh! let him go it!" These were the last words he uttered in the greatest debate of the *ante-bellum* days.

The victor bundled up his papers and withdrew, the assembly shouting: "Hurrah for Abe Lincoln as next President!" "Bully for old Abe!" "Lincoln for ever!" Excited crowds followed him about, reporters caught his slightest word, and by night time the bar-rooms, hotels, street corners, and prominent stores were filled with his admirers, fairly intoxicated with the exciting triumph of the day.

PROBLEMS FOR WRITING AND DISCUSSION

1. Edmund Wilson has said that Francis Grierson had a "special conception of Lincoln as the designated and conscious instrument through which larger forces were working. . . ." Does this conception come through in the essay here, and if so how does Grierson convey it to the reader?

2. Grierson witnessed this debate when he was ten and wrote about it when he was past fifty. How does this information affect your judgment of the essay's validity?

3. Why does Grierson say Lincoln and Douglas seemed predestined to meet and discuss this most important issue?

4. Grierson has been described as a master "at creating atmosphere, the atmosphere, hushed and foreboding, ominous and exalting, that precedes great events." Does he succeed in creating such an atmosphere in this essay? Where?

5. Most schoolchildren know of the Lincoln-Douglas debates and their place in history, but this account centers on the men as men rather than on their ideas. What essential difference between Lincoln and Douglas emerges in this essay?

6. The people, Grierson says, were "thrilled" to behold a man who reflected their own attributes. What attributes does he enumerate? Compare his conception of the American people with William Carlos Williams'. Is there any indication that Lincoln's audience was capable of behaving like the fickle mob Williams (p. 106) describes?

7. Despite differences in technique and purpose, do the essays on Washington and Lincoln point to any traits of leadership the two men had in common? On the basis of these two essays, what would you say chiefly distinguished Lincoln from Washington?

8. The Kennedy-Nixon debates took place on television before millions, the Lincoln-Douglas debates before possibly hundreds. Apart from the technical differences, what others were there? What do these differences reveal about the changes in American democracy?

The Last Full Measure

KEVIN CORRIGAN

> Kevin Corrigan (1926-), son of the first American Ambassador to Venezuela, entered the army during World War II after his freshman year at Amherst, saw action in Europe as an infantryman, returned to Amherst after the war, and was graduated in 1949. He has written articles and book reviews for a variety of magazines, including Modern Age, Social Order, and Catholic World; he is now an executive with the International Television branch of the American Broadcasting Company. The letter that follows was written to his brother Ed, an officer with another unit.

IDSTEIN, GERMANY, June 18, 1945

DEAR ED: —

You asked me to tell you about my officers. Here's a case I was planning to save until I saw you. His name was Harold D. Wilson. On graduation from Officer Candidate School he came to our outfit and took over the third platoon. He had gone to West Point for eight months but had not qualified in one subject, so they dismissed him. He went into the Army as an enlisted man in the AA. But he felt that he had let down the man who had sponsored his appointment, as well as his family, by not getting a commission. He wanted to be an infantry soldier and a combat man so he got himself into Infantry OCS at Fort Benning.

Although he was twenty-one, Wilson looked about seventeen or eighteen, had blond hair, baby-blue eyes, and about as much of a

From The Atlantic Monthly, *June 1946. Copyright 1946 by The Atlantic Monthly Company, Boston 16, Mass.*

beard as yours truly. His voice was high and his enunciation clear. When he intoned "Column right, MARCH" in his high little voice you had to smile and shake your head. He was very precise and GI. He was soon to fall heir to the name of "Little Boy Blue," and the name fitted him well. I liked him, but the thought of this almost ridiculous little character leading a platoon of men into combat was too much.

When we first came over, we took up mainly defensive positions, and he was careful in his preparations. In our first attack I didn't see him during the main assault, but after it was over, my squad was off by itself to the left flank. We were crowded into three little Kraut holes. Jerry laid a terrific barrage on us and then started to counterattack. Because of the terrain and thick woods we couldn't see over 20 yards and I thought it was the end.

Then Wilson came bouncing down the road paying no attention to the artillery. "What's going on here, you men?" he asked.

We explained the situation, which was obvious. He grabbed a burp gun I had picked up and started popping away single shot. Six of us were crowded into two small holes, so he said, "We'll have to improve this position by joining these holes. One of us will dig while the other two fire. We'll just sort of dig and fight here."

It was the right thing, but I wasn't thinking much about improving positions at the moment. I wondered what the hell he was doing there, anyway. It was the worst possible place to be at the moment and we weren't even in his platoon. It did make the men feel better to have an officer with them, but I thought he was crazy to be there. He had a piece of shrapnel in his leg from earlier in the day, but he didn't pay any attention to that. After we broke up the counterattack, we got the two holes together, and despite his wound he stayed there all night and pulled his guard. The impression of "Little Boy Blue" was undergoing quite a change.

As you know, we were on the defensive in that sector during the winter and our position on the hill grew worse as the entire line ebbed and flowed to the right and left of us. We sweat it out on the hill for about a week, expecting to be pushed off any time. Wilson kept saying, "We'll keep busy up here if it's doing nothing but melting snow to wash our feet." It sounded pretty silly, but he was right, for it was necessary to keep the men busy.

Wilson was always willing to take prisoners. Once while leading his men, and paying no attention to the enemy fire, he saw a Heinie behind a tree. He yelled, "I see you there hiding behind that tree. Come out, I see you."

One day in February the whole company marched into a couple of German machine guns, and one platoon was immediately cut up. It was before dawn and we stayed pinned down till dawn, when the very dangerous false report got around that we were supposed to pull out.

The men were on the verge of panic. Up stands Wilson and ignores the enemy fire and runs all over the place; gets protection on the flanks and gets the rest of the company and tells them they're going to attack with him. Everything is pretty active with heavy mortar and machine-gun fire, but he's running around to the platoons, shouting, "Here, here, you men, where are you going? You come right back here! Over there, Sergeant. Bring those men by you up here. We're going to attack these woods." His way from the first to the third is barred by a stream of machine-gun fire. He simply hurdles it.

He got things organized and by a miracle wasn't killed. He was hit in the face and leg by a Panzerfaust shell, but as usual, if a wound didn't kill him it couldn't stop him. He led the company into a smashing assault which led the division. Do you get the picture? This gentle guy with no fear. Quick to make decisions and quick to carry them out. He always fought "by the book." Once the company was moving through the attack and he stopped. "You men there. Pick those boards up. We may have to use them later." Always quick to search the dead. "Better look this man over—he may have something we need." Death didn't bother him, but he always had time for a kind word to the wounded.

Wilson became company exec, so he wasn't supposed to lead assaults any more. But one day we were going to attack a town at the bottom of a thickly wooded hill. He couldn't bear to stay behind, so he told our platoon leader, "Beck, I'll go to the bottom of the hill with you, but then I'll have to go back." We moved slowly through the woods, Beck getting maximum use from his scouts. Jerry started to mortar hell out of us. Wilson said, "Beck, we're going to have to move faster; it's costing us lives staying here." About that time Beck was killed, so Wilson took over. We started moving fast and the artillery and mortar fire falling behind us was terrific, but it was behind us.

We cut some barbed wire and moved as skirmishers through the woods. The underbrush was thick, and control was an almost impossible problem, but an effort was made through yelling, which, although it might not have been too effective for control, was good against the Heinies. As we approached the pillboxes, we started to receive fire and had to slow down, so the platoon following behind us came up into us to mess things up even more. We got to the edge of the woods and came upon a jungle of barbed wire. Jerry was laying down fairly intense grazing machine-gun fire. One gun was about 30 yards to the front and another off to the left. The flash was clear as hell.

Wilson had us lay down a base of fire. "Crawl right up there. Make some noise, you men—show them you're up here shooting at them. Show them you're *doughboys!*" After a while we silenced the machine guns. I don't know if we hit them or scared them. At any rate our rifle fire was effective. But because of the terrifically thick wire that was undoubtedly mined, Wilson decided to attack around to the right. "All right, you men. Everybody up. We're going around to the right. Come now, let's go."

We went through the woods far enough to the right to satisfy him; then he said, "All right, we're going out of these woods. Keep right on going across the clearing." As soon as we got out of the woods, of course some machine guns opened up on us. "That's all right, men, we'll go right across here in short rushes. Everybody up. Let's go now—short rushes." The men started some rushes. "Here, here, we can do better than that. Now give me some good rushes.

You there, soldier, that wasn't a rush at all—that was just a flop. Now you get right up and give me a nice rush."

Mind you, this isn't an umpire on maneuvers—this is a leader in combat. All the time he was standing up directing the thing. Why he wasn't killed I'll never know. Across the clearing was a tank trap. "Now let's see who's going to be the first man to the ditch." Once we got into the ditch—it was about 12 feet deep—he yelled, "All right now, we'll just dig each other right up out of here. Buddy up and help each other out of here."

Next we crossed a railroad track. During this time we were being fired at from a basement window. We spotted the window and poured an intense volume of fire through it, then started bouncing the rounds off the edges of the window. By the time a few of us were across the track, a white something cautiously appeared. One of the gunners, a corporal, came across the street and of course Wilson wouldn't let anyone shoot him.

Watching us keep coming despite his fire had scared this Kraut badly. He said his buddies were too scared to come out. The boys were ready to go over and dig them out, but Wilson said we would take them prisoners, so we had the corporal yell across the street and the other two finally came over, quite shaken. These men were from a fresh regiment that, less than a week before, had almost broken our regimental line, but now the M-1 rifle had taken the fight out of them.

We got into the house and cleared it, then Wilson told me to come along with him while he cleared the basement. I asked him if he didn't think it was better to drop a couple of grenades down the stairs first. "No, we won't mess it up. We'll go right down there." Down he went, and luckily there was no one there. The reason he had wanted to take the house was to be able to use the basement as protection against artillery.

When we got back upstairs we had two wounded men on our hands. There was a guy sniping at us with a machine carbine from one of the by-passed pillboxes. He was becoming too effective, so Wilson took two men upstairs to see if they could get him. By that time Wilson had a bullet hole through his helmet but luckily only a scratch on his forehead. He went to the window and started yelling to some men who were still on the other side of the railroad, telling them to come over at five-minute intervals.

Then he stepped back from the window and said he was hit. He said to the two men with him, "Now, don't worry. I'll be all right." He started to fade, so he had them slap his face—as if that could do any good! But he wasn't the type to accept death without a fight. When he realized that he had lost, he said, "God, help me through this" (and I'm sure He did). Then he kicked a heavy oak table across the room and was dead. There was another lieutenant in the house who took over, but the leader was dead and our spirit died with him.

That's the story of "Little Boy Blue." I haven't exaggerated. He was a mild-mannered little guy, who we would have said shouldn't be in the infantry had we seen him in Washington. He didn't chew tobacco, he didn't smoke, drink, or swear. But time and again he showed no fear. Maybe he had a complex, but I think it was more than that. He knew there was a job to do and wasn't sure it would be done if he didn't do it. He was the driving factor of the whole company. He was a good infantry soldier.

To my mind Wilson proves one big thing. Men in all divisions and companies are about the same. They all have their brave men and their cowards, but the big thing is the leader. A good leader is everything. Men will follow a good leader any place. If there is no leader, there is confusion and panic. If the leader is poor, the organization is poor. Once in a while an enlisted man will take over; but still, brave as he may be, he won't get the following a brave officer will get. Every company needs a Wilson, but the trouble is they don't last. If all leaders (squad, platoon, and company) had been on the ball, there wouldn't have been the need for such extreme leadership as Wilson's. I've seen brave men, but no one like "Little Boy Blue."

As ever,

KEVIN

PROBLEMS FOR WRITING AND DISCUSSION

1. What are the specific qualities of leadership that Wilson exhibited? Are they qualities noted as "American" in other essays in this part? Explain.
2. Does the writer's conclusion seem valid to you on the basis of the letter itself? Explain.
3. Does it seem ludicrous to compare Washington with Lieutenant Wilson or do the two have qualities in common as Williams (p. 106) and Corrigan picture them?
4. Bernard De Voto (p. 93) believed it was men's "response to the continent" that transformed them from Europeans into Americans. Is there anything about Lieutenant Wilson that justifies or contradicts this generalization?

Off Limits for Conscience

ALAN LEVY

Alan Levy (1932-), free-lance writer, was graduated from Brown University (1952) and the Columbia University School of Journalism (1953), after which he became a staff writer for the Louisville Courier-Journal. *During his years with the paper (1953-60), he covered the 1959 Berlin crisis and the Cuban revolution, winning a regional award for his reporting of the latter event. He has written on a variety of subjects for various magazines, including* The New Republic, Theatre Arts, *and* Horizon, *and he has published four books, among which is* Wanted: Nazi Criminals at Large *(1962).*

On Monday, August 6, 1945, Major Claude E. Eatherly, piloting a B-29 weather plane called the *Straight Flush,* found a hole in the clouds over Hiroshima. Eatherly recalls: "I sent my coded message which was the final 'go-ahead' to the bomb-carrying plane"—another B-29, the *Enola Gay,* cruising behind. Eatherly led the mission through the break in the overcast. The *Enola Gay* dropped an atomic bomb that killed 91,233 people and injured another 37,425.

Three days later, Eatherly led another mission—over Nagasaki. Again, the *Enola Gay* followed him and dropped a bomb. This time, 73,884 Japanese died. Five days later, World War II ended. Eatherly—27 years old and a onetime student-teacher from Texas—had lifted the curtain on the Atomic Age. He received the Distinguished Flying Cross. He and his crew were christened the "Victory Boys."

From The New Republic, *June 11, 1962. Copyright © 1962 by The New Republic, Washington 6, D. C.*

But on the island of Tinian, where they were awaiting their return home Eatherly would not speak to the other "Victory Boys" for days on end. His crew attributed his moodiness to battle fatigue, which Eatherly had suffered once before—in 1943—and licked. But this time it was different. Neither the world nor Claude Eatherly would ever be the same again: "I was unable to forget the act," he said later, "and . . . the guilt of the act has caused me great suffering." From the moment he had dispatched his historic command to the *Enola Gay,* Eatherly was numbered among the *victims* of Hiroshima.

The Air Force discharged him in 1947 as suffering from a "neurosis with psychotic manifestations." Eatherly blamed himself for acquiescing to the second mission: "After I saw the destruction at Hiroshima, I didn't want to go over Nagasaki. But I went." He drank heavily. He couldn't sleep. He took to stuffing money into envelopes and mailing them to Hiroshima. In 1950, he took an overdose of sleeping pills in a hotel room, but he lived.

In 1953, he forged a check and served nine months in a New Orleans jail. In 1957, he was accused of breaking into two post offices in West Texas. He also entered a grocery store, pointed a gun at the cashier, told him to put all the ready cash in a bag, and then he left without taking the money. When caught, as he always was, he told one district attorney that the Japanese were after him. On some occasions, he pleaded innocent by reason of insanity; in others, the cases were dropped when he agreed to enter a hospital. He has been in the Veterans Administration Hospital in Waco nine times.

In the fall of 1960, after being rebuffed in an effort to be discharged from the hospital, Claude Eatherly walked out of the psychiatric ward and escaped. Shortly before Christmas, 1960, however, he was arrested for a traffic violation in Dallas. In custody, he insisted that his guilt complex had "been getting better the last six months. All I want is a break." He told a court that he was learning to "live with" his problem though he "hadn't had any sleep in 15 years." A jury decided that he was insane. He was committed to the veterans hospital.

Claude Eatherly does not consider himself a madman. He views his decade of lawbreaking as part of "my determination to shatter the 'hero image' of me, by which society has sought to perpetuate its own complacency." He refers to "anti-social acts while in a confused state seeking punishment for myself." Noting that he spent nearly eight of the last 15 years in hospitals plus several days in jail, he remarks: "I always seemed happier in jails because I had a release of guilt by being punished." He sees himself as a symbol of the pacifist revolt:

> "To most people my method of rebellion against war is that of an insane person. No other way could I have made people realize that nuclear war is moral degeneration as well as physical destruction. It does not matter to me what people think of my moral character if it will only make them stop and think that they must not let the same thing happen to themselves and their children."

But he feels that his rebellion has been thwarted:

> ". . . I have been having such difficulty in getting society to recognize the fact of my guilt, which I have long since realized. The truth is that society simply *cannot* accept the fact of my guilt without at the same time recognizing its own far deeper guilt. But it is, of course, highly desirable that society should recognize this, which is why *my* . . . story is of such vital importance. Now I accept the fact that I am unlikely to bring about that recognition by getting into scrapes with the law."

If he is known at all in America, Eatherly is known as a case; elsewhere, he is a cause. John Wain, the British author, has even written a poem about him that reads, in part:

> Leave him; if he is sleeping, come away.
> But lay a folded paper by his head,
> nothing official or embossed, a page
> torn from your notebook, and the words in pencil.
> Say nothing of love, or thanks, or penitence;
> say only "Eatherly, we have your message."

Eatherly's sanity hearing in Texas last year was covered voluminously by the foreign press. A correspondent for a French newspaper wrote back: "Eatherly was probably the most intelligent person in the whole courtroom." Writing to President Kennedy, an Austrian pacifist, Günther Anders, called the Eatherly case "a moral scandal which threatens to go down in history as the Dreyfus Affair of the 20th Century." Eatherly's remorse is often contrasted with that of his Commander-in-Chief, Harry S. Truman, who said—as his 75th birthday approached in 1959—that he had "never lost any sleep" over the decision to bomb Hiroshima. In a letter to *The New Statesman and Nation,* Bertrand Russell asserted that:

"Eatherly is repentant and certified; Truman is unrepentant and uncertified. I have seen a number of Eatherly's statements explaining his motives. These statements are entirely sane. But such is the power of mendacious publicity that almost everyone, including myself, believed that he had become a lunatic."

I met Claude Eatherly briefly during one of his rare periods of freedom—at the 1958 Kentucky Derby, where he had been invited to a reunion of his crew members. He was a wiry, leathery man with a crinkly western smile. There was a savage, barely repressed mockery in his eyes and voice as he gave one fatuous statement to the local press. He was contending that Derby Day was far more exciting than August 6, 1945: "That fight was just routine. This is the Kentucky Derby. To us, it's more earthshaking."

On June 12, 1959—from Building 90 at the Veterans Administration Hospital in Waco—Eatherly replied to a sympathetic letter from Günther Anders. The two men struck up a correspondence and later, with Eatherly's tacit consent, Anders compiled their letters. Ironically, they were published first in German—under the title, *Off Limits for Conscience*—last year. This year, they were published in Britain as *Burning Conscience.* The slim volume has just been published in America.

Burning Conscience is no measure of the man's sanity, but it does hint at his infinite misery. It may be said, too, with some justice, that *Burning Conscience* isn't Claude Eatherly's book, but Günther Anders'. Of its 71 letters only 28 are by Eatherly. And because Anders is the more garrulous of the two their book makes particularly lumpish reading. Anders constantly lectures his captive audience. Much of *Burning Conscience* is Anders' advice to Eatherly on how he might sell his story to the movies without compromising his dignity: "I happened to see a review of a Bob Hope picture which must be simply nonsensical. I think he has to be eliminated from our consideration" (as producer of the Eatherly saga). And: ". . . the idea of Audie Murphy portraying you doesn't appeal to me at all. It is quite clear that the movie business hopes for a sensation because 'one hero portrays another hero.' I have never seen Audie Murphy in a picture; maybe he is an actor. . . ."

In 1960, when President Eisenhower's good-will visit to Japan (later cancelled) was threatened by student riots, a United States Senator asked Eatherly whether he would exert his prestige as a pacifist to quiet down the young Japanese. Eatherly obliged. As Anders notes: "How cynical that the man who is excluded from the outer world . . . as mentally ill is being regarded in the opportune moment to be sufficiently competent to influence the world. . . ."

When the pen is in Eatherly's hand, the book becomes an affecting, almost childlike, biography of a friendship between two grown-up pen pals who have never met, but who have the same obsession. For all its faults, *Burning Conscience* begins to document a story of which we have had only fragments.

Adolf Eichmann, whose achievements in mass murder dwarfed those of the *Enola Gay's* crew, held to the end that he "was merely a little cog in the machinery that carried out the directives and orders of the German Reich." His lawyer contended that Eichmann bore no more responsibility than the man who doomed Hiroshima. But Claude Eatherly would not have it that way. In a twisted, mocking way, the Texan shouldered responsibility which nobody says is his.

PROBLEMS FOR WRITING AND DISCUSSION

1. Levy wrote this essay as a book review of the Eatherly-Anders correspondence. Does this fact weaken the effectiveness of the essay? Why does Levy choose the German rather than the English title for his own title?

2. What is the effect of the statistics given in the first two paragraphs?

3. Why does Levy say that Eatherly was eventually "numbered among the *victims* of Hiroshima"?

4. Comment on the contrast Bertrand Russell draws between Eatherly and Truman. Kevin Corrigan concludes "The Last Full Measure" (p. 122) with the assertion that "a good leader is everything. Men will follow a good leader any place." Test both Eatherly and Truman by Corrigan's conclusion.

5. Levy ends the essay with an analogy between Adolf Eichmann and Eatherly. What moral point does Levy stress in making this analogy?

6. What are the reasons Eatherly gives for his behavior? Discuss his motives in the light of what Lincoln is quoted as having said about slavery (p. 115).

7. Compare the way Wilson shouldered his responsibility ("The Last Full Measure") with the "twisted mocking way" Levy says Eatherly has shouldered his. To what do you attribute this difference? Explain.

8. Defend or attack the inclusion of the Eatherly story in this book.

Part Two. The Forms to Which They Are Accustomed

1. FREE ENTERPRISE
2. EDUCATION
3. SCIENCE

1. Free Enterprise

Horatio Alger

FREDERICK LEWIS ALLEN

Frederick Lewis Allen (1890-1954) spent most of his working years as a journalist. He joined Harper's Magazine *in 1923 and became its editor-in-chief in 1941, a post he held until 1953. He wrote as well as edited and found time to produce five books. His first and best-known,* Only Yesterday *(1932), is a lively account of the 1920's and has sold over a half million copies. He followed it with* The Lords of Creation *(1935), a financial history of America from 1830 to 1935;* Since Yesterday *(1940), which focused on the depression years;* The Great Pierpont Morgan *(1949), a biography; and* The Big Change *(1952), an informal history of America since the twentieth century opened. Although dismissed by some historians as a "historical journalist," he wrote popular history in the best sense: it is both reliable and readable.*

In 1899 there died in New York a man who, though he had never made much of a study of economics and had a curiously immature mind, may have had a more pervasive influence on the thinking of American businessmen at the turn of the century than all the professors of economics put together. This man's name was Horatio Alger, Jr., and what he had done was to write more than a hundred books for boys—success stories called *Bound to Rise, Luck and Pluck, Sink or Swim, Tom the Bootblack,* and so forth—the total sales of which came to at least twenty million copies.

From The Big Change *by Frederick Lewis Allen. Copyright 1952 by Frederick Lewis Allen. Reprinted by permission of Harper & Row, Publishers.*

Horatio Alger was a creature of paradox. The unfailing theme of his books was the rise of earnest, hard-working boys from rags to riches; yet he himself did not begin life in rags and did not by any means achieve riches; during his later years he lived mostly in the Newsboys' Lodging House on one of New York's drearier streets. His paper-bound guides to success were, and are, generally regarded by educated readers as trash; they were literal, prosy, unreal, and unsubtle to a degree. Yet they were the delight of millions of American boys during the years between the Civil War and World War I, and it is possible that most of these boys got from Horatio Alger their first intelligible picture of American economic life.

The standard Horatio Alger hero was a fatherless boy of fifteen or thereabouts who had to earn his own way, usually in New York City. He was beset by all manner of villains. They tried to sell him worthless gold watches on railroad trains, or held him up as he was buggy-riding home with his employer's funds, or chloroformed him in a Philadelphia hotel room, or slugged him in a Chicago tenement. But always he was strong and shrewd and brave, and they were foolish and cowardly. And the end of each book found our hero well on the way toward wealth, which it was clear resulted from his diligence, honesty, perseverance, and thrift.

To the farmer's son, thumbing his copy of *Andy Grant's Pluck* by lamplight on the Illinois prairie, or to the country banker's son, scanning the *Brave and Bold* series in a Vermont village, the lesson of Horatio Alger seemed clear: business was a matter of trading among individuals and small groups of men, and if you worked hard and saved your money, you succeeded. The basic principles of economic conduct were the same as those laid down by Benjamin Franklin's Poor Richard:

"God helps them that help themselves."
"Early to bed, and early to rise,
  Makes a man healthy, wealthy, and wise."
"If we are industrious we shall never starve, for, as Poor Richard says, *At the working man's house, Hunger looks in; but dares not enter.*"

"A fat Kitchen makes a lean Will."

And, to sum up: "In short, the way to wealth, if you desire it, is as plain as the way to market. It depends chiefly on two words, *industry* and *frugality*."

There was no denying that the Alger thesis had a certain magnificent validity. Look at John D. Rockefeller, who had begun as a $4-a-week clerk in a commission merchant's house in Cleveland, and by the beginning of the twentieth century was becoming the richest man in the world. Look at Andrew Carnegie, who had begun at thirteen as a $1.20-a-week bobbin boy in a Pittsburgh cotton mill, and had become the greatest of steel manufacturers. Look at Edward H. Harriman, who had begun as a broker's office boy at $5 a week, and was building a railroad empire. And as for thrift, look at the great banker, George Fisher Baker, who not only had begun his career as a clerk, but during his early married life had imposed upon himself and his wife the discipline of living on half their income and saving the other half. These were only a few of the examples which proved the formula for success: begin with nothing, apply yourself, save your pennies, trade shrewdly, and you will be rewarded with wealth, power and acclaim. To which the natural corollary was: poor people are poor because they are victims of their own laziness, stupidity, or profligacy.

Naturally it was pleasant for successful businessmen to believe that these were, in fact, the first principles of economics. But, one might ask, hadn't they learned in the classroom that economics is just a little more complex than that?

To this question there are two answers. The first is that mighty few of the tycoons of 1900 had ever studied economics. Take, for instance, eight of the most successful of all: John D. Rockefeller, Carnegie, Harriman, and Baker, whom we have just mentioned; and also J. Pierpont Morgan, William Rockefeller, James Stillman, and H. H. Rogers. Of these eight, only Morgan had had anything approaching what we today would call a college education; he had spent two years at the University of Göttingen in Germany, where he had pretty certainly not studied anything that we would now classify as economics. And it is doubtful if even in the prime of life many of these men, or of their innumerable rivals and imitators, had much truck with economic science, or thought of professors of economics as anything but absurdly impractical theorists. A man who had come up in the world liked to describe himself as a graduate of the School of Hard Knocks. Education was all right in its way, and you sent your son to college if you could, if only because it was a good place to make useful contacts with the right people; but these college professors knew nothing about business, which was a battlefield for hard-shelled fighters. And anyhow the principles laid down by Ben Franklin, and somewhat foolishly simplified for boys by Horatio Alger, were fundamentally sound.

PROBLEMS FOR WRITING AND DISCUSSION

1. No sophisticated businessman today would admit to admiring the Horatio Alger stories or even to having read them. Has the "rags-to-riches" tradition lost its power over the American mind or is it that Alger's statement of that tradition has lost its attraction? On what evidence do you base your answer?

2. Are Horatio Alger's heroes peculiarly American boys or could they have flourished any time and anywhere? Why?

3. Does Allen's account of the Horatio Alger boy explain adequately why the "rags-to-riches" tradition acquired the hold it did over the American imagination? How can you make the explanation more adequate?

4. How would the Alger hero define success? How many of the persons depicted in Part I of this book would qualify as successful in terms of that definition?

5. Commager (p. 14) contends that Americans generally cannot understand the fear and desire which afflict other peoples of the earth. Does the popularity of the Horatio Alger legend explain their failure or simply illustrate it? Explain.

6. Discuss the possible contribution that the following may have made to the American belief that "success" was obtainable by "industry and frugality": (1) the American Revolution, (2) the open frontier, and (3) representative democracy.

FORD AND MASS PRODUCTION

My Philosophy of Industry

HENRY FORD

> Henry Ford (1863-1947) more than any other man created the big change Frederick Lewis Allen has written about: the technological and industrial revolution that came to America during the first half of the twentieth century. He was born on a Michigan farm and embodied to the end the virtues and views of rural America. "I still like boiled potatoes with the skins on," he once said, "and I don't want a man standing back of my chair at table laughing up his sleeve at me while I am taking the potatoes' jackets off." He believed the common man was good, that all aristocrats, bankers, and politicians were bad. He became in his lifetime both the symbol, as historian Ralph Gabriel has said, of "the Horatio Alger theory and ideal of the free individual" and the chief support of "an American belief as old as the eighteenth century that man by use of reason can change his environment."

Students of world progress recognize that there is a time for everything. Like the opening of a flower or the budding of a tree, certain events cannot be forced ahead of their time; nor, conversely, can they

From My Philosophy of Industry. *Reprinted by permission of Coward-McCann, Inc.*

be disregarded after the time for their appearance has come. Therefore it behooves the man—especially the young man—who wishes to have his part in the progress of this world, to watch the signs of the times and be ready at the proper moment to take his place in the procession of human events.

Not only in industry, but in all lines of work is this so. In the scheme of progress each unit has its logical place, which no other can fill. As a case in point, the automobile and the airplane could not be successfully developed until the internal combustion engine had been invented. Earlier engines, such as steam engines, were too heavy; they weighed too much per horsepower to be practical for use in these two new vehicles of transportation. But with the coming of the internal combustion engine it was possible to concentrate in a small place and a small weight an enormous amount of power. Thus it enabled us to develop the automobile, and, later on, the airplane. One invention makes way for another; one discovery lights up the path ahead so that he who runs may read—and lead.

Similarly, the development of industry was long delayed because one link in the chain of progress was missing. When that had been forged, industry shot ahead to its present high state of production. I refer to the matter of long-distance power transmission. Back in the days when machinery had to be run by steam or water power, cables and belts were the only means of power transmission. This meant that factories had to be located in the immediate neighborhood of the plant, or on the bank of the stream from which power was derived. The natural tendency was for industry to group itself around large sources of power. Thus centralization was brought about, and on its heels followed quantity production. The mere idea of quantity production was a great step forward, but its concentration was hampered by the very condition that had given rise to it. So long as centralization was necessary, so long as manufacturing could be carried on only by the limited number of factories that could crowd around the various sources of power, quantity production on the present scale was impossible.

Then within our knowledge—within our century—electricity was discovered. Electricity possessed this great advantage over all other kinds of power previously produced: it could be instantaneously transmitted over great distances by wire. Power could be generated in one spot and sent out to any number of factories all over the country. The necessity for centralization had been eliminated, and manufacturing went ahead on a larger scale than ever.

Light, heat, and power—think what has been accomplished by this one idea put into action! And the power age has barely begun. In our own shops we are constantly improving our method of manufacture, with an eye to efficiency, economy, and the safety and comfort of our employees. Belt transmission has been entirely supplanted by electrically driven machines, which frees us from the danger and annoyance of wheels and belts whirling overhead. Our furnaces, most of which are electrically heated, are so constructed and insulated that the men work in front of them without discomfort. There is no smoke or gas except in a few processes, and, in these, electric ventilators carry off all disagreeable odors and unhealthful fumes.

The increase in the scale of production does not mean that craftsmanship has gone. From the earliest times machines of some sort have been in use. It took craftsmen to make and use machines then, and it takes craftsmen now. The hand and the brain and the eye have functioned together ever since man came upon the earth. The hand-made age is still with us, but it has been refined and advanced until it stands on a higher plane than when men used wooden plows and primitive potters' wheels. We value the things of the past because of their association; they were steps toward those of the present. But as needs have grown, means of production have been increased and improved.

It has been asserted that machine production kills the creative ability of the craftsman. This is not true. The machine demands that man be its master; it compels mastery more than the old methods did. The number of skilled craftsmen in proportion to the working population has greatly increased under the conditions brought about by the machine. They get better wages and more leisure in which to exercise their creative faculties.

There are two ways of making money—one at the expense of others, the other by service to others. The first method does not "make" money, does not create anything; it only "gets" money—and does not always succeed in that. In the last analysis, the so-called gainer loses. The second way pays twice—to maker and user, to seller and buyer. It receives by creating, and receives only a just share, because no one is entitled to all. Nature and humanity supply too many necessary partners for that. True riches make wealthier the country as a whole.

Most people will spend more time and energy in going around problems than in trying to solve them. A problem is a challenge to your intelligence. Problems are only problems until they are solved, and the solution confers a reward upon the solver. Instead of avoiding problems we should welcome them and through right thinking make them pay us profits. The discerning youth will spend his time learning *direct methods,* learning how to make his brain and hand work in harmony with each other so that the problem in hand may be solved in the simplest, most direct way that he knows.

We can get rid of a tremendous number of the bothersome things of life if we put our minds to it. The number of needless tasks that are performed daily by thousands of people is amazing. It is the work of men with vision to trim out some of these dead limbs of life. Some of our industrial leaders have already done a good job in their own front yards, but the commons of life need attention too. Trimming out dead wood hurts no one. After all is said and done, our one great problem is the problem of life itself, of which industry is one of the tributary activities.

It is easier to denounce a wrong than to tackle the job of curing it. We cannot evade our job by blaming the past. The past took care of itself, and it depends on us to take care of the present. Many things that were thought in the past to be right we have found to be wrong. But—and remember this—none of the things believed to be thoroughly wrong have we found to be right. Even wrong things have to pass through a period of being thought right before they can be known as wrong. When we find out their nature, our responsibility begins. It is this generation's duty to the next to start at once to make room for the right thing.

Our fathers thought that life was hard, but we are beginning to see how preventable some of its hardships are. We have come to believe that there is no necessity for economic distress in a world so richly furnished with resources. Men are searching with sharp eyes for the defects in our system which prevent a man from working when he wants to work and his responsibilities require it. Economic stoppage is not natural. This defect is not in the created order of things; it is in the human order. Our selfishness, our lack of wisdom have created it. If we have established a money system which can be manipulated to the hurt of multitudes, it is as certain as fate that the system is doomed. The very discovery of insufficiency is its death warrant.

Some people think that everything will be rectified when war is abolished. Well, let nothing interfere with the abolition of war. But sound thinking insists that war will not be abolished until its roots are cut; and one of its main roots is a false money system and the high priests thereof. But more of that later. What causes war is not patriotism, not that human beings are willing to die in defense of their dearest ones. It is the false doctrine, fostered by the few, that war spells gain. It is this that makes war, and there are not enough pacifists who see it and attack it. The fact that pacifists are left in peace is proof they are not attacking the real causes of war. If pacifists spoke the truth, they would not be petted as they are today; theirs would be the hard lot of the martyrs of Truth.

We often speak of the ignorance of the past; but our distant forefathers were no more ignorant than we. They were grinding the grist of experience through the mills of the mind, and were discovering what was good and what was bad for them. That is all we are doing. What will be known in the future as the ignorance of this present generation is just the residue of discoveries which we shall not have time to make. Our responsibility is not to create a perfect world, but to establish our discoveries of what is right by weeding out what we have newly discovered to be wrong, leaving to the future its task of the same nature.

One of the principal duties that devolve during periods of change is the duty of *conscious allegiance*. To-day, conscious allegiance costs something. At the very first it means division between those who are loyal to moral convictions and those who are not. The majority of the people are naturally straddlers. They are not in the world to pioneer but to be as happy as possible. If pioneering in a cause brings discomfort, they would rather not be among the pioneers. They would rather stand on the side lines and, in the combat between truth and error, wait and see which proves the stronger. Though they may have a lazy faith that truth at last will win, they do not wish to lend a premature support. Yet majorities are essential, not to the truth, but to the acknowledgment of the truth. There are some opposites in the world that should never be reconciled. There are some programs that should never be harmonized. What frightens some people is that they want to be happy, to live and let live without being bothered. They would like to enjoy the world as it is, and if there are those who would improve the world, let them do so—but not in a way that interferes with their present happiness.

The most important work that faces the young generation to-day is making the world a better place to live in. There are thousands of great tasks waiting to be accomplished. There are innumerable opportunities in the three great arts—agriculture, industry, and transportation. The youth who can solve the money question will do more for the world than all the professional soldiers of history.

I have often said that mankind passes from the old to the new on a human bridge formed by those who labor in the three principal arts—agriculture, manufacture, transportation. We are a bridge generation. The complaints that we hear concerning the slowness of the world's change from worse to better come mostly from people who would rather be the crossing throng than help support the bridge upon which humanity passes. Fortunately for all of us, ours is not the choice.

There is a group of people who believe that the millennium will be brought about by a new system of distribution. They do not realize the fundamental truth that all things of value have always been distributed. The problem is to use them. It takes thinking, and there is no substitute for that. All the treasure chests of industry may be unlocked by this key. Look at our natural resources, our undeveloped water power, our unused forces of nature. Often a single right idea put into action is enough to make them mankind's slaves.

The truth of things escapes us, mostly because truth is so simple. Truth is a seed within itself; its nature is to reveal itself first to one or two, then ultimately to all. At a pace dependent upon our receptivity and in a manner measured by our mentality, we must do the work that destiny has given us if we would pass on to the next generation its rightful heritage. Don't be afraid of the changing order. It may look like chaos, but when the passing débris of the old has been cleared away, there will be found a thousand new opportunities teeming with promise and power.

Youth has one great element in its favor—it can live in the future. The world of to-morrow belongs to the young man of to-day; he can begin shaping the world now. No age has ever presented the tremendous opportunities of the present, but along with these opportunities are proportionate responsibilities. With the changing wheel of ambition, boys no longer regard the talkative professions as more important than the manual. They realize that there are gigantic tasks to be done and that these will be accomplished by doers rather than talkers. The man who does things is vastly more important to the world than the clerk who merely makes the record of others' achievements.

Youths have a tremendous advantage over their elders in possessing the power of vision without the drawback of retrospect. They bring fresh eyes and fresh minds to old tasks. They are not tied down by the traditions of the past; they are not slaves to the failures of others. Their concern is not so much with what could have been done in the past as with what can be done in the future. What they make of it will depend on what they make of themselves and the opportunities or tasks which are now before them.

Of course, education has its limits. Education and ability to do things are not interchangeable terms. You cannot educate brains into a man's head, but you can help him to make the most of the brains he has. A man who cannot think is not an educated man, no matter how many college degrees he may have acquired. One who can think things out usually can do them. An education which consists of signposts indicating the failures and fallacies of the past is doubtless useful. Many men are at work to-day on theories fundamentally wrong, ignorant that other men have followed that road and have had to come back. So schools are useful if they show the blind alleys of human endeavor. Then they must help to put men in possession of their own powers. But they cannot do this without the earnest desire of their students to be so helped. Inventors, by the way, are not made by education; but if they have enough education to spare them the mistakes of the past, it saves their time.

Most of us are doing two things—that by which the body is kept alive, and that by which the higher part of our nature lives. We go to the job to pay expenses and then we indulge ourselves in what we like to do and maybe were meant to do. The whole secret of a successful life is to find out what it is one's destiny to do, and then do it. Some day there may come to one the duty to do a disagreeable task, to take up a cause which will yield no reward—a cause which will at first surround one with misunderstanding and abuse, and which will make one look like a fool before men. One naturally shrinks from it. But when a man is sure of what he has to do, he should go ahead full speed. To be right means mainly to be in tune with destiny and willing to obey. It does not necessarily mean to be agreeable, nor to be agreed with, nor to be popular; it does mean to be useful in the purpose which destiny is trying to achieve in us and through us. If a man is right, he need not fear to stand alone; he is not alone. Every right idea that is put forth has many silent adherents.

There is a great deal of nonsense spoken about the "lonely heights"—they may seem to be lonely, but they are only silent. The loneliness comes when a man settles within himself whether he is to be a mere form following a conventional routine or whether he is to listen and obey the voice of a changeable life. It is lonely while he is deciding. If he decides to do what duty bids him, then he is no longer lonely. He comes at once into the fellowship of other people who are thinking as he is, but who have been waiting for a leader to declare them and their principles.

(For Problems in Writing and Discussion, see the end of the next essay.)

Henry Ford

ROGER BURLINGAME

Roger Burlingame (1889-), a native New Yorker, was graduated from Harvard in 1913 and worked for over a decade in publishing before turning to free-lance writing. He has written six novels but is better known as a biographer—of General "Billy" Mitchell, Henry Ford, Benjamin Franklin, and Elmer Davis—and even better known through March of the Iron Men *(1938) and* Engines of Democracy *(1940) as a historian of industrialism in America. More recently he has written* The American Conscience *(1957), an account of American behavior as "seen through the moral judgments of the people upon themselves"; the autobiographical* I Have Known Many Worlds *(1959); and* The Sixth Column *(1962).*

Mass production is peculiarly and almost uniquely American in its origins. The main reasons for this are, first: the American belief, in spite of many demonstrations to the contrary, that all men are created equal; and, second: the unparalleled need to supply a constantly migrating and constantly increasing agrarian population with goods produced under an acute labor shortage.

In European and Asiatic societies, tradition prescribed that the best things went to a privileged few. Clocks, watches, fine fabrics, shoes, and, later, sewing machines and bicycles were perquisites of an upper class and filtered slowly, if at all, down to the masses.

Reprinted from Henry Ford *by Roger Burlingame, by permission of Alfred A. Knopf, Inc., and The Hutchinson Publishing Group. Copyright, 1954 by Roger Burlingame.*

With abundance of labor many goods could be produced in limited quantities more or less by hand. In the United States, where everyone considered himself "as good as the next man," and where land fever and the pull of the frontier robbed the static centers of skilled workmen, machines had to be designed to multiply the productiveness of a few men and to keep the democracy supplied with what the "inalienable rights" demanded.

Through all of later American history, as social democracy became more and more complete, industry has been continuously occupied in turning luxuries into necessities. Early Connecticut clockmakers made it possible for timepieces—regarded abroad as property of the well-to-do—to become part of the furnishings of the humblest frontier cabins. Machine production plus installment-selling brought reapers, harvesters, and threshers to farmers penniless but for their land. Factory-made shoes and clothing raised the living standard of American "masses" above that of other peoples, and, finally, such astonishing luxuries as electric refrigerators, oil burners, radio, and television gained markets that to foreigners are truly fabulous.

It is largely to quantity production through semi-automatic machinery that Americans owe the rapid development of their country. With the coming of the twentieth century the enormous territory had been surprisingly integrated, considering the sparseness of its population in the frontier period; yet much of the land was still unexploited, almost unexplored. Cities and towns followed one another in long, straight lines along rivers and railroads: to these communities the rural population had flocked, leaving hundreds of ghost villages, lonely farms, or large barren stretches that were virtually wilderness. The railroads had killed the improvement of highways, and wagon roads had lapsed into conditions that, a half century later, are impossible to visualize.

By 1900, however, many Americans had had glimpses of other horizons. An entirely new taste of individual freedom—freedom to escape, to explore, to discover the allures of nature—had come in the nineties with the bicycle. Supposing that the bicycle was a social fixture, several eager promoters had started good-roads movements. Imported techniques of roadbuilding—notably McAdam's—were tried and proved successful. Finally, in the first year of the new century, road conditions and the possibilities of new frontiers in the interior were brought sensationally to public attention in the exploit of Roy Chapin, who drove a one-cylinder, curved-dash Oldsmobile buggy from Detroit to New York. "He was forced," Mr. Arthur Pound tells us, "to leave the muddy highways, and drive along the towpath of the Erie Canal, contesting with mule trains for the right-of-way."

Such things as this undoubtedly sank into the subconscious minds of Americans everywhere and prepared the way for the revolution. It is probable, for instance, that the great army of boys who followed automotive development with acute interest saw visions of their own futures, driving horselessly into far country. A child taught to believe that he might well one day become president was still easier to convince that he might one day drive and even own a car. On the surface, however, Roy Chapin's feat was regarded as a daring sporting effort—not quite so reckless as going over Niagara Falls in a barrel, but in that general category.

Even six years later, when 142,000 motor vehicles were registered in the United States, private ownership of a car was a mark of distinction or, perhaps, evidence of extravagant frivolity: indeed, as we have seen, business trends seemed to be toward increasing its luxurious characteristics. Keith Sward, writing of the early 1900's in *The Legend of Henry Ford,* says:

> In this day the rich themselves thought of the automobile as a luxury reserved for the few. . . . It was understood at the same time that the plain people of the country were to function as the tenders and repairers of the motor car. Guided by such a conviction, the Detroit *Saturday Night* said in 1909 that the best chauffeurs were to be recruited from the ranks of former coachmen. Such drivers, observed the *Saturday Night,* were dutiful members of the "servant class" who could be counted on to know "exactly what is expected of them by their masters."

Whatever may have been Henry Ford's motives during his company's experimental period, we may be sure that such statements as this must have exasperated him. Above all else, this man suspected and despised the rich and shied away from anything that smacked of luxury. It would have been wholly out of character for him to favor the production of expensive cars except for technical purposes. It must, therefore, have been a satisfaction to him that there was a sharp decline of sales when his $2,500 Model K was introduced and a quick up-curve when the cheaper Model N went on the market. It was obvious by 1907, though no suggestion of a "universal car" had yet engaged the public fancy, that the name of Ford was popularly associated with low-priced automobiles.

We may put our finger precisely on 1907 as the year in which revolution came. It seems, looking back on it, as if fate played then into Ford's hands—as if it were a wind of destiny that shook the stock market in March, brought the most hopeful securities to the ground, and sowed the seeds of October panic. The rich were hard hit. Low-priced cars were more than ever sought after. In the course of the year Ford production jumped to about eighty-five hundred, five times that of the previous year; and the great bulk of it consisted of the latest experimental light cars—Models N, R, and S, all selling for less than $1,000.

Watching these things, keeping careful track of costs, thinking of the future in terms of expansion beyond all dreams of the time in this first adolescence of the industry, Henry Ford evolved his great concept. It was in the light of this vision that he felt too confined in the Piquette-Beaubien plant, to which the company had moved when Strelow's Mack Avenue shop would no longer hold it. He planned for the purchase of the sixty-acre Highland Park race track, where he talked of building "the largest automobile factory in the world."

Various employees of the Ford Motor Company have claimed credit for the revolutionary idea. It has been said that it was not one man's brainstorm, but the result of the focusing of many minds. It is undoubtedly true that others contributed details of design and, especially, production methods. But no one can examine the records or analyze the reminiscences of Ford workers of the period without knowing beyond question not only that Henry Ford's was the master mind but that the whole of the broad project originated with him. Indeed, we find evidence of discontented and sometimes angry rumblings throughout the time when the plan was taking shape and, indeed, of the disgusted exit of two of the most important production men in the plant. And with Ford's contemplation of the new gigantic installations at Highland Park—to be financed entirely by the plowing back of profits—the waves of unrest spread out to the stockholders. So the project had far from unanimous support.

The project was Model T.

The way for the realization of Model T was now open. If the idea had occurred to Henry Ford before—as it probably had—there were difficulties to be overcome. He had not had full control. Malcomson, with whom he had shared equally the majority stockholding, was opposed to concentrating on a low-priced car. But here too the gods were conniving. Malcomson had sold out to Ford. Speculating in other directions, he had needed cash and, as the stock for which he had originally paid $12,000 was now worth $175,000, he was content. Albert Strelow and three minor stockholders had followed Malcomson's exit. Ford bought all of these shares. Those who like to play the game known as "the if's of history" enjoy speculating on the millions these men might have made had they remained aboard. Yet if they had stuck, perhaps there would have been no Model T. Poor Strelow put the $25,000 he received into a gold mine, which almost immediately turned out to be barren, and he was later reported standing in line for a lowly job with the company he had once partly owned.

By 1907, then, 58½ per cent of stock in the Ford Motor Company had been acquired by Henry Ford, giving him full power in the management of the company. In these fateful years some valuable technical assets had also arrived. To make crankshafts for Model N, Ford had hired a great, brawny, uncouth ox of a man named Walter Flanders, who, nevertheless, was original, ingenious, and highly versed in mass-production techniques. Also, working creatively in the company since 1904, another giant, physically and mentally, was a Dane named Charles Sorensen or "Cast-iron Charlie." This man, whose later contributions to the moving assembly were perhaps without equal anywhere, was an old friend of Henry's going back to the days of the Edison company. A third was the brilliant mechanic, P. Edward ("Pete") Martin.

These men and others picked by the chief's almost infallible instinct must, by the methods of economy and speed they installed—rearranging machinery, devising jigs and fixtures for accurate machine-tool work, dividing labor, and insisting on interchangeability—have led Ford over the months into his large, over-all view of the most adaptable product for full mass production. He was constantly moving through all the departments, watching every man and every machine. Like Frederick Taylor, the great inventor of scientific management, Ford had a passion for simplifying operations, for economy of time and materials, for eliminating little waste motions from each worker's performance.

It is remarkable how close all this came to the carefully worked-out plans of Taylor, because Ford had certainly not read Taylor's treatises. It must be assumed that the efficiency patterns came into the Ford plant with the factory men he hired, but in the use of them Ford exercised a critical judgment and creative force that everyone acknowledged. His power lay in an instant recognition of what was right and what was wrong in any new method. The reminiscences of the workers taken, after Ford's death, on tape recordings testify to the master's almost constant pressure, walking over miles of factory floor, stopping at every work center to watch or speak, to say no, to nod approval, to berate—perhaps fire on the spot—an inflexible perverse, or skeptical worker. A man in these times who hinted, even by the expression of his face, that he thought one of the master's schemes impossible was doomed.

> Mr. Ford [Charles Sorensen recalls] never caught me saying that an idea he had couldn't be done. If I had the least idea that it couldn't be done, I wouldn't announce myself on it to him. . . . I always felt the thing would prove itself.

Walter Flanders thought the Model T project was impossible. He did not think the Model T itself was impossible. He was willing to try that. But he thought the *project* would be fatal to the company. He thought Ford was crazy to pursue it and said so. He then walked out before Ford had a chance to invite his departure.

It was not Ford's determination to produce Model T—a simple, sturdy, utilitarian, low-priced job—that worried Flanders. It was his determination *to produce nothing but*. It was a profound obsession in the industry that no manufacturer could survive concentrating on a single model—that he must offer a choice and make annual changes. Today we may sympathize with this view. The industrialists of 1907 were merely thinking twenty years ahead of their time. Mass production of this highly complex machine had to be established first—not only technically but economically as well. We know now that a Model T project had to be injected into American society before the universal market and the universal desire could become facts. The *flexible* mass production that engineers are dreaming of in the 1950's will probably follow more flexible tastes of the future. But *inflexible* mass production had to precede it: neither the techniques nor the popular demand of the years immediately following 1907 would have permitted anything else. That was the fact: but of all the eager folk who were then engaged in pushing the horse off the American road, only Henry Ford knew it.

Against the advice, then, of those who should have known better —yet who, curiously enough, provided many of the technical needs of the scheme—Henry Ford announced that thereafter there would be only one Ford.

> I will build a motor car [he stated] for the great multitude. It will be large enough for the family but small enough for the individual to run and care for. It will be constructed of the best materials, by the best men to be hired, after the simplest designs that modern engineering can devise. But it will be so low in price that no man making a good salary will be unable to own one—and enjoy with his family the blessing of hours of pleasure in God's great open spaces.

Advertising men have done a great deal of talking about "psychology" and much solemn experimenting with it. Yet it would be hard to find in all their copy anything as appealing in its time as this simple, almost biblically worded statement. What American before 1910 could be indifferent to the vision of transporting his family, of a Sunday or holiday, into "God's great open spaces"? What head of a family would not be inflated by the prospect of running and caring for this family machine? What "equal" citizen would admit to making anything less than a "good salary"?

In his autobiography Ford recalls that his rivals were delighted by this announcement and by the news that he had bought the sixty acres at Highland Park for his production. The question, he says, asked so many thousand times since, was already being asked in 1908 and 1909: "How soon will Ford blow up?"

> It is asked [he adds] only because of the failure to grasp that a principle rather than an individual is at work, and the principle is so simple that it seems mysterious.

The principle was to decide on your design, freeze it, and, from then on, spend all your time, effort, and money on making the machinery to produce it—concentrating so completely on production that, as volume goes up, it is certain to get cheaper per unit produced. Changing your design every year means retooling your factory every year; it means not continuing one process long enough to study ways of making it more economical; it means constantly changing your orders for materials; it means that the customers have to learn new tricks; it means that salesmen have to keep changing their story; it means expensive advertising.

The "great multitude," Ford thought, was not interested in fashions or experiments; it did not care about pretty lines or colors in a car: it wanted something useful to drive to town or country, something that would meet any road conditions, something that took no thought to drive, no expense to maintain, no special skill to repair. And the multitude, Ford believed, *would want these things forever* and nothing else. This was the theory and philosophy of mass production carried to its extreme.

Workers still living remember Ford in his elation, the almost fanatical excitement of his drive as this concept came to full flower in his mind. He would look at the design for a cylinder block or differential or steering unit and say: "There! We won't change that until we've built a hundred thousand cars!" At the beginning he wanted to simplify the manufacture until skilled workers were eliminated—until, as one pattern-maker remembers, "he just took a man off the street and broke him in like a piece of machinery doing a certain job." This was not an effort to get cheap labor. It was simply that, for the tremendous production that he envisioned, there was not enough skilled labor in the world; also, production could never become fast enough until the worker's motions were almost automatic and without thought.

PROBLEMS FOR WRITING AND DISCUSSION

1. What attributes of American character discussed in Part I does Henry Ford manifest?

2. Is Ford's distinction between the "two ways of making money" valid? What is the "money question" the solution of which "will do more for the world than all the professional soldiers of history"?

3. What are the "real causes of war" which Ford says the pacifists fail to attack?

4. With the criteria Ford gives, would you know how to carry out your "duty of conscious allegiance"?

5. What, for Ford, is the chief value of education? Compare Ford's attitude with that of Agee (p. 191) and Kennan (p. 233).

6. What group does Ford probably have in mind when he refers to "people who believe that the millenium will be brought about by a new system of distribution"?

7. Ford suggests that the millenium will be effected when we solve "our one great problem": "the problem of life itself," to which industry is but a tributary. Does Ford suggest by what activities other than industry "the higher part of our nature lives"?

8. Ford says, "We are a bridge generation." Explain what he means. Is his metaphor for human life logically tenable? Is there evidence in this piece that Ford regards as parasitical those who do not support the bridge by laboring in "the three principal arts"? If you had to choose between "enjoying the world as it is" and supporting this bridge, which would you choose? Why?

Free Enterprise

9. What is Ford's "secret of a successful life"? How might Ford have rated the "success" of Abraham Lincoln, Harold Wilson, Grandma Moses (and of William Carlos Williams, Sevareid, and Commager—men who merely make "the record of others' achievements")?

10. Once a man has decided against being "a mere form following a conventional rule" and "decides to do what duty bids him," how does Ford say his loneliness is dispelled?

11. The people wait for a leader "to declare them and their principles," Ford declares by way of exhortation. Select from the essay comparable statements about "most people," "some people," or "the majority of the people." To whom is Ford addressing himself?

12. Ford speaks of "the processes of human events," a "scheme of progress," "the created order of things," and the "work destiny has given us," and of our being "right" when we are "in tune with destiny and willing to obey" it. Examine these phrases in context. Examine also what Ford says about the "nature of truth" and those who lazily believe that "truth at last will win." Then answer this question: Is Ford a fatalist or a rugged individualist? Indicate specifically the evidence on which you base your answer.

13. What is Burlingame's view of American mass production? Why does he call it "peculiarly and uniquely American in its origins"?

14. According to Burlingame, what led Ford to conceive of the Model T? Did fate or destiny play any part in Ford's success?

15. What light does Burlingame's sketch of Ford shed on Ford's philosophy of industry—that is, on what Ford meant by the "simplicity" of truth, by the "right" and the "wrong," by the harmonious working of brain and hand?

16. Burlingame describes Ford's desire to render the "worker's motions . . . almost automatic and without thought." Ford himself writes that economic "stoppage is not natural" but a "defect . . . in the human order." What dangers do you see in equating the "human order" with the natural or "created order" of things?

17. Ford once said, "History is more or less bunk," and intellectuals ridiculed him for the remark. How does this selection clarify what Ford meant? Does it indicate that his view of history, for his purposes, was not ridiculous?

The Personification of Corporation
THURMAN ARNOLD

Thurman Arnold (1891-) is perhaps most widely known for his work as an Assistant Attorney General of the United States in charge of antitrust actions from 1938 to 1943. His legal background suited him well for this post. Once a lawyer in and Mayor of Laramie, Wyoming, his home town, Arnold became dean of the College of Law, West Virginia University, in 1927, leaving three years later to teach at Yale, where he remained until entering government service. After a brief term (1943-1945) as an Associate Justice of the United States Court of Appeals for the District of Columbia, he returned to practicing law. Among his published works are The Folklore of Capitalism *(1937),* The Bottlenecks of Business *(1940), and* Democracy and Free Enterprise *(1942).*

One of the essential and central notions which give our industrial feudalism logical symmetry is the personification of great industrial enterprise. The ideal that a great corporation is endowed with the rights and prerogatives of a free individual is as essential to the acceptance of corporate rule in temporal affairs as was the ideal of the divine right of kings in an earlier day. Its exemplification, as in the case of all vital ideals, has been accomplished by ceremony. Since it has been a central ideal in our industrial government, our judicial institutions have been particularly concerned with its celebration. Courts, under the mantle of the Constitution, have made a living thing out of this fiction. Men have come to believe that their own

From The Folklore of Capitalism *by Thurman Arnold, Yale University Press, 1937. Reprinted by permission of the publisher.*

future liberties and dignity are tied up in the freedom of great industrial organizations from restraint, in much the same way that they thought their salvation in the future was dependent on their reverence and support of great ecclesiastical organizations in the Middle Ages. This ideal explains so many of our social habits, rituals, and institutions that it is necessary to examine it in some detail.

The origin of this way of thinking about organization is the result of a pioneer civilization in which the prevailing ideal was that of the freedom and dignity of the individual engaged in the accumulation of wealth. The independence of the free man from central authority was the slogan for which men fought and died. This free man was a trader, who got ahead by accumulating money. There was something very sacred in the nineteenth-century conception of this activity. In the 'seventies the most popular text in economics was one originally written by a clergyman, Bishop Francis Wayland, and revised in 1878 by A. L. Chapin, President of the Congregational College at Beloit. Joseph Dorfman, in his brilliant book on *Thorstein Veblen and His America*,[1] summarizes this philosophy of the holy character of the trader's function as follows:

> 1) "God has made man a *creature of desires*" and has established the material universe "with qualities and powers . . . for the *gratification of those desires.*" Desire is the stimulus to production and invention. 2) To satisfy desires, to obtain pleasures, man must by "irksome" labour force "*nature to yield her hidden resources.*" 3) *The exertion of labour establishes a right of PROPERTY in the fruits of labour*, and the "idea of *exclusive possession* is a necessary consequence." Originally the object belongs to the producer "by an intuitive conception of right, and the act of appropriation is as instinctive as the act of breathing." The right of property may be conceived as "a law of natural justice," as Bowen of Harvard put it, because "the producer would not put forth his force and ingenuity if others deprived him of their fruits." Thus is established 4) *"The Right of EXCHANGE."*

Here is the beginning of the religion of the essential dignity of an individual's accumulating wealth by trading which later became

---
[1] p. 23.

the mystical philosophy that put the corporate organization ahead of the governmental organization in prestige and power, by identifying it with the individual. Our fathers breathed this atmosphere in every day of their schooling. For a pointed summary of their attitude toward distribution of goods by so-called governmental organizations, we quote again from Mr. Dorfman's book:[2]

> Since socialism is the "utter negation" of the right of private property, "man is no more adapted to it than the barn fowl is to live in the water." Philanthropy or any other aid of the poor is a violation of the same laws of God and property. All attempts to "relieve the natural penalties of indolence and improvidence" bring about "unexpected and severe evil." The doctrine that the government should provide for the unemployed "is the most subversive of all social order." Even the claim of Ruskin that "all labours of like amounts should receive the same reward," means the suppression of "commercial law," which is "God's method." If labour and capital are free, as they are in the "order of nature undisturbed" under "the law of competition," then "the flow of each . . . toward an equilibrium, is as natural as that of waters of the ocean under gravitation." In reality the labourer has no complaint against the competitive system. As Perry put it, employer and employee "come together of necessity into a relation of mutual dependence, which God has ordained, and which, though man may temporarily disturb it, he can never overthrow."[3]

Here was the philosophy of the men who came later to dominate our large industrial organizations and also to work for them. There was nothing in that philosophy which justified far-flung industrial empires. Indeed, the great organization in which most men were employees, and a few at the top were dictators, was a contradiction of that philosophy. The great organization came in as a result of mechanical techniques which specialized the work of production so that men could not operate by themselves. Nothing could stop the progress of such organization, and therefore in order to tolerate it, men had to pretend that corporations were individuals. When faced

---

[2] pp. 24-25.

[3] The quotations in the above excerpts are selected from texts and articles current at Carleton College when Veblen was a student.

with the fact that they were not individuals, they did not seek to control, but denounced and tried to break them up into smaller organizations. Those who did not choose to dissent, however, sought refuge in transferring the symbolism of the individual to the great industrial armies in which they were soldiers.

It is a familiar social phenomenon to see the symbols of the habits of pioneer times transferred as a social philosophy to later institutions to prove that we still are following the examples of our fathers. . . .

It was this identification of great organizations with the dignities, freedom, and general ethics of the individual trader which relieved our federation of industrial empires from the hampering restrictions of theology which always prevent experiment. Men cheerfully accept the fact that some individuals are good and others bad. Therefore, since great industrial organizations were regarded as individuals, it was not expected that all of them would be good. Corporations could therefore violate any of the established taboos without creating any alarm about the "system" itself. Since individuals are supposed to do better if let alone, this symbolism freed industrial enterprise from regulation in the interest of furthering any current morality. The *laissez faire* religion, based on a conception of a society composed of competing individuals, was transferred automatically to industrial organizations with nation-wide power and dictatorial forms of government.

This mythology gave the Government at Washington only a minor part to play in social organization. It created the illusion that we were living under a pioneer economy composed of self-sufficient men who were trading with each other. In that atmosphere the notion of Thomas Jefferson, that the best government was the one which interfered the least with individual activity, hampered any control of our industrial government by our political government. We were slower, therefore, in adopting the measures of control of industrial organization than a country like England. The Government at Washington gradually changed into what was essentially a spiritual government whose every action was designed to reconcile the conflict between myth and reality which men felt when a creed of individualism was applied to a highly organized industrial world. Government in Washington was supposed to act so as to instil "confidence" in great business organizations. The Supreme Court of the United States, because it could express better than any other institution the myth of the corporate personality, was able to hamper Federal powers to an extent which foreigners, not realizing the emotional power of the myth, could not understand. This court invented most of the ceremonies which kept the myth alive and preached about them in a most dramatic setting. It dressed huge corporations in the clothes of simple farmers and merchants and thus made attempts to regulate them appear as attacks on liberty and the home. So long as men instinctively thought of these great organizations as individuals, the emotional analogies of home and freedom and all the other trappings of "rugged individualism" became their most potent protection. . . .

A similar complication of philosophy and dialectic attended the ceremonies of chivalry when the institutions which this mythology once described so vividly were disappearing. Such things are familiar in times of social change.

When the actual world is not at variance with men's belief, it is unnecessary to write or think much about it. People are not troubled by doubt in such times; therefore doctrine is not needed. When symbols or beliefs have no relation to what men see before them, regularity of doctrine becomes of paramount importance. Since observations in such a situation create only paralyzing doubt, men must drown their observations in doctrine and philosophy. Therefore, ceremonies grow in number and mystical literature increases by leaps and bounds, becoming more and more abstract as it grows. That this has happened to economic theory is obvious. The reasons why it has happened lie in the fact that where the fiscal religion becomes completely undescriptive of what is going on, ceremony is the only way of giving force to the creed.

This symbolism made practical legislation legalistic and complicated so that it would not contradict fixed beliefs. For example, the

Social Security Act was drawn to resemble an insurance corporation, because insurance corporations were supposed to be very pious and respectable individuals indeed. The Government put money in a huge reserve. This reserve had to be invested in its own bonds and therefore had no meaning whatever, except to make social security legislation look like an old-line insurance company. In other enterprises the Government found that by adopting the device of a government corporation it gave its activities a little of the freedom which was enjoyed by private corporations and escaped the rules and principles which hampered action when it was done by a government department instead of a government corporation. In other words, it gave the Government some of the robes of the individual.

There seemed no limit to the size of these industrial empires masquerading as individuals. Laws against monopoly and restraint of trade were easily evaded in the fairyland where men pretended that organizations were men who owned property. Nothing in the Middle Ages compares for sheer fantasy with the holding company, or with modern security manipulation by which control of large organizations may be obtained without investment risk. Equally fantastic was the notion that a corporation had the rights of a citizen of the state which incorporated it. This permitted the use of the sacred doctrine of states' rights to hamper regulation of industrial empires which had no connection with any particular state.

Organizations which exercise governing powers of a permanent character do not maintain their power by force. Force is entirely too exhausting. They do it by identifying themselves with the faiths and loyalties of the people. Therefore, the picture which people see of a society is always in terms of these faiths and loyalties. They do not examine anything, however obvious, which contradicts those faiths. Few educated men who opposed the holding-company bill could actually describe the structure of any of our great holding companies, but this did not interfere with their belief that an attack on that form of corporate structure was an attack on individualism. . . .

This book is not concerned with the unsolvable problem of whether America would have progressed faster or slower under some other set of myths. It does not attack the use of the corporate personality in folklore. The results have been the creation of one of the greatest productive machines that the world has ever known, and this perhaps is justification enough if anyone is interested in justifying what has happened. This book is concerned only with diagnosing the present difficulties which have come upon us now that the industrial feudalism is no longer protecting large groups of our citizens who demand security, and with trying to explain the ideological difficulties which prevent the creating of organizations which will give that protection. We cannot be practical about social problems if we are under the illusion that we can solve them without complying with the taboos and customs of the tribe. The corporate personality is part of our present religion. We must continue to refer to corporations as individuals in public discourse so long as the words have emotional relevance. Since, however, we must use the words and ceremonies, it becomes important that we be able to use them intelligently. It becomes necessary, therefore, to analyze a few of the principal rituals connected with the personification of corporate organization which are generally completely misunderstood.

The two most important ceremonies which have dramatized the rugged individualism of business organizations are those which surround the antitrust laws and the reorganization of insolvent corporations. The one is useful in times of prosperity. The other is called on in times of adversity. Both are designed to perpetuate the illusion that it is men, and not organizations, with whom the Government at Washington is dealing.

PROBLEMS FOR WRITING AND DISCUSSION

1. This selection was published in 1937. What evidence can you cite from the present to support Arnold's thesis? Is there evidence that his thesis is invalidated by developments since 1937?

2. From what peculiarly American ideal does the personification of corporations grow? What part would you say the Horatio Alger tradition Allen describes (p. 139) played in its growth?

3. What developments in industrial societies necessitated the pretense that corporations were individuals? What fallacies inhere in the analogy between individuals and corporations? How have the fallacies affected the role of government and courts in relation to corporations?

4. Do Henry Ford's remarks (p. 143) suggest an explanation for the personification of corporations that Arnold overlooks? Charles E. Wilson, a former corporation head and Secretary of Defense, is reported to have said, "What's good for General Motors is good for America." Is his remark one of the "ceremonial" attempts to reconcile myth and reality that Arnold describes? Explain.

5. Explain the analogy Arnold draws between the corporation and the church of the Middle Ages.

6. Does the modern industrial worker by his "irksome" labor establish "a right of Property in the fruits of labour"? Does he establish his right to exclusive possession of the resources with which he works? Speaking for the workers, Hoffer (p. 175) says, "We know that we shall manage to get our full share no matter what happens." What, in the modern technological economy, does the worker exclusively possess?

7. Compare Henry Ford's ideas on distribution of wealth and on the "natural order" with those described by Dorfman in the second passage Arnold quotes. If man's labor is part of a preordained "process" governed by "laws," what is incongruous in the nineteenth-century ideal of the "freedom and dignity of the individual engaged in the accumulation of wealth"?

8. Arnold writes, "The corporate personality is part of our present religion." Is our "present religion" the same as the *"laissez faire"* religion of the nineteenth century?

9. According to Arnold, the modern corporation has been made in man's image. Examine the advertising of a large corporation and discuss the kind of "image" it attempts to project.

10. By what means does our "industrial government" exercise its authority? Does Arnold challenge its exercise of authority openly or covertly? What is it for which Arnold suggests the operation of "natural law" has failed to provide?

11. When, according to Arnold, does "regularity of doctrine" become imperative? Does the American attempt to define a national character appear significant in the light of Arnold's observation?

Corporate Capitalism and "The City of God"
ADOLF A. BERLE, JR.

Adolf A. Berle, Jr., (1895-) has been a Professor of Corporation Law at Columbia University since 1927, taking extended leaves of absence to serve as a member of Franklin D. Roosevelt's "Brain Trust" in 1932, as Treasurer of the City of New York (1934-37), as Assistant Secretary of State (1938-44), and as Ambassador to Brazil (1945-46). Between tours of public duty he has written several books, among them The Twentieth Century Capitalist Revolution *(1954),* Tides of Crisis *(1957), and* Power Without Property *(1959). Central to his work is the role of the corporation in modern life. He is interested neither in attacking nor in defending the corporation, but in analyzing what it is, how it acts, and what it is becoming.*

In the fifth century A.D. one Augustine, Bishop of Hippo in North Africa, surveyed the wreck of the Roman Empire. It had broken into vast, unstable fragments. The Roman peace and the Roman imperial order had ceased to be the framework with which life could be formed. New institutions were appearing; old ones were breaking up. In the words of the Psalmist, the foundations of the earth were out of course, and whole peoples walked in darkness.

This prelate had had full measure of experience with the phenomena of power. As bishop, he had held some himself. As observer of the ebb of empire and of men who seized kingdoms or forged

From The Twentieth-Century Capitalist Revolution, *copyright, 1954, by Adolf A. Berle, Jr. Reprinted by permission of Harcourt, Brace & World, Inc., and Macmillan & Co. Ltd.*

them, he knew quite well that power was only half the story of human organization. Aside from its ecclesiastical implications his study, *The City of God,* was a striking and simple statement of a hypothesis of political science. Underlying, entering, complementing, ultimately controlling every tangible institutional organization of affairs there was inevitably a moral and philosophical organization which continued from age to age and which ultimately directed power. This philosophical content alone gave permanence to institutions; this philosophical organization survived institutional creation. This Augustine christened "The City of God." Because it worked directly on the minds of men wherever and however placed, it could exact action from them within any framework and thus guide any institution. It is, perhaps, the first great source book for the theory of dichotomy of power which has entered this study from time to time.

We have not, up to the present, been accustomed to think of the modern corporation as an institution at all, let alone a political institution. We have thought of it merely as an enterprise (or perhaps combination of enterprises) within a community. American political thought has been frightened, and corporations themselves have been frightened, at any suggestion that they might emerge as political institutions in their own and separate right. So we have not been accustomed to place over against each other, as necessarily interrelated facts, the pragmatic concept of the corporation and the philosophical concept of the desirable community. Corporate executives rather resent being assimilated to politicians; still more they resent being called to account by philosophers. They belong to one of the few groups in history to which political power came unsought, or at any rate as a by-product rather than a main objective. It is probable that when Mr. Harlow Curtice and Mr. Alfred P. Sloan, Jr., wrote in General Motors' Annual Report for 1953, that "with the elimination of controls and with the trend away from a centrally managed economy, industry is possessed of the opportunity to make its maximum contribution to the forward march of our country," they did not think they were talking politics at all. Still less, perhaps, would they consider they had assumed in substantial measure the philosophical burden of judging what is and what should be the "forward march" of a very great country. But they had done just that.

Herein lies, perhaps, the greatest current weakness of the corporate system. In practice, institutional corporations are guided by tiny self-perpetuating oligarchies. These in turn are drawn from and judged by the group opinion of a small fragment of America—its business and financial community. Change of management by contesting for stockholders' votes is extremely rare, and increasingly difficult and expensive to the point of impossibility. The legal presumption in favor of management, and the natural unwillingness of courts to control or reverse management action save in cases of the more elementary types of dishonesty or fraud, leaves management with substantially absolute power. Thus the only real control which guides or limits their economic and social action is the real, though undefined and tacit, philosophy of the men who compose them.

Fifteen hundred years ago, St. Augustine made the same observation concerning the men and groups who achieved power in the fragmented territories of the empire that had once been Rome. But he also knew, as the men in power in his time frequently did not, that whatever institutions they built derived permanence, continuity and significance from the philosophy more than from the power; and he endeavored, in the diffuse scholastic fashion of the time, to set the Christian philosophy over against the contemporary power institutions; and he gave impetus and direction to the whole of the Middle Ages.

The lesson, I think, is as valid for the twentieth as for the fifth century. Capitalism is not a way of life, but a method of achieving economic and social results—a method indeed evolving so rapidly that the capitalism of 1954 has but a bowing acquaintance with that of 1854 and little if any real resemblance to the capitalism of 1804. The institutional corporation collectivized capital, and like most collectivisms concentrated power into a small directing group. The aggregate of such groups—a couple of hundred or so—have proved to be the chief instruments of the twentieth-century revolution in the western world outside the Iron Curtain. As yet the community has not created any acknowledged referent of responsibility, no group from which they take their power mandate or get instructions in dealing with serious streams of events they can and do affect. There is no recognized body of doctrine by which they themselves must test their choice as they act from day to day.

PROBLEMS FOR WRITING AND DISCUSSION

1. Berle implies that the power of the modern corporation is both political and philosophical. Give examples other than the one example he gives to clarify what he means.
2. What does Berle see as the greatest weakness of the corporate system?
3. What does Arnold (p. 162) say about the internal control of corporations that corroborates Berle's charge that "institutional corporations are guided by tiny self-perpetuating oligarchies"?
4. Explain the relevance of Augustine's *The City of God* to Berle's central idea. At what point does the analogy between the institutions Augustine studied and the institutional corporations Berle studies break down? What does Berle mean by a "referent of responsibility"?
5. Henry Ford, though no philosopher, wrote *My Philosophy of Industry* (p. 143). Are there points of "doctrine" in the excerpt that you read which would serve as reliable philosophical guides to action? Explain.
6. Is the Horatio Alger formula for the accumulation of wealth (p. 139) commensurable with the Christian doctrine with which Augustine "gave impetus and direction to the whole of the Middle Ages"?
7. In support of his assertion that "nothing in the Middle Ages compares for sheer fantasy" with certain twentieth-century corporation phenomena, Arnold cites existing "laws" and "doctrines" to which the modern corporation has recourse for the appearance of legality. Would Berle consider these "laws" and "doctrines" a satisfactory "referent of responsibility"?
8. Compare what Berle and Arnold have to say about the "dichotomy of power" by which institutions preserve their position. Does Arnold explain the faiths and loyalties that lend corporations their philosophical justification? Does Berle? Explain.

9. Berle considers the institutional corporation a revolutionary collectivism and seems to deplore the lack of a "recognized body of doctrine" to guide its choices. According to Arnold, when does "regularity of doctrine" become "of paramount importance"? Does Berle intimate that the countries outside the Iron Curtain need an ideological scheme to square theory with actuality? (Note carefully his definition of "capitalism.")

10. As the writers in this Part see it, is the problem of modern industry essentially economic, political, or philosophical? Justify your choice by reference to specific writers.

The Workingman Looks at the Boss

ERIC HOFFER

> Eric Hoffer (1902-) is a California longshoreman who has written numerous articles on the workingman and two books, The True Believer *(1952)* and The Passionate State of Mind *(1955)*. The first has been described as "a series of short essays and apothegms on the characteristics of dedicated souls in politics and religion" and the second as more of the same. Hoffer's early life in New York was grim. Virtually blind from the age of seven to that of fifteen, and with no schooling, Hoffer had to fend for himself after his father, a German cabinetmaker, died. In Hoffer's words: "I knew several things: One, that I didn't want to work in a factory; two, that I couldn't stand being dependent on the good graces of a boss; three, that I was going to stay poor; four, that I had to get out of New York. Logic told me that California was the poor man's country." He has lived there ever since.

There are many of us who have been workingmen all our lives and, whether we know it or not, will remain workingmen till we die. Whether there be a God in heaven or not; whether we be free or regimented; whether our standard of living be high or low—I and my like will go on doing more or less what we are doing now.

This sober realization need not be unduly depressing to people who have acquired the habit of work and who, like the American workingman, have the ingredients of a fairly enjoyable life within their reach. Still, the awareness of being an eternal workingman

From "The Workingman Looks at the Boss," Harper's Magazine, March *1954*. Reprinted by permission of the author.

colors one's attitudes; and it might be of some interest to indicate briefly what the relations between management and labor look like when seen from his point of view.

To the eternal workingman management is substantially the same whether it is made up of profit-seekers, idealists, technicians, or bureaucrats. The allegiance of the manager is to the task and the results. However noble his motives he cannot help viewing the workers as a means to an end. He will always try to get the utmost out of them; and it matters not whether he does it for the sake of profit, for a holy cause, or for the sheer principle of efficiency.

One need not view management as an enemy or feel self-righteous about doing an honest day's work to realize that things are likely to get tough when management can take the worker for granted; when it can plan and operate without having to worry about what the worker will say or do.

The important point is that this taking of the worker for granted occurs not only when management has unlimited power to coerce but also when the division between management and labor ceases to be self-evident. Any doctrine which preaches the oneness of management and labor—whether it stresses their unity in a party, class, race, nation, or even religion—can be used to turn the worker into a compliant instrument in the hands of management. Both communism and fascism postulate the oneness of management and labor, and both are devices for the extraction of maximum performance from an underpaid labor force. The preachment of racial unity facilitated the exploitation of labor in our South, in French Canada, and in South Africa. Pressure for nationalist and religious unity served, and still serves, a similar purpose elsewhere.

Seen from this point of view, the nationalization of the means of production is more a threat than a promise. For we shall be bossed and managed by someone, no matter who owns the means of production—and we can have no defenses against those who can tell us in all truth that we, the workers, own everything in sight and they, our taskmasters, are driving us for our own good. The battle between socialism and capitalism is to a large extent a battle between bosses, and it is legitimate to size up the dedicated Socialist as a potential boss.

One need not call to mind the example of Communist Russia to realize that the idealist has the making of a most formidable taskmaster. The ruthlessness born of self-seeking is ineffectual compared with the ruthlessness sustained by dedication to a holy cause. "God wishes," said Calvin, "that one should put aside all humanity when it is a question of striving for his glory." So it is better to be bossed by men of little faith, who set their hearts on toys, than by men animated by lofty ideals who are ready to sacrifice themselves and others for a cause. The most formidable employer is he who, like Stalin, casts himself in the role of a representative and champion of the workers.

Our sole protection lies in keeping the division between management and labor obvious and matter-of-fact. We want management to manage the best it can, and the workers to protect their interests the best they can. No social order will seem to us free if it makes it difficult for the worker to maintain a considerable degree of independence from management.

The things which bolster this independence are not utopian. Effective labor unions, free movement over a relatively large area, a savings account, a tradition of individual self-respect—these are some of them. They are within the worker's reach in this country and most of the free world, but are either absent or greatly weakened in totalitarian states.

In the present Communist regimes unions are tools of management, worker mobility is discouraged by every means, savings are periodically wiped out by changes in currency, and individual self-respect is extirpated by the fearful technique of terror. Thus it seems that the worker's independence is as good an index as any for measuring the freedom of a society.

The next question is whether an independent labor force is compatible with efficient production. For if the attitude of the workers tends to interfere with the full unfolding of the productive process, then the workingman's independence becomes meaningless.

It has been my observation for years on the docks of San Francisco that, while a wholly independent labor force does not contribute to management's peace of mind, it can yet goad management to perfect its organization and to keep ever on the lookout for more efficient ways of doing things. Management on the San Francisco waterfront is busy twenty-four hours a day figuring out ways of loading and discharging ships with as few men as possible.

Mechanization became very marked on the waterfront after the organization of the present militant labor union in 1934. The fork lift and the pallet board are almost in universal use. There are special machines for handling sugar, newsprint, and cotton bales. There are new methods for handling coffee, rice, and wool. New arrangements and refinements appear almost every day. Here nobody has to be told that management is continually on the job. Certainly, there are other factors behind this incessant alertness, and some of them play perhaps a more crucial role in the process of mechanization. But it is quite obvious that a fiercely independent labor force is not incompatible with efficient production.

Contrary to the doctrine propounded by some in the heyday of the Industrial Revolution, mechanization has not taught docility to "the refractory hand of labor." At least here on the docks, no one worries lest the machines cut down our earnings. We know that we shall manage to get our full share no matter what happens. And it is a dull workingman who does not see in the machine the only key to the true millennium. For only mechanization can mitigate—if not cure—"the disease of work," as de Tocqueville calls it, which has tortured humanity since the first day of its existence.

It is true, of course, that the cleavage between management and labor is a source of strain and strife. But it is questionable whether tranquillity is the boon it is made out to be. The late William Randolph Hearst shrewdly observed that "whatever begins to be tranquil is gobbled up by something that is not tranquil." The constant effort to improve and advance is neither automatic nor the result of a leisurely choice between alternatives. In human affairs, the best stimulus for running ahead is to have something we must run from. The chances are that the millennial society, where the wolf and the lamb shall dwell together, will be a stagnant society.

PROBLEMS FOR WRITING AND DISCUSSION

1. Hoffer argues against the oneness of management and labor. Why? What relevance does Arnold's essay (p. 162) have to this point?
2. Discuss the validity of Hoffer's statement that "the preachment of racial unity facilitated the exploitation of labor in our South. . . ."
3. Why does Hoffer look upon mechanization as a blessing rather than a threat to the working man? Is his a commonly held view? Compare his view with Henry Ford's (p. 143).
4. Does Ford fit into Hoffer's category of ideal employers—"men of little faith, who set their hearts on toys"? Why or why not?
5. What would Hoffer think of Ford's distinction between the two ways of making money?
6. Hoffer says that "things get tough when management can take the worker for granted." Does Burlingame (p. 152) give evidence that Ford took the worker for granted in the way Hoffer fears?
7. What does Hoffer consider the principal advantage *to industry* of an independent labor force? Is he more cynical than Ford about efficiency? Explain.
8. Compare the opening two paragraphs of Hoffer's essay with the last paragraph of Ford's (p. 151). Would Hoffer agree that the "voice of a changeable life" is the best one to which the "eternal workingman" should listen? What, by implication, is Hoffer's attitude toward the Horatio Alger myth of self-realization?

Labor, Leisure, and the New Class

JOHN KENNETH GALBRAITH

> John Kenneth Galbraith (*1908-   *), *after receiving his doctorate from the University of California, spent a year in England at Cambridge, returning to teach at Princeton (1939-42) and later to become deputy administrator of the Office of Price Administration. He left government to be an editor of* Fortune *from 1943 to 1948 and then joined the faculty of Harvard University, where he remained until he accepted the ambassadorship to India in 1960. Among the more recent of his many books are* The Great Crash *(1955),* The Affluent Society *(1955), and* The Liberal Hour *(1960). He writes with wit and urbanity and has been called the "king of American capitalism's critics."*

I

The greatest prospect that we face—indeed what must now be counted one of the central economic goals of our society—is to eliminate toil as a required economic institution. This is not a utopian vision. We are already well on the way. Only an extraordinarily elaborate exercise in social camouflage has kept us from seeing what has been happening.

Nearly all societies at nearly all times have had a leisure class— a class of persons who were exempt from toil. In modern times and especially in the United States the leisure class, at least in any

---

The selection from John Kenneth Galbraith The Affluent Society, *1955, is reprinted by permission of and arrangement with Houghton Mifflin Company, the authorized publishers, and with the author.*

identifiable phenomenon, has disappeared. To be idle is no longer considered rewarding or even entirely respectable.

But we have barely noticed that the leisure class has been replaced by another and much larger class to which work has none of the older connotation of pain, fatigue, or other mental or physical discomfort. We have failed to appreciate the emergence of this New Class, as it may be simply called, largely as the result of one of the oldest and most effective obfuscations in the field of social science. This is the effort to assert that all work—physical, mental, artistic, or managerial—is essentially the same.

This effort to proclaim the grand homogeneity of work has commanded, for different reasons, the support of remarkably numerous and diverse groups. To economists it has seemed a harmless and, indeed, an indispensable simplification. It has enabled them to deal homogeneously with all of the different kinds of productive effort and to elaborate a general theory of wages applying to all who receive an income for services. Doubts have arisen from time to time, but they have been suppressed or considered to concern special cases. The identity of all classes of labor is one thing on which capitalist and communist doctrine wholly agree. The president of the corporation is pleased to think that his handsomely appointed office is the scene of the same kind of toil as the assembly line and that only the greater demands in talent and intensity justify his wage differential. The Communist officeholder cannot afford to have it supposed that his labor differs in any significant respect from that of the comrade at the lathe or on the collective farm with whom he is ideologically one. In both societies it serves the democratic conscience of the more favored groups to identify themselves with those who do hard physical labor. A lurking sense of guilt over a more pleasant, agreeable, and remunerative life can often be assuaged by the observation "I am a worker too" or, more audaciously, by the statement that "mental labor is far more taxing than physical labor." Since the man who does physical labor is intellectually disqualified from comparing his toil with that of the brainworker, the proposition is uniquely unassailable.

In fact the differences in what labor means to different people could not be greater. For some, and probably a majority, it remains a stint to be performed. It may be preferable, especially in the context of social attitudes toward production, to doing nothing. Nevertheless it is fatiguing or monotonous or, at a minimum, a source of no particular pleasure. The reward rests not in the task but in the pay.

For others work, as it continues to be called, is an entirely different matter. It is taken for granted that it will be enjoyable. If it is not, this is a source of deep dissatisfaction or frustration. No one regards it as remarkable that the advertising man, tycoon, poet, or professor who suddenly finds his work unrewarding should seek the counsel of a psychiatrist. One insults the business executive or the scientist by suggesting that his principal motivation in life is the pay he receives. Pay is not unimportant. Among other things it is a prime index of prestige. Prestige—the respect, regard, and esteem of others—is in turn one of the more important sources of satisfaction associated with this kind of work. But, in general, those who do this kind of work expect to contribute their best regardless of compensation. They would be disturbed by any suggestion to the contrary.[1]

Such is the labor of the New Class. No aristocrat ever contemplated the loss of feudal privileges with more sorrow than a member of this class would regard his descent into ordinary labor where the reward was only the pay. In the years following World War II a certain number of grade school teachers left their posts for substantially higher paid factory work. The action made headlines

---

[1] We have here an important reason why the income tax, despite high marginal rates and frequent warnings of the damage these may do in impairing incentives, has so far had no visibly deleterious effect. The surtax rates fall almost entirely on members of the New Class. These are people who, by their own claim except when they are talking about the effect of income taxes, are not primarily motivated by money. Hence the tax, which also does not disturb the prestige structure —people are rated by before-tax income—touches no vital incentive. Were high marginal rates to be placed on (say) the overtime income of automobile workers, we would expect a substantial withdrawal of effort. Here pay, as an incentive, remains important.

because it represented an unprecedented desertion of an occupation which was assumed to confer the dignity of the New Class. The college professor, who is more securely a member of the New Class than the school teacher, would never contemplate such a change even as an exercise in eccentricity and no matter how inadequate he might consider his income.

In keeping with all past class behavior, the New Class seeks energetically to perpetuate itself. Offspring are not expected to plan their lives in order to make a large amount of money. (Those who go into business are something of an exception at least partly because income, in business, is uniquely an index of prestige.) But from their earliest years the children are carefully indoctrinated in the importance of finding an occupation from which they will derive satisfaction—one which will involve not toil but enjoyment. One of the principal sources of sorrow and frustration in the New Class is the son who fails to make the grade—who drops down into some tedious and unrewarding occupation. The individual who meets with this misfortune—the son of the surgeon who becomes a garage hand—is regarded by the community with pity not unmixed with horror. But the New Class has considerable protective powers. The son of the surgeon rarely does become a garage hand. However inadequate, he can usually manage to survive, perhaps somewhat exiguously, on the edge of his caste. And even if, as a salesman or an investment counselor, he finds little pleasure in his work, he will be expected to assert the contrary in order to affirm his membership in the New Class.

II

The New Class is not exclusive. While virtually no one leaves it, thousands join it every year. Overwhelmingly the qualification is education.[2] Any individual whose adolescent situation is such that

---
[2] Political capacity is another qualification, and it is of especial importance to those who seek to make their escape after reaching their adult years. The intensity of the campaigns for local political offices—city councilors, school committeemen, sheriffs, and county supervisors—is to be explained by this fact as also is

sufficient time and money is invested in his preparation, and who has at least the talents to carry him through the formal academic routine, can be a member. There is a hierarchy within the class. The son of the factory worker who becomes an electrical engineer is on the lower edge; his son who does graduate work and becomes a university physicist moves to the higher echelons; but opportunity for education is, in either case, the open sesame.

There can be little question that in the last hundred years, and even in the last few decades, the New Class has increased enormously in size. In early nineteenth-century England or the United States, excluding the leisure class and considering the New Class as a group that lived on what it has carefully called earned income, it consisted only of a handful of educators and clerics, with, in addition, a trifling number of writers, journalists, and artists. In the United States of the eighteen-fifties it could not have numbered more than a few thousand individuals. Now the number whose primary identification is with their job, rather than the income it returns, is undoubtedly in the millions.

Some of the attractiveness of membership in the New Class, to be sure, derives from a vicarious feeling of superiority—another manifestation of class attitudes. However, membership in the class unquestionably has other and more important rewards. Exemption from manual toil; escape from boredom and confining and severe routine; the chance to spend one's life in clean and physically comfortable surroundings; and some opportunity for applying one's thoughts to the day's work, are regarded as unimportant only by those who take them completely for granted. For these reasons it has been possible to expand the New Class greatly without visibly reducing its attractiveness.

---

the enduring interest in appointive political office. Those who are already members of the New Class often fail to see how such posts are valued as an *entrée*. They look askance at the competition for such posts between the less well educated members of the community. They fail to realize that such posts provide the greatest opportunity for such individuals and that it is upon such people that we depend for much good (as well as some bad) civic enterprise. The union is another important opportunity for the individual of political capacity. Cf. the interesting sketches by Harvey Swados in *On the Line* (Boston: Atlantic-Little, Brown, 1957).

This being so, there is every reason to conclude that the further and rapid expansion of this class should be a major, and perhaps next to peaceful survival itself, *the* major social goal of the society. Since education is the operative factor in expanding the class, investment in education, assessed qualitatively as well as quantitatively, becomes very close to being the basic index of social progress. It enables people to realize a dominant aspiration. It is an internally consistent course of development.

Recent experience has shown that the demand for individuals in the occupations generally identified with the New Class increases much more proportionately with increased income and wellbeing. Were the expansion of the New Class a deliberate objective of the society this, with its emphasis on education and its ultimate effect on intellectual, literary, cultural, and artistic demands, would greatly broaden the opportunities for membership. At the same time the shrinking in the number of those who engage in work *qua* work is something to be regarded not alone with equanimity but with positive approval. For one of the inevitable outlets for the intellectual energies and inventiveness of the New Class will be in finding substitutes for routine and repetitive manual labor. To the extent that such labor is made scarce and more expensive, this tendency will, of course, be accelerated. To minimize the number of people doing such work is the counterpart of the goal of expanding the New Class.

It is a measure of how little we need worry about the danger from reducing the number of people engaged in work *qua* work that, as matters now stand, our concern is not that we will have too few available for toil but too many. We worry lest such technical advances as automation, an already realized dividend of the expansion of the New Class, will proceed so rapidly as to leave a surplus of those who still work. This, indeed, could be the greater danger.

III

I venture to suggest that the unprofessional reader will find rather reasonable and rational the ideas here offered. Why should men struggle to maximize income when the price is many dull and dark hours of labor? Why especially should they do so as goods become more plentiful and less urgent? Why should they not seek instead to maximize the rewards of all the hours of their days? And since this is the plain and obvious aspiration of a great and growing number of the most perceptive people, why should it not be the central goal of the society? And now to complete the case, we have a design for progress. It is education or, more broadly, investment in human as distinct from material capital.

But in the more sophisticated levels of the conventional wisdom, including, regrettably, some professional economists, any such goal will seem exceedingly undesirable. The production of material goods, urgent or otherwise, is the accepted measure of our progress. Investment in material capital is our basic engine of progress. Both this product and the means for increasing it are measurable and tangible. What is measurable is better. To talk of transferring increasing numbers of people from lives spent mostly in classical toil to lives which, for the most part, are spent pleasantly has less quantitative precision. Since investment in individuals, unlike investment in a blast furnace, provides a product that can be neither seen nor valued, it is inferior. And here the conventional wisdom unleashes its epithet of last resort. Since these achievements are not easily measured, as a goal they are "fuzzy." This is widely deemed to be a fatal condemnation. The precise, to be sure, is usually the old and familiar. Because it is old and familiar it has been defined and measured. Thus does insistence on precision become another of the tautological devices by which the conventional wisdom protects itself. Nor should one doubt its power.

Yet anyone who finds this analysis and these proposals sensible should not be entirely discouraged. We are here in one of the contexts where circumstance has marched far beyond the conventional wisdom. We have seen how general are the efforts to join the New Class and how rapid is its expansion. We are not here establishing a new economic and social goal but identifying one that is already widely if but tacitly accepted. In this situation the conventional wisdom cannot resist indefinitely. The economist of impeccable credentials in the conventional wisdom, who believes that there is no goal in life of comparable urgency with the maximization of total and individual real income, would never think of applying such a standard to himself. In his own life he is an exponent of all the aspirations of the New Class. He educates and indoctrinates his children with but one thing in mind. It is not that they should maximize their income. This is abhorrent. He wants above all that they will have an occupation that is interesting and rewarding. On this he hopes, indeed, that they will take their learned parent as their model.

PROBLEMS FOR WRITING AND DISCUSSION

1. Why have "social camouflage" and "obfuscation" attended the emergence of the New Class?
2. What, primarily, qualifies one to belong to the New Class? What privileges does membership bring?
3. What attributes of "class" (such as snobbery, internal conformity, self-justification) does the New Class display? Why does Galbraith say it is not exclusive?
4. Why did such a class not emerge before this era? Why has the leisure class in effect disappeared? What class did Henry Ford belong to? For whom did he design the Model T? (See Burlingame, p. 152).
5. On what ground would some "professional economists" dispute Galbraith's thesis? How would Galbraith call their bluff?
6. Members of the New Class (capitalist and communist) absolve their "democratic conscience" by identifying "with those who do hard physical labor." Why would Hoffer's dock worker (p. 175) find it difficult to assail this identification?
7. Why does Galbraith say that the "greater danger" is not that eventually there may be too few left to toil but that there may be too many?
8. The New Class Galbraith describes has resulted from the same technological revolution Berle (p. 170) credits with having "collectivized capital." If this new "collectivism" assures the unhampered "pursuit of happiness" to members of the New Class, is it merely a means of production

(as Berle says) or is it an end in itself—that is, a "way of life"? Who, besides Galbraith, has foreseen a classless society as the end-product of revolution?

9. In going to college and in choosing a profession, which motivates you more strongly: making money or finding "work" that is enjoyable in itself? Have you ever toiled, or do you expect ever to be a toiler? Are your parents members of the New Class? If so, are they first or second generation? Whether they are members or not, have they invested in "human capital"? Explain.

2. Education

Education

JAMES AGEE

James Agee (1910-1955) was born in Knoxville, Tennessee, and his years there served as background for two novels—The Morning Watch (1951) and A Death in the Family (1957), which was published posthumously and received the Pulitzer Prize. After his family moved to Maine, he entered Exeter and then Harvard. Two years after graduation from Harvard he published Permit Me Voyage, a book of verse. He worked for Fortune from 1932 to 1935 and for Time from 1939 to 1948. His managing editor said he was "the finest writer Time ever had." Interest in movies—he was film critic for Time—led him to Hollywood in 1948, and there he wrote the scripts for The Red Badge of Courage, The African Queen, and Night of the Hunter. The selection that follows comes from Let Us Now Praise Famous Men (1942), done with Walker Evans, the photographer, after the two men had lived in the rural South with the Gudgers, a family of sharecroppers. The prose in this book varies from the best of our time, as Agee's friend Dwight MacDonald has put it, to some of the best. "The content is as varied as the style," MacDonald goes on. "Much of it is close, minute description which blends lyricism with naturalism in an extraordinarily effective way." The book sold less than 600 copies the first year of publication. It has recently been reprinted and is now considered a classic.

In every child who is born, under no matter what circumstances, and of no matter what parents, the potentiality of the human race is born again: and in him, too, once more, and of each of us, our terrific responsibility towards human life; towards the utmost idea of goodness, of the horror of error, and of God.

Every breath his senses shall draw, every act and every shadow and thing in all creation, is a mortal poison, or is a drug, or is a signal or symptom, or is a teacher, or is a liberator, or is liberty itself, depending entirely upon his understanding: and understanding,[1] and action proceeding from understanding and guided by it, is the one weapon against the world's bombardment, the one medicine, the one instrument by which liberty, health, and joy may be shaped or shaped towards, in the individual, and in the race.

This is no place to dare all questions that must be asked, far less to advance our tentatives in this murderous air, nor even to qualify so much as a little the little which thus far has been suggested, nor even either to question or to try to support my qualifications to speak of it at all: we are too near one of the deepest intersections of pity, terror doubt and guilt; and I feel that I can say only, that 'education,' whose function is at the crisis of this appalling responsibility, does not seem to me to be all, or even anything, that it might be, but seems indeed the very property of the world's misunderstanding, the sharpest of its spearheads in every brain: and that since it could not be otherwise without destroying the world's machine, the world is unlikely to permit it to be otherwise.

In fact, and ignorant though I am, nothing, not even law, nor property, nor sexual ethics, nor fear, nor doubtlessness, nor even authority itself, all of which it is the business of education to cleanse

---

The selection from James Agee Let Us Now Praise Famous Men, *1942, is reprinted by permission of and arrangement with Houghton Mifflin Company, the authorized publishers.*

[1] Active 'understanding' is only one form, and there are suggestions of 'perfection' which could be called 'understanding' only by definitions so broad as to include diametric reversals. The peace of God surpasses all understanding; Mrs. Ricketts and her youngest child do, too; 'understanding' can be its own, and hope's, most dangerous enemy.

the brain of, can so nearly annihilate me with fury and with horror; as the spectacle of innocence, of defenselessness, of all human hope, brought steadily in each year by the millions into the machineries of the teachings of the world, in which the man who would conceive of and who would dare attempt even the beginnings of what 'teaching' must be could not exist two months clear of a penitentiary: presuming even that his own perceptions, and the courage of his perceptions, were not a poison as deadly at least as those poisons he would presume to drive out: or the very least of whose achievements, supposing he cared truly not only to hear himself speak but to be understood, would be a broken heart.[2]

For these and other reasons it would seem to me mistaken to decry the Alabama public schools, or even to say that they are 'worse' or 'less good' than schools elsewhere: or to be particularly wholehearted in the regret that these tenants are subjected only to a few years of this education: for they would be at a disadvantage if they had more of it, and at a disadvantage if they had none, and they are at a disadvantage in the little they have; and it would be hard and perhaps impossible to say in which way their disadvantage would be greatest.

School was not in session while I was there. My research on this subject was thin, indirect, and deductive. By one way of thinking it will seem for these reasons worthless: by another, which I happen to trust more, it may be sufficient.

I saw, for instance, no teachers: yet I am quite sure it is safe to assume that they are local at very least to the state and quite probably to the county; that most of them are women to whom teaching is either an incident of their youth or a poor solution for their spinsterhood; that if they were of much intelligence or courage they could not have survived their training in the State Normal or would never have undertaken it in the first place; that they are saturated in every belief and ignorance which is basic in their

---

[2] It may be that the only fit teachers never teach but are artists, and artists of the kind most blankly masked and least didactic.

country and community; that any modification of this must be very mild indeed if they are to survive as teachers; that even if, in spite of all these screenings, there are superior persons among them, they are still again limited to texts and to a system of requirements officially imposed on them; and are caught between the pressures of class, of the state, of the churches, and of the parents, and are confronted by minds already so deeply formed that to liberate them would involve uncommon and as yet perhaps undiscovered philosophic and surgical skill. I have only sketched a few among dozens of the facts and forces which limit them; and even so I feel at liberty to suggest that even the best of these, the kindly, or the intuitive, the socalled natural teachers, are exceedingly more likely than not to be impossibly handicapped both from without and within themselves, and are at best the servants of unconscious murder; and of the others, the general run, that if murder of the mind and spirit were statutory crimes, the law, in its customary eagerness to punish the wrong person,[3] might spend all its ingenuity in the invention of deaths by delayed torture and never sufficiently expiate the enormities which through them not by their own fault, have been committed.

Or again on the curriculum: it was unnecessary to make even such search into this as I made to know that there is no setting before the students of 'economic' or 'social' or 'political' 'facts' and of their situation within these 'facts,' no attempt made to clarify or even slightly to relieve the situation between the white and negro races, far less to explain the sources, no attempt to clarify psychological situations in the individual, in his family, or in his world, no attempt to get beneath and to revise those 'ethical' and 'social' pressures and beliefs in which even a young child is trapped, no attempt, beyond the most nominal, to interest a child in using or in discovering his senses and judgment, no attempt to counteract the paralytic quality inherent in 'authority,' no attempt beyond the most nominal and stifling to awaken, to protect, or to 'guide' the

---

[3] This is not to suggest there is a 'right person' or that punishment can ever be better than an enhancement of error.

sense of investigation, the sense of joy, the sense of beauty, no attempt to clarify spoken and written words whose power of deceit even at the simplest is vertiginous, no attempt, or very little, and ill taught, to teach even the earliest techniques of improvement in occupation ('scientific farming,' diet and cooking, skilled trades), nor to 'teach' a child in terms of his environment, no attempt, beyond the most suffocated, to awaken a student either to 'religion' or to 'irreligion,' no attempt to develop in him either 'skepticism' or 'faith,' nor 'wonder,' nor mental 'honesty' nor mental 'courage,' nor any understanding of or delicateness in 'the emotions' and in any of the uses and pleasures of the body save the athletic; no attempt either to relieve him of fear and of poison in sex or to release in him a free beginning of pleasure in it, nor to open within him the illimitable potentials of grief, of danger, and of goodness in sex and in sexual love, nor to give him the beginnings at very least of a knowledge, and of an attitude, whereby he may hope to guard and increase himself and those whom he touches, no indication of the damages which society, money, law, fear and quick belief have set upon these matters and upon all things in human life, nor of their causes, nor of the alternate ignorances and possibilities of ruin or of joy, no fear of doubtlessness, no fear of the illusions of knowledge, no fear of compromise:—and here again I have scarcely begun, and am confronted immediately with a serious problem: that is: by my naming of the lack of such teaching, I can appear too easily to recommend it, to imply, perhaps, that if these things were 'taught,' all would be 'solved': and this I do not believe: but insist rather that in the teaching of these things, infinitely worse damage could and probably would result than in the teaching of those subjects which in fact do compose the curriculum: and that those who would most insist upon one or another of them can be among the deadliest enemies of education: for if the guiding hand is ill qualified, an instrument is murderous in proportion to its sharpness. Nothing I have mentioned but is at the mercy of misuse; and one may be sure a thousand to one it will be misused; and that its misuse will block any more 'proper' use even more solidly than unuse and discrediting could. It could be said, that we must learn a certitude and correlation in every 'value' before it will be possible to 'teach' and not to murder; but that is far too optimistic. We would do better to examine, far beyond their present examination, the extensions within ourselves of doubt, responsibility, and conditioned faith and the possibilities of their more profitable union, to a degree at least of true and constant terror in even our tentatives, and if (for instance) we should dare to be 'teaching' what Marx began to open, that we should do so only in the light of the terrible researches of Kafka and in the opposed identities of Blake and Céline.

All I have managed here, and it is more than I intended, is to give a confused statement of an intention which presumes itself to be good: the mere attempt to examine my own confusion would consume volumes. But let what I have tried to suggest amount to this alone: that not only within present reach of human intelligence, but even within reach of mine as it stands today, it would be possible that young human beings should rise onto their feet a great deal less dreadfully crippled than they are, a great deal more nearly capable of living well, a great deal more nearly aware, each of them, of their own dignity in existence, a great deal better qualified, each within his limits, to live and to take part toward the creation of a world in which good living will be possible without guilt toward every neighbor: and that teaching at present, such as it is, is almost entirely either irrelevant to these possibilities or destructive of them, and is, indeed, all but entirely unsuccessful even within its own 'scales' of 'value.'

Within the world as it stands, however, the world they must live in, a certain form of education is available to these tenant children; and the extent to which they can avail themselves of it is of considerable importance in all their future living.

A few first points about it:

They are about as poorly equipped for self-education as human beings can be. Their whole environment is such that the use of the intelligence, of the intellect, and of the emotions is atrophied, and is all but entirely irrelevant to the pressures and needs which involve almost every instant of a tenant's conscious living: and indeed if these faculties were not thus reduced or killed at birth they would result in a great deal of pain, not to say danger. They learn the work they will spend their lives doing, chiefly of their parents, and from their parents and from the immediate world they take their conduct, their morality, and their mental and emotional and spiritual key. One could hardly say that any further knowledge or consciousness is at all to their use or advantage, since there is nothing to read, no reason to write, and no recourse against being cheated even if one is able to do sums; yet these forms of literacy are in general held to be desirable: a man or woman feels a certain sort of extra helplessness who lacks them: a truly serious or ambitious parent hopes for even more, for a promising child; though what 'more' may be is, inevitably, only dimly understood.

School opens in middle or late September and closes the first of May. The country children, with their lunches, are picked up by buses at around seven-thirty in the morning and are dropped off again towards the early winter darkness. In spite of the bus the children of these three families have a walk to take. In dry weather it is shortened a good deal; the bus comes up the branch road as far as the group of negro houses at the bottom of the second hill and the Ricketts children walk half a mile to meet it and the Gudger children walk three quarters. In wet weather the bus can't risk leaving the highway and the Ricketts walk two miles and the Gudgers a mile and a half in clay which in stretches is knee-deep on a child.

There was talk during the summer of graveling the road, though most of the fathers are over forty-five, beyond road-age. They can hardly afford the time to do such work for nothing, and they and their negro neighbors are in no position to pay taxes. Nothing had come of it within three weeks of the start of school, and there was no prospect of free time before cold weather.

Southern winters are sickeningly wet, and wet clay is perhaps the hardest of all walking. 'Attendance' suffers by this cause, and by others. Junior Gudger, for instance, was absent sixty-five and Louise fifty-three days out of a possible hundred-and-fifty-odd, and these absences were 'unexcused' eleven and nine times respectively, twenty-three of Junior's and a proportionate number of Louise's absences fell in March and April, which are full of work at home as well as wetness. Late in her second year in school Louise was needed at home and missed several consecutive school days, including the final examinations. Her 'marks' had been among the best in her class and she had not known of the examination date, but no chance was given her to make up the examinations and she had to take the whole year over. The Ricketts children have much worse attendance records and Pearl does not attend at all.

School does not begin until the children shall have helped two weeks to a month in the most urgent part of the picking season, and ends in time for them to be at work on the cotton-chopping.

The bus system which is now a routine of country schools is helpful, but not particularly to those who live at any distance from tax-maintained roads.

The walking, and the waiting in the cold and wetness, one day after another, to school in the morning, and home from schools in the shriveling daylight, is arduous and unpleasant.

Schooling, here as elsewhere, is identified with the dullest and most meager months of the year, and, in this class and country, with the least and worst food and a cold noonday lunch: and could be set only worse at a disadvantage if it absorbed the pleasanter half of the year.

The 'attendance problem' is evidently taken for granted and, judging by the low number of unexcused absences, is 'leniently' dealt with: the fact remains, though, that the children lose between a third to half of each school year, and must with this handicap keep up their lessons and 'compete' with town children in a contest in which competition is stressed and success in it valued and rewarded.

The schoolhouse itself is in Cookstown; a recently built, windowy, 'healthful' red brick and white-trimmed structure which perfectly

Education

exemplifies the American genius[4] for sterility, unimagination, and general gutlessness in meeting any opportunity for 'reform' or 'improvement.' It is the sort of building a town such as Cookstown is proud of, and a brief explanation of its existence in such country will be worth while. Of late years Alabama has 'come awake' to 'education,' illiteracy has been reduced; texts have been modernized; a good many old schools have been replaced by new ones. For this latter purpose the counties have received appropriations in proportion to the size of their school population. The school population of this county is five black to one white, and since not a cent of the money has gone into negro schools, such buildings as this are possible: for white children. The negro children, meanwhile, continue to sardine themselves, a hundred and a hundred and twenty strong, into stove-heated one-room pine shacks which might comfortably accommodate a fifth of their number if the walls, roof, and windows were tight.[5] But then, as one prominent landlord said and as many more would agree: 'I don't object to nigrah education, not up through foath a fift grade maybe, but not furdern dat: I'm too strong a believah in white syewpremcy.'

This bus service and this building the (white) children are schooled in, even including the long and muddy walk, are of course effete as compared to what their parents had.[6] The schooling itself is a different matter, too: much more 'modern.' The boys and girls alike are subjected to 'art' and to 'music,' and the girls learn the first elements of tap dancing. Textbooks are so cheap almost anyone can afford them: that is, almost anyone who can afford anything at all; which means that they are a stiff problem in any year to almost any tenant. I want now to list and suggest the contents of a

---

[4] So well shown forth in 'low-cost' housing.

[5] Aside from discomfort, and unhealthfulness, and the difficulty of concentrating, this means of course that several 'grades' are in one room, reciting and studying by rotation, each using only a fraction of each day's time. It means hopeless boredom and waste for the children, and exhaustion for the teacher.

[6] Their parents would have walked to one-room wooden schoolhouses. I'm not sure, but think it more likely than not, that many of the white children still do today.

few textbooks which were at the Gudger house, remembering, first, that they imply the far reaches of the book-knowledge of any average adult tenant.

The Open Door Language Series: First Book: Language Stories and Games.
Trips to Take. Among the contents are poems by Vachel Lindsay, Elizabeth Madox Roberts, Robert Louis Stevenson, etc. Also a story titled 'Brother Rabbit's Cool Air Swing,' and subheaded: 'Old Southern Tale.'
Outdoor Visits: Book Two of *Nature and Science Readers.* (Book One is *Hunting.*) Book Two opens: 'Dear Boys and Girls: in this book you will read how Nan and Don visited animals and plants that live outdoors.'
Real Life Readers: New Stories and Old: A Third Reader. Illustrated with color photographs.
The Trabue-Stevens Speller. Just another speller.
Champion Arithmetic. Five hundred and ten pages: a champion psychological inducement to an interest in numbers. The final problem: 'Janet bought 1¼ lbs. of salted peanuts and ½ lb. of salted almonds. Altogether she bought ? lbs. of nuts?

Dear Boys and Girls indeed!

Such a listing is rich as a poem; twisted full of contents, symptoms, and betrayals, and these, as in a poem, are only reduced and diluted by any attempt to explain them or even by hinting. Personally I see enough there to furnish me with bile for a month: yet I know that any effort to make clear in detail what is there, and why it seems to me so fatal, must fail.

Even so, see only a little and only for a moment.

These are books written by 'adults.' They must win the approval and acceptance of still other 'adults,' members of school 'boards'; and they will be 'taught' with by still other 'adults' who have been more or less 'trained' as teachers. The intention is, or should be, to engage, excite, preserve, or develop the 'independence' of, and furnish with 'guidance,' 'illumination,' 'method,' and 'information,' the curiosities of children.

Now merely re-examine a few words, phrases and facts:

The Open Door: open to whom. That metaphor is supposed to engage the interest of children.

Series: First Book. Series. Of course The Bobbsey Twins is a series; so is The Rover Boys. *Series* perhaps has some pleasure associations to those who have children's books, which no tenant children have: but even so it is better than canceled by the fact that this is so obviously not a pleasure book but a schoolbook, not even well disguised. An undisguised textbook is only a little less pleasing than a sneaking and disguised one, though. *First Book:* there entirely for the convenience of adults; it's only grim to a child.

Language: it appears to be a *modern* substitution for the word 'English.' I don't doubt the latter word has been murdered; the question is, whether the new one has any life whatever to a taught child or, for that matter, to a teacher.

Stories and Games: both, modified by a school word, and in a school context. Most children prefer pleasure to boredom, lacking our intelligence to reverse this preference: but you must use your imagination or memory to recognize how any game can be poisoned by being 'conducted': and few adults have either.

Trips to Take. Trips indeed, for children who will never again travel as much as in their daily bus trips to and from school. Children like figures of speech or are, if you like, natural symbolists and poets: being so, they see through frauds such as this so much the more readily. No poem is a 'trip,' whatever else it may be, and suffers by being lied about.

The verse. I can readily imagine that 'educators' are well pleased with themselves in that they have got rid of the Bivouac of the Dead and are using much more nearly contemporary verse. I am quite as sure, knowing their kind of 'knowledge' of poetry, that the pleasure is all theirs.

These children, both of town and country, are saturated southerners, speaking dialects not very different from those of negroes. *Brother* Rabbit! *Old Southern Tale!*

Outdoor Visits. Nature and Science. Book One: *Hunting.* Dear Boys and Girls. In this book you will read (oh, I will, will I?). Nan and Don. Visit. Animals and Plants that Live Outdoors. Outdoors. You will pay formal calls on Plants. They live outdoors. 'Nature.' 'Science.' Hunting. Dear Boys and Girls. Outdoor Visits.

Real Life. 'Real' 'Life' 'Readers.' Illustrated by *color* photographs.

Or back into the old generation, a plainer title: *The Trabue-Stevens Speller.* Or the *Champion Arithmetic,* weight eighteen pounds, an attempt at ingratiation in the word champion, so broad of any mark I am surprised it is not spelled *Champeen.*

Or you may recall the page of geography text I have quoted elsewhere: which, I must grant, tells so much about education that this chapter is probably unnecessary.

I give up. Relative to my memory of my own grade-schooling, I recognize all kinds of 'progressive' modifications: Real Life, color photographs, Trips to Take (rather than Journey, to Make), games, post-kindergarten, 'Language,' Nan and Don, 'Nature and Science,' Untermeyer-vintage poetry, 'dear boys and girls'; and I am sure of only one thing: that it is prepared by adults for their own self-flattery and satisfaction, and is to children merely the old set retouched, of afflictions, bafflements, and half-legible insults more or less apathetically submitted to.

PROBLEMS FOR WRITING AND DISCUSSION

1. How much of Agee's indictment of the educational system is supported by facts? To what extent are the "facts" subservient to a strong feeling? Explain.

2. In the specific locale Agee describes, what are the handicaps and shortcomings of both teacher and pupil? Although the selection was written at the end of the depression of the 1930's, discuss its relevance to texts, teachers, techniques, and community pressures you know of from your own experience.

3. What does "didactic" mean? Agee suggests that the only "fit" teachers may be artists—the least didactic kind. Is his suggestion irresponsible or is it intellectually provocative? Explain what he means by this suggestion and by saying that a man who would dare begin "what 'teaching' must be" would end up in a penitentiary with a "broken heart."

4. Analyze Agee's criticism of the books at the Gudger house. Agee complains that this assortment of books, despite ineffectual changes, is just the "old set." If Agee himself is a product of the educational "machine" with which the world will not permit one to tamper, what hope is there that bad systems of education do not altogether destroy individual potentiality?

5. Agee also complains that these books are written by adults to be taught by adults, and that their diction, while it flatters adults, lies to the children. In what ways? What are the alternatives to these faults?

6. Agee speaks of "responsibility" for the world as a corollary to individual potentiality. Does Agee fulfill his responsibility? What does he attack? What would he preserve?

Bringing Up Children—French Way, Our Way

LAWRENCE WYLIE

> Lawrence Wylie (1909-   ) was born in Indianapolis. After graduating from Indiana University he went east to Brown University, where he received his doctorate in 1940. While teaching at Haverford College he received a Social Science Research Council Fellowship (1950-51), a Ford Faculty Fellowship (1955-56), and a Guggenheim Fellowship (1957-58). He is at present the C. Douglas Dillon Professor of the Civilization of France at Harvard University. He has written Saint-Marc Girardin, Bourgeois (1947) and Village in Vaucluse (1957).

From our house we could hear the children down in the schoolyard, and it sounded as though our ruse had worked. We had lived in a village I will call Peyrane, a few miles east of Avignon, for two months, and our children had not learned French as fast as children are rumored to pick up a foreign language. On that Sunday morning, we had suggested that the two boys take their soccer ball down to the school, where they might attract some French friends to play with them.

To see what was up, I walked down and looked around the corner of the building. The situation was not what I had expected. An exciting soccer game was indeed in progress—but Jonathan and David were not picking up French phrases. On the contrary, all the children of the neighborhood were shouting at the top of their lungs:

From The New York Times Magazine, June 30, 1957. Reprinted by permission of the author.

"Keek eet to me!!! Keek eet to me!!!"

English had won this skirmish. However, I was somewhat consoled by the fact that the French children were learning English, for I was teaching English to the *classe des grands* as a part of my project to discover what goes on in a French village school. An assist on the soccer field was welcome.

In spite of their American aggressiveness, the boys did learn French before the village children learned English. Within five months, both of them could express themselves effectively, if not always grammatically, in the language. Little by little they came to prefer French to English, and French customs to their American ones. We tried to cling to some parental tenets from home—no eating between meals, getting to bed by 8 o'clock. As our children rejected these sacred institutions, they began to reject us, too. We were immigrants.

Perhaps if we had stayed in France longer, our family unit would have become French enough, that is, a sufficiently tight unit, to withstand this attack, but we were not put to the ultimate test. After almost a year in Peyrane, our leave was up and we left for home. When we stopped in Paris, our two children, so obviously American in appearance but with the most exaggerated of southern French accents, were a delight to French friends and to the *liftiers* of the Hotel Lutétia. The wonder grew to amazement among relatives back in this country at these two little boys who politely shook hands with everyone and who spoke French when they were playing together.

But this Gallic behavior did not last long. First went the handshake, which had caused American adults to laugh and to make coy remarks. Then it became apparent that the French language could not resist the corrosive influence of different surroundings. Day by day chunks of it dropped out and were replaced by English.

Since I am a language teacher and know how hard it is for adults to learn a foreign language, I hated to see the children lose this skill. French conversation at home, private lessons with French students from Bryn Mawr, play with French children discovered in the neighborhood—neither these nor other remedies worked. The children were not interested in an accomplishment that made them different from their friends. Then I read about James Grew, a teacher at Andover, who was successful in teaching French to small children in the grades, and this gave me an idea. If I could get the children's "peer group" to try to learn French, then my boys would be proud of their French.

I got permission from the principal and school board to teach French to the third grade of a Haverford school. I so enjoyed teaching this group that I have not been able to give it up. Year by year I have been promoted with them, so that now we are in the sixth grade together. I think the children have enjoyed the experience, too. Unhampered by the self-consciousness that characterizes high school and college students, they pick up phrases enthusiastically, accurately and rapidly. As the children became interested in French, of course, my immediate purpose was achieved: Jonathan's and David's attitude changed. The few words they had hung on to became important to them.

This avowedly narrow achievement turned out, of course, to be the least interesting aspect of my excursion into the third grade. Especially fascinating has been the contrast between teaching English to French children and teaching French to American children. Or rather, between teaching the children of Peyrane and teaching the children of Haverford, for it is not safe to generalize concerning French and American children simply on the basis of observation of the secular, public school of peasant Peyrane and the Quaker school of middle-class, suburban Haverford. Nevertheless, a comparison of the details of everyday routine in the classrooms of these two little schools does illuminate certain basic differences between the French and American patterns of life. These differences were glaringly apparent from the moment I entered the classroom.

When I walked into the Peyrane school, the children were sitting quietly waiting for me. As I reached the front of the room they all stood up and chorused "Bonjour, Monsieur"—or, after the first day, "Good afternoon, Mister Wylie." They remained standing, not stiffly, but politely, until I told them to sit down.

At Haverford, the reaction to my arrival depends on what the children have been doing before I get there. If they have been working on arithmetic, the welcome is overwhelming. But if they're all engaged in preparing the layout for the class newspaper, my arrival is scarcely noticed; it takes the combined efforts of the teacher and me to divert their interest to French.

Once the language class gets under way, the responsibility for its success in both schools is all mine, but in quite different ways. In Peyrane, the children sat patiently ready to carry out any instructions I might give them. The initiative was mine, and it was up to me to carry the class forward in the lesson, point by point. In Haverford, if I want to take the initiative, it is up to me to grasp it and hold it. One slip and it's lost, to be picked up by a child who will draw the attention of the class away from the lesson to himself. When I leave, I often feel that we have wasted almost half of our time and my energy trying to create an atmosphere in which learning is possible. When I left the classroom in Peyrane I often felt that we had covered a considerable amount of subject matter, but I was not sure how much the children really cared whether they covered it.

One reason for this is that the two groups differ in the amount of attention they want. The children of Peyrane seemed to prefer not to be noticed; they avoided calling attention to themselves. Most of the children in the Haverford class demand attention and develop their own means to get it. Helen jumps in her seat and waves her hand. She knows the answers to all questions and can scarcely bear not being called on. Jimmy rarely knows what the class is talking about, for he is absorbed in peculiar engineering feats with rubber bands and paper clips, clever feats that attract attention to him. Jane listens to the class, but she never knows the answer to a question. Nevertheless, she always puts up her hand to be called on. She would rather call attention to a lack of knowledge than fail to be noticed at all.

The difference between the two groups is most noticeable when the children are asked to act out make-believe situations: a child of Peyrane helps a lost American tourist find his way; a Haverford child shows a French visitor about his school. The Peyrane children hung back and had to be persuaded to take part in a skit, but once they accepted a role they were serious actors. Unembarrassed, they stood up and acted out their parts while the class listened to them almost respectfully. In Haverford every child begs to take part in a skit. But the more timid are embarrassed and forget their lines. Those who know the expressions we are practicing slow up the action by trying to think up an unusual way to twist them in order to make the rest of the class laugh.

Nevertheless, I am inclined to use such skits in Haverford classes much more often than in Peyrane. In Haverford, there is a constant need for the teacher to create motivation, and such attempts at dramatization are popular with the children. In Peyrane there is less pressure to make class exciting, for the children are willing to put up with the more traditional techniques of teaching.

Language learning is not new to them: the study of their own is stressed from kindergarten on. They are steeped in formal grammar. They are accustomed to memorizing quantities of material. They have heavy homework as early as the first and second grades. Work does not delight them, but they expect it. In Haverford, the mention of homework, of memorization, of quizzes, brings loud groans and mutinous threats. The teacher must find a gimmick to remove the onus of work from a project, or he must maneuver to make it appear, at least, to be a class decision, not a teacher decision. In both Peyrane and Haverford the ultimate decision is usually the teacher's. The difference is that in Peyrane the decision is immediate and forthright. In Haverford one must learn to manipulate the group.

Incidentally, the mention of grammar reminds me of one curious difference in the reaction of the children. The children of Peyrane were surprised to learn that English nouns have no gender, but they took it in their stride. In Haverford, the walls of the third grade classroom almost burst the day I confided to the class that some French words are masculine and others are feminine. The girls giggled. The boys howled. Sam Fox blushed, raised the cover of his desk and stuck his head beneath it. Johnny Woolman yelled and ran out into the hall. Tim Lindley and Jimmy Stout jumped up and started dancing around together. This was the best joke the third grade had ever heard. Now that these same children are in the sixth grade they have come to accept the idea, although the boys still find satisfaction in discovering that "stupidité" is feminine and "pouvoir" is masculine. Natch!

It is true that the Haverford children did not act with all their teachers as they did with me. I marveled at their third grade teacher who could quiet them with a glance; they all said that she had "magic eyes." The class *mystique* forced them to submit to her. I not only did not have magic eyes; I then believed I could dominate the children if I could make my subject interesting. I succeeded, but with a great loss of time. Four years' experience, delightful as it has been as a personal experience, has forced me as a teacher and as a parent to revise my belief in the value of permissiveness and contrived motivation.

It is different in Peyrane. The school is the school, and there is a behavior appropriate for children in the school no matter who is teaching. I did not feel that my skill had much to do with their reaction to me. The teacher supplies the knowledge, and the children are expected to supply their own motivation. They are conditioned by their home training to recognize that they are children and that adults, not children, make decisions. School is presented to them as a serious experience that they must accept, regardless of their individual feelings. Children must learn—and often learn by heart—their lessons. Horseplay is not appropriate in the classroom. The children love horseplay, but it is reserved for the school ground. To play a prank in a classroom would attract the attention of the teacher, and one wants to be forgotten by the teacher. It is best, it is safest, to do one's lesson quietly and to stay out of trouble.

This school experience seems to have no pernicious effect on the French child's character: he is in no way cowed. Rather, he is serious and dignified where such behavior is appropriate. Out of school he plays freely. In school he learns how to do tasks that are not glamorous but need to be done, without a teacher's having to seek ways to make them interesting. He learns that experience is compartmentalized, that each compartment has definite limits and requires appropriate conduct. The Peyrane child's sense of appropriateness is reflected in a social poise that is truly impressive.

The child of Haverford comes to school well aware of his importance. At home he has been, if not the center of the family attention, at least an equal partner in family affairs. School is a further opportunity for the expression of his personality, which he must learn to adapt to the collective personality of his class. He also acquires skills and knowledge in school subjects, but there is more emphasis on his development as a person than on his training as a scholar.

He is constantly called on to make decisions—individual and group decisions—which in another culture would be considered too complicated for a child of limited experience. Life presents itself as a total field in which his personality may unfold. Within that field he may devote himself in a large degree to what best suits him. He has a voice equal with his teacher's in deciding what country his school class will study in a class project, just as he has a voice equal with his parents in deciding where the family will spend its vacation. A parent or the teacher may determine the decision but only if he is skillful in persuading the group that his proposal is most attractive to them. The important thing is for each individual to have his say and for each decision to be a group decision.

This system makes for orderly or chaotic families and classrooms, depending on whether each group happens to have a leader with sufficient manipulatory skill. It prepares the child admirably, however, to meet the demands of social and political organizations in which persuasion, effective compromise, the individual vote, and the collective will to abide by group decisions are essential elements. It is not surprising that children raised under this system should grow up believing that the strength of our country lies in our political institutions.

In Peyrane, it is the wisdom of a decision, rather than its acceptance by a group, that is important. Experience, training, rational control tempered by love, are considered essential in making a wise decision, and since adults have more of these than do children generally, it is the adults who make the decisions.

This system works perfectly at home and at school. In adult social and political organizations the various adult wisdoms come into conflict, so that the organizations lead a stormy existence, but there is no such conflict in the smallest social unit. It would be hard to find better integrated, more sturdy, more smoothly functioning institutions than the classrooms and families of Peyrane. The scourges of nature and of man bring devastation, but the family endures. It is not surprising that a child of Peyrane grows up believing that the most important thing in life is the integrity of his family. In the long run, he believes this is more important for France as a nation than what goes on in Paris or Indochina or Algeria.

It has become stylish for American journalists and political scientists to look at French political behavior, shake their heads and moan, "France is sick!" French journalists and sociologists look at American family life, shake their heads and moan, "America is sick!" Surely both countries have their troubles, but it is a poor diagnosis that is based on only one symptom. If these diagnosticians were willing to have a look at the total pattern of a nation's behavior—including the more humble aspects, such as what goes on in the schoolrooms of Peyrane and Haverford—their diagnosis might not be so self-flattering, but it would make sense.

PROBLEMS FOR WRITING AND DISCUSSION

1. What basic differences did Wylie find between the French children of Peyrane and the American children of Haverford?
2. What accounts for the French children's desire for anonymity in the classroom? What admirable character traits did the French system seem to develop?
3. Does the American child's desire for attention reflect anything basic about the American family and, possibly, the American society itself? See

particularly the essays of William Miller and Henry Steele Commager (p. 225 and p. 14).

4. George Kennan (p. 233) argues that students interested in international affairs must "build within themselves . . . self-discipline and self-restraint." What hope do you see in the Wylie essay that we are moving in this direction?

5. What material in the essay indicates that Wylie himself is a product of the American pattern in family life and classroom?

6. Contrast Wylie's attitude toward "motivating" the student with Agee's (p. 191). Does the tendency to make work (here, schoolwork) seem like "play" appear to be a tendency with which you are familiar? Illustrate from your own experience.

The Catcher in the Rye Complex: Two Letters from an American at Cambridge

HENRY EBEL

Henry Ebel (*1938-*), upon graduating from Columbia College, where he had been editor-in-chief of the humor magazine Jester, received Columbia's Kellett Fellowship for two years of study at Clare College, Cambridge. He also held an honorary Woodrow Wilson Fellowship during *1959-60*. While holding two more fellowships, he has been working toward a doctorate in English at Columbia University. He has collaborated with David Diringer on one book, Writing: Its Origins and Early History (*1962*).

To the COLUMBIA UNIVERSITY FORUM:

December, 1959

"Emmanuel College . . . is also noted for its pleasant gardens, with a lovely reed-fringed lake and swans floating among the water lilies. John Harvard, who later founded the American University, had rooms there on F staircase. They are still preserved as he had them, with three mysterious bullet-holes in the oak panelling and a cut-out in the door labelled 'For the Cat.' Each year an American scholar occupies them."

My quotation is from a slick and breezy little booklet entitled *This Is Cambridge,* which the visitor or student at this 800-year-old institution can purchase for the rather exorbitant price of ten shillings sixpence (approximately $1.50). If a certain air of ambiguous mystery hovers over the account of John Harvard's rooms, it

From Columbia University Forum, *Winter 1961. Copyright © 1961 by Columbia University. Reprinted by permission of Columbia University.*

may be taken as symbolic of the general position of American students in the University. That position is nothing if not ambiguous.

One thing is clear—an American arrives at Cambridge with a series of distinct advantages: age, worldliness and money. He is generally older than the undergraduates among whom he moves, and he is generally more experienced. He has travelled less, perhaps, than many an English schoolboy of sixteen: but travel is by no means a guarantor of sophistication. The enthusiasm and the vigor of a good American college more than compensate, I think, for the short hop to Paris or Copenhagen; the ferment of New York makes Cambridge (or even London) look somewhat provincial by comparison.

Above all, the fellowship, scholarship or grant which an American at Cambridge may hold, or such private means as have made it possible for him to cross the Atlantic in the first place, give him a considerable advantage over most English students, if only in the unworried purchase of sherry, "biscuits," books and framed prints for his walls.

These are very considerable advantages. Add to them the fact that there is, on the surface at least, no language barrier; that the most nagging restraints and demands of an American university are almost completely lacking; that Cambridge is an exquisitely beautiful place—and one would expect to find the American student an integral, functioning member of Cambridge life, contented, respected and happy.

Yet what seems on the surface to be an earthly paradise is not necessarily that. American students at the Cambridge colleges are seldom wholly at ease or conspicuously happy; the American "community" sometimes looks suspiciously like a defensive huddle, a pale but unmistakable refraction of the Ivy League. (With some of the Ivy League's very worst features: the anemic, quasi-intellectual wit, the continual facetiousness, the peculiar mixture of knowingness and embarrassment.)

Part of this is undoubtedly traceable to the peculiar position in which Americans at Cambridge find themselves. They have all, to some extent, left fully formed lives behind them—a family, close friends, a recognized position of some sort at their respective universities—to which they will return within a year or two. They have already passed through the full cycle of undergraduate life, and are not, most of them, inclined to begin all over again by joining a dramatic society, a literary magazine, or the student newspaper; the "extracurricular" life of the University moves on without them—infantile, sometimes, but undeniably alive. As a result, the years an American spends at Cambridge often seem vaguely unreal: an interlude, if not an outright punishment.

This sense of isolation—undefined, vague, yet undeniably there—is immeasurably enhanced by a bridgeable but profound gulf between Americans and Englishmen: by the discovery which every American makes for himself, that beneath the similarity of language there exist astonishing divergencies of background and ways of thinking. The misunderstandings—the *snobismus* and the counter-*snobismus*—are perhaps more subtle than they were twenty or thirty or fifty years ago, less openly prejudicial. But this makes them all the more difficult to define, and all the more difficult to grapple with.

The assumption that cultural barbarism of some sort is implicit in American intellectual life seems nearly extinct among English academicians, if we except a few of the donnish wraiths who flit through the pages of the *Times Literary Supplement,* an occasional utterance by Mr. C. S. Lewis, or a random aside by this or that young Cambridge lecturer intent on proving that he is not in the *least* Red-Brick. But it has a residual tenacity among the less well-informed. One undergraduate told me, in a conversation of a few weeks ago, how amused he had been by the newspaper accounts of the Charles Van Doren affair. (He may have been reading Alistair Cooke's dispatches to *The Guardian* on this subject. In one of the most insensitive bits of journalism yet foisted on the English public, Cooke demonstrated how thoroughly vapid his irony really is.) I pointed out at length that the story seemed to me simply grave and tragic, and rather full of implications regarding the effects of television and the position of the intellectual; to which he replied simply that "that sort of thing couldn't happen over here"—that the subtle and not-so-subtle barbarities of television, like Napoleon and Hitler, would never set foot on this tight little island. (He may subsequently have had a good look at English commercial television: the enemy is no longer battering at the gates but safely within the parlor.)

Another undergraduate, a freshman, spent a week or two in New York City. He tells me (with a knowing leer) of the prostitutes in Times Square, the gross overt sexuality of American women, and the feverish love-lives of American undergraduates. There is a kind of envious appreciation mingled with his sarcasm; but whatever the particular nuances of his beliefs (and he is fairly intelligent), it is clear that his dominant impressions of the United States have little to do with matters of the spirit. And like so many Englishmen he has absorbed only one fact about American education: that the condition of the high schools is appallingly bad.

Thus, the American student who ventures further afield in the University than his own college, or who remains in his own rooms dispensing coffee and sherry, is confronted with the almost continual necessity to explain, to define, to correct. He is by no means received with hostility. Quite the contrary: the fact of being American makes him, frequently, the center of interest in a gathering. But even with sympathetic listeners it is an exhausting and discouraging role to play; and at the end of it there sometimes lies the knowing remark which says, in effect: "Oh, but you're one of the *good* ones." With a slow and insidious inevitability, the American student finds himself falling back upon his compatriots for real contact or communication.

What of the English undergraduate? Unless he has done National Service, he will probably be eighteen or nineteen upon arrival at Cambridge, and will probably come from a public school: grammar school boys are still distinctly in the minority at Cambridge, and, unless they have taken the trouble to affect public-school manners and accents, distressingly conspicuous. (Some of the more facile American theorizers about "class" would find it illuminating, I think, to see it at work.) Until coming up to Cambridge, then, the English undergraduate will probably have lived one of the oddest existences ever imposed on an adolescent male. If no longer quite so grim and bleak as that described by Orwell in *Such, Such Were the Joys,* it has still lost little of its original insularity.

A few of these undergraduates are intolerable snobs and *poseurs,* like some undergraduates everywhere but with more polish and self-assurance; a few appear to have had their development arrested at age thirteen, and move in an atmosphere of boyish messiness and *camaraderie*; most of the freshmen, at least, would probably regard the social and sexual exploits of their American counterparts with some awe. And yet, having taken all this into account, one's final judgment on them cannot help but be favorable. Even the freshmen make an impression of articulateness and intelligence which one would be hard-put to find among second- and third-year students at even an Ivy League university. They have an admirable command of the English language: one finds in them none of the tension between articulate (="intellectual") and popular speech, none of the linguistic embarrassment, which characterizes too many American students. The few who are exceptionally intelligent manage, at the same time, to be relaxed, witty and even (occasionally) charming. Indeed, it is difficult to escape the conclusion that the wit and charm which are the stamp of English intellectual life at its best, both in and out of print, have their source here: in this early, unforced familiarity with the English language.

If these undergraduates lack something which can be found among the students of an American college then it is a certain emotional fervor, an intensity (maligned word!), which is particularly evident at an urban school like Columbia. I had occasion, some time ago, to meet an undergraduate of Trinity College, Cambridge, who had recently paid an extended visit to the United States. He spoke with amused contempt of the prevailing *earnestness* (his word) of American academic life; and he touched on something which I believe is important. The minority who, at an American university, are deeply concerned with intellectual matters—in, above, and beyond their studies—do indeed tend to be earnest: or at least to clearly compartmentalize their serious thinking and discussion from moments of wit and playfulness. And this earnestness has its own virtue and its own vice. On the one hand, they "take themselves too seriously"—that is, they never take themselves lightly, which to my mind is the greater offense. Yet it must be admitted that numbers of them develop obsessions severe enough to warp their critical faculties, and fail to recognize that unfounded nonsense is unfounded nonsense even when it is shouted at the top of one's lungs.

More or less the same kind of balance holds true for the tone of intellectual and social life at Cambridge. Its virtue is that it tempers scholarship with civility; its vice that it enables a good many boys to cloak simple ignorance and stupidity in wit, articulateness, and charm.

As what I have said thus far implies, the prevailing atmosphere at Cambridge is relaxed, sometimes to the point of somnolence. Most of all is this so when winter has descended, bringing with it the Fen mists: a bleak syndrome of grayness, damp and cold. At least as much energy is expended on the indoor round of coffee- and sherry-drinking as on actual study, and the undergraduate or Research Student is soon highly adept at the gentle art of wasting time. Within a week of my own arrival at Cambridge two students informed me, under separate circumstances, that anyone who does not have "a good time" at Cambridge is wasting his years here; the same statement was subsequently echoed by the Tutor of one of the colleges. There is little pretense that work is primary and play to be fitted in only here and there, the almost universal practice being to reserve heavy study for vacations: and always to deny, as a matter of "face," that one does any work at all.

Yet this very somnolence, this relaxedness, this lack of aggravation, seems to deepen the sense of oppression, futility and *schmerz* felt, in varying degrees, by many of the Americans here. "It's a drag," one of them announced recently, "everything here is such a drag." And another greeted me with: "Well, are you getting everything you possibly can out of the Cambridge Experience?"—spoken with a mixture of bitterness and good humor. And so it goes. . . .

It is difficult to escape the conclusion that something is at least mildly wrong. Perhaps the mistake lies in assuming that an American student of evident intelligence and talent, given an adequate amount of money, will necessarily be happy here. But perhaps, too, a generation has been raised up which finds it difficult to be really happy anywhere: and toward this view I more and more incline. The precocious sense of disillusionment and worldliness which is *de rigueur* in the eastern American colleges—the *Catcher in the Rye* complex—is a difficult burden to bear even when it seems to be the universal order of society. Its most common manifestation is the quasi-erudite wisecrack—surely the most effective weapon ever devised against any overt expression of seriousness or feeling—accompanied by the sense, the mystique, of a private and literally incommunicable tragedy: or, in a less self-consciously dramatic form, of a vast inner life—intellectual, perhaps, or moral—which, though it never breaks through the knowing surface of banter and facetiousness, lurks iceberg-like beneath it all. This set of attitudes (I've done little justice to either their pervasiveness or their complexity) is a sad and slightly ludicrous affair when encountered on native ground. Transplanted across the sea, it becomes insidious and frustrating. It makes the very worst out of Cambridge; and rather than mitigating, it exaggerates, the obstacles Americans face here.

Those obstacles are considerable ones but they are by no means insurmountable. They don't justify a pose of bitterness and futility, a sense that one has somehow been "done in" by the world. The fault, as always, is not in our stars.

November, 1960

Perhaps it is taking something of an unfair advantage to treat oneself as a text. I can only say that my views remain, after a year, fundamentally unchanged. Here and there time has altered, not my opinions, but my emphases; looking over what I wrote a year ago, I see that in one or two places an additional word might be said.

First, a word more about the nature of the anti-Americanism in the English academic world (by which I mean Oxford and Cambridge), and the English upper class generally. It remains a quiet but firm article of faith among Tories, and neo-Tories; it is increasingly the secret vice of the English liberal.

Almost never does it take the form of personal discourtesy, and at no time that I can call to mind has it seemed to have a coherent rationale behind it. It is explainable only as a faint schizophrenia. On the one hand, there is a formal recognition that the first half of the twentieth century has brought a vigorous and sustained burst of artistic activity in the United States, such as no other nation can equal. Of the first four volumes issued in a British paperback series devoted to literary criticism, three are concerned with Henry James, Ezra Pound and Wallace Stevens; *The Penguin Book of Modern American Verse* seems (in Cambridge at least) to enjoy a phenomenally good sale. So much for good points. On the other hand there is the Bomb; there has been the occasionally phantasmagoric bungling of Mr. Herter and his Department (all the more lurid when described in the dry prose of the *Times*); there are the peculiarly insulated American air-bases, enclosed in miles of barbed wire; there are the American GI's, a thoroughly random sample of humanity which includes the intelligent and articulate, the loud and brash, and those conspicuous few who are little more than unlicked bear-whelps; and there is the American high-school system.

An American reader might be inclined to say simply (and correctly) that these two 'compartments' have nothing whatsoever to do with each other: but they live in a state of uneasy coexistence, in the minds of many intelligent Englishmen, and in a pinch, when instinctive reactions rather than sustained thought come into play, it is the latter 'compartment' which has to bear the weight of the adjective "American."

In itself all this might be no more than a prolegomenon to the observation that we all have our prejudices, and isn't it interesting how genuinely irrational they are? But this antagonism has a heavy bearing on the lives of those Americans who come to England neither as soldiers nor as whirlwind tourists, and who remain here for one to five years. It takes one man to hold a prejudice, but it takes two, ordinarily, to make an Anglophile, or to concoct that strange amalgam of self-consciousness, pride and self-dislike which animates a good many of us here in our relationships with Englishmen. It takes two to set up a more or less perverse quasi-relationship in which condescension (or mild contempt), prejudice, pride, snobbery, and inverted snobbery all find a place.

The English contribution to such a relationship is understandable, if not excusable. It is founded on the kind of ignorance which cannot be dispelled by newsreels and propaganda efforts, by USIA libraries, by joint communiqués, or (least of all) by the export in quantity of *Time-Life*. For better or worse, we have all become insulated against propaganda, whether it is instigated by the State Department or by Henry Luce. We cut off the feeling part of ourselves from it, and are "entertained" or "informed" but not deeply moved or changed. It is real knowledge, the knowledge of meaningful and *prolonged* human contact, which is needed, and in the case of America this is for most Englishmen impossible.

The American contribution to the same relation is more difficult to grasp, to pin down, to understand. Why should Americans still respond so strongly to the prejudice they may meet, why does it still get under their skins? Why did one young American, after two weeks in London, adopt a bowler, waistcoat and tightly-rolled umbrella, and proceed to deliver long disquisitions on the superior and mysterious ancestral wisdom of "the English." Why did another spend an inordinate amount of time carping about English roads, English inefficiency, English food, English weather, English social habits and English academic failings, as if these amounted to a personal insult? Why have I seen an expression of almost painful joy cross the face of a young American who was treated in a civil and courteous fashion by a book-seller? Why do so many conversations between Americans and Englishmen at Cambridge move on a level of innuendo, implication, veiled aggression and self-defense? Why do a few intelligent Americans (a *few*, thank God!) seem eager still, in the sixth decade of the twentieth century, to kiss the rod and thank the teacher?

No single direct answer to all these questions is possible. Each is a situation, each involves a human being; so that a flat judgment or a prescriptive exhortation must be either too facile or too pretentiously stern. Behind them, however, stands the single question of origins. Where and why do the feelings and habits I have discussed in these two letters have their beginnings?—the Anglophilia and the Anglophobia, the homegrown and exported *schmerz*? To *this* question I can, in a somewhat allegorical fashion, suggest an answer.

Take an intelligent American boy and expose him at length to a primary and secondary-school system in which he is "taught," by ordinarily unintelligent bureaucrats, material which becomes progressively more irrelevant to what is actually going on in his mind: which bores him to death with its own emended version of sweetness and light:

> The lavish illustrations, many of them in color, will not only delight the student's eye; they will aid him in catching the spirit of America. From the moment he looks at the handsome cover, with its vivid representation of typical Americana, he will be strongly influenced by the art work of the volume. In the eight pages of the Prelude, he will sense the American quality of varied regional scenes. In his study of the text selections, he will find the illustrations a powerful stimulus to comprehension and appreciation.

This is the preface to *The United States in Literature,* Chicago, 1952: designed for high school reading, and still, apparently, in print. The "text selections" include the prose and poetry of Donald Culross Peatie, Mary Johnston, Helen Grace Carlisle, Cale Young Rice, George and Helen Papashvily, Don Marquis, Ruth Suckow, Robert Haven Schauffler, Louis Adamic, M. M. Musselman, Sara Teasdale, John Mayo Gross, John Hay, Abram J. Ryan, John Bannister Tabb, and *Time* magazine. The names of William Faulkner, F. Scott Fitzgerald, T. S. Eliot, Ezra Pound, E. E. Cummings and Hart Crane do not occur. Only one of the serious poets whose work is included—Karl Shapiro—was born in the twentieth century. There are two poems by Shapiro, two by Emily Dickinson and two by Robert Frost, thus giving them equal weight with Philip Freneau, Bryant, Poe, Longfellow, Whittier, Holmes, and—John Bannister Tabb.

When he has completed his secondary school education, send our intelligent American boy to a good American college, where a systematic and (ordinarily) successful attempt is made to undermine such intellectual props as his previous training has erected. He may already have discovered for himself the somewhat dated iconoclasm of Mencken or Philip Wylie; introduce him now to the rather more relevant iconoclasm of the classroom, and of Mort Sahl; and against the excruciating dullness of Whittier and Longfellow *et al.*, and the boy's accumulated resentment against what passes on the high-school level for Literature, bring the forces of Eliot, Pound, Cummings, Hemingway.

> . . . but seeing he had been born
> In a half-savage country, out of date;
> Bent resolutely on wringing lilies from the acorn;
> Capaneus . . .

Having thus broken the ice of our young man's apathy, give him, within three years, the full weight of European literature and historiography (or at least of European "classics"). Set up in his mind a clear distinction between the two classes of Americans immortalized by Jules Feiffer: those who Have Been to Europe and those who Haven't. And set up, as the crowning reward for academic achievement, an extended stay at a university on the other side of the Atlantic. As a final touch, make him liable for the draft, and see to it that he reads the *New Yorker*.

Our fortunate young man, whether he makes it to Europe or not, will now go one of two ways: either he will achieve a reasoned and sure stabilization of his own feelings *vis-à-vis* the fact of being American—a confident transcendence of both banal "heritage"-worship and reactive iconoclasm—or he will succumb to some form of *schmerz*, to -philisms and -phobias, to the kind of chronic dissatisfaction which has no cause and no cure. Sad if he should take the latter path; but I am less inclined than I was a year ago to say it is his fault, and his alone. One cannot build conviction—much less "National Purpose"—on broken reeds, on chaos and confusion.

PROBLEMS FOR WRITING AND DISCUSSION

1. Ebel writes that the American comes to Cambridge with three advantages: "age, worldliness, and money"; yet the student is usually unhappy and isolated. Why?
2. How does the latent British anti-Americanism manifest itself? What explanations for it does Ebel give? Can you think of other plausible explanations that he does not mention?
3. To what extent does the American's own background and training contribute to his estrangement from the British student and educational milieu?
4. What does Ebel mean by the title of his essay? (You should be able to answer this question without having read J. D. Salinger's novel.)
5. What advantages, educational and social, over the American student does his British counterpart have? Compare his attributes with those Wylie observed in the French students (p. 204).
6. How do you account for Ebel's report that Americans, who have been cajoled and "motivated" in their pre-college days, seem excessively "earnest" as college students? What does Ebel consider the "danger" in their earnestness?
7. What is the difference between the undisciplined group of Haverford students and the time-wasting "relaxedness" of the English students?
8. Does Ebel's explanation of anti-Americanism abroad clarify or contradict Boorstin's explanation (p. 5) of the same phenomenon?
9. The "precocious sense of disillusionment and worldliness" which Ebel says is *de rigueur* for American undergraduates is seriously at odds with the optimistic Horatio Alger program of self-improvement once popular with young Americans (see p. 139). To what do you attribute the change? Are you yourself precociously disillusioned and worldly? What illusions have you lost? Where did you get them and how did you lose them?
10. Henry James (p. 82), T. S. Matthews (p. 99), and James Agee (p. 191), although American, reacted bitterly and hypersensitively to the philistinism that still, according to Ebel, typifies the picture of Americans harbored by educated Englishmen. Which of the writers whom you have read in this book fit that stereotype of the American philistine and chauvinist? Which seem to suffer from the Catcher-in-the-Rye complex? How would you characterize the rest?

Education and Some American Temptations
WILLIAM LEE MILLER

> William Lee Miller (1926-   ), Associate Professor of Social Ethics at the Divinity School of Yale University, is widely known for his articles on American life in The Reporter *magazine and for his contribution to a study of the place of religion in a free society, conducted by the Fund for the Republic (1958). He has published one book,* The Protestant and Politics *(1958).*

To say that American education has erred in the direction of the too "practical" service to limited ends is not to say that there is no error in the other direction. Education must have in it something of the intrinsically worthful, which is an end in itself and needs no further justification, but it must also have in it something instrumental, tested by its service to other ends of living. When education becomes entirely directed to ends-in-themselves, then it loses an enlivening tension with the claims of the real world that gives meaning to those ends. Though recognizing its point in the American context, one is not altogether in sympathy with the quotation attributed to a great old teacher: "Thank God I learned nothing *useful* at Yale!" Sometimes in such pronouncements one can detect a note of purely social snobbery. Whether or not that note is present, we do not want an education, unsullied by usefulness, that fashions and finishes gentlemen, who are presumed then to be just living bundles of intrinsically worthful ends. An Oxford don is reported to have said, when asked by the soldier what he was doing for the war effort, "Sir, I represent the civilization you are

From Education in the Nation's Service, *edited by August Heckscher, 1960. Reprinted by permission of the publisher, Frederick A. Praeger, Inc.*

fighting to defend." He gave a good reply, if he said it in the right tone of voice. Earnest devotion to one's intellectual work, in war time or any time, has its justification. But one would not sympathize with flippant or condescending notes in his remark. The civilization that education helps to maintain and create, worthwhile in itself, must also at the same time be aware of its relation to the war efforts, the life efforts, of men: it must do so, even to have its own meaningful content.

There is a point of tension between the instrumental and the intrinsically worthful that makes for an education better than that which resolves the tension in either direction.

But the effort to reach and maintain that enlivening point of tension is complicated, not only by our "practicality," but by the way "democracy" is misunderstood.

That misunderstanding of democracy and the conditions of a dynamic modern industrial society are linked together in our present American problem. The conditions of the mass society help pose the problem for the free society, but it is intensified by the way the free society (or "democracy") is interpreted. Nowhere is this more true than in the field of education.

We know that the difficulties of American education begin with the mass society in the most obvious sense, with numbers: the vast school population of forty-three million; the one in four Americans who spends his day in school; the growth of the American population a hundred-fold since the country's founding; the especially rapid rise in school population since World War II. This rapid growth and shift in school population, and the postponement of school building made necessary by World War II, combine with the difficulties of local financing to make the obvious and pressing shortages of classrooms and teachers. But of course the issue rests not just in the physical facts but in the way we interpret and respond to them. Our inability to deal with this problem despite the recognition of it on almost all sides for more than a decade, shows one fault in the mind of the democracy: its difficulty in adjusting its social philosophy and social action to new, collective and complex conditions. An excessive and unrealistic preoccupation with the dangers of "federal control," no doubt reinforced by a reluctance to pay necessary taxes, helps to inhibit the kind of large, new national financial commitment that the schools obviously need. One might say that we have been unable since World War II to get the needed federal aid to education partly because we have too many principles: principles of local control; principles of non-segregation (the Powell amendment); principles of separation of church and state (the aid to parochial schools issue).

The free society sometimes is understood not as a flexible ideal adaptable to new conditions but as a static set of rules requiring the relative simplicities of earlier days. One problem that the free society creates for itself has to do with power: the rightful defense of freedom becomes wrongfully identified with certain forms (for example, primarily local-state financing of schools) which do not altogether accord with changed patterns of life and power. The national mind nurtured in the pleasant atmosphere of American individualism has a hard time grasping the problems of a new situation, full of collective problems that that individualism overlooks.

But the free society's problem (in education, as elsewhere) is not only the relation of freedom to power, but also of freedom to truth and value. The difficulty is not only that we devotees of democracy have a hard time dealing with complex, collective life; it is also that we have a hard time advancing standards. The problems of education are not only those of providing money for buildings and teachers, it is also that of providing something to be taught by the teachers in the buildings. The free society has as much difficulty interpreting itself to do the latter as it does organizing itself to do the former. Democracy, misunderstood, can be destructive of serious discriminations about the content of life.

This misunderstanding would turn the initial relativism, which democracy requires, into a final relativism, which destroys the conviction and purpose, and the intellectual and ethical discrimination, without which democracy does not work. This thoroughgoing relativistic attitude about truth and value may not be explicit, but it is widely implied: "Who are you to say?" "The people like it,"

"We give the public what it wants," "It's a free country, isn't it?" It appears in education: "there is no aristocracy of subjects." Sometimes it attaches to the rule of numbers or of the majority (the "People," the "Public"): the democratic belief that it is right that the majority rule may turn into the optimistic assumption that the majority will rule what is right, and then finally into the nihilistic notion that there is no such thing as "right," but only what a majority rules. Sometimes it uses our celebration of individual freedom: we may insist not only on the individual's right to make his own error but also that he be free from the judgment that it is an error. Sometimes the claim of equality may be extended from the ultimate and personal dimension in which it is valid into other, proximate regions in which it is not. Sometimes the notion of "tolerance" is felt to mean that one should not hold firmly and clearly to anything, lest one become intolerant. Democracy, misunderstood, encourages its believers to make a premature compromise or toleration or equalization within themselves, to discount (too early) their own apprehension of the worthful, or true, and to bring therefore into the democratic dialogue an already marked-down position.

The correction of this fault does not lie in an "individualism" that encourages the eccentric, deviating, superficial opinion, the more different from the "crowd" the better: that, in fact, is another expression of the same underlying error, the one that tends to make indiscriminable all real choices and judgments. As the critics of conformity say, it too much unsettles the confidence in one's judgment, when the generality is against it, but as these critics usually do not say, it also too much reinforces one's confidence in one's own whim, when more carefully considered judgment is against it. What is lacking in either case is a sufficient sense of responsibility to a truth and value which the mind and conscience can, by effort, and always in part, discover and act upon (whether or not with others). Democracy requires responsible and thinking persons, with convictions, making up a public with a will.

The misconception of democracy we have been describing has a considerable effect on our education. Sometimes it causes the school to lose its educational focus, which is blurred by the intrusion of a whole range of extra-educational activities put there by a community that has "democratically" deprived itself of the power to discriminate among the purposes that are appropriate and inappropriate to the school. The misunderstanding of democracy also works to reinforce the bias toward the practical, the short-run, and tangible that we discussed above: it gives a decided advantage, in the contest for support, to those purposes that can be comprehended easily by many, and a decided disadvantage to that which can be understood only with time, difficulty and by few.

But the democratic fault probably has been most widely discussed recently with respect to the "gifted child," and to the need for "excellence." Thus the excellent Rockefeller Report on Excellence said that our society "has given too little attention to the individual of unusual talent or potentialities."

Much of the criticism, springing from events in the scientific competition with Russia, has emphasized the loss to the nation of intellectual resources needed for that contest. This approach is inadequate both because it is too instrumental and because it is too much motivated by comparison and fear. (How would we know what to do, Robert Hutchins recently asked, ironically, if we could not compare ourselves with the Russians?) Admiral Rickover's book of speeches on American education, though full of these matters of the cold war, ("lead time," "our first line of defense"), makes a broader point: that we need more highly educated persons not only to compete with the Soviets, but also to manage this complicated society: "at different levels of civilization, different degrees of popular education are needed." The numbers of persons, the using up of resources, the complicated elaboration of technology, all call for a larger component of creative intelligence.

But this, too, though important, is still an argument from the needs of the society. The neglect of the gifts of the gifted is vulnerable to the somewhat more fundamental argument, that has to do not with the loss to the society, but with the treatment of this child.

But then this "undemocratic" result does not apply only to the more gifted children; far from it. Sometimes educators, responding to the attacks of Arthur Bestor, Mortimer Smith, Admiral Rickover and the rest, claim that these critics are concerned only with the bright child. That is not so, and to say so is a revealing mistake. To imply that an intellectually substantial education is of importance only for a gifted minority is surely to show just that confusion, or loss, of standards to which a misunderstanding of democracy unfortunately sometimes leads.

The nature of our American democratic ethic helps to create these difficulties. Democracy of course is not the pure, perfect, final and uncomplicated arrangement oratory would suggest; in practice, it has its characteristic weaknesses. It creates problems for itself, and not least in education: while needing an educated citizenry, it may generate a pressure against the carrying out of educational ideals.

The discussion of this often centers around "equality." Dr. Conant's first report, on the high school, refers to our American understanding of "equality," in contrasting American with European educational history. "Equality" means for us not only political equality, but also "equality of opportunity"—an equal start in the competitive struggle—and the equal status of all honest labor. More education was an important means by which these ideals were to be realized, and from these ideals have come characteristic features of American education, like the "comprehensive high school" that Dr. Conant discusses. The point here is that the results of such an ideal are not only external; they are also internal—they are found in attitudes, ideas, dispositions.

The Rockefeller Report sees the problem as a "tug of war between equality and excellence in a democracy," in which the generality are continually able to rewrite the rules of the social contest in ways that may damage excellence and rule out distinguished attainment. Against this inclination the report urges an "express emphasis on excellence" as especially necessary in a democracy. Without disagreeing with this, one would want to say that it should not be seen primarily as a matter of one man against another, but rather of one ideal against others within each man. The "excellence" should not be thought of too much in the comparative—

one man excelling another; the fault should not be thought of just as that of the generality's restraint upon the best men, the individuals of ability. This outer, social phenomenon of democracy is linked to an inner, philosophical one, and the importance of the latter should not be missed. If there is an inclination toward the leveling of men, there is also a certain inclination toward the leveling of subjects, ideas, and values. Is that not the central difficulty?

But at the same time that the equalitarian bent of this American democracy may cause difficulties for the very education that the democracy needs, that bent also helps to prevent its education from falling into worse, and opposite, ills. For all our American difficulties, we do have at least the possibility of a productive tension between the discriminations of intellect and talent that education must recognize and encourage, on the one hand, and the claims of a people's real life that keep those discriminations limited and relevant, on the other. Men overestimate the larger worth of that in which they themselves can excel, and this is perhaps especially true of those who excel in intellectual work. It is important that they be reminded, as the Rockefeller Report says, there are many different kinds of excellence, that none can rest on laurels but each must continually reestablish its claim and that none can extend itself out beyond the range of its applicability to create any aristocracies. At its best, the spirit of democracy should strip away false and overextended claims for deference and authority in order that genuine merit and attainment may emerge. Instead of "democratically" leveling away standards and confusing goals, it can democratically encourage real goals and real attainment by anyone. It can combine excellence and inclusiveness, making these not oppose, but support each other. If the person has a worth beyond his service to society, and an "equality," or rather a unique place, in an order that transcends the distinctions of society, then the distinctions in attainment and in service to society can be admitted and used without jeopardizing anyone's ultimate standing. False distinction of class and family and group can be removed; real distinctions of merit can be admitted, but kept limited and relevant.

PROBLEMS FOR WRITING AND DISCUSSION

1. Miller contends that one of the problems of a free society has to do with power. What is the problem? Have you encountered elsewhere in this Part a discussion of the same problem? In what context?

2. "Democracy, misunderstood, can be destructive of serious discriminations about the content of life." What specific misunderstandings does Miller note? Can you add others from your own experience? Specifically in education, how or where do such misunderstandings of democracy reveal themselves most clearly, and how do they ultimately impair the "democratic dialogue"?

3. Discuss the Lincoln-Douglas debates (p. 115) in the light of what Miller says the democratic belief in the "rule of numbers" may degenerate into.

4. What alternative to the "levelling" of persons and subjects does Miller propose? How does Miller distinguish between "levelling" and "equality"? How does he reconcile the democratic ideal of equality and the "excellence" various critics of American education have stressed?

5. Miller notes the difficulty of American individualism in grappling with a "new situation full of collective problems." What other writers in this Part comment on the same difficulty as one inherent in our traditional philosophy?

6. Does Miller make precisely clear what the demands are of the new "collective problems" of our society? What concrete problems have you encountered in your own experience? What ones do you foresee?

7. Would Henry Ford (p. 143) have agreed with Miller that the "numbers of persons, the using up of resources, the complicated elaboration of technology, all call for a larger component of creative intelligence"? Would Ford have agreed generally with Miller about education?

8. Miller, like Agee, is interested not only in the "needs of society" but in the "treatment" of the child. Compare what you consider the educational ideal of Miller and Agee with the Emersonian ideal (quoted by Boorstin, p. 5) for the American scholar.

9. Like Agee (p. 191), Miller sees that individual freedom and potentiality entail responsibility, and, like Kennan (p. 233), he sees that one's education should be "relevant" to the content of life. Discuss (1) how your increasing freedom as an adult has made you aware of new responsibilities, and (2) how the courses you are taking are relevant to the world for which you will be responsible.

Training for Statesmanship

GEORGE F. KENNAN

George F. Kennan (1904-   ) entered the Foreign Service in 1926. After early assignments in Germany and the Baltic countries, he spent two years on Russian studies at the University of Berlin, then served in Moscow from 1933 to 1935 as aide to Ambassador Bullitt. He was in Prague when Czechoslovakia collapsed in 1938-39; during the remainder of the war he served variously in Berlin, Lisbon, London, and Moscow. In 1947 he became head of the State Department's Policy Planning Staff and two years later chief long-range adviser to the Secretary of State. He spent 1950-52 at the Institute for Advanced Study, leaving to become U.S. Ambassador to the Soviet Union. Among his books are American Diplomacy, 1900-1950 *(1951);* Realities of American Foreign Policy *(1954); two volumes on Soviet-American relations from 1917 to 1926; and* Russia and the West Under Lenin and Stalin *(1961). He left retirement in 1961 to become U.S. Ambassador to Yugoslavia.*

I

One can hardly complain today about the time and effort devoted in American colleges and universities to instruction in foreign affairs. I doubt whether there is a liberal arts curriculum in the country which does not offer courses or activities in this field, and many of the technical institutions also are beginning to include such courses.

From The Atlantic Monthly, *May 1953. Reprinted by permission of the author.*

There are people, I am sure, who would feel that the high volume of instruction in this field is in itself the guarantee of a fairly respectable measure of achievement. These people would argue that some instruction in international affairs is obviously better than none at all, and that therefore this impressive volume of activity must produce useful results, regardless of the content of the courses.

About this I have my doubts. I am not certain that there is any virtue in teaching people about international affairs—aside from such virtue as may reside in the tenor of the teaching itself. Since the amount of relevant factual material is infinite, embracing in the last analysis practically everything there is to know about the human family, international affairs is a field in which the pursuit of knowledge without understanding is peculiarly pointless and useless. This being the case, mere volume of instruction does not guarantee anything at all in the way of desirable results. In fact, if instruction does not proceed from a realistic understanding of the subject, it can be worse than useless. I think anyone who has lectured extensively about foreign affairs will have had the same experience I have had—of noting that the questions asked by simple and relatively uneducated people are often more sensible and penetrating than those asked by people who have had a good deal of teaching on these subjects but have been taught the wrong way.

Instruction in international affairs can be given for two different purposes. The first is to instill into the student the type of understanding of the subject needed by the man who is not going to make participation in international affairs his business in life but who wants to acquit himself creditably of his duties of citizenship. A man who wants to be a good citizen needs to be able to judge men and issues in national life. But there are few important issues of national policy that can be understood today except in relation to our international position. And even the quality of the statesmanship of our national leaders often becomes manifest primarily in their reactions to problems that are at least partly problems of international life. The conscientious citizen therefore obviously requires as broad and enlightened an understanding of this subject as he can get.

The second purpose which instruction in international affairs can serve is to prepare men for service in the foreign field, either in governmental or in other positions.

It is a mistake to think of international affairs as anything outside the regular context of life—as anything which a man could hope to understand without having to understand things much more basic. There is no such thing as foreign affairs in the abstract. The relations between nations are part of the whole great problem of politics—of the behavior of man as a political animal. They are inseparably connected with the fundamental human problem of power that lies at the heart of all politics: the problem of how the freedom of choice of the individual, or of the organized society, is to be limited in order to repress chaos and ensure the good order necessary to the continuation of civilization.

We Americans have a strange—and to me disturbing—attitude toward the subject of power. We don't like the word. We don't like the concept. We are suspicious of people who talk about it. We like to feel that the adjustment of conflicting interests is something that can be taken care of by juridical norms and institutional devices, voluntarily accepted and not involving violence to the feelings or interests of anyone. We like to feel that this is the way our own life is arranged. We like to feel that if this principle were to be understood and observed by others as it is by us, it would put an end to many of the misunderstandings and conflicts that have marked our time.

But we ignore the fact that power underlies our own society as it underlies every other order of human affairs distinguishable from chaos. Order and civilization are not self-engendering. They do not flow from themselves or even from any universal and enlightened understanding of political institutions in the abstract.

In our country, the element of power is peculiarly diffused. It is not concentrated, as it is in other countries, in what we might call the "pure form" of a national uniformed police establishment functioning as the vehicle of a central political will. Power with us does exist to some extent in courts of law and in police establishments, but it also exists in many other American institutions. It exists in our economic system, though not nearly to the degree the Marxists claim. Sometimes, unfortunately, it exists in irregular forces—in underworld groups, criminal gangs, or informal associations of a vigilante nature—capable of terrorizing their fellow citizens in one degree or another. Above all, it exists in the delicate compulsions of our social life, the force of community opinion within our country—in the respect we have for the good opinion of our neighbors. For reasons highly complex, we Americans place upon ourselves quite extraordinary obligations of conformity to the group in utterance and behavior, and this feature of our national life seems to be growing rather than declining. All these things can bring us to put restraints upon ourselves which in other parts of the world would be imposed upon people only by the straightforward exercise of the central police authority.

Now I am not taking exception to this curious diffusion, within American life, of the power to make men conform to given patterns of behavior. It has both advantages and dangers. It represents unquestionably a manner of protecting the interests of the individual against the more dangerous and humiliating forms of tyranny and oppression in normal times. But we must not permit this advantage to blind us to the fact that such a thing as power does exist and is, indeed, a necessity of civilization, flowing from certain facts about human nature—certain imperfections if you will—that are basic and that are not going to be corrected by any man-made device, whether institutional or educational. These basic facts provide one of the main keys to the understanding of history. They lie at the heart of our problem of living together as human beings within the borders of this land. And they also lie at the heart of our problem of living side by side with other human societies within the broader framework of this planet.

Whoever would understand foreign affairs, therefore, cannot and will not do it solely by understanding the intricacies of tariffs or the various classifications of treaties or the ways in which the United Nations Charter differs from the Covenant of the League of Nations or the techniques of sampling mass opinion. International affairs are primarily a matter of the behavior of governments. But the behavior of governments is in turn a matter of the behavior of individual man in the political context, and of the workings of all those basic impulses—national feeling, charity, ambition, fear, jealousy, egotism, and group attachment—which are the stuff of his behavior in the community of other men.

Whoever does not understand these things will never understand what is taking place in the interrelationships of nations. And he will not learn them from courses that purport to deal with international affairs alone. He will learn them, rather, from those things which have been recognized for thousands of years as the essentials of humanistic study: from history and from the more subtle and revealing expressions of man's nature that go by the names of art and literature.

II

I would say, therefore: Let the international affairs course stand as an addendum to basic instruction in the humanities. Let it stand as an exercise in which the student is told to take what he has already learned about the characteristics of the human animal and to note in what curious and marvelous ways they find their ultimate expression in the behavior of governments. Let foreign relations be viewed as one area—an extremely important one—in which these laws of nature work themselves out. But let the teaching of the subject not be permitted to obscure its basic components. Let no one be permitted to think that he is learned in something called a "science" of international relations unless he is learned in the essentials of the political process from the grass roots up and has been taught to look soberly and unsparingly, but also with charity and sympathy, at his fellow human beings. International affairs is not a science. And there is no understanding of international affairs that does not embrace understanding of the human individual.

Only if these principles are observed will we be able to free ourselves from the strain of utopianism that has been present in the teaching of international affairs in our country in recent decades. By this I mean teaching that portrays incorrectly the nature of our world environment and our relation to it and encourages students to disregard the urgent real requirements of international life in favor of the cultivation of artificial and impractical visions of world betterment. This argument about the philosophy of our approach to our problems of foreign relations is one that has been agitating our academic communities intensely in recent months. I am myself a partisan in the dispute. I shall only say here that further exposure to the bitter realities of the practice of international relations, in a place where these realities are about as bitter as they can conceivably be, has strengthened my conviction that the shortcomings in the teaching of international affairs, and primarily the leanings toward shallow and utopian interpretations, represent, in their ultimate effect, an important limitation of our ability to handle ourselves effectively in world affairs. Admittedly this is largely a question of general educational level, and not just of the philosophical tenor of courses on foreign affairs; but that is precisely my point. Until we can achieve a deeper and more realistic understanding generally, among the influential strata of this country, as to what is really involved in the process of international relations, I fear we shall not succeed in reducing appreciably the number of bewildering and painful surprises our people derive from the unfolding of international events.

If the young men of this day are to be trained to look clearly and intelligently on America's foreign relations, the teaching to which they are subjected must be stern and uncompromising. It must be founded in humility and renunciation of easy effects. It must exclude all that is Pollyannaish and superficial. It must reject utopianism and every form of idealism not rooted in an honest and unsparing recognition of the nature of man. It must free itself from the tyranny of slogans, fashionable words, and semantic taboos. It must proceed from a recognition that the understanding of this subject can never be more simply acquired than the understanding of its basic component, which is man himself.

III

So much for the teaching of the understanding of international affairs. Now a word about the teaching of the practice of it. There are a number of institutions in the country engaged, either entirely or partly, in this sort of teaching. I think they have done fine work. I think that they deserve every support. What I say is not in criticism of them but rather by way of defense of them against the pressures to which I know they must from time to time be subjected.

The participation of individual Americans in international activity takes a variety of forms, even within the framework of government work alone. The variety is so great that no institution could hope to give complete vocational training, in the strict sense of the word, for work in the international field. A man who enters the Foreign Service of the United States or who goes abroad in the employ of any great American concern, commercial or philanthropic, is apt to find himself dealing with the most amazing diversity of problems. This lies in the nature of international life and in the necessity—whatever the man's function—of reconciling conflicting national outlooks and customs.

As far as I can see, the qualities that enable people to measure up to these various functions are the general qualities of understanding, adaptability, tact, and common sense. Certainly that is true of the Foreign Service of the United States. To be useful in the tasks of service in the international field, a man requires dignity both of the intellect and of character. The two are linked in curious ways, but character, in my opinion, is unquestionably the more important.

As one who has been in charge of Foreign Service establishments at one time or another, I can say without hesitation that I would wish my subordinates to be well-disciplined both in mind and in character; but if I had to choose, I would take any day the man on whose character I could depend, even though I had to nurse him along in his thinking, rather than the man whose mind might have been trained but whose character was unformed or undependable.

The qualities of honor, loyalty, generosity, consideration for others, and sense of obligation to others have been the guts of usefulness and effectiveness in the Foreign Service as I have known it. This was true even in the more distant days when it was easier to be a part of government, when the relationship of the individual officer to his superiors rested on rather old-fashioned assumptions that made things simple and uncomplicated for both parties and permitted the officer to concentrate his attention almost entirely on the external aspects of his work. How much truer it is today, when so much more is asked of the individual and so little help is given him. In our present controversial age, when the growing awareness of the responsibilities of citizenship and the sudden impact of the hideous problem of human disloyalty are whipping our established institutions about like trees in a storm, the position of the professional civil servant can become the center of some of the most severe strains and tensions our society knows. In this day of bigness and impersonality, of security clearances and loyalty investigations, of swollen staffs and managerial specialists—in this day, in short, of the fading vitality of the individual relationship in government—it requires a special manliness and fortitude for the civil servant to stride confidently along the path of his duties, to retain his serenity of mind and confidence in the future, to find the deeper roots of understanding of his own country and the deeper sources of faith in the utility of what he is doing.

As I said in my talk before the Pennsylvania State Bar Association, there has been much discussion about Communist penetration into our government. But people seldom attempt to appraise the actual damage done thereby to our public policy. I have been fairly close to the policy-making processes in Washington for the past six years. With many of the decisions I have been personally in accord; with others, not. But I cannot recall a single major decision of foreign policy during that period which Communist influence could have had any appreciable part in determining. If, therefore, I were to be asked what part Communist penetration had played in creating our difficulties and perplexities of today in the field of foreign affairs, I would have to say that—as far as these past years are concerned—that part has been negligible, and I am sure it is negligible today.

On the other hand, I have seen serious damage done in these recent years to public confidence and to governmental morale by the mishandling of our own measures to counter precisely this problem of Communist penetration. Such damage has been done by the public discussion of things that should have been handled quietly and privately. It has been done by the inability of many people to distinguish between questions of loyalty and questions of opinion. It has been done by the workings of hastily devised and not fully appropriate procedures for testing and establishing the reliability of public servants. Finally, such damage has been done by the failure of many people to realize that what is important from the standpoint of personal loyalty is not the dusty record of actions committed ten to twenty years ago and now proven by hindsight to have been errors, but the picture of the living human being as he stands before us today, and the extent to which he now possesses wisdom and maturity and stability and all those other positive qualities which too often are acquired only through the process of painful error.

The result to date of all these deficiencies in the treatment of the subject of civic loyalty has been the creation of a situation which worries me precisely because it seems to me to play very dangerously into the hands of those men who have constituted themselves our adversaries in the international sphere. I can see no reason why malicious people should have any particular difficulty in rendering unavailable for service to this country almost any person whom they might select for this treatment. All that is necessary is to release a spate of rumors and gossip and demands for investigation. There are always tongues willing and eager to take up this cry and carry it further; something of it is bound to stick in the public mind; and in the end, if the public servant in question is not discouraged and demoralized, a portion of the public will at any rate have lost confidence in him, and his usefulness to the country will have been thereby reduced. Mind you, I am thinking here not only of the man's loss, which may be grievous. I am thinking of the country's loss, which is more grievous still. Are we so rich in talented public servants that we can afford to leave the ones we have vulnerable to this sort of danger?

In coping with the strains and trials that such conditions involve, the official will not be much helped by memorized facts or by acquired techniques. He will not be much helped by erudition, as distinct from understanding. He will be helped primarily by those qualities of courage and resolution that make it possible for men to have independence of character, to face the loneliness and opprobrium this sometimes involves, and to stand up for their friends and their beliefs and their sense of duty to the national tradition.

It is my impression, from the recollection of my days as an undergraduate, that understanding based on a firm grasp of the humanities, and character based on an uncompromising integrity in all personal associations, are the very essence of a liberal education and represent goals to which our colleges have clung in the face of very considerable pressures. This is my plea: Let those students who want to prepare themselves for work in the international field read their Bible and their Shakespeare, their Plutarch and their Gibbon, perhaps even their Latin and their Greek, and let them guard as the most precious of their possessions that concept of personal conduct which has grown up around the honor system, but of which the honor system is only a part and a symbol. Let them guard that code of behavior which means that men learn to act toward each other with honor and truthfulness and loyalty, to bestow confidence where confidence is asked, and to build within themselves those qualities of self-discipline and self-restraint on which the integrity of a public service must be founded.

If these things are clung to and cultivated, then our colleges will be doing what is most important to prepare their sons to confront the problems of international life, whether as citizens or as public servants. Whatever else can be taught them about the contemporary facts of international life will be a useful superstructure—but only that.

PROBLEMS FOR WRITING AND DISCUSSION

1. Why does Kennan say that "international affairs is a field in which the pursuit of knowledge without understanding is peculiarly pointless and useless"?

2. What is the danger in our continuing to study international affairs as a self-contained "science"?

3. What does Kennan see as our basic limitation in handling ourselves effectively in world affairs? How does the educational pattern contribute to this limitation?

4. How is the American attitude toward power indicative of something Arnold (p. 162) and others observe in the American character? Is Kennan's discussion of power relevant to the rest of the essay?

5. Clearly, Kennan has faith in what is sometimes called the "power" of books and of ideas and the "authority" inherent in character. Are *authority* and *power*—as Kennan uses the term—synonymous? Is there any difference between the various kinds of "power" he enumerates as "diffused" in America, and "power" in its " 'pure form' of a national uniformed police establishment functioning as the vehicle of a central political will"?

6. Kennan argues for training in the humanities for anyone interested in international affairs. Why? Does his concept fit in with the present trend in education as you know it? If you were preparing for a career in foreign service, would you follow Kennan's plan? Why or why not?

7. Compare what Kennan says about the place of international affairs in education with Herberg's theory of the role of religion in American life (p. 657).

8. Whereas Kennan is concerned with the political problem of how "to repress chaos and ensure the good order necessary to the continuation of civilization," Agee (p. 191) implies that the present "order" is not good but is preserved through the "world's misunderstanding." Nevertheless, what weapon do both men choose as the one most effective in dealing with their enemy? Do you think that they would agree on curricula?

9. Both Agee and Kennan suggest that the wrong kind of education may be worse than none at all. Particularize their reasons. Agee attacks the "murder of the mind and spirit," and Kennan is concerned lest the "dignity of intellect and of character" collapse under the perplexities of world affairs. Which man has more faith in the efficacy of education to strengthen and sustain mind and character?

10. Compare and contrast the picture of the American undergraduate as Ebel (p. 213) sees him and as Kennan would like to see him.

11. Is the mishandling of the subject of civic loyalty, as Kennan describes it, an instance of what William Miller (p. 225) calls democracy misunderstood? Explain. Compare Kennan's protest against public persecution with the protests of T. S. Matthews (p. 99), Arthur Miller (p. 59), and James Thurber (p. 34) in Part I.

3. Science

Understanding Science

JAMES B. CONANT

James B. Conant (1893-) was graduated from Harvard in 1913, received his doctorate there three years later and, after rising to chairman of the Department of Chemistry, became President of the University in 1933, a post he held until 1953. During World War II he was chairman of the National Defense Research Committee, which had much to do with development of the atomic bomb, and after the war he was a member of the general advisory committee of the Atomic Energy Commission until 1952. He served in Germany, first as U.S. High Commissioner and later as Ambassador to the new Federal Republic of Germany from 1953 to 1957. Since then he has given his time to improving American public education. Throughout his busy public and professional life he has always found time to write such books as On Understanding Science *(1947),* Modern Science and Modern Man *(1952),* Germany and Freedom *(1958),* The American High School Today *(1959), and* Slums and Suburbs *(1962).*

In my experience, a man who has been a successful investigator in any field of experimental science approaches a problem in pure or applied science, even in an area in which he is quite ignorant, with a special point of view. I designate this point of view "understanding science." Note carefully that it is independent of a knowl-

Reprinted from James B. Conant On Understanding Science, © *1947, by permission of the publisher, Yale University Press.*

edge of the scientific facts or techniques in the new area to which he comes. Even a highly educated and intelligent citizen without research experience will almost always fail to grasp the essentials in a discussion which takes place among scientists concerned with a projected inquiry. This will be so not because of the layman's lack of scientific knowledge or his failure to comprehend the technical jargon of the scientist; it will be to a large degree because of his fundamental ignorance of what science can or cannot accomplish, and his consequent bewilderment in the course of a discussion outlining a plan for a future investigation. He has no "feel" for the Tactics and Strategy of Science.

In the last five years I have seen repeated examples of such bewilderment of laymen. If I am right in this diagnosis (and it is the fundamental premise of this book), the remedy does not lie in a greater dissemination of scientific information among nonscientists. Being well informed about science is not the same thing as understanding science, though the two propositions are not antithetical. What is needed are methods for imparting some knowledge of the Tactics and Strategy of Science to those who are not scientists. Not that one can hope by any short-cut methods to produce in a layman's mind the same instinctive reaction toward scientific problems that is the hallmark of an investigator, but enough can be accomplished, I dare hope, to bridge the gap to some degree between those who understand science because science is their profession and those who have only studied the results of scientific inquiry—in short, the laymen.

But even if we agree that it is not more knowledge about science (more facts and principles) but some understanding of science that is required by the general public our pedagogic problem is not solved. For there are two ways of probing into complex human activities and their products: one is to retrace the steps by which certain end results have been produced, the other is to dissect the result with the hope of revealing its structural pattern and exposing the logical relations of the component parts, and, incidentally, exposing also the inconsistencies and flaws. Philosophic and mathematical minds prefer the logical approach, but it is my belief that for nine people out of ten the historical method will yield more real understanding of a complex matter.

For example, consider our form of government here in the United States with its complicated interplay of state and federal relations so baffling to even a highly educated visitor from another democratic nation. In one sense, only a few lawyers, statesmen, and political scientists understand the American Commonwealth. The rest of us can find time only to try to obtain some understanding by the study of a few books. Shall we follow Lord Bryce, for example, in looking for insight into the American constitution, or read Beard balanced by Charles Warren? For me, the answer is easy; if I have to choose, the historian's story will provide more understanding than the statesman's analysis. Whether this is true for a large majority of students, only the teachers of political science and history could say. But I venture the analogy to illustrate two ways in which an understanding of science may be to some degree attained by a relatively small amount of study. You may turn to the philosopher's interpretation or you may study examples of science in the making.

As far as the scientific education of the layman is concerned, I believe there is no real choice. It may be a toss-up as to whether the political scientist or the historian can give the better understanding of our government in a limited amount of time; but the odds are all against the philosopher, I believe, who has a parallel assignment in regard to science. To be sure, he has had a clear field for the most part, for the histories illustrating the Tactics and Strategy of Science are as yet unwritten. But in spite of this lack of competition I doubt if the philosophical treatments of science and scientific method have been very successful when viewed as an educational enterprise. No one questions of course the importance of this type of penetrating analysis. There must be constant critical appraisal of the progress of science and in particular of scientific concepts and operation. This is one of the prime tasks of philosophers concerned with the unity of science and the problems of cosmology. But when learned discussions of these difficult matters are the sole source of popular knowledge about the ways of science, education in science may be more handicapped than helped by their wide circulation. I am inclined to think that, on the whole, the popularization of the philosophical analysis of science and its methods has led not to a greater understanding but to a great deal of misunderstanding about science.

To illustrate, let me . . . refer to *The Grammar of Science*. Throughout the volume Karl Pearson refers to science as the classification of facts, and in his summary of the first chapter he writes as follows: "The scientific method is marked by the following features: (a) careful and accurate classification of facts and observation of their correlation and sequence; (b) the discovery of scientific laws by aid of the creative imagination; (c) self-criticism and the final touchstone of equal validity for all normally constituted minds." With (b) and (c) one can have little quarrel since all condensed statements of this are by necessity incomplete, but from (a) I dissent entirely. And it is the point of view expressed in this sentence that dominates Pearson's whole discussion. It seems to me, indeed, that one who had little or no direct experience with scientific investigations might be completely misled as to the nature of the scientific method by studying this famous book.

If science were as simple as this very readable account would have us believe, why did it take so long a period of fumbling before scientists were clear on some very familiar matters? Newton's famous work was complete by the close of the seventeenth century. The cultured gentlemen of France and England in the first decades of the eighteenth century talked in terms of a solar system almost identical with that taught in school today. The laws of motion and their application to mechanics were widely understood. Yet it was not until the 1770's that the common phenomenon of combustion was formulated in terms of comparable clarity; it was not until much later still that the concept of heat as a "mode of motion" was accepted. Spontaneous generation of life, you will recall, was an open question as late as the 1870's. Seventy-five years ago the Professor of Natural Philosophy at Harvard told his classes that "people now accept the undulatory theory of light because all those who formerly accepted the corpuscular theory are dead." The implied prophecy in this bit of skepticism turned out to be not far from the mark. Only within the lifetime of many of us has it been possible to develop concepts which take care of relatively simple facts concerning the emission and absorption of radiant energy. Darwin convinced himself and later the scientific world and later still the educated public of the correctness of the general idea of evolution because of a theory as to the mechanism by which evolution might have occurred. Today, the basic idea of the evolutionary development of higher plants and animals stands without question, but Darwin's mechanism has been so greatly questioned as to have been almost overthrown. And we are no nearer a solution of the problem of how life originated on this planet than we were in Darwin's day.

The stumbling way in which even the ablest of the early scientists had to fight through thickets of erroneous observations, misleading generalizations, inadequate formulations, and unconscious prejudice is the story which it seems to me needs telling. It is not told in courses in physics or chemistry or biology or any other of the natural sciences as far as I am aware. Take up a textbook of any of these subjects and see how very simple it all seems as far as method is concerned, and how very complicated the body of facts and principles soon becomes. Indeed, before you have got far in a freshman course you will find the harassed professor under pressure to be up to date bringing in subjects which cannot be adequately analyzed by the class at hand. Having insufficient knowledge of other disciplines, and particularly mathematics, the students have to take on faith statements about scientific laws and the structure of matter which are almost as dogmatic as though they were handed down by a high priest. Let me hasten to add, I am not blaming the teachers of these subjects. I have done the same in my time, and as an author of textbooks I am sinning in the same way today. For there is no other method of presenting factual knowledge in these subjects in this day of a vast interrelated and highly complicated fabric of physics, chemistry, and biology.

Let me now be specific as to my proposal for the reform of the scientific education of the layman. What I propose is the establishment of one or more courses at the college level on the Tactics and Strategy of Science. The objective would be to give a greater degree of understanding of science by the close study of a relatively few historical examples of the development of science. I suggest courses at the college level, for I do not believe they could be introduced earlier in a student's education; but there is no reason why they could not become important parts of programs of adult education. Indeed, such courses might well prove particularly suitable for older groups of men and women.

The analogy with the teaching of strategy and tactics of war by examples from military history is obvious. And the success of that educational procedure is one reason why I venture to be hopeful about this new approach to understanding science. I also draw confidence from the knowledge of how the case method in law schools and a somewhat similar method in the Harvard Business School have demonstrated the value of this type of pedagogic device. The course would not aim to teach science—not even the basic principles or simplest facts—though as a by-product considerable knowledge of certain sciences would be sure to follow. Of course, some elementary knowledge of physics would be a prerequisite, but with the improvement in the teaching of science in high schools which is sure to come, this should prove no serious obstacle.

If one is content to give up the objectives of even a broad survey course—which are, to convey the basic facts and principles of science—one has a free hand in choosing the case histories. How they would in fact be chosen would depend on the inspiration of the teacher. All I can give in these lectures is one man's view, with the warning that it is based on no experience whatsoever with the type of teaching I suggest. Like many teachers of physics and chemistry and biology, I have from time to time quarried out bits from the history of a special science to assist my exposition. I have seen others go much further in the same direction with considerable success. But I must freely admit that what I am proposing represents a tremendous extrapolation from any educational experiments of which I am aware. Therefore, I warn that I may be peddling a rope of sand. But at all events, in so doing I shall have the satisfaction of answering for myself the question, "What is science?" not in analytical but in historic terms.

The case histories would almost all be chosen from the early days in the evolution of the modern discipline. Certain aspects of physics in the seventeenth and eighteenth centuries; chemistry in the eighteenth and nineteenth; geology in the early nineteenth; certain phases of biology in the eighteenth; others in the nineteenth. The advantages of this method of approach are twofold: first, relatively little factual knowledge is required either as regards the science in question or other sciences, and relatively little mathematics; second, in the early days one sees in clearest light the necessary fumblings of even intellectual giants when they are also pioneers; one comes to understand what science is by seeing how difficult it is in fact to carry out glib scientific precepts.

A few words may be in order as to the principles which would guide me in selecting case histories for my hypothetical course in the Tactics and Strategy of Science. I should wish to show the difficulties which attend each new push forward in the advance of science, and the importance of new techniques: how they arise, are improved, and often revolutionize a field of inquiry. I should hope to illustrate the intricate interplay between experiment, or observation, and the development of new concepts and new generalizations; in short, how new concepts evolve from experiments, how one conceptual scheme for a time is adequate and then is modified or displaced by another. I should want also to illustrate the interconnection between science and society about which so much has been said in recent years by our Marxist friends. I should have very little to say about the classification of facts, unless it were to use this phrase as a straw man. But I should hope that almost all examples chosen would show the hazards which nature puts in the way of those who would examine the facts impartially and classify them accurately. The "controlled experiment" and the planned or controlled observation would be in the forefront of every discussion. The difference in methods between the observational sciences of astronomy, geology, systematic biology on the one hand, and the experimental sciences of physics, chemistry, and experimental biology on the other should be emphasized.

To what extent a course in the Tactics and Strategy of Science should take cognizance of the existence of problems in metaphysics and epistemology would depend on the outlook of the instructor and the maturity and interest of the student. Obviously the course in question would not be one on the metaphysical foundations of modern science; yet the teacher can hardly ignore completely the influence of new scientific concepts on contemporary thinking about the structure of the universe or the nature and destiny of man. Nor can one fail in all honesty to identify at least vaguely those philosophic problems which have arisen when man has sought to examine critically the basis of his knowledge about "the external world." Perhaps in collaboration with a colleague from the department of philosophy the instructor would wish to suggest the reading of extracts from the writings of certain philosophers. If so, the existence of more than one school of thought should certainly be emphasized.

As I shall show in subsequent chapters, a discussion of the evolution of new conceptual schemes as a result of experimentation would occupy a central position in the exposition. This being so, there would be no escape from a consideration of the difficulties which historically have attended the development of new concepts. Is a vacuum really empty, if so, how can we see through it? Is action at a distance imaginable? These questions at one time in the forefront of scientific discussion are well worthy of careful review. The Newtonian theory of gravitation once disturbed "almost all investigators of nature because it was founded on an uncommon unintelligibility." It no longer disturbs us because "it has become a common unintelligibility." To what extent can the same statement be made about other concepts which have played a major part in the development of modern science? When we say that the chemists have "established" that chlorophyll is essential for photosynthesis and that they also have "established" the spatial arrangements of the carbon, hydrogen, and oxygen atoms in cane sugar, are we using the word "establish" in two different senses? These and similar questions should be explored in sufficient degree to make the student aware of some of the complexities which lie hidden behind our usual simplified exposition of the basic ideas of modern science in an elementary course.

However, I cannot emphasize too often that the course in question must *not* be concerned with the fruits of scientific inquiries, either as embodied in scientific laws or theories or cosmologies, or in the applications of science to industry or agriculture or medicine. Rather, the instructor would center his attention on the ways in which these fruits have been attained. One might call it a course in "scientific method" as illustrated by examples from history, except that I am reluctant to use this ambiguous phrase. I should prefer to speak of the methods by which science has been advanced, or perhaps we should say knowledge has been advanced, harking back to Francis Bacon's famous phrase, the advancement of learning.

PROBLEMS FOR WRITING AND DISCUSSION

1. What does Conant mean by the phrase "understanding science"?
2. What method does Conant propose to use in helping the layman understand science? Why does he prefer this method to that of philosophical analysis? Does Conant discredit or disparage philosophical formulations?

3. Conant "dissents entirely" from a feature of the scientific method noted by Karl Pearson. Does he say explicitly why? Explain.

4. What are the implications for the atomic age of Conant's observation that "only within the lifetime of many of us has it been possible to develop concepts which take care of relatively simple facts concerning the emission and absorption of radiant energy"?

5. Does Conant imply that "understanding science" will lessen the bewilderment of laymen in areas other than scientific areas? To what extent might it?

6. Distinct as their areas of interest are, do Conant and Kennan share any common concern in their educational proposals?

7. What does the term "Tactics and Strategy of Science" suggest about Conant's conception of man's relation to the natural order of things? Does his analogy between "understanding science" and understanding the American commonwealth seem valid to you? Do you think the natural order of things and the human order, studied by the same approach, will yield equally satisfactory results? Give instances to support your answer.

A Scientific Experiment

BENJAMIN FRANKLIN

Benjamin Franklin (1706-1790) was born in Boston. He moved to Philadelphia when seventeen. Seven years later he was the city's leading printer and remained so until 1748, when, at the age of forty-two, he retired to devote himself to science. But from 1754 until his death one public mission after another —first for Pennsylvania, later for the United Colonies, later still for the United States— made demands on his time. Franklin excelled as businessman, inventor, writer, and statesman, but his international fame stemmed first from his electrical experiments, and science, as Carl Becker has remarked, was "the one mistress to whom he gave himself without reserve and served neither from a sense of duty nor for any practical purpose."

In 1746, being at Boston, I met there with a Dr. Spence, who was lately arrived from Scotland, and show'd me some electric experiments. They were imperfectly perform'd, as he was not very expert; but, being on a subject quite new to me, they equally surpris'd and pleased me. Soon after my return to Philadelphia, our library company receiv'd from Mr. P. Collinson, Fellow of the Royal Society of London, a present of a glass tube, with some account of the use of it in making such experiments. I eagerly seized the opportunity of repeating what I had seen at Boston; and, by much practice, acquir'd great readiness in performing those, also, which we had an account of from England, adding a number of new ones. I say

From Benjamin Franklin, Autobiography *(1771).*

much practice, for my house was continually full, for some time, with people who came to see these new wonders.

To divide a little this incumbrance among my friends, I caused a number of similar tubes to be blown at our glass-house, with which they furnish'd themselves, so that we had at length several performers. Among these, the principal was Mr. Kinnersley, an ingenious neighbor, who, being out of business, I encouraged to undertake showing the experiments for money, and drew up for him two lectures, in which the experiments were rang'd in such order, and accompanied with such explanations in such method, as that the foregoing should assist in comprehending the following. He procur'd an elegant apparatus for the purpose, in which all the little machines that I had roughly made for myself were nicely form'd by instrument-makers. His lectures were well attended, and gave great satisfaction; and after some time he went thro' the colonies, exhibiting them in every capital town, and pick'd up some money. In the West India Islands, indeed, it was with difficulty the experiments could be made, from the general moisture of the air.

Oblig'd as we were to Mr. Collinson for his present of the tube, etc., I thought it right he should be inform'd of our success in using it, and wrote him several letters containing accounts of our experiments. He got them read in the Royal Society, where they were not at first thought worth so much notice as to be printed in their Transactions. One paper, which I wrote for Mr. Kinnersley, on the sameness of lightning with electricity, I sent to Dr. Mitchel, an acquaintance of mine, and one of the members also of that society, who wrote me word that it had been read, but was laughed at by the connoisseurs. The papers, however, being shown to Dr. Fothergill, he thought them of too much value to be stifled, and advis'd the printing of them. Mr. Collinson then gave them to *Cave* for publication in his Gentleman's Magazine; but he chose to print them separately in a pamphlet, and Dr. Fothergill wrote the preface. Cave, it seems, judged rightly for his profit, for by the additions that arrived afterward they swell'd, to a quarto volume, which has had five editions, and cost him nothing for copy-money.

It was, however, some time before those papers were much taken notice of in England. A copy of them happening to fall into the hands of the Count de Buffon, a philosopher deservedly of great reputation in France, and, indeed, all over Europe, he prevailed with M. Dalibard to translate them into French, and they were printed at Paris. The publication offended the Abbé Nollet, preceptor in Natural Philosophy to the royal family, and an able experimenter, who had form'd and publish'd a theory of electricity, which then had the general vogue. He could not at first believe that such a work came from America, and said it must have been fabricated by his enemies at Paris, to decry his system. Afterwards, having been assur'd that there really existed such a person as Franklin at Philadelphia, which he had doubted, he wrote and published a volume of Letters, chiefly address'd to me, defending his theory, and denying the verity of my experiments, and of the positions deduc'd from them.

I once purpos'd answering the abbé, and actually began the answer; but, on consideration that my writings contain'd a description of experiments which any one might repeat and verify, and if not to be verifi'd, could not be defended; or of observations offer'd as conjectures, and not delivered dogmatically, therefore not laying me under any obligation to defend them; and reflecting that a dispute between two persons, writing in different languages, might be lengthened greatly by mistranslations, and thence misconceptions of one another's meaning, much of one of the abbé's letters being founded on an error in the translation, I concluded to let my papers shift for themselves, believing it was better to spend what time I could spare from public business in making new experiments, than in disputing about those already made. I therefore never answered M. Nollet, and the event gave me no cause to repent my silence; for my friend M. le Roy, of the Royal Academy of Sciences, took up my cause and refuted him; my book was translated into the Italian, German, and Latin languages; and the doctrine it contain'd was by degrees universally adopted by the philosophers of Europe, in preference to that of the abbé; so that he lived to see himself the last of his sect, except Monsieur B——, of Paris, his *élève* and immediate disciple.

What gave my book the more sudden and general celebrity, was the success of one of its proposed experiments, made by Messrs. Dalibard and De Lor at Marly, for drawing lightning from the clouds. This engag'd the public attention every where. M. de Lor, who had an apparatus for experimental philosophy, and lectur'd in that branch of science, undertook to repeat what he called the *Philadelphia Experiments*; and, after they were performed before the king and court, all the curious of Paris flocked to see them. I will not swell this narrative with an account of that capital experiment, nor of the infinite pleasure I receiv'd in the success of a similar one I made soon after with a kite at Philadelphia, as both are to be found in the histories of electricity.

Dr. Wright, an English physician, when at Paris, wrote to a friend, who was of the Royal Society, an account of the high esteem my experiments were in among the learned abroad, and of their wonder that my writings had been so little noticed in England. The Society, on this, resum'd the consideration of the letters that had been read to them; and the celebrated Dr. Watson drew up a summary account of them, and of all I had afterwards sent to England on the subject, which he accompanied with some praise of the writer. This summary was then printed in their Transactions; and some members of the Society in London, particularly the very ingenious Mr. Canton, having verified the experiment of procuring lightning from the clouds by a pointed rod, and acquainting them with the success, they soon made me more than amends for the slight with which they had before treated me. Without my having made any application for that honour, they chose me a member, and voted that I should be excus'd the customary payments, which would have amounted to twenty-five guineas; and ever since have given me their Transactions gratis. They also presented me with the gold medal of Sir Godfrey Copley for the year 1753, the delivery of which was accompanied by a very handsome speech of the president, Lord Macclesfield, wherein I was highly honoured.

PROBLEMS FOR WRITING AND DISCUSSION

1. Would Conant (p. 247) have approved of the Kinnersley demonstrations for purposes of educating the layman?
2. On the basis of your readings in Section I, account for the reactions of Abbé Nollet and, initially, of the Royal Society to Franklin's observations.
3. Franklin is often said to be the embodiment of American practicality. What was practical about Franklin's experiments? Did practicality motivate Franklin to perform these experiments?
4. How does Franklin's attitude toward his findings corroborate what Conant says of "the special point of view" of experimental researchers?
5. Franklin was a diplomat as well as an experimental scientist. In his dealings with fellow scientists abroad, does he reveal attributes of character Kennan (p. 233) considers requisite for diplomatic success? Explain.

Science

E. B. WHITE

E[lwyn] B[rooks] White (1899-) was born in Mount Vernon, New York, and was educated at Cornell University. He was writing automobile advertising when he joined The New Yorker in 1926, working part time at thirty dollars a week. "I hung on to my advertising connection because I had no confidence in the world of letters." His stories, essays, captions, verses, and tag lines for fillers "brought the steel and music to the magazine," as one friend put it, and his column of "Notes and Comment," according to James Thurber, "did more than anything else to set the tone and cadence of The New Yorker and to shape its turns of thought." Among his many books are Every Day is Saturday (1934), Quo Vadimus (1939), One Man's Meat (1942), The Wild Flag (1946), The Second Tree from the Corner (1954), The Points of My Compass (1962), and several volumes for children. He lives at present in Maine, and from there occasionally sends off a "Letter from the East" to the magazine he did so much to shape.

From science we get intimations of doom, and from science we get the facts to refute them. We read, for instance, that in the upper reaches of the stratosphere there is a little wall of ozone an eighth of an inch thick, and it is all that separates us from destruction by the sun. Dr. Charles G. Abbot, in a report to the Smithsonian In-

From Every Day Is Saturday *by E. B. White. Copyright 1934 by Harper & Row, Publishers, Incorporated. Reprinted by permission of the publishers.*

stitute, points out that if this slender sheath should ever fold up (these balloonists should really be more careful!) we would all be wiped out instantly. On the other hand, we recall reading some time ago a most absorbing statement on the mechanism of sensation by Professor Henri Piéron. Dr. Piéron explained that between us and reality there stands an insurmountable barrier beyond which our knowledge and consciousness may never pass. All that we see, hear, touch, taste, smell, feel, think, or know, are merely shadows, symbols of objects but not the objects themselves—such stuff as dreams are made on. How strange it all is: between us and the death-dealing rays of the sun there stands a tiny wall which (science hastens to add) is not a wall at all, but a mere symbol of a wall, saving us from the sun, which is no sun but a mere shadow—a shadow waiting to deal death, and death is but a dream.

PROBLEMS FOR WRITING AND DISCUSSION

1. White wrote this brief essay in 1934, eleven years before the explosion of the first atomic bomb. Does the paradox of his first sentence still apply? Explain.
2. White points out the logical absurdity of conflicting statements on the universe. On the basis of what Conant says, do you think White understands science? Explain.
3. Does the logical absurdity invalidate the two sets of "facts" White brings together, or does it support Conant's contention (p. 247) that metaphysics and epistemology are inseparable adjuncts to science in the "advancement of learning"? Explain.

The Encouragement of Science

J. ROBERT OPPENHEIMER

J[ulius] Robert Oppenheimer (1904-   ) was born in New York City. He entered Harvard in 1922 and completed work for a degree in physics in three years. He did advanced work in England at Cambridge and in Germany at Göttingen, where he received his doctorate. He returned to America in 1928 and accepted concurrent appointments at the California Institute of Technology at Pasadena and at the University of California in Berkeley. In 1943 he became the first director of the Los Alamos project and was of key importance in the development of the first atomic bomb. He went to Princeton in 1947 as Director of the Institute of Advanced Study, a position he still holds. He continued to advise various government agencies on scientific matters until 1954 when, though found to be loyal, he was deprived of his security classification for having "consistently placed himself outside the rules which govern others." The decision was widely criticized at the time. The steady demands for his presence at scientific and other public meetings suggest, however, that it did little to diminish respect for his integrity and ability. Many of his speeches and essays have been collected in The Open Mind *(1955).*

We are here tonight to honor you and to celebrate the high promise of your future as scientists. We are happy to be with you.

From The Open Mind, *copyright © 1955 by J. Robert Oppenheimer. Reprinted by permission of Simon and Schuster, Inc. ["The Encouragement of Science" was delivered as an address to the winners of the annual Westinghouse Science Talent Search on March 7, 1950, in Washington, D.C.—Eds.]*

We think of that future with respect and curiosity. We think of the discoveries which you will make. We think of the questions to which we today have no answer and to which you will come to know an answer. Even more, we think of the answers that we have today and of the new questions that you will put to those answers. We think of how altered and how deepened our knowledge of the world will be before you are through with it. My first wish to you is that you may make and that you may share in the making of great and beautiful discoveries which enrich our knowledge of the world of nature and of man. I have a second wish for you; but that must come at the end of my talk.

I do not propose to talk to you of such topics of the day as the hydrogen bomb and the statutory provisions of the National Science Foundation. If these matters are not in a very different state when you shall have come to assume the full responsibilities of citizenship, you will have reason to reproach your elders for your inheritance.

Science has profoundly altered the conditions of man's life. During the last centuries, the discoveries in science and their applications to practice have changed the material conditions of life. They have changed as well many matters of the spirit. They have changed the form in which practical problems of right and wrong come before us; they have changed the focus of moral issues, both for the individual and for governments. They have given us new methods for defining the meaning of problems that face us and for judging whether or not our solutions are just.

The most manifest of the changes are the material ones. Yet even here it takes a certain perspective to see their true extent. Advances in the study of man and other living forms have extended our life span by decades. Discoveries in physical science have immeasurably lightened our toil and enriched our lives. They have given leisure to an ever-widening group of men. They have made a reasonable education not a special privilege but a common right. They have made the world, in its physical dimensions, a small place, and established the means by which people in remote parts of the earth can communicate with each other, can get to know each other, and can learn to work together. They have put at the disposal of everyone the resources of physical power, of ease and of knowledge that were in the past reserved for the few.

Not all the changes in material well-being that science offers are realities. Yet the very fact that they are possibilities has changed the nature of the responsibility which we bear, both as individuals and as a community of men and women banded together in government. In the Greek cities, political democracy and civilization itself appeared possible only on the basis of a slave economy. Technology, born of science, has altered that; it has enabled mankind, as it has forced mankind, to deal with the issues of slavery as a moral issue. Poverty has always been an ugly thing, and in its extremes a desperate one. Today it is an evil, in the sense that it lies within human hands and human hearts to abate it. Science can provide us, for the first time in history, with the means of abating hunger for everyone on earth.

Perhaps nowhere has the impact of science more clearly altered the specific terms of a great political issue than in the effects of scientific development on warfare. This is a can of worms with which I have myself unhappily been engaged for some years. It would not be honest to say—as it would be folly not to hope—that the very terror of modern weapons would in itself put an end to war; it would not even be honest to say that because of this terror the abolition of war and the maintenance of peace have become the one absolute, final objective of all political decisions. There are other things in man's life—his freedom, his decency, his sense of right and wrong—that cannot so lightly be subjected to a single end. But what we need to remember is that war today has become, and is increasingly becoming, something very different from what it was a century ago or a millennium ago. We need to recognize the new situation as new; we need to come to it with something of the same spirit as the scientist's when he has conducted an experiment and finds that the results are totally other than those that he had anticipated.

Four months before Hiroshima, in the last days of his life, President Roosevelt's thoughts turned to these questions. In the last words that he wrote, in words he did not live to speak, the President looked to the future, to the atomic age. He looked to the past, to the days of the founding of the Republic. He wrote:

"Thomas Jefferson, himself a distinguished scientist, once spoke of the 'brotherly spirit of science, which unites into one family all its votaries of whatever grade, and however widely dispersed throughout the different quarters of the globe.'

"Today science has brought all the different quarters of the globe so close together that it is impossible to isolate them one from another.

"Today we are faced with the pre-eminent fact that, if civilization is to survive, we must cultivate the science of human relationships—the ability of all peoples, of all kinds, to live together and work together, in the same world, at peace."

Science has greatly extended the range of questions in which man has a choice; it has extended man's freedom to make significant decisions. Is there anything in the methods of science itself, or in the spirit of science, which can help in the making of these decisions? To what extent is there a play on the word *science* which can mislead us and take us up false roads when we speak of this science of human relationships? Is there anything we can learn from the relevance of science to politics?

If we are to answer these questions and answer them honestly, we must recognize important and basic differences between problems of science and problems of action as they arise in personal or in political life. If we fail to recognize these differences, we shall be seeking magic solutions and not real ones. We shall delude ourselves into laying aside responsibility, which it is an essential part of man's life to bear.

In most scientific study, questions of good and evil or right and wrong play at most a minor and secondary part. For practical decisions of policy, they are basic. Without them political action would be meaningless. Practical decisions and, above all, political decisions can never quite be freed from the conflicting claims of special interest. These too are part of the meaning of a decision and of a course of action, and they must be an essential part of the force of its implementation.

Political decisions are unique acts. In politics there is little that can correspond to the scientist's repetition of an experiment. An experiment that fails in its purpose may be as good or better than one that succeeds, because it may well be more instructive. A political decision cannot be taken twice. All the factors that are relevant to it will conjoin only once. The analogies of history can provide a guide, but only a very partial one.

These are formidable differences between the problems of science and those of practice. They show that the method of science cannot be directly adapted to the solution of problems in politics and in man's spiritual life. Yet there is relevance of a more subtle but by no means trivial kind.

In trying more fully to explore this relevance, I should like to start with a text. This text is a letter written by Thomas Jefferson to a young man who had inquired of him as to the usefulness of his studies of science. It was written in the middle of the year 1799, the year in which Napoleon abolished the Directory and began to assume dictatorial power in France, the year before Thomas Jefferson was elected for the first time as President of the United States. Jefferson and the diverse brave and hopeful men who with him laid the foundations of our own government had learned much from the peoples of other nations. Many of their highest political ideals and their most powerful political instruments were built on the experience, the insight and wisdom of European scientists and philosophers. Even today we need to remember that this was so, that there may be much we can learn from others, and that we should be glad to learn, as in turn by example we should be glad to teach.

Jefferson's letter starts with a survey of the subjects in science which he believes young Munford ought to pursue. I will quote one characteristic passage which may strike a familiar and homely note for you:

". . . the science of calculation also is indispensible as far as the extraction of the square and cube roots: Algebra as far as the quadratic equation and the use of logarithms are often of value in ordinary cases: but all beyond these is but a luxury; a delicious luxury indeed; but not to be indulged in by one who is to have a profession to follow for his subsistence."

But that is not really the part of Jefferson's letter which I commend to you. Here it is:

"I am among those who think well of the human character generally. I consider man as formed for society, and endowed by nature with those dispositions which fit him for society. I believe also, with Condorcet, as mentioned in your letter, that his mind is perfectible to a degree of which we cannot as yet form any conception. It is impossible for a man who takes a survey of what is already known, not to see what an immensity in every branch of science yet remains to be discovered, and that too of articles to which our faculties seem adequate."

And later, in the same letter, still more explicitly:

". . . and it is still more certain that in the other branches of science, great fields are yet to be explored to which our faculties are equal, and that to an extent of which we cannot fix the limits. I join you therefore in branding as cowardly the idea that the human mind is incapable of further advances. This is precisely the doctrine which the present despots of the earth are inculcating, and their friends here re-echoing; and applying especially to religion and politics; 'that it is not probable that any thing better will be discovered than what was known to our fathers.' We are to look backwards then and not forwards for the improvement of science, and to find it amidst feudal barbarisms and the fires of Spital-fields. But thank heaven the American mind is already too much opened, to listen to these impostures; and while the art of printing is left to us, science can never be retrograde; what is once acquired of real knowledge can never be lost. To preserve the freedom of the human mind then and freedom of the press, every spirit should be ready to devote itself to martyrdom; for as long as we may think as we will, and speak as we think, the condition of man will proceed in improvement. The generation which is going off the stage has deserved well of mankind for the struggles it has made, and for having arrested that course of despotism which had overwhelmed the world for thousands and thousands of years. If there seems to be danger that the ground they have gained will be lost again, that danger comes from the generation your contemporary. But that the enthusiasm which characterises youth should lift its parracide hands against freedom and science would be such a monstrous phaenomenon as I cannot place among possible things in this age and this country."

To me there are two striking impressions which this letter of Jefferson's makes, even beyond its eloquence and its beauty. The first is that the letter is pervaded with the idea of progress, that ideal that owes so much to the development of science and that in turn has provided the great enriching human faith in which scientific discovery and invention have flourished. Jefferson is confident that an increased understanding of the world will lead to progress; he is convinced that the barbarisms of the past cannot stand up against inquiry and understanding and enlightenment; he is confident in man and sure that as men know more they will act more wisely and live better. In our contemporary expressions of hope that catastrophe can be averted and civilization yet be saved, that confidence has lost much of its robustness.

The second point is that for Jefferson there is something in the ways of science that is relevant to political life. Even in religion and politics, he holds that it is probable that things better will be discovered than what was known to our fathers. This conviction that new knowledge is possible, and that not all the answers are known, is of course the stuff of the day-to-day life of the scientist. Science itself does progress; new knowledge is possible; and new knowledge, because it does not destroy or ignore the old, can only increase our understanding. The very idea of the development of science is an example of progress, and of progress which in no true sense can ever be reversed. But this is only part of the story. It is true, as Jefferson knew, that in the large, science has flourished in conditions of human freedom, and that its growth is parallel to the growth of democratic institutions. Today, looking back on more than a century and a half of further history, we can be even more sure of this. We have seen not only the inspiring example of science and democracy flourishing together, but the tragic examples of their foundering together. We express the hope that of this tragedy we shall soon have seen the end.

What are these lessons that the spirit of science teaches us for our practical affairs? Basic to them all is that there may be no barriers to freedom of inquiry. Basic to them all is the ideal of open-mindedness with regard to new knowledge, new experience and new truth. Science is not based on authority. It owes its acceptance and its universality to an appeal to intelligible, communicable evidence that any interested man can evaluate.

There is no place for dogma in science. The scientist is free to ask any question, to doubt any assertion, to seek for any evidence, to correct any error. Where science has been used in the past to erect a new dogmatism, that dogmatism has found itself incompatible with the progress of science; and in the end, the dogma has yielded, or science and freedom have perished together.

Our own political life is predicated on openness. We do not believe any group of men adequate enough or wise enough to operate without scrutiny or without criticism. We know that the only way to avoid error is to detect it, that the only way to detect it is to be free to inquire. We know that the wages of secrecy are corruption. We know that in secrecy error, undetected, will flourish and subvert.

Let me be clear. Science is not skepticism. It is not the practice of science to look for things to doubt. It was not by a deliberate attempt of skepticism that physicists were led to doubt the absolute nature of simultaneity, or to recognize that the ideas of strict causality embodied in classical physics could not be applied in the domain of atomic phenomena. There is probably no group of men who take more for granted in their daily work than the scientists. Common sense and all that flows from it are their principal basis for what they do in the laboratory and for what they make of it on paper. But for scientists it is not only honorable to doubt; it is mandatory to do that when there appears to be evidence in support of the doubt. In place of authority in science we have and we need to have only the consensus of informed opinion, only the guide of example. No scientist needs to order his colleagues to use a new technique of experiment or to enter a new field of discovery. If he has done this, it will be an invitation to his fellows to follow.

These, then, are some of the attitudes of mind, these are some of the disciplines of spirit which grow naturally in the scientist's world. They have grown there in part as a result of a humane and liberal tradition in political life and in part as a cause of that. The open mind, the reliance on example and persuasion rather than on authority—these are the heritage of the centuries in which science has altered the face of the earth. Science can help in diverse ways in preserving and extending this heritage. Its very universality speaks across frontiers to make truth manifest in lands otherwise darkened; its material applications create the preconditions—in leisure, in education, in means of communication—for the converse of men with one another. Science provides the material and the intellectual basis for a world in which example and understanding can help all men to improve their lot and fulfill their hopes. Today we need to remember that our country, founded on these practices and grown strong by their exercise, owes its strength to them. In this time of crisis, we need to cherish that strength.

And this brings me to my second wish for you. I wish you not only the joy of great discovery; I wish for you a world of confidence in man and man's humanity, a world of confidence in reason, so that as you work you may be inspired by the hope that what you find will make men freer and better—in which, working as specialists in what may be recondite parts of the intellectual life of the time, you are nevertheless contributing in a direct and basic way to the welfare of mankind.

PROBLEMS FOR WRITING AND DISCUSSION

1. How have the discoveries of science changed "many matters of the spirit"? Name specific issues, formerly economic or political merely, that technological advances have compelled men to confront as moral issues.
2. Have the conditions Oppenheimer refers to in his second paragraph changed substantially? Should these conditions persist into the maturity of your generation, how would you undertake to improve the heritage you leave your children?
3. How do the material changes Oppenheimer enumerates support Hoffer's expectation of a "millenium" for the "eternal workingman" (p. 175)?
4. Do science and democracy flourish together? How do you explain America's frantic competition with the Soviet Union for supremacy—or simply equality—in technological achievement? What in the nature of scientific study (noted by Oppenheimer himself) enables it to survive in an ideological climate hostile to the arts and to political change?
5. Does Oppenheimer believe the "terror of modern weapons" should dictate political decisions? What objectives other than mere survival does he hold important? What sentence in the quotation from Jefferson best expresses the choice between survival and freedom that Oppenheimer himself approves?
6. Why does Oppenheimer caution that "the method of science cannot be directly adapted to the solution of problems in politics and in man's spiritual life"?
7. Although Oppenheimer is aware of what science can and cannot do, what is the "subtle relevance" he sees of science to political life?
8. Oppenheimer shares with Henry Ford (p. 143) (as well as Jefferson) the ideal of progress. Which declaration of that ideal do you find more inspiring? Give your reasons.
9. It is probable that Jefferson, in true eighteenth-century style, used the word *science* to mean knowledge or learning, as Conant uses Sir Francis Bacon's phrase "the advancement of *learning*." For all the enthusiasm the phrase has inspired, does it seem to you that the human condition (that is, the total balance of misery and happiness, of hope and disappointment) has been altered by the advancement of learning?
10. "Science is not based on authority." Would Franklin (p. 257) have understood this assertion? What, according to Oppenheimer, happens when science is used to "erect a new dogmatism"? Conant, in his proposals, promised that he would want "to illustrate the interconnection between science and society about which so much has been said in recent years by

our Marxist friends." What, presumably, might Conant (p. 247) have intended to illustrate?

11. Does Oppenheimer equate openmindedness with skepticism? If every man may not "doubt" the findings of science, is not science "based on authority"? What answers to this question would William L. Miller (p. 224), Benjamin Franklin, and E. B. White (p. 262) be likely to give?

12. "The open mind, the reliance on example and persuasion rather than on authority" are the "disciplines of the spirit" that Oppenheimer says science inculcates. How do you reconcile his assertion with Kennan's charge (p. 233) that Americans, because they fear power, naïvely trust to example and persuasion?

13. Like other writers in this Part and in Part I, Oppenheimer strongly implies that, because technology has facilitated One World, each man who is born is morally responsible for what happens everywhere in that world. Does the magnitude of such a responsibility explain the retreat into self-conscious preciosity Ebel (p. 213) says "seems to be the universal order of society"? Do young Americans particularly, because technology has placed in their hands the means to alleviate "evils," feel as though they had, as Ebel puts it, somehow been "done in" by their world?

A Vapor Moving North-Northwest

DANIEL LANG

Daniel Lang (1915-   ) has written widely on the atomic age, most notably in The New Yorker *and in three books:* Early Tales of the Atomic Age *(1949),* The Man in the Thick Lead Suit *(1954), and* From Hiroshima to the Moon *(1959). His work has been translated into at least a dozen languages, including Hindi, Korean, and Japanese. A graduate of the University of Wisconsin (1935), he has been a war correspondent for* The New Yorker *(during World War II) and has contributed verse and fiction to the same magazine and to* Story. *Typical of his versatility is* A Summer's Duckling *(1963), a story for children.*

A few moments after the underground nuclear blast known as Project Gnome went off, at noon on a Sunday last month [December 1961], in a flat and chilly stretch of desert southeast of Carlsbad, New Mexico, all of us who were watching the event from a mound of bulldozed earth four and a half miles due south of ground zero—some four hundred foreign observers, congressmen, government scientists, local citizens, photographers, and reporters—could tell that something had gone wrong. What gave us this impression was not the broad blanket of dust that the explosive—deep below in a formation of salt rock—had jolted out of the desert. Nor was it the bouncing we took—the result of a violent earth tremor that had been caused by the nuclear charge, which was one-fourth as powerful as the Hiroshima bomb. (In the immediate vicinity of the

From The New Yorker, *January 6, 1962. Reprinted by permission,* © *1962 The New Yorker Magazine, Inc.*

explosion, the desert leaped three feet, and it has yet to descend to its former level.) We had been told to expect these things. Rather, it was the sight of thick and steadily thickening white vapor at the scene of the firing that made us think that plans had miscarried. The vapor was puffing up through an elevator shaft that dropped twelve hundred feet to an eleven-hundred-foot tunnel, at the end of which the explosive, and also much of the project's experimental equipment, had been installed. As we watched the vapor slowly begin to spread, like ground fog, and, rising, vanish into the air, we knew we were witnessing something that we had been practically assured wouldn't happen—venting, or the accidental escape of radio-activity into the atmosphere. "The probability of the experiment venting is so low as to approach the impossible," the Atomic Energy Commission had stated in a comprehensive pamphlet it had published on Project Gnome. Indeed, at a briefing held the previous evening in Carlsbad, where Gnome's headquarters were located, one of the speakers had warned that the shot was just a small one and might well disappoint us as a spectacle. It was the excitement of its underlying idea that made it worthwhile for us to be at the proving ground, we had been told, for Project Gnome marked the opening of the Plowshare Program—a series of nuclear blasts whose purpose, as the name implied, was to turn the atom to peaceful ways. Any number of benefits, we were informed, could flow from these blasts: harbors might be carved out of wasteland in Alaska; oil might be dislodged from shale; abundant sources of water under great mountains might be freed; diamonds might be made out of ordinary carbon.

We were in no danger—the wind was blowing the vapor to the north-northwest of us—but the feeling seemed to take hold that this wasn't necessarily the Prophet Isaiah's day. Before the explosion, a gala mood had prevailed on our barren mound. Local ranchers, their big Stetsons bobbing, had heartily declared that it was a great day for these parts. The operators of nearby potash mines—the world's largest producers of this chemical—had agreed. Their wives, modishly clad, had greeted each other effusively. And Louis

M. Whitlock, the manager of the Carlsbad Chamber of Commerce, had assured me, "This bomb is for the good of mankind, and we're for it," as we awaited the explosion. Representative Ben Franklin Jensen, of Iowa, a Republican member of the House Appropriations Committee, had also caught the proper spirit. "There are certain things you just have to spend money on, and Plowshare is one of them," he told me. The foreign visitors lent a certain glamour to the occasion. There was Professor Francis Perrin, for instance—a small, goateed man with elegant manners who is the High Commissioner of France's Commissariat à l'Energie Atomique. The science attaché of the Japanese Embassy was there, too—a young chemist named Dr. Seiichi Ishizaka. Chatting with him shortly before the venting, I had gathered that his government was of two minds about the wisdom of the day's explosion. "Japan is curious," he had told me, smiling politely. The bustle of the many journalists on the scene had added to the festive air. The local people had been fascinated by their activities, clustering around each time Dr. Edward Teller, the widely celebrated father of the H-bomb, who is also the father of Plowshare, posed for television crews. On the high-school platform in Carlsbad during the previous evening's briefing, he had, in response to a reporter's question, agreed that the Plowshare Program was "too little and too late," and had gone on to say, "Plowshare had to wait for permission from the Kremlin, which it is giving in a slightly ungracious manner."

Now, as the insidious gases continued to escape from the shaft, the gala mood faded. An A.E.C. official, speaking over a public-address system from a crudely constructed lectern, announced that all drivers should turn their cars around to facilitate a speedy retreat from the test area. An evacuation, he said, might be in order. A short while later—about half an hour after the detonation—the same official, a calm, affable man by the name of Richard G. Elliott, announced that, according to word from a control point a hundred yards forward, the venting had created a radioactive cloud, low and invisible, which was moving in the general direction of Carlsbad, twenty-three miles away to the northwest. The invisible cloud, which was being tracked by an Air Force helicopter equipped with radiation counters, was expected to miss the town, but it would pass over a section of the highway on which we had driven from Carlsbad. The state police had consequently been instructed to throw up a roadblock there. Until further notice, the only way to reach Carlsbad would be to head southeast and follow a detour of a hundred and fifty miles. Some spectators left at once to take this round-about route, figuring that they might as well get the trip over and done with, rather than face an indefinite delay. Some other spectators also departed hurriedly; they suspected the A.E.C. of being excessively cautious, and hoped to use the direct highway to Carlsbad before the police could organize their blockade. As things turned out, a few of these motorists did elude the police, only to be intercepted eventually in Carlsbad itself. Seven cars were found to be contaminated; the A.E.C. paid to have them washed down. Two of the passengers, according to the A.E.C., showed slight, easily removable, traces of radioactivity, one on his hand and the other on his clothing and hair. As for the cloud, the helicopter that had started tracking it had been forced to return to base when the craft's instruments showed that it was being contaminated. Another machine took its place, and the pilot of this kept the cloud under surveillance until darkness forced him to give up his mission; the cloud was then five miles north of a small town called Artesia, about sixty miles north-northwest of the test site; it had hovered briefly over the eastern edge of the town, and continued in its north-northwesterly path. At the time he took his leave of the cloud, the pilot reported, its radiation was diminishing steadily— a process attributable to nature, rather than to Gnome's artificers.

Fortunately, the countryside over which this gaseous debris was being wafted was only sparsely populated. In fact, this was one of the reasons the explosive had been set off in this particular area. In spite of the reassurances about venting in the pamphlet, the A.E.C. and its chief contractor for Plowshare—the University of California's Lawrence Radiation Laboratory, in Livermore, California—had had this eventuality very much in mind when they planned Gnome.

Many precautions had been taken. The tunnel was packed with bags of salt and blocks of concrete, designed to arrest the spread of radioactivity. Wind patterns had been analyzed by the United States Weather Bureau during the entire week before the shot. The day's detonation had, in fact, been delayed four hours until the winds were considered to be blowing in a safe direction. Ranchers for five miles around had been evacuated, tactfully, by being asked to join the Gnome spectators; their cattle, less privileged, had simply been driven off to roam different pastures for the day—or for however long it might take the United States Public Health Service to certify the cleanliness of their familiar acres. The Federal Aviation Agency had been asked to order planes in the area to maintain a certain altitude until further notice. The dryness of the salt formation notwithstanding, the United States Geological Survey had made ground-water surveys of the surrounding area for six months before the shot and would continue to do so for at least a year afterward, in order to keep tabs on any underground movement of radioactive material. Seismic effects had also been anticipated. A special bill had been put through Congress to assure the potash industry of suitable indemnification in the event of damage. On the day of the detonation, no potash miners were on hand to chip at the rose-colored walls of their rough corridors. Nor were tourists permitted to explore the Carlsbad Caverns, thirty-four miles to the east of the detonation site. Acting on behalf of Project Gnome, the Coast and Geodetic Survey had placed a seismograph inside the Caverns. A member of the Caverns' staff—a naturalist from the National Park Service—was on hand to measure seismic effects in his own way; he watched to see if the blast would ripple one of the still, subterranean ponds that had been created over millennia, partly by drops of water from the cave's stalactites. (It didn't.) In retrospect, perhaps the most significant of all the precautions taken was the relatively last-minute reduction of the yield of the explosive from ten kilotons, as originally planned, to five kilotons. "Whoever made *that* decision, I'd like to shake his hand," an A.E.C. official told me the day after the shot.

Those of us who, like me, were waiting for the roadblock to be lifted, passed the time as best we could. We discussed our reactions to the blast for a while, but, oddly, this soon began to pall. Some of us wandered over to a chuck wagon that the A.E.C. had thoughtfully laid on, and bought ourselves coffee and sandwiches. Now and then, we heard new announcements, of varying interest, on the public-address system. One dealt with the far-flung network of seismic recording stations that had been organized by the Department of Defense. A colonel mounted the lectern to tell us that the network appeared to have functioned well. (He didn't know then that Gnome's seismic signal had been recorded in Scandinavia and Japan.) The firing, the colonel added, had taken place "at exactly one four-thousandth of a second after noon." Returning to the lectern, Elliott told us that, according to the instruments, the radiation at the bottom of the shaft now came to a million roentgens an hour, while on the ground at the top of the shaft the count was ten thousand roentgens an hour—twelve and a half times the lethal exposure for a healthy man.

After a while, some of us went and sat in our cars to read or doze or just get out of the cold. Those who didn't could stare at the shaft, from which vapor was still issuing, or, if they preferred, scan the desert, stubbled with tumbleweed and greasewood and cactus. Only the distant sight of a potash refinery relieved the terrain. Bluish-white smoke was pouring from its tall chimney, its furnace having been left unbanked on this day of days. The refinery lay due northwest, near the Carlsbad road, so I knew that the radioactive gases were bound to mingle with the vapors of the tall chimney. Like my fellow-spectators, though, I had no idea when that would come to pass.

The technical objectives of the day's blast, which were almost entirely in the hands of Livermore scientists, were well planned, it had been impressed on me in the course of the briefings before the shot. The central purpose was to see what happened when an atomic explosive was set off in a salt formation—what is called phenomenology. The Livermore people hadn't previously had a chance for such a test, their underground efforts thus far having been limited to military shots in the volcanic tuff of the Nevada test site—a substance that doesn't retain heat nearly as well as salt does. And heat was the key to much of what the researchers were seeking to learn. Gnome would enable them to carry out a heat-extraction experiment, for example—the general idea being to investigate the possibility of tapping for productive uses the inferno of superheated steam and other forms of energy that would result from the detonation. This energy, it was hoped, would be contained in a cavity in the salt that the explosive, low though its yield was, would create in about a tenth of a second. The cavity, if it didn't collapse, would be eggshaped and glowing, and it would be about a hundred and ten feet in diameter; six thousand tons of molten salt were expected to run down its sides and compose a pool thirty-five feet deep. The cavity would also be "mined," by remote control, for radioactive isotopes—unstable atoms that are produced by a nuclear explosion, a fair percentage of which are valuable in scientific research, medical treatment, and industrial processes. (One of them, strontium 90, which is greatly feared in fallout, may someday be used in long-lived batteries to power unmanned weather stations in godforsaken regions, a Livermore expert told me.)

For pure researchers, it was thought, Gnome's most interesting data might be gained from the large numbers of neutrons—uncharged particles that are part of the atomic nucleus—that would be produced by the blast. In the instant of the explosion, I had been told, Gnome would release as many neutrons as a laboratory apparatus could release in several thousand years. So plentiful would they be, in fact, that only one out of ten million could be studied. Even so, much new light might be shed on such matters as the different velocities of neutrons and the interaction of these particles, which are usually emitted in bursts that last less than a hundred-millionth of a second, an interval of time that is known in scientific shoptalk as "a shake."

But these technical objectives of Project Gnome were only a part of the Plowshare Program, and the Plowshare Program was something more than a scientific enterprise—a fact that had become apparent in the days immediately preceding the desert shot, when Carlsbad had been rife with briefings, interviews, and informative handouts. The case for Plowshare, in the opinion of some of the foreign observers and other people I talked with, seemed to rest on a variety of grounds. I learned, for example, that the proposed series of blasts had been approved by the A.E.C. four years before, which raised the question of why they were being started at this particular time. Plowshare officials readily acknowledged that the complete answer certainly included the state of international affairs. Was Plowshare, then, a solid program or a passing, virtuous response to the Russian resumption of atmospheric testing? Perhaps Plowshare's name was partly to blame for this questioning attitude. "It sounds a little too much like magic," a foreign scientist remarked. "So many swords are being made just now."

In any event, a day or two before the shot, I discussed Plowshare in Carlsbad with two of its overseers, both of whom were strongly in favor of the program, as one would expect, but in a fairly thoughtful, unmagical way. One of them was John S. Kelly, a bespectacled, mild-mannered man of thirty-nine who is the director of the A.E.C.'s Division of Peaceful Nuclear Explosives. He saw Plowshare's explosives as scientific and engineering tools. It excited him, he said, to contemplate the excavation jobs that might be performed in the future, like blasting lakes out of the wilderness and breaking up ore deposits that could be leached out. Plowshare represented a continuation of the whole history of explosives, Kelly said. Certainly explosives could be harmful, he conceded, but on the other hand gunpowder had done away with the feudal system and TNT had made possible the mining of fossil fuels.

"But can we afford to guess wrong with nuclear explosives?" I asked. "Don't they represent an ultimate kind of energy?"

"Why not use them for our ultimate good?" Kelly replied.

For an undertaking concerned with the peaceful uses of the atom, I remarked, Plowshare appeared to have its ambiguities. The fissionable material and the equipment for the Gnome explosive, I mentioned, had been taken from our armaments stockpile; the explosive was being concealed from the public gaze, the same as a weapon is; men in uniform had come to Carlsbad for the shot, and were participating actively in its preparation; and among those prominently involved were people from Livermore, which was noted primarily as a center of weapons design.

Kelly was quick to grant that the line between the peaceful and the military sides of the atom was fuzzy. It would be nice, he said, if the two functions could be neatly demarcated, for in that case the Plowshare Program, living up to its name more fully, could have postponed the blasts until war was an obsolete institution. But that wasn't the way things were, in Kelly's view. "We may have to take our peaceful uses when we can," he said.

The other official I talked with was Dr. Gary H. Higgins, the director of the Plowshare Division of the Lawrence Radiation Laboratory. Higgins is a soft-spoken chemist of thirty-four, whose desk in his Carlsbad office was adorned, when I saw it, with a small ceramic gnome he had bought in a department store. Like Kelly, he believes that nuclear explosives have a great peacetime future. "Within five to fifteen years, they'll be basic to our industrial economy," he told me. "They'll help us get at raw materials we need for our growing population. It may take us time to make use of them. After all, forest husbandry developed only when the nation was practically deforested." He was delighted that the United States was moving ahead with Plowshare, but not, he told me, because it relieved him of his weapons duties at Livermore. The two kinds of work, he felt, were not pure opposites; there was a difference between weapons and war, he said, just as there was between a police force and murder. But whether an idea like Plowshare or an arms race was to dominate our lives in the years ahead was another matter. It depended, Higgins thought, on whether mankind could eventually achieve an immense self-consciousness. "It would not cater to the oversimplified images that religion and ethics tend to give us," Higgins said. "It would enable us to recognize our weaknesses. We'd know our motives for acting the way we do, and what else is it that counts but intent, whether shots are called Plowshare or something else?"

It was almost four hours after the detonation when I left the bulldozed mound in the desert. The roadblock hadn't yet been lifted, but to a number of us that didn't matter. We were chafing to get away, although not for any sensible reason I heard expressed. Perhaps the others felt, as I did, a sense of rebellion and indignation at being trapped by a mysterious, invisible antagonist. In the distance, the refinery's tall chimney continued to surrender its thick plume of smoke, giving no sign, of course, whether there had yet been any mingling with the radioactive cloud. Absurdly, I felt like going to the refinery to find out. Around us, shadows were beginning to fall on the desert, making it seem more limitless than ever, and underscoring our marooned condition.

At any rate, when a rancher who was among the spectators mentioned to some of us that certain back roads might bring one out on the Carlsbad highway three or four miles beyond the police blockade, I was off at once, in a car with two other men—Ken Fujisaki, a young correspondent for a Tokyo newspaper, the *Sankei Shimbun*, and David Perlman, a reporter for the San Francisco *Chronicle*. The rancher, who himself was in no hurry to leave, had said he hadn't used those particular back roads in fifteen years, but at the time this remark had struck us as irrelevant. Our immediate goals were a windmill and a gas well—two landmarks that, the rancher had said, might soon guide us on our way to Carlsbad.

"How would you like to spend two weeks in a fallout shelter?" Perlman, who was driving, asked me as he impatiently started the car.

After a ten-minute drive over a bumpy, rutted road, we were at the gas well. We were also at a dead end. As we were looking at each other in puzzlement, we heard the honk of a car horn behind us, and discovered that we had been leaders of men. Nine other cars had followed us to the dead end; we had been too intent on our flight from safety to notice them. One of the vehicles was a small orange government truck, and another was a sports car—a dirty, white Triumph whose driver wore goggles. Some of us got out of our cars, conferred ignorantly, and decided to go back and follow a dirt road that had intersected the one we were on. This road also came to a dead end. Backtracking, we tried another, and then another. The fourth ran parallel to a ranch fence, on the other side of which were cattle and horses. Beyond the field they were in we could see the Carlsbad highway, only a couple of miles off. The fence seemed to run on endlessly, leading nowhere. Our caravan halted, and a few of us climbed a stile to seek advice at the ranch. We found a young Mexican hand, who obligingly corralled the animals, and opened a gate into a muddy, reddish road that crossed the field. In no time we were on the highway to Carlsbad. To get there, we had gone east, north, west, and northeast. Now we passed the potash refinery, its tall stack still smoking. I looked at it as long as I could. No police intercepted us. When we reached the Project Gnome office in Carlsbad, we learned that the roadblock had been called off fifteen minutes after our departure. Perlman asked that he be gone over with a radiation counter. He proved to be fine, which meant the rest of us were.

When I arrived at my motel, the manager phoned me. He was a transplanted Englishman with whom I had made friends. Since I was leaving the next day, I thought perhaps he was calling to say goodbye, but it was Project Gnome that was on his mind.

"I'm sick in bed, you see, so *I'm* quite all right, but it's the staff—" he began. A guest, he said, had told the cashier in the restaurant not to touch the money of anyone who had been to the test. The cashier had become hysterical. Then a policeman had come and collected two other members of the staff to have them "counted" at the Gnome office; the two had been spectators at the shot and had been among those who eluded the roadblock.

"There's no need for any concern, is there?" the manager asked me uneasily. "I mean, those men out there know what they're doing, don't they?"

I could hear him breathing at the other end of the phone, waiting for my answer.

"Of course they do," I said. "Of course everything's all right."

PROBLEMS FOR WRITING AND DISCUSSION

1. What effect does Lang gain by describing the gala setting for the underground nuclear explosion?
2. Why does Lang quote the remarks of Representative Jensen, Dr. Ishizaka, and Dr. Teller?
3. Discuss the implications of the spectators' reactions to the news that a radioactive cloud had escaped.
4. What ironical effect does Lang achieve in outlining the precautions taken by the A.E.C. and Plowshare to see that the experiment was a safe one?
5. Why does Lang quote the colonel who says the explosion has taken place "at exactly one four-thousandth of a second after noon"?
6. What were the scientists hoping to learn from this experiment? Why does Lang say that the Plowshare Program "was something more than a scientific enterprise"?
7. Discuss the significance of the exchange between Lang and John S. Kelly, or of that between Lang and Dr. Gary H. Higgins.
8. After the experience, one reporter asked Lang, "How would you like to spend two weeks in a fallout shelter?" After reading Lang's essay, how would you?
9. Explain the significance of Lang's encounter with the motel manager.
10. What would you say is Lang's dominant purpose in this "report"?
11. E. B. White (p. 262) sees that science holds out hope and doom for mankind simultaneously. Does Lang's essay add weight to White's idea? Explain.
12. Conant (p. 247) says that laymen need some knowledge of the "Tactics and Strategy of Science" before they can understand science properly. Daniel Lang is a science reporter, not a scientist. Do you think he understands science, or has he "failed to grasp the essentials" of Project Gnome?

Science and Social Change

BRUCE STEWART

> Bruce Stewart (1919-   ), a native of Texas, has taught at Missouri Valley College and at the University of Kansas and is presently a member of the Department of Natural Science of Michigan State University. He has published many essays and a textbook on the social relations of science.

"Why is there so much social change today and so little in ancient times? The most probable answer, the result of quite extensive study, is mechanical invention and scientific discovery."—WILLIAM F. OGBURN.

People today look upon science with ever deepening ambivalence. On the one hand it promises a material paradise, and on the other it threatens a nuclear inferno beyond Dante's wildest dreams. The scientists themselves have not been able to escape from this dilemma, even though some have struggled heroically to do so. In one breath they will agree that science is transforming our society and with the next they will attack the idea of technologically determined change as a form of communism. The fears and myths surrounding the relationship of science and social change have long obstructed a straightforward approach to the problem. C. P. Snow has recently tried to exorcise this specter:

> One has to be ludicrously frightened of the shadow of Marx not to see earthy roots for the major transformations in scientific history. I am sometimes irritated that the West is so nervous of Marxist thought that we are unconsciously obfuscating ourselves.

The scientists are, of course, not averse to taking credit for the great blessings of science and its practical utilization in technology,

From Bulletin of the Atomic Scientists, September 1961. Reprinted by permission of the publisher.

but the discredit for the ever-menacing demons they may have unleashed is very bothersome. Many have tried to divest themselves of responsibility, and the most common rationale for this has been, "We discover, you employ." According to this view, the scientist only pursues truth, discovering new concepts, new forces, and new instruments. Other parts of society decide whether these shall be used for good or for ill. There is both truth and fiction in this hypothetical separation of powers. A great lack of knowledge and sophistication is required to blame the scientists for the misuse of technical discoveries, and the same is no less true of a belief that scientists can intervene and guarantee a quick and sane solution to these problems.

On the other hand, sociologists such as R. K. Merton have shown the tremendous impact which culture has upon science and its practitioners. The interests of the culture indeed determine what kind of truths the scientist will pursue, and the naive vision of scientists working in their ivory towers, uncontaminated by social controversy around them, has been shattered. Merton described the situation in *Social Theory and Social Structure*.

> The intensified division of labor has become a splendid device for escaping social responsibilities. As professions subdivide, each group of specialists finds it increasingly possible to pass the buck for the social consequences of their work on the assumption, it would seem, that in this complex transfer of responsibility there will be no hindmost for the devil to take. When appalled by the resulting social dislocations, each specialist, secure in the knowledge that he has performed his task to the best of his ability, can readily disclaim responsibility for them. And of course, no one group of specialists, the engineer any more than the others, alone initiates the consequences.

It is quite unrealistic to suppose that the scientists can avoid affecting public issues. Anything they say affects public issues. Anything they do *not* say affects these issues, for action is taken in default of their contribution. The effort to strip off their prestige as scientists when speaking about these matters, while commendable, is not likely to be entirely successful, nor should it be, for scientists often know more about some aspects of certain subjects than do laymen.

However, it is not the scientist's chief responsibility to give opinions on subjects where he has no special knowledge. Considered rationally, *the main function of the scientist would be to bring to public problems those mental qualities and attitudes which have made him successful in science:* critical analysis of old concepts, constant search for new and superior theories, insistence that all these be based on evidence rather than generalized idealism and that they be accepted on the basis of predictive and analytic success, not on the strength of their tradition or the power of their special interests. Perhaps the scientist cannot originate social concepts but he can encourage the general expression of new ones and support the testing of those which show promise. This role is one which the scientists, social as well as natural, have avoided and which they have failed to assume.

How does one prove that such a failure has indeed occurred? First by the absence of widespread criticism of traditional ideas and the general noncirculation of radically different ones. This is the null hypothesis of the statistician. Simultaneously, there is an almost unchallenged currency of traditional beliefs, later to be illustrated. This unbalanced picture can scarcely be explained on any other grounds. Few surveys are available on the subject, but a 1937 survey by A. Kornhauser indicated that the engineers were more conservative than the big industrialists and only a little less so than the small businessmen. Probably the reactions of scientists are not greatly different from those of the general population, which has been shown to have a remarkable schizophrenia about its general principles and its specific practices. For example, an overwhelming majority favors freedom of speech, but most people are opposed to free expression for "radical groups." The more specific and operational the question of free expression of ideas that tend to threaten the status quo, the greater the resistance.

Why have scientists failed to perform the critical function of encouragement and rational support of new ideas? Probably the most important reason is that they shrink from the consequences. It is all very inspiring to speak of free inquiry, fearless search for truth, challenging old concepts and proposing new ones, but when this process threatens powerful interests and long cherished beliefs, then the scientific ideal shrivels under the hot glare of danger, passion, and antipathy. Scientists can suffer this prospect of alienation little better than can others. The attempt often follows to rationalize science into a position of harmony with the conservative faith. George Sarton, whose perspective in science was very broad, took pains to demolish this harmony and to assert the revolutionary effect of science:

> The resistance to scientific novelties was due to an intuitive, if unconscious, appreciation of their revolutionary nature. The slightest and most innocent scientific innovation is but a wedge which is bound to penetrate deeper and deeper, and the advance of which will soon be impossible to resist. Conservative people are undoubtedly right in their distrust and hatred of science, for the scientific spirit is the very spirit of innovation and adventure into the unknown. And such is its aggressive strength that its revolutionary activity can neither be restrained nor restricted within its own field.

The scientists are aware, at least intuitively, of de Santillana's dictum: "Deviations from what is considered the essential orthodoxy have never, of course, escaped punishment since the beginning of history." Although we are thousands of years from the beginning of history, the situation has not changed very much; punishments are still things to be avoided, and material rewards are perhaps even more to be sought. Threats by scientists to depart from orthodoxy are met with much agitated buzzing, so that the results are often very amusing. For example, in 1943 J. B. Conant wrote "Wanted: American Radicals" for *Atlantic Monthly,* an article which included an opinion by the author that all private property should revert to the state once every generation. One observer described the consequences as follows: "Conant was promptly set upon and badly stung by a majority of the various fellows, overseers, trustees, faculty members, and vintage graduates who uphold the

Harvard tradition." Conant spoke no more about the need for American radicals and for property confiscation.

On the ubiquitous subject of war and militarism, H. Brown and J. Real have recently commented in *Community of Fear* about the growing conservatism and special interests of many scientists:

> Tens of thousands of scientists and technicians have devoted all of their professional lives to the invention and construction of weapons. A majority of those who went to work *after* World War II are convinced that weaponry is a way of life. . . . Although these men are not generally openly political, they are in every sense the paramilitary-civilian soldiers. They have spent most of their adult lives in the direct or secondary employment of one or another of the services, and their sympathy for and concurrence with their uniformed colleagues are often marked and open. Should a showdown between the military and civilian sectors occur, this group could be relied upon to staunchly back the handlers of the weapons they have so devotedly evolved.

If this picture is accurate, many scientists threaten to become the modern merchants of death who were the cause of so much concern 30 years ago. In a similar way, the special interests of industry and government can exert a regimenting effect upon the scientists in their employ, and there may be the same reluctance to think or say anything which can be construed as biting the hand that feeds them. This feeling contributes to the support of feudalism, monarchy, or communism, but is scarcely consistent with scientific objectivity.

More money and fame for scientists is not necessarily an unmixed blessing, for there is inevitably some sense of *quid pro quo*, no matter how diffused it may be, and a scientist can betray his calling to the extent that he gives hostages to fortune. Subsidies may easily become golden threads which tie down the exploring Gulliver to set ideas, set values, or set subjects of inquiry. As Ruskin observed, "Some slaves are bought with money and others with praise. It matters not what the purchase money is. . . . The fact of slavery is in being driven to your work without thought at another's bidding." This is far from saying that discoveries which are sought by society cannot be good discoveries, but it would be more accurate to conclude that new concepts which are resisted or rejected by society are not necessarily bad concepts. The unquestioned tendency in scientific history to so regard many of them is invalid as well as dangerous. No one should know this better than today's scientists, yet far from being a new group of independent thinkers, the scientists show many signs of deepening the schizophrenia caused by the tug of war between scientific philosophy on the one hand and special interest and super-specialization on the other.

There are, of course, cases where modern scientists have publicly supported unorthodox social views, and perhaps among the most notable of these was Einstein's support of socialism. This has been either ignored or treated as an instance where a scientist was expressing faulty conclusions outside his specialty. The occurrence is very enlightening on several counts. First it illustrates what might be called the double standard of concept testing. For unorthodox beliefs such as socialism the degree of critical skepticism is high and there is a rigorous demand for supporting data. For the culturally accepted belief, in this case capitalism, criticism is not only unnecessary but unwelcome. Postulates are readily accepted without evidence. The occurrence also illustrates the difficulties which are to be experienced by involvement in social controversy. However, *the reluctant scientist has one legitimate misgiving about his colleagues becoming the partisans of some organized doctrine* (other than the accepted ones, of course). Alliance with any doctrine is unscientific and when it occurs, properly neutralizes much of the scientist's message. This leads to a still more important conclusion.

Poincaré observed that "In science it is necessary to be independent—utterly independent." But it is very difficult to be independent where there is great pressure to conform to dogmas such as capitalism, socialism, communism, democracy, and Americanism. These doctrines are not objectively derived concepts founded in causal dynamics but rather a compound of the purely descriptive, the idealistic, the mythological, and the opportunistic. They may be well adapted for developing true believers and conducting propaganda campaigns, but they are poor instruments for analyzing, predicting, and ultimately controlling social change. There are several preconditions for the growth of scientific objectivity and successful control. We must sit down before many unpleasant facts which we have heretofore swept under the rug and learn how concepts may best be changed. In addition, social theory must be dusted free of its academic cobwebs, and as L. Hogben demanded, "get to grips with live contemporary issues if it ever hopes to enjoy the prestige of the natural sciences." Finally, we must distinguish sharply between our personal norms and our objective estimate of probable developments, for this is the first essential of any science.

Modern social scientists have been captivated by the desire to imitate experimental physics, whereas the more important parallel with early astronomy has been slighted. The mass movements of society, which increasingly assume a broad pattern, are largely beyond experimental control, like the movements of celestial bodies, and yet macroscopic laws can be detected. Moreover it is possible to test these laws in an empirical manner—by their ability to explain observed phenomena which have hitherto seemed unconnected or not satisfactorily accounted for, and by their ability to predict future events, new and unsuspected relationships, and to suggest productive lines of inquiry. If man is ever able to control the movements of celestial objects, it can only be as a result of comprehending their laws of motion. Likewise if man is ever able to control the large scale changes in his society, this too can only become possible after a thorough understanding of these laws. Poincaré sardonically remarked that we cannot understand an elephant by restricting ourselves to thin slices of him seen under a microscope. This enormous organism called society can only be understood by a fearless study from all points of vantage, not the least important of which is macroscopic analysis designed to detect dependable regularities. We have shrunk from the task of applying and systematically following up the consequences of radical new concepts.

The revolutionary impact of science is compelling us to conform to new circumstances of which we may have little appreciation. If we were rational creatures we would not wait to be dragged blindly into the future but would try to anticipate these tremendous changes by means of some new concepts. This recognition does not, of course, exclude or minimize other dynamic processes besides science in man and in the environment, some of which have in fact given rise to science. Examples of these radical changes which will require new solutions are the maladjustments of automation, and the technology which triggered and is now impelling the rise of undeveloped countries; however it is more instructive to concentrate upon one which now occupies much of our time and thought: the changing role of war. Although man's traditional attitudes toward war and the methods and circumstances under which it is employed have been deeply implanted by the centuries, they are now being revolutionized by science. Thus far we have shown little capacity to anticipate the social consequences of these scientific changes and to bring our thinking into harmony with them.

The tragicomic efforts of the military, the superpatriots, and the civil defense advocates to preserve our old beliefs about preparedness and how to win wars may contribute to our amusement, to our expenditures, and perhaps even to the next war, but they can make no difference in the final result, though they may modify our path to that end. The campaign to move the population underground illustrates this power of conservative thinking. Yet if satellite bombs which will sear five states are soon to appear, we might dig deeper holes to live in but we would not be likely to survive on a diet of rocks. We are not even close to any discovery which would free us from our dependence upon the land, which can be thoroughly poisoned or burned. New pathways must be broken, which in dangerous territory always involves frightening risk. In the event of war, says C. P. Snow, "We have a certainty of disaster. Between a risk and a certainty a sane man does not hesitate."

The dilemma of Nobel has been magnified as manyfold as the power of the atom exceeds the power of dynamite. The costs of failure to bring our social thinking into harmony with the upheavals being caused by science are becoming more suicidal. Nevertheless there are powerful influences which stand in the way of any new exploration, as George Sarton so acutely described:

> Even now there are too many people, good citizens, pillars of society, who are afraid of science because they are afraid of truth; they will not face the facts of life. In order to cure a disease we must first understand it; the same is true of social diseases. In order to heal them we must first know them as well as possible. The Renaissance was an age of superstition, but so is our own, under the surface; science has made gigantic progress in certain fields, but in others, *e.g.* politics, national and international, we are still fooling ourselves.

Indeed we are, and furthermore we will not tolerate anyone pointing out instances of this self-deceit. These troublemakers are no longer burned, they are simply buried alive so deeply by the mass media they cannot be heard, and few people take any notice of them.

The work of Fromm and Russell illustrates an effort to explore new concepts about war instead of being forcibly abducted into the future, which is now the case whether one agrees with them or not. The very mention of unilateral nuclear disarmament arouses strong negative feelings, but this reaction only illustrates the point at issue. Unilateral nuclear disarmament is by no means either logically indefensible or communistic, but the mass media are not free to treat this proposal as any more than a crackpot idea, for it promises only to diminish their profit and increase their troubles. Here again, the absence of any general criticism of established beliefs and dissemination of outrageous proposals, even when both are made available, proves the null hypothesis with regard to press freedom. It also provides a good example of what has already been called the double standard of concept testing. Finally, it cannot be overemphasized that any scientific analysis of nuclear disarmament and similar subjects of controversy must not allow an objective prognosis of probable developments to be influenced by what appears to be the most rational procedure.

The conclusion that science will *ultimately* proscribe war, however probable, gives no assurance about the *next* war. In fact a nuclear war would be a most compelling stimulus for the survivors to scrap old beliefs and to accept new ones which could effectively prevent its recurrence. H. G. Wells anticipated many modern developments of this kind in a most remarkable book written, be it noted, in 1913. He predicted that atomic energy would be released in 1933. He foresaw the public battles over its control and utilization; he commented on the futile attempt to "put this explosive new wine into old bottles," and he despaired about "this profound, this fantastic divorce between the scientific and intellectual movement on the one hand, and the world of the lawyer-politician on the other." He forecast that "By the spring of 1959 from nearly 200 centers . . . roared the unquenchable crimson conflagrations of the atomic bombs. . . ." Wells was just six years too early in his first prediction—the release of atomic energy. Will he be just six years too early in the last? It should be a matter of considerable interest to future historians to observe whether atomic war had to become inescapable before we were willing to inject the spirit of science into the world of the lawyer-politician-soldier.

The common picture of the scientist as a genius in his field and an illiterate outside it is a menace to the extent that it is true and to the extent that it blocks a more constructive attitude. The chief social function of scientists is to emphasize the applicability of scientific methods and attitudes to national and world problems, particularly in the criticism of old concepts and in the proposal and testing of new ones. Opposition to this process is to be expected, but its productive benefits must be communicated in every possible way. Natural scientists may lack some revelant knowledge but the essentials are not difficult to gain. Moreover, it is surprising how little attention has been given to the interaction of science and society and to the exploration of new ideas and procedures. The main task is not to become steeped in more specialized social lore but to seek out and try new concepts. In this territory the scientist is no more a helpless neophyte than are the keepers of the established wisdom. The philosophy of his discipline (if he is indeed true to it) provides the most reliable means yet found to advance into the future—into that exciting realm which nobody knows.

PROBLEMS FOR WRITING AND DISCUSSION

1. Why, according to Stewart, are scientists especially conservative? Is their conservatism comparable to the "conservative wisdom" among economists to which Galbraith (p. 180) refers?

2. Does the passage quoted from Merton's *Social Theory and Social Structure* describe the situation Stewart says it does? What is its relevance to Stewart's argument?

3. Does Stewart justify his belief that "more money and fame for scientists is not necessarily an unmixed blessing"?

4. What are the pressures in America that force the scientist to conform to dogmas? Does Stewart's example of J. B. Conant convince you that scientists cringe under pressure? Does the argument that follows the example convince you? Why or why not?

5. Does Stewart himself use a "double standard of concept testing" when he talks about Einstein's courageous stand on an unpopular issue and then about "socialism" as one of several compounds of the "idealistic, the mythological, and the opportunistic"? Explain.

6. Is the scientific approach to projects that Conant (p. 247) describes comparable with the approach "to public problems" Stewart advocates for the scientist? Would Oppenheimer (p. 264) agree that the "mental qualities and attitudes which have made him successful in science" assure the success of the scientist in understanding public—that is, political—problems?

7. The scientist in public issues, according to Stewart, should search for "theories . . . based on evidence rather than generalized idealism." Thurman Arnold (p. 162) insists that we "cannot be practical about social problems if we are under the illusion that we can solve them without complying with the taboos and customs of the tribe." Which suggestion indicates greater wisdom? Why?

8. How does one determine the "predictive" success of social theories? How can one "test" those "which show promise"? Keep in mind what Oppenheimer says about the number of times a political decision can be made.

9. Stewart deplores the "absence of widespread criticism of traditional ideas and the general noncirculation of radically different ones." What "traditional ideas" does he criticize and what "radically different ones" does he circulate?

10. Is Stewart's analogy between astronomy and social science a valid one? With what "laws" of societies' motions are you familiar? How does Stewart suggest we grasp conceptually the "enormous organism called society"?

11. The remark of C. P. Snow is relevant to a contemporary public issue and indicates a political decision. To what issue, judging from the context in which it appears, would you say Snow's remark refers and what choice, by implication, has Snow made? Do you agree with Stewart that the lawyer-politician-soldier is responsible for this public crisis and that only the scientific spirit can rescue us?

How Human Is Man?

LOREN EISELEY

Loren Eiseley (1907-) was born in Lincoln, Nebraska, attended the University of Nebraska, and received his doctorate from the University of Pennsylvania. He has taught at the University of Kansas and Oberlin College and was Chairman of the Department of Anthropology at the University of Pennsylvania before becoming Provost of the university in 1959. He has since retired as Provost to become University Professor in the History of Science. His collection of essays in The Immense Journey *(1957) led one critic to remark: "No other writer since Hudson, to my knowledge, evokes with such authority and persuasion man in Nature, and the awesome Nature of man."* Darwin's Century *(1958), a study of the concept of evolution as it developed in the nineteenth century, was followed by* The Firmament of Time *(1960) and by* Francis Bacon and the Modern Dilemma *(1963).*

Some time ago there was encountered, in the litter of a vacant lot in a small American town, a fallen sign. This sign was intended to commemorate the names of local heroes who had fallen in the Second World War. But that war was over, and another had come in Korea. Probably the population of that entire town had turned over in the meantime. Tom and Joe and Isaac were events of the past, and the past of the modern world is short. The names of

From The Firmament of Time *by Loren Eiseley. Copyright © 1960 by Loren Eiseley. Reprinted by permission of Atheneum Publishers and Victor Gollancz, Ltd.*

yesterday's heroes lay with yesterday's torn newspaper. They had served their purpose and were now forgotten.

This incident may serve to reveal the nature of what has happened, or seems to be happening, to our culture, to that world which science was to beautify and embellish. I do not say that science is responsible except in the sense that men are responsible, but men increasingly are the victims of what they themselves have created. To the student of human culture, the rise of science and its dominating role in our society presents a unique phenomenon.

Nothing like it occurs in antiquity, for in antiquity nature represented the divine. It was an object of worship. It contained mysteries. It was the mother. Today the phrase has disappeared. It is nature we shape, nature, without the softening application of the word mother, which under our control and guidance hurls the missile on its path. There has been no age in history like this one, and men are increasingly brushed aside who speak of the possibility of another road into the future.

Some time ago, in a magazine of considerable circulation, I spoke about the role of love in human society, and about pressing human problems which I felt, rightly or wrongly, would not be solved by the penetration of space. The response amazed me, in some instances, by its virulence. I was denounced for interfering with the colonization of other planets, and for corruption of the young. Most pathetically of all, several people wrote me letters in which they tried to prove, largely for their own satisfaction, that love did not exist, that parents abused and murdered their children and children their parents. They concentrated upon sparse incidents of pathological violence, and averted their eyes from the normal.

It was all too plain that these individuals were seeking rationalizations behind which they might hide from their own responsibilities. They were in the whirlpool, that much was evident. But so are we all. In 1914 the London *Times* editorialized confidently that no civilized nation would bomb open cities from the air. Today there is not a civilized nation on the face of the globe that does not take this aspect of warfare for granted. Technology demands it.

In Kierkegaard's deadly future man strives, or rather ceases to strive, against himself.

But crime, moral deficiencies, inadequate ethical standards, we are prone to accept as part of the life of man. Why, in this respect, should we be regarded as unique? True, we have had Buchenwald and the Arctic slave camps, but the Romans had their circuses. It is just here, however, that the uniqueness enters in. After the passage of three hundred years from Bacon and his followers—three hundred years on the road to the earthly Paradise—there is a rising poison in the air. It crosses frontiers and follows the winds across the planet. It is man-made; no treaty of the powers has yet halted it.

Yet it is only a symbol, a token of that vast maelstrom which has caught up states and stone-age peoples equally with the modern world. It is the technological revolution, and it has brought three things to man which it has been impossible for him to do to himself previously.

First, it has brought a social environment altering so rapidly with technological change that personal adjustments to it are frequently not viable. The individual either becomes anxious and confused or, what is worse, develops a superficial philosophy intended to carry him over the surface of life with the least possible expenditure of himself. Never before in history has it been literally possible to have been born in one age and to die in another. Many of us are now living in an age quite different from one into which we were born. The experience is not confined to a ride in a buggy, followed in later years by a ride in a Cadillac. Of far greater significance are the social patterns and ethical adjustments which have followed fast upon the alterations in living habits introduced by machines.

Second, much of man's attention is directed exteriorly upon the machines which now occupy most of his waking hours. He has less time alone than any man before him. In dictator-controlled countries he is harangued and stirred by propaganda projected upon him by machines to which he is forced to listen. In America he sits quiescent before the flickering screen in the living room while horsemen gallop across an American wilderness long vanished in the past. In the presence of so compelling an instrument, there is little opportunity in the evenings to explore his own thoughts or to participate in family living in the way that man from the early part of the century remembers. For too many men, the exterior world with its mass-produced daydreams has become the conqueror. Where are the eager listeners who used to throng the lecture halls; where are the workingmen's intellectual clubs? This world has vanished into the whirlpool.

Third, this outward projection of attention, along with the rise of a science whose powers and creations seem awe-inspiringly remote, as if above both man and nature, has come dangerously close to bringing into existence a type of man who is not human. He no longer thinks in the old terms; he has ceased to have a conscience. He is an instrument of power. Because his mind is directed outward upon this power torn from nature, he does not realize that the moment such power is brought into the human domain it partakes of human freedom. It is no longer safely *within* nature; it has become violent, sharing in human ambivalence and moral uncertainty.

At the same time that this has occurred, the scientific worker has frequently denied personal responsibility for the way his discoveries are used. The scientist points to the evils of the statesmen's use of power. The statesmen shrug and remind the scientist that they are encumbered with monstrous forces that science has unleashed upon a totally unprepared public. But there are few men on either side of the Iron Curtain able to believe themselves in any sense personally responsible for this situation. Individual conscience lies too close to home, and is archaic. It is better, we subconsciously tell ourselves, to speak of inevitable forces beyond human control. When we reason thus, however, we lend powers to the whirlpool; we bring nearer the future which Kierkegaard saw, not as the *necessary* future, but one just as inevitable as man has made it.

PROBLEMS FOR WRITING AND DISCUSSION

1. Are Eiseley and Stewart (p. 287) writing about the same contemporary dilemma? Would the involvement of scientists in the non-scientific problems of society restore the "individual conscience"?

2. What does Eiseley see as one of the basic differences between antiquity and the present? Does the role science plays in this difference augur well for the future?

3. Eiseley says that personal adjustments are often not "viable" in times of rapid technological changes. Explain.

4. What are the dangers to Americans in a society in which man "has less time alone than any man before him"?

5. Is it true, as Eiseley says, that man today is dangerously close to being "not human"? Do Americans fit this category? Has any other writer you have thus far read suggested, in a different connection, the same idea?

6. A whirlpool has a vortex into which it sucks whatever enters its periphery—unless what enters has sufficient strength to struggle out again. How does Eiseley's metaphor intensify man's present danger?

7. Eiseley, like Stewart, notes that whoever speaks of a "road into the future" other than the one we are on is "brushed aside." In what follows this observation, does Eiseley suggest an alternate route for human society? How does his alternative differ from Stewart's?

8. Eiseley says that once the "power torn from nature" enters "the human domain it partakes of human freedom. It is no longer safely *within* nature. . . ." In the light of this observation, does Franklin's experiment in the eighteenth century (p. 257) retrospectively gain significance?

9. "There is a rising poison in the air"—"a vapor moving north-north-west." Is it wise in the circumstances to encourage science as Oppenheimer (p. 264) suggests? Explain.

Part Three. "...These Truths"

1. LIBERTY AND EQUALITY
2. THE POLITICAL BANDS
3. THE WIDE WORLD

1. Liberty and Equality

The Declaration of Independence

> *Thomas Jefferson (1743-1826) wrote the Declaration of Independence in a second-floor apartment he had taken in a house on the outskirts of Philadelphia to escape "the excessive heats of the city." He worked swiftly and probably took no more than a day to complete a first draft. He edited and rewrote the draft drastically in making a fair copy. Congress, after it received the paper in late June, revised the document further, cutting it by a fourth, making it in a real sense a Declaration that drew its authority from "the harmonizing sentiments of the day," as Jefferson later remarked. The Declaration of Independence that emerged from Congress on July 4, 1776, had become what Jefferson intended it to be—"an expression of the American mind."*

IN CONGRESS, JULY 4, 1776, THE UNANIMOUS DECLARATION OF THE THIRTEEN UNITED STATES OF AMERICA

When in the Course of human events, it becomes necessary for one people to dissolve the political bands which have connected them with another, and to assume among the Powers of the earth, the separate and equal station to which the Laws of Nature and of Nature's God entitle them, a decent respect to the opinions of mankind requires that they should declare the causes which impel them to the separation.

We hold these truths to be self-evident, that all men are created equal, that they are endowed by their Creator with certain unalienable Rights, that among these are Life, Liberty and the pursuit of Happiness. That to secure these rights, Governments are instituted among Men, deriving their just powers from the consent of the governed, That whenever any Form of Government becomes destructive of these ends, it is the Right of the People to alter or to abolish it, and to institute new Government, laying its foundation on such principles and organizing its powers in such form, as to them shall seem most likely to effect their Safety and Happiness. Prudence, indeed, will dictate that Governments long established should not be changed for light and transient causes; and accordingly all experience hath shown, that mankind are more disposed to suffer, while evils are sufferable, than to right themselves by abolishing the forms to which they are accustomed. But when a long train of abuses and usurpations, pursuing invariably the same Object evinces a design to reduce them under absolute Despotism, it is their right, it is their duty, to throw off such Government, and to provide new Guards for their future security.— Such has been the patient sufferance of these Colonies; and such is now the necessity which constrains them to alter their former Systems of Government. The history of the present King of Great Britain is a history of repeated injuries and usurpations, all having in direct object the establishment of an absolute Tyranny over these States. To prove this, let Facts be submitted to a candid world.

He has refused his Assent to Laws, the most wholesome and necessary for the public good.

He has forbidden his Governors to pass Laws of immediate and pressing importance, unless suspended in their operation till his Assent should be obtained; and when so suspended, he has utterly neglected to attend to them.

He has refused to pass other Laws for the accommodation of large districts of people, unless those people would relinquish the right of Representation in the Legislature, a right inestimable to them and formidable to tyrants only.

He has called together legislative bodies at places unusual, uncomfortable, and distant from the depository of their Public Records, for the sole purpose of fatiguing them into compliance with his measures.

He has dissolved Representative Houses repeatedly, for opposing with manly firmness his invasions on the rights of the people.

He has refused for a long time, after such dissolutions, to cause others to be elected; whereby the Legislative Powers, incapable of Annihilation, have returned to the People at large for their exercise; the State remaining in the mean time exposed to all the dangers of invasion from without, and convulsions within.

He has endeavoured to prevent the population of these States; for that purpose obstructing the Laws for Naturalization of Foreigners; refusing to pass others to encourage their migration hither, and raising the conditions of new Appropriations of Lands.

He has obstructed the Administration of Justice, by refusing his Assent to Laws for establishing Judiciary Powers.

He has made Judges dependent on his Will alone, for the tenure of their offices, and the amount and payment of their salaries.

He has erected a multitude of New Offices, and sent hither swarms of Officers to harass our People, and eat out their substance.

He has kept among us, in time of peace, Standing Armies without the Consent of our legislature.

He has affected to render the Military independent of and superior to the Civil Power.

He has combined with others to subject us to a jurisdiction foreign to our constitution, and unacknowledged by our laws; giving his Assent to their acts of pretended Legislation:

For quartering large bodies of armed troops among us:

For protecting them, by a mock Trial, from Punishment for any Murders which they should commit on the Inhabitants of these States:

For cutting off our Trade with all parts of the world:

For imposing Taxes on us without our Consent:

For depriving us in many cases, of the benefits of Trial by Jury:

For transporting us beyond Seas to be tried for pretended offences:

For abolishing the free System of English Laws in a Neighbouring Province, establishing therein an Arbitrary government, and enlarging its boundaries so as to render it at once an example and fit instrument for introducing the same absolute rule into these Colonies:

For taking away our Charters, abolishing our most valuable Laws, and altering fundamentally the Forms of our Governments:

For suspending our own Legislatures, and declaring themselves invested with Power to legislate for us in all cases whatsoever.

He has abdicated Government here, by declaring us out of his Protection and waging War against us.

He has plundered our seas, ravaged our Coasts, burnt our towns, and destroyed the Lives of our people.

He is at this time transporting large Armies of foreign Mercenaries to compleat the works of death, desolation and tyranny, already begun with circumstances of Cruelty & perfidy scarcely paralleled in the most barbarous ages, and totally unworthy the Head of a civilized nation.

He has constrained our fellow Citizens taken Captive on the high Seas to bear Arms against their Country, to become the executioners of their friends and Brethren, or to fall themselves by their Hands.

He has excited domestic insurrections amongst us, and has endeavoured to bring on the inhabitants of our frontiers, the merciless Indian Savages, whose known rule of warfare, is an undistinguished destruction of all ages, sexes and conditions.

In every stage of these Oppressions We have Petitioned for Redress in the most humble terms: Our repeated petitions have been answered only by repeated injury. A Prince, whose character is thus marked by every act which may define a Tyrant, is unfit to be the ruler of a free People.

Nor have We been wanting in attention to our British brethren. We have warned them from time to time of attempts by their legislature to extend an unwarrantable jurisdiction over us. We have reminded them of the circumstances of our emigration and settlement here. We have appealed to their native justice and magnanimity, and we have conjured them by the ties of our common kindred to disavow these usurpations, which, would inevitably interrupt our connections and correspondence. They too have been deaf to the voice of justice and of consanguinity. We must, therefore, acquiesce in the necessity, which denounces our Separation, and hold them, as we hold the rest of mankind, Enemies in War, in Peace Friends.

We, therefore, the Representatives of the united States of America, in General Congress, Assembled, appealing to the Supreme Judge of the world for the rectitude of our intentions, do, in the Name, and by Authority of the good People of these Colonies, solemnly publish and declare, That these United Colonies are, and of Right ought to be Free and Independent States; that they are Absolved from all Allegiance to the British Crown, and that all political connection between them and the State of Great Britain, is and ought to be totally dissolved; and that as Free and Independent States, they have full power to levy War, conclude Peace, contract Alliances, establish Commerce, and to do all other Acts and Things which Independent States may of right do. And for the support of this Declaration, with a firm reliance on the protection of Divine Providence, we mutually pledge to each other our lives, our Fortunes and our sacred Honor.

PROBLEMS FOR WRITING AND DISCUSSION

1. A few days before Jefferson sat down to write the Declaration, George Mason, a friend in Virginia, completed a draft of a Declaration of Rights for Virginia. His first draft, which appeared in the *Pennsylvania Evening Post* for June 6, read:

> That all men are born equally free and independent and have certain inherent natural rights, of which they can not, by any compact, deprive or divest their posterity; among which are the enjoyment of life and liberty, with the means of acquiring and possessing property, and preserving and obtaining happiness.

The assumption seems reasonable that Jefferson took Mason's sentence and rewrote it for *his* Declaration. Compare the two versions and try to determine why Jefferson, as a writer, made the changes he did and what was gained by them.

2. Upon what philosophical assumptions does Jefferson rest the "rectitude" of American intentions?

3. George Santayana, an American expatriot and philosophical essayist, once called the Declaration "a salad of illusion." Do you think he referred to its philosophical assumptions or to the grievances Jefferson lists? Why?

4. Jefferson's main task was to persuade "a candid world" that America was justified in what she was doing. As an argument, is the Declaration successful? Would its form serve other people who are ready "to dissolve the political bands which have connected them with another, and to assume among the Powers of the earth, the separate and equal station to which the Laws of Nature and of Nature's God entitle them"? Do you know if it has served as a model for other people?

5. Does the Declaration seem today to be a sound "expression of the American mind"? Discuss events in recent history that illustrate American adherence to or departure from the "truths" which Jefferson held to be "self-evident."

6. Compare Boorstin's remarks (p. 5) about the American character with that "character" as it is revealed in the Declaration. Boorstin says we are a nation of "antis." Does the Declaration bear this out? Does Boorstin's belief that Americans should go about their own business reflect the sentiments expressed in the Declaration?

Contributions of the West to American Democracy

FREDERICK JACKSON TURNER

Frederick Jackson Turner (1861-1932) was a young unknown historian from the University of Wisconsin when in 1893 he read a paper before the American Historical Association that reshaped the interpretation of the American experience. The title of the paper was "The Significance of the American Frontier in American History," and its thesis was that the abundance of free land along the steadily westward-moving American frontier had from the earliest settlements been mainly responsible for the growth of American democracy. Turner's "frontier thesis" swiftly replaced the long-held belief that American characteristics had evolved from those Anglo-Saxon institutions imported from Europe. General acceptance of Turner's argument has declined of late, as David Potter's essay (pp. 328-45) suggests, but it still has its warm adherents. The essay that follows was published a decade after Turner produced his thesis.

Western democracy has been from the time of its birth idealistic. The very fact of the wilderness appealed to men as a fair, blank page on which to write a new chapter in the story of man's struggle for a higher type of society. The Western wilds, from the Alleghenies to the Pacific, constituted the richest free gift that was ever

From The Frontier in American History *by Frederick Jackson Turner. Copyright 1920 by Frederick Jackson Turner. Copyright renewed 1948 by Caroline M. S. Turner. Reprinted by permission of Holt, Rinehart and Winston, Inc.*

spread out before civilized man. To the peasant and artisan of the Old World, bound by the chains of social class, as old as custom and as inevitable as fate, the West offered an exit into a free life and greater well-being among the bounties of nature, into the midst of resources that demanded manly exertion, and that gave in return the chance for indefinite ascent in the scale of social advance. "To each she offered gifts after his will." Never again can such an opportunity come to the sons of men. It was unique, and the thing is so near us, so much a part of our lives, that we do not even yet comprehend its full significance. The existence of this land of opportunity has made America the goal of idealists from the days of the Pilgrim Fathers. With all the materialism of the pioneer movements, this idealistic conception of the vacant lands as an opportunity for a new order of things is unmistakably present. Kipling's "Song of the English" has given it expression:—

> "We were dreamers, dreaming greatly, in the man-stifled town;
> We yearned beyond the sky-line where the strange roads go down.
> Came the Whisper, came the Vision, came the Power with the Need,
> Till the Soul that is not man's soul was lent us to lead.
> As the deer breaks—as the steer breaks—from the herd where they graze,
> In the faith of little children we went on our ways.
> Then the wood failed—then the food failed—then the last water dried—
> In the faith of little children we lay down and died.
>
> "On the sand-drift—on the veldt-side—in the fern-scrub we lay,
> That our sons might follow after by the bones on the way.
> Follow after—follow after! We have watered the root
> And the bud has come to blossom that ripens for fruit!
> Follow after—we are waiting by the trails that we lost
> For the sound of many footsteps, for the tread of a host.
>
> "Follow after—follow after—for the harvest is sown:
> By the bones about the wayside ye shall come to your own!"

This was the vision that called to Roger Williams,—that "prophetic soul ravished of truth disembodied," "unable to enter into treaty with its environment," and forced to seek the wilderness. "Oh, how sweet," wrote William Penn, from his forest refuge, "is the quiet of these parts, freed from the troubles and perplexities of woeful Europe." And here he projected what he called his "Holy Experiment in Government."

If the later West offers few such striking illustrations of the relation of the wilderness to idealistic schemes, and if some of the designs were fantastic and abortive, none the less the influence is a fact. Hardly a Western State but has been the Mecca of some sect or band of social reformers, anxious to put into practice their ideals, in vacant land, far removed from the checks of a settled form of social organization. Consider the Dunkards, the Icarians, the Fourierists, the Mormons, and similar idealists who sought our Western wilds. But the idealistic influence is not limited to the dreamers' conception of a new State. It gave to the pioneer farmer and city builder a restless energy, a quick capacity for judgment and action, a belief in liberty, freedom of opportunity, and a resistance to the domination of class which infused a vitality and power into the individual atoms of this democratic mass. Even as he dwelt among the stumps of his newly-cut clearing, the pioneer had the creative vision of a new order of society. In imagination he pushed back the forest boundary to the confines of a mighty Commonwealth; he willed that log cabins should become the lofty buildings of great cities. He decreed that his children should enter into a heritage of education, comfort, and social welfare, and for this ideal he bore the scars of the wilderness. Possessed with this idea he ennobled his task and laid deep foundations for a democratic State. Nor was this idealism by any means limited to the American pioneer.

To the old native democratic stock has been added a vast army of recruits from the Old World. There are in the Middle West alone four million persons of German parentage out of a total of seven millions in the country. Over a million persons of Scandinavian parentage live in the same region. The democracy of the newer West is deeply affected by the ideals brought by these immigrants from the Old World. To them America was not simply a new home; it was a land of opportunity, of freedom, of democracy. It meant to them, as to the American pioneer that preceded them, the opportunity to destroy the bonds of social caste that bound them in their older home, to hew out for themselves in a new country a destiny proportioned to the powers that God had given them, a chance to place their families under better conditions and to win a larger life than the life that they had left behind. He who believes that even the hordes of recent immigrants from southern Italy are drawn to these shores by nothing more than a dull and blind materialism has not penetrated into the heart of the problem. The idealism and expectation of these children of the Old World, the hopes which they have formed for a newer and freer life across the seas, are almost pathetic when one considers how far they are from the possibility of fruition. He who would take stock of American democracy must not forget the accumulation of human purposes and ideals which immigration has added to the American populace.

In this connection it must also be remembered that these democratic ideals have existed at each stage of the advance of the frontier, and have left behind them deep and enduring effects on the thinking of the whole country. Long after the frontier period of a particular region of the United States has passed away, the conception of society, the ideals and aspirations which it produced, persist in the minds of the people. So recent has been the transition of the greater portion of the United States from frontier conditions to conditions of settled life, that we are, over the large portion of the United States, hardly a generation removed from the primitive conditions of the West. If, indeed, we ourselves were not pioneers, our fathers were, and the inherited ways of looking at things, the fundamental assumptions of the American people, have all been shaped by this experience of democracy on its westward march. This experience has been wrought into the very warp and woof of American thought.

Even those masters of industry and capital who have risen to power by the conquest of Western resources came from the midst of this society and still profess its principles. John D. Rockefeller was born on a New York farm, and began his career as a young business man in St. Louis. Marcus Hanna was a Cleveland grocer's clerk at the age of twenty. Claus Spreckles, the sugar king, came from Germany as a steerage passenger to the United States in 1848. Marshall Field was a farmer boy in Conway, Massachusetts, until he left to grow up with the young Chicago. Andrew Carnegie came as a ten-year-old boy from Scotland to Pittsburgh, then a distinctively Western town. He built up his fortunes through successive grades until he became the dominating factor in the great iron industries, and paved the way for that colossal achievement, the Steel Trust. Whatever may be the tendencies of this corporation, there can be little doubt of the democratic ideals of Mr. Carnegie himself. With lavish hand he has strewn millions through the United States for the promotion of libraries. The effect of this library movement in perpetuating the democracy that comes from an intelligent and self-respecting people can hardly be measured. In his "Triumphant Democracy," published in 1886, Mr. Carnegie, the ironmaster, said, in reference to the mineral wealth of the United States: "Thank God, these treasures are in the hands of an intelligent people, the Democracy, to be used for the general good of the masses, and not made the spoils of monarchs, courts, and aristocracy, to be turned to the base and selfish ends of a privileged hereditary class." It would be hard to find a more rigorous assertion of democratic doctrine than the celebrated utterance, attributed to the same man, that he should feel it a disgrace to die rich.

In enumerating the services of American democracy, President Eliot included the corporation as one of its achievements, declaring that "freedom of incorporation, though no longer exclusively a democratic agency, has given a strong support to democratic institutions." In one sense this is doubtless true, since the corporation has been one of the means by which small properties can be aggregated into an effective working body. Socialistic writers have long been fond of pointing out also that these various concentrations pave the way for and make possible social control. From this point of view it is possible that the masters of industry may prove to be not so much an incipient aristocracy as the pathfinders for democracy in reducing the industrial world to systematic consolidation suited to democratic control. The great geniuses that have built up the modern industrial concentration were trained in the midst of democratic society. They were the product of these democratic conditions. Freedom to rise was the very condition of their existence. Whether they will be followed by successors who will adopt the exploitation of the masses, and who will be capable of retaining under efficient control these vast resources, is one of the questions which we shall have to face.

This, at least, is clear: American democracy is fundamentally the outcome of the experiences of the American people in dealing with the West. Western democracy through the whole of its earlier period tended to the production of a society of which the most distinctive fact was the freedom of the individual to rise under conditions of social mobility, and whose ambition was the liberty and well-being of the masses. This conception has vitalized all American democracy, and has brought it into sharp contrasts with the democracies of history, and with those modern efforts of Europe to create an artificial democratic order by legislation. The problem of the United States is not to create democracy, but to conserve democratic institutions and ideals. In the later period of its development, Western democracy has been gaining experience in the problem of social control. It has steadily enlarged the sphere of its action and the instruments for its perpetuation. By its system of public schools, from the grades to the graduate work of the great universities, the West has created a larger single body of intelligent plain people than can be found elsewhere in the world. Its political tendencies, whether we consider Democracy, Populism, or Republicanism, are distinctly in the direction of greater social control and the conservation of the old democratic ideals.

To these ideals the West adheres with even a passionate determination. If, in working out its mastery of the resources of the interior, it has produced a type of industrial leader so powerful as to be the wonder of the world, nevertheless, it is still to be determined whether these men constitute a menace to democratic institutions, or the most efficient factor for adjusting democratic control to the new conditions.

Whatever shall be the outcome of the rush of this huge industrial modern United States to its place among the nations of the earth, the formation of its Western democracy will always remain one of the wonderful chapters in the history of the human race. Into this vast shaggy continent of ours poured the first feeble tide of European settlement. European men, institutions, and ideas were lodged in the American wilderness, and this great American West took them to her bosom, taught them a new way of looking upon the destiny of the common man, trained them in adaptation to the conditions of the New World, to the creation of new institutions to meet new needs; and ever as society on her eastern border grew to resemble the Old World in its social forms and its industry, ever, as it began to lose faith in the ideals of democracy, she opened new provinces, and dowered new democracies in her most distant domains with her material treasures and with the ennobling influence that the fierce love of freedom, the strength that came from hewing out a home, making a school and a church, and creating a higher future for his family, furnished to the pioneer.

She gave to the world such types as the farmer Thomas Jefferson, with his Declaration of Independence, his statute for religious toleration, and his purchase of Louisiana. She gave us Andrew Jackson, that fierce Tennessee spirit who broke down the traditions of conservative rule, swept away the privacies and privileges of officialdom, and, like a Gothic leader, opened the temple of the nation to the populace. She gave us Abraham Lincoln, whose gaunt frontier form and gnarled, massive hand told of the conflict with the forest, whose grasp of the ax-handle of the pioneer was no firmer than his grasp of the helm of the ship of state as it breasted the seas of civil war. She has furnished to this new democracy her stores of mineral wealth, that dwarf of those of the Old World, and her provinces that in themselves are vaster and more productive than most of the nations of Europe. Out of her bounty has come a nation whose industrial competition alarms the Old World, and the masters of whose resources wield wealth and power vaster than the wealth and power of kings. Best of all, the West gave, not only to the American, but to the unhappy and oppressed of all lands, a vision of hope, and assurance that the world held a place where were to be found high faith in man and the will and power to furnish him the opportunity to grow to the full measure of his own capacity. Great and powerful as are the new sons of her loins, the Republic is greater than they. The paths of the pioneer have widened into broad highways. The forest clearing has expanded into affluent commonwealths. Let us see to it that the ideals of the pioneer in his log cabin shall enlarge into the spiritual life of a democracy where civic power shall dominate and utilize individual achievement for the common good.

PROBLEMS FOR WRITING AND DISCUSSION

1. How does Turner differentiate American democracy from others which have preceded it? How does he distinguish Western democracy from all others?
2. What does Turner mean by the "idealism" of the West? What does he mean by its "materialism"?
3. On what aspect of pioneer life does Turner put the greatest stress? Does De Voto's essay (p. 93) on camping strengthen or weaken Turner's argument? Does Sevareid's essay (p. 45) on a small Western town verify what Turner says about the American West and "social mobility"?
4. Turner uses the word *farmer* to describe Jefferson. Would Viereck (p. 324) approve of this epithet?
5. Would Turner consider George Washington, who was born on the western edge of Virginia, a product of the frontier? In the light of William Carlos Williams' sketch of Washington (p. 106) would you consider him a frontiersman? Explain.
6. The Declaration of Independence postulates that liberty and equality are principles of "Nature and of Nature's God." Is Turner convinced that the rights of free men are "unalienable"?
7. What difficulty does Turner see confronting Western democracy? Does this same difficulty—in different forms, perhaps—exist for your genera-

tion? (The readings under "Free Enterprise," Section 1 of Part II, should help clarify your views here.)

8. Turner wrote his essay in 1903. Does his view of the corporation seem dated? Does what he says about the persistence of American frontier ideals after the frontier had closed ramify Arnold's thesis (p. 162) of the personification of corporations? Would Arnold agree that the corporation " 'has given strong support to democratic institutions' "? Berle (p. 170) warns that the only ethical control of corporations lies in the ideals and tacit assumptions of the men who direct them. Is Turner more optimistic about the "masters of industry" than Berle?

9. Compare the situation and philosophy of Henry Ford (p. 143) with those of the "masters of industry" Turner cites. Do the "masters of industry" today still rise from the ranks of the workingmen? Would Galbraith (p. 180) agree with Andrew Carnegie that the treasures of the land are "used for the general good of the masses and not made the spoils . . . of a privileged hereditary class"?

10. Like Henry Ford (p. 180) and Oppenheimer (p. 264), Turner is concerned that the "individual achievement" be utilized "for the common good." Compare these views from an industrialist, a scientist, and a historian. Do their views have a common origin in the expectations of American democracy Turner describes? Would Ford and Oppenheimer agree that "civic power" should determine the individual contribution?

11. Turner emphasizes the magnitude of the American wilderness that lent scope to the dreams and designs of all who contemplated it or confronted it. Does Henry James (p. 82) understand the effect of sheer size upon Americans? Does his evaluation of its effects correspond in any way with Turner's?

12. Turner cites the "system of public schools" as a means by which American democracy insures "greater social control and the conservation of old democratic ideals." Compare Turner's expectations of the public schools with those of Agee (p. 191) and Lipset (p. 348).

13. Turner notes that the "idealism and expectation" of immigrants to America "are almost pathetic when one considers how far they are from the possibility of fruition." Are the "aloneness" of Kazin's parents (p. 64) and the disillusionment of T. S. Matthews (p. 99) understandable partly as the result of "idealism and expectation"?

The Aristocratic Origin of American Freedom
PETER VIERECK

> *Peter Viereck (1916-), poet, historian, and polemicist, was graduated from Harvard in 1937, attended Oxford the following year, then returned to Harvard to receive his doctorate in 1942. He taught at Harvard, Smith, and the U.S. Army University in Florence, Italy, and spent three years in the army before going to Mount Holyoke College, where he currently teaches Russian history. In 1949 he won the Pulitzer Prize for poetry, as well as a Guggenheim Fellowship. In addition to several volumes of verse, he has written historico-philosophical works, the best known of which are* Conservatism Revisited: The Revolt Against Revolt, 1815-1949 *(1949) and* Shame and Glory of the Intellectuals *(1953).*

The palaces of Thomas Jefferson and the founding fathers—examine them yourself any day at the Williamsburg restoration—hardly look like log cabins. Not even to the disciples of Turner. Let us have no Rousseauistic myths, no noble savages. American freedom, the Conservation of 1776, did not spring from the Wholesome Plebeian Poverty of any westward-facing man-with-the-hoe.

Whether for better or for worse, American freedom was founded in the Europe-styled, lackey-tended, varlet-scrubbed châteaux of noblemen like Jefferson. For he, too, was one of Hamilton's "well-born"; today our folksy-progressive prejudices would call them

From Shame and Glory of the Intellectuals *by Peter Viereck, Beacon Press, 1953. Reprinted by permission of the author.*

"un-American," "the idle rich," "effete easterners," and, worst of all, "lacking the common touch."

For the crucial first six decades, from the 1770's till the Jacksonian revolution that followed 1828, the American government was not only extremely conservative. It was a closed, hierarchical "government by gentlemen." Power alternated between two rival groups of almost equally conservative gentlemen: Hamilton's élite of northern merchants versus Jefferson's élite of intellectual lawyers and southern planters. Yet neither group neglected our Bill of Rights; they managed to increase, and not only preserve, the liberties bequeathed by our founders.

By 1828 the foundations of American liberty had already been laid, without benefit either of Turner's westward movement or of the A.D.A. The western log cabins and Jackson's proto-New-Deal did indeed contribute to American freedom by diffusing it: from aristocratic republic to—or, rather, toward—mass democracy. An exciting gain. But also a depressing potential danger to liberty; reread Ortega y Gasset on "the mass-man."

The concept of civil liberties is aristocratic. It bravely defies democratic majority rule. If you insist on civil liberties, and there are few things more worthy of insistence, then you must be prepared to say: "Even if a fairly elected, democratic majority of 99 per cent wants to lynch all Negroes, Jews, Catholics, labor leaders, or bankers, it is our moral and legal duty to resist the majority, though we die in the attempt." Guarding the Bill of Rights even against majorities and even *against the people's will,* the American Constitution performs an aristocratic function.

The familiar contribution to freedom made by the log cabin and by the human Grass Roots of the West was valuable and necessary. Yet secondary. It merely broadened the primary impulse of freedom bequeathed by the palaces of our aristocratic Conservers of 1776.

Today Americans will be better and not worse democrats if they reject not entirely our original aristocratic heritage and if they reflect occasionally upon the subtle disadvantages as well as the obvious advantages of majoritarianism. Democracy, yes. In Sandburg's phrase, "the people, yes." But not an egalitarianism in which "bricklayers lord it over architects." [1]

The inner aristocrat may be defined as the man who enforces his civilized standards from within, by cultural and ethical self-discipline. The inner plebeian, the mass-man, is he who only obeys standards physically forced upon him from without. To the plebeian, be he a millionaire or pauper, life is not a challenge to transcend himself and to carry a great heritage forward. It is a vast garbage pile in which he is ceaselessly rooting—like a wart-hog—for more swill. Economics, which Ruskin called "the gospel of Mammon," is the Good Tidings of the plebeian. It is this latter view of "life" that a great aristocratic artist meant when he said, "As for *living,* our servants can do that for us." The inner plebeian is ruled only by his snout. And therefore only by the knout. And therefore the mass-man is a totalitarian, tending toward a communazi dictatorship of lynch law, whereas to the inner aristocrat the civil liberties of his opponents are sacred, even against a mass majority of 99.9 per cent.

Because the American context is unique in all recorded history, aristocracy must take a unique form in America today. It must abandon the analogies with Old World class lines. I am prepared undemocratically to defend aristocratic class lines as performing necessary functions, beneficial to society as a whole, in certain European historical contexts of the past. But the American context is universal suffrage, fluid class lines, a "new" country without a Middle Ages, without hereditary nobility, and without any élite trained in *noblesse oblige,* as opposed to a plebeian money-bags "élite."

In this very exceptional, very American context, there is only one cure for the quantitative, antiqualitative vulgarism that en-

---

[1] Every variation on this theme is examined in one of the most challenging books of our era: Erik von Kuehnelt-Leddihn, *Liberty or Equality* (Caldwell, Idaho: Caxton Printers, 1952). For originality of approach to an old theme, it is equaled only by the very different and equally brilliant book by Eric Hoffer, *The True Believer* (New York: Harpers, 1951).

dangers all democracy. The cure is not to retreat into un-American class lines in order to make *some* men aristocrats. The cure is to subordinate economics to cultural values and to subordinate external coercion to internal self-discipline, in order to make all men aristocrats.

PROBLEMS FOR WRITING AND DISCUSSION

1. Viereck here presents a point of view that challenges the Turner view of American democracy (p. 315). In what specific way does Viereck deny Turner's basic idea? What tone does Viereck employ?
2. Viereck was born in New York City in the twentieth century, while Turner was born in the rural environment of the mid-nineteenth century. In what ways do their backgrounds perhaps shape their interpretations of the American experience?
3. What does Viereck mean by "egalitarianism" and "Rousseauistic myths"?
4. Reread the paragraph beginning: "The concept of civil liberties is aristocratic." Is the paragraph logically developed? How does Viereck distinguish between the "mass-man" and the "inner aristocrat"? How does he finally limit the meaning of "aristocracy"?
5. According to Viereck's concept of civil liberties, was Lincoln [as Grierson (p. 115) and Jaffa (p. 360) present him] an aristocrat?
6. Viereck cites Ortega y Gasset on the dangers of the "mass-man." What other writers in this book discuss these dangers? Are they saying the same thing as Viereck?
7. Compare Viereck's approach to the American dream with that of MacLeish (p. 439).
8. Compare what Viereck says of "majoritarianism" with what William L. Miller (p. 224) sees as a misunderstanding of democracy. Is Viereck's cure for the "vulgarism" that endangers all democracy comparable with Miller's cure for the "levelling" tendencies in education?
9. Do you see an analogy between the "inner aristocrat" and the "inner plebeian" Viereck defines and the members of the New Class and the "toilers" Galbraith (p. 180) describes?
10. Can you give instances illustrating Viereck's assertion that "the mass-man is a totalitarian"?

Abundance, Mobility, and Status

DAVID POTTER

David M. Potter (1910-   ) attended Emory University as an undergraduate and received his doctorate from Yale in 1933, whereupon he returned to the South to teach at the University of Mississippi (1936-38) and at Rice Institute (1938-42). He came back to Yale in 1942 as Professor of American History and remained there until 1961, when he moved to Stanford University. Between 1949 and 1951 he was editor of the Yale Review. *Among his books are* Lincoln and His Party in the Secession Crisis *(1942) and* People of Plenty: Economic Abundance and the American Character *(1954), which many historians consider one of the best and most original books on the American character written in the last decade.*

Abundance has influenced American life in many ways, but there is perhaps no respect in which this influence has been more profound than in the forming and strengthening of the American ideal and practice of equality, with all that the ideal has implied for the individual in the way of opportunity to make his own place in society and of emancipation from a system of status.

The very meaning of the term "equality" reflects this influence, for the connotations to an American are quite unlike what they might be to a European. A European, advocating equality, might very well mean that all men should occupy positions that are on roughly the same level in wealth, power, or enviability. But the

Reprinted from People of Plenty *by David M. Potter by permission of The University of Chicago Press. Copyright 1954 by The University of Chicago.*

American, with his emphasis upon equality of opportunity, has never conceived of it in this sense. He has traditionally expected to find a gamut ranging from rags to riches, from tramps to millionaires. To call this "equality" may seem a contradiction in terms, but the paradox has been resolved in two ways: first, by declaring that all men are equal in the eyes of the law—an explanation which, by itself, could have satisfied only the more legalistic type of mind; and, second, by assuming that no man is restricted or confined by his status to any one station, or even to any maximum station. Thus equality did not mean uniform position on a common level, but it did mean universal opportunity to move through a scale which traversed many levels. At one end of the scale might stand a log cabin, at the other the White House; but equality meant that anyone might run the entire scale. This emphasis upon unrestricted latitude as the essence of equality in turn involved a heavy emphasis upon liberty as an essential means for keeping the scale open and hence making equality a reality as well as a theoretical condition. In other societies, liberty—the principle that allows the individual to be different from others—might seem inconsistent with equality—the principle that requires the individual to be similar to others; but in America "liberty," meaning "freedom to grasp opportunity," and "equality," also meaning "freedom to grasp opportunity," have become almost synonymous.

In short, equality came to mean, in a major sense, parity in competition. Its value was as a means to advancement rather than as an asset in itself. Like an option in the world of business, it had no intrinsic value but only a value when used. Since the potential value could be realized only by actual movement to a higher level, the term "equality" acquired for most Americans exactly the same connotations which the term "upward mobility" has for the social scientist.

Understanding equality or mobility in this way, one can readily see the effect of abundance upon it. Alexis de Tocqueville perceived the relationship very clearly and stated it forcibly when he observed that "the chief circumstance which has favored the establishment and the maintenance of a democratic system in the United States is the nature of the territory that the Americans inhabit. Their ancestors gave them the love of equality and of freedom; but God Himself gave them the means of remaining equal and free by placing them upon a boundless continent." Clearly, Tocqueville did not really mean that the Americans needed a boundless continent to assure them of equality in the sense of being on a common level. He meant that a boundless continent enabled them to fulfil the promise of mobility. Democracy made this promise, but the riches of North America fulfilled it; and our democratic system, which, like other systems, can survive only when its ideals are realized, survived because an economic surplus was available to pay democracy's promissory notes.

Throughout our history the development of new geographical areas and new segments of the economy has offered those instances of advancement to which we point when offering illustrative proof that our system of equality enables anyone to succeed. What we mean, more nearly, is that our system of equality removes certain negative impediments to success, and then our positive access to a larger measure of abundance permits fulfilment of the success promise.

The point may seem self-evident when stated, but it is a fact which we have consistently and effectively suppressed in the national consciousness. Thus during the Depression, when economic access to advancement was lacking, men nevertheless tended to blame themselves as guilty in failing to achieve it, for they still had their freedom from legal restraints, and they had been taught to believe that this was all that they needed. As long as they continued to enjoy exemption from the negative impediments, the set of their mind was such that they did not recognize that the exemption had no meaning except in conjunction with positive opportunity.

Today our somewhat disillusioned intellectuals tend to emphasize the fact that the American dream of absolute equality and of universal opportunity was never fulfilled in the literal sense, and they often play up the discrepancy between the realities of American life and the beliefs of the American creed. Discrepancy there is, was, and perhaps ever shall be, and it must be confronted in any analysis; but the recognition of it should not obscure another primary fact, namely, that American conditions, in addition to encouraging a belief in mobility, actually brought about a condition of mobility far more widespread and pervasive than any previous society or previous era of history had ever witnessed.

The classic illustration, always cited in this connection, is the frontier, and it is indeed true that the existence of the frontier presented people with a unique opportunity to put behind them the economic and social status which they held in their native communities and to acquire property and standing in the newly forming communities of the West. But, while we constantly remind ourselves that the West offered abundance in the form of free land and provided the frontier as a locus for the transformation of this abundance into mobility, we often forget that the country as a whole offered abundance in the form of fuel resources, mineral resources, bumper crops, industrial capacity, and the like, and provided the city as a locus for the transformation of this abundance into mobility. More Americans have changed their status by moving to the city than have done so by moving to the frontier. The urban migration is almost as great a factor in American development as the westward migration, and more young men have probably followed Horace Greeley's example in moving from a rural birthplace to a metropolis than have followed his precept to go west and grow up with the country.

In America, the processes of an expanding economy—expanding geographically to open new territorial areas, expanding technologically to open new realms of production—have provided a constant supply of advantageous positions to which enterprising people could advance from less favored beginnings and have also provided, until 1921, a steady flow of immigrants to insure that the lower economic ranks need not be left empty by the ceaseless trend upward. Each wave of immigrants, in turn, was likely to move up as succeeding waves came in at the bottom. If opportunity, operating from above, has exerted a drawing force, pulling individuals upward, immigration, operating from below, has exerted a thrusting force, pushing them upward. But it is the factor of abundance, like the steam alternately generated and condensed in an engine, which has simultaneously exerted the force of drawing and that of thrusting.

There is a real question how much of the rapid transformation of America has been marked by actual mobility in the sense of advancement by the individual through the ranks of society from one status to another and how much has been a mere change in the manner of life and standard of living of classes which retain pretty much the same relative position. The middle-class city dweller of today has a money income that would have connoted wealth to his frugal, landowning, farm-dwelling forebear of the nineteenth century, and his facilities for living make his forebear's life seem Spartan by comparison; but his standing in the community is no higher and is, in fact, considerably less independent. Improvements in the standard of living of society at large should not be confused with the achievement of separate social advancement by individuals.

But even allowing for this distinction, it bears repeating that America has had a greater measure of social equality and social mobility than any highly developed society in human history. In terms of geographical movement ("horizontal mobility," as it is sometimes called), it has been characteristically American for the individual to make his life in a place distant from his family home, which is to say that he achieves his own status instead of receiving one which is entailed upon him. In terms of economic and social ups and downs ("vertical mobility," so called) America has been the country where the cycle "from shirtsleeves to shirtsleeves" was three generations, which is to say that status has changed readily and rapidly. In America, education has been more available to people with native ability; professional and business opportunities have been more available to people with education; wealth has been more available to people who excelled in business and the professions; and social fortresses have yielded to the assaults of wealth more readily than in any other country. At every stage, the channels of mobility have been kept open. As for social distinctions, certainly they exist; but, whatever their power may be, social rank can seldom assert an open claim to deference in this country, and it usually makes at least a pretense of conformity to equalitarian ways. Certain conspicuous exceptions, such as the treatment of American Negroes, qualify all these assertions but do not invalidate them as generalizations.

Americans have attached immense value, of course, to this condition of equal opportunity. It has, they feel, enabled men and women in this country, more than anywhere else in the world, to find, develop, and exercise their best potentialities as human beings. Such opportunity has not only meant fulfilment for the individual; it has also been of great value to society: it has enabled the nation to make the optimum use of its human resources by recruiting talent from the whole body of the population and not merely from a limited class, and thus it has strengthened the arts, the sciences, the economic enterprise, and the government of the country.

Moreover, American society, as a society of abundance, especially needed men who would accept the challenge of mobility. Historically, as new lands, new forms of wealth, new opportunities, came into play, clamoring to be seized upon, America developed something of a compulsion to make use of them. The man best qualified for this role was the completely mobile man, moving freely from one locality to the next, from one economic position to another, or from one social level to levels above. The rapidity of economic change required a high degree of convertibility, of transmutability, in the economic elements which it employed, and the system of mobility imparted this necessary flexibility in the human resources which were needed. In a country where the entire environment was to be transformed with the least possible delay, a man who was not prepared to undergo personal transformation was hardly an asset. Hence mobility became not merely an optional privilege but almost a mandatory obligation, and the man who failed to meet this obligation had, to a certain extent, defaulted in his duty to society.

Because of these values and these compulsions, America not only practiced a full measure of mobility and social equality but also developed a creed of equality and articulated a myth to accompany the creed.

The myth of equality held that equality exists not merely as a potentiality in the nature of man but as a working actuality in the operation of American society—that advantages or handicaps are not really decisive and that every man is the architect of his own destiny. It asserted the existence in the United States of a classless society, where no one is better than anyone else and merit is the only recognized ground of distinction. Despite their patent implausibility, these ideas received and still retain a most tenacious hold. Americans are notoriously unresponsive to the concept of class warfare, and American workers, while fully alert to the protection of their economic interests, have never accepted identity as members of a working class in the way in which workers in England and other countries have. As Margaret Mead observes, "the assumption that men were created equal, with an equal ability to make an effort and win an earthly reward, although denied every day by experience, is maintained every day by our folklore and our day dreams." American fondness for the underdog is perhaps not so much a matter of sympathy for causes which are losing (America cares little for causes which are lost) as of desire to see the creed of equality proved by the success of those who appear less than equal.

So long as these beliefs can be maintained intact—so long as they approximate reality closely enough to be convincing—they exercise an immense moral power. From them are derived many of the attitudes that make for decency in American life. The optimism with which Americans have confronted the future; the confidence with which they have grappled with difficult problems; their conviction that merit will be rewarded and that honest work is the only reliable means to attain success; their integrity in social relations; and their respect for the human dignity of any man or woman, regardless of that person's social credentials, are all by-products of the ideal of full equality in a classless society. But, with all its value, this ideal has never been maintained without a certain cost, for it breeds great expectations, and, in so far as these expectations fail of realization, social and personal tensions result. As we move past the mid-point of the twentieth century, it is becoming increasingly clear that the ideal confronts two serious and growing difficulties. One of these difficulties is that we really cannot attain a classless society, and the other is that we have sacrificed some very valuable qualities of the now repudiated status system in an effort to attain it.

Belief in a classless society in the literal sense was an illusion from the beginning, for, as Pitirim A. Sorokin has remarked, "unstratified society with real equality of its members is a myth which has never been realized in the history of mankind. . . . The forms and proportions of stratification may vary, but its essence is permanent." But Sorokin also mentions that a large measure of mobility will produce the illusion that there are no strata, and America has apparently had in the past more than enough mobility to sustain the illusion. Today the degree of mobility is apparently somewhat reduced, and a growing awareness of the invisible barriers of social class has resulted.

The existence of social class in this sense has been fully demonstrated by a number of intensive social studies which analyze the structure of the American system of social hierarchy and which seek to define its strata in precise terms. The foremost of these in exhaustiveness of investigation is W. Lloyd Warner's analysis of a New England coastal town, in the "Yankee City" volumes which began to be published eleven years ago, but there are several others, including Warner's own survey of "Jonesville," a middle western community; August de B. Hollingshead's analysis of the youth of "Elmtown"—the same middle western town; Davis, Gardner, and Gardner's investigation of a southern community in their volume, *Deep South*; Robert and Helen Lynd's two volumes on *Middletown*; and James West's *Plainville, U.S.A.*; not to mention John Dollard's *Caste and Class in a Southern Town*, published in 1937. In some respects, these studies remain controversial: for instance, disagreement prevails as to whether the so-called "classes" are objective, self-conscious social groupings or whether they are mere classificatory devices for the investigator. To state it in another way, there is a lively dispute as to whether social distinctions are aligned along an unbroken gradient from the top to the bottom of society or whether they shape society into a number of levels, like stair steps. But, in any case, the studies all demonstrate abundantly that social inequalities prevail and that these inequalities can be correlated with factors such as occupation, income, education, and area of residence and can be verified by various statistical procedures. One characteristic of these strata, quite generally recognized, is that the bulk of the population falls within the middle class and another large group within the upper zone of the lower class. For instance, the middle classes of "Yankee City" and "Jonesville" contain 38 and 42 per cent of the population, respectively, while the upper-lower group accounts for 28 and 41 per cent, respectively. Another tendency which seems evident, though it cannot be verified by any such clear-cut enumeration, is that the ease of mobility from class to class appears to be diminishing, and the barriers between classes are growing increasingly difficult to pass.

The existence of social strata in America is, to repeat, in no sense unique, for such strata have existed in every advanced society, and society has always accommodated itself to them. But, though class divisions are nothing new, there are certain elements in the stratification of today which set it apart from earlier class stratification and which make the American situation essentially unique.

One of these elements is the fact that social barriers in this country are a violation of our national ideals, and therefore the mere awareness of them impairs public morale. Whereas other societies accept them as part of the order of nature, we have refused to recognize them and have conducted life on the theory that they do not exist. Hence our people are not prepared to encounter them and are less able psychologically to adjust to them, with the result that, when such barriers do force themselves upon public against the society which, as they feel, betrayed them with a false notice, many people either lose confidence in themselves or rebel promise. In America some of the ripest recruits for Marxism have been the idealists who loved the doctrine of equality too well and who would not compromise with the realities of a society which merely offered a relatively closer approach to equality than other stratified societies afford. But the problem created by social rebels is less serious than the problem of men and women who are personally broken and defeated by a system which sets one standard for what people shall attempt and another for what they may attain. Thus there was much point in certain questions posed by Margaret Mead in 1942: "Has the American scene shifted so that we still demand of every child a measure of success which is actually less and less possible for him to attain? . . . Have we made it a condition of success that a man should reach a position higher than his father's when such an achievement (for the many) is dependent upon the existence of a frontier and an expanding economy?" [1]

This conflict between the ideal and the actuality, which is one of the peculiarly American aspects of social stratification, has been clearly recognized by all students of the subject; but there is another aspect which has been generally overlooked, though it is of marked importance. This is the fact that American social distinctions, however real they may be and however difficult to break down, are not based upon or supported by great disparities in wealth, in education, in speech, in dress, etc., as they are in the Old World. If the American class structure is in reality very unlike the classless society which we imagine, it is equally unlike the formalized class societies of former times, and thus it should be regarded as a new kind of social structure in which the strata may be fully demarked but where the bases of demarcation are relatively intangible. The factor of abundance has exercised a vital influence in producing this kind of structure, for it has constantly operated to equalize the overt differences between the various classes and to eliminate the physical distance between them, without, however, destroying the barriers which separate them. The traditional dissimilarities in

---

[1] *And Keep Your Powder Dry* (New York: William Morrow & Co., 1942), pp. 68-69.

social demeanor, in education, in dress, and in recreation made class distinction in the past seem natural and perhaps, in a pragmatic sense, justifiable, while the social chasm between, for instance, an upper class which attended school and a lower class which did not diminished the element of what might be called "invidious proximity." Where extremes of wealth and poverty, education and ignorance, privilege and exploitation prevail, resentment is directed against these conditions themselves and not against class distinctions, which are a mere recognition of the conditions. If the poor, the hungry, the ragged, the unlettered man complains, his complaint is not that he is excluded from select society, in his starved, ill-clad, ignorant condition; it is rather that he is denied decent food, decent garments, and a chance to learn. But when, living in a society that practices outward uniformity, he gains a satisfactory income, acquires education, dresses himself and his wife in the standard clothes worn by all the members of the community, sends his children to school—and then finds himself the object of class discriminations imposed at close quarters and based upon marginal, tenuous criteria, which are, in any case, probably invisible to his eyes, then the system of classes itself, no longer natural, no longer inevitable, begins to seem unjust and hateful.

If this analysis is accurate, it means that abundance has brought about an entirely new sort of inequality. By diminishing the physical differentials, the social diversity, and the real economic disparities that once separated classes, it has made any class distinction or class stratification seem doubly unfair and discriminatory. In proportion as it has solved the problem of class differentials, it has accentuated the problem of class distinctions.

Thus the goal of social equality in a classless society, which abundance seemed to make possible and which the mobility drive promised to achieve, has been sought at a substantial cost. By presenting an unattainable ideal as if it were a reality, the mobility drive has created damaging psychological tensions; by eliminating class diversity without being able to abolish class distinctions, abundance has only made subjective discrimination more galling, while making objective differentials less evident. But, in addition to these costs, the quest for equality has exacted a still more serious price: while it could not fulfil its promise to create a classless society, it has destroyed the one value which seemed inherent in the traditional class society—namely, that sense of the organic, recognized relationship between the individual and the community which was defined by the individual's status. To speak of our social structure today as a "status system," which Warner does, seems in some ways a perversion of the original term, for the actual effect of our system is to deny assured status to all except the members of the top class. Status, truly understood, implies a condition of corporate membership in the group and thus a sense of belonging in the community. It implies also a condition of dependence by the group upon the individual for the performance of certain specific work and thus makes possible a sense of worth for the individual and a pride in performance, no matter how humble his labor. The principle of true status assures the individual that he may lead a meritorious and respected life in the station where circumstances have placed him, regardless of what that station may be. Peter Drucker describes the values of status eloquently but without exaggeration when he says: "Social status and function are terms of relationship, of 'belonging,' of identification, of harmony. 'Status' defines man's existence as related in mutual necessity to the organized group. 'Function' ties his work, his aspirations and ambitions to the power and purposes of the organized group in a bond that satisfies both individual and society. . . . Together, status and function resolve the apparently irresolvable conflict between the absolute claim of the group—before which any one man is nothing in himself and only a member of the species—and the absolute claim of the individual, to whom the group is only a means and a tool for the achievement of his own private purpose. . . . Without . . . [status], man is either the 'caged spirit' of Oriental philosophy, senselessly and meaninglessly caught in a senseless and meaningless life, or just 'Homo Sapiens' and one of the . . . brutish apes. But the group's own cohesion and survival also depend on the individual's status and function; without it, the group is a mere herd, never a society."[2]

In America, of course, status, as fixed differential social position, has long been in disrepute. Ever since the Revolutionary War, it has borne the hateful implications of privilege and subservience; it connoted the attitude of English common folk who were supposed to pray,

> "God bless the squire and his relations,
> And keep us in our proper stations."

Thus status incurred obloquy, and even the party of conservatism—that is, the Republican party—rejected it. Probably nothing has contributed more to the weakness of the conservative position in the United States than the fact that this principle, which the great conservative leaders like Edmund Burke and Benjamin Disraeli have recognized as the foundation stone of conservatism, has been so sharply rejected by American conservatives that it fell by default to the opposition. Ultimately, Franklin Roosevelt did more to give men a sense of status than all the Republican Presidents since Lincoln.

The heavy emphasis which America has placed upon mobility of course necessitated this rejection of status, for the two are basically contradictory. Whereas the principle of status affirms that a minor position may be worthy, the principle of mobility, as Americans have construed it, regards such a station both as the penalty for and the proof of personal failure. This view is often pushed to a point where even the least invidious form of subordination comes to be resented as carrying a stigma, and certain kinds of work which are socially necessary are almost never performed except grudgingly. The individual, driven by the belief that he should never rest content in his existing station and knowing that society demands advancement by him as proof of his merit, often feels stress and in-

---

[2] *The New Society: The Anatomy of the Industrial Order* (New York: Harper & Bros., 1949), pp. 151-54.

security and is left with no sense of belonging either in the station to which he advances or in the one from which he set out.

After nearly two hundred years, these difficulties now begin to be recognized, and there is a dawning realization that both our insistence upon mobility and our denial of status have been carried to excess. The fierceness of the mobility race generates tensions too severe for some people to bear, and fear of failure in this race generates a sense of insecurity which is highly injurious. Denial of status deprives the individual of one of his deepest psychological needs. Few societies have ever attempted to dispense with it, and most of them have acted to assure the individual of a certain niche in society, even if they were not prepared to offer a minimum wage or a more abundant life. Even where status appears to have been ejected, it sometimes comes in again by the back door: for instance, Americans who repudiated status in terms of an existing social order very often embraced mobility as leading to secure and desirable status in the social order of the future. In a country which possessed so little but could legitimately anticipate so much, it became genuine realism for the pioneer to identify himself with the prosperous future community which he was building rather than the squalid temporary settlement in which he lived. The imperceptible way in which the drive of mobility merges with the anticipation of status is suggested by the appeal used by a life insurance company which sells policies to provide for the future education of children and advertises with the picture of a small boy, over the caption, "He is going to college already."

It follows, then, that even where status has been publicly renounced, individuals continue to manifest, in a variety of ways, a deep psychological craving for the certitudes which it offers. The hazards and insecurities resulting from absence of status have sometimes caused an impulse, as Erich Fromm expresses it, to "escape from freedom." At times the appetite for the assurances which status gives has taken a pathological turn and contributed to the rise of the Fascist and Nazi and Communist dictatorships.

Anyone who supposes that these phenomena were exclusively Italian or German or Russian has only to read *The Authoritarian Personality,* by T. W. Adorno and his associates (New York: Harper & Bros., 1950), in order to see how corrosive an effect the frustrated craving for status has had upon personality in the United States.

In this connection, however, one should take the precaution of noting that the mobility drive and the doctrine of equality were not the only factors in the destruction of status, although they caused it to be repudiated morally. A fully articulated status system rested, technologically and socially, upon two bases which have now been very seriously impaired. One of these was the workman's satisfaction in and identification with his work. However humble his position, the craftsman knew that his community, with its economy of scarcity, needed his work, and, since it was his own work in the craft sense, he could regard his product as an extension of himself. The age of abundance, however, requiring a greater volume of processed goods, utilized machinery to meet the demand and made the former craftsman a more productive but less creative and less essential attendant upon the machine. The other basis was the position of the family as a matrix within which status was contained. Biologically and psychologically the family was a unit, and, so long as its members worked together, cultivating the crops, tending the animals, preparing the food and clothing, and practicing the handicrafts of early America, it was socially and economically a unit as well. The completeness of its integration assured to each member strong ties of relationship with the group. But again the age of abundance, arising from industrial growth and in turn stimulating further industrialization, caused a transformation. By compelling the individual to work outside the family, it divorced the family from the economy. For instance, it even took children, who had previously worked within the family, and made them work in the factory. The horror of child labor, as Drucker has observed, was not that it caused children to work (they had always worked) but that it deprived even those who most needed it of the protecting status found in the family relationship. By diffusing the focus which the family had given to social organization, the new economy made status a matter of several fragments—a man's status among his fellow-employees, his status in his neighborhood, his status at the bank—rather than one of a single, homogeneous social relationship. In this case the original whole was far greater than the sum of the subsequent parts.

The tenor of all these observations may seem, at first glance, utterly pessimistic. In summary, they seem to mean that the economic potentialities of our continent have caused us to subordinate other values to the realization of maximum wealth; that, in the process, we have committed ourselves to an impossible ideal— the ideal of mobility for everyone—with the consequence of causing tensions and insecurity for the individual; that we have made class distinctions more galling than ever by maintaining discriminations after the actual differences between classes have dwindled away; and that we have deprived men and women of the psychological values inherent in status. While abundance was producing these results through its emphasis on the mobility drive, it was at the same time striking at the foundations of status by substituting machine production for craft production and by bringing into operation an economy of which the family was not part. In short, everything would seem to lead to the conclusion that abundance has exacted a heavy psychological penalty for the physical gains which it has conferred.

In so far as there has been real damage, it would be fatuous to suppose that it can be to any great extent undone. No future policy is likely either to restore on a large scale the satisfactions of craftsmanship (which ought not to be idealized too much) or to give back to the family its function as a unifying focus for the multiple facets of life. Nor can we grasp either horn of the dilemma when bidden to choose between completely fulfilling the promise of equality, which is impossible, or abandoning it, which is unthinkable.

But, despite these factors, there is valid ground for hope that the same abundance which, in its developing stage, accentuated some of these conditions will, in its stage of fulfilment, ameliorate the same conditions.

What abundance did, in the period when its potentialities were being rapidly developed, was to throw out of balance the equilibrium between two forces, both of which are essential to a healthy society—the principle of mobility, which involves the welfare of man as an independent individual, and the principle of status, which involves his welfare as a member of the community. It destroyed this balance by making a good standard of living available for any man, while perpetuating a low standard as usual for most men. The continued low standard was the penalty for lack of mobility, and, as a consequence, mobility became mandatory. At the same time, the changes in the potential living standard began to make the system of status seem evil, for the status system had always consigned the vast majority to a life of bare sufficiency in an age when this was all that the existing economy would allow; but the growth of abundance, by making insufficiency unnecessary, made this aspect of status an avoidable one, thus making status itself seem needlessly harsh and unjust. In these circumstances, society exalted mobility inordinately, at the corresponding sacrifice of status.

Though these were the conditions, historically, under which abundance first began to make itself felt, it is important to recognize that they are not the conditions of abundance today. In our present economy, where there are fewer undeveloped opportunities demanding to be exploited, society does not need a population of mobile individuals as urgently as it did formerly. At the same time, the wide prevalence of a high standard of living means that the individual is no longer required to become mobile in order to share in the benefits which the economy has to offer. In proportion as this condition develops, mobility ought to become optional rather than obligatory. Where mobility was once the price of welfare, we now have a larger measure of welfare without mobility than any previous society in history, and this may enable us to relax the tensions of mobility, keeping it as an instrument for the self-fulfilment of the individual but dispensing with it as a social imperative.

In a comparable way, the fulfilment of abundance can free status of its one great historic blemish—its condemnation of the vast majority to a life of want. This opens the way for a more beneficent form of status which would emphasize the concepts of membership, of identity, of place in the community, and would minimize the hierarchical aspects, as, indeed, the new abundance has already minimized them by diminishing the physical differences in standards of dress, of diet, of housing, and of recreation among the various elements in society.

Admittedly, this restoration of the balance between mobility and status is still to be attained, and the consequences both of the excessive mobility drive and of lack of status are still conspicuous in our society. But there are some indications already that the emphases are beginning to change. Personnel offices in large business enterprises throughout the country are constantly at work to create a relationship which will give to employees a sense of membership and permanence in the organization; labor unions are concentrating their attention upon pensions, seniority, and the general question of tenure. In both cases, self-interest may be the motive, but, in so far as the efforts succeed, mobility will be diminished and status will be enhanced.

But, however these trends may work themselves out, it seems reasonably clear already that the present phase of abundance has begun to restore a balance by tending toward a permissive mobility, free of psychological tensions, and toward voluntary status, free of economic penalties. Thus there is every prospect that abundance will be a vital factor in controlling the status and mobility adjustments of the future, as it has been in determining the compulsion toward mobility and the repudiation of status which are such crucial factors in the American society of the present.

PROBLEMS FOR WRITING AND DISCUSSION

1. According to Potter, how do Americans understand the term *equality*? In what sense are *liberty* and *equality* synonymous in American thought?

2. Potter says our democratic system "survived because an economic surplus was available to pay democracy's promissory notes." Explain.

3. Does Potter's discussion of the effects of mobility on American democracy substantiate Turner's frontier thesis (p. 315)? What effects of abundance of land and resources does Potter treat more fully? What, according to Potter, facilitated the "optimum use" of human resources of which Henry Ford dreamed (p. 143)? Ford talked about increasing the productivity of the craftsman. What does Potter say has happened with the increase of his productivity?

4. How is the self-reproach and guilt of Americans who do not "succeed" a vestige of the nineteenth-century philosophy that not only Potter but Allen (p. 139) and Arnold (p. 162) describe?

5. Why does Potter distinguish between the rise in the general national standard of living and the "separate social advancement by individuals"?

6. Despite the "myth of equality," Potter stresses the existence of social strata in America but calls the stratification "essentially unique"—"an entirely new sort of inequality." What distinguishes it from the class distinctions in the Old World, for example? Why do social discriminations in this new "inequality" seem particularly unjust?

7. Arnold shows that the myth of the corporation as a free individual came into being once the worker had lost his economic independence. When, presumably, and for what reasons did the "myth of equality" develop? Are the personification of the corporation and the myth of equality traceable to postulates in the Declaration of Independence?

8. The myth of equality, Potter says, is still close enough to reality to "exercise an immense moral power." What commendable American attitudes does he give it credit for? What irreparable damage? Like Potter, Arnold and Berle (p. 170) recognize the "immense moral power" exerted by the myths of corporate institutions. What at best do they credit to these myths? What at worst?

9. Potter links "parity of competition" with the concomitant that "merit is the only recognized ground of distinction" in America. Do William L. Miller's educational ideals (p. 224) illustrate this aspect of the myth of equality?

10. Potter notes that the "rapidity of economic change" demands a corresponding "flexibility in the human resources." What, according to Eiseley (p. 299), results from the perpetual need to adapt to new circumstances?

11. According to Galbraith (p. 180), has the "upward mobility" Potter describes slackened in America? What, in Galbraith's theory, guarantees fluidity? Presumably, when would it cease? Does Galbraith see the same stratification of society Potter sees? Do both agree upon the consequences of a man's failure to move upward or to be discontented with the level he has attained?

12. The term *status* or *status seeker* is widely used in America today. Is Potter's meaning of *status* the popular one with which you are familiar? Can you illustrate from your own experience how the emphasis of Americans on mobility causes them to reject the idea of status? How has modern technology diminished the status of the working man? What attempts other than those Potter names are being made today to restore it? (You might consider the prevalence of the term *togetherness*, advertising appeals, the television voices that come "right into your living room" or invite you to be a "guest," etc.)

13. Until the balance is restored between mobility and status—that is, between the promise of self-realization and contented reconciliation to one's place in an organic whole—what may we expect to characterize the American scene? Do you see evidence of Americans' readiness to "escape from freedom"? Consider not only political and economic refuges but the early domestic arrangements Mead (p. 24) describes and the prevalence of seemingly aimless crime and gang activity among American youth.

14. Potter calls status the cornerstone of conservatism. What is the irony of Franklin Roosevelt's role in developing status in America? How is the *conserving* power of status comparable with the "aristocratic" preservation of civil rights about which Viereck writes (p. 324)? Potter says that "some of the ripest recruits for Marxism have been the idealists who loved the doctrine of equality too well." Compare his assertion with Viereck's: "the mass-man is a totalitarian."

15. Does Potter clarify what the new bases of class distinction are now that the old bases are gone? What, conceivably, in American society (besides the "plebeian money-bags 'élite' " Viereck cites) could become the differential for a new hierarchy?

Equal or Better in America

SEYMOUR MARTIN LIPSET

> Seymour Martin Lipset (1922-   ), educated at City College in New York and at Columbia University, was Ford Research Professor of Political Science and Sociology at Yale (1960-61) and is currently Professor of Sociology and Director of the Center for Comparative Research at the University of California at Berkeley. Among his published works are Social Mobility (1959) with Reinhard Bendix, and Political Man (1960).

There has been a quite extraordinary number of books published recently which seek to analyze American society. Among the most widely-read and talked about have been the works of Vance Packard, especially *The Status Seekers; The Power Elite* by C. Wright Mills; *The Organization Man* by William H. Whyte; *Image of America* by R. L. Bruckberger; *America as a Civilization* by Max Lerner; and *The Self-Conscious Society* by Eric Larrabee. These and other works arrive at roughly two sorts of conclusions:

On the one hand, our society is shown to be suffering from elaborate corruption in business practices, and in labor and law enforcement practices; from a growing concentration of business power; from the influences of mass media operated by entertainment tycoons seeking to satisfy the lowest common denominator in popular taste; and from a wasteful expenditure of resources in products designed only for conspicuous consumption and enhancement of social status.

From Columbia University Forum, *Spring 1961, Copyright © 1961 by Columbia University. Reprinted by permission of Columbia University.*

On the other hand, ours is shown to be an affluent, highly democratic society in which the distribution of income, status symbols and opportunities for social mobility is becoming more even-handed all the time; in which tolerance for differences in culture, religion and race is growing; and in which there is an increasing demand for the best in art, literature and music. This outburst of self-criticism and self-analysis has been brought on, I believe, by anxiety over traits and trends which we Americans find hard to reconcile, but which form around two basic American values which are not entirely compatible and never have been. These are Equality and Achievement.

When I say that we value Equality, I mean that we believe all persons must be given respect simply because they are human beings; we believe that the differences between high- and low-status people reflect accidental, and perhaps temporary, variations in position—differences which should not be stressed in social relationships. The emphasis on equality has pervaded much of American culture. It was reflected in the introduction of universal suffrage in America long before it came in other nations; in the fairly consistent and extensive support for a unitary school system at all levels so that all might have a common background; and in the pervasive antagonism to any domination by an elite in the fields of culture, politics or economics. Foreign visitors throughout the nineteenth and twentieth centuries have constantly remarked in their writings on the aggressive equalitarianism of the American people.

Most foreign observers have also been impressed by the value we have put on Achievement—by our belief that everyone, regardless of his background, should try to "succeed." Until the emergence of the Communist states, there had been no other society which compared with America in the emphasis placed on "getting ahead." The strength of the value of Achievement is closely related, of course, to the importance of the value of Equality. The ideal of equality helped to institutionalize the idea that success should be the goal of all, no matter the accidents of birth, class or race. In societies where social status has been more obviously related to inherited qualities, there is necessarily less emphasis on achievement.

Historically, the relation between the forceful American themes of equality and achievement has been close and complex. Tocqueville, for example, noted that equalitarianism maximizes competition among the members of a society, and that the abolition of hereditary privilege opens "the door to universal competition." A detailed analysis of the descriptions of American society written by foreign visitors in the late nineteenth century shows that these commentators generally agreed that "social and economic democracy in America, far from mitigating competition for social status, intensified it." Some European socialists, in particular, were surprised to find American workers so deeply involved in conspicuous consumption—that is, imitating the middle-class style of life—and reported that the very feeling of equality itself presses workers in America to "make a show," since in America a worker could hope to demonstrate his achievements to others.

But if equalitarianism has encouraged competition for status, for advancement, it has also made individuals extremely uncertain about their social position; that is, it makes them uncertain just how much they *have* achieved, and leaves them insecure about their prospects to maintain or pass on their achieved higher status to their children. In fact, many of the foreign visitors who have been so impressed with the equalitarianism of social relations in America, have also suggested that it is precisely because of the emphasis on equality and opportunity that Americans have been more status-conscious than those who live in the more aristocratic societies of Europe. Many have reported that it has been easier for the *nouveaux riches* to gain acceptance in English high society than in American. English observers, from Harriet Martineau and Frances Trollope in the 1830's to James Bryce in the 1870's and Denis Brogan in recent years, have described the way in which the very absence of a legitimate aristocratic tradition, in which social rankings are unquestioned, forces Americans to emphasize status. In a more class-conscious society, everyone is aware of class distinctions and can therefore ignore them on many occasions: they will remain what they are. But in a social system in which such distinctions conflict with the basic belief that all are socially equal, those with a claim to higher status must assert that claim in a variety of ways or lose their right to it.

In all societies committed to equalitarianism, the "successful"—those who have achieved status—will seek to undermine the aims of the equalitarian society in order to retain and pass on their privileged position. This inherent challenge to the abolition of class limits has been checked in part in America by the recurrent victories of the forces of equality in the political order. Much of American political history, as Tocqueville pointed out over 130 years ago, can be interpreted as a struggle between proponents of democratic equality and would-be aristocracies of birth and wealth. In terms of political parties, the linkage of the Democrats to the working-class and lower-status ethnic groups makes them the dominant party—according to the polls, a large majority think of themselves as Democrats and the election registration rolls also indicate a large Democratic advantage. This creates major difficulties for the Republicans, who are identified in the public mind as the party of wealth and big business. In America, to be identified with the common man is a considerable advantage. In recent decades, whenever a majority of voters choose on the basis of *domestic* issues, as they seem to do in state and Congressional elections, they choose the equalitarian Democrats. The Republicans are well aware of their disadvantage in this and seek in their campaign tactics to place the emphasis on other issues, particularly foreign policy matters, or on the personal qualities of candidates.

The ideal of a traditional elite governing our own country is clearly anathema to our equalitarian ethos. This seems to be the opposite of the British situation, in which political observers suggest that the situation which Bagehot described still exists to some extent, that a large segment of the lower strata believe it proper that members of leading families, who are accustomed to ruling, should in fact rule. Thus the Anglo-Canadian political sociologist,

Robert MacKenzie, has suggested that the Tories, unlike the Republicans, are actually advantaged by the fact that they are identified with traditional wealth and authority.

The stress on equality and achievement has also meant that in comparison with, say Britain, America is what one might call a particularly "ends-oriented," rather than "means-oriented," society. In a country which places an extreme emphasis on the importance of success, people are led to feel that the game must be won, no matter what methods are employed to win it. The worst thing that can happen, they feel, is to lose, to be perceived to be a failure. In contrast, the ethos of the more rigidly stratified or aristocratic societies stresses the value of playing the game well, and implies that one must conform to the behavior appropriate to one's station. Such societies usually contain special sets of goals for each stratum within them. And consequently a worker who is the son of a worker is less likely to feel himself a personal failure than would a man with a comparable background in America—the American's values insist on the progressive achievement of higher status for all. This does not mean that people in more rigidly stratified societies such as Britain do not resent having low status, but rather that each man is less likely to feel the need to do something extraordinary about it himself. Deprived people in such countries have rather tended to try to improve their situation collectively through class political movements.

Sociological students of crime have suggested that the much greater prevalence of organized vice and racketeering in America, as compared with that in England and other well-to-do countries of northern Europe, reflects the greater pressure on those with deprived social backgrounds to find individual ways of succeeding when the more legitimate fields are closed to them. Columbia sociologist Daniel Bell has pointed out that the rackets have attracted members of minority ethnic groups who are denied other opportunities. He suggests that the rackets must be seen as one of the principal "ladders of social mobility in American life."

Public opinion studies of situations in which officials have been clearly involved in corrupt activities but still retain widespread electoral support indicate that many Americans will knowingly tolerate such practices if they are accompanied by accomplishments, by getting things done. This is not a new phenomenon; many nineteenth-century foreign travellers were disturbed by the ready public acceptance of those who succeeded regardless of the means they had employed to get ahead. Thus Charles Dickens reports as typical of opinion in the mid-nineteenth-century America which he visited the following comments about a man who had succeeded by dubious methods, but was held in high repute:

> "He is a public nuisance, is he not?"
> "Yes, sir."
> "A convicted liar?"
> "Yes, sir."
> "He has been kicked, cuffed, and caned?"
> "Yes, sir."
> "And he is utterly dishonourable, debased, and profligate?"
> "Yes, sir."
> "In the name of wonder, then, what is his merit?"
> "Well, sir, he is a smart man."

Much of the unique character of the American labor movement may be interpreted in the same way. For workers, as for other Americans, the emphasis on ends, on pecuniary success, combined with the absence of the kind of class consciousness characteristic of less equalitarian societies, has helped to foster acceptance, if not approval, of various devices to permit union officials to "get ahead." In no other country do heads of unions earn as much in relation to the earnings of their members as in the United States. The incomes of major American labor leaders astonish Europeans, who think of such officers as the leaders of a lower class who should reflect the status of their class. The same emphasis on success has meant an acceptance of the right of union officials to be private businessmen, even to be employers. The job of a union leader is regarded by many workers as a means of getting ahead, not as a way of life. There is no reason, therefore, why a union leader should not get as much as he can for himself and his family, as long as he does not injure his members' interests.

The ends-orientation of Americans, as contrasted with the greater stress on means in societies which retain elements of aristocratic norms, is reflected also in the tactics and strategy of the American labor movement as a body. In contrast to most European unions, American unions have had little interest in radical political ideologies or programs which are concerned with changes in the overall social system or the class order. But while ideologically conservative and often narrowly self-interested in their objectives, the American labor movement has in some ways been more violent and militant in its tactics than have the seemingly more Marxist-oriented unions in other industrial nations. American unionists have not been loath in the past to use physical violence, up to and including the dynamiting of buildings, in the struggle for their ends—higher wages and better working conditions. They have employed mobsters in labor disputes (as have employers), and even today they are freer with the use of the strike weapon than any other set of non-Communist Western unionists. American labor has been brutally aggressive, much like American industry.

While I have argued that pressures which come from the interplay of the ideals of Equality and Achievement account for the prevalence of certain forms of deviant or nonconformist behavior, it is also possible that these same basic values contribute to the American over-sensitivity to the judgment of others, to our tendency to conformism and "other-directedness."

It is strange how frequently commentators on the American scene have remarked upon this quality of the national character. Most of the English travellers in America from 1785 to 1835 mentioned "the acute sensitiveness to opinion that the average American revealed." But though most of the nineteenth-century travellers disliked the "other-directed" behavior which they reported, many pointed out that there is an intimate relationship between such behavior and the basic American values—values which the more liberal among them approved. They suggested that it is the very emphasis on equality, the dislike of pretensions to permanent status, that makes Americans so sensitive to the opinions of others. Summarizing the remarks of various British writers on America, an American, John Graham Brooks, wrote some fifty years ago:

> One deeper reason why the English are blunt and abrupt about their rights . . . is because class lines are more sharply drawn there. Within these limits one is likely to develop the habit of demanding his due. He insists on his prerogatives all the more because they are narrowly defined . . . In a democracy everyone at least hopes to get on and up. This ascent depends not upon the favor of a class, but upon the good-will of the whole . . . To make one's self conspicuous and disagreeable is to arouse enmities that block one's way.

But America's is not the first social system to call forth comments suggesting that conformism may stem from a conflict between stratification and equalitarian values. In Plato's *Republic* we find a description of the consequences of equalitarian democratic life that reads as if it came from one of the travellers' reports on America. Plato writes that in such societies fathers fear their sons, schoolteachers flatter their pupils, the old seek to imitate and win the good opinion of the young, and equality prevails in the relations of men and women. And according to Plato, the main result of all these things is to make the souls of the citizens extremely sensitive.

Above all, equalitarianism seems to promote consideration for the rights and feelings of others. This is seen in extreme form in the efforts in schools to avoid hurting the feelings of the less bright or popular students by various practices designed to avoid public invidious distinction. At the same time, it intensifies the strength of the achievement value, which demands that all strive by every means possible to secure or maintain a status above the average. While one may point to the kindliness and idealism of Americans as desired consequences of the central unifying values of the society, one may look on corruption and conformism as unanticipated but inherent consequences of these values. America presses students, ethnic groups, businessmen, union leaders, politicians, and scholars to "innovate"—to get ahead. And then we wonder why there is cheating on exams, rackets among low-status ethnic groups, embezzlement in white-collar jobs, dictatorships in unions, and graft among politicians. Though we deplore the fact that there seems to be too much conformism in the way people behave and speak, we should not forget what many of the nineteenth-century foreign travellers to America knew, that an open and necessarily ambiguous class structure made status-striving, the desire to get ahead, tantamount to conformity. It seems to me that the growing strength of the same values of Achievement and Equality in the Soviet Union has had similar consequences. In Russia, for example, cheating on examinations and bribery of university admissions officers are now something of a scandal, and the upper strata can give Americans lessons in status-seeking, conformist behavior and in conspicuous consumption.

All this is not to say that corruption and conformism are necessary consequences of equalitarian democracy. There is in fact much evidence that America is in other ways becoming a more moral and less conformist society. Our concern with Equality is reflected in the field of race relations; as Gunnar Myrdal pointed out twenty years ago, the most important single argument of the Negroes is the fact that their second-class citizenship violates a basic postulate of the American Creed. The successful efforts to spread and equalize educational opportunities are clearly linked to the belief in equal opportunity.

Through much of American history, those advocating public education argued that such measures were essential to making equality a reality. And by the mid-Nineteen-Fifties, American education crossed two historic benchmarks: a majority of all high school students now actually graduate, and a majority of such graduates go on to institutions of higher learning. The equalization of educational opportunities has meant that an ever-increasing proportion of the population is now exposed to, in Eric Larrabee's words, that "modest range of cultural experience that the arts represent." Book sales have increased remarkably; the annual expenditure has almost doubled since 1950. Popular magazines have become better. According to C. J. McNaspy, the Metropolitan Museum of Art in New York had almost four million visitors in 1959, twice the figure at the Louvre, and three times the number to visit the Metropolitan twenty years earlier. *The Times Literary Supplement* is rightly impressed by the presence of over one thousand community symphony orchestras in the United States; there were less than 100 in 1920.

America is not a simple country to understand. Jennie Lee, Aneurin Bevan's wife, and a British Left Socialist leader in her own right, once wrote of her despair that after five trips to this country she felt it was impossible to "get any coherent picture of America . . . And the more Americans explained America to me, the more blurred the picture became." What is confusing is the fact that the institutions and practices of this country fluctuate between the two related values, which are also polarities, Equality and Achievement. Tocqueville could see the latter value as causing Americans to shun public affairs as "a troublesome impediment, which diverts them from their occupation and business," yet he could also call attention to the amazing propensity of Americans to form voluntary associations of all kinds to achieve socially desirable ends. The seeming contradiction between the emphasis on success, and the felt acceptance even by the very successful of the value of Equality can be seen in some measure in American patterns of philanthropic giving. Foreign travellers in the nineteenth century noted this trait to give away wealth, long before there were income and inheritance taxes.

It is easy to discuss American culture from an integrated positive or negative point of view as some of the books mentioned in the beginning of this essay do: to stress the extent to which it has become a corrupt, irresponsible mass society characterized by a high degree of conformity; or conversely, to emphasize the extent to which it has expanded the possibilities for all to partake in the "higher life," by increasing access to the preconditions for individual freedom and self-expression—greater education, more leisure from petty routine tasks, and greater economic security. To recognize that many of the social supports of what we like and dislike are often rooted in identical institutions and values is difficult. But such recognition does not mean we must passively accept the bad because of its ties to the good. Rather it implies the need for a constant struggle to preserve and extend these positive institutions, for only through the efforts to maintain and extend Equality have the corrupting effects of the necessary emphasis on Achievement been prevented from dominating the society.

PROBLEMS FOR WRITING AND DISCUSSION

1. In what ways, according to Lipset, are Equality and Achievement incompatible, and what are the effects of this incompatibility on Americans?

2. Compare the effects Lipset describes of "aggressive equalitarianism" on achievement with those Potter describes (p. 328). What effects of uncertain status other than those Potter cites does Lipset note? Do both writers see good as well as bad effects proceeding from the tension between the American ideals of Equality and Achievement? Explain.

3. How does Lipset interpret the appeal of the two major political parties in America? What does he see as the key to American political history?

4. "In America, to be identified with the common man is a considerable advantage." Did Henry Ford (p. 143) identify himself with the common man? Did Roosevelt, according to Potter? Compare this identification with the one Galbraith (p. 180) says members of the New Class make.

5. Explain Lipset's use of the terms *ends-oriented* and *means-oriented*. Discuss "ends-oriented" activities in politics, business, and education, substantiating Lipset's examples with your own.

6. How is the "ends-orientation" of Americans reflected in the American labor movement? Are Lipset's remarks about the labor movement in general verified by Eric Hoffer's views (p. 175) on the workingman in particular?

7. Lipset uses a term David Riesman has made popular in America: *other-directedness*. What is meant by it?

8. What, according to Lipset, has been the effect of equalitarianism on education in America? Compare what he says with what Wylie (p. 204) and William Miller (p. 224) say on the same subject.

9. Compare Boorstin's ideas (p. 5) on American "over-sensitiveness to the judgment of others" with those of Lipset.

10. How does Lipset explain the high incidence of crime and rackets in America? How does Potter (p. 328)?

11. What, according to Lipset, do the American and communist societies have in common? How do these societies differ from those in which class distinctions are traditional and taken for granted? What difference in point of attack is there between the "deprived people" of Britain and of America, for example? Does Potter make the same observation?

12. In "societies which retain elements of aristocratic norms," says Lipset, labor movements are often propelled by "radical ideologies" that seek to overturn the existing order. Why is American labor more "conservative"? How, in the light of Lipset's essay, are the "aristocratic norms" Viereck (p. 324) advocates typically American? How is Viereck's fear of "mass-man" typical? How is Lipset's conclusion in his final three sentences typically American?

Lincoln and the Declaration

HARRY V. JAFFA

Harry V. Jaffa (1918-) has been teaching political science at The Ohio State University since 1951. Among his major publications are two books on Lincoln: Crisis of the House Divided *(1959) and, with co-editor Robert W. Johannsen,* Speeches and Writings of Lincoln and Douglas in the Ohio Campaign of 1859. *In addition, he is at work on two more books on Lincoln, one dealing with Lincoln's term in Congress during the Mexican War and the other with the Civil War as the culmination of "fourscore and seven years."*

Lincoln firmly believed that the spread of slavery had to be halted by a principle that treated slavery as a wrong *everywhere*. In this Lincoln may seem doctrinaire or opportunistic, as he seems to Douglas' defenders. Yet no one was, in general, more prone than Lincoln to follow that dictate of prudence, by which one attempts always to remove evils without shocking the prejudices that support them—allowing time and circumstances rather to wear down the prejudices. No one was more intolerant of mere "pernicious abstractions" that set people by the ears for no practical ends. But Douglas' doctrine of letting the people of a territory decide whether or not they wanted slavery involved the specific repeal of the Missouri Compromise, a compromise that, in the minds and hearts of a great majority of the North, canonized a great national principle: the principle that, wherever the national territory had not already been infected with the virus of slavery, it should not be

From The Anchor Review No. 2, 1957. Copyright 1957 by Doubleday & Company. Reprinted by permission of the author.

permitted to enter. This principle was merely a corollary of that supreme axiom of our national existence: "That all men are created equal." To Lincoln, the repeal of the Missouri Compromise involved the repudiation of the Declaration of Independence.

What the Declaration of Independence meant to Lincoln is difficult for us, who are no longer accustomed to live among sacred things, to appreciate. It must suffice for the present to say that for Lincoln it embodied the principle of distributive justice: that for the sake of which our Union and our laws existed and were instituted. The key to Lincoln's policy must be found, above all, in the relation of this principle to the Constitution and the Union.

"Our government," Lincoln said over and over, "rests upon public opinion. Whoever can change public opinion can change the government practically just so much." What Lincoln understood by public opinion, however, was not what Dr. Gallup tries to measure. Over and again, in the debates against Douglas, Lincoln said: ". . . he who molds public sentiment goes deeper than he who enacts statutes and pronounces decisions. He makes statutes or decisions possible or impossible . . ." But public opinion is not, primarily, opinion about individual statutes or decisions: "Public opinion, on any subject, always has a 'central idea' from which all its minor thoughts radiate." The central idea at the founding of our government, from which all minor thoughts radiated, was "the equality of all men." The repudiation of this "central idea" meant to Lincoln not merely the possible opening of the Nebraska Territory to slavery, but the changing of the entire basis of our national existence. In Aristotelian terms, it meant the substitution of a new end—a different conception of the ultimate political good—for the original one. The following is perhaps Lincoln's classic statement of what our central national political idea meant. It is from his speech on the Dred Scott decision:

> Chief Justice Taney, in his opinion in the Dred Scott case, admits that the language of the Declaration is broad enough to include the whole human family, but he and Judge Douglas argue that the authors of that instrument did not intend to include Negroes, by the fact that they did

not at once actually place them on an equality with the whites. Now this grave argument comes to just nothing at all, by the other fact, that they did not at once, or ever afterwards, *actually place all white people on an equality with one another*. And this is the staple argument of both the Chief Justice and the Senator, for doing this obvious violence to the plain, unmistakable language of the Declaration. I think the authors of that notable instrument intended to include all men, but they did not intend to declare all men are equal in all respects. They did not mean to say all were equal in color, size, intellect, moral developments, or social capacity. They defined with tolerable distinctness, in what respects they did consider all men created equal—equal in "certain inalienable rights, among which are life, liberty, and the pursuit of happiness". This they said, and this they meant. They did not mean to assert the obvious untruth, that all were then actually enjoying that equality, nor yet that they were able to confer it immediately upon them. In fact they had no power to confer such a boon. They meant simply to declare the right, so that the enforcement of it might follow as fast as circumstances should permit. They meant to set up a standard maxim for free society, which could be familiar to all, and revered by all; constantly looked to, constantly labored for, and even though never perfectly attained, constantly approximated, and thereby constantly spreading and deepening its influence, and augmenting the happiness and value of life to all people of all colors everywhere.

"A standard maxim," "familiar to all," "revered by all," "constantly looked to": it is impossible not to recognize the similarity of expression to that of the greatest of all lawgivers:

And these words, which I command thee this day, shall be in thine heart:
And thou shalt teach them diligently unto thy children, and shalt talk of them when thou sittest in thine house, and when thou walkest by the way, and when thou liest down, and when thou risest up.

It was impossible to place the slavery question on the footing Douglas wished to put it without repudiating the Declaration of Independence—or, which came to the same thing, without caricaturing it into Douglas' interpretation: so that "all men are created equal" was said to mean that "all British subjects on this continent were equal to British subjects born and residing in Great Britain." For whatever private expressions of repugnance to slavery Douglas' biographers may dig up, the fact remains that all his public expressions were calculated to gain acceptance of the proposition that slavery was a matter of moral indifference. This, to Lincoln, meant inscribing new words in the heart of America, in place of the old ones.

Douglas stumped up and down the country, asserting his humanity by saying that "we ought to extend to the Negro race, and to all other dependent races, all the privileges, and all the immunities which they can exercise consistently with the safety of society . . ." From this Lincoln would not have dissented. But, in answer to the question, what are those rights and privileges? Douglas answered: "Each state, and each territory, must decide that for itself: We of Illinois have decided for ourselves. We tried slavery, kept it up for twelve years *and, finding that it was not profitable,* we abolished it *for that reason.*" This, as Lincoln repeatedly charged—not the safety of society, but the profitability of slavery—was to be made the measure of the Negro's rights. Whether or not Lincoln was just in ascribing a positive zeal for slavery to Douglas, he was undoubtedly right in implying that there was no practical difference between a position of alleged neutrality and one of positive zeal. The following is from Lincoln's Peoria speech:

> *This declared indifference, but, as I must think, covert real zeal for the spread of slavery, I can not but hate. I hate it because of the monstrous injustice of slavery itself. I hate it because it deprives our republican example of its just influence in the world—enables the enemies of free institutions, with plausibility, to taunt us as hypocrites—causes the real friends of freedom to doubt our sincerity, and especially because it forces so many really good men amongst ourselves into an open war with the very principles of civil liberty—criticizing the Declaration of Independence, and insisting that there is no right principle of action but self-interest.*

According to Lincoln, the unique value of the American Union lay in its incorporating a moral principle: change the principle by virtue of which the Union constitutes a moral association of a certain kind, and you have dissolved the Union. Lincoln did, at one time, say that he would consent even to the extension of slavery, rather than see the Union dissolved, just as he would consent to any great evil in order to avoid a greater one. What he meant, however, was that he would consent to practical compromises, such as those of 1820 and 1850, which did not imply more than a readjustment of the *modus vivendi*. But the compromise Douglas offered the southern radicals in 1854 was not one in which a lesser evil was accepted, but one in which what had heretofore been regarded as evil was now acknowledged not to be an evil at all. If such an acknowledgment was once made, there would be no grounds for resisting the evil in the future. As Lincoln correctly predicted, such an appetite as that which Douglas appeased grows by what it feeds upon. Before the Repeal of the Missouri Compromise all the southern leaders had asked for was acknowledgment of their rightful claims in the national territory. Soon thereafter, they were demanding congressional protection for slavery in that territory. And, as Lincoln forcefully pointed out, if there was no moral difference between taking slaves and hogs to Kansas, if both were equally property, there was no moral reason why both should not be bought on the cheapest market—and as slaves might be bought cheapest on the coast of Africa, he was certain that demands for revival of the slave trade would also soon be made. Once the premises were firmly fixed, it was only a question of time until the public mind could be brought to accept all the consequences. The only point at which resistance to all these consequences could be made, Lincoln believed, was at the point which established their premises. This was Douglas' Nebraska Bill.

Lincoln's attitude toward this whole problem is, again, suggestive of one of the central themes of Aristotle's *Politics*. Aristotle asks, by virtue of what is it that the identity of a *polis* is established? It is not because men inhabit a certain place, Aristotle says, because a wall could be built around the Peloponnesus—but that would not make those so embraced fellow citizens. Similarly, it is not any particular group of citizens; for the citizens who comprise a city are always changing, like the water in a river. A *polis,* Aristotle says, is a partnership or association, a partnership in a *politeia*. And the *politeia* is the form of the *polis*, as the soul is the form of the body. Therefore the *polis* is no longer the same when the *politeia* changes, any more than a chorus is the same when the persons who have comprised a tragic chorus now constitute a comic chorus. I have had to use the Greek word *politeia*, because it is usually translated *constitution*, as in the expression *American Constitution*. But the Constitution is a set of laws, albeit fundamental laws. However, the *politeia* is not the laws, but is rather the animating principle of the laws, by virtue of which the laws are laws of a certain kind. Consequently, Aristotle says, "the laws should be laid down, and all people do lay them down, to suit the *politeiai* and not the *politeiai* to suit the laws." This relationship is beautifully expressed in a fragmentary writing of Lincoln's in which he draws an analogy based on a verse in the Book of Proverbs: "A word fitly spoken is like apples of gold in pictures of silver":

> Without the Constitution and the Union, we could not have attained the result; but even these are not the cause of our great prosperity. There is something back of these, entwining itself more closely about the human heart. That something is the principle of "Liberty to all"—the principle that clears the path for all—gives hope to all—and, by consequence, enterprise and industry to all. The expression of that principle, in our Declaration of Independence, was most happy, and fortunate . . . The assertion of that principle, at that time, was the word "fitly spoken," which has proved an "apple of gold" to us. The Union, and the Constitution, are the pictures of silver, subsequently framed around it. The picture was made, not to conceal, or destroy the apple; but to adorn and preserve it. The picture was made for the apple—not the apple for the picture.

To preserve that apple of gold Lincoln joined battle with Douglas.

There is one thing more that must be emphasized in order to understand why Lincoln believed such a fight was so essential in 1858. Lincoln's concern with world freedom has appeared in many of the passages I have read. And, of course, no one who has heard or read the Gettysburg Address can ever forget it. Lincoln did, indeed, believe that our Union was the "last, best hope of earth" that men might live under free institutions. Whether the political order Lincoln believed to be the best, and freest, was, or is, the best and freest possible, need not be disputed for present purposes. Few, however (outside the Iron Curtain) would doubt that the future of mankind's freedom did then, as it does now, rest largely with this Union. Lincoln never felt that any price was too high to pay to preserve the Union. He might have doubted this had the welfare of Americans alone been at stake. But to Lincoln the ultimate responsibility of American statesmanship was always, not to Americans, but to the world. Standing in Independence Hall, Philadelphia, in 1861, on his way to take office, Lincoln made it clear that he would make no concession, even to save what men might call the Union, that involved a repudiation of the Declaration of Independence. For, Lincoln implied, the Declaration of Independence, although proclaiming the *rights* of humanity as the just basis of every political order, laid upon the first nation dedicated to the justice it proclaimed a *duty* that took precedence of every right. In his words at that time, the Declaration of Independence "gave liberty not alone to the people of this country, but hope to all the world, for all future time. It was that which gave promise that in due time the weights would be lifted from the shoulders of all men, and that all should have an equal chance."

PROBLEMS FOR WRITING AND DISCUSSION

1. Why does Jaffa say that we are no longer accustomed to "live among sacred things"?

2. What did Lincoln mean by "public opinion"? Does his view differ from that of Lippmann (p. 381)?

3. How does Grierson's essay (p. 115) reinforce Jaffa's analysis of Lincoln's views?

4. Summarize Lincoln's concept of equality as drawn from the Declaration of Independence. Does it differ from Potter's (p. 328) and Lipset's (p. 348) views of what equality means to Americans? Is Viereck (p. 324) in his

discussion of civil rights close to Lincoln in the discussion of rights Jaffa quotes?

5. On what basis did Douglas discuss slavery? On what basis did Lincoln oppose him? Lincoln said at Gettysburg: "Four score and seven years ago our fathers brought forth on this continent a new nation, conceived in liberty and dedicated to the proposition that all men are created equal." To what in that sentence would Douglas have objected?

6. Lincoln and Douglas, both successful politicians, represent two divergent tendencies in American politics throughout its history. Which type has been the more effective in achieving its ends? Were Lincoln and Douglas (to use Lipset's terms) "ends-oriented" or "means-oriented"? Explain.

7. Discuss Jaffa's use of Aristotle's *Politics*. What central point does Jaffa make about the word *politeiai*? How is Lincoln's discussion of "apples of gold" analogous to Aristotle's ideas?

8. Is the duty Lincoln saw for Americans different from the duty Stevenson (p. 478) sees?

9. Do you feel as Lincoln felt that "the ultimate responsibility of American statesmanship" is "not to Americans, but to the world"? Do events in American history indicate that since the Civil War American statesmanship has served our "self-interest" or the "world"?

10. Americans have been accused of not tending to their own business and of trying to impose upon the world their way of life. Does "our central national political idea" make an assumption about the way all men should, ideally, live? Is the American Union still the "last, best hope of earth"?

11. What is the effect of comparing Lincoln's phrases with those of "the greatest of all lawgivers"? Lincoln believed that because it contained a "standard maxim for free society" the "language of the Declaration is broad enough to include the whole human family." Yet Jaffa notes that rather than see the Union dissolved Lincoln would have tolerated the extension of slavery. Why? Today we face the proposition that, from the American point of view, one world cannot exist half slave, half free. To preserve the human community as a whole, would you tolerate the extension of "slavery"?

The American Immigrant and Ideologies

OSCAR HANDLIN

> *Oscar Handlin (1915-) was born in Brooklyn, New York, went to Brooklyn College, then moved on for his doctorate to Harvard, where he has taught American social history since 1939. Coincidentally, Handlin directs the Center to Study the History of Liberty in America. In addition to editing* The Library of American Biography *and* The Harvard Guide to American History *(1954), he has written a great many historical works.* The Uprooted *(1951), which received the Pulitzer Prize, is perhaps the best known.*

That systems of ideas have power we know. They can move men to action and can influence the destinies of whole peoples. Yet the means by which they are communicated and spread are not often understood; and the question of means may, in this context, be critical.

Consideration of the problem of the diffusion of ideologies has been shaped largely by the point of view of the intellectuals who are most directly and most consciously concerned with it. The spread of ideas, from their perspective, is a process that operates through argument and conviction. Conceptions are examined and compared by logical men who choose among them. An idea thus moves through the conquest of opinion. This is the guiding premise of our efforts at propaganda and information.

It is well recognized, of course, that the process of conviction is not altogether rational; the past century has made abundantly clear the necessity for taking account of the nonrational aspects of

---

From "The American Immigrant and Ideologies," by Oscar Handlin, Confluence, *Vol. 2, No. 3 (September 1953). Reprinted by permission of the author.*

human behavior. Nevertheless, discussion of the problem still rests largely on the assumption that ideologies are spread by some sort of debate, as a result of which men come to believe in the superior merit of one set of ideas over another.

This assumption conditions much of the current concern over the ideological aspects of the present world conflict. The necessity of a war for men's minds—the very phrase itself—reflects the notion that persuasion and the will to believe are the primary elements in the acceptance or rejection of an ideology.

Whatever its validity for the intellectuals, this assumption is certainly questionable when it comes to the broader strata of society which are the stakes of today's war of ideas. In the conflict now in progress the minds at issue are not simply, nor even primarily, the minds of the intellectuals, but those of men whose most deeply held beliefs are acquired not by argument and conviction, but by inherited tradition. It would be deceptive to think of the diffusion of ideologies among them as the product of the same process that animates the intellectuals.

The vast bodies of peasants throughout Europe and the Near and Far East who are only now being touched by the dominant strains of modern politics are an example. These people existed under ways of life fixed for generations, and integral with those ways of life were ideologies millennial in their firmness. It is shortsighted in the extreme to regard current alterations in their modes of thinking as if those were induced by any specific or immediate system of propaganda. If the ideologies of Russian or Indian peasants have shifted in the last half century, it was not through the impact of doctrines imparted through books or speeches, but through some deeper change in the structure of their societies. Marx in Russia or India is but vaguely the recognizable figure of the German nineteenth-century socialist.

The anthropologists whose work brought them into immediate contact with variant systems of beliefs have been most sensitive to the dimensions of the problem. Most often they have been disposed to regard ideologies as inextricably linked to the social and cultural milieu of the group involved, and therefore not subject to ready change. Some anthropologists, indeed, have accepted a kind of relativism on the basis of which every people's system of beliefs is deemed appropriate by the mere fact of its existence.

From this point of view alterations are almost impossible of achievement, and the diffusion of ideologies is a slow glacial process that can be only slightly affected by policy. In general the anthropologists have been inclined to recommend that the social and cultural structure of a society, including its ideology, be accepted without direct efforts toward immediate alteration.

Such a course has obvious liabilities as far as policy is concerned. To put it most concretely and most bluntly, it surrenders the hope of transforming the basic value systems of the great masses of people who must be our allies in the near future. It involves the incalculable risk of materially strengthening groups whose ideas are fundamentally divergent from our own, and who would therefore in the future make unreliable partners. If it is not possible to spread the notions of democracy to men brought up in a patriarchal or traditional society, have we any assurance that the collaborators our aid now brings us will ever acquire an interest in our ultimate objectives?

Without in the least minimizing the real difficulties involved it may yet be that the problem is soluble. The American experience offers suggestive clues as to the nature of an operation in the present, for the essence of that experience was the spread of a complex of ideas to large groups of men initially hostile to it.

The American ideology, general to the nation despite the diversity of its people, is not simply a common heritage in the narrow sense; the bulk of Americans today do not have a common heritage. The antecedents of that ideology lie back in the eighteenth century, but the process by which it reached the mass of the population was slow, and extended through the nineteenth and early twentieth centuries. In the course of diffusion it encountered great resistance, with the outcome often uncertain. Comprehension of the factors that enabled it to take hold may throw light on some of the crises we must anticipate in the near future.

Let our point of approach be the 1830's in the United States. In that decade there could be said to be a well-defined American ideology, compounded from the doctrines of the eighteenth-century enlightenment, from the forms American religion took in its development from Calvinism, and from the terms in which the descendants of Europeans explained their contact with the wilderness. The elements of that ideology were an implicit acceptance of the idea of progress and of man's perfectibility, a firm faith in the power of reason to transform the world, and the confidence that evil was a product of defective human institutions that could be rectified by human effort. The external expressions of this ideology took form in the years that followed and played a significant part in the life of the nation. On one level they included the certainty that the individual, by his striving, could assure himself of his proper goal, mundane success; on another they included the conviction that society could be reformed by organized movements to eliminate its imperfections. These ideas and the overt forms in which they were embodied were involved in all the crucial issues of the next hundred years.

In the century after 1830 some thirty-five million immigrants came to the United States. Among them were a handful of intellectuals who brought with them ideas close to those they discovered in the New World. But the great, the overwhelming, mass of newcomers were peasants displaced from the soil their families had inhabited for generations. They carried with them ideologies that had been firmly fixed for centuries and that were altogether different from those prevalent here. The peasants had no conception of the meaning of progress, reason was to them a feeble instrument, and evil was an omnipresent and conscious force of the universe. By contrast with the Americans these people were likely to be pessimists; their reliance was upon the power of faith and religion as a means to salvation, for they believed that the world in which they lived was not one that was capable of true reformation, much less perfection. Instead their earthly existence was only the prelude to a more significant life that began after death.

Yet the newcomers became a part of American society in the fullest sense; they did not remain sojourners, but lost their strangeness as a process of accommodation made familiar the ways of life and thought in their new home. Furthermore, they acquired the privileges of citizenship and before long were able to act as conscious and direct participants in the politics of the country.

The old Americans accepted democracy as a matter of course. Since man was essentially good and reasonable, he was capable of guiding his own actions in affairs of state as in other aspects of his life. As he cast his ballot he made the choices most in accord with his own interest and with the interests of the whole society. For the peasant, by contrast, reason was fallible and man imbued with evil, and democracy was therefore a rank delusion. Each individual occupied that status in life to which he had been called, and it made no more sense that a husbandman should vote on foreign policy than that a ruler should plow. More concretely, nothing in their experience in the Old World had prepared these people for the conception of citizenship they discovered in the United States; nor had they any inkling of the means by which they themselves would come to be the governors rather than the governed. Yet these peasants, as removed from political democracy as their counterparts in Egypt or India today, within a remarkably short time became habituated to the instruments and manners of popular control of government.

That happy outcome was not simply the product of persuasion or education. The immigrants did not accept the new ideas as a result of argument and debate; indeed, the effort to thrust strange conceptions upon them evoked only stubborn conservatism. This was a lesson painfully and invariably learned by the political reformers who occasionally accompanied the peasants in the migration to the United States.

The small groups of political malcontents from Ireland, Germany, Italy, Poland, and eastern Europe who drifted to the New World in the nineteenth century were members of the middle classes moved by political grievances against the undemocratic governments under which they lived. They had been far removed from the peasants at home and only approached them through the bonds of common language and common situation in the United States.

The émigrés conceived their role to be simply that of educating and leading a peasant following. They were, after all, educated, or at least literate, and capable of dealing with the native Americans on terms of relative equality. Furthermore, their ideas were already closer to those most prevalent here, and were expressed in the common nineteenth-century language of democracy, liberalism, and nationalism. The very motives for their emigration were such as to attract universal sympathy. Yet, in the decades of adjustment, the émigrés discovered they were not capable of supplying the mass leadership. Their most hopeful schemes came to nought in the face of the apathy or hostility of those they presumed to guide. They were no more capable of arguing the peasants over to their beliefs in the New World than in the Old.

Paradoxically, in fact, the political refugees remained less at home in the United States than other immigrants. The émigrés were often insensitive to the shadings of difference between their ideas and those they encountered in America. Their vision was limited by the ideals for which they had fought in Europe, and often those proved but slightly relevant to the problems of the New World. Their situation as a minority within a minority in the United States constrained them to attempt to exercise control by means which were sometimes undemocratic and often self-frustrating. In the end they were driven to a succession of intellectual and political compromises in the effort to hold their following. Only the very exceptional individual among them—such a man as Carl Schurz—was able to locate himself in a pattern of American ideas and values; and he did so by decisively fixing his sights on this side of the Atlantic. On the other hand, the great mass of immigrants, once they discovered they had access to power, learned to work toward a definition of their own interest and toward a perception of the ideological necessities of their situation.

The political involvement of the immigrants began at the comprehensible local level; while the issues of national policy still lacked meaning, those of the urban ward or rural county had a direct relevance to industrial laborers or subsistence farmers. These folk sought protection from the government against the hazards of the economic and social order, substitutes, as it were, for the traditional communal safeguards of the family and village that no longer existed in America. Their ideal was thus a policy of patronage.

Through much of the nineteenth century they found themselves in opposition to the dominant currents of American liberalism, in which laissez-faire elements were strong and which held to the ideal of a polity of regulation. The immigrants were therefore likely to find attractive the leadership of bosses and other political adventurers who could make meaningful promises to them.

The inadequacy of favors as the basis for political decision became increasingly evident, however, to the immigrants and, more so, to their children. After 1890 there was a search for more generalized concepts of political action to replace the free food basket of the ward boss. There followed a succession of experiments with labor and social legislation from which emerged the ideal of a polity of welfare, an ideal which could engage the interest and the loyalty of the immigrants and their children.

In the process American liberals discovered new dimensions to their conceptions of state action. By the 1930's such terms as "progressive" and "reform," which fifty years earlier had evoked no response from the immigrants, were now meaningful embodiments of their own hopes. And, although the connotations of the terms had changed enough to permit the kind of action these people desired, they rested still on an ideological base of optimism, progress, rationality, and reform. The change had meanwhile won the immigrants over to the basic ideology. Comparable developments in other aspects of American life illustrated the same kind of mediation.

Most critical in the pattern of adjustment was the attitude of the natives. Through most of the nineteenth century they approached the immigrants with confidence that any individual was capable of being an American and exercising the privileges of citizenship. At no point was there any serious disposition to limit political rights; indeed, in many states for a time citizenship was not even a prerequisite for voting. These practices reflected the assumption that any man, whatever his background and previous ideology, simply by exposure to American life became American.

This belief was perhaps naïve. On occasion bitter conflicts followed disillusion when newcomers, given the powers of citizens, acted not as other Americans, but in accord with their own divergent ideas. There were crises, for instance, in the 1850's and in the 1890's that produced short-lived nativist movements. In both cases the objective was to limit the political power of the newcomers. Both movements quickly collapsed. They failed partly because they were contradictory to the very democratic ideology they aimed to preserve. They failed also because the immigrants were accommodating themselves to American democracy and in other crises demonstrated their capacity for dealing with the real problems of life in the United States. Apart from these brief aberrations Americans clung to their faith in the open quality of their Americanism, except for the interval when racism clouded that faith.

Precisely that faith spread the American ideology through the great mass of the immigrants. The fact that they were treated as citizens capable of acting deliberately in the affairs of the nation to which they had come was a challenge to which the newcomers responded by so acting. That created a situation in which the ideology they encountered, at first strange, became ever more meaningful, not through argument, but through its appropriateness to the way of life in which they were involved. Furthermore, the fluidity of the ideology and of the society persuaded the immigrants that their own hopes and needs could be encompassed within the existing order. Inherited ideas then lost their relevance as the transplanted peasants absorbed the new ideology through having lived it in practice.

It was critical, of course, that these peasants were transplanted, that they moved into the society the ideology of which they absorbed. The problem is certainly different and more difficult when it comes to spreading the same ideology to peasants still fixed in their own society and still surrounded by the institutions and forms that support a divergent, indeed hostile, system of ideas. Yet it is possible to suggest a similar process of diffusion even under these conditions.

In the nineteenth century the same spirit that convinced Americans it was safe to leave their gates unguarded and to admit to the United States whoever chose to come there also drove them to an aggressive effort to spread their ideas to every corner of the world. The most important expression of this desire was the overseas missionary movement, which took form shortly after 1800 and by mid-century had carried bands of men and women to the remotest ends of the earth—to the jungles of India and Siam, along the coast of Africa, and deep down the rivers of South America.

The motives which sustained this movement were complex. But its impulses were truly popular, springing from some deep urgings of the American spirit. The movement drew its strength not from a handful of wealthy individuals, but from the contributions of thousands of relatively poor people. In the farmhouses of rural New England the housewives contributed each their mite to the salvation of the unknown souls in the outer darkness. They did so because it was an intimate concern of theirs that hundreds of millions of people remained unenlightened.

It is difficult now to assess the success of the missions. Yet there is considerable evidence of their genuine influence in many parts of the world. That influence was not the product of the particular theological doctrines the missionaries bore with them. It was, rather, the product of the diffusion of a way of life. The missionaries took with them more than tracts and Bibles; they carried with them also agricultural techniques, clothing, and the methods of modern medicine and hygiene. To the people among whom they came these were all inextricably bound together. As men learned to live the round of life the missionary practiced, they accepted also his ideology.

The weakness of the missions was a product of the inflexibility that limited their ability to adjust to the social and cultural needs of the peoples among whom they were planted. Yet they enjoyed enough openness of approach to exercise perceptible influence throughout the world.

There may be in these American experiences a clue to the general problem. The simple erection of steel mills and the building of railroads will no more bring democracy with them than will the export of slogans through the most skillful propaganda. Our ideas will have meaning and relevance throughout the world only as they explain a way of life. The diffusion of the ideology is thus bound in with diffusion of the way of life, in the fullest sense.

There are indications enough that men everywhere are prepared to accept both. If American movies are attractive, if *Reader's Digest* shows a remarkable penetrative power, even if Coca-Cola replaces the traditional wines, those are all signs of that readiness.

It is true that little in the background or antecedents of the peasant people has prepared them for either the way of life or the ideology. But just as men who have never seen the sea still recognize it at the first glimpse, so too those without a previous conception of democracy know it for the good it is at the first experience of it.

In that context the earlier adjustment of the millions of immigrants who were peasants, like those we seek now to influence, is instructive. For the immigrants also did not know in advance what they sought in the New World, other than a refuge from the Old, yet here they learned to recognize the worth of what they found.

Like them, the multitudes now who know only the unhappiness of their present situation may find in the new ideology and the new way of life a new "America" that will give them the dignity that is worth fighting for, and make of them the most valuable of allies.

PROBLEMS FOR WRITING AND DISCUSSION

1. Handlin declares that "the bulk of Americans today do not have a common heritage." *Did* the bulk of Americans in 1830? Do you think the

relative homogeneity of population (in the formed states) in 1845 may have facilitated Lincoln's task? Why?

2. What are the elements of American ideology that Handlin enumerates as already formulated by 1830 which have persisted to the present (and which have been discussed by writers you have read so far in this book)?

3. Name the outstanding ideological differences between the "natives" of 1830 and the immigrant groups which settled in America during the nineteenth and twentieth centuries. How does Handlin explain the failure of reforming attempts by political émigrés of countries from which these groups came?

4. Does Kazin's essay (p. 64) illustrate what Handlin describes as the "process of accommodation" by which these groups were "Americanized"? How did the naïve confidence of the natives that "any individual was capable of being an American" assist and accelerate this process?

5. Today, is spreading American ideology "by exposure" as simple as it was in the past? What major difficulty does Handlin note? By analogy, with what precedent does he predicate the possibility of success?

6. What fallacy, as Handlin sees it, inheres in the expression "a war for men's minds"?

7. Why does Handlin say that neither the building of steel mills (in itself) nor the export of propaganda will effectually win converts to American thought?

8. What does Handlin mean by the anthropologists' "relativism"? Why, for the making of policy, does it have liabilities?

9. Thousands of Americans, Handlin says, animated by a concern "that hundreds of millions of people remained unenlightened," contributed their "mite" to foreign missions. Does Handlin himself display missionary zeal?

10. Handlin has faith that "at the first experience" of democracy those who have hitherto been unable to conceive of it will "know it for the good it is." Yet he says that the diffusion of ideology is "bound in with diffusion of the way of life." Does he not, then, agree with the anthropologists? Does he share the "relativism" and disinterestedness of the anthropologists? Explain.

11. Does Handlin, in adhering to "the hope of transforming the basic value systems of the great masses of people who must be our allies in the near future," tacitly assume (as Lincoln did) that America represents the "last, best hope of earth"? Explain.

2. The Political Bands

The Democratic Malady

WALTER LIPPMANN

> Walter Lippmann (1889-   ), a distinguished journalist, was educated at Harvard and not long after graduation became one of the original editors of The New Republic when it was founded in 1914. He resigned two years later to serve as assistant to the Secretary of War, rejoined the magazine in 1919 for two more years, then left to become editor of the New York World. In 1931 he began to write a syndicated column on national affairs that still appears regularly. Among the better known of his many books are Public Opinion (1922), A Preface to Morals (1929), The Good Society (1937), and The Public Philosophy (1955).

The unhappy truth is that the prevailing public opinion has been destructively wrong at the critical junctures. The people have imposed a veto upon the judgments of informed and responsible officials. They have compelled the governments, which usually knew what would have been wiser, or was necessary, or was more expedient, to be too late with too little, or too long with too much, too pacifist in peace and too bellicose in war, too neutralist or appeasing in negotiation or too intransigent. Mass opinion has acquired mounting power in this century. It has shown itself to be a dangerous master of decision when the stakes are life and death.

The errors of public opinion in these matters have a common characteristic. The movement of opinion is slower than the movement of events. Because of that, the cycle of subjective sentiments

---
From The Public Philosophy by Walter Lippmann, by permission of Little, Brown and Co.—Atlantic Monthly Press. Copyright 1955, by Walter Lippmann.

on war and peace is usually out of gear with the cycle of objective developments. Just because they are mass opinions there is an inertia in them. It takes much longer to change many minds than to change a few. It takes time to inform and to persuade and to arouse large scattered varied multitudes of persons. So before the multitude have caught up with the old events there are likely to be new ones coming up over the horizon with which the government should be preparing to deal. But the majority will be more aware of what they have just caught up with near at hand than with what is still distant and in the future. For these reasons the propensity to say No to a change of course sets up a compulsion to make mistakes. The opinion deals with a situation which no longer exists.

When the world wars came, the people of the liberal democracies could not be aroused to the exertions and the sacrifices of the struggle until they had been frightened by the opening disasters, had been incited to passionate hatred, and had become intoxicated with unlimited hope. To overcome this inertia the enemy had to be portrayed as evil incarnate, as absolute and congenital wickedness. The people wanted to be told that when this particular enemy had been forced to unconditional surrender, they would re-enter the golden age. This unique war would end all wars. This last war would make the world safe for democracy. This crusade would make the whole world a democracy.

As a result of this impassioned nonsense public opinion became so envenomed that the people would not countenance a workable peace; they were against any public man who showed "any tenderness for the Hun," or was inclined to listen to the "Hun food snivel."[1]

In order to see in its true perspective what happened, we must remember that at the end of the First World War the only victorious powers were the liberal democracies of the West. Lenin, who had been a refugee in Switzerland until 1917, was still at the very beginning of his struggle to become the master of the empire of the Romanoffs. Mussolini was an obscure journalist, and nobody

---
[1] Cf. Harold Nicholson, *Peacemaking*, Chap. III.

had dreamed of Hitler. The men who took part in the Peace Conference were men of the same standards and tradition. They were the heads of duly elected governments in countries where respect for civil liberty was the rule. Europe from the Atlantic to the Pripet Marshes lay within the military orbit of their forces. All the undemocratic empires, enemy and ally, had been destroyed by defeat and revolution. In 1918—unlike 1945—there had been no Yalta, there was no alien foreign minister at the peace conference who held a veto on the settlement.

Yet as soon as the terms of the settlement were known, it was evident that peace had not been made with Germany. It was not for want of power but for want of statesmanship that the liberal democracies failed. They failed to restore order in that great part of the world which—outside of revolutionary Russia—was still within the orbit of their influence, still amenable to their leadership, still subject to their decisions, still working within the same economy, still living in the same international community, still thinking in the same universe of discourse. In this failure to make peace there was generated the cycle of wars in which the West has suffered so sudden and so spectacular a decline.

Public opinion, having vetoed reconciliation, had made the settlement unworkable. And so when a new generation of Germans grew up, they rebelled. But by that time the Western democracies, so recently too warlike to make peace with the unarmed German Republic, had become too pacifist to take the risks which could have prevented the war Hitler was announcing he would wage against Europe. Having refused the risk of trying to prevent war, they would not now prepare for the war. The European democracies chose to rely on the double negative of unarmed appeasement, and the American democracy chose to rely on unarmed isolation.

When the unprevented war came, the fatal cycle was repeated. Western Europe was defeated and occupied before the British people began seriously to wage the war. And after the catastrophe in Western Europe eighteen agonizing months of indecision elapsed before the surprise and shock of Pearl Harbor did for the American people what no amount of argument and evidence and reason had been able to do.

Once again it seemed impossible to wage the war energetically except by inciting the people to paroxysms of hatred and to utopian dreams. So they were told that the Four Freedoms would be established everywhere, once the incurably bad Germans and the incurably bad Japanese had been forced to surrender unconditionally. The war could be popular only if the enemy was altogether evil and the Allies very nearly perfect. This mixture of envenomed hatred and furious righteousness made a public opinion which would not tolerate the calculated compromises that durable settlements demand. Once again the people were drugged by the propaganda which had aroused them to fight the war and to endure its miseries. Once again they would not think, once again they would not allow their leaders to think, about an eventual peace with their enemies, or about the differences that must arise among the Allies in this coalition, as in all earlier ones. How well this popular diplomacy worked is attested by the fact that less than five years after the democracies had disarmed their enemies, they were imploring their former enemies, Germany and Japan, to rearm.

The record shows that the people of the democracies, having become sovereign in this century, have made it increasingly difficult for their governments to prepare properly for war or to make peace. Their responsible officials have been like the ministers of an opinionated and willful despot. Between the critical junctures, when public opinion has been inattentive or not vehemently aroused, responsible officials have often been able to circumvent extremist popular opinions and to wheedle their way towards moderation and good sense. In the crises, however, democratic officials—over and above their own human propensity to err—have been compelled to make the big mistakes that public opinion has insisted upon. Even the greatest men have not been able to turn back the massive tides of opinion and of sentiment.

There is no mystery about why there is such a tendency for popular opinion to be wrong in judging war and peace. Strategic and diplomatic decisions call for a kind of knowledge—not to speak of an experience and a seasoned judgment—which cannot be had by glancing at newspapers, listening to snatches of radio comment, watching politicians perform on television, hearing occasional lectures, and reading a few books. It would not be enough to make a man competent to decide whether to amputate a leg, and it is not enough to qualify him to choose war or peace, to arm or not to arm, to intervene or to withdraw, to fight on or to negotiate.

Usually, moreover, when the decision is critical and urgent, the public will not be told the whole truth. What can be told to the great public it will not hear in the complicated and qualified concreteness that is needed for a practical decision. When distant and unfamiliar and complex things are communicated to great masses of people, the truth suffers a considerable and often a radical distortion. The complex is made over into the simple, the hypothetical into the dogmatic, and the relative into an absolute. Even when there is no deliberate distortion by censorship and propaganda, which is unlikely in time of war, the public opinion of masses cannot be counted upon to apprehend regularly and promptly the reality of things. There is an inherent tendency in opinion to feed upon rumors excited by our own wishes and fears.

At the critical moments in this sad history, there have been men, worth listening to, who warned the people against their mistakes. Always, too, there have been men inside the governments who judged correctly, because they were permitted to know in time, the uncensored and unvarnished truth. But the climate of modern democracy does not usually inspire them to speak out. For what Churchill did in the Thirties before Munich was exceptional: the general rule is that a democratic politician had better not be right too soon. Very often the penalty is political death. It is much safer to keep in step with the parade of opinion than to try to keep up with the swifter movement of events.

In government offices which are sensitive to the vehemence and passion of mass sentiment public men have no sure tenure. They are in effect perpetual office seekers, always on trial for their political lives, always required to court their restless constituents. They are deprived of their independence. Democratic politicians rarely feel they can afford the luxury of telling the whole truth to the people.[2] And since not telling it, though prudent, is uncomfortable, they find it easier if they themselves do not have to hear too often too much of the sour truth. The men under them who report and collect the news come to realize in their turn that it is safer to be wrong before it has become fashionable to be right.

With exceptions so rare that they are regarded as miracles and freaks of nature, successful democratic politicians are insecure and intimidated men. They advance politically only as they placate, appease, bribe, seduce, bamboozle, or otherwise manage to manipulate the demanding and threatening elements in their constituencies. The decisive consideration is not whether the proposition is good but whether it is popular—not whether it will work well and prove itself but whether the active talking constituents like it immediately. Politicians rationalize this servitude by saying that in a democracy public men are the servants of the people.

This devitalization of the governing power is the malady of democratic states. As the malady grows the executives become highly susceptible to encroachment and usurpation by elected assemblies; they are pressed and harassed by the higgling of parties, by the agents of organized interests, and by the spokesmen of sectarians and ideologues. The malady can be fatal. It can be deadly to the very survival of the state as a free society if, when the great and hard issues of war and peace, of security and solvency, of revolution and order are up for decision, the executive and judicial

---

[2] "As we look over the list of the early leaders of the republic, Washington, John Adams, Hamilton, and others, we discern that they were all men who insisted upon being themselves and who refused to truckle to the people. With each succeeding generation, the growing demand of the people that its elective officials shall not lead but merely register the popular will has steadily undermined the independence of those who derive their power from popular election. The persistent refusal of the Adamses to sacrifice the integrity of their own intellectual and moral standards and values for the sake of winning public office or popular favor is another of the measuring rods by which we may measure the divergence of American life from its starting point." James Truslow Adams, *The Adams Family* (1930), p. 95.

departments, with their civil servants and technicians, have lost their power to decide.

PROBLEMS FOR WRITING AND DISCUSSION

1. Does Lippmann see American democracy as unique or simply as illustrative of a worldwide pattern? Explain.
2. Lippmann argues that governments are usually wiser than the governed, at least at "critical junctures" in history. Is this a valid assumption? What proof does Lippmann offer that it is?
3. Why, according to Lippmann, are the people compelled to make mistakes?
4. That "the people" may often be wrong is not a novel idea. Why do you think that Lippmann, a distinguished journalist, writes on this subject? What influence in contemporary American life does he counteract?
5. Does Lippmann, as Riesman (p. 488) says intellectuals do, help destroy utopian thinking? If so, does he in the act of destroying challenge any of Jefferson's assertions in the Declaration?
6. Lippmann implies that the special knowledge needed for decisions of war and peace could not be acquired by the public even if the public were disposed to hear it. Does he propose an alternative to the dilemma?
7. Which of these alternatives might Lippmann approve: (1) modernized methods of manipulating popular opinion; (2) integrity of leadership to withstand pressure; or (3) tenure of public office independent of the electorate? Explain your answer.
8. Lippmann compares democratic officials to "the ministers of an opinionated and willful despot." Do Viereck (p. 324) and William L. Miller (p. 225) complain of the same despotism? Explain.
9. Lipset (p. 348) summarizes Plato's description of equalitarian societies as ones in which "fathers fear their sons, school teachers flatter their pupils, the old seek to imitate and win the good opinion of the young, and equality prevails in the relations of men and women." Could you, from your reading of Lippmann's essay, and from your own observation and knowledge of history, describe the "devitalization of leadership" in such a society? Explain.

Democracy: Its Presumptions and Realities

LEARNED HAND

> *Learned Hand (1872-1961), one of the most distinguished and literate American jurists, studied philosophy at Harvard with William James and George Santayana and received his law degree from the Harvard Law School in 1896. He was appointed United States District Judge in the Southern District of New York in 1909 and Judge of the United States Circuit Court, Second Circuit, in 1924, serving there until his retirement in 1951. He wrote nearly two thousand decisions during his judicial career, many of them based on concepts then new but now accepted; he has been called "a genuine architect of the law."*

The fathers who contrived and passed the Constitution were wise in their generation; as time passes, we come more and more to realize their powers of divination. And yet, as has been so often observed, they were curiously blind to the way in which the government they set up was to work; they apparently had no intimation of the role that party was to play. In this they were proper children of their time; for, though Britain was already in fair train to develop party out of faction, the spirit of the century chose to ignore it. If you set men free from the restraint of prince and priest, and gave them an opportunity to decide their own fate, they would almost automatically come to an understanding of their true needs, and the needs of one were the needs of all. True, the fathers were deeply preoccupied with the possibility that their work might be overthrown by faction and popular tumult, or by the despotism which these en-

From the Federal Bar Journal, *Vol. I, No. 1 (March 1932). Reprinted by permission of the publisher.*

gender, and against these they provided the elaborate system which we have come to know so well. But, given time, with its opportunity for deliberation, the mass of mankind was assumed to be, broadly speaking, homogeneous; at least, government as a compromise between more or less permanent and competing groups, seems not to have been contemplated. This was a strange inadvertence. Even while the Constitution was being framed, Hamilton at least understood that to pass it he must secure the concurrence of special interests which, though they overlapped, he drew into concert by holding out a different bait to each. Perhaps the greatest testimony to his genius is the skill with which he welded them together, and passed what would probably have failed to command a majority of the votes of even the limited numbers who then had the suffrage. But that the work of government should be carried along by the same means by which it had been instituted, nobody seems to have foreseen. Within a decade all were undeceived, since when we have become accustomed to parties as essential to our institutions.

A party system was still compatible with the underlying ideas of the eighteenth century, out of which it had developed. The government, by which I mean those who have present power, is to be watched and checked by an opposition which will succeed, when it can demonstrate that those who now hold office are not acting for the public weal and that it is likely to do better. This presupposes rather that that weal is a matter on which all judge alike, and in which all share in the same way, than that society will array itself into classes, pressing their several demands, indifferent to the general welfare, and establishing an equilibrium only by compromises in which they alone share. Bipartisan democracy presupposes the individual, whose welfare is identical with that of the community in which he lives, the absence of coherent social classes, a basic uniformity of interest throughout.

It seems a strange idea to us now. We have come to think of the problem of democracy as that of its minorities, a repellant notion, which has predisposed many peoples to throw it over and meet the difficulties by substituting less responsive control, exempt from the discord and distraction of purpose that is apparently inherent in a representative state. Even here among us, if your experience is like mine, there is an undercurrent of protest, a discontent which I cannot help finding ominous. In what I have to say, I want to suggest that the result is not as bad as it seems, and that, good or bad, we still derive from it advantages which are irreplaceable in any other system. If you insist, I shall ask no more than that you agree with Dean Inge that even though counting heads is not an ideal way to govern, at least it is better than breaking them. We do more than count; we measure political forces by the aggressiveness and coherence of conflicting classes, and this, though it may be the despair of the reformers, I should like to put in a more respectable light. It may not be an ideal, I shall argue that it is a tolerable, system; that it can insure continuity and give room for slow change, since it allows play to the actual, if unrecognized, organs of society.

One difficulty at any rate in the traditional theory is inherent; it arises from our necessary preoccupations and our incapacity to understand and deal with the multitude of questions that increasingly call for answer in a desperately complicated world. I do not know how it is with you, but for myself I generally give up at the outset. The simplest problems which come up from day to day seem to me quite unanswerable as soon as I try to get below the surface. Each side, when I hear it, seems to me right till I hear the other. I have neither the time nor the ability to learn the facts, or to estimate their importance if I knew them; I am disposed to accept the decision of those charged with the responsibility of dealing with them. My vote is one of the most unimportant acts of my life; if I were to acquaint myself with the matters on which it ought really to depend, if I were to try to get a judgment on which I was willing to risk affairs of even the smallest moment, I should be doing nothing else, and that seems a fatuous conclusion to a fatuous undertaking. Because, if all were done, for what after all does my single voice count among so many? Surely I can play my part better in the society where I chance to be, if I stick to my last, and leave governing to those who have had the temerity to accept the job. Distracted by the confusion, and conscious that I can reach no sound opinion, I turn away from any share in it and go about my business. I am aware of those protests of my youth, lingering in my memory, calling upon me to gird my loins and fall to. But then I reflect; excellent citizens banded to secure good government; youths full of aspiration and high resolve, ready to turn their swords against the giants; election returns leaving all outside the breastwork, shining examples of the noble dead. This is not an uncommon mood; indeed the apathy of the modern voter is the confusion of the modern reformer. I live where that apathy seems to have attacked even the deepest ganglia; no disclosures, no scandals, can stir the voters from their inertia. Doubtless things might become uncomfortable enough to arouse them, but, given reasonable opportunity for personal favors, and a not too irksome control, they are content to abdicate their sovereignty and to be fleeced, if the shepherds will only shear them in their sleep.

That was not the presupposition of our traditional democracy, which assumed an intelligent attention and capacity in public affairs, and a will directed towards the general good. We have surely outgrown the conditions it assumed, and the theory has ceased to work. In Europe they have tried another scheme, partly on paper, partly in practice. Recognizing that most men are bound in the end to look out for themselves, and to know more about their own affairs than anything else, they have either deliberately or by unconscious acceptance, recognized that government will inevitably react to the pressures of economic or social classes, which thus have become internal organs of the state. True, there must be some central control, a brain, as it were, where cross-impulses may neutralize each other; and indeed, so far as this has been omitted, as in theory at times it appears to have been, the machinery is incomplete. But granted such a nexus, there is much in modern politics which seems to present just that picture. I think that in spite of our reluctance, we are coming to the same situation here; have come to it, indeed.

It would indeed be the plainest folly to pretend that such a system works for the best; we see about us everywhere evidences to the contrary. We lose the forest for the trees, forgetting, even so far as we think at all, that we are trustees for those who come after us, squandering the patrimony which we have received. It seems scarcely better statecraft to turn over a society to the scramble of organized minorities than to leave it to be looted by bands of mercenaries under partisan chiefs. We must confess our apostasy; but before we abandon the ritual, is it not best to consider in what the faith has failed, and whether we may not use the old formulas with another meaning? The notion of a common will has teased political philosophers from the outset. It gets its completest expression in the Hegelian state which made its highest bid for dominance during the Great War and failed; the state, as an entity, an organism apart from those who compose it, a creature to which they owe unquestioning allegiance, and which may dispose of them at its own inscrutable pleasure. In theory that form of idolatry has never got much hold on men who speak English; in practice, the modern cult of the nation is hardly distinguishable; it veils itself behind the fiction of a common will. Just where that will resides, or how it is made manifest, is not too plain; like other deities, it is wise not to expose itself too freely. Is it for example to be found in a referendum? Perhaps so; I can think of no complete incarnation. If you put a question for categorical answer to a multitude, you may say that the majority has expressed itself. You may be wrong; in any case your assurance is factitious; men seldom have anything that can truly be called an opinion. Their leaders take sides as their interests direct, and they follow because they are used to follow. Indeed it may be better so. You remember Private Willis in *Iolanthe*: "But then the prospect of a lot of dull M.P.'s in close proximity, each thinking for himself, is what no man can face with equanimity." We recently had a referendum in New York about extending the forest preserve. The city voted for it by a large majority; yet as I walk the streets I do not see afforestation written with conviction on the harried faces of my fellow citizens. I suspect that the powers sent out word—for what subtle reason I do not know—that that amendment was to pass, and pass it did. Was there a common will in New York about adding to the forest preserve? I doubt it. Moreover, granting that at times we do so get an expression of a genuine opinion, belief, attitude—call it what you will—it must be sporadic and limited; one cannot carry on government by referendum—surely not among one hundred and twenty million people. They must act by deputy, and how much common will is there then?

You are familiar enough with the mechanism. Every man who aspires to office wants, if he is worth his salt, to be returned. Why else should he go in; why accept an interruption in his normal vocation, long enough to disrupt it, but not to achieve substantial results elsewhere? And how can he be returned? He looks upon an inert mass of constituents, who care little for themselves as citizens at large, but very much for this measure or that, which affects them in their livelihood. Make me prosperous in my job, and I will take care of myself in my other relations. How much of the history of tariff legislation, for instance, can be written in those words? To promote their special interests they form groups with inconveniently long memories, before which their memories as undifferentiated voters are like the spring snows. The common will, as the official sees it, is not common at all; it is a complex of opposing forces, whose resultant has no relation to the common good, but which will nevertheless decide whether he goes back or not. That mechanical equation is his master; he is not the mouthpiece of the people's voice, or any other Hegelian Absolute, realizing its eternal essence in the solution of opposites. And so the common good is squeezed out, and enterprises of great pith and moment fall by the way. The more compact, determined, and relentless the groups with which he must deal, the more they have to say in his fate. He must pick his way nicely, must learn to placate though not to yield too much, to have the art of honeyed words but not to seem neutral, and above all to keep constantly audible, visible, likeable, even kissable. There are indeed more exhilarating moments when he may strike boldly, but they are not frequent and the effect is apt to be transitory; they are not so good as a supply of advice to mothers which comes in every evening just after bed-time stories.

That, I agree, is not a pretty picture; it did not intrude into the inspired reveries of Thomas Jefferson, though it has hag-ridden the thoughts of his political descendants, and gives them pause. Is there any answer? I suspect not; but there may be solace. After all, silken purses come only from busy silk worms; we must weave with what we have. The millennium is still beyond the horizon; just beyond, if you insist, but not yet in sight. Have we the qualities of our defects? In the first place, why must we hold altogether illegitimate the advantage that cohesion, assiduity, and persistence bring in government as elsewhere? By what right do we count those who have not the energy or intelligence to make themselves felt, equivalents of those who have? I have yet to learn that political masses must be weighed by counting molecules and disregarding atomic weights. In any society, I submit, the aggressive and insistent will have disproportionate power. For myself, I confess I should like it otherwise; I prefer the still small voice of reason, but then I am timid and constitutionally incompetent in such matters. But, though I would build the world anew and nearer to the heart's desire, if I could, I do not propose to cry for the moon. In a world where the stronger have always had their way, I am glad if I can keep them from having it without stint.

It seems to me, with all its defects, our system does just that. For, abuse it as you will, at least it gives a bloodless measure of social forces—bloodless, have you thought of that?—a means of continuity, a principle of stability, a relief from the paralyzing terror of revolution. I have been where this was not true; in lands where one felt the pervasive foreboding of violence, of armed suppression, the inability of minorities to exert just those peaceful pressures, that seem to us so vicious; where government is conducted not by compromise, but by *coup d'état*. And I have looked back with contentment to my own country, distracted as she might be by a Babel of many voices, uncertain of her purposes and her path; where yet there can be revolution without machine guns, and men may quit a public office and retain a private life. Given an opportunity to impose our will, a ground where we may test our mettle, we get the sense that there is some propriety in yielding to those who impose upon us. There has been an outlet, a place of reckoning, a means not of counting heads, but of matching wits and courage. If these are fairly measured, most of us acquiesce; we are conscious of a stronger power which it is idle to resist, until we in turn have organized in more formidable array and can impress ourselves in turn. And so I will not declaim against the evils of our time, the selfishness of class struggle, the disregard of the common good. Nor will I forsake the faith of our fathers in democracy, however I must transmute it, and make it unlovely to their eyes, were they here to see their strangely perverse disciple. If you will give me scales by which to weigh Tom and Dick and Harry as to their fitness to rule, and tell me how much each shall count, I will talk with you about some other kind of organization. Plato jumped hurdles that are too high for my legs; maybe you can help me over, or lower them. But unless you do, I will stand in the place that I am accustomed to. I will say that there must be a trying-out of men, according to their qualities as God has made them; that it is a precious inheritance, which we must not abjure, that that chance exists; that we must write down our miscarriages to our own flaccid selves. Meanwhile we shall not bottle up the gases and prepare for the inevitable explosion.

And so when I hear so much impatient and irritable complaint, so much readiness to replace what we have by guardians for us all, those supermen, evoked somewhere from the clouds, whom none have seen and none are ready to name, I lapse into a dream, as it were. I see children playing on the grass; their voices are shrill and discordant as children's are; they are restive and quarrelsome; they cannot agree to any common plan; their play annoys them; it goes so poorly. And one says, let us make Jack the master; Jack knows all about it; Jack will tell us what each is to do and we shall all agree. But Jack is like all the rest; Helen is discontented with her part, and Henry with his, and soon they fall again into their old state. No, the children must learn to play by themselves; there is no Jack the master. And in the end slowly and with infinite disappointment they do learn a little; they learn to forbear, to reckon with another, accept a little where they wanted much, to live and let live, to yield when they must yield; perhaps, we may hope, not to take all they can. But the condition is that they shall be willing at least to listen to one another, to get the habit of pooling their wishes. Somehow or other they must do this, if the play is to go on; maybe it will not, but there is no Jack, in or out of the box, who can come to straighten the game.

We are meeting tonight just ninety-one years from the day on which one[1] first saw the light, who for far more than the ordinarily allotted span has played a high and shining part among us. Seventy years after he lay mortally wounded, as they thought, on a defeated field, he was still in the service of his country, lending luster to that court which we all delight to honor. At last he has sheathed his sword, and takes his leisure like the gallant soldier that he is. Another[2] takes his seat, happily his rightful heir, his one authentic successor. There is no tribute we can give him which he has not had; no honor which we shall do more than repeat. What perhaps we can do is to try to understand his message, the upshot of his life. In this we are apt to go astray; we have no right to impute to him the version we may carry off, for he wrote not for the mass. Them that have eyes to see, let them see; them that have ears to hear, let them hear. It is a hard saying, and most of all do I doubt my own capacity as interpreter. And yet, in one way or another, we must all assume that role; for we cannot ignore what he said; we must read and write our own gloss. To me at any rate it seems that the message is not unlike in spirit what I have been trying to say. Man may be a little lower than the angels, but he has not yet shaken off the brute. His passions, his thinking, his body carry their origins with them; and he fails, if he vaingloriously denies them. His path is strewn with carnage, the murderer lurks always not far

---

[1] Oliver Wendell Holmes (1841-1935), Associate Justice of the United States Supreme Court. This address by Judge Hand was delivered on the occasion of Justice Holmes' ninety-first birthday, at the twelfth annual dinner of the Federal Bar Association, March 8, 1932, in Washington.

[2] Associate Justice of the United States Supreme Court Benjamin Cardozo (1870-1938).

beneath, to break out from time to time, peace resolutions to the contrary notwithstanding. What he has gained has been with immeasurable waste; what he shall gain will be with immeasurably more. Trial and error is the confession, not indeed of an impotent, but of a wayward, creature, blundering about in worlds not realized. But the Absolute is mute; no tables come from Sinai to guide him; the brazen sky gives no answer to his prayers. He must grope his way through the murk, as his remote forerunners groped, in the dank, hot world in which they moved. Look where he will, there are no immutable laws to which he can turn; no, not even that in selfless abnegation he must give up what he craves, for life is self-assertion. Conflict is normal; we reach accommodations as wisdom may teach us that it does not pay to fight. And wisdom may; for wisdom comes as false assurance goes—false assurance, that grows from pride in our powers and ignorance of our ignorance. Beware then of the heathen gods; have no confidence in principles that come to us in the trappings of the eternal. Meet them with gentle irony, friendly skepticism, and an open soul. Nor be cast down; for it is always dawn. Day breaks forever, and above the eastern horizon the sun is now about to peep. Full light of day? No, perhaps not ever. But yet it grows lighter, and the paths that were so blind will, if one watches sharply enough, become hourly plainer. We shall learn to walk straighter. Yes, it is always dawn.

PROBLEMS FOR WRITING AND DISCUSSION

1. What, according to Hand, was the "strange inadvertence" of the framers of the Constitution?

2. Explain Hand's statement: "Bipartisan democracy presupposed the individual, whose welfare is identical with that of the community in which he lives, the absence of coherent social classes, a basic uniformity of interest throughout."

3. Hand says that "the apathy of the modern voter is the confusion of the modern reformer." Explain what he means. Do you think that the

modern voter is apathetic? Who are the modern reformers? Is Hand an apathetic voter or a modern reformer?

4. Hand says that we come to think of the problem of democracy as that of its minorities and consider this a "repellant notion." Is Hand himself repelled by the notion? How does he justify the exercise of power by vocal, self-interested minorities? What "notion" of government repels him much more strongly?

5. Hand declares that "men seldom have anything that can truly be called an opinion." Is Hand, a distinguished jurist, simply cynical about men, or is he an accurate observer? Does he dislike the "Babel of many voices" that he believes is mistaken for the expression of opinion?

6. Referring to what were then pre-World War II European states, Hand notes that they have admitted representation on the basis of organized economic and social classes. What do Potter (p. 328) and Lipset (p. 348) say about American equality that may explain our reluctance to admit the pressure of "economic and social classes" as political entities?

7. Does Hand agree with Lippmann (p. 381) about the reliability of public opinion and about the role of the politician in America? Does he agree that the malady of democracy is the "devitalization of leadership"?

8. Why is "counting heads" (or molecules) in itself a meaningless basis upon which to determine the "will of the people"? In Hand's understanding of our system, may "the consent of the governed" be tacit?

9. Hand prefers the "still small voice of reason" to the "aggressive and insistent" voices of "political masses." Yet, despite its shortcomings, Hand accepts and justifies the American system. Why? In so doing, has he forsaken "the faith of our fathers in democracy"?

10. When Hand declares "there is no Jack, in or out of the box, who can come to straighten out the game," is he issuing a warning that is as relevant to American democracy today as it was in 1932, before the rise to power of Hitler? Explain.

11. In his tribute to Holmes, Hand declares that "there are no immutable laws" to guide us. Does Hand, then, reject "certain unalienable rights" with which man's creator endowed him, or does he affirm the self-reliance these rights entail? Explain. (It is interesting in this connection to compare President Kennedy's final sentence in his inaugural address, p. 508.)

On the Publick

JAMES FENIMORE COOPER

> James Fenimore Cooper (*1789-1851*) spent most of his adult life in New York. Author of the Leatherstocking Series, of which the most famous is, perhaps, The Last of the Mohicans (*1826*), he was a belligerent man who found the time and energy—both between and during novels—to engage in libel suits against newspapers that criticized his work. A soul as contentious and conservative naturally appealed to H. L. Mencken, who nearly a century after the appearance of The American Democrat (*1838*), said: "Cooper was probably the first American to write about Americans in a really frank spirit. What he discovered, searching the national scene, was that the democratic panacea, after all, was a fraud like any other." There is no certainty that Cooper would have agreed with Mencken's judgment.

There is a disposition, under popular governments, to mistake the nature and authority of the publick. Publick opinion, as a matter of course, can only refer to that portion of the community that has cognizance of the particular circumstances it affects, but in all matters of law, of rights, and of principles, as they are connected with the general relations of society, the publick means the entire constituency, and that, too, only as it is authorized to act, by the fundamental laws, or the constitution. Thus the citizen who asserts his legal rights in opposition to the wishes of a neighborhood, is not opposing the publick, but maintaining its intentions, while the particular neighborhood is arrogating to itself a power that is confided to the whole body of the state.

From The American Democrat. *Cooperstown, N.Y.: H. and E. Phinney, 1838.*

Tyranny can only come from the publick, in a democracy, since individuals are powerless, possessing no more rights than it pleases the community to leave in their hands. The pretence that an individual oppresses the publick, is, to the last degree, absurd, since he can do no more than exercise his rights, as they are established by law; which law is enacted, administered and interpreted by the agents of the publick.

As every man forms a portion of the publick, if honest and influenced by right principles, the citizen will be cautious how he takes sides against particular members of the community, for he is both deciding in his own case, a circumstance under which few make impartial judges, and combining with the strong to oppress the weak.

In this country, in which political authority is the possession of the body that wields opinion, influences that elsewhere counteract each other, there is a strong and dangerous disposition to defer to the publick, in opposition to truth and justice. This is a penalty that is paid for liberty, and it depends on the very natural principle of flattering power. In a monarchy, adulation is paid to the prince; in a democracy to the people, or the publick. Neither hears the truth, as often as is wholesome, and both suffer for the want of the corrective. The man who resists the tyranny of a monarch, is often sustained by the voices of those around him; but he who opposes the innovations of the publick in a democracy, not only finds himself struggling with power, but with his own neighbors. It follows that the oppression of the publick is of the worst description, and all real lovers of liberty should take especial heed not to be accessaries to wrongs so hard to be borne. As between the publick and individuals, therefore, the true bias of a democrat, so far as there is any doubt of the real merits of the controversy, is to take sides with the latter. This is opposed to the popular notion, which is to fancy the man who maintains his rights against the popular will, an aristocrat, but it is none the less true; the popular will, in cases that affect popular pleasure, being quite as likely to be wrong, as an individual will, in cases that affect an individual interest.

It ought to be impressed on every man's mind, in letters of brass, "*That, in a democracy, the publick has no power that is not expressly conceded by the institutions, and that this power, moreover, is only to be used under the forms prescribed by the constitution. All beyond this, is oppression, when it takes the character of acts, and not unfrequently when it is confined to opinion.*" Society has less need of the corrective of publick opinion, under such a system, than under a narrow government, for possessing all the power, the body of the community, by framing the positive ordinances, is not compelled to check abuses by resisting, or over-awing the laws. Great care should be had, therefore, to ascertain facts, before the citizen of a free country suffers himself to inflict the punishment of publick opinion, since it is aiding oppression in its worst form, when in error, and this too, without a sufficient object.

Another form of oppression practised by the publick, is arrogating to itself a right to inquire into, and to decide on the private acts of individuals, beyond the cognizance of the laws.

Men who have designs on the favor of the publick invite invasions on their privacy, a course that has rendered the community less scrupulous and delicate than it ought to be. All assumptions of a power to decide on conduct, that is unaccompanied by an authority to investigate facts, is adding the danger of committing rank injustice, to usurpation. The practice may make hypocrites, but it can never mend morals.

The publick, every where, is proverbially soulless. All feel when its rights, assumed or real, are invaded, but none feel its responsibilities. In republicks, the publick is, also, accused of ingratitude to its servants. This is true, few citizens of a democracy retaining the popular favor, without making a sacrifice of those principles, which conflict with popular caprices. The people, being sovereign, require the same flattery, the same humoring of their wishes, and the same sacrifices of truths, as a prince.

It is not more true, however, that the people in a democracy, are ungrateful, than that monarchs are ungrateful. The failing is common to all power, which, as a rule, is invariably as forgetful of services as it is exacting. The difference in the rewards of the servants of a prince, and the rewards of the servants of a democracy, is to be found in the greater vigilance of the first, who commonly sees the necessity of paying well. No dignities or honors conferred on a subject, moreover, can raise him to a level with his master, while a people reluctantly yield distinctions that elevate one of their own number above themselves.

In America, it is indispensable that every well wisher of true liberty should understand that acts of tyranny can only proceed from the publick. The publick, then, is to be watched, in this country, as, in other countries kings and aristocrats are to be watched.

The end of liberty is the happiness of man, and its means, that of leaving the greatest possible personal freedom of action, that comports with the general good. To supplant the exactions of the laws, therefore, by those of an unauthorized publick, is to establish restraints without the formalities and precision of legal requirements. It is putting the prejudices, provincialisms, ignorance and passions of a neighborhood in the place of statutes; or, it is establishing a power equally without general principles, and without responsibility.

Although the political liberty of this country is greater than that of nearly every other civilized nation, its personal liberty is said to be less. In other words, men are thought to be more under the control of extra-legal authority, and to defer more to those around them, in pursuing even their lawful and innocent occupations, than in almost every other country. That there is much truth in this opinion, all observant travellers agree, and it is a reproach to the moral civilization of the country that it should be so. It is not difficult to trace the causes of such a state of things, but the evil is none the less because it is satisfactorily explained. One principal reason, beyond a question, is the mistake that men are apt to make concerning the rights and powers of the publick in a popular government.

The pretence that the publick has a right to extend its jurisdiction beyond the reach of the laws, and without regard to the principles and restraints of the fundamental compact that binds society together, is, indeed, to verify the common accusation of the enemies of democracy, who affirm that, by substituting this form of government for that of a despotism, people are only replacing one tyrant by many. This saying is singularly false as respects the political action of our institutions, but society must advance farther, the country must collect more towns, a denser population, and possess a higher degree of general civilization, before it can be as confidently pronounced that it is untrue as respects the purely social.

The disgraceful desire to govern by means of mobs, which has lately become so prevalent, has arisen from misconceiving the rights of the publick. Men know that the publick, or the community, rules, and becoming impatient of any evil that presses on them, or which they fancy presses on them, they overstep all the forms of law, overlook deliberation and consultation, and set up their own local interests, and not unfrequently their passions, in the place of positive enactments and the institutions. It is scarcely predicting more than the truth will warrant, to say, that if this substitution of the caprices, motives and animosities of a portion of the publick, for the solemn ordinances of the entire legal publick, should continue, even those well affected to a popular government, will be obliged to combine with those who wish its downfall, in order to protect their persons and property, against the designs of the malevolent; for no civilized society can long exist, with an active power in its bosom that is stronger than the law.

PROBLEMS FOR WRITING AND DISCUSSION

1. What does Cooper consider the malady of a democratic state? What is paradoxical about it?

2. Does Cooper argue that a true democrat must always side with the majority? If the true democrat does not, how may popular opinion label him? Would Viereck (p. 324) welcome such a "true democrat" to his "aristocracy"?

3. Although Cooper admits the solidity of "political liberty" in America, what does he say about "personal liberty"? Compare the pressures Cooper

describes with the contemporary pressures Potter (p. 328) and Lipset (p. 348) say the ideals of Equality and Achievement have created.

4. Has the invasion of privacy Cooper condemns lessened or increased in America? Describe from your own knowledge and experience an instance in which the "prejudices, provincialisms, ignorance and passions" of the public usurped the authority of "statutes."

5. Explain Cooper's statement: "The publick, every where, is proverbially soulless. All feel when its rights, assumed or real, are invaded, but none feel its responsibilities." Does Hand (p. 388) concur in this evaluation? What is the difference between Cooper's and Hand's *attitudes* toward the public?

6. Hand says the European democracies, recognizing "that most men are bound to know more about their own affairs than anything else," have allowed self-interested groups as "organs of the state," neutralizing these "impulses" in a central "brain" of government. Compare Hand's description with Cooper's opening assertions about "publick opinion." Does Cooper admit "publick opinion" as an organ of the state? Compare what Cooper says about the Constitution with what Lincoln (Jaffa, p. 360) considered the "word fitly spoken." What "apple of gold" does Cooper cherish?

7. The "publick," Cooper says, "is to be watched, in this country, as, in other countries kings and aristocrats are to be watched." Were the founding fathers in the Bill of Rights aware of the dangers of mob rule?

8. Cooper declares that, in a democracy, "Tyranny can only come from the publick." Examine the Salem "trials" (p. 54 and p. 59 in Part I) as instances of Cooper's statement. Compare also Cooper's observations on the dangerous pressures of public opinion with those made by Boorstin (p. 5), Kennan (p. 233), Viereck, and Lipset.

9. Discuss Cooper's remarks on the fate of "public servants" with those of Lippmann (p. 381).

10. Discuss Lincoln's stand on slavery in the light of Cooper's final statement: "no civilized society can long exist, with an active power in its bosom that is stronger than the law." Do Arnold (p. 162) and Berle (p. 170) suggest that there is today "an active power" in American democracy "stronger than the law"? In science, what powers operate at present outside the compass of the law?

11. In the next to last paragraph of this essay, Cooper sees the increase of population and urban communities as a hopeful sign for man's social liberty. Would Lewis Mumford, who wrote on sprawling suburbia (p. 76), share his optimism?

The Price of Union

HERBERT AGAR

>Herbert Agar (1897-   ), after receiving his doctorate from Princeton in 1922, and after a stint at preparatory teaching, went in 1928 to London where, among other things, he was the overseas correspondent for the Louisville Courier-Journal. In 1934 his history of the American Presidency, The People's Choice, won the Pulitzer Prize; in 1940 he became the editor of the Courier-Journal. He has produced a steady flow of books on the American past, including A Time for Greatness (1942), The Price of Union (1950), and A Declaration of Faith (1952). During World War II he was special assistant to American Ambassador Winant and head of the London Office of War Information. Since the war he has lived in England, where he continues to write about the American political scene.

In 1788, when Alexander Hamilton, James Madison, and John Jay were struggling to persuade the New York convention to ratify the Constitution of the United States, young De Witt Clinton composed a prayer for the Opposition: "From the insolence of great men—from the tyranny of the rich—from the unfeeling rapacity of the excise-men and tax-gatherers—from the misery of despotism—from the expense of supporting standing armies, navies, placemen, sinecures, federal cities, senators, presidents, and a long train of

The selections from the Introduction and Chapter XXXV of Herbert Agar, The Price of Union, 1950, *are reprinted by permission of and arrangement with Houghton Mifflin Company, the authorized publishers, and with Eyre & Spottiswoode (Publishers) Ltd., which published the book under the title* The United States: the President, the Parties and the Constitution.

405

etceteras, Good Lord deliver us." There speaks the deep American distaste for government, the belief that it is evil and that it must be kept weak.

The proposed constitution seemed weak enough to its friends— too weak for safety in the opinion of Hamilton. The thirteen states were left with all the powers which would normally concern "the lives, liberties and properties of the people," while the delegated powers of the Union were divided among the Executive, the Legislature, and the Judiciary in the belief that they would check each other and prevent rash or oppressive deeds. Yet behind this modest proposal Clinton saw threats of insolence, rapacity, misery, needless expense, and all the corruptions of history. There is little doubt that he spoke for the majority in New York; and many citizens would still agree with him. A constant factor in American history is the fear of Leviathan, of the encroaching state.

We can trace this fear from prerevolutionary days, and we can trace the forces which have nevertheless caused Leviathan to grow steadily more ponderous. War and industrial revolution promote strong government. Foreign dangers, business depressions, sectional or class strife—whenever these are acute the people look to central power for help. Yet they have not abandoned hope that life might sometime be peaceful and that government might become frugal and unassuming, as Jefferson promised. And they have not abandoned the constitution which seemed to many of those who wrote it to err on the side of weakness, to put the liberties of the citizen before the safety of the commonwealth. Yet by unwritten means, out of simple self-protection, that constitution has been given strength and flexibility to meet the threats and disasters of a hundred and sixty years. The result is one of the most interesting forms of government the world has seen, and in the light of its problems one of the most successful.

The special problems of the American Government derive from geography, national character, and the nature both of a written constitution and of a federal empire. The government is cramped and confined by a seemingly rigid bond; yet it must adapt itself to a rate of change in economics, technology, and foreign relations which would have made all previous ages dizzy. In good times the government must abide by the theory that its limited sovereignty has been divided between the Union and the several states; yet when the bombs fall or the banks close or the breadlines grow by millions it must recapture the distributed sovereignty and act like a strong centralized nation. The government must regard the separation of its own powers, especially those of the Executive and the Legislature, as an essential and indeed a sacred part of the system; yet when the separation threatens deadlock and danger it must reassemble those powers informally and weld them into a working team. Finally, the government must accept the fact that in a country so huge, containing such diverse climates and economic interests and social habits and racial and religious backgrounds, most politics will be parochial, most politicians will have small horizons, seeking the good of the state or the district rather than of the Union; yet by diplomacy and compromise, never by force the government must water down the selfish demands of regions, races, classes, business associations, into a national policy which will alienate no major group and which will contain at least a small plum for everybody. This is the price of unity in a continent-wide federation. Decisions will therefore be slow, methods will be cumbersome, political parties will be illogical and inconsistent; but the people remain free, reasonably united, and as lightly burdened by the state as is consistent with safety.

It may be asked, if the inevitable problems are so acute and so contradictory why not change the form of government? The answer is that the American political system with all its absurdities is one of the few successes in a calamitous age. Step by step, it has learned to avoid many of the worst mistakes of empire, in a nation which would stretch from London to the Ural Mountains and from Sweden to the Sahara; it has learned to circumvent threats of secession (the mortal illness of federalism) before they appear; it has learned to evade class warfare (the mortal illness of liberty), and to the dismay of its critics it shows no sign of moving toward class parties. Once, in the midst of the long period of learning, the political system failed totally. The result was civil war. The system must always fail partially, since politics cannot rise above the mixed nature of man. "Government is a very rough business," said Sir George Cornewall Lewis to the young Gladstone; "you must be content with very unsatisfactory results." In a world condemned to such results the American political system deserves attention—especially that part of the system which combines compromise with energy, minority rights with government by a majority which may live thousands of miles away. This is the special province of the unwritten constitution.

The written constitution has been unofficially revised, without the change of a word or a comma, in several ways. First, the government which had been planned as a very loose federation grew steadily more centralized. Not even the most power-fearing statesmen could prevent this drift.

Second, the office of the presidency was captured by the emerging democracy—much to the surprise of the Fathers, who thought they had put it beyond the clutches of what they called the "mob." The President, thereafter, was the one man elected by all the voters,* so when the country became a thorough democracy the President became the voice of the people. For the most part the members of the Senate and of the House must represent their own states and districts. It is not waywardness which makes them do this; it is the nature of the federal system. The representatives from Delaware do not and should not spend their time serving the interests of Idaho. Yet there may be occasions when the welfare of the national majority conflicts with that of Idaho. It then becomes the duty of the congressmen from Idaho to argue for their own region and to ask for compromise. But the President talks for the nation.

Third, when the President became the voice of the people it was important that his voice carry weight. Under the written constitution, as interpreted from the days of Madison (who came to the White House in 1809) to those of J. Q. Adams (who left it in

---

* Except for the Vice-President, who does not matter unless the President dies.

1829), not even the most popular President could impose a national policy. The Congress was "a scuffle of local interests," and could make only desultory policy. So the nation drifted: in and out of war, in and out of depression, in and out of sectional strife. Thus came the demand for the third unwritten change, which stabilized the others and saved the system from stagnation: the modern political parties.

These parties are unique. They cannot be compared to the parties of other nations. They serve a new purpose in a new way. Unforeseen and unwanted by the Fathers, they form the heart of the unwritten constitution and help the written one to work.

It is through the parties that the clashing interests of a continent find grounds for compromise; it is through the parties that majority rule is softened and minorities gain a suspensive veto; it is through the parties that the separation of powers within the federal government is diminished and the President is given strength (when he dares use it) to act as tribune of the people; it is through the parties that the dignity of the states is maintained, and the tendency for central power to grow from its own strength is to some extent resisted. It is through the parties, also, that many corruptions and vulgarities enter the national life, and many dubious habits—like that of ignoring issues which are too grave for compromise.

The parties are never static. They are as responsive to shifting conditions as the Constitution of Great Britain. Above all, they are not addicted to fixed ideas, to rigid principles. It is not their duty to be Left, or Right, or Center—but to be all three. It is not their function to defend political or economic doctrines, but to administer the doctrines chosen by the majority, with due regard to special interests and to the habits of the regions.

Third parties may preach causes and adhere to creeds. They may educate the public and thus mold history. But the two major parties have a more absorbing, a more subtle, and a more difficult task. The task is peculiar to a federal state covering so much land and containing so many people that its economic and cultural life cannot and should not be merged. Over such an area, where there is no unity of race, no immemorial tradition, no throne to revere, no ancient roots in the land, no single religion to color all minds alike—where there is only language in common, and faith, and the pride of the rights of man—the American party system helps to build freedom and union: the blessings of liberty, and the strength that comes from letting men, money, goods, and ideas move without hindrance.

Although the major parties do not stand for opposed philosophies and do not represent opposed classes, there are traditional differences which divide them. On the whole, it is roughly true that the ancestors of the Democratic Party are Thomas Jefferson and his friends, who made a political alliance in the seventeen-nineties and who came to power in 1801. And it is roughly true that the ancestors of the Republican Party are Alexander Hamilton and his friends, who formed the dominant group in the Cabinets of the first two Presidents (1789-1801).

Broadly speaking, and subject to many qualifications, the Jeffersonians drew their strength from the landed interests (the small farmers and in some cases the great plantation owners) and from the mechanics and manual workers of the towns, whereas the Hamiltonians drew their strength from the business and banking and commercial communities, from the middle-class workers who associated their interests with these communities, and from some of the richest owners of plantations. There are so many exceptions to the above statements that it would be misleading to take them literally; yet in a very general sense they tend to be true. Some such alignment existed in most sections of the country, not only in the days of Jefferson and Hamilton, but in the days of Andrew Jackson and Henry Clay and Daniel Webster (1820-1850), and in the days of Bryan and McKinley, and in the days when Woodrow Wilson ran against Theodore Roosevelt and Taft, and again in the days of Franklin Roosevelt. Yet the alignment is insignificant compared to the fundamental forces which make the party system.

Another tendency toward strict party alignment stems from the Civil War—a tendency which cuts across and confuses the alignment which has just been described. The Republican Party was the party of Union during the Civil War, the party of Northern victory. As a result the farmers of the Middle West and of New England, for whom the Union was a sacred cause, long tended to vote the Republican ticket. So did the Negroes, for whom Northern victory meant release from slavery. And so did the veterans of the Union armies, for whom the Republican Party meant generous pensions. And on the other side the states of the Confederacy formed the "solid South" wherein only the Democratic Party was respectable. It is the remnants of such wartime passions which explain the Georgia judge who said, "I shall die a penitent Christian, but meet my Maker as an impenitent Democrat."

Yet in recent years Franklin Roosevelt won the whole of the Middle West for the Democrats, and the whole of New England with the exception of Maine and Vermont. And in two elections he received most of the Negro votes. And in 1928 (under very exceptional circumstances, to be sure) Herbert Hoover, the Republican candidate, received the votes of Virginia, Tennessee, Texas, North Carolina, and Florida—all parts of the "solid South."

The meaning and the purpose of the national parties cannot be sought in traditional alignments or old animosities, and still less in economic or political creeds. They can only be understood in the light of the regional problem created by America's size, and of the constitutional problem created by the separation of powers.

The American political system sometimes fails lamentably. Although on the whole it promotes freedom and union, too many citizens have a sham freedom, and too often the Union is used to press colonial servitude upon entire regions. Yet we must remember, as Denis Brogan says, that when the Constitution went into effect in 1789 "there was still a King of France and Navarre, a King of Spain and the Indies, a Venetian and a Dutch Republic, an Emperor in Pekin; a Pope-King ruled in Bologna, a Tsarina in Petersburg and a Shogun in Yedo, not yet Tokio and not yet the residence of the Divine Mikado."

The form of government which has weathered the wars, revolutions, and economic collapses ravaging the world during this century and a half must satisfy some deep need of man. And it must have resilience and adaptability. The unwritten constitution supplies the latter qualities.

During Grover Cleveland's first term in the White House, James Bryce published his remarkable book, *The American Commonwealth*. Surveying the party system from the English point of view, and with quiet surprise, he made the classic statement of the difference between the Republicans and the Democrats.

> What are their principles [he wrote], their distinctive tenets, their tendencies? Which of them is for free trade, for civil-service reform, for a spirited foreign policy . . . for changes in the currency, for any other of the twenty issues which one hears discussed in the country as seriously involving its welfare? This is what a European is always asking of intelligent Republicans and intelligent Democrats. He is always asking because he never gets an answer. The replies leave him in deeper perplexity. After some months the truth begins to dawn on him. Neither party has any principles, any distinctive tenets. Both have traditions. Both claim to have tendencies. Both have certainly war cries, organizations, interests, enlisted in their support. But those interests are in the main the interests of getting or keeping the patronage of the government. Tenets and policies, points of political doctrine and points of political practice, have all but vanished. They have not been thrown away but have been stripped away by Time and the progress of events, fulfilling some policies, blotting out others. All has been lost, except office or the hope of it.

This is a true description of the parties as they were, and as they still are; but Bryce's explanation of how they came to be that way is misleading. He assumes that if the American parties were healthy they would resemble the parties of Great Britain. They would have "principles" and "tenets," and would thus be forced to take sides on all "the twenty issues that one hears discussed." And he assumes that "Time and the progress of events" have deprived the parties of their principles, leaving them with nothing but "office or the hope of it." But this is too short a view; Lord Bryce was confused by the brief history of the Republican Party, which possessed principles in 1856 and none in 1886. He thought this was a sign of failure and decay; but in fact it was a sign of health: 1856 had been the exception and the danger; 1886 was the reassuring norm.

The purpose—the important and healthy purpose—of an American party is to be exactly what Lord Bryce describes, and by implication deplores. The party is intended to be an organization for "getting or keeping the patronage of government." Instead of seeking "principles," or "distinctive tenets," which can only divide a federal union, the party is intended to seek bargains between the regions, the classes, and the other interest groups. It is intended to bring men and women of all beliefs, occupations, sections, racial backgrounds, into a combination for the pursuit of power. The combination is too various to possess firm convictions. The members may have nothing in common except a desire for office. Unless driven by a forceful President they tend to do as little as possible. They tend to provide some small favor for each noisy group, and to call that a policy. They tend to ignore any issue that rouses deep passion. And by so doing they strengthen the Union.

The decisive American experience—the warning against politics based on principles—took place between 1850 and 1860. A subtle and healing compromise had been effected in 1850; yet year by year, whether through fate or through human folly, it slowly disintegrated. The best men watched in anguish but could not halt the ruin. In the name of principles and distinctive tenets the Whig Party was ground to bits. A new party was born which met Lord Bryce's requirements. The Republicans knew exactly where they stood on the major issue and would not give an inch. Finally, the same "principles" broke the Democratic Party, and the Union of 1789 perished.

The lesson which America learned was useful: in a large federal nation, when a problem is passionately felt, and is discussed in terms of morals, each party may divide within itself, against itself. And if the parties divide, the nation may divide; for the parties, with their enjoyable pursuit of power, are a unifying influence. Wise men, therefore, may seek to dodge such problems as long as possible. And the easiest way to dodge them is for both parties to take both sides. This is normal American practice, whether the issue turns section against section, like "cheap money"; or town against country, like Prohibition; or class against class like the use of injunctions in labor disputes. It is a sign of health when the Democrats choose a "sound-money" candidate for the presidency and a "cheap-money" platform, as they did in 1868; or when they choose a "wet" Eastern candidate for the presidency and a "dry" Western candidate for the vice-presidency, as they did in 1924. It is a sign of health when the Republicans choose a "sound-money" platform but cheerfully repudiate it throughout the "cheap-money" states, as they did in 1868.

A federal nation is safe so long as the parties are undogmatic and contain members with many contradictory views. But when the people begin to divide according to reason, with all the voters in one party who believe one way, the federal structure is strained. We saw this in 1896, during the last great fight for "free silver." To be sure, there remained some "gold Democrats" and some "silver Republicans" in 1896; yet the campaign produced the sharpest alignment on principle since the Civil War. And the fierce sectional passions racked the nation. Luckily, the silver issue soon settled itself, and removed itself from politics, so the parties could relapse into their saving illogicality.

The faults of such irrational parties are obvious. Brains and energy are lavished, not on the search for truth, but on the search for bargains, for concessions which will soothe well-organized minorities, for excuses to justify delay and denial. Unofficially, and in spite of any constitution, successful federal politics will tend to follow Calhoun's rule of concurrent majorities. Every interest which is strong enough to make trouble must usually be satisfied before anything can be done. This means great caution in attempting new policies, so that a whole ungainly continent may keep in step. Obstruction, evasion, well-nigh intolerable slowness—these are the costs of America's federal union. And the endless bartering of minor favors which we saw at its silliest in President Arthur's Congress is also part of the price. And so is the absence of a clear purpose whenever the President is weak or self-effacing, since the sum of sectional and class interests is not equal to the national interest, and the exchange of favors between blocs or pressure groups does not make a policy.

Yet no matter how high one puts the price of federal union, it is small compared to the price which other continents have paid for disunion, and for the little national states in which parties of principle can live (or more often die) for their clearly defined causes. And the price is small compared to what America paid for her own years of disunion. The United States, of course, may some day attain such uniformity (or have it thrust upon her) that she will abandon her federal structure; but until that happens she will be governed by concurrent majorities, by vetoes and filibusters, by parties which take both sides of every dangerous question, which are held together by the amusements and rewards of office-seeking, and which can only win an election by bringing many incompatible groups to accept a token triumph in the name of unity, instead of demanding their full "rights" at the cost of a fight.

The world today might do worse than study the curious methods by which such assuagements are effected.

PROBLEMS FOR WRITING AND DISCUSSION

1. Agar says Americans have always feared "Leviathan." How, then, have they allowed the growth of a relatively strong federal government? What concomitantly does Agar say has strengthened with its growth?

2. Do any contemporary domestic events indicate the continuing American distrust of centralized government?

3. What dichotomy of power in Agar's judgment has made the American "one of the most interesting forms of government the world has seen, and . . . one of the most successful"?

4. By what means is unity achieved in this "continent-wide federation" of diverse groups and interests? Compare the means Agar describes with what Hand (p. 388) calls the "bloodless measure" of stability and continuity American government has insured.

5. How does Agar justify the compromises with idealism the American political system must make? Is his notion of the "nature of man" comparable with Hand's?

6. When Agar says that the "written constitution has been unofficially revised," does he mean that Americans have violated the constitution? What specific changes does Agar discuss? What forms the "heart" of the "unwritten constitution"?

7. How do the modern political parties help to build "freedom and union"? Should they not, theoretically, tend toward discord and hatred?

8. What essential services do parties render government? How do these functions differ from those of political parties in England and Europe that Potter (p. 328), Lipset (p. 348), and Hand (p. 388) describe? Is the function of the American third party similar to that of foreign political parties?

9. Lippmann (p. 381) argues that public opinion often is too slow to react to an impending crisis. Agar, in effect, agrees. What is the difference in their attitudes?

10. Hand questions the existence of popular "will." Agar assumes that the President gives voice to it. Which view do you think is accurate? Does Agar agree with Lippmann that an official elected by all the people must be subservient to mob rule? What change in the office of President has kept local interests subordinate to national?

11. Agar and Handlin (p. 368) both comment on the lack of a common heritage for Americans. What, according to each, takes the place of tradition and makes for "freedom and union"?

12. Compare Agar's analysis of the two major American parties with that of Lipset. Does either writer find party distinctions significant? How do their functions, as Agar sees them, make it impossible for the two major parties to differ substantially from each other?

13. Explain what Agar means by saying that "in a large federal nation, when a problem is passionately felt, and is discussed in terms of morals, each party may divide within itself, against itself." Why is it dangerous to the federation when the voters "begin to divide according to reason"? What are the dangers of the basic irrationality of party allegiance in America?

14. How can the American politician "tend to ignore any issue that rouses deep passion" and at the same time strengthen the Union? Why does Agar say the American system "failed" at the time of the Civil War? Does Jaffa's essay on Lincoln (p. 360) make you suspect the accuracy of Agar's view? Does anything in recent American politics illustrate the dodging of important issues "as long as possible"? Explain.

15. Agar proposes that a government which has weathered the storms that have ravaged "the world during this century and a half must satisfy some deep need of man." Presumably, what "deep need" does it satisfy? Does Agar think of the American Union as Lincoln did, or as Handlin does? Explain.

How I Became President

HARRY S. TRUMAN

Harry S. Truman (1884-), thirty-third President of the United States, was born in Lamar, Missouri. After high school he tried a variety of jobs before taking over management of the family farm from 1906 to 1917. He served as a captain of a field artillery company during World War I, and upon discharge he ventured briefly and unsuccessfully into business, then entered politics. Shortly after being elected a judge of the Jackson County Court in 1922, he attended the Kansas City School of Law (1923-25). He served as presiding judge of the court until 1934, when he went to the United States Senate. His chairmanship during World War II of the Special Committee to Investigate the National Defense Program won him a national reputation that led to the vice-presidency in 1940. He became President on the death of Franklin D. Roosevelt in 1945 and was elected to that office in 1948. Since retiring from public life he has written the autobiographical Years of Decision *(1955) and* Years of Trial and Hope *(1956).*

During the first few weeks of Franklin Delano Roosevelt's fourth administration, I saw what the long years in the presidency had done to him. He had occupied the White House during twelve fateful years—years of awful responsibility. He had borne the burdens of the reconstruction from the great depression of the 'thirties. He

From Harry S. Truman Memoirs, Vol. I, *published by Doubleday & Company, 1955. Copyright © 1955 Time Inc.*

shouldered the heavier burdens of his wartime leadership. It is no wonder that the years had left their mark.

The very thought that something was happening to him left me troubled and worried. This was all the more difficult for me because I could not share such feelings with anyone, not even with the members of my family. I kept saying to myself that this man had often demonstrated amazing recuperative powers. Only a few months earlier, during the closing days of the 1944 presidential campaign, he had ridden for four hours in an open car through a driving rain in New York City and had seemed none the worse for it.

Knowing something of the great responsibilities he was forced to carry, I did not want to think about the possibility of his death as President. The rumors were widespread but not publicly discussed. But there had always been baseless rumors about Franklin D. Roosevelt.

We all hoped that victory against our enemies was near. Under Roosevelt's inspiring leadership the war was approaching its climax. The things he stood for and labored for were about to be realized. The world needed his guiding hand for the coming transition to peace.

On February 20, 1945, while I was presiding over the Senate, a rumor that the President was dead swept through the corridors and across the floor. I left my place at once and headed for the office of Les Biffle, Secretary of the Senate. As I entered, I said to Biffle, "I hear the President is dead. What will we do? Let's find out what happened."

Biffle called the White House and was informed that it was Major General Edwin M. Watson—"Pa" Watson, the appointment secretary to the President—who was dead. He had died at sea aboard the U.S.S. *Quincy* while returning with President Roosevelt from the Yalta conference. And later that same day I received a wireless message from the *Quincy*. In it President Roosevelt asked me for my opinion and advice about his appearing before a joint session of Congress to make a personal report on the results of his just completed conference with Churchill and Stalin.

I met the President a week later and was shocked by his appearance. His eyes were sunken. His magnificent smile was missing from his careworn face. He seemed a spent man. I had a hollow feeling within me, for I saw that the journey to Yalta must have been a terrible ordeal.

I tried to think how I could help him conserve his strength. With Mrs. Roosevelt and their daughter Anna, who was the President's close confidante, I had already discussed the problem of the strain of appearing before Congress. I recalled the expressions of pain I had seen on the President's face as he delivered his inauguration speech on January 20 on the south portico of the White House. Apparently he could no longer endure with his usual fortitude the physical pain of the heavy braces pressing against him.

With that in mind, and in order to spare him any unnecessary pain, I urged that he address Congress seated in the well of the House, and I explained that I had already cleared this unusual arrangement with the congressional leaders. He had asked for no such consideration, but he appeared relieved and pleased to be accorded this courtesy.

I shall never forget that day. The President's appearance before a joint meeting of the Senate and the House was a momentous occasion both for him and for the country. He was to report directly to Congress on the outcome of the deliberations at Yalta—deliberations that were bound to have a profound effect on the future peace of the world. He was anxious for bi-partisan support and wanted the full and sympathetic backing of Congress on foreign policy.

The speech was arranged for Thursday, March 1, 1945, and Mrs. Roosevelt, as well as Anna and her husband, Colonel Boettiger, were with him as he drove from the White House. Princess Martha and Crown Prince Olaf of Norway were also in the presidential party, which reached the Capitol just a little after noon.

The President was met in the same way he had always been met. Formerly, however, he had spoken from the rostrum of the House of Representatives, with the stenographers for the Congressional Record in their usual places before him, and with the presiding officers of the Senate and the House side by side behind. This time, however, the microphone-laden table that had been set up for his use stood in the well of the House chamber within little more than arm's length of the first curved row of seats.

The chamber was filled as he entered, and Speaker Rayburn and I, together with the others who had met him, followed him in and took our places on the rostrum. The justices of the Supreme Court were in the places they always occupy on such occasions. The rows of seats were solidly filled with senators and representatives. I vaguely caught a glimpse of the many members of the diplomatic corps. Here and there a uniform was visible, and I remember looking up into the gallery for Mrs. Roosevelt and daughter, and for Mrs. Truman and our daughter, while the audience, which had risen in honor of the President as he entered, resumed their seats. The President looked about him and at the papers that lay before him.

Even before Speaker Rayburn let the gavel fall and introduced "the President of the United States," it was plain that this appearance of the nation's leader before Congress was to have about it an unusual atmosphere.

"Mr. Vice-President, Mr. Speaker, and members of the Congress," he began. "I hope that you will pardon me for the unusual posture of sitting down during the presentation of what I want to say, but I know that you will realize it makes it a lot easier for me in not having to carry about ten pounds of steel around on the bottom of my legs, and also because of the fact that I have just completed a 14,000-mile trip."

Everyone present was intent on his words, but unhappily the famous Roosevelt manner and delivery were not there. And he knew it. He frequently departed from his prepared script. At one point he brought in a mention of "a great many prima donnas in the world who want to be heard," and he interrupted his text at another point to warn his listeners that "we haven't won the war." But these attempts to get away from his excellent script with light-hearted references and more thoughtful asides were not of much help.

Congress was stirred. Many members of both houses were awed by his dramatic display of sheer will power and courage, and there were very few who were critical of what he said.

I saw the President immediately after his speech had been concluded. Plainly, he was a very weary man.

"As soon as I can," he said to me, "I will go to Warm Springs for a rest. I can be in trim again if I can stay there for two or three weeks."

He left Washington for the South on March 30, 1945.

I never saw or spoke with him again.

Shortly before five o'clock in the afternoon of Thursday, April 12, 1945, after the Senate adjourned, I went to the office of House Speaker Sam Rayburn. I went there to get an agreement between the Speaker and the Vice-President on certain legislation and to discuss the domestic and world situation generally. As I entered, the Speaker told me that Steve Early, the President's press secretary, had just telephoned, requesting me to call the White House.

I returned the call and was immediately connected with Early.

"Please come right over," he told me in a strained voice, "and come in through the main Pennsylvania Avenue entrance."

I turned to Rayburn, explaining that I had been summoned to the White House and would be back shortly. I did not know why I had been called, but I asked that no mention be made of the matter. The President, I thought, must have returned to Washington for the funeral of his friend, Bishop Atwood, the former Episcopal Bishop of Arizona, and I imagined that he wanted me to go over some matters with him before his return to Warm Springs.

On previous occasions when the President had called me to the White House for private talks he had asked me to keep the visits confidential. At such times I had used the east entrance to the White House, and in this way the meetings were kept off the official caller list. Now, however, I told Tom Harty, my government chauffeur, to drive me to the main entrance.

We rode alone, without the usual guards. The Secret Service had assigned three men to work in shifts when I became Vice-President.

However, this guard was reinforced, as a routine practice, during the time President Roosevelt was away on his trip to Yalta and again when he went to Warm Springs. A guard had been placed on duty at my Connecticut Avenue apartment, where I had lived as Senator and continued to live as Vice-President, and another accompanied me wherever I went. These men were capable, efficient, self-effacing, and usually the guard who was on duty met me at my office after the Senate had adjourned. But on this one occasion I slipped away from all of them. Instead of returning from Speaker Rayburn's office to my own before going to the car that was waiting for me, I ran through the basement of the Capitol Building and lost them. This was the only time in eight years that I enjoyed the luxury of privacy by escaping from the ever-present vigil of official protection.

I reached the White House about 5:25 P.M. and was immediately taken in the elevator to the second floor and ushered into Mrs. Roosevelt's study. Mrs. Roosevelt herself, together with Colonel John and Mrs. Anna Roosevelt Boettiger and Mr. Early, were in the room as I entered, and I knew at once that something unusual had taken place. Mrs. Roosevelt seemed calm in her characteristic, graceful dignity. She stepped forward and placed her arm gently about my shoulder.

"Harry," she said quietly, "the President is dead."

For a moment I could not bring myself to speak.

The last news we had had from Warm Springs was that Mr. Roosevelt was recuperating nicely. In fact, he was apparently doing so well that no member of his immediate family, and not even his personal physician, was with him. All this flashed through my mind before I found my voice.

"Is there anything I can do for you?" I asked at last.

I shall never forget her deeply understanding reply.

"Is there anything *we* can do for *you*?" she asked. "For you are the one in trouble now."

The greatness and the goodness of this remarkable lady showed even in that moment of sorrow. I was fighting off tears. The overwhelming fact that faced me was hard to grasp. I had been afraid for many weeks that something might happen to this great leader, but now that the worst had happened I was unprepared for it. I did not allow myself to think about it after I became Vice-President. But I had done a lot of thinking about it at the Chicago convention. I recall wondering whether President Roosevelt himself had had any inkling of his own condition. The only indication I had ever had that he knew he was none too well was when he talked to me just before I set out on my campaign trip for the vice-presidency in the fall of 1944. He asked me how I was going to travel, and I told him I intended to cover the country by airplane.

"Don't do that, please," he told me. "Go by train. It is necessary that you take care of yourself."

Sometime later, too, Mrs. Roosevelt had seemed uneasy about the President's loss of appetite. She remarked to me at a dinner shortly after the elections, "I can't get him to eat. He just won't eat."

She was very devoted to the President, as he was to her. Mrs. Roosevelt was also close to the President in his work. In a way, she was his eyes and ears. Her famous trips were taken at his direction and with his approval, and she went on these long, arduous journeys mainly in order to be able to inform and advise him.

But now, as I stood there with her, I was thinking of a letter I had written to my mother and my sister a few hours earlier. They had not received it yet—would not receive it until this terrible news of the President's death had reached them. But once my letter had arrived, they would know how little I had anticipated this overwhelming hour.

Dear Mamma & Mary [I had written]: I am trying to write you a letter today from the desk of the President of the Senate while a windy Senator . . . is making a speech on a subject with which he is in no way familiar. The Jr. Sen. from Arizona made a speech on the subject, and he knew what he was talking about. . . .

We are considering the Mexican Treaty on water in the Colorado River and the Rio Grande. It is of vital importance to Southwestern U.S. and northern Mexico. Hope we get it over some day soon.

The Senators from California and one from Utah and a very disagreeable one from Nevada (McCarran) are fighting the ratification. I have to sit up here and make parliamentary rulings—some of which are common sense and some of which are not.

Hope you are having a nice spell of weather. We've had a week of beautiful weather but it is raining and misting today. I don't think it's going to last long. Hope not for I must fly to Providence, R.I., Sunday morning.

Turn on your radio tomorrow night at 9:30 your time, and you'll hear Harry make a Jefferson Day address to the nation. I think I'll be on all the networks, so it ought not to be hard to get me. It will be followed by the President, whom I'll introduce.

Hope you are both well and stay that way.

Love to you both.

Write when you can.

Harry

That is what I had written only a few hours earlier, but now the lightning had struck, and events beyond anyone's control had taken command. America had lost a great leader, and I was faced with a terrible responsibility.

It seems to me that for a few minutes we stood silent, and then there was a knock on the study door. Secretary of State Stettinius entered. He was in tears, his handsome face sad and drawn. He had been among the first to be notified, for as Secretary of State, who is the keeper of the Great Seal of the United States and all official state papers, it was his official duty to ascertain and to proclaim the passing of the President.

I asked Steve Early, Secretary Stettinius, and Les Biffle, who now had also joined us, to call all the members of the Cabinet to a meeting as quickly as possible. Then I turned to Mrs. Roosevelt and asked if there was anything she needed to have done. She replied that she would like to go to Warm Springs at once, and asked whether it would be proper for her to make use of a government plane. I assured her that the use of such a plane was right and proper, and I made certain that one would be placed at her disposal, knowing that a grateful nation would insist on it.

But now a whole series of arrangements had to be made. I went to the President's office at the west end of the White House. I asked Les Biffle to arrange to have a car sent for Mrs. Truman and Margaret, and I called them on the phone myself, telling them what had happened—telling them, too, to come to the White House. I also called Chief Justice Harlan Fiske Stone, and having given him the news, I asked him to come as soon as possible so that he might swear me in. He said that he would come at once. And that is what he did, for he arrived within hardly more than fifteen or twenty minutes.

Others were arriving by now. Speaker Rayburn, House Majority Leader John W. McCormack, and House Minority Leader Joseph W. Martin were among them. I tried personally to reach Senator Alben W. Barkley, Senate majority leader, but I could not locate him. I learned later that word of the President's death had reached him promptly and that he had gone at once to see Mrs. Roosevelt. In fact, he was with her in the White House while the group about me was gathering in the Cabinet Room.

There was no time for formalities and protocol. Among the people there were a score or so of officials and members of Congress. Only three women were present—Mrs. Truman and Margaret and Secretary Frances Perkins.

The Cabinet Room in the White House is not extensive. It is dominated by the huge and odd-shaped table, presented to the President by Jesse Jones, at which the President and the members of the Cabinet sit, and by the leather-upholstered armchairs that are arranged around it.

Steve Early, Jonathan Daniels, and others of the President's secretarial staff were searching for a Bible for me to hold when Chief Justice Stone administered the oath of office.

We were in the final days of the greatest war in history—a war so vast that few corners of the world had been able to escape being engulfed by it. There were none who did not feel its effects. In that war the United States had created military forces so enormous as to defy description, yet now, when the nation's greatest leader in that war lay dead, and a simple ceremony was about to acknowledge the presence of his successor in the nation's greatest office, only two uniforms were present. These were worn by Fleet Admiral Leahy and General Fleming, who, as Public Works Administrator, had been given duties that were much more civilian in character than military.

So far as I know, this passed unnoticed at the time, and the very fact that no thought was given to it demonstrates convincingly how firmly the concept of the supremacy of the civil authority is accepted in our land.

By now a Bible had been found. It was placed near where I stood at the end of the great table. Mrs. Truman and Margaret had not joined me for over an hour after I had called them, having gone first to see Mrs. Roosevelt. They were standing side by side now, at my left, while Chief Justice Stone had taken his place before me at the end of the table. Clustered about me and behind were nine members of the Cabinet, while Speaker Rayburn and a few other members of Congress took positions behind Chief Justice Stone. There were others present, but not many.

I picked up the Bible and held it in my left hand. Chief Justice Stone raised his right hand and gave the oath as it is written in the Constitution.

With my right hand raised, I repeated it after him:

"I, Harry S. Truman, do solemnly swear that I will faithfully execute the office of President of the United States, and will to the best of my ability, preserve, protect and defend the Constitution of the United States."

I dropped my hand.

The clock beneath Woodrow Wilson's portrait marked the time at 7:09.

Less than two hours before, I had come to see the President of the United States, and now, having repeated that simply worded oath, I myself was President.

PROBLEMS FOR WRITING AND DISCUSSION

1. This section of the *Memoirs* of Truman recounts one of the most dramatic moments in recent American history. How does the tone in which the selection is written reflect the drama?

2. What characteristics of Truman do tone and selection of detail reveal? Truman was reared in a small town similar to Eric Sevareid's. Does this selection indicate qualities similar to those of the inhabitants of such towns as Sevareid describes (p. 45)?

3. Does Truman, as he reveals himself in this selection, illustrate Commager's analysis of American character (p. 14)? Does he reveal typical American traits that Commager overlooks?

4. How do Truman's tie with his family and Roosevelt's with his differ from the family relationships of more recent generations depicted in Mead's essay (p. 24)?

5. How does Truman stress the importance and oppressiveness of the Presidency? Agar (p. 405) says that in the early nineteenth century "not even the most popular President could impose a national policy." Is it apparent from what Truman says that Roosevelt considered the "imposing" of national policy one of his duties? What light does Lippmann (p. 381) throw on the difficulties Roosevelt may have encountered?

6. What does Truman's sudden elevation to the Presidency reveal to you about the way the American political system functions in emergencies? What does Truman find significant in the absence of military men from his swearing into office? What other characteristics of American political life are evident from Truman's description of the people who attended the ceremony and the way in which it was conducted?

7. Does "The Price of Union" (p. 405) give any hint of why Truman was chosen by President Roosevelt to become his Vice-President? How does Roosevelt's urgency to appear before both houses of Congress illustrate what Agar says about the interrelation of executive and legislative powers in the American federation?

The Art of the Primary

THEODORE H. WHITE

> Theodore H. White (1915-   ), novelist and journalist, became the chief of Time's China bureau shortly after he graduated from Harvard in 1938. He returned to America in 1946 and, with Annalee Jacoby, wrote his first book, Thunder Out of China (1946). In 1948, the year his edition of The Stillwell Papers was published, he traveled to Europe as a correspondent for The Reporter, and while there completed Fire in the Ashes (1953). He returned to America to become national correspondent for The Reporter, then occupied a similar post with Collier's until that magazine ceased publication in 1956. Since then he has published two novels and, in 1961, a book that has already been called a classic in political reporting, The Making of the President 1960.

A primary fight, at any level, is America's most original contribution to the art of democracy—and, at any level, it is that form of the art most profanely reviled and intensely hated by every professional who practices politics as a trade.

In theory a primary fight removes the nomination of candidates from the hands of cynical party leadership and puts it directly in the hands of the people who make the party. When, indeed, theory matches fact (for, in some states, primaries are absurdly meaningless), primary contests result in disastrous and unforgettable explosions. A genuine primary is a fight within the family of the party—and,

---

From The Making of the President 1960 by Theodore H. White. Copyright © 1961 by Atheneum House, Inc. Reprinted by permission of the publisher, and by permission of Jonathan Cape Ltd., publisher, Atheneum Press, Inc., proprietors.

like any family fight, is apt to be more bitter and leave more enduring wounds than battle with the November enemy. In primaries, ambitions spurt from nowhere; unknown men carve their mark; old men are sent relentlessly to their political graves; bosses and leaders may be humiliated or unseated. At ward, county or state level, all primaries are fought with spurious family folksiness—and sharp knives.

Bosses and established leaders hate primaries for good reason; they are always, in any form, an appeal from the leaders' wishes to the people directly. Primaries suck up and waste large sums of money from contributors who might better be tapped for the November finals; the charges and countercharges of primary civil war provide the enemy party with ammunition it can later use with blast effect against whichever primary contender emerges victorious; primary campaigns exhaust the candidate, use up his speech material, drain his vital energy, leave him limp before he clashes with the major enemy.

And whatever ill can be said of local primaries can be multiplied tenfold for the Presidential primaries. For the amount of money used in a series of Presidential primaries across the breadth of this land is prodigious; the stakes of the Presidency are so high and dramatic that a horde of self-winding citizens and amateurs suddenly insists on participation; and the wreckage that a primary usually leaves of a well-organized local machine is as nothing compared to the wreckage that two political giants from alien states can make of an instate organization, whose private ambitions they abuse and whose delicate local balances and compromises they completely ignore as they strive for power to command the whole country.

Yet, when all is said, there remains this gross fact: were there no Presidential primaries, the delegates sent to the National Conventions would be chosen by local party bosses, and the decision of the Convention, made blind by inability to measure candidates' voting strength, would rest in the back room, with the bosses. When, for a period of thirty-five years, from 1865 to 1900, the choice of Presidential candidates was left to the bosses in convention assembled, their selections resulted in such mediocre leadership of this country that it could be truly written that "No period so thoroughly ordinary had been known in American politics since Christopher Columbus first disturbed the balance of American society." It was only with the turn of the twentieth century that the Presidential primary was introduced, soon to spread over the union. Many states in the next half-century experimented with the Presidential primary—some making it a permanent feature of their politics, some finally abolishing it, most of them altering its rules from decade to decade. By 1960, only sixteen states still retained a legal, open primary, in which all seekers for the Presidency of the United States, of either party, might offer themselves to the people directly. These sixteen states were as diverse in their politics and sociologies as the diversity of American civilization itself; they had been chosen by no superior reason or plan. Altogether to the foreign eye they must have seemed the most preposterous field of battle on which men who aspire to the leadership of American freedom and control of its powers should choose to joust. Yet these states were, and remain, vital to the play of American Presidential politics.

For John F. Kennedy and Hubert Humphrey there was no other than the primary way to the Convention. If they could not at the primaries prove their strength in the hearts of Americans, the Party bosses would cut their hearts out in the back rooms of Los Angeles. Thus, as they approached their combat, they had a sense of multiple audience—first, the folksy audience of the primary state to be won directly, along with the local delegates that could be harvested in the primary victory (this, of course, was the least of their considerations); next, the national audience, as the nation first paid its attention to the combat and assessed the men; and, last, there were the bosses of the big Eastern states and the smaller organized states who would coldly watch the race to observe the performance of political horseflesh.

Of the sixteen primary states, Hubert Humphrey had by late winter chosen five as his field of battle; of the same sixteen, John F.

Kennedy had similarly chosen seven. And they were first to clash head-on in Wisconsin on April 5th.[1]

Of all fifty states of the union, Wisconsin is probably that state in which professional politicians most hate to tempt a primary. It was Wisconsin, as a matter of fact, that in 1903 first invented the Presidential primary, which so many other states have since copied. And the political philosophy that inspired that revolutionary invention has made and left Wisconsin in political terms an unorganized state, a totally unpredictable state, a state whose primaries have over many quadrennials proved the graveyard of great men's Presidential ambitions.

It is worth examining the roots of Wisconsin's political philosophy and its kinship with that of a sister state, California. It would have been difficult at the end of the nineteenth century to pick two states more thoroughly Republican or more thoroughly corrupt than Wisconsin and California. The ownership and management of the political machinery of these states by their railways, their bankers and their industries had become so knavish that from within the Republican Parties they owned, there burst forth twin revolutions, with twin leaders who were to blow fresh air through the entire American political system. If today, half a century later, the maverick politics of Wisconsin and California remain alike, as do their magnificently decent and efficient systems of state government, it is a tribute to the ability, in our political system, of individual men to change the life of their communities. Decades after their death, both Wisconsin and California are better states to live in because fifty years ago Hiram Johnson of California and Robert LaFollette of Wisconsin decided to make them better.

---

[1] The actual technical opening of the 1960 campaign was, to be sure, the New Hampshire primary of March 8th. In previous years—as in the Eisenhower-Taft clash of 1952, or the Kefauver-Stevenson clash of 1956—the technical opening of the season in New Hampshire had been its true political opening, for the New Hampshire primaries in those years were battles. But in 1960 Kennedy's over-the-border strength from Massachusetts made any challenge to him in his New England backyard political folly. Kennedy won, contested only by a ballpoint pen manufacturer, by a margin of 9 to 1 in what was, politically, a trumpet flourish for national publicity but of no real meaning.

The philosophy of Robert LaFollette saw the state of Wisconsin as servant of the people and the open choice of state government as the citizens' prime right and responsibility. The source of all evil, by his philosophy, lay in political bosses, the pressure groups that controlled the bosses and the system of patronage and machine-made convention candidates who did their will. Over thirty years of furious political activity, Robert LaFollette succeeded in changing the politics and constitution of his state so thoroughly that professional politicians still shudder at his memory.

Candidates in Wisconsin are today still chosen not by conventions but by wild open primaries. Organized, incorporated, legal party machinery is forbidden (as in California), and the formal receptacles of party responsibility are denied official recognition. Patronage in Wisconsin (as in California) is almost negligible—the Governor of Wisconsin has only eight major patronage jobs at his disposal. Paid political advertising is forbidden in newspapers and magazines, over radio and TV, for twenty-four hours before election day. No political candidate can hire cars to haul voters to the polls, or pay poll workers. And, above all, when it comes to the sacred office of the Presidency and the Presidential primary, the maximum is achieved in frustrating political discipline and party control: in a Presidential primary voters may vote, without regard to their registration, either in the primary of their own party or of the opposition party, so that crossover Republicans may frustrate Democratic aspirants they hate, or crossover Democrats may frustrate Republicans they hate. This system so nearly approaches anarchy that there is much talk among the best of men in Wisconsin of abolishing the crossover privilege (as, indeed, California did six years ago when it abolished cross-filing in primaries, a Hiram Johnson legacy similar to the LaFollette legacy).

Having thoroughly disorganized formal party politics in Wisconsin, the LaFollette family went on, in 1934, officially to divorce their Progressive wing from the Republican Party, and establish a Wisconsin Progressive Party that was to dominate the state's politics for the next twelve years. In Wisconsin, Progressives were the first party, Republicans the second and the Democrats a poor third.

The Republican Party rested heavily on old colonial American stock, the suburban middle class, big industry and farmers of German origin, and chose through the open primaries, now horrible leaders like Joseph McCarthy, and now fundamentally decent men like Alexander Wiley. The Democratic Party became a fossilized, parochial group in the industrial cities along Lake Michigan, a receptacle for crumbs of Washington patronage, regarded in the words of one of its leaders as "little more than a Polish-Irish marching society." As late as 1938, Democrats could claim only 8 per cent of the general vote. The dominant party, the Progressives, combined many elements: intellectuals of the campus and the middle class, proud of LaFollette's innovations and achievements; working-class voters in the largely Germanic big cities, tinged heavily with Teutonic beer-hall socialism (Milwaukee for decades elected a Socialist Mayor); and in the countryside the predominantly Scandinavian farming vote, oriented toward a more puritan Danish-American socialism.

It was the collapse of the Progressives immediately after World War II that upset this pattern of Wisconsin politics—that plus the rise of Joe McCarthy. Though at war's end the son of the great LaFollette rejoined the Republican Party, which his father had dominated a generation before, not even his LaFollette name could lead the basically decent voting elements of the Progressives back to the party whose standard bearer was now McCarthy. The homeless drift of these scores of thousands of Progressives coincided, moreover, with the citizen revival in the Democratic Party. The nationwide surge of citizen participation in politics, which in the past decade has become one of the Democratic Party's greatest promises and problems, had begun early in the upper Midwest. Hubert Humphrey and his citizen groups had triumphed in 1948, to take over the Minnesota Democratic Party; in the same year G. Mennen Williams, Neil Staebler and Walter Reuther had taken over the Michigan party. In 1952 Adlai Stevenson's campaign beckoned thousands of high-minded amateurs to new enthusiasm for politics and new participation; and though Stevenson's influence in reshaping the structure of American democracy was nationwide, nowhere was it more permanently effective in changing the nature of a state party than in Wisconsin. (Madison, Wisconsin, is not only the state capital, it is the capital of Stevensonian strength across the country.) The new young men of the Wisconsin Democracy, largely amateurs in 1952, and the old homeless Progressives, thus began to pour in on the fossilized sectarian Democrats of the lake shore to obliterate older Democratic leadership. By the midfifties they had taken over the Democratic Party. In 1957, for the second time in the century, one of them—William Proxmire—became a United States Senator; in 1958, again for the second time in the century, one of them—Gaylord Nelson—became Governor. Democrats were fashionable, full of vigor, victorious.

In March, as the primary approached, Wisconsin still lay beneath its snow. The snow stretched in a crystal carpet all across the hills as the plane flew west from New York, a white blanket across the slopes of the Appalachians, embroidered by the black of leafless trees; the snow covered the gray ice of the frozen lakes, just beginning to show the seams and cracks of coming thaw; the snow covered Wisconsin.

Under the snow it is impossible to tell poor farm from rich farm, for snow forces farmers to shelter their automobiles and equipment indoors; the snow gives a white uniformity to the landscape, to dairy farm and corn farm, to German-American and Polish-American homestead, to Anglo stock and Scandinavian stock, to Catholic and Protestant.

The campaign was about to begin.

PROBLEMS FOR WRITING AND DISCUSSION

1. Why, according to White, do professional politicians hate primaries—especially presidential ones? Does White share their hatred?

2. When White refers to political bosses, does he have in mind the political leaders of which Lippmann writes (p. 381) or the aristocrats Viereck defends (p. 324)?

3. How does White's definition of a primary as a family fight reinforce what Agar says (p. 405) of the in-party splits on issues? Does White, like Agar, regard these fights as, on the whole, a symptom of the party's health?

4. White calls primaries "an appeal from the leader's wishes to the people directly." Would Hand (p. 388) accept the primary as an authentic "referendum"? How might Lippmann evaluate this appeal to the people's wishes?

5. Cooper (p. 399) takes the public's "ingratitude" to its "servants" in his stride, and White refers jocularly to "old men" being sent "relentlessly to their political graves." In the vigor of change that characterizes politics (as well as every other aspect of American life), what is sacrificed and what, if anything, is preserved? Does Americans' willingness to "scrap" their leaders reflect an aspect of equalitarianism?

6. White observes not only the tremendous expense of the primary but also the havoc it works on candidates and on existing state organizations as "two political giants from alien states . . . strive for power to command the whole country." How does Agar clarify the function of this seemingly "preposterous field of battle on which men who aspire to the leadership of American freedom and control of its powers . . . choose to joust"?

7. Lippmann and Cooper complain of the tyranny of public opinion, and White notes that had Kennedy and Humphrey not proved "their strength in the hearts of Americans," the party bosses would have "cut their hearts out in the back rooms. . . ." Does Lippmann, Cooper, White, or Hand (who also speaks of the "responsive control" of the public) propose any basic alteration in the political system? Explain.

8. Why are California and Wisconsin ideal (yet terrifying) states for a Presidential primary?

9. Compare White's description of the historical development of these two states with the general comments Handlin (p. 368) makes on the maturing of native leadership after a period of bossism. How does La Follette's philosophy illustrate the general American aversion to authority?

10. Does Agar's explanation (p. 405) of splits over issues within the major political parties clarify the "crossing over" of voters in primaries that White describes? How does White's description of the three parties in Wisconsin in the early part of the century illustrate what Handlin says of the political alignment of immigrant groups and their eventual assimilation as "citizens" and what Agar says not only of the Democratic and Republican parties but of the occasional third party in American politics and its function? (Note especially the "reasoning" propensity and the ideological dedications of Progressive Party membership.)

11. Does White agree with Hand on the political apathy of Americans? Explain.

12. Why, in a piece given over to detailed description of historical facts and the practical working of politics, does White spend two paragraphs describing the snow that covered Wisconsin in March of 1960?

3. The Wide World

The National Purpose

ARCHIBALD MacLEISH

Archibald MacLeish (1892-   ), like many intellectuals in the 1930's, was sharply critical of America, but with the rise of Nazism he sought "in the American past a credo and fortress," to use the words of Merle Curti. A Librarian of Congress (1939-44) and an Assistant Secretary of State (1944-45), MacLeish has been a professor at Harvard, except for the war years, since 1942. His life has been filled with awards—the Pulitzer Prize for poetry (1932, 1953, and 1958), the National Book Award for Poetry (1953), and the Antoinette Perry Award for Drama (1958)—and with writing. The most recent of his nearly two score of books are Freedom Is the Right to Choose *(1951), the play* J.B. *(1958), and* Poetry and Experience *(1961).*

That something has gone wrong in America most of us know. We are richer than any nation before us. We have more Things in our garages and kitchens and cellars than Louis Quatorze had in the whole of Versailles. We have come nearer to the suppression of grinding poverty than even the nineteenth-century Utopians thought seriously possible. We have wiped out many of the pests and scourges which afflicted humanity. We have lengthened men's lives and protected their infancy. We have advanced science to the edges of the inexplicable and hoisted our technology to the sun itself.

We are in a state of growth and flux and change in which cities flow out into countryside and countryside moves into cities and

From Life, *Vol. 48, May 30, 1960. This article appeared as one of a series titled "The National Purpose." Reprinted by permission of Houghton Mifflin Company.*

new industries are born and old industries vanish and the customs of generations alter and fathers speak different languages from their sons. In brief, we are prosperous, lively, successful, inventive, diligent—but, nevertheless and notwithstanding, something is wrong and we know it.

The trouble seems to be that we don't feel right with ourselves or with the country. It isn't only the Russians. We have outgrown the adolescent time when everything that was wrong with America was the fault of the Russians and all we needed to do to be saved was to close the State Department and keep the Communists out of motion pictures. It isn't just the Russians now: it's ourselves. It's the way we feel about ourselves as Americans. We feel that we've lost our way in the woods, that we don't know where we are going— if anywhere.

I agree—but I still feel that the diagnosis is curious, for the fact is, of course, that we *have* a national purpose—the most precisely articulated national purpose in recorded history—and that we all know it. It is the purpose put into words by the most lucid mind of that most lucid century, the 18th, and adopted on the Fourth of July in 1776 as a declaration of the existence and national intent of a new nation.

Not only is it a famous statement of purpose: it is also an admirable statement of purpose. Prior to July 4, 1776, the national purpose of nations had been to dominate: to dominate at least their neighbors and rivals and, wherever possible, to dominate the world. The American national purpose was the opposite: to liberate from domination; to set men free.

All men, to Thomas Jefferson, were created equal. *All* men were endowed by their Creator with certain inalienable rights. Among these rights were life, liberty, and the pursuit of happiness. It was the existence of these rights which justified American independence from King George and justified also the revolution which would have to be fought for that independence. It was the existence of these rights which would provide a foundation for the government to be established when independence was secure.

We not only *have* a national purpose: we have a national purpose of such aspiration, such potentiality, such power of hope that we refer to it—or used to—as the American Dream. We were dedicated from our beginnings to the proposition that we existed not merely to exist but to be free, and the dedication was real in spite of the fact that it took us three generations and a bloody war to practice our preachment within our own frontiers. It was real in spite of the fact that its practice is still a delusion in numerous pockets of hypocrisy across the nation.

To be free is not, perhaps, a political program in the modern sense, but from the point of view of a new nation it may be something better. The weakness of political programs—Five Year Plans and the like—is that they can be achieved. But human freedom can never be achieved because human freedom is a continuously evolving condition. It is infinite in its possibilities—as infinite as the human soul which it enfranchises. The nation which seeks it and persists in its search will move through history as a ship moves on a compass course toward a constantly opening horizon.

And America did move steadily on before it lost headway in the generation in which we live. The extraordinary feel of liveness which the Americans communicated, whether agreeably or not, to their early European visitors came from that sense of national expectation. We were never a very philosophical people politically after Jefferson and his contemporaries left us. We were practical men who took instruction from the things we saw and heard and did. But the purpose defined in our Declaration was a reality to us notwithstanding. It gave us *aim* as the continent gave us *scope*, and the old American character with its almost anarchic passion for idiosyncrasy and difference was the child of both. Those Missouri militiamen Parkman describes in *The Oregon Trail* slogging their way West to the war with Mexico, each in his own rig and each in his own way, could have constituted an army nowhere else. When, at Sacramento, a drunken officer commanded his company to halt and a private yelled "Charge!" the company charged, knocking five times their number of Mexicans out of prepared entrenchments.

The anarchy didn't matter because they were all headed in the same direction and the name of that direction was West—or freedom. They had a future in common and they had a purpose in common and the purpose was the enfranchisement of men—of all men—to think for themselves, speak for themselves, govern themselves, pursue happiness for themselves, and so become themselves.

Why then do we need to rediscover what our national purpose is? Because the words of the Declaration in its superb housing in the National Archives have become archival words, words out of history? Because the Bill of Rights of the American Constitution belongs, like the Magna Carta, in an airtight case? No one who reads the newspapers could think so. There has never been a time when courts and Congress devoted more of their attention to the constitutional guarantees of individual freedom than they do today, and as for the Declaration of Independence, its language is more alive in the middle of the twentieth century than it was in the middle of the nineteenth or even when it was written. It is not Communism, however Communism may attempt to exploit them, which has begotten the new nations of Asia and Africa or the new nationalistic stirrings in South America and the Caribbean and even in Europe. The Marxist dream is a dream of economic machinery, not of living men: of a universal order and system, not a proliferation of nationalities. No, the dream which has set the jungle and the cane on fire is different and older. It is Thomas Jefferson's dream—the dream which he and his contemporaries believed would change the world. It *is* changing the world—and not later than one might expect. Two hundred years is a short time in the history of institutions.

If the American Dream is out of date today it is out of date only in America—only in America and in the Communist countries in which the political police have extinguished it. But is it really out of date in America? Is its power to direct and draw us really so faint that we are lost in the blaze of our own prosperity and must enlist the aid of learned men to tell us where the future lies? That, I think, is a question for debate in these discussions.

Have we lost our sense of purpose or have we merely lost touch with it? Have we rejected the arduous labor to which our beginnings committed us? Or are we merely confused and bewildered by the volcanic upheavals which have changed the landscapes of our lives? Or is it neither rejection nor confusion? Is it nothing more than the flatulence and fat of an overfed people whose children prepare at the milk-shake counter for coronary occlusions in middle age? Are we simply too thick through the middle to dream?

I doubt for myself that we have rejected the American Dream or have even thought of rejecting it. There are minorities, of course, who have little enthusiasm for the actualities of the American commitment to freedom, but this is largely because they do not understand what the struggle it culminated was all about. Certain areas on the fringes of Europe were preserved by their geographical location from the necessity of living through the crisis of the Western mind which we call the Reformation, and American stock from these areas tends to find the master-mistress idea of the American Revolution—the idea which raised it from a minor war for independence to a world event—incomprehensible if not actually misguided. It is not a question of religion. Catholics from the heart of the European continent understand Jefferson as well as any Protestant. It is a question of geography. Men and women whose ancestors were not obliged to fight the battle for or against freedom of conscience cannot for the life of them understand why censorship should be considered evil or why authority is not preferable to freedom.

But all this does not add up to a rejection of the American dedication to liberty—the American dedication to the enfranchisement of the human spirit. The Irish Catholics, who are among the most persistent and politically powerful advocates of increasing censorship in the U.S., and who are brought up to submit to clerical authority in matters which the American tradition reserves to the individual conscience, are nevertheless among the most fervent of American patriots. And if their enthusiasm for freedom of the mind is restrained, their passion for freedom of the man is glorious. Only if a separate system of education should be used to perpetuate the historical ignorance and moral obtuseness on which fear of freedom of the mind is based would the danger of the rejection of the American Dream from this quarter become serious. As for the rest, the only wholehearted rejection comes from the Marxists with their curiously childish notion that it is more realistic and more intelligent to talk about economic machinery than about men. But the Marxists, both Mr. Hoovers to the contrary notwithstanding, have no perceptible influence on American opinion.

I cannot believe that we have *rejected* the purpose on which our Republic was founded. Neither can I believe that our present purposelessness results from our economic fat and our spiritual indolence. It is not because we are too comfortable that the dream has left us. It is true, I suppose, that we eat better—at least more—than any nation ever has. It is true too that there are streaks of American fat, some of it very ugly fat, and that it shows most unbecomingly at certain points in New York and Miami and along the California coast. But the whole country is not lost in a sluggish, sun-oiled sleep beneath a beach umbrella, dreaming of More and More. We have our share, and more than our share, of mink coats and prestige cars and expense account restaurants and oil millionaires, but America is not made of such things as these. We are an affluent society but we are not affluent to the point of spiritual sloth.

Most American young women, almost regardless of income, work harder in their homes and with their children than their mothers or their grandmothers had to. For one thing, domestic servants have all but disappeared and no machine can cook a meal or mind a baby. For another, there are more babies than there have been for generations. For still another, the rising generation is better educated than its parents were and more concerned with the serious business of life—the life of the mind. To watch your daughter-in-law taking care of her own house, bringing up four children, running the Parent-Teacher Association, singing in the church choir, and finding time nevertheless to read the books she wants to read and hear the music she wants to hear and see the plays she can afford to, is a salutary thing. She may think more about machines and gadgets than you ever did but that is largely because there are more machines and gadgets to think about. No one who has taught, as I have been doing for the past ten years, can very seriously doubt that the generation on the way up is more intelligent than the generation now falling back. And as for the materialism about which we talk so much, it is worth remembering that the popular whipping boy of the moment among the intelligent young is precisely "Madison Avenue," that mythical advertising copy writer who is supposed to persuade us to wallow in cosmetics and tail-fin cars. We may be drowning in Things, but the best of our sons and daughters like it even less than we do.

What then has gone wrong? The answer, I submit, is fairly obvious and will be found where one would expect to find it: in the two great wars which have changed so much beside. The first world war altered not only our position in the world but our attitude toward ourselves and toward our business as a people. Having won a war to "make the world safe for democracy," we began to act as though democracy itself had been won—as though there was nothing left for us to do but enjoy ourselves: make money in the stock market, gin in the bathtub, and whoopee in the streets. The American journey had been completed. The American goal was reached. We had emerged from the long trek westward to find ourselves on the Plateau of Permanent Prosperity. We were *there*! It took the disaster of 1929 and the long depression which followed to knock the fantasy out of our heads but the damage had been done. We had lost touch with the driving force of our own history.

The effect of the second war was different—and the same. The second war estranged us from our genius as a people. We fought it because we realized that our dream of human liberty could not survive in the slave state Hitler was imposing on the world. We won it with no such illusions as had plagued us twenty-five years before: there was another more voracious slave state behind Hitler's. But though we did not repeat the folly of the '20s we repeated the delusion of the '20s. We acted again as though freedom were an accomplished fact. We no longer thought of it as safe but we made a comparable mistake: we thought of it as something which could be protected by building walls around it, by "containing" its enemy.

But the truth is, of course, that freedom is never an accomplished fact. It is always a process. Which is why the drafters of the Declaration spoke of the *pursuit* of happiness: they knew their Thucydides and therefore knew that "the secret of happiness is freedom and the secret of freedom, courage." The only way freedom can be defended is not by fencing it in but by enlarging it, exercising it. Though we did defend freedom by exercising it through the Marshall Plan in Europe, we did not, for understandable reasons involving the colonial holdings of our allies, defend freedom by exercising it in Asia and Africa where the future is about to be decided.

The results have been hurtful to the world and to ourselves. How hurtful they have been to the world we can see in Cuba, where a needed and necessary and hopeful revolution against an insufferable dictatorship appears to have chosen the Russian solution of its economic difficulties rather than ours. We have tried to explain that ominous fact to ourselves in the schoolgirl vocabulary of the McCarthy years, saying that Castro and his friends are Communists. But whether they are or not—and the charge is at least unproved—there is no question whatever of the enormous popular support for their regime and for as much of their program as is now known. Not even those who see Communist conspiracies underneath everyone else's bed have contended that the Cuban people were tricked or policed in their enthusiasm for their revolution. On the contrary the people appear to outrun the government in their eagerness for the new order. What this means is obvious. What this means is that the wave of the future, to the great majority of Cubans, is the Russian wave, not the American. That fact, and its implications for the rest of Latin America, to say nothing of Africa and Asia, is the fact we should be looking at, hard and long. If the Russian purpose seems more vigorous and more promising to the newly liberated peoples of the world than the American purpose, then we have indeed lost the "battle for men's minds" of which we talk so much.

As for ourselves, the hurt has been precisely the loss of a sense of national purpose. To engage, as we have over the past fifteen years, in programs having as their end and aim not action to further a purpose of our own but *counter*action to frustrate a purpose of the Russians is to invite just such a state of mind. A nation cannot be sure even of its own identity when it finds itself associated in country after country—as we have most recently in South Korea and Turkey—with regimes whose political practices are inimical to its own.

What, then, is the issue in this debate? What is the problem? Not to *discover* our national purpose but to *exercise* it. Which means, ultimately, to exercise it for its own sake, not for the defeat of those who have a different purpose. There is all the difference in the world between strengthening the enemies of our enemies because they are against what we are against, and supporting the hopes of mankind because we too believe in them, because they are our hopes also. The fields of action in the two cases may be the same: Africa and Asia and Latin America. The tools of action— military assistance and above all economic and industrial and scientific aid—may look alike. But the actions will be wholly different. The first course of action surrenders initiative to the Russians and accepts the Russian hypothesis that Communism is the new force moving in the world. The second asserts what is palpably true, that the new force moving in the world is the force we set in motion, the force which gave us, almost two centuries ago, our liberating mission. The first is costly, as we know. The second will be more costly still. But the second, because it recaptures for the cause of freedom the initiative which belongs to it and restores to the country the confidence it has lost, is capable of succeeding. The first, because it can never be anything but a policy of resistance, can only continue to resist and to accomplish nothing more.

There are those, I know, who will reply that the liberation of humanity, the freedom of man and mind, is nothing but a dream. They are right. It is. It is the American dream.

PROBLEMS FOR WRITING AND DISCUSSION

1. MacLeish says that "something has gone wrong in America." What? Does he tell what the symptoms of the malady are? What is our national purpose, according to MacLeish? How is it unique?

2. What does MacLeish see as the weakness of programs capable of being achieved? Why is "American Dream" a fit name for our national purpose?

3. As the Declaration gave us "aim," MacLeish says, "the continent gave us scope" and from the two American character was born. Compare MacLeish's explanation of its origins with the frontier and abundance theories of Turner (p. 315) and Potter (p. 328). Would they agree that the aim of those who went west was the "enfranchisement" of all men "to think for themselves, speak for themselves, govern themselves, pursue happiness for themselves, and so become themselves"? Would De Voto (p. 93)?

4. Does MacLeish believe we are "simply too thick through the middle to dream"? Does T. S. Matthews (p. 99)?

5. Compare what MacLeish says of the immigrant groups from certain areas of Europe with what Handlin says of them (p. 368). What battle must men pass through to understand the American dream?

6. MacLeish cites Jefferson's dream—not communism—as the chief force behind the nationalistic stirrings in the new nations. What evidence does he offer? What is his chief objection to the "Marxist" dream?

7. MacLeish belittles the influence of Marxists in America, and he identifies them contemptuously as those who believe "it is more realistic and more intelligent to talk about economic machinery than about men." What happens to the freedom of man when he is subsumed into a mechanistic universe run by "laws" of history? What evidence does Eiseley (p. 299) see that men everywhere, not just Marxists, are becoming cogs in machinery? How does his essay reinforce MacLeish's appeal?

8. What, according to MacLeish, was our basic mistake after each world war? Compare his explanation with that of Lippmann (p. 381).

9. Lippmann criticizes the tyranny of the public over its leaders. Is MacLeish, in effect, making an appeal for American leadership? Explain the differences in their reasoning.

10. Freedom is never accomplished, MacLeish asserts. "It is always a process." Unlike a mechanistic process, it relies continually on self-initiated action. What is wrong, as MacLeish sees it, with mere *counter*-action? Does MacLeish say concretely how our "actions will be wholly different" from our enemies' or from our own counteractions?

11. MacLeish is a poet, playwright, essayist, and teacher; he is not a political commentator. By Kennan's standards (p. 233), is he competent to understand political problems? Is he competent by Stewart's standards (p. 287)?

12. Compare MacLeish's version of the American dream with Lincoln's (p. 360) and with Handlin's (p. 368). Is Matthews, for all his disillusionment with America, really rid of the dream that animates so many American writers, scientists, and leaders? Explain.

The Shape of the U.N.

E. B. WHITE

[For biographical detail, see page 262.]

Turtle Bay, December 1, 1956

My most distinguished neighbor in Turtle Bay, as well as my most peculiar one, is the U.N., over on the East River. Its fame has soared in the past month, on the wings of its spectacular deeds, and its peculiarities have become more and more apparent. Furthermore, the peculiarities have taken on an added importance, because of President Eisenhower's determination to make United States foreign policy jibe with the U.N. Charter. In many respects, I would feel easier if he would just make it jibe with the Classified Telephone Directory, which is clear and pithy.

The Charter was a very difficult document to draft and get accepted. The nations were still at war and the founding fathers were doubtful about whether a world organization could be made to work at all, so they inserted a clause or two to cover themselves in case it didn't. Every member went in with his fingers crossed, and the Charter reflects this. It derives a little from the Ten Commandments, a little from the Covenant of the League of Nations, and a little from the fine print on a bill of lading. It is high in purpose, low in calories. Portions of it are sheer doubletalk and, as a result, support double-dealing, but membership in a league is an exercise in double-dealing anyway, because the stern fact is that each sovereign nation has one foot in, one foot out. When the United States, for example, found itself up to its neck in the Middle East dilemma,

"The Shape of the U.N." (Turtle Bay, Dec. 1, 1956) from The Points of My Compass by E. B. White. Copyright © 1956, 1962 by E. B. White. Originally published in The New Yorker without its postscript, and reprinted by permission of Harper & Row, Publishers.

it subscribed to the Charter's pledge to suppress aggression in the common interest; it also issued an order to the commander of the 6th Fleet: "Take no guff from anyone!" You won't find such words in the Charter, but they are implicit in the Charter, and that is one of its peculiarities.

In shape the U.N. is like one of the very early flying machines—a breath-taking sight as it takes to the air, but full of bugs. It is obviously in the experimental stage, which is natural. Since many readers have probably never examined the Charter, I will give a quick rundown, covering merely the Preamble and Chapter One, where the gist of the political structure is to be found.

The Preamble awards honorable mention to the following: human rights, equal rights, justice, respect for treaties (the Charter itself is a treaty, so it is just whistling to keep up its courage here), tolerance, peace, neighborliness, economic and social advancement. The Preamble is *against*: war, and the use of armed force except in the common interest.

Chapter One deals with (1) Purposes, (2) Principles. The *purposes* are, in summarized form: to maintain peace; to suppress aggression; to develop friendly relations among nations on the principle of equal rights and self-determination (which I presume includes cannibalism); to cooperate; to harmonize actions of nations. The *principles* are: sovereign equality; members shall fulfill obligations in good faith; settle disputes by peaceful means; refrain from the threat or use of force against the territorial integrity or political independence of any state; cooperate; and never, never intervene in matters which are essentially within the domestic jurisdiction of any state.

As you can see, the thing has bugs. There are some truly comical ones, like Chapter I, Article 2, Paragraph 5, which, if I interpret it correctly, commands a member to help deliver a public whipping to himself. But I shall not dwell on the funny ones. Let us just stare for a few moments at two of the more serious bugs.

One: In a fluid world, the Charter affirms the *status quo*. By its use of the word "aggression" and by other devices it makes the *status quo* the test of proper international conduct.

Two: Aimed at building a moral community, of peace, order, and justice, the Charter fails to lay down rules of conduct as a condition of membership. Any nation can enjoy the sanctuary of the Charter while violating its spirit and letter. A member, for example, is not required to allow the organization to examine its internal activities. Mr. Shepilov can come to Turtle Bay, but can Mr. Hammarskjöld go to Budapest? The world waits to see. Even if he makes it, he will arrive awfully late.

Despite its faults, the U.N. has just emerged from a great month in world history, and emerged all in one piece. It pulled England and France out of a shooting war and sent the constabulary to replace them in Egypt. It failed in Hungary, but in the General Assembly the Soviet Union took a rhetorical shellacking that really counted. The U.N. is our most useful international device, but it is built on old-fashioned ideas. The Charter is an extremely tricky treaty. Its trickiness is dangerous to the world because, for one thing, it leads idealistic nations like ours into situations that suddenly become sticky and queer. This very thing happened when, in order to "condemn aggression" in the Middle East, in conformity with our Charter obligations, we deserted England and France and took up with the dictator of the Arab world and his associate the Soviet Union.

Some people, perhaps most people, think words are not really important, but I am a word man and I attach the very highest importance to words. I even think it was dishonest to call the world organization the "United Nations," when everybody knew the name was a euphemism. Why start on a note of phonyness, or wistfulness? The newspapers, with their sloppy proofreading, sometimes call the world organization the United Notions, sometimes the Untied Nations. Neither of these typos would make a serviceable title, but curiously enough, both are pat. Dr. Luns, of the Netherlands, recently described the U.N. Charter as "the expression of an attitude of mind." He said some countries used it merely as a juke box—they put in their nickel and the box would light up and play. That is about it. The Charter is an accommodating box and can produce a remarkable variety of tunes.

When Hungary erupted, the world was shocked beyond measure at what was taking place. But under the Charter of the United Nations the Hungarian government was in a position to put up just as noisy an argument as the oppressed people who were in rebellion. "Nothing contained in the present Charter shall authorize the United Nations to intervene in matters which are essentially within the domestic jurisdiction of any state." (Chapter I, Article 2, Paragraph 7). And when the U.N. wanted to send observers in, it received a polite no. This is palpably ridiculous, and it boils down to a deficiency in the Charter, a deficiency that is in the nature of an eleven-year-old appeasement. The Charter says that a member shall encourage "respect for human rights." That is laudable but fluffy. One way a Charter can advance human rights is to insist that the rights themselves (such as they are) remain visible to the naked eye, remain open to inspection. One of the preconditions of membership in the United Nations should be that the member himself not shut his door in the face of the Club. If the member won't agree to that, let him look elsewhere, join some other club.

Many will argue that if you are dealing with Iron Curtain countries, you have to take them on their own terms or you don't get them at all. That may be true. But who agreed to that amount of appeasement in the first place? And were they right? The appeasement was agreed to eleven years ago by charter writers who were trying to put together a world organization while a world war was still in progress. Their eye was not always on the ball, and they were looking back more than ahead. They were playing with century-old ideas: nonaggression (which is undefinable), self-determination (which includes the determination to send people to the salt mines), sovereign equality (which means that all nations are equal in the sight of God but the big ones are equal in the Security Council). The Charter bravely tries to keep these threadbare ideas alive, but they will not stay alive in the modern world of hydrogen and horror, and unless the Charter is brought up to date, it may fail us.

Much has happened in eleven years. Almost everything that has happened indicates that the United Nations should never have admitted the Communist nations on *their* terms; that is, freedom to operate behind a wall. If nations are to cooperate, the first condition must be that they have social and political intercourse. The Soviet Union held out for cooperation without intercourse, which is a contradiction in terms and which is as unworkable for nations as for spouses. A marriage can be annulled on the ground of denial of intercourse. A world organization can blow up on account of it.

The subtlest joker in the Charter is the word "aggression." There are other jokers, but none so far-reaching. When the United States was confronted with the Middle East crisis, it was surprised and bewildered to discover itself backing Nasser and Russia against France and England. One reason for this queer turn of events was that Britain and France had "aggressed," and therefore had violated the Charter of the United Nations. Actually, our government did not take its stand solely, or even principally, on the basis of its U.N. membership, but it did use its U.N. membership to justify its decision and lend it a high moral tone.

The word "aggression" pops up right at the very beginning of the Charter: Chapter I, Article 1, Paragraph 1. Aggression is the keystone of the Charter. It is what every member is pledged to suppress. It is also what nobody has been able to define. In 1945, the founding fathers agreed among themselves that it would be unwise to include a definition of aggression in the Charter, on the score that somebody would surely find a loophole in it. But in 1954 a special U.N. committee was appointed to see if it could arrive at a definition of aggression. The committee was called the United Nations Special Committee on the Question of Defining Aggression. It huffed and it puffed, but it did not come up with a definition, and around the first of last month it adjourned. So one of the great peculiarities of the Charter is that all nations are pledged to oppose what no nation is willing to have defined. I think it can fairly be said that the one subject the seventy-nine members of the United Nations are in silent agreement on is aggression: they are agreed that each nation shall reserve the right to its own interpretation, when the time comes.

This isn't surprising. To define aggression, it is necessary to get into the realm of right and wrong, and the Charter of the United Nations studiously avoids this delicate area. It is also necessary to go back a way. Webster says of aggression, "A first or unprovoked attack." And that, you see, raises the old, old question of which came first, the hen or the egg. What, we must ask, came first in the Middle East clash between Arab and Jew? You could go back two thousand years, if you wanted to. You could certainly go back beyond October 29, 1956, when the Israelis came streaming across the Sinai desert.

Not only has no member, in eleven years, accepted a definition of aggression, no member has admitted that it has committed an aggressive act, although many members have used arms to get their way and at least one member, the U.S.S.R., employs the threat of force as a continuing instrument of national policy. The Charter of the U.N. is a treaty signed by sovereign nations, and the effect of a treaty written around the concept of aggression is to equate the use of arms with wrongdoing and to assume that the world is static, when, of course, that is not so—the world is fluid and (certainly at this point in history) riddled with revolutionary currents at work everywhere. The tendency of any document founded on the idea of nonaggression is to freeze the world in its present mold and command it to stand still.

The world has seen a lot happen lately; it hasn't been standing still. And you will get as many definitions of aggression as there are parties to the event. Ask the delegate of the Soviet Union what happened in Hungary and he will say, "Remnants of Fascist bands aggressed." And he will cite Chapter I, Article 2, Paragraph 4: "All members shall refrain . . . from the threat or use of force against the territorial integrity or political independence of any state." Ask a citizen of Budapest what happened and he will say, "We couldn't take it any longer. We threw stones." And he will cite the Preamble on fundamental human rights and the dignity and worth of the human person. Under the Charter, it is possible to condemn both these aggressive acts—you just take your choice. Is the aggressor the man who throws stones at a tank, or is the aggressor the man who drives the tank into the angry crowd? The world was quick to form an opinion about this, but it got little help from the Charter. The Charter affirms the integrity of Hungary as a political entity, and officially designates both the Hungarian government and the Soviet government as "peace-loving." But that's not the way it looked to most of the world.

When the Israelis were asked what had happened, Eban replied, "The Israeli forces took security measures in the Sinai Peninsula in the exercise of Israel's inherent right of self-defense" (Chapter VII, Article 51). When the Arabs were asked what had happened, the heads of the Arab League issued a statement applauding Egypt's "glorious defense of the safety of her territories and sovereignty" (same chapter, same verse).

Neither England nor France has admitted to an aggression, although the two nations mounted an assault and carried it out—two permanent members of the Security Council shooting their way into Egypt before breakfast. It is, in fact, inconceivable that any nation will ever admit to having aggressed.

In the *Herald Tribune* the other morning, Walter Lippmann wrote, "In the past few days, the U.N. has been pushed into a position where its main function seems to be that of restoring conditions as they were before the explosion." That is certainly true, and one reason for it is that the Charter condemns aggression, sight unseen, and then turns over to the forum the task of studying the events leading up to the tragedy and the atmosphere in which it occurred. To condemn aggression is to decide *in advance of an event* the merits of the dispute. Since this is absurd, the subject of aggression should not be made part of a charter. The business of a charter is not to decide arguments in advance, it is to diagram the conditions under which it may be possible, with luck, to settle the argument when it arises. Surely one of those conditions is the right to observe at close hand.

Another peculiarity of the U.N. is its police. These are now famous, and rightly so. A couple of weeks ago, ninety-five Danish and Norwegian riflemen, wearing emergency blue, dropped out of the sky to keep the peace of the world. They were the advance unit of the United Nations Emergency Force. The men were reported looking "tired," and I should think they might. One editorial writer described them as "symbolic soldiers"; the label is enough in itself to tire a man. The *Times* correspondent in Abu Suweir, where the troops landed, described the policemen's task as "most delicate."

Their task is more than merely delicate; it is primeval. This force (it now numbers about two thousand) is the true dawn patrol, and these Scandinavian riflemen are dawn men. They are the police who are charged with enforcing the laws that do not yet exist. They are clothed with our universal good intentions, armed with the hopes and fears of all the years. They have been turned loose in a trouble spot with the instructions "Enforce the absence of law! Keep us all safe!" Behind them is the authority of the United Nations, all of whose members are "peace-loving" and some of whose members have just engaged in war. It is a confusing scene to a young policeman. It is confusing for people everywhere. One of the first things that happened on the arrival of UNEF was that General Burns, the commander, had to fly back to First Avenue to find out what the Chief of Police had in mind. Another thing that happened was that the Secretary General of the U.N. had to fly to Cairo to get permission from the Egyptian government to let the world be policed in its bailiwick.

It is confusing, but it is not hopeless. Police (so-called) have sometimes been known to antedate the laws that they enforce. It is again a case of the egg and the hen—law enforcers preceding law itself, like the vigilantes of our frontier West.

The U.N. has from the very start stirred people's imaginations and hopes. There seems little doubt that the very existence of a world organization is a help. I read in the *Times* magazine section the other day a good analysis of the U.N. by Ambassador Henry Cabot Lodge, who praised it because it "mobilizes world opinion" and because it shows "midnight courage." All this is certainly true. The U.N. is the shaky shape of the world's desire for order. If it is to establish order, though, it will have to muster the right words as well as the midnight courage. The words of the Charter are soft and punky. The Charter makes "aggression" synonymous with "wrongdoing" but drops the matter there, as though everyone understood the nature of sin. Yet it would appear from recent events that the users of force rarely think they are aggressing, and never admit they are. To simplify an idea this way is bad writing.

A league of sovereign nations—some of them much sovereigner than others—is not in a good position to keep order by disciplining a member in the middle of a fracas. Discipline can mean war itself, as we saw in Korea, and the U.N. is physically puny. But a league *is* in a position to do other things. One thing it can do is lay down conditions of membership. In its own house the U.N. has unlimited power and authority. Its bylaws should not appease anybody or make life easy for bad actors. The U.N. swings very little weight in Moscow or in Budapest, but it swings a lot of weight in Turtle Bay, and that's where it should start to bear down. Whether the U.N. could have been effective in Hungary is anybody's guess, but certainly its chances of operating effectively, for human rights and humankind, were diminished by the softness of the Charter and the eleven-year-old accommodation to the Communists, who from the very start showed that they intended to eat their forum and have it, too. Munich has nothing on San Francisco in this matter.

Ambassador Lodge, in his article, pointed out that the U.N., contrary to what a few Americans hope and a few Americans fear, is not a world government. He wrote, "As for the future, a world government which free men could accept is as far off as a worldwide common sense of justice—without which world government would be world tyranny."

True enough. And the world is a long way from a common sense of justice. But the way to cut down the distance is to get on the right track, use the right words. Our Bill of Rights doesn't praise free speech, it forbids Congress to make any law abridging it. The U.N. could profit from that kind of tight writing. The Charter sings the praises of the dignity of man, but what it lacks is a clause saying, "A member shall make no move abridging the right of the Secretary General to stop by for a drink at any hour of the day or night."

P.S. (May 1962). The Goa episode was a perfect demonstration of the pleasures and paradoxes of membership in a league of nations. When India, a peace-loving member, decided the time had come to tidy up its coastline, it took Goa from Portugal by force of arms, an operation that struck other members as in violation of the Charter (Chapter I, Article 2, Paragraph 4: "All Members shall refrain in their international relations from the threat or use of force against the territorial integrity or political independence of any State."). Mr. Nehru's explanation of the Goa adventure was that it was not an aggressive act, since it was "right"—an interesting new sidelight on the meaning of aggression. The Soviet Union, another peace-lover, came to India's defense; it said the seizure of Goa wasn't aggression because it was "inevitable," it was "historic." This left Western nations, including the United States, pointing to the simple words about not using arms. It also left them in bed with colonialism for a few moments, while India and Russia waved the anti-colonial flag and pretended they didn't smell gunsmoke.

Goa was "historic," all right. But everything that happens is historic, because everything that happens is a part of history. It is not unlikely that some similar episode, involving the use of guns by a lover of peace, will ignite the great fire of nuclear war. This may turn out to be so historic it won't even be remembered.

The United Nations has managed to survive for seventeen years. It is a more flexible organization than the old League—more accommodating, more ambitious, more daring. Under Dag Hammarskjöld it was sometimes breathtaking. Hammarskjöld was a sort of Paladin, roaming the world, doing good according to his lights, far, far from home. And behind it, it has a far stronger desire of people to cooperate for peace, a far greater sense of urgency. The U.N. was designed not to establish order but to prevent trouble and preserve peace. It is not, as some seem to believe, an embryo government; it is simply a pistol-packing trouble-shooter. Many groups, searching for an approach to world government, advocate "strengthening" the U.N., to make it a "limited world government," its function the control of arms; and, in a sense, this is now the avowed policy of the United States in its program for general and complete disarmament under a U.N. Peace Force. I think this is idle talk. Strengthening the U.N. would not turn it into a government. Short of knocking the whole thing apart and starting fresh, there would be, I think, no way to build the U.N. into a government, even if its members wanted that, and most of them don't.

Nevertheless, the U.N. is so useful, it should strive to strengthen itself and put its own house in better order, not in the hope of becoming a government but with the intention of improving its services, lessening its capacity to cause trouble, and promoting liberty. The Charter should be re-examined. The Charter is eloquent on the subject of human rights and fundamental freedoms, but it does not spell them out in the places where they would count, such as in Chapter II, where the question of membership is dealt with. Since 1945, the U.N. has almost doubled its membership, and the newly admitted states have been taken into the fold without presenting any credentials. They merely advertised themselves as "peace-loving" and were accepted as peace-loving by the others. Red China wants in, and the question of admitting China is as vexing as it is persistent. It would be a whole lot easier for the United States, for example, to make out a case against the admission of Red China if Chapter II offered any guidelines, but it doesn't.

Here are a few elementary matters that might well be considered for inclusion in the Charter. (1) A nation that jams the air shall not be eligible for membership. (2) A member of the U.N. that jams the air shall be expelled. (3) A nation that builds a wall to prevent people from leaving the country shall not be eligible for membership. (4) In the case of members whose press is run by the government, the privilege of using the forum shall carry with it the obligation to report fully the proceedings of the forum, in the home press. Failure to publish the proceedings revokes the privilege of the forum and is ground for suspension. (5) Member states shall grant the Secretary General and his aides free access to the country at all times.

To inject such democratic things into the Charter would require a two-thirds vote in the General Assembly. Moreover, even if an amendment that favored an open society over a closed society were to pass in the Assembly, it could be vetoed by any of the five permanent members of the Security Council. (Among its other defects, the Charter is virtually amendment-proof.) The U.N. was, of course, not created to praise liberty; yet the lovers of liberty should occasionally try to write their love into the document. Amendments ought to be proposed from time to time, if only to place the proprietors of closed societies in the unwholesome and embarrassing position of having to stand up before the crowd and defend darkness. The U.N. should do more than try to preserve the peace. If it seriously hopes to save future generations from the scourge of war, it should come out in favor of light, in favor of openness, and get it into the Charter.

PROBLEMS FOR WRITING AND DISCUSSION

1. Where does the weight of White's criticism fall: on the hypocrisy of United Nations' members, on unhalted aggression, or on the wording of the United Nations Charter? To what does he attribute the fault he attacks?

2. What quarrel does White have with each of the following terms: *common interest; United Nations; sovereign equality; self-determination; peace-loving; internal jurisdiction; aggression*?

3. Does the failure to define "aggression" operate to the disadvantage of the Iron Curtain countries or of "idealistic nations like ours"? What examples does White give? What is the force of the analogy he makes between marriage and the world organization?

4. What two concrete improvements in the United Nations Charter does White propose be made?

5. A brief look at the opening paragraphs of Hand's (p. 388) and Agar's (p. 405) articles will remind you that the founding fathers of America, like those of the United Nations, were doubtful that their new organization would work at all. What parallels can you draw between the problems of American federation and of the world organization? Does the Preamble of the United Nations Charter assume the homogeneity of national interests as Hand says the American "fathers" assumed that "the mass of mankind was . . . homogeneous"? What major difference does White point to between the United Nations Charter and the American Bill of Rights?

6. White notes that "self-determination" may mean anything from cannibalism to the "determination to send people to the salt mines." Lincoln put the rights of the Negroes to life, liberty, and the pursuit of happiness before the right of a majority to determine for themselves the question of slavery. Does White's interest in the *way* things are determined within the borders of member nations presuppose (like Lincoln's concern with the *way* Negroes were regarded—that is, as men or as chattels) a sense of right and wrong, a sense of "common justice"? Does *law* of any kind presuppose these things? Does the Declaration assume a law of Nature and Nature's God? Explain.

7. Does White reveal any implicit hope that the "revolutionary currents" that keep the world from being static may move toward a sense of common justice if the world is not tyrannized into a status quo (with the unwitting help of "idealistic nations")? Compare the tenor of his conclusion with those of Hand, MacLeish (p. 439), and Handlin (p. 368).

8. What in particular pains White about the plight of the UNEF? Does he mitigate the hopelessness of its task by suggesting the role it may play in shaping the "world's desire for order"?

Our National Talent for Offending People

D. H. RADLER

D[onald] H[oward] Radler (1926-   ) was born in New York City and graduated from Kenyon College, but since 1958 he has been a resident of Central America, where he acts as correspondent for about forty newspapers and magazines, concentrating on medicine (Medical World News), politics (The Reporter), and human interest (San Francisco Chronicle). Speaking fluent, unaccented Spanish, he has traveled throughout twelve Latin American countries. Among his books is El Gringo: The Yankee Image in Latin America (1962). In addition, he has published more than one hundred articles in such magazines as Harper's and Scientific American.

Despite what the hit-and-run newspaper pundits write after a one- or two-week flying visit, we *are* in trouble in Latin America and all of our money isn't helping our cause here. And odd as it may seem to the nation that gave birth to Madison Avenue, one strong reason we aren't liked in Latin America is simply that we aren't very likable. In fact, it almost seems that Americans here are intent upon—and eminently successful at—losing friends and alienating people.

Since I live in Honduras and know it better than the other Latin American countries, I'll use Honduras as my main example. What happens here, however, is not very different from what happens elsewhere south of the border.

Here we are known primarily through two banana companies (Standard Fruit Company and the larger United Fruit Company),

From "Our National Talent for Offending People," **Harper's Magazine**, *August 1961. Reprinted by permission of the author.*

a handful of State Department personnel, and the American publications that are read here—chiefly, *Time* magazine's Latin American edition, in English. Many, many Latin Americans know English—a fact we tend to forget when we talk about them in their presence. English is taught in the schools here and is spoken, or at least understood, by many ordinary citizens, not just by the Stateside-educated business and professional men and politicians. When I first came to La Esperanza, one of the most remote towns in the country, the tax collector greeted me: "Good! Now I've got a chance to practice my English." He had never been to the States, didn't plan to go, but wanted to improve his English "because it's an important language." How many Americans feel that way about Spanish, spoken by well over two hundred million people?

To Hondurans and other Central Americans, the banana companies represent American capitalism; the Embassy and Consulate stand for American government; the press, notably *Time,* says what the American people think about their neighbors to the South. All have failed to present our country effectively. It is worth examining why.

Initially, the banana companies came here under concessions from local governments granting them huge acreages in return for their investments, especially the construction of much-needed railroads.

Honduras, perennially the leader in efforts toward Central American federation, hoped for an east-west rail link to encourage union. By 1924 it had awarded nearly 200,000 acres of rich banana land to United Fruit alone, as compensation for future railroad construction. Today, Honduras possesses 900 miles of railroad—but they are all within the banana zone and Tegucigalpa remains one of the few national capitals in the world without rail communication.

On the other hand, the banana companies have turned useless jungles and swamps into productive farms. They have built homes, hospitals, schools, and clubs; have maintained vast health and sanitation programs, virtually eradicating malaria in their own areas; have consistently paid their men more than any other rural workers in the country. In addition, the taxes and wages they pay are larger by far than those of any other industry in the country—United Fruit alone contributes almost one-sixth of Honduras' gross national product.

UF has also endowed and helped support the Central American School of Agriculture at Zamorano, near Tegucigalpa; maintains a vast collection of economic tropical crops at Lancetilla, near the port of Tela; has sent out, free, millions of seedlings to spread new and better fruits, vegetables, and timber trees throughout the American tropics.

Why, then, is there such feeling against the Company? Part of the answer is sheer size—UF is the dominant factor in the national economy. Operating throughout Guatemala, Costa Rica, Panama, Colombia, Ecuador, and the Dominican Republic, it is known as *el pulpo*, "The Octopus." Another reason lies in its special contracts with the government. Hondurans charge that these agreements have subjected their national resources to foreign control and their local politics to foreign interference.

It is conceivable that different policies could have made UF, which has done much for Honduras, a welcome partner. Instead, the Company seems consistently to have pursued a course calculated to make it—and American industry in general—warmly disliked.

No attempt has been made to let Hondurans purchase stock in the local Companies, thus allowing them participation in ownership if not control; no director or top executive of the present Company is a Latin American, few even have much tropical experience. Local managers are all Americans, as are most department heads and other executives. For years, executive trainees have been shipped in from the States rather than recruited locally. (This year, at last, some graduates of the UF-endowed Zamorano agricultural school are being trained by the Company for senior agricultural positions. But all "dollar employees"—those hired in the States—are paid on a higher wage scale than those hired locally.)

Instead of integrating its American personnel into the local community, United Fruit maintains Company towns. Housing and other facilities, including, for example, use of Company vehicles, are a function of position—which means that the American *jefes* conspicuously have the best. As a direct result of this segregation, many Company people, and even more of their wives, speak Spanish poorly or not at all, even after years of residence here. Their parties and leisure activities might well take place back home: the Latin hosts feel shut out on their own home ground.

The Company does nothing to discourage this effective *apartheid* —it maintains no orientation program for American employees, doesn't demand Spanish language ability or teach the language (except in a few essential cases of men who will supervise farm workers speaking only Spanish), in no way rewards employees who adapt to the local environment and make friends for the Company. Instead, UF runs an American school for all U. S. children as well as some Latins—who are chastised for speaking even a word of Spanish, "because we're teaching English here!"

Recently, UF has given much proud publicity to a plan for transferring the ownership of its land to local farmers if they agree to raise bananas on it. UF will buy their product, ship and market it, thereby "going into partnership" with the nationals in the countries where it operates. However, labor leaders point out that the Company will thus avoid most of its current legal obligations to maintain schools and hospitals, provide labor benefits such as vacation with pay, terminal leave, etc. Government agronomists note that most of the land in question is now unsuitable for production of the market-favorite Gros Michel banana because of a soil fungus imported by UF on planting material in years past. Other critics wonder why the company is not extending its "partnership plan" to its highly productive, low-cost producing zone on Panama's west coast.

The irony of such close-fisted policies is that they are not paying off. Toward the end of 1958 the Company's stock sold at $52 and was considered an eminently blue chip. In May of this year, it was selling at less than half that price. The pessimism of investors is matched by the hostility of Central Americans to North American industry in general.

If anything, our diplomats do worse. Our Embassy in Tegucigalpa occupies a huge, luxurious, high-walled modern fortress. In sharp contrast to most of the other embassies of the old capital, it reeks of money and power.

One former Ambassador made a policy of accompanying President Ramón Villeda Morales on his frequent trips around the country, apparently intending to create an image of American-Honduran solidarity. Instead, sensitive local people predictably interpreted this as U. S. domination over their government. As one Honduran put it, "Uncle Sam gives us money with no strings attached—then he attaches 'the tick' to the President's back to see that we spend it right!"

Recently, a Tegucigalpa university student told me that he and his fellow students are "tired of having every government decision checked with your Embassy." Whether this actually happens or not is unimportant—the significant thing is that the students *think* it happens, and resent it. Remember that in Latin America, the students are both active and potent politically—their weight has often swung revolutions one way or another. (In 1959, for example, Colonel Armando Velásquez Cerrato led a rebellion against the Honduran government. The police defected to him; the army wavered; the revolution failed when the students took up arms in support of the government.)

No U. S. group in Honduras addresses itself to student opinion. The Communists do—all the time. Is it any wonder that the students are influenced by them?

"We have few real Communists in our group," a student friend told me, "but annoyance with American meddling and patronizing American attitudes causes many of us to accept the Communist vocabulary: Yankee Imperialism, Dollar Diplomacy, and the rest. And remember—we are the real future leaders here. Anyone with a university education is still so rare that he is automatically on top of the heap in the professions, in business, or in politics."

Our consulate in San Pedro Sula, second city and economic capital of the country, is also big and expensive by local standards. Awaiting retirement, the consul is fairly inactive, but several vice-consuls have left their mark on the community. There was one, for example, who

(1) replaced without notice the popular director of the U. S. cultural center because she was a German, not an American, causing vigorous student protest;

(2) demanded that students at the center, for course credit, must listen to the Voice of America;

(3) established a conversational English course based on reading from *Time* (whose negative attitude toward Latin America we will examine shortly);

(4) called a popular local businessman "a dog-thief and an ex-Nazi" when a watchdog lent him by this man doggishly ran home;

(5) earned the local name of "The Ugly American"—and a promotion to a major European capital as senior information officer.

It would appear that a great many of our diplomats here are neither selected for nor trained in diplomacy—or in the language and customs—or in an acceptable attitude toward the people whose friendship they are supposed to win. The rare effective U. S. spokesman—such as a political officer I met in Mexico City who had married a Latin, brought his children up to be bilingual, and settled into the life of the country—is shortly transferred elsewhere on the State Department's rigid rotation schedule.

The Russians, who lack official representation here, have been represented by Cuban emissaries—tall, handsome, bearded, and uniformed Latins who are obviously "brothers" of the Hondurans and whose friendship missions take them into the *cantinas* and football stadia of the people rather than the loftier confines of diplomatic circles. This approach is reflected in the very language of the Russians as compared with ours: *e.g.,* in an early exchange over Cuba, Khrushchev said, "We will help our Cuban brothers . . ."; Eisenhower declared, "The U. S. will not permit. . . ."

If American business and government are failing to make friends for us in Latin America, their impact is no greater than that of *Time* magazine, which, on the record, has made us a host of enemies. One high-ranking Honduran government official told me that America would be much better liked "if *Time* printed no Latin American edition at all."

It's easy to see why. Here in Honduras, after a stormy history of dictatorship, revolution, and more dictatorship, the people finally have a freely elected, genuinely democratic government. President Ramón Villeda Morales, a leading physician and ardent humanist, took office in December 1957. Consider *Time's* coverage of the events leading up to the election, beginning with its issue of September 23, 1957:

> "Three years ago Honduras' Liberal Party Chief Dr. Ramón Villeda Morales, 48, nicknamed 'Little Bird,' had a badly busted wing. . . . Last week he was riding high. . . .
> "For the last eight months Villeda has been serving as Honduras' Ambassador to Washington. *The stay in the U. S. apparently had done him good* [italics mine]. Washington received him warily, largely because of his leftist campaign oratory in '54, *e.g.,* promising *campesinos* an eight-hour day at double and triple pay."

U. S. workers have long had an eight-hour day—and triple the 1954 Honduran average is still only $1.50 a day, which many Hondurans are now getting, thanks to Villeda's having fulfilled the promise *Time* called "leftist." The article concluded: "But Villeda Morales proved himself a much sobered man." The implication that the Honduran presidential candidate was a wild-eyed leftwinger, but saw the light after eight months in Washington, is not a pretty compliment to a probable chief of state.

Then, on October 7, 1957, *Time* reported:

> "Villeda had won the [Honduran presidential] election in 1954 on a wild-eyed program promising double and triple wages to farmhands. . . . But eight months in Washington . . . had a steadying effect. . . . He announced that he was categorically opposed to Communism."

Here we go one step further, to the clear implications that Villeda had been pro-Communist (there is no record that he ever was); and that his stay in Washington had set him straight.

Time continued: "The Assembly . . . can either name Villeda President or schedule elections, which he claims to prefer. . . ." Why "claims"? This implies that Villeda is no democrat, really wants the presidency any way he can get it. But in Honduras in 1957, Villeda could have won any election—why *not* prefer it?

Despite *Time,* Villeda became president. He went to work on health, welfare, education, and transportation for his country's nearly two million people. He built schools, health centers, roads, and bridges, gave workers a realistic labor code. *Time* reported not a word of this. Then Villeda announced plans for a hydroelectric plant on the turbulent Rio Lindo. *Time* declared, October 20, 1958:

> "The [World] Bank argued that roads are more important than a big dose of power for a primitive country, gave Honduras a $5,000,000 highway loan, hoping to encourage a big road-building program. The effect was just the opposite."

As a matter of fact, in that first year in office, Villeda built or started building more miles of road than Honduras had previously had in its entire 139-year history. He is now building the Rio Lindo hydroelectric plant as well, with $16 million loaned by the Export-Import Bank and other banks which agree that power is essential to Honduras' further development.

On January 11 of last year, *Time* continued its curious brand of "reporting" from Honduras. Under the heading of "Letdown," its story began with a pat on the back for President Morales, saying that two years after he took office, "Honduras is free and politically stable—no small merit in a country whose history counts 135 revolutions." But *Time* swung immediately into: "Nonetheless, Honduras is a troubled land, suffering, as Tegucigalpa's *El Cronista* put it last week, with 'spiritual helplessness and a chronic economic depression'." And, it added, "Communists are beginning to elbow their way into the nation's press." *Time* failed to note that *El Cronista,* the authority it quoted a few lines earlier, is the principal Communist-dominated newspaper in the country. It has been frantically and unpopularly supporting—and receiving substantial financial aid from—Fidel Castro's Cuban revolutionary government. Concluding the same story, *Time* declared: "The longer he flutters, the less Little Bird looks like the stormy petrel he seemed before taking office."

But Villeda, in addition to his clear record of social accomplishment, has meanwhile successfully handled a half-dozen armed rebellions from the extreme right; replaced an entire recalcitrant national police force with a loyal civil guard; effectively countered constant Communist agitation throughout the country—without declaring a "state of siege" such as neighboring Guatemala, Nicaragua, and El Salvador have found necessary. Furthermore, he has avoided major strikes in the ailing banana industry, the mainstay of the nation's economy, and he has attracted substantial capital investment from abroad in a period when such investment has been on the decline throughout most of Latin America because of political instability.

Were *Time's* needless flippancy aimed only at Villeda, one might see it as an isolated prejudice but the magazine—which is read throughout Latin America as the voice of the U. S.—maintains the same smug, belittling attitude toward virtually everything Latin American, except, perhaps, its dictators. Items:

BRAZIL (January 16, 1956): ". . . Foregoing his gimpy English, the President-elect talked to Ike in Portuguese, translated by . . ." [*For that matter, what of Ike's non-existent Portuguese?*]

COSTA RICA (June 23, 1958): *Ex-President José Figueres, one of Latin America's most respected democrats and a firm friend of the U. S., was asked to tell our House of Representatives why the U. S. is disliked south of the border. He did.* Time *reported:* ". . . . outspoken Pepe so exaggerated and overstated his case that great pieces of his statement ended up sounding sadly like the *Yanqui*-baiting he deplores. . . ." *Don Pepe is and was outspoken—that's why he was asked to give the talk in the first place—but there was little in his statement that is exaggerated or overstated, unless any criticism of the U. S., even by invitation, must necessarily be so characterized.*

VENEZUELA (July 21, 1958): Time's *first reference to Presidential Candidate Rómulo Betancourt, another leading liberal with pro-U. S.*

leanings: "Key to the political puzzle was beefy Rómulo Betancourt, 50, top man of the leftist Democratic Action. . . . Betancourt now takes a carefully statesmanlike line."

BOLIVIA (March 2, 1959): "Last week a U. S. Embassy official added up the results [of U. S. aid to Bolivia] and made a wry face. 'We don't have a damn thing to show for it,' he said. 'We're wasting money. The only solution to Bolivia's problems,' he went on to wisecrack, 'is to abolish Bolivia. Let her neighbors divide up the country and the problems'."

Time's story not only enraged Bolivians but set off anti-American riots in which several people were hurt, significant property damage was done, and U. S. prestige was badly deflated. On March 16, calling the story "The Fanned Spark," *Time* reported: "This rueful jest, repeated by a U.S. official in La Paz and quoted in *Time's* March 2 issue, was turned last week into the spark for three days of anti-U. S. violence. . . . The U. S. position [was] that there was 'no evidence' that the statement was ever made. . . ."

These examples could easily be multiplied. Surveying the Latin American edition of *Time* over the past four years, one finds a consistent tone of smug superiority, a persistent flow of ridicule for virtually everything Latin American. Of course, there are occasional favorable stories in *Time*. Its longer "cover stories" on Latin America—for example, the one on Betancourt of Venezuela in February 1960—sometimes show signs of more responsible editing and writing than do its week-to-week reports. But *Time's* favors are rarely bestowed on any performance south of the border that doesn't neatly mirror *Time's* version of life in the U.S.

Even then the *Time* style intrudes. For instance, in a story commending Brazil, *Time* couldn't resist discussion of the country's "Johnny-come-lately industries." In general, towns smaller than Rio de Janeiro or Buenos Aires are described as "sleepy"; nations less developed industrially than Mexico or Colombia as "backward" or "primitive"; plans for local development as "starry-eyed"; appeals to the U. S. as "dollar-hungry"; dealings with governments *Time* does not approve of as "Red-lining."

So much for our major press representation in Latin America. Along with the often greedy, thoughtless behavior of American business here and the weirdly "Ugly American" performances of so many of our government people, *Time* must bear responsibility for jeopardizing our relations with Latin America.

Meanwhile, the average Americans who come here make matters worse. In general, they are badly informed before they come and they make a bad impression when they arrive. Then, while they are here, they send more misinformation back home. Talking in New York recently with a director of a large, world-wide U. S. corporation, I was shocked to hear that his men had reported that anti-Yankee feeling is dead in Latin America, except for Cuba. "We don't have a thing to worry about," he smilingly told me. But his men, dressed in business suits, arriving by plane and traveling by car in the big cities, see only the glitter—and talk only with their Latin American counterparts. Educated, traveled, and wealthy, these Latins know what side their imported melba toast is buttered on. If they know of anti-gringo sentiments, they're altogether too smart to talk about it.

But on the walls of the millions of thatch-roofed shacks of the peasants, Fidel's picture hangs alongside that of Christ and the Virgin, replacing such former local heroes as Francisco Morazán, martyr to Central American unity. (In San Pedro, Morazán's statue recently sported the red-paint legend, "Viva Castro! Yanquis go home!") And in the field commissaries of the banana companies and in the candlelit *cantinas* of the poor, a word against Castro is still tantamount to suicide. (I know this because I've been there. Unfortunately, most of our pulse-takers haven't.)

There are obvious historical, political, and economic reasons for anti-gringo feelings, chief among them the size, wealth, and good fortune of the United States. But the hostility toward us could be diminished if the Americans who come here were the sort of people Latins could like and respect. With few exceptions, they usually manage to make enemies instead of friends.

We do this by acting as if we are better than anyone else. We know little of Latin American history, geography, politics, or economics, apparently because we don't think it's worth learning; we speak Spanish poorly or not at all because "they'll understand English if I holler loud enough." We describe ourselves as democratic and ask Latin Americans to emulate us— yet Americans here usually stick to the big cities and ride the best and most private transportation. If they enter a Latin home, it is a high-class home, comfortably reminiscent of upper-middle-class homes in the States. We seem unable to tolerate the natural smell of a man who never heard of deodorants.

During and after World War II, the British criticized us for brashness, forwardness, loudness. But today in Latin America we make enemies by seeming to be too reserved, too preciously withdrawn. An ex-European, now a Honduran citizen, told me: "You Americans have had it too good. You're starting to act like the Germans before they set out to take over the world. You really believe you're better than anyone else. But the day of the superman is over—that's why nobody likes you."

But I don't think most Americans down here are irrevocably arrogant, even if they appear to be. I think they're afraid. They seem to be frightened and embarrassed by people who use warm *abrazos* in place of cold handshakes, who express their emotions frankly instead of rationalizing around every bush. Weaned on canned "self-help" and "popularity" formulas, and babied along on condensed, homogenized food, clothing, and culture, they are repelled and even terrified by people who eat food as it comes from the ground, wipe their fingers on their rough denim pants, and make music and poetry with their own mouths and hands instead of by proxy.

I know a big, strapping American woman who has lived peaceably in the tropics for three or four years who—in broad daylight—left a friend's house by the back door to avoid passing four or five Latin workers, employees of the same company as her husband. She was afraid even to walk past them (although, husky as she is, she might well have whipped the whole crowd had the need arisen). I know another woman who has always done her own cooking "because if that Indian got mad at me some day, she might poison the food."

I know several American managers, foremen, etc., who refuse to discipline their crews or express disapproval of poor work "because I don't want to wind up with a machete in my back." This, despite the countless managers and foremen who have got on with the job for years without becoming emergency clinic statistics. Anyone who has lived here and used his eyes could cite dozens of similar cases of imagined fears.

It sometimes seems to me that fear, not arrogance, is what makes some American companies abroad exclude local people from stock ownership or executive responsibility. And perhaps it is a kind of fear that causes our diplomats to be woefully undiplomatic, and publications such as *Time* to adopt an attitude of smugness about everything American (the known) and of flippancy toward everything Latin (the unknown).

In the first half of this century, we were supremely unafraid—in Latin America, the dictators owned the people, and, as often as not, we owned the dictators. (For example, the old Cuyamel Fruit Company, which later merged with United Fruit, openly supported the Bonilla coup in Honduras, and received notoriously preferential treatment in return.)

Today, Latin America has only three dictators—after centuries of oppression, the people have, in the last dozen years, affected a series of social and political revolutions in this half of the hemisphere. In 1948, Costa Rica put down a would-be dictator, Calderón Guardia; in 1952, Bolivia overthrew its ancient oligarchy; Argentina rid itself of Juan Perón in 1955; in 1956, Peruvian Dictator Manuel Odría quit; Honduras installed Villeda Morales in 1957; in 1958, Columbia replaced Dictator Rojas Pinilla with Alberto Lleras Camargo, one of the world's most distinguished and effective democrats; that same year, Venezuelan Dictator Pérez Jiménez fled, was replaced by freely-elected Rómulo Betancourt; in 1959, Castro swept Batista out of Cuba; having betrayed the revolution, he may soon suffer the same fate himself.

Sadly enough Americans often seem less comfortable in the new rather rough-and-ready atmosphere of emerging democracy than they were before Latin Americans began gaining control of their own destinies. A fruit company executive who travels constantly told me that he likes the Dominican Republic best of all: "The people there don't dare steal anything from an American or give him a hard time or they'll end up in jail for life. It may be tough on them but it's sure good for us!" Our Ambassadors still seem to get on famously with such people as Nicaraguan Dictator Luis Somoza, son of the infamous, assassinated "Tacho."

Of course Americans back home approve in principle when brutal dictators are overthrown; but those on the spot too often find their neat and privileged world shattered—and they are unwilling or unable to come to terms with the more demanding one that replaces it.

Certainly it would be naïve to argue that all the problems of the United States in Latin America spring from defective personal relations. No matter how sympathetic or concerned Americans in Latin America may be, our relations will still founder if obtuse and greedy policies are pursued by our government and our corporations. But until the Americans now in Latin America overcome their provincial fear of the new and different, they will seem arrogant—and they will be fondly hated. And even the most enlightened policies designed in Washington or New York will be undermined.

Hypocritical calculations by Madison Avenue public relations experts won't work. Nor will the patent absurdity of "going native." Instead we must look upon our Latin American neighbors simply as people like ourselves—less fortunate geographically and historically perhaps, and for the moment in need of our financial and technical aid. But they are becoming equal partners in the Western Hemisphere, and they demand to be treated as such.

Have we become so affluent and pampered a people, so lacking in adventure and warmth, that we will be unable to meet this direct human challenge? I do not think so, but if we are to succeed in Latin America, we must shuck off the habits of the past; and we must do it soon.

PROBLEMS FOR WRITING AND DISCUSSION

1. Despite the "popularity formulas" of Madison Avenue on which Americans are weaned, Radler says Americans lose friends and alienate people. Explain in detail how American capitalism, American government, and American public opinion "have failed to present our country effectively."

2. Does the operation of United Fruit display any characteristics of the American corporation pointed out by Arnold (p. 162) and Berle (p. 170)? Have Latin Americans personified our corporations?

3. *Time,* like Coca-Cola, apple pie, and *The Readers' Digest,* is a national institution in America. Does the disservice it performs to America south of the border justify the view of the American press Matthews (p. 99) has?

4. What explanation of economic and political *apartheid* does Radler give? The secret of freedom, Thucydides knew, is courage. Radler asks, "Have we become so affluent and pampered a people, so lacking in adventure and warmth, that we will be unable to meet this direct human challenge?" What answers would MacLeish (p. 439) and Kennedy (p. 508) give? Would Stevenson (p. 478) second their voices?

5. Does Radler's picture of America's effect in Honduras invalidate Handlin's expectation (p. 368) that to see the American way of life is to know immediately the "good" that it is?

6. In the remarks of college students and other educated Hondurans whom Radler quotes, is there evidence that, as MacLeish contends, it is not communism but Jefferson's dream that has begotten the "new nationalistic stirrings in South America and the Carribean"?

7. Fear is often given as the force behind theories of racial supremacy. Do you think that, in addition to the fear Radler hypothesizes in Americans, our seeming arrogance in Latin America is also motivated by the assumption that "industry and frugality" account for success and idleness and dissipation for poverty?

8. Compare the insights into American character (as it is seen by foreigners) given elsewhere in this book—for example, by Boorstin (p. 5), Commager (p. 14), Henry James (p. 82), Matthews, Ebel (p. 213), and Kennan (p. 233)—with Radler's picture of our offensive qualities. In what ways have the very richness of our resources and our luck in historical time and geographical place contributed to the difficulties of our dealing with the rest of the world?

9. Has our simultaneous commitment to Latin America on the one hand and to the United Nations' "principle" of nonaggression on the other

embarrassed us in ways E. B. White does not describe (p. 449)? White says that one of the conditions under which arguments may be settled is "the right to observe at close hand" the elements of the argument. Does the United States honor this right in her relations with Latin America?

10. In a declaration of independence from "Yankee imperialism," what grievances might Latin America list? What historical or ideological advantages over the United States have kept the communist slate clean in Latin America?

America Under Pressure

ADLAI E. STEVENSON

> Adlai E. Stevenson (1900-   ) was graduated from Princeton in 1922, returning to work on the family newspaper in Bloomington, Illinois, before taking his law degree at Northwestern University in 1926. He practiced law in Chicago from 1927 to 1941, except for two years in Washington as special counsel for the Agricultural Adjustment Administration (1933-35). Since 1941 he has given most of his time to public service—as assistant to the Secretary of the Navy (1941-44), Assistant Secretary of State (1945), delegate to the General Assembly of the United Nations (1946-47), and governor of Illinois (1949-53). He ran twice—in 1952 and 1956—for the Presidency and since 1960 has represented the United States in the U.N. Among the more recent of his books are Friends and Enemies (1958) and Putting First Things First (1960).

The quality of the electorate, the news it will listen to, the leads it will follow, the inconveniences and difficulties it is prepared to face—these are the measure of effective democracy. Even within our system of checks and balances, vigorous and effective government is not impossible. Our republican institutions are now among the oldest continuous political institutions in the world. They could not have survived from a rural, decentralized community to the modern world of cities and industrial concentrations without im-

From "America Under Pressure," Harper's Magazine, August 1961. Reprinted by permission of Adlai E. Stevenson and Opera Mundi, Paris.

mense powers of adaptation. These have made it possible for great Presidents to reshape popular thinking and introduce eras of great reform. They have done this by developing a close dialogue with a responsive public opinion and thus imposing political vision and direction on the chaos of separate interests and rival lobbies which make up—inevitably—so much of Congressional politics.

This is as it should be. For interests deserve representation, and the compromises of countervailing power make for healthier social conditions than stifling unity imposed from above by single party rule. But the national purpose is more than a sum of these compromises—just as the citizen is more than a member of his own lobby. He is neighbor, parent, worshiper, and patriot as well. The great social purposes of a community—its security, the quality of its life and education, the beauty of its public monuments, its images of greatness, its communion with past and future—all these must be expressed in the political dialogue—and cannot be if the citizens themselves succumb to what I regard as, historically, the three great distempers of the public mind—reaction, complacency, and mediocrity.

Take first the issue of reaction. America is not in temperament essentially conservative. We have no feudal past such as anchors so many communities in unworkable institutions and outdated ideas. We were born in the morning of popular government and national liberation and some of that fresh light still falls on our faces.

We turn most naturally to the future. We live in hope, not fear. All this is true. But it also is true that the challenge presented by Soviet power is a new challenge. It is that of an apparently implacable power pressing in on us from a steadily widening foreign base and threatening, as we see it, all that is most precious in our way of life. This is new to us.

It is not, however, new to others. Between the seventeenth and the early twentieth century, this was precisely the type of pressure that Western nationalism, mercantilism, colonialism, and capitalism exercised on Asia, Africa, and in a rather different form on Latin America. Westerners in those days appeared—to Turks or Arabs or

Indians or Chinese—to have the characteristics we see in Communists today. They seemed implacable men convinced of their own mission and superiority. Their power was growing. Their influence was spreading—and with their influence went the destruction of ancient and cherished beauties, institutions, and beliefs.

Under this disturbing pressure—which we in the West are only now beginning to appreciate, from experiencing it ourselves—peoples and societies reacted in opposite ways. In India, for example, a long line of philosophers and reformers—from Sir Ram Mohan Roy in the 1820s to Pandit Nehru in our own day—met the Western encroachment with intelligence, balance, and a readiness to judge their own traditions constructively in the light of its challenge. On these foundations they built a philosophy and then a movement which were able to reverse British pressure, re-create Indian society, and achieve independence in modern terms. But during the same period, other Indian groups took on opposite line. Leaders hankering for old glories and unchanged feudal society brought about the disasters of the Mutiny. Extreme Hindu groups took to terrorism and murder in the name of the traditional gods. On the morrow of independence, such a terrorist killed Gandhi, the father of the nation. From such sterile reaction, no gain came—no nation building, no emancipation, nothing but counter-violence and hate. In short, the way of reaction proved to be the way of destruction.

Now let us look at another instance—this time between nations, not within the same community. When in the nineteenth century, Western pressure in the Far East became irresistible, the Manchu leaders of China refused to recognize the fact. The regime of the Empress Dowager took refuge in an ever deeper conservatism. The modernization of any part of the state was virtually made impossible by the stagnant, backward-looking court. Then rule by eunuchs and assassination—typical of all China's worst periods—continued while the Western powers filched away ports, treaties, territories, customs, concessions, spheres of interest, and turned the proud empire into the sick man of Asia—everyone's butt and everyone's prey.

During the same years, the leaders of Japan looked at Western civilization squarely and in an intense revolutionary effort took over from it what was necessary to keep it out. As a result, while China still drifted on, as storm-tossed and rudderless as a junk in a typhoon, Japan rose to modern power in a generation. Once again, the way of sterile reaction brought disaster, while change and adaptation ensured the power to survive.

Or let us take a more recent instance—the response to Communist pressure given by Hitler's Germany. Allegedly to keep the Communists out, Hitler adopted all communism's most reactionary techniques—the single party, the single ideology, tyranny, total censorship, total police power, government by torture and murder. And the result? After a ruinous war, half Europe fell under Communist control—a warning against those self-styled defenders of freedom against communism who care nothing about killing freedom in the process of conducting their "defense."

These are not remote historical analogies. They are relevant to our experience here and now. The central traditions of our country are liberal, generous, and forward-looking. But, in times of stress our history has continued to throw up groups of irreconcilable reactionaries whose solution to the problems of the age lies in violence, hysteria, distrust, and fear-mongering. The Know-Nothings, the Ku-Klux Klan, the McCarthyites, the White Segregationists—all these are recurrent manifestations of the spirit of irrational reaction. I do not know whether our new tensions are breeding—in the John Birch Society—yet another outburst of this destructive and defeatist spirit. But I do know that history gives us only one verdict on the outcome of looking in times of crisis to a fearful and backward conservatism. The outcome is quite simply defeat. Men do not overcome their crises by running away from them backward. No cosy retreats from a challenging future can be looked for in an outgrown past. Times of challenge are times for new frontiers, not last ditches.

Yet reaction is not our chief danger. The greater risk in our present crisis is not that public opinion will react with a blind and backward-looking conservatism, but that it may not react at all. Complacency, not frenzied John Birchery, may be our chief weakness, and it is easy to understand why this is so. We are the wealthiest society in depth that the world has ever seen. More people enjoy more comfort than at any previous time. Yet there is no guarantee that whole communities are any more immune than families or classes from the typical temptations of affluence. Inertia, indifference, exaltation of the pleasure principle, a falling away in curiosity and human sympathy—all these afflict so-called "Café Society." They can afflict general society as well.

Three-quarters of mankind still live in a poverty so grinding, in such pitiful conditions of health and livelihood, that the framework of their brief lives is not very distant from Hobbes' definition: "nasty, brutish, and short." But when Hobbes wrote, the rich minority contrived to overlook the spectacle. In France, the Court played at shepherds and shepherdesses while the peasants ate grass. Today we in America are the rich minority of world society. Are we any less prone than they to while away our most precious gift of time in pursuit of distractions fully as trivial as those of Le Trianon or Le Hameau? Indeed, we have in television an instrument of mass entertainment that does not even demand that we dress up as shepherds ourselves. We can watch other people doing it for us and sink to an even greater passivity of mind and spirit. A nation of viewers, gazing at what FCC Chairman Newton Minow calls the "wasteland" of the television screen, is not likely to widen its sympathies or feel its instincts of justice and compassion deeply stirred. Yet no wealthy group in the modern age has finally resisted the inroads of popular misery and revolt while clinging to all the trivia of a self-indulgent existence. History is neither made nor changed by the complacent and the comfortable. On the contrary, it is made against them and at their expense.

This complacency in our society has its bearing on a third weakness in popular opinion today—the risk of mediocrity. Our tradition was founded and constantly renewed by great leaders responding to a popular demand for great action. Washington and Jefferson guided and canalized the general revolt against colonial rule. Lincoln directed the energies of a mighty nation at war with itself over the great principles of human freedom. Theodore Roosevelt and

Woodrow Wilson caught the reforming tide set flowing by popular disgust at the raw money-grubbing capitalism of our "Robber Baron" epoch. Franklin Roosevelt mobilized popular despair over the Depression behind his New Deal, and Harry Truman caught up the expectations and hopes of the immediate postwar years into the superb strategy of the Marshall Plan. In every case a ferment among the people enabled leaders of stature to direct that ferment into new, imaginative, and epoch-making acts of policy.

Against this background, our present predicament is deeply disturbing. The need for great acts of statesmanship is more urgent than ever before. Wherever we look there confronts us a stark crisis, demanding greatness for its resolution. And most of them have nothing directly to do with communism. They would exist in any case. All that communism does is, by its extra pressure, to make their resolution more urgent.

In our domestic economy, we have not been able to reconcile the need for economic growth with the desire for price stability. While Western Europe has achieved rates of growth double and treble ours, we have lagged behind with a 2 per cent rate that does not fully absorb our rising population. This in turn aggravates the problem of our growing level of built-in unemployment. Bold new measures of replacing and retraining, new restraints on wage increases and speculation, more competition for greater efficiency are clearly needed to reverse these trends.

We add to our population a city the size of Philadelphia every year. These millions will swell the millions already crowding into our vast urban concentrations, there to live with all the discomforts of congestion, commuting, and declining civic services, caught between an urban life without community and a nonurban life without access to natural life and beauty. Only heroic measures of urban renewal, metropolitan planning, and nation-wide conservation can save our national life from foundering in a series of shapeless, soulless urban sprawls.

The challenge abroad is if anything tougher. We have used up the momentum the Marshall Plan gave to bolder Western association. The trade areas we call the Six and the Seven are still divided in Europe. The exchange reserves of the non-Communist countries are inadequate to cover their rising trade. Their capital assistance to developing areas, though considerable, has been undirected and unco-ordinated—and often wasted. Their trade policies, particularly in regard to slumping commodity prices, have often undone the work their aid was supposed to accomplish.

All these facts point toward a unified North Atlantic economy and community, which by freer competition and expanding internal trade would pile up capital for use in the developing world, and by its prosperity attract the trade of other nations. Such a community would also be politically cohesive enough to roll back Soviet pressure in Europe, compete with it successfully in the developing world, and provide within the wider framework of the United Nations a first concrete example of the kind of confederal association under law which the nations of the world must ultimately achieve if they are to avoid the final horrors of atomic war.

These are not remote needs. They are immediate necessities. But how are we to rally public opinion for such great tasks? Our complacency threatens to breed mediocrity of aim—"You never had it so good"; mediocrity of response—"I'm all right, Jack"; mediocrity of vision—our monument, in the poet's phrase, "a thousand lost golf balls." In the past, social discontent was the fuel of the engine of progress. Today, we have never needed creative change more urgently. Yet we were never so lacking in divine discontent.

Of course, we must not restore genuine misery in order to restore general momentum. We must somehow find, in alert, educated, responsible public response, an alternative to the old discontented pressures for change. In every soul, I believe, there lies not only the desire to be left in peace but also the desire to feel part of a great adventure. It was the glory of Athens—prototype of all free societies—that by the spontaneous will of the citizens, it could outface the might of Persia and outthink the leaden discipline of the Spartans. We carry in our minds echoes of Pericles' great Funeral Oration:

"We admit anyone to our city and do not expel foreigners for fear that they should see too much, because in war we trust to our bravery and daring rather than stratagems and preparations. Our enemies prepare for war by a laborious training from boyhood; we live at our ease, but are no less confident in facing danger. . . . We love the arts, but without lavish display, and the things of the mind but without becoming soft."

So long as this temper prevailed, Athens proved invulnerable. Its voice remained the voice of confidence, of excellence, of a community attuned to greatness, drawing its reforming energies not from the miseries of past and present, but from a high vision of the future. During its greatest days, it proved once and for all that free societies can show this vitality, that free societies can be the history-making forces in the world.

But today our society is far indeed from a Periclean spontaneity and vitality. Reading further in Thucydides, I found this disturbing comparison of Athenians with Spartans:

"They—the Athenians—are always thinking of new schemes and are quick to make their plans and to carry them out. You—Sparta—are content with what you have and are reluctant to do even what is necessary. They are bold, adventurous, sanguine; you are cautious and trust neither your power nor your judgment."

Today, who is Sparta, who is Athens? Who has the initiative? Who is making the schemes? Who is bold and adventurous? Who is cautious and "reluctant to do even what is necessary"? Have free men become the conservatives and the Communists the adventurers and innovators? Can there be more to Khrushchev's confidence that he will "bury us" than brash self-assertion? Has he captured a sense of history that we in the West have lost?

I hope I know the answer to these questions. I hope that I can say that while free society may have slumbered for a little and rested and drawn breath, it is ready again for great purposes and great tasks, and that its creative imagination, rearoused and refreshed, is equal to all the crisis and challenge of our perilous days.

PROBLEMS FOR WRITING AND DISCUSSION

1. What basic threats to America does Stevenson see? Stevenson speaks of "responsive public opinion" as a desirable element in effective democracy. Compare his estimate with those of Abraham Lincoln (p. 360) and Walter Lippmann (p. 381).

2. Stevenson, like Lippmann, says that the "need for great acts of statesmanship is more urgent than ever before." What, unlike Lippmann, does Stevenson assume to be the relation between these acts and public opinion?

3. Is the lack of status (*i.e.*, of a secure, indispensable relation to a human community) that Potter (p. 328) and Lipset (p. 348) describe destructive of the "democratic dialogue" Stevenson and others consider essential to American political health?

4. What particular "pressure," according to Stevenson, will crush America unless she responds? Does Stevenson's analogy between this pressure and the one Western "isms" formerly exerted upon Asia, Africa, and Latin America illustrate that "the way of reaction" is "the way of destruction"? Does the analogy break down when it sustains the full weight of pressure America bears today?

5. What did Japan do once she had risen "to modern power"? Does Stevenson foresee the danger of America's destruction if she, like Japan, adopts the methods of her enemy?

6. Since Stevenson noted the signs of reaction in America, have developments or events given further grounds to his fears?

7. Are complacency and mediocrity in America related? Compare the dangers of affluence Stevenson describes with those Radler sees (p. 462). MacLeish asks (p. 439) if we are "too thick through the middle to dream." Does he find the "young generation" complacent and resigned to mediocrity? Does Mumford (p. 76) amplify what Stevenson says about "our vast urban concentration"? Explain.

8. Stevenson notes that the national purpose is greater than the sum of its compromises among rival interests. Hand (p. 388) and Agar (p. 405), like Stevenson, commend the "republican institutions" that have achieved a working balance among these interests. How do they also envision a national purpose?

9. What *does* Stevenson see as our national purpose? Have time and the creation of destructive forces invalidated comparisons with the past, such as Stevenson's reference to the spirit of the Athenians and Spartans? If so, what substitute for vigorous spirit in the "pursuit of freedom" do you advocate?

10. Like Stevenson, MacLeish says that if the "Russian purpose seems more vigorous and more promising to the newly liberated peoples of the world than the American purpose, then we have indeed lost the 'battle for men's minds' . . ." Is Stevenson more concrete in proposing actions we may take to change our present course of mere "*counter*actions"?

11. What reasons, other than economic ones, does Stevenson have for urging "a unified North Atlantic . . . confederation"? Compare his hope with E. B. White's (p. 449).

12. Although Stevenson says we today lack the "divine discontent" that formerly inspired our progress, what faith in humanity does he express? Do Oppenheimer (p. 264), Eiseley (p. 299), Hand (p. 388), and MacLeish share his faith? Did Jefferson (p. 309) and Lincoln? Explain.

The Search for Challenge

DAVID RIESMAN

David Riesman (1909-   ), author of the ubiquitous terms inner-directed *and* other-directed, *graduated from the Harvard Law School and remained long enough in the legal profession to serve, first, as law clerk to Justice Brandeis and, later, as Deputy Assistant District Attorney of New York County. He turned to teaching—at the University of Chicago—in 1946 and is currently a Professor of Sociology at Harvard. Among his several books are* The Lonely Crowd *(1950), in collaboration with Nathan Glazer and Reuel Denney;* Faces in the Crowd *(1952), with Nathan Glazer; and* Individualism Reconsidered *(1954), a collection of essays.*

I want to discuss the problem of discovering challenge in what Galbraith calls the "affluent society," challenge when the older challenges based on the subsistent society and the struggle for sheer survival are no longer imperative. One of the perspectives I want to use is cross-cultural, and we shall look at an anthropological example. Another is historical, and we shall look at ourselves as we were in an earlier day—this, too, is cross-cultural. The third perspective is genetic, in which I shall ask what sorts of challenges are requisite at what stages of one's own life cycle. This is a vast topic. I don't bring to it the erudition of a Toynbee or an Alfred Kroeber, but on the contrary I shall bring to it some observations and free associations in the hope of stimulating further thinking.

From "The Search for Challenge, 1960," New University Thought, *Vol. I, Spring 1960. Reprinted by permission of New University Thought Publishing Co., Chicago.*

Periodically throughout Western history men have imagined that collective as well as individual life could be better, or at least less bad. In times of chaos and of war they dreamed of social stability and hierarchy, as Plato did in *The Republic*, or as Sir Thomas More did in his *Utopia*. Myths of heaven refracted the popular weariness of toil, short life, illness and social disorganization. Periodically, too, men could be mobilized for revolt against plainly oppressive conditions, once these conditions had lightened enough to make them seem less than divinely given. For the ills that have plagued man have been such nightmares that men at all but the lowest levels of brutishness could grasp the possibility of being less badly off, once they *were* less badly off. Today, however, we are faced with a paradox: the United States and a few other rich countries have caught up with many Utopian ideals while at the same time literal belief in heaven has almost vanished. In this country people suffer less from nightmarish misery than from the more subtle disorders previously buried by the harsh struggle for existence.

We can see an analogue to this development in the short career of psychoanalytic therapy, which is about 50 years old. When Freud began, patients came to him who were suffering from hysteria, from paralyzed arms, from inability to talk, from obvious symptoms. By helping them internalize what they had externalized, that is, what they had (so to speak) thrown into an arm, it was relatively easy and even speedy to cure them. Today, in contrast, one sees such cases only, for instance in this country, among immigrant Poles in Pittsburgh or among rural southerners in West Virginia. Many therapists go through their entire lives without ever seeing such a case. People come to analysis today who do not suffer from an external subsistence problem, from a paralysis. Their limbs work and their sexual organs work, but somehow life doesn't live up to its billing for them; they carry on an unrepressed interior dialogue, but it bores them. Often, I might add, all they do is include the analyst in the dialogue and bore him. They need, usually without knowing it, a new vision and not merely a new way of talking about themselves; in fact, I was talking the other day with an analyst who said that patients talked today, as was no surprise, very freely indeed about any of the things that in Freud's day they would have considered private and intimate.

Yet, as we all know, most of the rest of the world would trade places any day with the rich American and trade its miseries for his neuroses. An ironic instance are the Manus whom Margaret Mead revisited several years ago, twenty-five years after her first field trip in 1928. When she had first been there the Manus had been a Stone Age people; then had come World War II and their island had been a staging area for American troops. When she arrived, the Manus had just finished throwing out a Catholic mission on the ground that the mission was trying to get them to adjust slowly to the ways of the West, whereas they wanted to take over the distance to modernity in one big jump. They thought the white people in the mission were patronizing them, holding out on them, trying to ration the blessings of industrial society. You can imagine the position of the mission which was saying in effect, "It isn't just so wonderful to be Westernized, and take it easy." For the Manus the effort to act like Americans was a heroic challenge; one, in fact, which produced a revolutionary leader, Paliau, a man of enormous strength and determination. For him, it was a new religion to become Americanized.

The Manus, like many South Pacific peoples, had had their craze of cargo cults in which traditional objects had been thrown in the ocean in the fond belief that planes or boats would come, piled high with the white man's goods, if only the Manus would propitiate the cargo by appropriate action. Even where the cargo cult does not take such open and violent form, it exists. A few years ago I met a Burmese doctor who had come to the University of Chicago to study technological change. I asked him why he, a gentle and speculative man, had left his homeland on such a quest; and he replied that once the peasants in the rice fields had seen American movies and Cadillacs they would never be quiet again until they had them too. In his book *The Passing of Traditional Society*, Daniel Lerner discusses interviews which were done a few years ago in seven countries of the Middle East. In these the theme that life in America is more modern and, hence, better comes up again and again—whatever the political hostilities towards America, one finds this lure among Egyptians and Syrians and others who are politically, ideologically, violently antagonistic to America and yet admire it. The dream of America—the dream of plenty—is shared by people at all levels, and it is also rejected on religious and traditional grounds by many who are obviously and plainly influenced by it. The conflicts are only about the rate of speed with which one should move to plenty and the mode, and the Malthusian handicaps and how they are to be overcome, and the values to be reintegrated by doing so. And all this is new and exciting to peoples to whom it happens, but it is not new to the West—we have had it.

In fact, we can today in some considerable degree measure the backwardness of a social class or a nation by the extent to which America provides it with a model of Utopia. For the intellectuals of Europe and of India, for instance, America is more to be feared than admired, distrusted than copied. The collapse of the image of America as a vision of Jeffersonian equality and of orderly democracy has been enormously rapid and is not merely the result of Communist propaganda. One factor is the shutting off of immigration after the first World War, which doused the hopes of millions of south Europeans and Levantines that they might find a personal Utopia in the United States; and in these interviews of Professor Lerner's one finds this also coming up again and again—people who have uncles in America from Syria or Turkey and who would like to come here and can't.

The more vociferous Americans themselves, moreover, in desperate search of a self-justifying ideology, have been tempted to identify *the* American way with their own tendentious misinterpretations of our economy as one of free enterprise, or to boast of American technological virtuosity or of the workingman's standard of living. This last might appear to appeal to workingmen in some places, but it does not appeal to the elites whose own frustrated materialism is all too well acted out on their behalf by strident Americans.

I have in the last years talked to a good many non-Americans who, like the Burmese doctor, are visiting this country in the hope of hastening the economic development of their own land, and they have gone home again with an ambivalent feeling: can they reduce poverty, cut the birth rate, start cumulative economic growth, all without arriving at the American destiny—that is, arriving at the place we are now, from which the next steps are opaque—once the novelty wears off?

I would be giving the wrong impression if I were understood to contend that there is no Utopianism in present-day America. There are first of all many conservative people, maybe some here, who find in the American past an adequate image for the future: they contend that if only we balanced our budgets, spanked our kids, worked hard and uncomplainingly, tore down all the teachers colleges—all would be well. And there are many others who find in the huge distance we still have to travel towards economic, and especially towards racial equality, enough challenge for their lifetimes—and in a sense it is enough. Likewise, the effort of the Communist bloc to overtake America has given still other Americans of both major parties the short-run aims of a coach whose all too confident team has lost a game—the feeling that with a little discipline and locker-room talk, along with better scouting and recruiting for scientists, all will be recouped. Perhaps the major benefit thus provided for Americans is the renewed conviction that there is a game and that winning it can give meaning to life. In my opinion none of these, not even the generous one of getting rid of the residues of inequality, is sufficient to mobilize social energies to take the next obscure steps in American life that would bring us a measure of international security and more adequate social goals for an age of plenty.

In this situation many of the most sensitive and truly disinterested young people have given up the larger societal goals to pursue what I might call the Utopianism of private life. It is in the family first of all, and beyond that in the circle of friends and neighbors, that one looks for Jeffersonian simplicity, an idyll of decency, generosity, and sensibility. Much of the confusion in current discussion is due to failure to distinguish between the high quality of these personal goals of young people and the low quality of our social aims. That is, if one is looking at the texture of individual life in

America, this country is harboring, despite all surrounding miasmas, extraordinarily fine enclaves whose tone, though not ascetic, has something in common with the outlook of Utopian colonies in the last century, or with Hopi pueblos, or with the spirit of some of our great 19th Century dissidents, whether Melville or Whitman, William James or Bellamy. In many past epochs of cultural greatness the dichotomy between an avant-garde few and the brutalized many was taken for granted and would occasionally perpetuate itself for long periods. But in the United States today the contrast between the private Utopianism that I have spoken of and the general low level of vision in the general population and in its political activities seems to my mind both less tolerable and less viable for the long term. With the growth of interdependence within and between nations, private virtues, if they do not actually become public vices, become almost irrelevant—beautiful gardens at the mercy of fall-out. I don't expect every young person to take part in the development of a more inclusive Utopia than "familism," but I would like to see a better proportion achieved between private and public visions; indeed, I believe that private life would be enriched and in a way become more meaningful if the two spheres were both more forcefully cultivated.

When I spent a summer in the Soviet Union twenty-seven years ago, I met many eager young Communists who had enthusiastically junked all private aims in the communal enterprise of "building socialism." Amid a Philistine culture made desolate with slogans, they *were* building socialism in an all too literal sense, *i.e.*, they were building dams, railroads, factories, and machine tractor stations and Communist Party apparatus. They brought to their work the zeal of pioneers and, as a blueprint for their own activities, the model of American industrial achievement. At the Stalingrad tractor plant, then barely beginning to produce, I saw fanatical young Stakhanovites (and I guess the term "Stakhanovite" is unknown to many undergraduates today; that is a kind of Russian version of an Eagle Scout) working with tremendous zeal in the midst of a mass of sullen peasants, new to industry and by no means reconciled to its restrictions. I had gone over with a group of American students, some of whom found this spectacle in contrast to the America of the depression marvelously exhilarating. It was a battle with simple rules and clear goals, or so it seemed, and, in fact, the reports from Stalingrad in *Pravda* and *Isvestia* were couched in the language of battle—so many tractors had been turned out that week on the Stalingrad front, or there were that many defeats in the battle for electrification, and so on. I thought then, and I still think now, that the tasks confronting Americans are more exhilarating but also more problematical. It would be child's play for us to build the Turk-Sib railway or the Dneprostroi dam, although, as I shall indicate later, every child should have this opportunity. We have to make our own model of the future as we go, in a situation which is new historically.

It is at this point that the Communists have done us an immense and possibly fatal disservice by so largely discrediting secular Utopias at the very time when religion no longer offers an illuminating other-worldly Utopia but has also become an adjunct to private life. While it is helpful for people to realize that fanaticism in pursuit of Utopian goals is a danger, allowing people to express their worst impulses while defeating their best hopes, the reaction among contemporary non-Communist intellectuals has gone much too far. Today the most influential Utopian writings are satiric anti-Utopias such as *Brave New World* or *1984*, which extrapolate, in the former case largely from the United States and in the latter largely from the Soviet Union, to their visions of a more total despair.

The Poles and for a time the Hungarians who rose against the terror could express in the writings of students and intellectuals a kind of minimum-decency platform—humane and sensible, but Utopian only in contrast to Stalinism. They have been like hysterics recovering from paralysis in the early days of psychoanalysis; and as the hysterics, once cured, could continue to operate on the moral capital of Victorianism, so these Polish and Hungarian revisionists can draw on the moral capital of pre-war Social Democracy; hence can project into the future their recall of the slightly less gruesome past, just as heaven is often the retroactive image of a childhood Eden.

As I have said, however, we Americans have caught up with our future at the very historical moment when the Communist example has done much to dampen Utopian thinking; such thinking, I need hardly say to you, is never easy. All literature shows that writers can more readily picture terrors than delights. For one thing, as Margaret Mead pointed out, we can all empathize with terrors, whereas delights, if they go beyond platitude, differentiate us. I have been struck all my life with how difficult it is for people—even storytellers and artists—to imagine nonexistent things: to imagine, for instance, nonexistent animals; they can only put parts together which are already available and come up with a centaur or a unicorn, much as science fiction for the most part is more science than fiction. Now that we can draw on the world storehouse of cultures through our knowledge of anthropology and history we can in imagination make unicorns, *i.e.*, fit pieces of culture together, but we find it hard to invent new ones.

And yet on the whole, social science, while enabling us to draw on a far wider spectrum of human experience than any one culture has ever had available to it, may have contributed to the decline of Utopian thinking. To free themselves from moralism and the kind of shallow evolutionism one can find in Herbert Spencer, social scientists in our time largely have eschewed either looking at evolution or engaging in prophecy. Somebody asked me recently whether sociologists weren't "do-gooders" and I said I was afraid that that was a thing of the past. The most frequent device for saving thought and conscience here is to say that the social scientist when he makes proposals for change, rather than presenting limited alternatives to a powerful decision-maker, is simply a citizen. As a scientist that is not his business. And science increasingly has become his business, and a business carried on in a business-like way, making measurements and keeping up with what is euphemistically called "the literature." Utopianism reappears in disguised forms, to be sure, as for instance in the belief that if vaster sums were spent on the sciences, prediction and control could take the place of prophecy; there is also the narrower Utopian hope that if each subdivision of science pursues its private aims, some later ecumenical movement may reunite the scattered findings within a grand scheme. (The very largeness of the branches of social science in so vast a country as this means that men can live their whole intellectual lives within the boundaries of a single subdiscipline.) Moreover, as more and more people go to college and more and more people teach those who go to college, intellectuals are increasingly becoming attached to universities; and this is an ambivalent trend in the light of the experience of the past that many of the most seminal ideas have come from outside the academy. And social science, like other intellectual activities, has been steadily democratized, in the sense that its concepts and findings are regarded as valid only if they can be taught to any competent graduate student. Thus, analysis of social wholes, entire cultures, which remains something of an art, is not a game at which any number can play and it tends to be deprecated and hence postponed until that quite distant and hardly foreseeable day when it can be handled in terms available to anybody. Thinking, that is, about a whole society is not something that can readily be democratized. And as for Utopian thinking, most of us after childhood form categorical images of our society and, while aided by images of hell we can imagine things being worse, we cannot imagine them being significantly better.

In addition, although the first explorations into social science often made men hopeful, as they made Condorcet or Marx hopeful (although not Malthus), later immersion tends to make people less hopeful, for it destroys the illusion that the masses have noble dreams which the capitalists or the bureaucrats repress. It shows how immense and how far-reaching are the changes in men's hopes and desires that would be necessary for the creation of a better world: we do not stand outside the portals of heaven only because some vested interests bar the way. And market research is frequently interpreted in such a way as to confirm the status quo; it makes, when conducted by politicians, things that might be worth doing "politically impossible." Let me take a trivial illustration: we go to people for instance and ask them if they would like a small car, and they say "no," or they say "yes" in such a way as to mean "no." Then we proceed to make many big cars, thus changing the visual landscape and people's expectations of what a car looks like and thus prove that people don't like small cars. Even so, a change in circumstances, let us say a slight recession, can show how evanescent was the earlier preference, especially among educated people who, having gone to college, have opinions and tastes which fluctuate more rapidly than do those of lesser learning. And, of course, market and public opinion research often can serve, if well done, to show that people no longer believe what they are supposed to believe and this can be emancipating.

Nevertheless, it seems to me that over-all the tendency of the effect on us of increasing knowledge of man is to curb radical departures of thought in the social sphere, less I think because of McCarthyite opposition than because we ourselves want to feel we are sensible, calm, well-organized people. The great achievement of the physical sciences, in my judgment, is not their ability to codify and measure —this is a detail, though important—but their ability to go beyond common or even uncommon sense to hold ideas—like the concept of the wavicle—which are paradoxical or contradictory and which bear no relation to daily sense experience. (It would be better, on second thought, to speak not of daily sense experience but rather of our cultural and linguistic codification of reality: those categorical imperatives which result from our specific and historical way of seeing as well as from perspectives framed by the human condition as such.) . . . .

I want to mention one example of approaching Utopia through the techniques of social science—an example that, I fear, shows how little these techniques can contribute at present. I have in mind a recent study done at The University of Michigan for the Michigan Bell Telephone Company in which a group of articulate adults were invited to let their imaginations roam free, and to tell trained interviewers what sort of things they would like to see in the "world of tomorrow." Out of 126 interviews, mainly with well-educated respondents, there were, in fact, few suggestions which were at all visionary. Respondents want a machine which will bring them the morning newspaper from the doorstep. They want conveyor-belt highways and drive-in supermarkets and automatic car controls. They want a personal air-conditioning unit inside their clothes. (This reminded me of Aldous Huxley's novel, *Antic Hay*.) Or they want a machine which will bring them any sight, sound, smell, or climate they choose without having to go out to find it. They want to be able to bring back fond memories at will, and to erase annoyances at will. One wants a device to look a doctor over without going to his office, another a device to make it easy to complain to a supercilious sales person, or another a gadget to allow one safely and anonymously to bawl out somebody. One wistfully asks, and here is one of the few quasi-political suggestions, for some means of making suggestions to the legislative government (that's his term) and still another says, "I want to be able to visit relatives and friends without missing church." One wants "more variety in my daily living—a surprise every day."

If such wishes can be called Utopian at all, they are once more very private; they are seldom connected with any plan for the development of the individual's powers, let alone any plan for society more extensive than that of the person who wanted whole cities covered with plastic to keep out the weather. Many of the suggestions represent what I have sometimes called the cult of effortlessness. I speak of it as a cult, for I don't believe that most Americans not presently overworked seek this nirvana with steady passion. But it is striking that in the interviews, and perhaps reflecting their relaxed form, no one seems to wish for obstacles, for challenges, for things that take time and require effort. . . .

Colleges are sometimes criticized as breeding discontented intellectuals who are too good for this world, whether "this world" is the graduate school to which they go on or a career in business or the professions. But I would be much happier if more colleges put more of this kind of pressure on later life to live up to college; that is, if more people got out of college who insisted that the world live up to the expectations created by college. I think one reason such insistence is muted is that people, once in a job and in a marriage, have no financial leeway to make a radical break and therefore the criticisms they might otherwise make simply don't occur to them; and this again goes back to my thought that if one had a period of compulsory service doing such work as building mountains, one could then later in life have a claim on society on the basis of that service. Now, actually, our society is rich enough so that we don't need that basis, we don't need it, that is, economically although we do need it psychologically or politically. Today, if people find their job undemanding, their temptation is not to seek for a demanding job or to struggle politically for a world in which jobs are more demanding and more interesting and in which industry and the professions do less in the way of stockpiling talent than they now do. Rather I think people flee into what I have called the Utopianism of private life, of domesticity. The trouble with this is that it puts too much of a burden on domesticity, because if one wants to live at the height of the times in work, one has to in leisure and vice versa.

To return to the beginning, it comes as a surprise to Americans that when we are faced with plenty we still find problems no less grave. It still takes nine months to produce a baby; it still takes time to develop anything worth while, whether this be a painting or a friendship or a talent or an interest. Walt Whitman wrote: "It is provided in the essence of things that from any fruition of success, no matter what, shall come forth something to make a greater struggle necessary."

PROBLEMS FOR WRITING AND DISCUSSION

1. State and explain the paradox confronting America today. In what sense are the troubles of Americans "more subtle" than those of human beings in other places and at other times?

2. What is the great attraction of America, according to Riesman? Is "freedom" one of the concerns of the Manus in wanting to become Americanized? Was it for Kazin's parents (p. 64) or for the immigrants Turner (p. 315) and Handlin (p. 368) describe? Radler says that the image of America as a utopia lingers even with those "who are politically, and ideologically, violently antagonistic to America . . ." Does his claim invalidate MacLeish's assertion that it is the American dream rather than the communist that inspires newly liberated peoples (p. 439)?

3. Why among some foreigners is America feared and distrusted? Riesman cites two main causes. Does Radler (p. 462) give further insights?

4. What utopianism still exists in America today? Why does Riesman find it ineffectual? Its major benefit, he says, may be in providing Americans with "the renewed conviction that there is a game and that winning it can give meaning to life." Stevenson (p. 478) says that in every soul there is the desire to participate in a great adventure. Does Riesman go further than Stevenson in suggesting how Americans may engage in an adventure that would make life meaningful? Explain.

5. What does Riesman mean by "the Utopianism of private life"? With what does Riesman contrast this form of utopianism? Does Mead (p. 24) substantiate Riesman's charge of "familism"? Is Hand's retreat (p. 388) from zealous causes and historical complexities an instance of private Utopianism? Does the young mother MacLeish describes (p. 439) who cares for four children and reads the books she wants to read show signs of it? Explain.

6. Why is Riesman critical of Huxley's *Brave New World* and Orwell's *1984*?

7. Why has communism helped to "dampen Utopian thinking"? What other decline, according to Riesman, makes the decline of faith in secular utopias crucial?

8. Why does Riesman, himself a sociologist, wonder whether the social scientists have not contributed to the decline in utopian thinking? Does Riesman share Stewart's faith (p. 287) that social scientists can understand the "enormous organism" of society? Does he think such understanding can ever be democratized? Would William L. Miller (p. 225) and Agee (p. 191) agree with Riesman about the tendencies of intellectual activity in America? Compare Riesman's hopes for science with Conant's (p. 247) and Oppenheimer's (p. 264), and his reaction to the complexities of the subject to be encompassed with Hand's.

9. What does Riesman say we need "psychologically and politically" in American life? In what way is Riesman's summation of the problem analogous to Potter's (p. 328)? In what way does it differ?

10. There is much talk today of the bad effects of "togetherness" and of complacency. To what does Riesman attribute these tendencies?

11. Like Stevenson (p. 478), Riesman notes the absence of "oppressive conditions" that once stimulated Americans to better themselves. What other authors in this book have noted and explained the effects of affluence on the drive to achieve?

12. Riesman says "men could be mobilized to revolt" against their oppressive conditions only after these conditions "had lightened enough to make them seem less than divinely given." How do Handlin and MacLeish, in their descriptions of non-native American groups, illustrate what Riesman means?

13. Riesman says Americans need a "new vision." MacLeish says we have that vision in the American dream. Which man do you think is right?

14. Riesman takes his point of departure from Galbraith. Does Galbraith (p. 180) describe "private Utopianism" in members of the New Class?

15. Do you belong to the "cult of effortlessness"? What "delights" (other than those the citizens of Michigan envisioned) can you imagine in a utopian future? What "terrors"?

16. Have your expectations of life been stimulated by college? Do you hope for a "demanding job" or for a chance to "struggle politically"? Explain.

Remarks at the Peace Banquet

WILLIAM JAMES

> William James (1842-1910), brother of the novelist Henry James, received a medical degree in 1869. His interests, however, centered in psychology and philosophy, both of which he taught at Harvard. His Principles of Psychology (1890) and The Will to Believe (1897) embraced the existence of positivism and metaphysics, a dualism resolved by the concept for which he is best known. This concept, set forth in Pragmatism (1907) and defended in The Meaning of Truth (1909), is that the validity of an idea is tested by its consequences in experience. Always altruistically concerned with political questions, and convinced empirically of man's martial propensities, he proposed an alternative to warfare in "The Moral Equivalent of War" (1910).

I am only a philosopher, and there is only one thing that a philosopher can be relied on to do. You know that the function of statistics has been ingeniously described as being the refutation of other statistics. Well, a philosopher can always contradict other philosophers. In ancient times philosophers defined man as the rational animal; and philosophers since then have always found much more to say about the rational than about the animal part of the definition. But looked at candidly, reason is one of the very feeblest of Nature's forces, if you take it at any one spot and mo-

From "Remarks at the Peace Banquet," The Atlantic Monthly, December 1904. Reprinted by permission of Paul R. Reynolds & Son, 599 Fifth Avenue, New York 17, N.Y.

ment. It is only in the very long run that its effects become perceptible. Reason assumes to settle things by weighing them against one another without prejudice, partiality, or excitement; but what affairs in the concrete are settled by is and always will be just prejudices, partialities, cupidities, and excitement. Appealing to reason as we do, we are in a sort of a forlorn hope situation, like a small sandbank in the midst of a hungry sea ready to wash it out of existence. But sandbanks grow when the conditions favor; and weak as reason is, it has the unique advantage over its antagonists that its activity never lets up and that it presses always in one direction, while men's prejudices vary, their passions ebb and flow, and their excitements are intermittent. Our sandbank, I absolutely believe, is bound to grow—bit by bit it will get diked and breakwatered. But sitting as we do in this warm room, with music and lights and the flowing bowl and smiling faces, it is easy to get too sanguine about our task, and since I am called to speak, I feel as if it might not be out of place to say a word about the strength of our enemy.

Our permanent enemy is the noted bellicosity of human nature. Man, biologically considered, and whatever else he may be in the bargain, is simply the most formidable of all beasts of prey and, indeed, the only one that preys systematically on its own species. We are once for all adapted to the military status. A millennium of peace would not breed the fighting disposition out of our bone and marrow, and a function so ingrained and vital will never consent to die without resistance, and will always find impassioned apologists and idealizers.

Not only men born to be soldiers, but noncombatants by trade and nature, historians in their studies, and clergymen in their pulpits, have been war's idealizers. They have talked of war as of God's court of justice. And, indeed, if we think how many things beside the frontiers of states the wars of history have decided, we must feel some respectful awe, in spite of all the horrors. Our actual civilization, good and bad alike, has had past wars for its determining condition. Great-mindedness among the tribes of men has always meant the will to prevail, and all the more so if prevailing included slaughtering and being slaughtered. Rome, Paris, England, Brandenburg, Piedmont—soon, let us hope, Japan—along with their arms have made their traits of character and habits of thought prevail among their conquered neighbors. The blessings we actually enjoy, such as they are, have grown up in the shadow of the wars of antiquity. The various ideals were backed by fighting wills, and where neither would give way, the God of battles had to be the arbiter. A shallow view, this; for who can say what might have prevailed if man had been a reasoning and not a fighting animal?

But apart from theoretic defenders, and apart from every soldierly individual straining at the leash and clamoring for opportunity, war has an omnipotent support in the form of our imagination. Man lives *by* habits, indeed, but what he lives *for* is thrills and excitements. The only relief from habit's tediousness is periodical excitement. From time immemorial wars have been, especially for noncombatants, the supremely thrilling excitement. Heavy and dragging at its end, at its outset every war means an explosion of imaginative energy. The dams of routine burst, and boundless prospects open. The remotest spectators share the fascination. With that awful struggle now in progress on the confines of the world, there is not a man in this room, I suppose, who doesn't buy both an evening and a morning paper, and first of all pounce on the war column.

This is the constitution of human nature which we have to work against. The plain truth is that people *want* war. They want it anyhow; for itself; and apart from each and every possible consequence. It is the final bouquet of life's fireworks. The born soldiers want it hot and actual. The noncombatants want it in the background, and always as an open possibility, to feed imagination on and keep excitement going. Its clerical and historical defenders fool themselves when they talk as they do about it. What moves them is not the blessings it has won for us, but a vague religious exaltation. War, they feel, is human nature at its uttermost. We are here to do our uttermost. It is a sacrament. Society would rot, they think, without the mystical blood payment.

We do ill, I fancy, to talk much of universal peace or of a general disarmament. We must go in for preventive medicine, not for radical cure. We must cheat our foe, politically circumvent his action, not try to change his nature. In one respect war is like love, though in no other. Both leave us intervals of rest; and in the intervals life goes on perfectly well without them, though the imagination still dallies with their possibility. Equally insane when once aroused and under headway, whether they shall be aroused or not depends on accidental circumstances. How are old maids and old bachelors made? Not by deliberate vows of celibacy, but by sliding on from year to year with no sufficient matrimonial provocation. So of the nations with their wars. Let the general possibility of war be left open, in Heaven's name, for the imagination to dally with. But organize in every conceivable way the practical machinery for making each successive chance of war abortive. Put peace-men in power; educate the editors and statesmen to responsibility. Foster rival excitements and invent new outlets for heroic energy; and from one generation to another, the chances are that irritations will grow less acute and states of strain less dangerous among the nations. Armies and navies will continue, of course, and will fire the minds of populations with their potentialities of greatness. But their officers will find that somehow or other, with no deliberate intention on any one's part, each successive "incident" has managed to evaporate and to lead nowhere, and that the thought of what might have been remains their only consolation.

The last weak runnings of the war spirit will be "punitive expeditions." A country that turns its arms only against uncivilized foes is, I think, wrongly taunted as degenerate. Of course it has ceased to be heroic in the old grand style. But I verily believe that this is because it now sees something better. It has a conscience. It knows that between civilized countries a war is a crime against civilization. It will still perpetrate peccadilloes, to be sure. But it is afraid, afraid in the good sense of the word, to engage in absolute crimes against civilization.

PROBLEMS FOR WRITING AND DISCUSSION

1. In the definition of man as a rational animal, *animal* denotes the genus to which man belongs; *rational* differentiates him from others of the genus. Does James, by saying philosophers have always said more about man's rationality than about his animality, imply that the emphasis has been wrong? Does he imply further that war stems from man's animality? Why does an animal fight? Why, according to James, does man?

2. Discuss James's comment that "man lives *by* habits, indeed, but what he lives *for* is thrills and excitement" in the light of what Lippmann (p. 381) says it takes to rouse Americans to fight.

3. If we are, as James says, "once for all adapted to the military status," what strategy against our "enemy" is possible? Do Americans evince romantic illusions about war? Explain.

4. Riesman (p. 488) observed that the Russians used military terminology to describe the socialization of their country. Do such phrases as "the struggle for freedom," "the battle for men's minds," or Conant's "Tactics and Strategy of Science" indicate that we have sublimated our "bellicosity" in civilized activities?

5. May the apathy, complacency, and lack of direction and of vision in Americans of which Riesman and others have complained be the results of our having nothing tangible left to "fight" for? MacLeish says freedom is possible only in the exercise of it. Aside from fighting wars for freedom and living in one's private utopia, in what ways may one exercise "freedom" in order to be aware of it?

6. Is the "vague religious exaltation" James says is inherent in war, or in the thought of it, akin to the great adventure Stevenson (p. 478) believes men desire?

7. E. B. White (p. 449) says that the United Nations Charter makes "aggression" its major foe and implies, thereby, that it is "wrong." By not defining "aggression," does the United Nations enable its members to indulge in this "vague religious exaltation" in a context where civilized nations feel it a "crime" to war against each other? Review those United Nations actions with which you are familiar. How many times have "punitive expeditions" been directed against one of the "sovereign" member nations? How often against "uncivilized foes"? (George Orwell's *1984* gives fictional insight into the world situation James foresees.)

8. What "new outlets for heroic energy" have opened up since James delivered these remarks in 1904 at the World's Peace Congress? May it be, as Mead suggests (p. 24), that the human race, having earthly utopias in its grasp, is consolidating for some great adventure into the unknown?

(Riesman [p. 488], for example, concludes that further features of an earthly utopia are all but inconceivable. In fact, he praises the physical scientists for being able to do what the social scientist cannot—that is, to "go beyond common or even uncommon sense to hold ideas . . . which . . . bear no relation to daily sense experience." They have evolved concepts which explain the unimaginable. Would James consider their achievement an instance of pure "rationality"?)

Inaugural Address, 1961

JOHN F. KENNEDY

John Fitzgerald Kennedy (1917-   ), thirty-fifth President of the United States, was graduated cum laude *from Harvard (1940). After seeing action in the Navy in World War II, he entered politics and served his native state of Massachusetts as a member of the House of Representatives (1947-53) and then as a Senator (1953-61), before being elected President. He has published three books:* Why England Slept *(1940), written as a senior thesis at Harvard and recently reissued as a paperback; the Pulitzer Prize-winning* Profiles in Courage *(1956); and* Strategy of Peace *(1960).*

We observe today not a victory of party but a celebration of freedom—symbolizing an end as well as a beginning—signifying renewal as well as change. For I have sworn before you and Almighty God the same solemn oath our forebears prescribed nearly a century and three-quarters ago.

The world is very different now. For man holds in his mortal hands the power to abolish all forms of human poverty and all forms of human life. And yet the same revolutionary beliefs for which our forebears fought are still at issue around the globe—the belief that the rights of man come not from the generosity of the state but from the hand of God.

We dare not forget today that we are the heirs of that first revolution. Let the word go forth from this time and place, to friend and foe alike, that the torch has been passed to a new generation of

---

Delivered at the Capitol in Washington, D.C., January 20, 1961.

Americans—born in this century, tempered by war, disciplined by a hard and bitter peace, proud of our ancient heritage—and unwilling to witness or permit the slow undoing of those human rights to which this nation has always been committed, and to which we are committed today at home and around the world.

Let every nation know, whether it wishes us well or ill, that we shall pay any price, bear any burden, meet any hardship, support any friend, oppose any foe to assure the survival and the success of liberty.

This much we pledge—and more.

To those old allies whose cultural and spiritual origins we share, we pledge the loyalty of faithful friends. United, there is little we cannot do in a host of new cooperative ventures. Divided, there is little we can do—for we dare not meet a powerful challenge at odds and split asunder.

To those new states whom we welcome to the ranks of the free, we pledge our word that one form of colonial control shall not have passed away merely to be replaced by a far more iron tyranny. We shall not always expect to find them supporting our view. But we shall always hope to find them strongly supporting their own freedom—and to remember that, in the past, those who foolishly sought power by riding the back of the tiger ended up inside.

To those peoples in the huts and villages of half the globe struggling to break the bonds of mass misery, we pledge our best efforts to help them help themselves, for whatever period is required—not because the Communists may be doing it, not because we seek their votes, but because it is right. If a free society cannot help the many who are poor, it cannot save the few who are rich.

To our sister republics south of our border, we offer a special pledge—to convert our good words into good deeds—in a new alliance for progress—to assist free men and free governments in casting off the chains of poverty. But this peaceful revolution of hope cannot become the prey of hostile powers. Let all our neighbors know that we shall join with them to oppose aggression or subversion anywhere in the Americas. And let every other power know that this hemisphere intends to remain the master of its own house.

To that world assembly of sovereign states, the United Nations, our last best hope in an age where the instruments of war have far outpaced the instruments of peace, we renew our pledge of support—to prevent it from becoming merely a forum for invective—to strengthen its shield of the new and the weak—and to enlarge the area in which its writ may run.

Finally, to those nations who would make themselves our adversary, we offer not a pledge but a request: that both sides begin anew the quest for peace, before the dark powers of destruction unleashed by science engulf all humanity in planned or accidental self-destruction.

We dare not tempt them with weakness. For only when our arms are sufficient beyond doubt can we be certain beyond doubt that they will never be employed.

But neither can two great and powerful groups of nations take comfort from our present course—both sides overburdened by the cost of modern weapons, both rightly alarmed by the steady spread of the deadly atom, yet both racing to alter that uncertain balance of terror that stays the hand of mankind's final war.

So let us begin anew—remembering on both sides that civility is not a sign of weakness, and sincerity is always subject to proof. Let us never negotiate out of fear. But let us never fear to negotiate.

Let both sides explore what problems unite us instead of belaboring those problems which divide us.

Let both sides, for the first time, formulate serious and precise proposals for the inspection and control of arms—and bring the absolute power to destroy other nations under the absolute control of all nations.

Let both sides seek to invoke the wonders of science instead of its terrors. Together let us explore the stars, conquer the deserts, eradicate disease, tap the ocean depths and encourage the arts and commerce.

Let both sides unite to heed in all corners of the earth the command of Isaiah—to "undo the heavy burdens . . . [and] let the oppressed go free."

And if a beachhead of cooperation may push back the jungles of suspicion, let both sides join in creating a new endeavor—not a new balance of power, but a new world of law, where the strong are just and the weak secure and the peace preserved.

All this will not be finished in the first 100 days. Nor will it be finished in the first 1,000 days, nor in the life of this Administration, nor even perhaps in our lifetime on this planet. But let us begin.

In your hands, my fellow citizens, more than mine, will rest the final success or failure of our course. Since this country was founded, each generation of Americans has been summoned to give testimony to its national loyalty. The graves of young Americans who answered the call to service surround the globe.

Now the trumpet summons us again—not as a call to bear arms, though arms we need—not as a call to battle, though embattled we are—but a call to bear the burden of a long twilight struggle year in and year out, "rejoicing in hope, patient in tribulation"—a struggle against the common enemies of man: tyranny, poverty, disease and war itself.

Can we forge against these enemies a grand and global alliance, north and south, east and west, that can assure a more fruitful life for all mankind? Will you join in that historic effort?

In the long history of the world, only a few generations have been granted the role of defending freedom in its hour of maximum danger. I do not shrink from this responsibility—I welcome it. I do not believe that any of us would exchange places with any other people or any other generation. The energy, the faith, the devotion which we bring to this endeavor will light our country and all who serve it—and the glow from that fire can truly light the world.

And so, my fellow Americans: ask not what your country can do for you—ask what you can do for your country.

My fellow citizens of the world: ask not what America will do for you, but what together we can do for the freedom of man.

Finally, whether you are citizens of America or citizens of the world, ask of us here the same high standards of strength and sacrifice which we ask of you. With a good conscience our only sure reward, with history the final judge of our deeds, let us go forth to lead the land we love, asking His blessing and His help, but knowing that here on earth God's work must truly be our own.

PROBLEMS FOR WRITING AND DISCUSSION

1. By what means does Kennedy appeal to "public opinion"? Does he limit his appeal solely to American citizens? Explain.
2. Kennedy offers aid to our friends, a warning to our enemy. But he also suggests a meeting ground for the opposing nations. What is this ground?
3. In dealing with enslaved peoples, Kennedy speaks in moral terms. With our potential enemy he speaks of a "world of law." Is the shift significant?
4. Kennedy assures Latin America of our help in "casting off the chains of poverty." Why does he refer to these rather than political chains?
5. Kennedy speaks of Americans as "heirs of . . . *revolution*" who will "oppose any *foe*" on behalf of liberty. He speaks of *"defending* freedom," of an *"alliance* for progress," of a *"peaceful revolution,"* of a *"beachhead* of cooperation" and of a "trumpet" which summons us to fight the *"enemies* of man."* Is Kennedy's metaphoric vocabulary significant in the light of William James's analysis of human nature (p. 502)? What paradox inheres in the term *Peace Corps*?
6. Aside from the remarks Kennedy addresses directly to "those nations who would make themselves our adversary," what implicit warning to such nations does he issue in his remarks to the "new states" of the world and to "our sister republics" to the south?
7. Examine Kennedy's argument for national military strength. Is it logically tenable?
8. Kennedy says, "If a free society cannot help the many who are poor, it cannot save the few who are rich." Stevenson (p. 478) says that "we in America are the rich minority of world society" in danger of being engulfed by the majority as we indulge ourselves. Is it significant that both American leaders have spoken of a new *frontier*? How is their thinking typically American both in this regard and in the national purpose they enunciate?
9. Compare Kennedy's speech with the Declaration of Independence (p. 309) and with Lincoln's words on slavery (p. 360). Is the "central

notion" of all three the same? Lincoln says the principle of "Liberty to all" is the golden apple for which the picture (the Constitution) was made. Does Kennedy indicate what world picture this apple of gold will fit into? Or is the apple made to fit into the existing picture?

10. Echoing Lincoln's words on the American Union, Kennedy calls the United Nations "our last best hope." He speaks of enlarging "the area in which its writ is run" and of "a new world of law." To your knowledge, have steps been initiated to do either in line with E. B. White's hope (p. 449) that the "writ" may be rewritten and that eventually the UNEF may have something to enforce besides the "absence of law"? Explain.

11. Is Kennedy's stoic expectation "of a long twilight struggle year in and year out" reminiscent of Hand's (p. 388) and MacLeish's (p. 439) closing exhortations? Explain.

Part Four. The Pursuit of Happiness

1. POPULAR TASTES
2. THE ARTS
3. RELIGION

ed by anyone who is honest with himself, and secondly because Conservative philosophy

1. *Popular Tastes*

Proof That We Are Not Barbarians

RUSSELL LYNES

> Russell Lynes (1910-   ) was born in Great Barrington, Massachusetts. He was graduated from Yale in 1932 at the depth of the Depression but managed to find work at Harper and Brothers, the publishers, where he remained until 1936. Between 1937 and 1944 he was assistant principal and then principal of the Shipley School, Bryn Mawr, Pennsylvania. He joined Harper's Magazine in 1944 and is currently its managing editor. The best known of his several books are Highbrow, Lowbrow, Middlebrow *(1949) and* The Tastemakers *(1957).*

"Culture" in America is a fighting word. At the mention of the state of American culture people choose up sides, for it is unlikely that there has ever been a nation as concerned about its cultural facade as ours.

Listen, for instance, to what the returning traveler says about our pavilion at the Brussels Fair: It makes a mockery of what we are pleased to call the American Way of Life or it inspires confidence in our concept of the pursuit of happiness. To one traveler it is imaginative and inspired, to another it is frivolous and misleading. It is the same with every attempt to define our culture. We argue and we complain; we pat ourselves on the back and we heap ashes on our heads. But no one could say we are indifferent, and we are very likely to be partisan. The fact is that for a long time we have been trying to make our culture fit a pattern. We are now beginning to discover that we must find a pattern to fit it.

From The New York Times Magazine, *July 6, 1958. Reprinted by permission of the author.*

Take an example. Not long ago, I sat next to an attractive woman at dinner who could have been the prototype for what Jacques Barzun has called "the professional European." "I don't understand you Americans," she said, though she is married to an American and by now is presumably one herself. "You give money to rebuild European opera houses destroyed in the war, and yet you have no national opera company of your own."

I suggested that in America we believe that cultural institutions are the responsibility of the community, not of the Federal Government, and that the strength of our culture is the diversity of its support. "Ah," she said, "but Americans have no culture."

Americans should be used to hearing such statements from Europeans; they have been saying that we have no culture since they first started coming here as tourists nearly a century and a half ago. In the vocabulary of European clichés used to describe America, there are all sorts of words and phrases for our industry and adventurousness, for our ingenuity, classlessness and casual manners. But the European is reluctant to admit that we have any culture or any cultural institutions worth his attention.

It has long been fashionable in certain intellectual circles in America to look at our culture through European eyes and to measure what goes on here in terms of what used to go on there. Each generation, for a century and more, has had its share of expatriates who went to Europe to absorb the older culture and who came home in hopes of making European standards our standards. It is only quite recently that the study of American culture as a phenomenon distinct from European culture has become intellectually respectable.

This respectability takes two principal forms of expression. There are those who deplore our culture as "mass culture," geared to the lowest common denominator of taste and education; they believe that everything that is precious and "serious" is sacrificed to the commercial maw of the communications media. This attitude is popular in university and college circles at the faculty level—especially in the language, English and art departments. You will also find it in some highbrow coteries, though by no means in all.

There is, in fact, an increasingly sharp distinction between those who deplore American mass culture, its size, shape, texture and quality, and those whom John Kouwenhoven has defined as the "neo-Pollyanna" school of cultural observers. This is a group of intellectuals who are determined to find something good or something interesting in all things American. The two groups might be called the "Oh-the-pain-of-it" and the "Oh-the-joy-of-it" schools of thought.

The Pain and Joy groups leave most Americans somewhere in between. Many of them merely shrug their shoulders and say that good old America is all right with them. But there are many others who are fascinated by the seeming contradictions in our culture. They deplore some of it and delight in some of it. But whatever the quality, of one thing we may be sure: America is on a sort of cultural bender.

In his preface to "The Meaning of Culture," John Cowper Powys quoted this definition: "Culture is what is left over after you have forgotten all you have definitely set out to learn." By this definition, it is the residue and not the effort that matters, whereas the only way that we have of measuring American culture at this moment is in the amount of effort that we, as a nation, are putting into it. It will take several generations before we will know whether the residue was worth the effort.

Culture does not lend itself to statistical analysis, but cultural effort does. We know how many new books are published each year in America (about 10,000) and how this compares with publishing twenty-five years ago (about 7,000). We know that some 350,000,000 books (of which 275,000,000 are paperbacks) are bought by Americans each year. This is about three books to each person. We are told that 17 per cent of Americans now read books today compared with 22 per cent before television.

On the other hand, a quarter of a century ago there were some 600 museums serving the public; now there are 2,500. We now have thirty major symphony orchestras and 650 professional and semi-professional orchestras, not including those in colleges. There are 2,300 community and civic theatres in America and some 100,000 theatrical groups in social clubs and industrial organizations, in addition to some 25,000 high schools that produce plays.

Looked at in these terms, it seems a wonder that we have any time left over from culture to get any work done. Add to these figures the explosion that has taken place in college and university populations since World War II (I grant you it's like adding apples and oranges), and more Americans seem to be involved in cultural activities than there are Americans. Such is the way of statistics.

But statistics aside, one need look only at his own community to see the cultural pot seething with activity. Those who ride the New York subways cannot but be struck with the number of people reading books ranging from Mickey Spillane to difficult philosophical treatises. A trip to the Metropolitan Museum of Art on a Sunday afternoon finds you there with as many as 30,000 people who also thought it a good idea to expose themselves to art. Look at the number of off-Broadway theatres experimenting with unconventional plays, and look, too, at their account books; if they are not rich, they are at least not broke.

You will find the same kinds of things wherever you travel in America. You will find a successful opera company in Santa Fé and a distinguished experimental theatre in Dallas. You will find suburban groups organizing art exhibitions. You will find music festivals in Aspen, Colo., and Newport, R. I., and Lenox, Mass., and a dozen other places. And everywhere people are taking cultural courses.

There is no question that our cultural statistics are impressive, but then so are those of other nations. The English publish twice as many books a year as we do and the Russians claim to publish three times as many. It is always easier to be impressed with one's own statistics than with somebody else's and comparisons can be misleading. We, for example, read a great many more magazines than the British who publish a great many more "dime novels" (to use a pre-inflationary phrase) than we do. But the danger with statistics of this sort is that they are likely to make us complacent (if they happen to be on our side) or competitive (if they happen to favor our rivals). In neither case do they really have anything to do with quality, and culture is a qualitative and not a quantitative word.

The real culture of America must be measured by its feel and not by its weight, by its texture and not by its size. And in the long run (to change the metaphor), it is the echo, not the shout, that matters.

Fortunately, the state of our culture is subjected to constant criticisms from within. It doesn't (or at least it shouldn't) make much difference to us what the professional Europeans say about our culture; they certainly aren't interested in what we say about theirs. But the attacks that are leveled at American culture from those who are part of it and are most concerned with its directions keep our culture lively.

Just as in our body politic the conflicting interests of our minorities assure a kind of vital, if sometimes aggravatingly slow, progress, so the minorities in our body cultural assure intellectual vitality which is not likely to stagnate or become smug. Nor does it allow any one group of self-styled arbiters of culture to take over and tell the rest of us what we ought to like.

Let's look at some of these conflicting opinions, at what the pain-of-it-all and the joy-of-it-all groups find dismaying and encouraging about the state of our cultural health.

The Pain group, as I have already suggested, is primarily concerned with the debilitating effects of "mass culture." Mass culture, the argument runs, is the result of the commercial hunger of mass communications. It is culture controlled by "ratings" and popularity polls. It shuns the experimental in the arts (especially where television and the movies are the media involved) because the investment of money is too great to risk on anything but tested formulas. The result is that we have a sort of mail-order-catalogue culture in which every style for every taste is pre-tested in the market place to assure acceptance by the largest possible number of people.

Mass culture is culture that will offend no one, surprise no one, raise no one's sights and stir no one's emotions, whatever it may do to his sentiments. Such are the demands for entertainment of this sort that even what is proved to be foolproof (or, to put it another way, proved to be sure-fire with fools) soon wears itself out. But the media cannot be stopped and to assure a continuous flow of the innocuous to the public, the media seduce the potentially "serious" writer from his proper work and, with blandishments of cash, make him turn to producing "tripe."

The result of this commercialization of culture, the argument goes, is to lull the public into a kind of cultural coma and to cheapen and prostitute the creative artist. The middle-man in this "pandering to popular taste" is the editor of the mass magazine, the agency that handles the account of the big television sponsor and the network and movie moguls who, out of greed, encourage such cheapening of standards.

The Joy group looks at mass culture from a quite different point of view. In the past, they say, most Americans had no opportunity whatever to enjoy the talents of our most able performers, dramatic artists and musicians. Not only do the mass media bring to millions of Americans first-rate talent and exposure to the arts (as, for example, in mass magazines that publish our ablest writers and all sorts of paintings, including the most *avant-garde*), but they also provide a certain amount of exposure to the experimental and the exotic through such television shows as "Omnibus," "Sunrise Semester" and an increasing number of unsponsored educational programs and stations.

The fact that such shows do not have the ratings of Ed Sullivan . . . is not a reflection on American taste. The fine arts have never commanded the same audiences as the popular arts and the wonder of it is that there are so many millions of Americans who enjoy the good things set before them.

Somewhere in every discussion about American culture today the word "conformity" is bandied about. The Pain group views with alarm the conformity which it sees everywhere—in dress, in the kinds of houses people live in, in the kinds of food they buy from supermarkets, in their cars and in their consciences. The Joy group construes the same manifestations of our culture in a diametrically opposite manner. There is a difference, they say, between conformity and individualism. Conformity of a sort is essential to making the wheels of our civilization turn; people must conform somewhat or they wouldn't be able to work together in harmony.

Individualism, on the other hand, is in evidence everywhere. Look, they say, at what is happening in the mass-produced suburbs; everyone is making changes in his house to defeat the established patterns. Look at the supermarkets and the odd and interesting kinds of food that they make available to everyone who wants to experiment. And so on. The coin of conformity seems to have heads on both sides.

The promise of our culture seems to lie somewhere between the alarm of the Pain group and the euphoria of the Joy group. In my opinion, and in the opinion of a good many other observers, if you add up the pro and con columns of our cultural effort, the pro column has the edge.

In the con column, in addition to the attacks against mass culture that I have mentioned, you will find wasted educational effort. You will find cluttering up our educational institutions many thousands of young men and women to whom education is not an intellectual exercise or an expansion of horizons but a waiting game. B. A. and Ph. D. degrees, instead of being intellectual achievements, are only job tickets.

In this same column, you will find "projectitis" among scholars: that is, the scholar with the biggest project involving the most people and for which he can get the most money from a foundation achieves a kind of preferred academic status. It substitutes group-thinking for individual exploration. You will find, in spite of concerted effort to the contrary in recent months, the sacrifice of the bright, eccentric student to the standards of achievement of the average and below-average student. The premium is on "well-roundedness." You will find group journalism in which "slant" takes the place of opinion and is passed off as truth. You will find a great deal of what passes for cultural activity to be merely social climbing.

But in the pro column you will find genuine enthusiasm, excitement and curiosity. People have been getting up at the crack of dawn to listen to television lectures on literature. They have been going out evenings to extension courses in everything from the Art of the Short Story to Paleontology. Record companies can scarcely find enough music, new or old, to satisfy the tremendous range (from pre-Palestrina to post-Bartók) of the public taste.

In much the same kind of dilemma, publishers of paperback books comb libraries for more "significant" books of philosophy, sociology, history, the physical sciences and the arts with which to satisfy a public that is hungry for something more than whodunits.

The current boom in the art market is more than just a hedge against inflation; it reflects a reaction against what sometimes seems like the tyranny of machine-made materialism. The growth of our colleges and universities is not just a demographic phenomenon; at least part of it is a genuine search by the young for intellectual values in an era when such values seem to have been overrun by what the sociologists call status symbols. Three-hundred-horsepower parlors bedecked with tinsel are not enough.

There is no question that we create much that is tawdry, flashy and phony—as what nation doesn't? But there is also no question that our arts—fine and popular—are enjoying a new kind of vitality. It comes, I believe, from a new self-confidence. We no longer worry about being the stepchild of Europe. For a long time, it seemed as though we were connected with European culture by a one-way street with all the ideas coming our way.

Now ideas seem to flow out rather more than they flow in. Our novelists are eagerly read everywhere. Our painting and sculpture and our architecture not only command respect but strongly influence the visual arts of other countries. Our playwrights fill foreign theatres and our musicians fill foreign concert halls and opera houses. Our ballet plays to respectful and enthusiastic audiences, and above all, our jazz has become a universal language. Our present danger is not that we underestimate the vitality of our cultural production as we once did, but that we become complacent and chauvinist about it.

Anyone can add his own items to the pro and con columns and arrive by his own arithmetic at almost any conclusions he pleases about the state of our culture. But he cannot truthfully say that our culture is any one thing or that it is dominated by any one group. No one can honestly contend that materialism has driven out humanism or that science in one of its greatest ages of exploration has slammed the door on the arts. No one can say that mass audiences have silenced the intellectuals any more than he can demonstrate that highbrows control the public taste.

Ours is a "You-name-it-we-have-it" kind of culture. It is a vast market place of conflicting tastes, conflicting ambitions and conflicting needs. In guaranteeing "the pursuit of happiness," we recognize that not every man's happiness is measured by the same yardstick. We may do our damnedest to convince him that our yardstick is better than his, but we do not beat him over the head with it.

We cajole and seduce, but we do not coerce or command. Out of the crowd that the *voyeurs* of culture call "the mass," many single voices are heard. So long as this is true, what we have is not a "mass culture," but neither is it an aristocratic culture. It is a highly competitive culture, perhaps the first of its kind, and unless it succeeds, perhaps the last.

PROBLEMS FOR WRITING AND DISCUSSION

1. Lynes says that probably no nation has ever been "as concerned about its cultural façade as ours." To what broad picture of American self-consciousness does Lynes's conjecture add?

2. If, as Lynes says, our cultural assets outweigh the deficiencies, why are Americans preoccupied with culture?

3. Describe the premises and arguments of the Pain and the Joy groups to which Lynes refers. He says anyone "can add his own items to the pro

and con columns and arrive ... at almost any conclusions" about American culture. From your own "addition," at what conclusion do you arrive?

4. Neither Kristol nor Morris (p. 529 and p. 560) is part of a "college circle," yet each finds fault with American culture. Would Lynes take issue with them? Explain.

5. Lynes says that the "real culture of America must be measured by its feel and not by its weight, by its texture and not by its size." Which measurement does he use in arguing that the "pro column has the edge" over the "con"? How would Kristol evaluate the statistics Lynes gives?

6. Why does Lynes deny that we have a "mass culture"? What analogy with democratic political assumptions does Lynes make? Are political assumptions valid ones on which to base an evaluation of cultural phenomena?

7. What would Kramer (p. 627) say to Lynes's statement that "we no longer worry about being the stepchild of Europe"?

8. Lynes says that rather than impose an alien pattern upon our culture we must find a pattern that fits it; yet he says, finally, that ours is a "you-name-it-we-have-it" culture, a "vast market place of conflicting tastes, conflicting ambitions and conflicting needs." Does he, then, discover its "pattern"? Justify your answer.

9. Is there anything in his wording which suggests that Lynes "patterns" American culture and predicts its "success" on the economic bases of *laissez-faire*? On what bases does an economy succeed or fail? Does culture "succeed" or "fail" on the same bases? What would Langer (p. 634) say?

10. Lynes notes that mass media of entertainment, the "commercial maw," require constantly to be fed with new material, since they "wear out" what they use. Does an art museum, a library, or a symphony orchestra have the same problem? Do you see a need to distinguish between mass entertainment and permanent works of art? Explain.

High, Low, and Modern

IRVING KRISTOL

> *Irving Kristol (1920-) has been managing editor of* Commentary *(1947-50), co-editor of* Encounter *(1953-58), and an editor of* The Reporter *(1959-60). In addition to his editorial work, he has written essays for the above magazines and for* Harper's, Partisan Review, The New Republic, *and various other journals. He is presently vice president of Basic Books, Inc.*

Rimbaud was unquestionably a great poet. But was he a highbrow? He would generally be so classified today—and yet, the more one considers the matter, the odder it looks. His contemporaries—even his admiring ones, to say nothing of his depreciators—certainly did not see anything "high" about this adventurer-bohemian who experimented with vice as energetically as with poetic forms. He himself would have been more than a little astonished at the description. "High" was where the *Académie Française* was located; Rimbaud was somewhere below, roaming among the cities of the plain.

The term itself, "highbrow," was first publicised in Van Wyck Brooks' historic essay, *America's Coming-of-Age*, which appeared in 1915. It is worth remembering that this essay was by way of being a manifesto of "the modern" in literature and art, and that it was, among other things, *an attack* on the highbrow. By this term, Brooks meant the American equivalent of the French Academy—the "genteel tradition" of letters represented by the New England "Brahmins": Longfellow, Emerson, Lowell, Howells, Aldrich, and co. "High-

From Encounter, *Vol. 83, August 1960 (London). Reprinted by permission of the publisher and the author.*

brow" culture was "high" culture, that dominating influence on American letters which placed the greatest emphasis, not on creativity itself, but on (1) the continuity of a cultural tradition and (2) the moral role played by art and the artist in the nation's life.

The young moderns, as we know, rejected this notion of cultural statesmanship. They were heirs to a literary tradition only in the sense that it was, in fact, their property—but this property could be used or abused at their pleasure, for they recognised no obligation to it. And they utterly rejected the idea that they were, in any sense, guardians of public morality. This morality wore a Victorian aspect; and so far from preserving it, the young moderns set out to subvert it by every means at their command. It was not, of course, that they —the majority at any rate—were against morality *per se*. What they wanted was to enlarge the moral sense so as to bring into the lives of men (and the arts of men), a freedom, an irreverence, an uninhibitedness, a candour (especially in matters of sex) that had hitherto been lacking.

And no one can say they have not succeeded.

Just as there is a distinction to be made between "highbrow" culture, properly speaking, and the "modern" movement which replaced it, so is there a distinction to be made between the "popular culture" of the last century and the "mass culture" of our own.

In the beginning there was only Culture, as defined by tradition and authority. There was never any ambiguity as to who had Culture and who did not—it was entirely a matter of education (though sometimes of self-education). Nor was there any doubt as to who had more or less of it: a man who knew Greek and Hebrew as well as Latin was more Cultured than one who merely knew Latin. Popularisations of this Culture were sometimes provided for the improvement of the uneducated; but not very often.

The uneducated had their entertainments and diversions—singing, dancing, cock-fighting, drinking, fornication, and an occasional festivity at the church. Existing as they did without benefit of anthropology, it never occurred to them or anyone else that this kind of thing could be regarded as Culture, or even as a Sub-culture. But with the spread of printing and literacy in the 18th and 19th century, something that could really be called "popular culture" began to emerge and multiply. It was epitomised by the sentimental romance, the Gothic horror tale, the penny-dreadful Western, the inspirational success story, popularisations of scientific and religious matters, the vast literature of self-improvement, self-help, self-education. There was inevitably some confusion as to whether certain commodities were Culture or "popular culture," especially since the novel, as a literary form, itself emerged from "popular culture" and has never disengaged itself from it. But, on the whole, it was pretty clear what was what and who was who. Nor was there much self-consciousness about the difference. One fails to find, in the 19th century, any serious concern with "popular culture" as a problem. Educated people could ignore it, when they did not surreptitiously enjoy it.

And why not? It was limited in scope, unpretentious in its manner. Most important, it was a highly moral enterprise, in ostensible intent if not always in calculated effect. It accepted the conventional canons—as established by "high culture"—of good and evil, success and failure, in order to weave its narrative around them. Whatever its offence to intelligence and good taste, it did not represent any kind of threat to the moral and political order.

We, in contrast, are very sensitive to "popular culture" as representing just such a threat. To be more exact, we are on the defensive against "mass culture," which is what "popular culture" has become. Whereas "popular culture" was the culture of a class (the uneducated), "mass culture" is a culture shared, to a greater or lesser degree, by everyone. We all watch the same TV shows, read the same advertisements, see the same movies. As a result of the increase in popular wealth, popular taste now has a coercive power such as civilisation has never before witnessed. By its sheer massive presence, "mass culture" tends to crowd culture of any other kind to the margins of society.

One does not want to sound like a prig or a snob. Day-dreams and diversions are the stuff most people's daily lives are made of;

the sentimentality, the inanity, the vulgarity of "mass culture" only become objectionable when they impose themselves upon society with such vigour as to set the tone, suggest the values, establish the context of life both private *and* public. And this is undeniably what is happening in the modern democracies.

And yet one wonders: is it that "mass culture" is so powerful, or that its opposition is so impotent? A clue is provided by the tendency—not in itself so very surprising—of "mass culture" to degenerate into pornography. Now, pornography is, or need be, a problem of no great importance; one certainly would not want to do without it entirely. But what is revealing, as concerns both pornography itself and the larger problem of mass culture, is the complete inability of the "natural" leaders of opinion in the community— the educated class in general, the intellectuals in particular—to deal with this problem.

What is pornography? The fact that we ask this question in genuine puzzlement is itself a cultural phenomenon of the greatest symbolic significance. It testifies to the fact that the educated class has lost its footing. And this, in turn, is connected with the fact that the educated class of to-day is not "highbrow" at all, but post-highbrow, i.e., "modern." Its difficulties in reaching firm opinions on the "mass culture" which it apprehensively confronts, derive from its kinship with it. As Leslie Fiedler has pointed out in ENCOUNTER (August, 1955):

> It has been charged against vulgar art that it is sadistic, fetishistic, brutal, full of terror; that it pictures women with exaggeratedly full breasts and rumps, portrays death on the printed page, is often covertly homosexual, etc., etc. About these charges there are two obvious things to say. First, by and large, they are true. Second, they are also true about much of the most serious art of our time. . . . There is no count of sadism and brutality which could not be equally proved against Hemingway or Faulkner. . . . Historically, one can make quite a convincing case to prove that our highest and lowest arts come from a common antibourgeois source . . . ; and there is a direct line from **Hemingway to O'Hara to Dashiell Hammett to Raymond Chandler to Mickey Spillane.**

The educated class of to-day, formed by the "modern" revolt against the "highbrow," is faced with the difficult task of rejecting pornography without repudiating itself. And the only reason this question of pornography is so provocative is that the startling lack of a ready answer makes it so.

The problem of differentiating between art and pornography has never been easy, if only because some pornographers are awfully talented. In our day, the task is well night impossible, and few there are (and these not necessarily the best equipped) who can face it. Thus, most members of the educated class in America will concede that pornography ought to be the object of legal sanctions. But these same people have never defined what pornography is; have never made any effort to discover such a definition; have resisted all urgings that they make such an effort. And, indeed, anyone who displays a genuine concern for the issue is regarded suspiciously as an enemy of art, an enemy of promise, an enemy of the free in spirit.

Instead of facing up to the issue, an elaborate ideology of evasion has been constructed. This ideology employs various arguments, as the occasion allows, but it relies primarily on the arguments from ignorance: We do not know what pornography is, because standards of propriety and decency are always changing. We do not know what the effects of pornography are upon the consumer; it is always possible that, by the vicarious discharge of sadistic aggressions, an individual's mental health may be, if not improved, then at least maintained in equilibrium. We do not know whether comic books that glorify brutality actually make children more brutal. We do not know—oh, there is so much we do not know! Only the other day a prominent American political scientist at one of our best universities argued before the Federal Communications Commission that it should not interfere with certain "objectionable" TV programmes until a massive (and, needless to say, expensive) study had been made to determine what effects, if any, such programmes had upon children.

No one can deny that all these arguments from ignorance have an element of truth in them. The only thing wrong with them is that they are impossible to live by. As cautions, they have their merit. But as guides, they lead nowhere. What they add up to is the assertion that we can never be sure of the difference between right and wrong, good and evil. True enough; but that is not the same thing as saying there is *no* difference between right and wrong, good and evil. And if such a distinction is made, it will have a bearing upon how we operate—or allow to operate—our mass entertainment media, our journalism, our book publishing, our educational system.

But who is going to make this authoritative distinction? And how?

In the United States, the American Civil Liberties Union is always appearing in court to defend provocatively illustrated magazines, reeking with sadism and sly perversion, against police prosecution; its plea is that such legal action is an interference with literary freedom. And when the prosecuting attorney denies that these sheets can be regarded as literature at all, the ACLU retorts (and I quote): "It is submitted, however, that any differences are those of taste." And it goes without saying that *de gustibus non* . . . etc. The net result is that the laws against pornography in the United States are enforced in an utterly capricious manner. Edmund Wilson's *Memoirs of Hecate County* is banned in New York State; *Playboy* circulates freely. This is what is bound to happen when the definition of "literature" is something that literary men, as a matter of æsthetic and political principle, refuse to essay.

Here we return to that central fact of the modern cultural situation: the destruction of the older "highbrow" élite whose declared purpose, and recognised function, was to "maintain standards." To some extent this élite was robbed of its authority by the rise of the "scientific expert" as the authoritative figure, in place of the "educated man." And the scientist naturally has a scepticism towards standards in general, emphasising their "relative" nature. But mainly it was overthrown by the advent of "the modern" in arts and letters—a movement which denied the very legitimacy of this kind of authority, and which insisted that to be genuinely creative the artist had to be free to create his own standards, as well as his own art.

In those cases where fragments of the older élite still survive and exercise some influence (notably in England), they are regarded as figures of fun, rather ludicrous anachronisms. One has only to mention the name of Lord Reith to a London literary audience to evoke a smile—because Lord Reith, as Director-General of the BBC in its formative years, put great emphasis on "maintaining standards." His BBC was exceedingly proper and unadventurous, respectful toward constituted authority and the taboos of middle-class morals. He was, moreover, solemnly patronising of his audience. If the BBC provided a Light Programme, it was not merely because ordinary people wanted and deserved a spot of fun; the Light Programme had to be slanted in such a way that, in theory, it gently led its listeners upwards toward the slightly more serious Home Programme; and the Home was similarly inclined towards the Third Programme, at which apex one was fortunate enough to listen to either the bland chatter of Oxford dons or learned sermons on Original Sin.

Lord Reith is gone, and his spirit only intermittently flutters over the air-waves. Instead of the stuffy Establishment of yesteryear there is Commercial Television à l'Américaine and a BBC television that is scarcely to be distinguished from the commercial variety. Already parents are indignant at the things their children (and, more rarely, themselves) are exposed to. A huge (and expensive) study by the Nuffield Foundation of the effects of TV on children came up with no definite conclusions; but people do not always need a social scientist to tell them what is happening in their homes. Those same sophisticates who were irritated to death by Lord Reith and all he stood for, are now outraged by commercial television and all it stands for. But no one knows quite what to do. . . . To be sure, one can always blame America; but not, convincingly, for long.

It is impossible genuinely to mourn the passing of the Mandarins and Brahmins of the older "highbrow" élite. Not all the things said against them were true or fair, by a long shot. But they not only deserved their fate; they positively courted it. Their notion of defending standards came to mean, in practice, a vigilant hostility to creative talent, as against mere mimicry. Above all, they seemed unaware of the fact that young people needed something more in life than the benevolent assurance that they would soon be middle-aged. And so they ended (or are ending) their days as sullen and sneering fulminators against modern "degeneracy" as exemplified by T. S. Eliot, Picasso, Stravinsky, etc.—their only audience, ironically, the popular press.

But now that they are gone, who is to do their job? *Someone* has to be able to say, with assurance and a measure of authority, what is culture and what is not, what is decent and what is not. There must be some group or class that is admittedly competent to decide —not without error, but more wisely than anyone else—questions of moral and cultural value. Otherwise, a necessary and vital element of order in the life of a society will be lacking.

Recently, in the United States, religious leaders, educators, and spokesmen for parents' organisations complained to the Federal Communications Commission that there was too much violence on TV. To which they received the official rejoinder that there is a great deal of violence in *Hamlet* too—and how could the United States Government lay down one rule for *Hamlet* and another for *Peter Gunn*? How could the United States Government set itself up as an arbiter of taste? This was, presumably, reserved for the advertising agencies who are the only ones to show a passionate interest in the subject.

In England, the London County Council has withdrawn the tax exemption previously granted to the London Library, a private subscription library much used (and much beloved) by scholars, writers, and educated people generally. The Council authorities declared that some people enjoyed going to the movies, others enjoyed going to a library, and why should the pleasure of one be privileged above that of the other? Why indeed? Who is going to come out and say that, as a matter of principle, people who read good books in their leisure time should be privileged as against people who go to the movies? And who, if he does say this, will be listened to?

What it comes down to is this: we seem to have manœuvred ourselves into a situation in which the men of letters, the "intellectual" class, jealous of their own hard-won freedom from previous restrictions and suspicious of the state's meddling with questions of art, have made it extremely difficult for society as a whole to give official recognition to *Hamlet* as against, say, *Headquarters Detective*. Such instances of official recognition do exist, to be sure. But most of them go back some years, and are survivals rather than precedents.

Not only is there no class of people which can be regarded as both representing and forming "public opinion" on matters of culture. The very idea that such a class *might* exist is fast becoming nebulous. For instance, a prominent American sociologist, until recently a dean in a major university, conducted a study of American reading habits, and arrived at the following conclusions:

> Not only does the frequency of book-reading vary markedly, it is also unevenly distributed among the constituent groups of the community. For a variety of reasons some kinds of people read a great deal more and some not much. The major factor which differentiates readers from non-readers in research to date is education—in the limited sense of number of years of formal schooling. The more years of schooling the individual has, the more likely he is to read books. In one national survey only twelve per cent of the college-educated had not read a book in the preceeding year as against seventy-five per cent of those with only grammar school education or less.
>
> Now, this might mean several things. It might mean that additional schooling has improved the individual's basic reading skills, or that it has developed his reading habits, or that it has produced in him the types of interests which are ordinarily satisfied by books, or even that the people who go on to further schooling already have a reading disposition which formal education only reinforces.

The ignorance is feigned, one knows. Our sociologist is not really puzzled as to why educated people read more books than noneducated people. He simply believes that he *ought* to be puzzled—and that is what is really interesting. For what it means is that the very existence of "culture" in the traditional sense of the term, the very idea of "the cultivated man," is but dimly apprehended. In place of a prescriptive definition of "culture" we have an anthropological-sociological one. "Culture" is whatever people do—some employ "reading skills" directed towards books, others presumably employ "viewing skills" directed towards TV; and the empirical fact that "reading skills" seem to be connected with education is a statistical correlation that needs further research to be explained.

Ludicrous as this is, it is but a *reductio ad absurdum* of a recognisable tendency, within all the Western democracies, for education —even higher education—to divorce itself from the task of forming character, habits, and tastes. Sometimes this is done candidly in the name of vocational training. At other times it proceeds under the guise of allowing "free development" to the students' natural bent. The end result is the same: the disappearance of a class of people which—by virtue of being educated—shares a cultural patrimony and is accepted by the community as providing spokesmen for this patrimony.

Even in those places where it is still taken for granted that education has something to do with reading books, what is ignored is that the educated person is one who has learned how to read, enjoy, and profit from *certain kinds* of books—kinds that are defined by the cultural tradition. Future historians may yet decide that one of the crucial events of our century, perhaps decisive for its cultural *and* political destiny, was the gradual dissolution and abandonment of the study of the classics as the core of the school curriculum. We all know the many reasons (some of them cogent enough) why this happened. But we fail to appreciate sufficiently the extent to which it destroyed a vital constituency of any well-ordered society; and the manner in which our failure to define a new core for the educational process helped open the way to what can only be called the subversion of public morality in the democratic nations.

Public morality? The phrase sounds almost archaic. Most young people today, if asked what it meant, would probably refer vaguely to prohibitions against necking on the beach during daylight, or perhaps to the disapproval that attaches to a public official who appropriates public funds for his private pleasure. Yet until not so very long ago, anyone who had ever given thought to the matter would have asserted, as a matter of course, that the ultimate basis of popular government was what in America was called republican morals, and in England civic virtue. As Edmund Burke put it: "Men are qualified for civil liberty, in exact proportion to their disposition to put moral chains upon their appetites; in proportion as their love of justice is above their rapacity; in proportion as their soundness and sobriety of understanding is above their vanity and presumption. . . ." Similar sentiments were expressed by Madison, Jefferson, and Washington. If Burke was no believer in popular government, it was because he placed a lower estimate on the average man's moral capacities than did the Founding Fathers of the United States. There was no disagreement between them, however, on the fact that self-government was a distinctively moral enterprise.

This moral component of political life has, over the past decades, been depreciated. Ours is an age that is hypnotised by Impersonal Forces. We instinctively regard ourselves as their creatures, and we find our freedom in cajoling, mollifying, and humouring them. Much of our political activity can be described, without malice, as efforts to build socialism without socialists, communism without communists, democracy without democrats. Whenever we discuss the prospects for democracy in one of the new nations of Africa or Asia, we analyse the rate of economic growth, the efficiency of the civil service, the loyalty of the armed forces, the number of schools per ten thousand children, etc. We never enquire whether the people display those particular dispositions of mind and character that make popular government workable.

What are these dispositions? This is a large question, and any short answer will be inadequate. But it is not too gross an oversimplification to say that included among them must be: a veneration for the rule of law as against the rule of men; a reliance on common reason as the dominant human motive, as against superstition or passion; a sense of community that transcends class divisions and the recognition of a common good beyond individual benefits; a scrupulous use of liberties towards these ends for which those liberties were granted; a distribution of wealth and inequalities according to principles generally accepted as legitimate; moderation in the temper of public debate and public demeanour; etc. In every historical case one can think of, these attributes have been prior and prerequisite to democratic government. When they did not exist, or where they did not exist sufficiently strongly, democratic government faltered. And if a democratic government fails to sustain and encourage them, it is undermining its own foundations.

For, in the end, democratic government is governed by reasonable public opinion. And reasonable public opinion is not merely one that may be "well-informed" on matters within its comprehension and relevant to its judgment. It is, by definition and above all, an opinion that *wants* to be reasonable and truthful. This is the moral fundament of democracy; and it is this moral fundament that is under constant assault by much of that "mass culture" which is now being distributed through the mass media.

Take advertising, for instance, which plays so dominant a role in modern life that large numbers of people cannot bring themselves to read a magazine or watch a TV show that is not adorned with the familiar ads—they feel it is not really directed at them, that there is something "queer" about it. The bulk of advertising consists of lies, spiced with half-truths. The advertiser knows this; the advertising agencies know it; the consumers know it; the toddling infants know it. The "advertising game" is quite literally that —an effort to sell commodities by producing the most attractive, the most ingenious, the most beguiling hokum. Since everyone understands it is hokum, there is little substance to the nightmarish dread, evoked by some writers, of a society eventually to be ruled by a self-appointed élite of "hidden persuaders." The importation of advertising techniques into political campaigns is a disaster, not because they will produce a political Svengali, not because they play upon credulity, but because they create a universal disbelief and cynicism. Political rhetoric is debauched; the statesman's plea becomes indistinguishable from the huckster's "pitch;" persuasion merges into demagoguery—and is calmly accepted as indispensable to "politics."

Another instance: popular journalism. We are all well aware that a large section of the popular press makes no effort to report the news honestly. Frequently this is a result of political bias; more frequently it flows from a knowledge of what will capture the interest and titillate the prejudices of its readers. This phenomenon is now so common as to seem unremarkable—it is accepted as part of the democratic scheme of things and is shrugged off with an expression of "democratic faith:" in a free competition between truth and falsehood for dominion over the minds of men, truth will eventually win out.

Yet no sensible man, contemplating the history of the human race, could seriously claim that truth always prevails over falsehood. And it is interesting to observe that this was *not* the claim of those who founded and formulated the philosophy of liberal democracy. What they said was that in a free competition between truth and *error*, the victory would finally be on the side of truth. The difference is by no means negligible. It is possible for truth to debate with error, to define itself in the very process of this debate, and for public opinion to be enlightened by the spectacle. But deliberate and cynical falsehood does not merely controvert truth; it challenges the idea which is at the heart of popular government: that the recognition of truth is not only a human but also a civic obligation. There is no such thing as a democratic right to lie, or a democratic freedom to lie. Such a liberty is reserved for a despotic society, whose State has its reasons that the citizen knoweth not. In contrast, democracy has an organic relation to enlightenment and truth.

Yet it is just this relation which is now being cavalierly discarded. Thus, Mr. Francis Williams, an experienced and eminent British journalist on the Left, has made a distinction . . . between "serious" and "mass circulation" newspapers, allocating to the former the business of "informing and persuading public opinion" and to the latter the task of "expressing the emotions—and often no doubt the prejudice, ignorance, and silliness—of its readers." This is an entirely novel conception of the function of a free press, and it implies an entirely novel conception of democracy as that system of society which allows people to give the freest expression to their emotions, their ignorance, their silliness. It is doubtful that such a society could exist; but it is certain that (a) no rational argument could be made in its defence, and (b) no popular government could long survive in it.

It is often said that "mass culture" is the price we pay for democracy. That all depends, of course, on what we mean by democracy.

If we mean by democracy nothing more than government which is freely consented to by the people, then this may well be so. In that case, one can either deny that "mass culture" poses any problem at all, and attribute our unease to the influence of "pre-democratic" standards of taste and culture upon our laggard imaginations; or one can seek reassurance in the belief that "mass culture" is only a passing phase of democratic evolution, and that in due course of time the level of popular taste and judgment will rise to nobler heights. Both alternatives involve an act of faith in The People, resting on the premise that what emerges from them is necessarily good and/or necessarily self-correcting.

This may be called the Populist religion of democracy, and there is no question but that it is the most common in our day. This can be seen from the frequency with which our publicists and statesmen make appeal to "the democratic faith" and "the democratic creed" as against other faiths and creeds, notably Communism. It is also interesting to observe that when the advertising and television industries feel the need to perform acts of "public service" they conceive of their mission as "selling" this democratic faith to all and sundry.

Like all political religions, this one is relatively invulnerable to rational examination and critique. But, again like all political religions, it has to face the test of reality. And the reality seems to be that this idea of popular government, in so far as it is most loyally put into practice, has a tendency to become unpopular—there is certainly more open dissatisfaction with "the democratic faith" in America to-day than there was fifty years ago, when the barest hint of scepticism was tantamount to treason. Nor is there anything paradoxical about this state of affairs; it simply reflects the fact that what people want (or think they want) is not inevitably identical with—and may even contradict—what they need (*i.e.*, what will truly satisfy them).

But this is not the only conception of democracy. And though it is now sovereign as an ideology, it is not the idea on which democracy in America and Britain was founded and which, to a greater or lesser degree, still rules the actual operations of government. That this is so in the United States is demonstrable by pointing to the existence of the Supreme Court—nine judges, appointed for life, with the power to nullify legislation (no matter how popular) that, in their considered opinion, is "unconstitutional" (a concept more vague than precise). There can be no doubt that, were a constitutional convention to be held to-day, no such thing as a Supreme Court could be set up—it would be regarded as flagrantly "undemocratic." (In those newer nations of Africa and Asia which have patterned themselves after the American system, either there is no such court or its powers are more formal than real.) Yet the Supreme Court, as originally established, has become an almost sacred institution, with which no politician dares tamper. In part, this is the sanctity that comes naturally with age. But in larger part, it is a tacit recognition that democratic government is something more than government that is popular in its origin: it is government that seeks justice as its aim.

It might be said that this is not a unique characteristic of democratic government, but is rather claimed by governments of all kinds. And it is indeed so. What this emphasises is merely that democracy is not a self-justifying system of government; that it is not divinely ordained, any more than absolute monarchy is; and that the problem of reconciling popular government with good government is a very real one.

And it is when one takes this problem seriously that one must take "mass culture" seriously. We have more evidence than we need or like that popular government can be oppressive, capricious, inadequate to its responsibilities. We have abundant testimony, too, to the truth that institutional safeguards, needed as they are, are not sufficient by themselves to protect a people against its own imprudence, its own passions. For these institutions cannot work unless they are respected, unless their legitimacy is freely acknowledged. And such respect and acknowledgment can only come from a people whose moral sense is sufficiently firm to know, not only that right and wrong exist, but that the distinguishing between them is not something they can achieve instinctively and unaided.

In the measure that people are encouraged to believe that what they want coincides with what they ought to want; in the measure that the mass media conceives it as its function to pander to "the prejudice, ignorance, and silliness" of its audience—in just such a measure is the moral fibre of democracy corrupted.

Apologists for the crudities of "mass culture" are fond of pointing out that it is really nothing new—that the favourite sport of the English people, until it was abolished by law in 1835, was bear-baiting. Quite true. But what is overlooked is that, before 1835, there was hardly a thoughtful man who believed the mass of the English people to be ready for self-government by universal suffrage. This is not because (as our text-books say) the very idea of democracy was novel and unfamiliar. Any educated person of that day knew a great deal about Periclean Athens and the Greek city-state. What he could not see was any resemblance between the Athenians who took part in popular assemblies and the Englishmen who took part in bear-baiting.

According to the Greek philosophers, the virtuous man was the man who exercised "self-government" over himself—over his passions, his impulses, his prejudices, his reasonings. Without such self-government in the individual, there could be no self-government in the state. Modern popular government is, of course, necessarily different from the Greek version. It involves large and representative republics rather than small and direct democracies. Only a utopian could expect virtuous men to be counted in the millions and tens of millions; the very difficulty of educating such a large number precludes it. But it is not utopian—or at least was not thought so by the thinkers of the 18th and 19th centuries who fathered the democratic idea—to believe that even such large numbers, suitably enlightened by instruction and example, could attain to a general level of decency and responsibility that allowed (though it could not, naturally, guarantee) virtuous and wise leadership to be exercised over them.

Whether such leadership will be forthcoming is the critical question that faces modern democracy. We know perhaps too well that democracy is government of, by, and for the people. What we need to remember is that, according to Thomas Jefferson, democracy was also a system in which "the natural aristocracy" of talent and virtue would find its most perfect fulfilment and satisfaction.

PROBLEMS FOR WRITING AND DISCUSSION

1. How has the meaning of the term "highbrow" shifted since the "moderns" made their revolt? Does Kristol approve of the original aim of their revolt? Explain.

2. What distinction does Kristol make between the "popular culture" of the nineteenth century and the "mass culture" of today? How is the distinction relevant to his main idea? Does Lynes (p. 519) preserve such a distinction?

3. What does Kristol see as the threat of "mass culture"? How would he judge Fishwick's attempt (p. 548) to elevate Billy the Kid to the rank of a Faust? Does Langer (p. 634) see "mass culture" as a comparable threat?

4. Why does Kristol find "of the greatest symbolic significance" the failure of educated men to define pornography?

5. Explain what Fiedler means by saying that "vulgar art" and "serious art" today both originate in an "antibourgeois source." What was "bourgeois" in the genteel tradition of England and America in the nineteenth

century? Kristol says that the original "highbrows" emphasized "(1) the continuity of a cultural tradition and (2) the moral role played by art . . . in the nation's life." What does Kristol himself emphasize? Does he see the dangers of an elite? Is he essentially in agreement with Mandel (p. 614)?

6. What ideological evasion do the "moderns" make to avoid definitive judgments on mass culture? Although the arguments in this "evasion" contain elements of truth, what, according to Kristol, is wrong with them? Compare what he says with Handlin's complaint (p. 368) against the relativism of anthropologists; with Riesman's charge (p. 488) that social scientists retreat into noncommittal specialism; and with E. B. White's insistence (p. 449) that the United Nations' weakness is its failure to define right and wrong. How have the ideals of equality, of scientific objectivity, and of artistic freedom contributed to modern man's timidity in making moral judgments?

7. Why does Kristol say that we are "hypnotized by Impersonal Forces" today? Compare his explanation with Eiseley's (p. 299).

8. Does Kristol's apprehension of the "art" of the masses resemble Cooper's (p. 399), Lippmann's (p. 381), and Viereck's (p. 324) apprehension of public opinion and the mass-man? Is it akin to Stevenson's fear (p. 478) of "mediocrity"?

9. "In place of a prescriptive definition of 'culture' we have an anthropological-sociological one." What is it, according to Kristol? Why does he call it a *"reductio ad absurdum"* for education "to divorce itself from the task of forming character, habits, and tastes"? What writers in the "Education" section of Part II lend support to Kristol's argument?

10. Does Kristol shed light on why Matthews (p. 99) left America for England? (Remember, however, that Kristol himself makes little if any distinction between England and America.) Do Kristol's remarks on British television throw light on the anti-Americanism Ebel (p. 213) senses at Cambridge?

11. What are the roles of advertising and popular journalism in the decline of cultural and moral standards? As Kristol sees it, what is the most invidious effect of the introduction of advertising appeals into the political sphere? Does he consider the "right to lie" a corollary of freedom of speech?

12. Why would the Supreme Court—if it had to be set up today—be considered "undemocratic"? Why, nevertheless, according to Kristol, is it "sacred" today?

13. What relation does Kristol see between education and "public morality" and between "public morality" and "self-government"? Is Kristol the first to perceive these relationships? Does Kristol assume that democracy is "divinely ordained"? Does he then dispute the claim of Jefferson

(p. 309) that Americans were acting in accord with the "Laws of Nature and of Nature's God"? What does Kristol say about the "organic relation" between truth and democracy that reconciles him with Jefferson?

14. What "dispositions of mind and character," in Kristol's opinion, "make popular government workable"? Compare what he considers requisite with what other writers in this book [Jefferson and Kennedy (p. 508), for example] have assumed.

15. What does Kristol mean by the "Populist religion of democracy"? Why does it fail the "test of reality"? Does Turner (p. 315) have more faith in the people's instinctive pursuit of what is right than Kristol has?

16. What does the "natural aristocracy" forseen by Jefferson and hoped for by Kristol have in common with the leadership Lippmann (p. 381) longs for, the "aristocracy" Viereck extols (p. 324), and the one Mandel (p. 614) says has traditionally been allied with art?

17. Kristol says that what people think they want and what "will truly satisfy them" are two different things. Does Mead (p. 24) make the same point about American young people? Is Kristol's observation confirmed by Langer's explanation (p. 634) of our "need" for art? Explain.

Billy the Kid: Faust in America

MARSHALL FISHWICK

> Marshall William Fishwick (1923-) is a native Virginian who was graduated from the University of Virginia (1943), wrote a book entitled The Virginia Tradition (1956), and teaches American Studies at Washington and Lee University in Lexington, Virginia. Another of his interests, however, is the American hero, both real and imagined, as seen in his book American Hero: Myth and Reality (1954).

> Scruples, or the perplexity of doubt,
> Torment me not, nor fears of hell or devil,
> But I have lost all peace of mind . . .
>   GOETHE'S "FAUST."

> Billy the Kid, he met a man
> Who was a whole lot badder.
> He didn't kid. Now Billy's dead
> And we ain't none the sadder.
>   WESTERN BALLAD.

Billy the Kid went straight to hell, and knew just what he was doing, too. He sold his soul to the devil, having killed twenty-one men before he was twenty-one—not counting Indians and Mexicans. Restless but damned, he roamed the American Southwest, goaded on by fate, living a full life before he was old enough to vote. After the devil had given him his due the law caught up with him; he died just as he should have, with his boots on and his guns blazing. Now he is paying for his crimes in hell. Here, in essence, is the

From The Saturday Review, *Oct. 11, 1952. Reprinted by permission of* The Saturday Review *and the author.*

Faustian legend moved to America and retitled Billy the Kid's saga: certainly the most important desperado tale in our culture.

Billy's contemporaries in the Southwest of post-Civil War days understood its importance even before he came to terms with cosmic justice. Legends about him flourished long before a sheriff's bullet snuffed out his life. When Pat Garrett hid in a dark room and ambushed Billy on July 14, 1881, he knew full well he was performing the most important act of his life. He described all the minute details as if he had been involved in some superhuman situation, one which posterity would long remember and debate. He sought political office on the basis of having fired the bullet that got Billy. And by one of history's interesting little turns, he met his death in the form of lead slugs, just as had Billy. The editor of the *Santa Fe Weekly Democrat* closed his account of Billy's death with a paragraph demonstrating his grasp of the Faustian drama involved:

> No sooner had the floor caught his descending form which had a pistol in one hand and a knife in the other, than there was a strong odor of brimstone in the air, and a dark figure with wings of a dragon, claws of a tiger, eyes like balls of fire, and horns like a bison hovered over the corpse for a moment. With a fiendish laugh he said, "Ha ha! This is my meat!" and then sailed off through the window. He did not leave his card, but is a gentleman well known to us by reputation, and thereby hangs a "tail."

Yet William H. Bonney was not the type of person one would pick out as a deadly killer. The two pictures extant show a frenzied but not a cunning or diabolic expression. Small of stature, Bonney weighed about 140 pounds and was five feet eight inches tall. He fits the folklorists' category labeled the Unpromising Hero. Unassuming and quiet, he moved like a panther, peering nervously out of gray eyes. His face was long, his hair light brown, his skin colorless, his hands and feet delicate. Dixon Wecter described Billy as an adenoidal farm boy with a rifle, the type visualized by the Western cliché "dirty little killer." Other writers have called him the most desperate white man on the border, and a scourge to his fellow man. But such indictments don't explain why Billy remains the most fascinating bad man in American history, and the basis of a whole series of legends and shrines.

One major thing his career points up is that law-abiding citizens get a delicious vicarious thrill from a killer's bloody progress. Movie makers discovered long ago that it was to escape the pettiness of their drab existence, not to see it portrayed or justified, that Americans came servilely to the silver screen. Hero makers knew this centuries before movies were invented. Two contemporary characters who are almost sure to start a conversation in any company are Al Capone and John Dillinger. Spilling a little blood always livens up an evening.

To what extent do the Kid's history and his legend overlap? No one can give a precise answer to this question now. The legendary veneer has all but hidden the historical truth underneath. Today scholars are even quibbling about whether or not "Bonney" was Billy's real name. Tabulating the various claims for the title "Billy the Kid" is a research project in its own right. Despite all this controversy there is no doubt of Billy's authenticity and cussedness. The blood he spilled liberally in the Southwest was real blood, and underneath all the legend there is enough verifiable truth to reconstruct a scant life history.

William H. Bonney was born in New York City (of all places) on November 23, 1859, the son of William H. and Kathleen Bonney. During the Civil War they moved to Coffeyville, Kansas, where the father died. Moving to Colorado, the mother married a man named Antrim, after which the family went to Silver City, New Mexico. After that, killing and Billy became synonymous, and the facts are hard to extract. Billy's first victim is said to have been a blacksmith who insulted his mother. In 1875 the youth and a partner supposedly killed three Indians for the furs they were carrying. In 1877 Bonney turned up in the rugged Pecos Valley, where he was employed by an English rancher and newcomer, J. H. Tunstall.

Quickly he was sucked into the famous Lincoln County war which raged in the 1870's. He probably saw Tunstall killed by a posse of the Murphy faction, and Tunstall's partner McSween shot,

Bible in hand, before his burning house. Such sights aroused the latent savagery inside Billy. He became a ruthless killer, putting his rare nimbleness of mind and body to effective use. Stories of his incredible speed and accuracy with a gun began to grow. Some said he practised shooting by picking snowbirds off fenceposts at a gallop. In any case, he definitely picked off Sheriff James A. Brady and a deputy, and refused to accept amnesty when urged to do so by Governor Lew Wallace.

When the warfare died down Billy concentrated on cattle stealing with such success that leading ranchers, headed by John Chisum, persuaded a brave Irishman named Pat Garrett to become sheriff and track down Billy's gang. He managed to capture Billy in 1881, and a jury promptly condemned him to death. But the Lincoln jail could not hold Billy. Despite handcuffs and leg irons he killed his two guards and escaped. Two and a half months later he was trapped at Pete Maxwell's house in Fort Sumner and ambushed in a pitch-black room by Garrett. This is the bald outline of Billy's career as it was written in ink, lead, and blood. The story does not stop there; it goes on, filling books, theatres, and movie houses, and proving a fertile seedbed for the American imagination.

There are many stories about the girl Billy was visiting at the Maxwells' when Pat Garrett ambushed and killed him at midnight. The kindest thing Billy's girl friend said to the sheriff was that he was too cowardly to meet Billy face to face; most of the other things are unprintable. Apparently pumping lead into his enemies was not Billy's only accomplishment. "In every *placeta* in New Mexico," attests Walter Noble Burns, "girls sing to their guitars songs of Billy the Kid. A halo has been clasped upon his scapegrace brow. The boy who never grew old has become a sort of symbol of frontier knight-gallantry, a figure of eternal youth riding forever through a purple glamour of romance." Like Faust, whose heir he is, he is sinister as well as gallant, dashing across the plains with his leg thrown across his horse's saddle, an arm protruding from beneath the horse's neck, deadly pistol glistening.

Like the historical Faust who actually lived in Germany, Billy the Kid was not so much invented as endowed with traits of the great folk heroes of earlier cultures. His birth, coming of age, initiation, consecration, "inthronization," and his mysterious death and burial all fit the age-old pattern. Yet the transformation of Bonney's legend into history was not a job for the centuries. Here is a man who jumped from history into legend so rapidly that no one has figured out just what happened. But it does seem certain that four little-known Americans deserve more credit for the transition than Billy himself. This quartet was not of the literati, but this doesn't seem to have hurt them. A fallen politician, a Texas cowpoke, a lawyer who preferred the outdoors to the court room, and an itinerant journalist gave Billy his immortality. Ash Upson, Charlie Siringo, Emerson Hough, and Walter Noble Burns were their names. Hero making was their specialty.

Ash Upson deserves the lion's share of credit in Billy the Kid's apotheosis. He is the major architect of the Kid's legend. He discovered Billy's literary possibilities, sought out the man who killed him, and with him collaborated on the most influential book about Billy the Kid. He raised Billy to an heroic level. Marshall Ashmum Upson was born in Wolcott, Connecticut, in 1828, and like Ben Franklin and Mark Twain got most of his education in a print shop. James Gordon Bennett's *New York Herald* provided his first reporter's job. After that he drifted westward. In 1867 he established the *Albuquerque Press,* which he published for two years, and later the *Las Vegas Mail.* For a while he dabbled in politics, but unfavorable publicity arising from his part in state speculation drove him back to the printer's case. In 1881 he became a boarder in the house of Pat Garrett, who in the same year shot Billy the Kid. When a few months later Garrett decided to write a book about the Kid, both to exonerate himself from charges that he had shot Bonney unfairly and to cash in on the wide interest in the shooting, what was more natural than to turn to his literary friend and housemate Upson for aid?

On March 12, 1882, the *Daily New Mexican* announced that the book was ready for sale, fifty cents a copy postpaid. Authoritatively entitled "The Authentic Life of Billy the Kid, the Noted Desperado of the Southwest," this slim volume of 137 pages is the fountainhead of most later Billy the Kid literature. It set the standard pattern of the Kid's career from which few have deviated. We cannot analyze it as if it were an historical monograph; it is more literary than historical. It does for New Mexico what Mark Twain's "Roughing It" did for Nevada: elevates it to a realm of the metaphor and well-turned phrase.

Some of the toughness of Billy got into the prose, and some of the plainness of Pat Garrett. The book is considerably less Victorian than anything else Upson ever wrote. Partiality to Billy is written on every page. "All who ever knew Billy will testify that his polite, cordial, and gentlemanly bearing invited confidence and promised protection—the first of which he never betrayed, and the latter he was never known to withhold." Enter the legend that Billy was a chivalric knight-errant, not a mere killer. "If purity of conversation were the test, hundreds of the prominent citizens of New Mexico would be taken for desperadoes sooner than young Bonney." Add a dash of Sir Galahad. "The aged, the poor, the sick, the unfortunate and helpless never appeal to Billy in vain for succor." Enter the Robin Hood motif. "Billy was, when circumstance permitted, scrupulously neat and elegant in dress." Add a dash of Beau Brummel. And so it goes, until a full-fledged hero emerges in the last chapters.

Upson was enormously pleased with his job with Billy the Kid. "I am now engaged in getting together data for a full history of the county," he wrote his sister enthusiastically in 1882, "The Indian Wars, the Harold War, several less important vignettes, and the great cattleman's war from 1876 to 1880. This will be published by subscription." It never was. Professor Maurice G. Fulton, Upson's biographer, tells of reports that Ash left a trunk full of papers and clippings, but he has been unable to locate it. Some idea of Upson's rapid decline in his later years can be gained from his obituary published in the *Roswell Register* for October 31, 1894. "He lived for forty years in violation of every law of health, and nothing but an incomparable vitality kept him alive for years. His many friends will regret to learn of his death, although it was not unexpected." He left as his contribution to the American scene the fascinating figure of a young American Faust galloping over the Southwestern plains to a blood-filled Walpurgis Night.

Like Walt Whitman, Charles Siringo preferred to find out about life first hand. He knew; he suffered; he was there. In all his writing Siringo played on the same three themes: his own experience as cowboy and detective, the role of tough men in the West, and the innate greatness of Billy the Kid. These things sustained him for years and carried him from Texas, where he was born in 1855, to Hollywood, where he was technical adviser on Western movies until his death in 1928. Numerous real cowhands have vouched for the authenticity of Siringo's stories and history. "A Texas Cowboy" became the cowboy's Bible. Written with a glow and a glee, it holds its own today in both cloth and paper-back editions. Had Siringo's book been the only one to deal with the Kid, Bonney would on its strength alone have gained a place of notoriety among Southwest outlaws. A high point of the book is Siringo's tale of meeting Billy on the LZ Range in the winter of 1878-79. He also knew Pat Garrett, who filled his mind with details of Billy's early career. The meeting with Billy kept magnifying in importance in Siringo's mind, until when he put out "A Lonestar Cowboy" in 1919 he added new details about giving the Kid his new ten-dollar meerschaum cigar holder, for which Billy gave him in return "a finely bound novel which he had finished reading." (To envisage Billy as a collector of the bindings requires vision.) A year later Siringo put out a book devoted entirely to hero-worship, called "History of Billy the Kid," in which he reveals his deep admiration for his killer-hero with details of his own campaign to place a lasting monument at the grave of the Kid.

No one got the story of Billy over to so many people as well as Charlie Siringo. He is by far the most important disseminator of the legend to the average American reader and, through his work in Hollywood, the average American movie-goer. Realizing how many Americans get into these two categories, one can call him the popularizer of Billy to mass audiences. His importance as a hero-maker far surpasses his importance as a writer or historian. As J. Frank Dobie (who knows more about Siringo than any one else) has pointed out, "He had almost nothing to say on life, he reported actions. He put down something valid on a class of livers, as remote now from the Atomic Age as Rameses II." Instead of hindering us their remoteness attracts us all the more. The fact that there can never be another Billy the Kid with a gray horse, blazing six shooters, and open range to cavort in gives him a distantness and mystery that enhances him beyond believing.

Raised on a mild, rolling corn-belt farm, Emerson Hough spent the best years of his life courting the wild and wooly West. He was born in Newton, Iowa, and graduated from the state university's law school in 1880. In 1883 he set up his law office in the little town of White Oaks, New Mexico, but was never too concerned with the law. Hough spent his time seeking out characters in the bloody Lincoln County war and collecting tales of the struggle in the back country. The local color of New Mexico fascinated him, and provided him with the basic material for a successful writer's career. Before his death in 1923 he had twenty-nine books to his credit, none so important to American letters as an eight-page article for a magazine. "The True Story of a Western Bad Man," published in the September 1901 *Everybody's Magazine*, is one of the shortest prose pieces to play a major role in the creating of an American hero.

In essence Hough put horns and tails on our juvenile killer, and saw the outlines of a pitchfork where others had only seen a fast-moving six-shooter. It was Faust gone Western that Hough envisioned. He sharpened up the image in his best-selling "The Story of the Outlaw: A Study of the Western Desperado" (1907). In a chapter called "The Man Hunt" he pictures brave Pat Garrett tracking down his *fiendus Americanus* in barren New Mexico. We can practically smell the sulphur when Billy's riddled body sinks to the floor. Instead of hurting Billy's reputation, Hough's accounts made him seem more wicked and hence vastly more interesting.

With his boy's love of the forests and the beckoning roads, Hough brought his own bumptious enthusiasm and energy to bear on his stories. He did such a good job of damning Billy the Kid that he helped damn him right into immortality.

The fourth hero-maker did not invent, but revived, the Kid's saga. Born in Lebanon, Kentucky, in 1872, Walter Noble Burns got printer's ink in his blood even before high-school days were behind him. In subsequent years his Westward urge carried him to newspaper jobs in St. Louis, Kansas City, Chicago, Denver, and San Francisco. Between jobs he decided to try the life on the rolling sea, and made a long whaling voyage aboard the brigantine *Alexander*. Experiences in the South Sea, Behring Sea, and Arctic Ocean were the basis of his first book, "A Year with a Whaler" (1913). He also tried his hand at soldiering, serving with the First Kentucky Infantry in the Spanish American War. He struck his best vein, however, when he left the sea and the West Indies and concentrated on the Western plains. "Tombstone," "The One Way Ride," and "The Robin Hood of El Dorado" were books all widely acclaimed before his death in 1932; but his "Saga of Billy the Kid" (1926) marked his real contribution to the mythology of the West.

This pivotal volume ended the lull that had set in with Bonney material after Siringo stopped writing about 1920. Perhaps it is more accurate to say that Burns restated the story in such a contemporary fashion that dozens of movie, comic, and pulp writers have drawn from him as a thirsty man draws water from a well. "The Saga of Billy the Kid" is required reading for the student of the heroic process in America. Burns sees that Bonney's story is folklore in the making, related to the Homeric succession. "A hundred years or so from now," he predicts, "Billy the Kid will appear in fireside tales." To such ancient rogues as Robin Hood, Claude Duval, Dick Turpin, and Fra Diavolo he compares Billy, whose legend he believes is destined to "a mellow and genial immortality." Burns contributes sizably to that legend by his apt choice of words, tales, and comparisons. To him Billy is a genius "painting his name in flaming colors with a six-shooter across the sky of the Southwest."

His is a unique and extraordinary personality, "frozen egotism plus recklessness and minus mercy." He is "not of the stuff of ordinary men," but has instead the "debonair courage of a cavalier" and "the afflatus that made him the finished master." He is "born to battle and vendetta, to hatred and murder, to tragic victory and tragic defeat." He is, in short, more of a god than a man.

As much as any other writer Burns sensed the cosmic qualities involved in Billy's Faustian career. "Opposite him played Death," he states dramatically. "It was a drama of Death and the Boy. He laughed at Death. Death was a joke. He waved Death a jaunty goodbye and was off to new adventures." This is fine writing, much better than that of the earlier hero makers. Burns turned a mean metaphor, and carried a formidable arsenal of adjectives. Billy was an ideal subject for him, a man whose bizarre life and death challenged his powers as a writer. As his 1926 title indicated, he intended to write a saga; if he did not do that, he at least added much to the saga that was already thriving.

So much for book sources of the Kid's legend. As any student of American culture knows, this gives only a partial view, since much legendizing is on the oral level also. The troubadour's note is probably more telling in the long run than the printer's touch. Legends passed down orally in America from one generation to another form a Homeric succession that is independent of the printing presses. Stories of Billy's charm, courage, Faustian abandon, and dramatic death are indispensable if he is to be a folk hero. "As each narrative adds a bit of drama here and a picturesque detail there," writes B. A. Botkin, "one wonders what form these legends will assume as time goes by, and in what heroic proportions Billy the Kid will appear in fireside fairy tales a hundred years or so from now."

In many ways William H. Bonney symbolized the whole pastoral epoch doomed by the railroad, tractor, and homesteader. He died grimly with both guns roaring defiance and death. If his particular crimes are dated, his appeal is not. Twentieth-century readers like their heroes raw, with a little blood on them. Having read the tough novels of Hemingway, Caldwell, and Faulkner, and seen such tough movie idols as Bogart, Cagney, and Raft, they are naturally attracted to this early killer. He got through all the scrapes the movies have later contrived, without a fall guy or double; even with mirrors the movie fictionists haven't been able to improve on his reality.

Like Faust, Billy the Kid sensed the drama in his own evil career, and even enjoyed his predicament. When, says the legend, the Las Vegas judge sentenced him to be hanged, he wanted to make sure his pronouncement of death sank in. "You are sentenced to be hanged by the neck until you are dead, dead, dead," intoned the judge. To which Billy quickly replied, "And you can go to hell, hell, hell!" Faust could not have improved on that line.

After Billy had been shot the townsmen dragged the body across the street to a carpenter's shop, where the young villain was stretched out on a bench. Candles were placed beside him, casting flickering shadows on the face of the hardened killer. The next day they buried him in a borrowed white shirt too large for the slim boy, placing him in a plain wooden coffin. Admirers scraped together $208 for a simple gravestone, later splintered and carried away by relic hunters. He had been on this earth exactly twenty-one years, seven months, and twenty-one days—long enough to supply the basis for an American legend.

The Kid had a lurking devil in him, sometimes debonair and impish, sometimes bloodthirsty and fiendish, as circumstances prompted. History favored the worser angel, and the Kid fell. His damnable life ended with a deserved death. Since God condemned, Americans have been content to forgive. May God have mercy on his soul.

PROBLEMS FOR WRITING AND DISCUSSION

1. Fishwick speaks of Billy the Kid's life as fitting the "age-old pattern." What does he mean?

2. Is Billy the Kid a genuine folk hero? If so, what would you call Lincoln and Washington?

3. Billy the Kid was a killer; yet a recent television series portrayed him as a hero working on the side of law and justice. How does Fishwick help you to understand the reasons for portraying him as a hero?

4. What is there about Billy the Kid—both the man and the legend—that reveals him to be a product of the West about which De Voto (p. 93) and Turner (p. 315) write? Does the absence of Billy the Kid or characters like him from Turner's essay weaken Turner's thesis about the role of the West in shaping American ideals?

5. Why does the West, embodied in part by such men as Billy the Kid, Jesse James, Wyatt Earp, and others, hold such obvious fascination for many Americans? Is there something basic about Americans to be learned from this attraction? What explanation would William James (p. 502) give?

6. Fishwick describes several men who bear a large responsibility for creating the Billy the Kid myth. What characteristics do they have in common?

7. Writing of Hough's account, Fishwick says: "He did such a good job of damning Billy the Kid that he helped damn him right into immortality" (p. 556). Explain.

8. To what extent does the legend of Billy the Kid illustrate Lynes's contention (p. 519) that ours is a "you-name-it-we-have-it" kind of culture?

9. Who on the modern American scene with characteristics similar to the real Billy the Kid has a chance of becoming enshrined in legend? Does your choice—or failure to make a choice—tell you something about the changes that have occurred in America since the nineteenth century?

10. What does Fishwick mean when he says: "Since God condemned [Billy the Kid], Americans have been content to forgive"?

11. What do you make of the basic comparison in the essay? Was Billy the Kid, as Fishwick describes him, a Faust figure? Or is the subtitle meant ironically?

12. In the versions of the legend best known to educated men, those of Marlowe and Goethe, Faust is torn by an internal moral struggle and awareness of his relation to cosmic forces of good and evil. Does the omission of this feature from the legend of Billy indicate the amorality of mass culture Kristol (p. 529) describes? Fishwick notes Billy's identity with the heroes of Hemingway, Caldwell, and Faulkner. Like them, would Billy have his origin in an "antibourgeois source"?

Abuse of the Past—Norman Rockwell

WRIGHT MORRIS

>Wright Morris (1910-   ) has been writing fiction for more than twenty years. From his early experimental work, he has continued to write about America, often focusing on the Nebraska country in which he was born and reared. His reputation grew steadily, and in 1957 he won the National Book Award for The Field of Vision. Since then he has written Love Among the Cannibals (1957); The Territory Ahead (1958), a study of the artist-writer in America; Ceremony in Lone Tree (1960); and What a Way to Go (1962). Few novelists, it has been said, have "so clear a vision of the essence of the American experience."

When we think of Don Quixote most of us will visualize the lean seedy figure in the pen drawings of Doré, an erect spindly wraith, seated on his bony nag, followed by the slouched, melancholy Sancho. If the pan is on his head it seems a small detail, just another crazy part of a witless old man. We see him spear in hand, we see him tilting windmills, we see him thrown from his ridiculous horse, but I think we never see him as he wished to see himself—*invisible*. He is all too visible, and in every inch mad as a coot. The element of humor in it appeals to us, but the element of wonder, I'm afraid, escapes. The golden Helmet of Mambrino is a piece of nonsense. We are all Sanchos at heart.

If we now conjure up the picture I have in mind, it will be a new one. Let us imagine Don Quixote, crowned with the battered

From The Territory Ahead *by Wright Morris, Harcourt, Brace, 1958. Reprinted by permission of the author.*

barber's basin, attended by his everfaithful Sancho, as he would appear on a cover of the *Saturday Evening Post,* as he would appear through the eyes and technique of Norman Rockwell.

I doubt that such an illustration exists, but I think that most Americans, at the suggestion, could supply it: a very lifelike figure—resembling somebody we know, a neighbor or a member of the family—on a horse that we had seen that morning, drawing the milk cart, wearing the basin in which we had, as a boy, washed our feet. I am not invoking this picture to ridicule it. Quite the contrary, since if we hope to understand the "imagination in America" we must start, if not end, with this master of verisimilitude, with this artist who, above all others, *heightens* the appearance of reality.

In speaking of the future of the novel James said: "Beginnings, as we all know, are usually small things, but continuations are not always strikingly great ones. . . ." In the beginning was Norman Rockwell. The continuations have not been strikingly great. From such a fact there is more to be gleaned than the usual sophisticated despair, or ironic amusement.

We can say, first, last, and always, that Norman Rockwell has been true to his beginnings, to his trust in his own and American sentiment. He is a genre painter; he uses graphic means to tell a story. His technique may be described as the most perfect where it dissolves, imperceptibly, into anecdote. This anecdotal picture that tells a simple story is the father of the story that gives us the simple picture, the *same* picture, as a rule—an unadorned, unpretentious, photographically convincing portrayal of *real* life.

In a period of forty years Rockwell has supplied the *Post* with more than three hundred of its covers. He has taught a generation of Americans to see. They look about them and see, almost everywhere they look, what Norman Rockwell sees—the tomboy with the black eye in the doctor's waiting room; the father discussing the Facts of Life with his teen-age son; the youth in the dining car on his first solo flight from home; and the family in the car, headed for an outing, followed by the same family on the tired ride home.

The convincing *realism* of the details, photographic in its accuracy, is all subtly processed through a filter of sentiment. It is this sentiment that heightens the reality, making it, for some, an object of affection, for others—a small minority—an object of ridicule. It all depends on that intangible thing the point of view.

Countless young men and women at the beginning of careers in art, have tried, and usually failed, to explain *their* point of view to a puzzled mother, a skeptical father. What can be wrong—Father would like to know—with Norman Rockwell, who is so obviously *good*? The answer is his very *goodness,* of course, but this usually ends the argument. Discussion leads nowhere. The two points of view go their different ways.

After considerable exposure to "modern" art, in museums, fashion magazines, the world of advertising, and everyday living, that mythic figure, the man in the street, will still go along with Norman Rockwell. And so—whenever they can get him—will the *Saturday Evening Post.* In that respect, the times have not changed. A vote for Norman Rockwell is a vote for the *real* America. It is the nature of his gift that his very technique appears to dissolve into the subject, leaving the deposit of sentiment we like, otherwise no trace. After we have recognized the figures as our neighbors, and the street they live on as our own, we are left precisely where we came in—at the beginning. It is the nature of the genre piece to limit itself to clichés.

But if this charge is leveled at Norman Rockwell, it is leveled in suspension and will never reach him. Norman Rockwell is not there. In the picture we attack there is only ourselves. This is why such an attack gets us fighting mad. That row of photographs we keep on the piano has been maligned. However, this will help to explain the almost total absence of transitional material between Grant Wood's "Iowa Gothic"—which is true to the Rockwell tradition—and the sort of painting that most young people are doing today. It was easier to leap directly into the arms of God or the Devil than fight across the no man's land of raw-material clichés. A clean break—on such a battlefield—was the only one possible.

The extent to which this gap remains—and will continue to remain, we can feel with assurance—is evident in Rockwell's painting of Jennifer Jones in *The Song of Bernadette.* When the movie was released, Twentieth Century-Fox turned to Norman Rockwell, the illustrator, rather than to the resources of the movie camera, to portray and advertise the star in the leading role. That the movie industry should choose Norman Rockwell is both a testimony to his craft and a revealing commentary on the prevailing American taste. Our *realistic* front still has its soft, yellow-filter sky.

A more recent example, in the form of a tribute, were Rockwell's portraits of the Presidential candidates. It was left to Rockwell, in this sense, to reveal what the camera angles concealed, and to give the people—insofar as they were self-evident—the facts. Mr. Rockwell's Stevenson is the most instructive: we see the wit and intellectual cut down to our size, not cut down with malice, but, rather, with affection, as the neighbors of a "famous" man know him to be a simple, regular guy. Mr. Stevenson emerges as the man we usually find behind a drug counter, shrewd in his way, of independent mind, and willing to both take and give advice. He is one of us, not at all the sort of egghead we had heard about.

Scrutinized, held under the light that we find the most illuminating—the soft-sharp lens of Rockwell's craft—our raw material is seldom raw at all. It is hardly material. The clinical word for it is cliché. In the beginning, this credo reads, was the cliché. The raw-material effect is like the tinseled snow hung on the rootless trees at Christmas, stimulating the sensation without the embarrassment of the facts.

The paradox of our situation might be put like this: having either exhausted, or depleted, the raw material that appeals to us, we needed a technician to create the illusion that it was still there. Rockwell is that technician. He understands the hunger, and he supplies the nourishment. The hunger is for the Good Old Days— the black-eyed tomboy, the hopeless, lovable pup, the freckled-faced young swain on his first date, the kid with white flannels at his first prom—sensations we no longer have, but still seem to want, dreams of innocence, as a rule, before they became corrupt.

This entire genre world, crowded with the artifacts that give it pathos and conviction, is generally inhabited by children, friendly animals, loving mothers, and wise old ladies and gentlemen. The beginnings of life come in for sentimental comment—often touching and penetrating—the Huckleberry Finn myth of our lost youth, the territory of dreams that always lay ahead. But what that territory turned out to really *be*, neither Mark Twain nor Rockwell will tell us. It is a world of onsets, maiden speeches, first blushes, first impressions, and new departures; a universe of firsts: first dog, first kiss, first heartbreak, and first love. At the end of this journey, somehow sweetened by a life that has evaded both realization and comment, we find the very old engaged in prayer, dozing with kittens, tolerating youngsters, or humorously caught in one of the innocent traps of life: a barber chair, a rumble seat, a train coach shared by a pair of young lovers, or a bench where the squirrels rifle our pockets while we sleep.

Between our first love, which is implicitly our last, and our last nap, which is implicitly forever, there is very little. What there is can be summed up in a word. *It's a joke, son.* In what is perhaps his most revealing work—one in which he portrays his full range of types—Rockwell illustrates the joke in question making its rounds. Here is *la ronde,* the permissible *ronde* American. It is clear that a good joke is something that good Americans can exchange. The democratic process can be seen at work as this joke makes its rounds from man to man, woman to woman, level to level, until it finally comes full circle—back, that is, to the man on whom the joke was played. They are all, needless to say, *good* American types. The democratic process is also at work, since we see no black men, no yellow men, no obvious Jews, Italians, or roughnecks—just plain folks, one of us. What the joke is we can almost guess. It is one that is funny to all these people. And it goes without saying that it is not *dirty*, though it might have an edge. It is basically good-hearted, basically good clean fun.

This interlude between first love and last breath is an illustrated version of Old Macdonald, forever down on his farm, where funny things are forever happening. Sex raises its adolescent murmur, not its ugly head. In this panel of profiles, this great family portrait, Rockwell gives us the long span of a lifetime between the first and the last joke we have heard. In this report, consciously or otherwise, a note of comment can be detected that is usually conspicuously absent from his work. His people are always, we might say, *comfortably* real. But in this portrait they verge on the uncomfortable. The raw material is so raw it almost speaks for itself. The effect—the cumulative effect, since we deal here with a group portrait—is something more than the sum of its parts. If the eye remains on the page, and slowly follows the joke through all of its phases, a disquieting, nonhumorous impression builds up. How does it happen? It is clear that they are all just goodhearted folks. But it is also clear, increasingly, that they have nothing else on their minds, that until the joke came along they had nothing else to *exchange*. It is the joke that binds them together in brotherhood. Missing from this tableau is the dirty-minded lowbrow who would have spoiled all the fun, and the egghead who might have used it for his own ends. The joke comes full circle pretty much as it was told.

In a series of 1957 calendar illustrations, entitled "The Four Seasons," Mr. Rockwell supplies us with a credo that lucidly sums up his function as an artist. This is his statement:

> In a world that puts such importance on the pursuit of youth, it is good to consider, occasionally, the charms—and the comforts—of maturity. For whatever else may be said, maturity fosters familiarity which in turn gives feelings of security and understanding that are valuable in these days of continuing change. I have tried to show these feelings in the paintings for the new Four Seasons calendar.
>
> My pictures show two people who, after living together for many years, have reached the stage of sympathy and compatibility for which all of us strive. They know their weaknesses and their strengths. They are comfortable and secure in their relationships with each other. And while Mother presumably takes Father's strong points for granted, she's still trying tolerantly to keep him on the straight and narrow when signs of frailty appear.
>
> Paintings like these are fun to do. While they are humorous, they are also human, and the subtle touch of forbearance evident in each of them is something all of us can learn. I can only hope you'll enjoy looking at these pictures as much as I have enjoyed working on them.

Perhaps the reader can visualize the "subtle touch of forbearance" in these illustrations. It verges closely—in the words of a recent parody in *Punch*—on the Brighter Side of the Bubonic Plague. Maturity—whatever else may be said—seen through the forbearance of Mr. Rockwell seems to be an adolescent pipe dream of the genial aspects of senility. The pursuit of youth is made more visible, rather than less, in these gentle fuddy-duddies, Mom and Pop, and their pathetic inability to grow *up*. A certain aging has taken place, but such growth as we observe is downward and backward. That Mother takes Father's strong points for granted is obvious, desperately so—because Father's *strong* points are touchingly invisible. A genial pathos, sentimentally evoked, would seem to be the mortar that binds them together, and provides the comfort in what we describe as their "relationship." That hard-work marriage has given way to the slogans inscribed on the insurance posters, where the happy smiling couple are preserved, safe from *old* age, in the amber of leisure. Nothing will touch them but the postman, with his monthly retirement check.

All of the durable clichés we have already described are served up afresh in these four tableaux. "Winter" shows us the calendar being nailed to the wall, one that features a pin-up girl discreetly censored—not the sort of tempting dish that men or boys, if the distinction exists, pin up for real delectation. "Spring" finds Father down with a cold, lovingly wrapped up in Mother's patchwork quilt, his feet in a pan of water as she spoonfeeds him what is so obviously good for him. "Summer" finds him in the yard, in a state of collapse, after a tussle with the lawn mower, while Mother, with a compassionate gaze, stands waiting to pour him a glass of lemonade. In all these pictures a cat, symbol of the loving home, is conspicuously evident, and proves, in his kittenish ways, to be as young in heart as his masters.

The date beneath these illustrations is 1957—but they are daydreams from a timeless past: only Mother's somewhat battered leather moccasins indicate that the time is the present. Immortal moths escape from the holes in Father's pair of red flannels, indicating that with "Autumn" something called Winter is near. The mature round of life—American style—in this manner comes full cycle, leaving the reader prepared and expectant for the new calendar that will usher in the New Year. We are free to rest assured that Mother will keep Father on the straight and narrow path.

We might say that Mr. Rockwell's special triumph is in the conviction his countrymen share that this mythic world he evokes actually exists. This cloudland of nostalgia seems to loom higher on the horizon, as the horizon itself, the world of actual experience, disappears from view. The mind *soars off*—in the manner that highways, with new model cars, soar off into the future—leaving the drab world of commonplace facts and sensations behind. In soaring into the past, rather than the future, Mr. Rockwell is true to himself and his public, since that is where the true territory ahead actually lies. In knowing this he illustrates, with admirable fidelity, the American Land of Heart's Desire.

If we now return to our imaginary painting, Mr. Rockwell's conception of Don Quixote, the pathetic old man, with the brass basin on his head, in the charge of the shrewd but loyal Sancho, we will sense to what extent he will reveal more than the obvious humor of it. There would be a touch of pity, a touch of pathos, and a quantity of good-humored affection—but of wonder, that transforming element, not a drop. He is a childish old man with bats loose in his belfry—not unlike one we have in the family— and we identify ourselves with Sancho, rather than with him, with poor old Sancho, who, like ourselves, has to humor him. As for that helmet on his head, it is plainly a barber's basin. We all know that. We are Sanchos to the core, and he speaks with our voice when he cries that he can no longer bear in patience the wind and the lies, the buggery and humbuggery that the old man gives out. There is pity for an old fool, humor for a young one, and between the two of them, a joke, a good, clean joke.

Pathos—the only serious sentiment we will permit ourselves, without embarrassment—might reveal itself unconsciously in this portrait, as a touch of malice revealed itself in "The Joke." Rockwell plainly knows, as he assumes we do, that the dream is in the past. The Great Good Place is back there at the beginning, where it has always been. The faces in "The Joke," all meant to be contemporaries, have the cracker-barrel look of period pieces, *characters* in the sense that time will no longer alter them. Many of these people are Rockwell's Yankee neighbors—or reasonable facsimiles of them—but they are selected for what they represent, and they represent the past. The present exists, if at all in Rockwell, as a frame that heightens the nostalgia—the doctor's crisp waiting room where the tomboy with her black eye smilingly waits.

How many American fathers—if not mothers—would like to have had a girl like *that,* not like the jitterbugging, all-too-sex-conscious little number he has, not like the present, that is, but more like the imagined past.

In "Thanksgiving, 1951"—one of the most successful of his *Post* covers—Rockwell portrays an old lady and a small boy, the permissible extremes of our awareness, seated at a table in a "rough" railroad restaurant, saying grace. The youths and elderly men who surround them are all touchingly aware, and properly *touched.* The central figures, the old lady and the boy, have been lifted from some genre piece of the past, lock, stock, and barrel, and show no taint of existing in the world where we find them. The boy wears what such little boys were wearing during World War I. The old lady has her alligator bag, her umbrella, and her sewing reticule on the floor at her side. No cliché has been evaded. Every cliché is treated with the utmost respect. Through the window a modern locomotive steams in the yard.

How times have changed! we exclaim, and see our *self* as that pious unspoiled boy, and this fragment of the past as the real past that is gone.

But these characters appear out of neither the past nor the hidden byways of the present, but, rather, out of the thin air of our imaginative need for them. That tomboy, with her blackened eye, and that puzzled teen-ager getting the Facts of Life, are meticulously illustrated daydreams to put the sad daily facts out of mind. These fantasies, generated on the trains whisking urban fathers to their homes in the suburbs, are meant to be fictions, lacking any connection to real life. It was in the past—just yesterday, that is—that there were giants in the earth, dreams in our hearts, love in our homes, religion in our churches, honor in our markets, and a future of such promise that the very thought of it brings an ache to the throat, and the eyes grow dim. In youth and age—a hopeful look forward or a yearning glance backward—Rockwell sustains the sentimental extremities of our lives. In between, making its eternal round, filling up the big central gap in our existence, is the joke. Stop me if you've heard this one, says the joker—but of course nobody does. After all, what else is there? *La ronde* is *le rire*.

If we now return to our imagined Don Quixote, the relationship between technique and raw material is made clear. The raw material is what counts. Technique is the way we gloss or heighten it with sentiment.

> "Do you know what I think, Sancho?" said Don Quixote. "I think that this famous piece of that enchanted helmet must by some strange accident have fallen into the hands of someone who did not know, and was incapable of estimating, its worth, and who, seeing that it was of the purest gold and not realizing what he was doing, must have melted down the other half for what he could get for it, while from the remaining portion he fashioned what appears, as you have said, to be a barber's basin."

Having melted down the other half, from the remaining portion Rockwell has fashioned what appears to be a barber's basin. It is the basin as *basin* that interests us, and no transformation is desired. Such magical properties as it might possess transport us into the past, rather than into the future. It is the key, the Open Sesame, to our nostalgia. The battered basin, the bony nag, the old man with the bats loose in his belfry, are so many strings around our memory fingers, the unbroken ties we retain with the past. They transport us, rather than transform us, and it is the past, not the future, that beckons.

The element of folk wisdom in this pattern generates much that is good in our writing, but we are apt to overlook the crippling power of the cliché. The Helmet of Mambrino, shorn of its magic, hangs affectionately on that nail in the kitchen—because it is a basin, an *old* basin, not because it has unusual properties. It does not change us so much as remind us—what we want is not change but reminiscence—and, needless to say, what we want is what we get.

Among our many native gifts, which are large, is one that is seldom singled out for comment. It is the faculty, one might say the intuition, we have by which we transform adult works of art, few as they are, into children's books. We transform them into books that are *safe*. *Moby Dick* and *Huckleberry Finn* are not merely safe for boys to read, but are even read by them. They are adventure stories, on the shelf with *Treasure Island* and *Tom Swift*. It would seem to be here, and here alone, that the transforming powers of the Helmet of Mambrino are part of our tradition. We transform the adult into a child. It is the converse of transforming the present into the past. In either case we get back to the beginnings, back to the innocence before it was corrupted, back to that time when the world and ourselves were young.

A boy's-eye view of the world, enchanted in *Tom Sawyer*, disenchanted in *Huckleberry Finn*, is wonderfully blended in the art of Norman Rockwell and seasoned to taste. Here we can often have it both ways. The grown-up world impinges on the past only to heighten its flavor, the purity of the enchantment, the sweet pathos of the light that failed. Old folks—people who once again are notoriously childlike—reappear to reaffirm, in their seasoned wisdom, the youthful dreams. At the extremities of our life, two aspects of the childlike meet. It is the childish dream—somewhat battered by the interlude of life—that once again, in its wisdom, dominates our lives. An old man's gnarled hand, one finger clutched by a boy's small hand, sums it all up. The beginning and the ending of the dream are thus made one.

Mark Twain, the one who didn't like books, would have seen eye to eye with Norman Rockwell, since it is Twain's eyes through which Rockwell customarily sees. It is the world of Tom Sawyer, Huck Finn, and Aunt Sally brought up to date. It is still the old battle of Aunt Sally and her civilizing ways, all of it under the watchful eyes of grownups who are still—bless their hearts—children at heart themselves. They have grown up, but we have no idea how they got that way. They are included in the picture to frame and heighten what came *first*. Childhood came first, of course, and young dreams, and all those promises that men fail to live by—but back then they were real, back *then* we believed in them. Whereas, if you look around you now—but of course we don't. *It's a joke, son.* It's much better to look, as we do, into the mythic past.

A world of beginnings, of exemplary firsts, is what we find, in various formations, in the works of Wolfe, Hemingway, Fitzgerald, and Faulkner. Their work spans, oddly enough, the period between Rockwell's first *Post* cover and his last. The battle is still the same old battle of Aunt Sally and her civilizing ways. It is nostalgia, in one form or another, that challenges the ability of each writer to function, as it determined the style and substance of Rockwell's craft. Here in America we begin, and occasionally we end, with the abuses of the past.

PROBLEMS FOR WRITING AND DISCUSSION

1. Explain Morris' remark that a "vote for Norman Rockwell is a vote for the *real* America." What does the description of Norman Rockwell's portrait of Adlai Stevenson explain about American taste in politics as well as in other things?

2. What paradox does Morris point to when he says that "having exhausted, or depleted, the raw material that appeals to us, we needed a technician to create the illusion that it was still there"?

3. What does Norman Rockwell, as Morris sees him, have in common with some best-seller authors? What does his art have in common with the "worst" of American art that Kramer (p. 627) says is mistaken for the presentation of the *real* America?

4. If Rockwell's "clichés" express sentiments that heighten reality, why is Morris critical of them? Does Morris think that Rockwell's work does reflect reality?

5. The four well-known modern American novelists Morris names all create the worlds of "beginnings." "It is nostalgia," says Morris, "which challenges the ability of each writer to function." What mythic properties do Americans nostalgically search for in their "beginnings"?

6. Do Rockwell's drawings illustrate Kronenberger's point (p. 573) that when we joke about ourselves we usually flatter ourselves? Is there anything terrifying in the innocence of the democratic joke Morris says is passed from old to young and from young to old? Explain.

7. What do you suppose Norman Rockwell would have done with Billy the Kid?

8. What would be missing in a Rockwell portrait of Don Quixote? What, by implication, is missing in the Americans who are "all Sanchos at heart"?

The American Sense of Humor

LOUIS KRONENBERGER

> *Louis Kronenberger (1904-   ) came to New York City, after graduation from the University of Cincinnati, to work in publishing (1926-35). He later wrote for* Fortune *(1936-38), and then became* Time's *drama critic, a post he held for some twenty years. He taught or lectured at a variety of colleges and universities before settling at Brandeis University in 1953 as its Professor of Theater Arts. He has written novels,* The Grand Manner *(1929) and* Grand Right and Left *(1952); a cultural history of eighteenth-century England,* Kings and Desperate Men *(1942); and a biography,* Marlborough's Duchess *(1958). In the preface to* Company Manners *(1954), he explains that he writes about the America he knows best—the "professional and intellectual world of the urban middle and upper-middle class."*

There is perhaps nothing we Americans feel more certain of than our sense of humor. In partial proof we can point to a vital humorous tradition and to a long, still-flourishing line of humorists. For the rest, it is indisputable that we have a famous method of joking. That method—very logical in a young, expansive, bumptious people—has been one of overstatement and exaggeration, of the tall tale and the woolly yarn, of bringing to our jests something of that giantism that has molded our dreams: we even joke, as it were, in six figures. Ours has been, almost entirely, a humor of release rather

From **Company Manners**, Copyright © *1951, 1953, 1954* by Louis Kronenberger. Reprinted by permission of *The Bobbs-Merrill Company, Inc.*

than reflectiveness, a fizz rather than a *fine*. There is little that is wise, there is little that is melancholy, about American humor—little, even, that can be called rueful. Possibly the best thing about it is the disbelief that gets hitched on behind the bragging, the "Sez you" that is tossed after the "And I said to him." But the snorting has much the same crudity as the boastfulness. We meet the braggart too much on his own terms: for though a world of humor can be insinuated into a mock bow, not much is possible to a Bronx cheer. Nor is the breezy manner at all a mask of seriousness. It's precisely because we are not, in the best sense, a serious people that we have ceased, in the best sense, to be a humorous one. At our worst, we have made our humor the handle of our acquisitiveness, a trick way of getting our foot in the door. Not only do we precede the moment of sale with the one about the two Irishmen, but signing on the dotted line is itself a quip.

It is because there is no longer a deeply self-critical quality in our humor that it is so much less cathartic. Our humor has become a confederate of our faults rather than their prosecutor. This has partly to do with our being such cocks of the walk, such top dogs in the struggle of life. The underprivileged, the downtrodden, the disreputable crack jokes that tell consciously against themselves or that make a sad fun of their betters. "If this is how Her Majesty treats her prisoners," said Oscar Wilde, standing handcuffed in the pouring rain, "she doesn't deserve to have any." With such humor there will often go a certain self-pity as well, or a certain twisted contempt—the sharper's contempt for the sucker, the rogue's for the gull. But the humor of such people, even where it is cruel, is the badge of their humanity, of what makes them despise, equally, their victim and themselves. Such people have usually suffered enough, sinned enough, faced the truth about themselves enough, to *feel* the joke. In most good jokes about crooks, about failures, about trades or races or groups that are looked down on or discriminated against, there is an element to be shared, as it were, between *professionals*: they share and react to the joke as two artisans share and react to a piece of technical skill. Americans, in this sense, seldom "experience" a joke; they merely get the point of it.* Their jokes have become a kind of surface communication—the latest gag is a way out of having to find something to talk about, or a mere preamble to getting down to business. The breezy approach enables one, without changing the tone of one's voice, to change the basis of one's talk. Our national joke is the one about the traveling salesman and the farmer's obligingly innocent daughter—and fittingly so, since that is our dream *business* relationship as well as sexual one.

Yet even here we have covered up our tracks, transposed our symbol; for the difference between us and more serious or self-accepting races is that where their jokes are a way of acknowledging their true motives, ours are frequently a way of trying to conceal them. We try to suggest that there is a strong playful element in all our business dealings, but increasingly, I think, there is a certain self-seeking in all our playfulness. We "entertain" clients; we hand over tricky contracts with a "better have a damn smart lawyer give *this* the once-over"; we crack wise to take advantage of an employee—"Gotta chain you to the galleys tonight"; we make gags as a way of minimizing resentment. Originally much of this sprang from something genuinely friendly and democratic in American life, but more and more—and all the more for having the appearance of real humor—it is becoming a device.

We possess a certain natural good humor, but no great sense of humor about ourselves, no very rueful appreciation of our plights. We are not at all an ironic people, so that once our humor loses its disinterestedness it tends to become cynical and hard-boiled, a sort of cold chuckle. Our breezy averageness robs us, moreover, of stance and style. No American, faced with the proofs of his grandscale buccaneering, would confess himself like Clive, "amazed at my own moderation." Our modern sports-jacket approach to the world—so youthful, playful, *un*-businesslike—is a touch misleading. To begin with, though it seems to break with a stuffy, over-solemn tradition, it is much more the product of an *arriviste* business class that never

---

* Which is not unrelated to our already obsessive and yet increasing enjoyment of the gag—a form of humor that for the most part has point *without* substance.

knew any such tradition and that, finding shirt sleeves comfortable, have gone on to make them respectable.

As for our brand of humor, the tall tale of the nineteenth century, being the expression of a young, healthy, hell-raising frontier people, gave something new and exhilarating to the humor of the world. Our contributions in the twentieth century—the gag, the wisecrack, the comeback, the nifty, the clincher—are nowhere so good. As long as it was expertly used—indeed, scrupulously stylized—in old vaudeville routines; as long, too, as it represented a second stage of American humor, a kind of retort on the tall tale's boastfulness, the American gag had its real virtues. But we have turned the gag into a mechanical, ubiquitous, incessant national tool so brassy as to be vulgar, so unchanging as to be dull. As for the comeback, though fond of it, we have never been very good at it; in terms of cussing and repartee alike, our truck drivers are mere duffers by comparison with even the average cockney. After all, the essence of a good comeback is a certain delayed sting, a certain perfection of surface politeness. Two Frenchmen who had been brilliant and bitterly hostile rivals at school went on to become a famous general and a distinguished cardinal. The cardinal, seeing the general, after many years, on a railway platform, approached him haughtily and said, "Mr. Stationmaster, when does the next train leave for Bordeaux?" The general paused, smiled, said, "At half past two, madame." By comparison, how very American at bottom is the most famous of modern comebacks; how lacking in all subtlety and in final wit is Whistler's "You will, Oscar, you will."

There is a reason, I think, why our comebacks are so crudely, so overtly abusive. The comeback flowers best in a class-ridden society where people must preserve at least the *form* of knowing their place and are thus driven in their retorts into understatement, or double meanings, or irony. Or it flowers in a cultivated formal society, where the urbanity of the language is wholly at variance with the brutality of the sentiment. In a democracy, where one is free to speak one's mind, one is prevented, as it were, from being insolent. We heckle rather than insinuate, and we *borrow* forms of abuse rather than invent them. We have even a sort of defensive guile about our lack of polish and sublety in these matters. "An epigram," Oscar Levant once said, "is a wisecrack that has played Carnegie Hall." But it is not, and in his heart Mr. Levant must be quite aware that it is not.

That our humor isn't deep or cleansing would seem belied by a great many things—though it is perhaps just those things that bear out my contention. We are humor-conscious much as we are culture-conscious; we are extremely worried that we won't seem to show sense of humor enough (particularly as a "sense of humor" has become a synonym for being a good sport). We joke incessantly—but partly from having reduced an attitude to a mere habit, and partly because, conversationally, we have so little to say. We shop for humor, we constantly listen to humor—on radio and TV, at movies and shows; but that is from lacking more serious cultural interests and from being so bored with ourselves when left alone. We have, generally, a brisk manner; we many of us lead bustling lives; we are still a "youthful" and often boisterous, slangy, sassy nation; and all this would seem to make us notably humorous. But a moment's reflection (a rare American trait) would suggest that humor is not a matter of being brisk, but of being reflective.

And though we once were open and hearty, were we ever—at any significant level—deeply humorous? In fact, could we have been? I say this rather to characterize than disparage us: humor, for one thing, isn't all pure gain; and for another, though purgative and health-giving, it often bulks largest in people who themselves are not healthy. Humor must largely constitute an appreciation, even an airing, of one's own and one's community's and one's country's faults, rather than a tribute to their virtues; or if that comes too close to defining satire, then humor is a gay confession and a wry acceptance of what makes us fools and sinners, goatish as well as godlike. Humor simultaneously wounds and heals, indicts and pardons, diminishes and enlarges; it constitutes inner growth at the expense of outer gain, and those who possess and honestly practice it make themselves more through a willingness to make themselves less.

Perhaps no young race can, in the very best sense, *be* humorous, for the crueler, cruder, more boyish, prankish, exuberant forms of humor neither greatly express nor truly educate. And it has been our misfortune as we have grown older not to have had, in our personal lives, misfortune enough, not to have been compelled to reflect or made to suffer. Creatures of noise and hurry, of hope and assurance, we have not had the time, we have never felt the need, to think hard on our problems or to confess our weaknesses. We have kept certain dead donkeys in our stables so as not to have to flay the living ones—and certain standard "goats" as well. Our national jokes are the umpire, the Milquetoast, the henpecked husband, the interfering mother-in-law, longhairs and sissies (whom we don't accurately define), suckers for gold bricks (the fool, not the knave!) and not the city slicker but the hick. All the symbols of push, of philistinism, of sharp practice—the joiner, the yes-man, the salesman, the Chamber of Commerce—are satiric figures created by an enlightened minority and objects of laughter to but a relative few. We laugh at polish (that is to say, Harvard) rather than push, at highbrows sooner than louts. Our humor is largely at the expense of what it is safe and indeed quite proper to despise: of what we don't want to be, can afford not to be, can with impunity make fun of. Even corruption thrives as a joke at the expense of those who *can't* horn in on it. We don't make fun of ourselves—only of our minorities and failures, of those who don't conform or assert themselves or measure up. Our humor, where it is directed inward and not at mere "goats," is almost completely flattering. We kid ourselves for being such reckless spenders and sports, such suckers for a good-looking girl, such soft touches for a hard-luck story; or, worse, we jest about what is wrong in terms that would make it seem right—just overgrown "boys" at reunions and conventions; just "cards" for perpetrators of various cruelties. We are really apologists for ourselves, as opposed to races that, like Negroes and Italians, have humility, or, like the Spaniards and Scots, have pride. In any important context, we tend to fear and fight off humor: Adlai Stevenson's Presidential campaign was a real anomaly and one that the nation felt sure could backfire.

No doubt humor, in the personal sense, is a distillate of suffering and, in the poetic sense, of melancholy; and it is no coincidence that we so often find it among the have-not races. More fortunate races, given to contemplate their blessings and to wonder how much they truly bless, are more likely to become ironic than humorous. America, in the deep sense, has neither irony nor humor. It is, on the one hand, still too naive; on the other, too shallow; in its ambitions and aggressions it is too much consumed with self-importance. Americans don't habitually see the wry humor of their plight, the sad irony of their triumphs; they go right on affirming the values that, even at the beginning, they hardly so much chose as had foisted upon them. They are only saved morally in the degree that they are so genuinely and wistfully lost. They haven't the melancholy of humor, but are the more lost, and more melancholy, for lacking it.

If we lack profound humor for lacking this poetic sense of melancholy, we lack it too from having so largely ceased to be spectators of life. We are much more a part of the game itself, or of the crowd who themselves insist on being looked at. And we seem destined to become a less humorous people because our twin gospels of Belonging and of Getting Ahead foster a sense of self-importance. Says a character in Sholom Aleichem: "I was, with God's help, a poor man." Americans, far from savoring such remarks, would quite fail to grasp their meaning. Humor, to most Americans, is not an inward way of looking at life, but an outward, good-guy way of living it. Humor, to most Americans, means grinning rather than getting sore when somebody hits you with a snowball, or laughing at yourself when you lose out through carelessness or anger. Humor, in other words, is for most Americans a matter of conduct rather than character, of the proper reaction rather than the owned-up-to-motive, and is but another facet of conformity. It is also a tactic at the other fellow's expense—a way of side-stepping sensibility and shame rather than feeling them. We hope—indeed often expect—that the wronged person will laugh the thing off so that we can join in, that *his* "seeing the humor in it" will take us off the spot. Increasingly, our humor shows a vital lack of criticism and insight, fails to educate either the heart or the mind; it is chiefly a salve or poultice for easing tensions, preventing scenes and snarls. Humor, it seems to me, has become a kind of national front, as politeness is with the French.

And as our humor grows more tactical, so our satire grows concessive rather than corrective. Doubtless most races get a certain pleasure out of joshing their own weaknesses and (as with the British on the subject of their insularity) are really bragging where they would seem to be self-critical. Self-satire is necessarily ambiguous; it provides those who indulge in it with some of the relief of the confessional, and it goes far toward disarming other people. Yet it is seldom practiced as a calculated maneuver. But what appears to be happening in America seems at least partly calculated; it constitutes confession *in lieu of* contrition; it is almost a way of serving notice on people that we may misbehave. We announce that we are part of the rat race as we might announce that we are part of the general public; we dub ourselves bastards as fair warning that we may be expected to behave as such. A single word like *integrity* proves, I think, extremely enlightening. It became, some time back, the cliché word for whoever felt guilt about leading a double life or for selling out. Today it is the cliché word for making fun of that attitude of guilt; from being an all-too-facile form of lament, *integrity* has become an equally facile form of lampoon. The word no longer has any dignity. And at least one reason why it no longer has any is that the man who begins by suffering from divided aims soon hardens into satirizing (and, in reality, writing off) his own dilemma. I was told of a playwright who asked another playwright at the opening of a third playwright's dismally bad show whether he was going backstage to congratulate the author. When his friend said no, what on God's earth could he congratulate him for, the first man sniffed, "Hell, you guys with your integrity" and strode backstage.

We are often, I think, quite literally trying to make capital of our sense of humor, to turn it into a social sheath for an antisocial dagger. Indeed, a man who uses his sense of humor at the cost of his *decency*, who has grown callous enough to satirize so as not to feel guilt or shame, is in the truest sense decadent; his is no better, though it is doubtless different, than the cold amusement of the ruffian. And it seems to me that the American sense of humor is being thus perverted—though there is still a great deal that is healthy and benign about it. But we must take care that it doesn't become for us the form of outlet, the kind of compensation, that sentiment is among the Germans—that, in the very act of letting something flow, it doesn't let a great deal more dry up. Without wishing to make too much of such standard cracks as "I'm a hack" or "I'm a Simon Legree"—or of ignoring the element of guilt involved—it is yet true that this kind of thing has become so constant a tactic as to be by now a mere habit, a way of making things less culpable or monstrous by giving them not just the air but the actual status of a joke. The point about classic satire is not that in actual practice it necessarily proves corrective but that at least the satirist is himself disinterested, that it is not face-saving only. "I laugh," said Figaro, "in order that I need not weep." "I laugh," says part of America today, "in order that I need not blush."

PROBLEMS FOR WRITING AND DISCUSSION

1. Why does Kronenberger say that "America, in the deep sense, has neither irony nor humor"?

2. Kronenberger admits the distinctive contribution of the American tall tale to world humor and admits even that the gag, originally, had "its real virtues." Why then does he find the contemporary brand of American humor sterile?

3. Does Kronenberger's charge that we are "humor conscious much as we are culture-conscious" explain why our humor should become more defensive as [according to Kouwenhoven (p. 585) and Kramer (p. 627)] we are liberated from our bondage to foreign opinion?

4. Kronenberger says that Americans "seldom 'experience' a joke; they merely get the point of it." Examine a series of cartoons from popular magazines and newspapers; or study the "jokes" designed for large television audiences. Do they "reveal" our motives or "conceal" them, as Kronenberger says?

5. Explain what Kronenberger means by saying our humor is "tactical" rather than "cathartic," abusive rather than humanizing, "a matter of conduct rather than character"? How does it become the "handle of our acquisitiveness"?

6. Kronenberger refers several times to Americans as a young, naïve, bumptious people without a "distillate of suffering" to afford them either profound humility or great pride. Does Morris make the same point about Americans? If Americans are still childlike after two hundred years of national life, what hope is there that they will ever grow up?

7. What, according to Kronenberger, has arrested our development toward mature humor? As the conditions of American life that stunt our growth intensify, do you believe, with Kronenberger, that our humor will become decadent before it arrives at the age of discretion?

8. Have writers other than Kronenberger noted that Americans are "bustling" but bored, culture-conscious yet lacking in "serious cultural interests"? What does Ebel (p. 213) say of American earnestness? What does Stevenson (p. 478) fear from our "spectator" attitude in front of television sets? What does Mead (p. 24) foresee for the young married couple in domestic bondage? What does Kristol (p. 529) see as the threat of "mass culture"? Do Galbraith (p. 180) and MacLeish (p. 439) agree that the "bustling" of the modern Americans leaves them no leisure for reflection?

9. Kronenberger refers to our "twin gospels of Belonging and of Getting Ahead" as enemies of the self-critical and truly confessional spirit of humor. Why? Do you recognize these "twin gospels" as ones Potter (p. 328) and Lipset (p. 348) describe? Explain.

10. How is Kronenberger's discussion of the fate of the word *integrity* relevant to his final point that, as politeness is to the French and sentiment to the Germans, humor is to us a "national front"? Is Kronenberger ultimately interested in our improving our humor or our character?

11. In what you have read of the dissemination of American culture, technology, advertising techniques, and popular entertainment throughout the world, do you find evidence that the world shows signs of growing "young" along with us? What happens to the "fears and desires" of man when his belly is full and he has mastered what Kristol calls the "viewing techniques"—when, in other words, he is nourished by bread and circuses?

2. *The Arts*

Art in America

JOHN A. KOUWENHOVEN

John A. Kouwenhoven (1909-   ) was graduated from Wesleyan University in 1931 and took his doctorate at Columbia. He then taught at Columbia (1936-38) and at Bennington (1938-41) before joining Harper's Magazine. *He remained with* Harper's *until 1954, though after 1946 editorial work was blended with teaching at Barnard College, where he is currently a full professor. He has written* Adventures of America, 1857-1900 *(1938),* Made in America: The Arts in Modern Civilization *(1948),* The Columbia Historical Portrait of New York *(1953), and* The Beer Can on the Highway *(1962).*

To many Americans the arts have always seemed to have little connection with our everyday life. Architecture, painting, literature, and the other arts have been regarded as rather remote subjects, no direct concern of ours. As a people we have been proud of American civilization and of its political and social institutions, but we have been less confident about our performance in the arts. There have been many respected American architects, painters, and poets, to be sure, but their total achievement, regarded from the conventional critical and historical points of view, has appeared to be only a somewhat crude dispersal of the western European tradition. There are, for example, still relatively few institutions in our educational system where American art and literature are not regarded as mere appendages to other—and, on the whole, weightier—matters.

From "Art in America" from Made in America *by John A. Kouwenhoven. Copyright 1948 by John A. Kouwenhoven. Reprinted by permission of Doubleday & Company, Inc.*

Most historical and critical studies of the development of the arts in America have been based on some variant of John Fiske's theory of "the transit of civilization." Culture, the theory goes, is brought here from Europe by "carriers"—artists, writers, and musicians who migrate to this country from the Old World or natives who return after studying abroad. Thus American culture is regarded as an extension of western European culture, subject only to certain influences—usually thought of as more or less regrettable—inherent in the American environment.

The principal cramping or limiting influences to which culture has been subjected in America, according to this theory, have been the lack of leisure among a people engaged in conquering the wilderness, the gross materialism fostered by the frontier and by industrial capitalism, and the reputed anti-aesthetic bias of our Puritan intellectual inheritance. What is more, all three of these influences have been pictured as interacting with one another in a diabolic circle: Puritanism encouraging (if it did not actually breed) materialism, the frontier strengthening both, and everything conspiring to make leisure impossible.

Yet if we accept the view that American art is an integral part of a western European tradition which, in spite of national variants, is essentially a unity, we inevitably encounter a problem. On the one hand we find that although all the trends and movements and fashions of European art may be traced in work done by Americans, there is nevertheless a quality in the total sum of our painting, our architecture, our music, or our literature which is distinct from the comparative unity of tradition among the arts in the various countries of Europe. As Henry James noted, without enthusiasm, in the book which sums up the impressions he received during a visit to the United States after living abroad for almost a quarter of a century, the way things were done in America was "more different from all other native ways, taking country with country, than any of these latter are different from each other."

On the other hand, however, it is frequently said that in spite of this distinctively American element the arts have been inadequately representative of our national character. In one way or another almost everyone, native or foreign, who has commented on our artistic history has borne witness to the disparity between our achievements in the arts and in the realms of politics, economics, and social organization. That is what Jay B. Hubbell meant when he said that our literature "has always been less American than our history"— an observation that might be applied with equal force to any of our fine arts. For, as Stuart Sherman once summed the matter up, the national genius has never expressed itself "as adequately, as nobly, in music, painting, and literature, as it has, on the whole, in the great political crises." And thus the theory of a transplanted culture leads us at last to the paradoxical conclusion that though art in America is American it is singularly less so than the acts and institutions which embody our history. Fruitful as the study of the interrelationship between American and European art can be, therefore, it clearly must abandon the theory that one is merely a maimed offshoot of the other. There is obviously something left out of our concept of the arts if they are unrepresentative of the civilization which produced them.

What has been left out is a tradition which was developed by people "who didn't know anything about art" but who had to deal with the materials of a new and unprecedented environment—a tradition which not only modified and obstructed the traditions carried over from western Europe but which contributed directly, as we shall see, to the evolution of new forms of artistic expression.

Men everywhere and at all times instinctively seek to arrange the elements of their environment in patterns of sounds, shapes, colors, and ideas which are aesthetically satisfying, and it is this instinct which underlies the creation of techniques and forms in which the creative imagination of the artist finds expression. In a given culture, such as that of western Europe, certain of these techniques and forms are more relevant than others to the life of the people, and from time to time these become institutionalized as schools of painting and sculpture, orders or styles of architecture, and types of music and literature. As long, therefore, as we are discussing a single, comparatively unified culture like that of western Europe from the Middle Ages to the Industrial Revolution, it is the tradition composed of these dominant techniques and forms which we have in mind when we talk about the arts. But in another culture, in a different kind of civilization, quite different forms and techniques might be in the ascendancy, and some of the arts which were most highly developed in western Europe might be relatively unimportant. The criteria of historical and critical judgments appropriate to the products of the western European tradition would not be adequate to the understanding or appreciation of an art produced in a different tradition. The capacity to enjoy and understand the music of Beethoven or Mozart, for example, is rooted in attitudes and sensibilities which provide little or no basis for an understanding or appreciation of the music of southern Asia.

So much is pretty obvious. Yet for a hundred and fifty years the historians and critics of American culture have, in effect, been applying the established western European criteria of value to the products of a civilization which has had less and less in common with that which produced the forms and techniques from which those criteria were deduced. To the cultural achievements, and specifically to the arts, of a civilization whose dynamics originate in technology and science, they have sought to apply the standards which were appropriate to those of civilizations founded upon agriculture or handicraft commerce.

The civilization which took form in the United States during the first century after the Declaration of Independence was, more than that of any European nation, the unalloyed product of those forces which throughout the world were creating what Charles Beard calls "technological civilization": that is, a civilization founded on power-driven machinery which indefinitely multiplies the capacity for producing goods, and upheld and served by science in all its branches. At most this civilization is two hundred years old, and there has never before been any order comparable to it.

Many people, including a good many historians, like to think of the United States as having been a nation of farmers and handicrafters, relatively untouched by the so-called Industrial Revolution, during a great part of its formative period. And it is, of course, true that until about the time of the Civil War the nation's economy was predominantly based upon agriculture. But it is easy to overestimate the agrarian aspects of our early history, and it is well to be reminded that in significant respects our civilization has from the beginning been dependent upon technology.

The least mechanized of all aspects of our society—the lives of men and women on the advancing frontier—depended upon the machine-made rifles and revolvers which enabled the pioneers to kill game and outfight the Indians, upon the steamboats and railroads which opened up new country for settlement, and upon the telegraph which made rapid intercommunication possible. It was technological civilization which made it possible for our people to conquer the wilderness and which ultimately built all our continental diversities into what the Civil War made clear was an indisseverable union. And as this civilization spread westward across the New World it was free, in a way that it could not have been free in any European country, to develop with relatively little interference from the habits of mind and social conventions which had been developed in earlier civilizations, and which, like the artistic monuments they had created, persisted in Europe.

It is this fact which gives special significance to the study of American arts. As this book will try to make clear, it is not primarily because they are American that they are worth our notice—though the author does not happen to be one of those who think it a mark of superior intelligence to be less interested in the work of their countrymen than in that of their fellow human beings beyond the seas. Their importance lies in the fact that because they are American, and because America is—for a number of fortuitous reasons—the only major world power to have taken form as a cultural unit in the period when technological civilization was spreading throughout the world—because of both these facts the arts in America reveal, more clearly on the whole than the arts of any other people, the nature and the meaning of modern civilization.

As a matter of fact, with the Declaration of Independence there had been an abrupt and rapid orientation of the American environment away from the cultural heritage of Europe. As democratic political ideals evolved in practice and as technological civilization developed, the social environment became increasingly unlike that which had produced the western European patterns. The need for appropriate new patterns became greater and greater.

Many Americans were aware of the need for new forms—for what they called a national literature, or art, or architecture. At first they tended to think in nationalist terms for the obvious reason that nationalism stood foremost in the consciousness of a people who had just fought a war for political independence. The answer to our needs seemed to many to be simply that we produce American versions of Shakespeare and paint pictures the way the European masters did—but of American subjects. Many of our early writers, on the other hand, began with a youthful determination to "forget Europe wholly," as James Russell Lowell urged in *A Fable for Critics*, and to write of native matters only, shaping their literature to the scale of the vast new continent, just as many painters like Bierstadt tried to develop an appropriate American art by simply increasing the size of their canvases. But they soon discovered that they could not forget Europe, and most of them found that they really didn't want to. The comfortable thing to do, then, was to relax into something approximating Longfellow's ultimate assumption that since Americans were really only "English under another sky" our literature needn't be expected to differ much from theirs. Of course, he added, the English stock in America was being mixed with other nationalities, and our English thoughts and feelings would therefore be tempered by German "tenderness," Spanish "passion," and French "vivacity." But he obviously assumed that we would remain essentially English, and that all that the writer and artist need do was carry on the old traditions. After all, he concluded, "all literature, as well as all art, is the result of culture and intellectual refinement."

Lowell stuck with the problem more tenaciously than that. "It is all idle to say that we are Englishmen," he wrote in 1854, because "we only possess their history through our minds, and not by life-long association with a spot and an idea we call England. History without the soil it grew in is more instructive than inspiring." But in everything that concerned art it seemed to Lowell that the Europeans had us at an immense disadvantage, for they were able to absorb cultural influences through their pores, as it were, from the whole atmosphere that surrounded them, while it required "weary years" for Americans to acquire these things from books and art galleries. The only good which might come of all this, he added rather lamely, was that, having been "thrown back wholly on nature," our literature might ultimately have a fresh flavor.

The nearest Lowell ever came to an answer which would prove fruitful to other writers and to himself was in his *Bigelow Papers*. Defending his use of dialect in these humorous poems and sketches of Yankee character, he declared in the preface to the second series (1867) that the first postulate of an original literature is that a people should use their language "as if it were a living part of their growth and personality, not as the mere torpid boon of education or inheritance." And in these dialect pieces Lowell did manage to capture some of the life and vigor and originality of native speech. But his formal poetry and essays were not much affected by this excursion into the vernacular; as far as style and manner are concerned, they could as well have been written in Cambridge, England, as in Cambridge, Massachusetts, and one feels that this, after all, was really the goal which Lowell wanted to achieve after the original nationalistic fervor wore off.

The quest for a national tradition in this spurious sense ended inevitably in failure. But all during the early years of the Republic we, and our European critics as well, debated the question of American art as if the problem were one of cultural independence. We argued stoutly that we could achieve it; most of the Europeans who came over here to inspect the strange new Republic argued that we could not. Yet both, by implication at least, recognized that beneath the surface manifestations of our society there were the elements of an indigenous culture—something singularly and essentially non-European expressed in our everyday life.

Many of the hundreds of books about America which issued so profusely from the pens of European visitors during the nineteenth century penetrated the truly American character of our life with surprising keenness. But their authors frequently disliked it. It was alien to them and came as a point-blank challenge to the culture which had shaped their own lives. There were, of course, numbers of visitors who—like Harriet Martineau and Alexander Mackay—liked much of what they found here; and a good deal of debate was carried on throughout the nineteenth century between our champions and our detractors. But those who had a vested interest in the survival of the ideals and customs of the older culture were frankly apprehensive about the growing influence of American ways. Here too, however, it was in terms of politics that the conflict was expressed. Captain Marryat, the popular English novelist whose *Diary in America* created a storm of protest among the Americans when it appeared in 1839, frankly anounced that it had been his object "to do injury to democracy." And Mrs. Trollope, who emigrated from England to Cincinnati, where she kept a shop in frontier days, professed that her chief purpose in writing the *Domestic Manners of the Americans* (1832) had been to encourage the English people "to hold fast by a constitution that insures all the blessings which flow from established habits and solid principles," and to save them from the tumult and degradation incident to "the wild scheme of placing all the power in the hands of the populace."

Both these writers were keen observers of men and affairs, and their books are a vivid record of what they saw and how they felt about it. They saw men living under democractic institutions without the restraints imposed by an established social order, and they detested it. What little they found to praise was mostly confined to the longer-settled regions along the Eastern seaboard, where English manners and customs had retained the greatest influence and where the American phenomena were most effectively diluted.

American people, still acutely aware of the newness of their nation, were eager to read what anyone wrote about them; hundreds of thousands of copies of books similar to Captain Marryat's and Mrs. Trollope's were sold and read in this country. Like other people, Americans don't enjoy being disliked; so the reaction to such attacks was immediate. Those whose cultural environment was least like that of Europe and who had therefore little emotional attachment to the manners and customs which the visitors were defending, turned bitterly against them, scorning their lack of understanding and their injustice, and were confirmed in distrust of the culture which such critics represented. It was this attitude, for example, which in 1835 led James Hall, the Cincinnati editor, to praise James K. Paulding on the grounds that his novels were "free from the blight of foreign influence."

Those, on the other hand, who still cherished in their homes furniture brought from the old country, whose education was patterned as closely as possible on that of their English cousins, or whose business or profession kept them in close contact with European society, tended often to react more with shame, or at worst with the anger which springs from shame. To them the long series of European attacks was a stimulus to mend their manners, to ape the ways of the older culture, and to adopt its externals so studiously that in the future they would appear less gross. Here was one of the sources of that development of conflicting traditions within American culture which this book will trace.

Both types of response to the travelers' criticisms were unfortunate. Both hastened the already widening split between two divergent streams of national life. As we look at various aspects of our civilization we shall discover, over and over again, tragic evidence of how much it cost those who turned their backs on Europe to lose fruitful contact with the essential humanity embodied in the living masterpieces of Western culture; and just as vividly we shall become conscious of the enervation and sterility which resulted from rootless imitation in this country of alien modes and surfaces. But it may also become clear that what seemed superficially to be a conflict between Europe and America was in reality quite another thing; that it was in essence only a more clear-cut and high-lighted version of a conflict which also existed within European culture itself.

It was easy, indeed almost inevitable, in nineteenth-century America to assume that art had little relation to the affairs of everyday life. Anyone familiar with American history will recall how remote Edgar Allan Poe and Henry James found themselves from the predominant concerns of their fellow Americans. But one need not assume—as some people do—that the things which interested Poe and James were of more aesthetic importance or of greater human value than those which preoccupied their countrymen. The world from which they were remote was, after all, the world of Abraham Lincoln.

Actually the chasm between art and everyday life may well prove to have been merely one manifestation of the catastrophic split which cut right through the whole of nineteenth-century society, both here and abroad. The conflict between the new science and the traditional religion produced an apparently unbridgeable gap between what man knew and what he believed. The development of industrial capitalism tended to divorce the production and distribution of goods from the political system, thus forcing men as unregulated economic beings to commit barbarous injustices which as political beings they had to cope with in terms of an inadequate traditional system. And finally, the tradition of western European art, like that of the Church, seemed to be seriously at odds with the social forces emerging chaotically from the Industrial Revolution.

So irreconcilable have art and technology seemed that many who believe in the creative discipline of form still cut themselves off deliberately from important areas of contemporary experience. On of the most influential modern critics holds that such willful isolation is imperative for the artist. Scientific knowledge, according to Mr. I. A. Richards, has made it impossible for us to believe countless poetic statements about God, the universe, and human nature. Furthermore, scientific knowledge, he maintains, is not of a kind upon which we can base an organization of the mind as "fine" (to use his own exceedingly vague term) as that which is based on prescientific thought. The solution which he offers—and which some of our most talented artists and writers have tried to accept—is that we must cut poetic and literary statements "free from belief, and yet retain them in this released state as the main instruments by which we order our attitudes to one another and to the world."[1]

For all its pseudo-scientific trappings, this is Victorian sentimentality in modern dress. So long as men persist in ordering their attitudes toward life in harmony with concepts which they merely wish were true, they will face life with emotional insecurity and dread. Only when men reckon with one another and the world in terms which take courageous account of what they *know* can they face life or death without fear.

Such wistful and perilous withdrawal from reality is evidence of a split between art and everyday life which, to many people, has seemed more complete in our generation than in any other in history. Actually that split, as has already been suggested, and as succeeding chapters will try to make clear, is illusory. What we really have to reckon with is a conflict between two civilizations—one maturing, the other powerless to die. If in the United States for a century and a half the arts have seemed more strikingly unrepresentative of national life than in the countries of Europe, that is because here the art forms inherited from the older culture have had to cope with

---

[1] One of the bluntest expressions of this point of view, in this instance with Marxist overtones, was contained in Kenneth Burke's demand, in *Counter-Statement* (1931), "that the aesthetic ally itself with a Program which might be defined roughly as a modernized version of the earlier bourgeois-Bohemian conflict." That program, designed to combat the "practical" values which the economic system imposes upon our society, should foster the following qualities: "inefficiency, indolence, dissipation, vacillation, mockery, distrust, 'hypochondria', non-conformity, bad sportsmanship." Mr. Burke did not defend these qualities as either admirable or "good" in themselves, but he urged adoption of the total attitude they reflect "because it could never triumph."

the new civilization in its most uninhibited aspects. What we have overlooked is the concomitant fact that in the United States—for that same reason—the new civilization has been freest to evolve its own artistic expression.

It is time we considered the frequently crude but vigorous forms in which the untutored creative instinct sought to pattern the new environment. It is in this unpretentious material that we may find the clearest expression of the vital impulses upon which the future of modern civilization depends.

PROBLEMS FOR WRITING AND DISCUSSION

1. According to the "transit of civilization" theory, what has "cramped" the development of American culture? What, according to Kouwenhoven, does the theory fail to explain?

2. Kouwenhoven cites the often remarked "disparity between our achievements in the arts and in the realm of politics, economics, and social organization." Does Kouwenhoven in the course of his essay suggest the reason for this disparity? Does the "culture-consciousness" in America which Lynes (p. 519) and Kronenberger (p. 573) note suggest that Americans themselves are aware of this disparity? Explain.

3. What unique characteristic of our civilization, according to Kouwenhoven, makes the cultural criteria of Europe inapplicable to American art? Does what Kouwenhoven says about the American frontier seem incongruous with Turner's thesis (p. 315)?

4. Why does Kouwenhoven say that "the arts in America reveal, more clearly on the whole than the arts of any other people, the nature and meaning of modern civilization"?

5. Why did initial attempts by Americans to find new expressive forms in the arts fail at the same time that democratic political ideals were actualized and economic strides made?

6. Beyond the immediate effects, what serious influence on the future of the arts in America did the attacks by foreigners upon American culture have?

7. Discuss Kouwenhoven's attempt to defend the American society from which James and Poe were "remote." In the light of Henry James's essay on Saratoga (p. 82), how "remote" do you think James was?

8. Why, to Kouwenhoven, is the "chasm between art and everyday life" that still characterizes the American scene significant of a conflict implicit in the plight of modern man everywhere? What other writers in the text describe a comparable conflict?

9. Why does Kouwenhoven call I. A. Richards' advice to the artist "Victorian sentimentality in modern dress"?

10. What, to Kouwenhoven, is the most pernicious effect of the divorce between what men *know* and what "they merely wish were true"? Does Morris (p. 560) comment on the same thing? Is the alternative to this divorce of artistic conception from reality the dilemma of the "educated man" that Kristol (p. 529) describes?

11. Kouwenhoven denies that there has to be a "split" between art and everyday life. He suggests that we look to the "crude but vigorous forms" with which the American imagination, uninhibited by the forms of an older civilization, has patterned its "new environment." If American civilization is "the unalloyed product" of the technological revolution, where is it likely American artists who do *not* divorce themselves from reality will find their "new forms"? Will these be forms of human feeling, as Langer (p. 634) says artistic forms are? Do you find evidence in the arts to confirm Eiseley's charge (p. 299) that man is approaching a "non-human" condition? Explain.

12. Would Kouwenhoven's generalizations about American art—that it is original and not a modification of European originals—hold for the American political tradition? If so, how?

Beat Literature and the American Teen Cult

JAMES F. SCOTT

> *James Scott (1934-   ) holds a doctorate from Kansas University (1960) and teaches English at Saint Louis University. His special interest is modern literature, on which he has published scholarly articles.*

From a remarkable variety of sources we are now told that the so-called "Beat movement" in American literature is about to expire. Whether this forecast will ultimately prove correct is slightly irrelevant. The striking thing is the untoward haste with which the American public has sought to dispose of these postwar prodigals, who have already been honored with quite an array of wishfully premature epitaphs. Surely the presence of the scraggly citizens of Greenwich, North Beach and Venice West must be highly embarrassing. Perhaps even more embarrassing is that popular journalism seems at a loss to account for them. A typical observer wonders, "What have we done to deserve this?"[1] While in this frame of mind, we can do little more than wish the Beats embalmed and interred with all deliberate speed.

The Beats do not really defy analysis. It's just that gasps of dismay are more heartening than close scrutiny. For in spite of their freewheeling eroticism and the vendetta they have sworn against both razor and scrub brush, the Beats are less alien to American culture than we would like to suppose. They are as unpopular among the rank and file of Americans as Benedict Arnold among the DAR, but

---

From American Quarterly, *Summer 1962. Reprinted by permission of the publisher and the author.*

[1] Paul O'Neill, "The Only Rebellion Around," *Life*, XLVII (November 30, 1959), 130.

society's strident outbursts against them often leave the impression of a harassed magician trying desperately to exorcise a demon without admitting, even privately, that his own magic has accidentally called it forth. This self-deception probably accounts for the irrelevance of much criticism of Beat literature.

Majority opinion notwithstanding, the failure of the Beats as literary artists has little to do with their widely publicized moral depravity and social negativism. Genius is not an exclusive possession of the righteous, nor is an artist obliged to edify the local chamber of commerce. No. The literary failure of the Beats is simply a bankruptcy of imaginative insight born of their willingness to nourish, direct or even properly motivate their creative faculties. But this failure of the Beat imagination, I fear, is related to a larger failure of American culture. More specifically, the Beat conception of the creative process, shot through with inconsistency and naïveté, is an indirect yet almost inevitable result of powerful social forces now active beneath the surface of American life, forces which glorify immaturity and thus obscure an essential distinction between adolescent spontaneity and adult creativity. In other words, the Beat movement represents the first incursion into serious literature of an already well entrenched popular mystique which accords exaggerated significance to the vision and values of adolescence. Furthermore, the reluctance of many editors and supplement writers to refer Beat literature to this larger frame of reference is almost more disturbing than the Beats themselves, because it measures the reluctance of the American public to examine those cultural pressures that have caused the Beat movement to move.

The continuing popularity of the fuzzy and convenient "youth must have its fling" interpretation of the Beats typifies a general retreat from careful inquiry. This shibboleth is unsuitable because the Beats' rebellion is not merely a temporary evasion of responsibility. Rather, it is a way of art and life which permanently consecrates the pose and gestures of adolescence. For though most full-fledged Beats are well beyond teen-age (some will never see thirty again), their patterns of behavior often reveal regressive adolescent traits, such as the use of special speech and dress as badges of identity and status or the compulsive hostility to authority, which causes all questions of value to be referred to the judgment of a select peer group. Going somewhat further, Ned Polsky identifies among many Beats of Greenwich Village a "persistence in more or less chronic form of some psychic states characterizing . . . adolescent pathology."[2] But even when pathology is not involved, the Beats—especially the literate and literary Beats—strenuously cling to an adolescent outlook which regards discipline or concentration as repressive and intelligence as a general nuisance. And though they profess to find this same view in the aesthetic radicalism of Whitman and the social iconoclasm of Thoreau, what the Beats really respect is not Whitman and Thoreau (neither of whom is immature) but an image of Whitman and Thoreau distorted by the eyes of adolescence. The tragicomic predicament of the Beats is that, having forsworn maturity, they have truncated their own creative life.

Unfortunately, however, the self-conscious cultivation of juvenility is not restricted to the isolated cadres of Beatdom. In fact, the emergence of an American teen cult is one of the most disturbing events of our generation. Undergirded by popular psychology, exploited by commercial advertising, and dramatized by the public arts, the sentimental enshrinement of adolescent values has come to touch nearly all areas of American life. Not only is the adolescent patronized in the permissive home and the "progressive" school; his attitudes and beliefs now threaten to become normative for the whole adult population.

The growing "adolescent directedness" of today's adults is reflected conspicuously in their almost obsessive concern with how the American teen-ager feels about the world. When Eugene Gilbert initiated his column, "What Young People Think," in the middle 1950s, he could hardly have foreseen that within five years this piece would become one of the most popular syndicated features of the Associated Press. And Gilbert's whirlwind success is certainly not an isolated event. Writing in 1958, Dwight MacDonald turned to the

---

[2] "The Village Beat Scene: Summer 1960," *Dissent,* VIII (Summer 1961), 339.

Readers' Guide to Periodical Literature to prove that the American people had developed an overblown interest in adolescence.[3] At that time, the number of entries under "adolescence" had jumped from 16 in 1941-43 to 51 in 1955-57, and the entries under "teen-age" had mushroomed from 2 in 1941-43 to 11 in 1955-57. Already, little tidbits like "What Makes Teen-Agers Swoon" had become a regular part of American magazine fare.[4] But the teen cult has since entered a new phase. The use of the word "adolescence," which sounds faintly clinical and has little commercial appeal, has declined in favor of the more attractive term "teen-age." Although *Readers' Guide* for 1959-61 contains only 24 references to adolescence, a glance at the entries under "teen-age" reveals 13 cross references embracing the whole spectrum of adolescent activity—teen drinking, teen marriage, teen parties, teen reading, to cite only a few samples. If he so wishes, the American adult can now use even the most fashionable magazines to participate vicariously in the life of the teenager, whose every thought, deed and desire has been elaborately chronicled.

Another index of the adolescent leaning of our culture is the tendency of adults to appropriate for their own enjoyment forms of entertainment once pitched exclusively to the young. The present enthusiasm of TV audiences for westerns is a case in point. Attaching the tag "adult" to such shows as "Gunsmoke" or "Tales of Wells Fargo" betokens more than semantic sleight of hand on the part of the television industry. It indicates the advertisers' sensitivity to a pronounced change in the public attitude toward the old horse opera. As late as a decade ago, the most popular western movies were still oriented to the taste of an audience not beyond the earliest teens.[5] The crooning cowboy, for example, was obviously an adolescent's hero, whose behavior invariably followed conventions

---

[3] "Profiles: A Caste, A Culture, A Market—I," *New Yorker*, XXXIV (November 22, 1958), esp. 67-68.

[4] *McCall's*, LXXXIII (December 1955), 38 ff.

[5] Films analogous to the TV western can, of course, be found in the 1930s and 1940s, though they are decidedly a minority of those produced.

which the elders of American society thought conducive to the moral uplift of impressionable youngsters. Though he might turn the full fury of his sixguns upon a gang of cattle rustlers, he would never smoke, drink, gamble or express so much as a trace of sexual interest in the damsels who lavished affection upon him. But this atmosphere of sentimental fantasy has now vanished, a fact which suggests the western is no longer an instrument used by adult society to inculcate Boy Scout ideals in the young. Instead, the new TV western (and the movie western as well) affects a superficial "realism," discarding stock features of the old cowboy movie, like that of the hero who outspokenly advertises his teetotalism. The strategy underlying this metamorphosis of convention, it seems, is to reduce the embarrassment of the older adolescent or the adult when he sits down to watch a show which is still palpably childish in everything but a few incidental motifs. A truly adult western—one, like "The Ox-Bow Incident" or "Treasure of Sierra Madre," which asks from an audience the full engagement of mature ethical judgment—has yet to win a place on American television screens. And the "adult" western in its present form is nearly as shallow and stereotyped as the Gene Autry and Hopalong Cassidy films of yesteryear. Really, the changes recently wrought in the western signify only that in the last decade American adults have become willing to surrender many once powerful authority symbols in exchange for the privilege of glutting themselves upon entertainment suited to the mentality of the late adolescent.

Furthermore, the sentimentalizing of adolescence is currently one of the most striking features of the public arts. The recent cinematic version of James Cozzens' *By Love Possessed* markedly exemplifies this fact, the more so because the novel itself flays all forms of sentimentality, especially feckless sentiment squandered upon unworthy adolescents. Except for Ann Winner, whose role is minor, there is scarcely a sympathetic portrait of adolescence in Cozzens' elaborate chronicle of the contemporary New England Brahmins. Ralph Detweiler is shiftless and irresponsible; Warren Winner is positively vicious; Joan Moore, though pathetic, hardly commands respect. Helen Detweiler's suicide, the ultimate catastrophe of the novel, is directly occasioned by Ralph's moral cowardice, which impels him to betray his sister's ill-founded trust in his good nature. And the sentimentalizing of youthful folly draws Cozzens' most caustic thrusts, as reflected, for example, in Julius Penrose's fierce outburst against our "age . . . of capital F Feeling—[our] century of the gulp, the lump in the throat, the good cry." The film script of *By Love Possessed*, however, is remarkable for its complete inversion of this attitude, a transformation complete enough to approach parody. Two changes are particularly noteworthy, one in the presentation of character and another in the arrangement of plot. First of all, Ralph is metamorphosed into Arthur Winner's son, who is by no means an indolent delinquent but a quick-witted, charming figure, probably more intelligent than his father and surely more likeable. And the young man's alleged "rape" of Veronica Kovacs is motivated, not as in the novel by his inability to control an erotic urge, but by an almost praiseworthy defiance of an adult society too prim and stuffy to allow any genuine impulse or emotion. Finally, the plot of Cozzens' novel is wrenched so that Arthur Winner, the movie character, whose approach to life is drearily bookish, appears to be educated in humanity by the imagination and energy of his son. According to the film, Arthur's decision not to expose Noah Tuttle results obliquely from the son's challenge of the father's cold, legalistic cast of mind. The movie thus conveys the decided impression (at which Cozzens would doubtlessly wince) that the world would be a better place if we could all somehow recapture the outlook of the eighteen-year-old.

These and other related phenomena seem to declare that many Americans, gainsaying their maturity, now unabashedly seek to recover the worldview of adolescence. The reasons for this are not easy to discern. Whatever they may be, however, the canonization of immaturity thus producd must perforce shake familial control, reduce the role of discipline in the formation of character, minimize the worth of patiently acquired learning and finally accredit to America's "typical teen-ager" a monopoly upon insight, inventiveness and vigor.

The public, of course, indulges its esteem for adolescence only within a carefully circumscribed frame of reference, never permitting it to undercut certain consensually validated symbols of adult prestige. In most respects, the place of the parent, the teacher and the clergyman is still sacrosanct. But herein lies a paradox. For while we formally honor the home, the school and the church, we continue to revel emotionally in a puerile worldview which renders these professed values meaningless, almost dishonest. And our divided loyalties cloud the development of mature insight into inherited codes of behavior, insight necessary to keep our institutions from turning into mere repositories of cultural fossils.

At the moment, this ambiguous commitment of the American people to the aggressive "spontaneity" of teendom on the one hand and to the reassuring stability of tradition on the other has its most adverse effect in the confused and confusing directives that devolve from it upon American youth. Currently fashionable counsel to the rising generation, disseminated through all the mass media, might (allowing for a trace of hyperbole) be summarized thus: Listen to mom and dad, even though their minds are darkened by middle age; study diligently in school, even though effective living requires only a bright, bacteria-free smile; respect Moses and the Commandments, even though a shiny, up-to-date Savior would at least have the decency to be beardless and would probably come only to lead a songfest at the local church. Obviously, this tissue of contradictions will withstand little battering, hardly the utterance of a cynical "pooh!" And this circumstance, I think, provides a clue to the coming of the American Beatnik.

Naturally, the current surfeit of adolescent sentiment cannot have caused the Beat movement directly. But it has contributed to the atmosphere in which Beat literature flourishes, because it gravely impairs genuine understanding of creative endeavor and thus deprives the adult world of all defenses against the Beats except aimless ridicule and ill formulated disgust. For by comparison with what presently passes for the public conscience, even the logic of Beatdom looks cogent and persuasive. Confronted by the muddle of conflicting public values, the Beats have simply shattered the moral frame of reference imposed by convention and then deified the adolescent element already permeating American life. In this sense, at least, the Beats are very much our spiritual sons, though we may still prefer to regard them as something visited upon us by a peculiarly malevolent conjunction of the stars.

Actually, whatever coincidence is involved in the coming of the Beats is not stellar, but historical. Wars and rumors of wars, so often destructive of mushy idealism, have figured importantly in the stentorian nay-saying of the Beat writers. Moreover, the current international situation, especially the threat of nuclear holocaust, has also helped give the Beat *nego* its decidedly adolescent accent. The dreadful promise of the hell bomb makes it rather easy for the Beats to assume their posture of rebelliousness and irresponsibility. Since the elder generation gave us Hiroshima, the Beats feel free, like the disaffiliate canine hero of Lawrence Ferlinghetti's "Dog," to regard every symbol of authority as "just another fire hydrant." Similarly, since the prospect of atomic destruction is still with us, the Beats absolve themselves of all social and political concern. Like Ray Smith of Jack Kerouac's *The Dharma Bums,* they have all seen in the sky the mystic writing which tells them, "This [the atomic bomb] is the Impossibility of the Existence of Anything." And accepting this fact as the consummate wisdom, they feel no incentive to grow up mentally. Thus has the anxiety accompanying a special historical occasion distilled from the total atmosphere of American culture, tainted with a profoundly negative bias and finally crystallized into dogma a set of values which militates against both intellectual and aesthetic maturity.

The hallmark of the Beat mystique, whether applied to critical intelligence or creative imagination, is the scaling down of everything to adolescent proportions. Nowhere is this demonstrated more pointedly than in the supposed Zen Buddhist influence upon Beat literature and life. Within the arcanum of Buddhist tradition, the doctrine and practice of Zen is entirely respectable, as its anti-rationalism and radical individualism are absorbed into a higher synthesis of human feeling. But washed upon the shores of San Francisco Bay, the Beat Buddha has undergone a disconcerting sea change.[6] Somehow there has vanished the exacting Zen ritual which, according to its practitioners, resolves the persistent Western dualism of Hebraic spirit and flesh, Hellenic subject and object. Even when the Beats nominally preserve Buddhist ideology, the distortion is egregious. Who would recognize the Zen concept of absolute absorption into the life experience after Kerouac has translated it into the patois of Sal Paradise, narrator of *On the Road*? "The only people for me," says Sal, "are . . . the ones who never yawn or say a commonplace thing, but burn, burn, burn like fabulous yellow roman candles exploding like spiders across the stars." Here the metaphor of the fireworks display suggests the essentially adolescent cast of Kerouac's Zen. The figure of the Zen lunatic also appears in this novel, transmogrified into the "HOLY GOOF," Dean Moriarity. But though Dean is wholly goofy, his irrationalism is adolescent, not Oriental. His chief diversions, far from philosophic but very sophomoric, are knocking in car fenders and knocking over high school girls. Sitting beneath a Bodhi tree, Dean would look more incongruous than Voltaire must have seemed under the tutelage of the Jesuits. "Beat Zen," admits Alan Watts, in spite of his sympathy for the movement, ". . . confuses 'anything goes' at the existential level with 'anything goes' on the artistic and social levels."[7] To put the matter a bit less kindly, the Beat attitude dissolves the wisdom of the East into exhibitionism, restlessness and maundering sexual-

---

[6] To my knowledge, the only serious student of Zen among the Beat writers is Gary Snyder, a talented poet and capable Orientalist, whose sensitive translation of Han-Shan's "Cold Mountain Poems" appeared in *Evergreen Review*, II (Autumn 1958), 69-80. Although the Beats apparently consider Snyder their compatriot (Kerouac even produced a fictionalized biography of his career in *The Dharma Bums*), Snyder's respect for intelligence and learning is foreign to Beatdom and his association with the movement seems accidental, probably only temporary.

[7] *Beat Zen, Square Zen, and Zen* (San Francisco: City Lights Press, 1959), p. 17.

ity, all of which are directly related to the Beats' glorification of adolescence.

Carried into aesthetics, this wallowing in the world of adolescence, even if we waive its ethical and social implications, is prejudicial to artistic excellence. Gregory Corso, in "Variations upon a Generation," speaks earnestly of creating a new kind of poetic statement "whose objectivity will be the accuracy of its introspection," but his published work gives little evidence that he has achieved this goal. Quite innocently he asks a critic, "Do you think I need form?"[8] As for Kerouac, self-appointed philosopher of Beatdom, he has already answered this question in the negative. "Remove literary, grammatical, and syntactical inhibition,"[9] he tells his would-be protégés. Thus unfettered, the literary tyro may then experiment with the process of "scoping," which Kerouac defines as "not 'selectivity' of expression but following free deviation (association) of mind into limitless blow-on subject seas of thought, swimming in seas of English with no discipline other than rhetorical exhalation and expostulated statement."[10] Alas . . . Beguiled by dubious Reichian assumptions which reinforce their adolescent contempt for discipline, the Beats persistently ignore the fact that the creative process presumes not only the interplay of powerful unconscious drives but also the imposition of exceptional psychic controls, capable of balancing, integrating and rendering socially intelligible a highly unstable compound of essentially private images. And conceiving of creativity exclusively as an emancipation from form, the Beats have produced a literature which tends either toward unregulated proliferation of incident or unintelligible subjective ecstasy.

Both of these faults are conspicuous in what is perhaps the most durable literary accomplishment of the Beat movement, Allen Ginsberg's "Howl." Their presence illustrates how the elevation of ado-

---

[8] Quoted by Carolyn Gaiser, "Gregory Corso: A Poet the Beat Way," *A Casebook on the Beat*, ed. Thomas Parkinson (New York: Thomas Y. Crowell Co., 1961), p. 274.

[9] "Belief & Technique for Modern Prose," *Evergreen Review*, II (Spring 1959), 57.

[10] "Essentials of Spontaneous Prose," *Evergreen Review*, II (Summer 1958), 72.

lescent impulse to the level of an aesthetic deforms poetic expression. Admirable in its compassionate perception of postwar frustration and disenchantment, "Howl" probably contains the stuff of greatness. But its jumbled profusion of experience and its spurious mysticism, especially marked in sections one and three respectively, detract measurably from its worth. Ironically, the most successful part of the poem in no way reflects Ginsberg's pet theories about the "Meaning Mind practiced in spontaneity [that] invents forms in its own image."[11]

Section two of "Howl"—an anguished attack upon the bases of modern materialism—is quite traditional in structure and owes much of its impact to a litanic repetition which creates a sense of robot activity. This part of the poem is organized around a few carefully chosen allusions (the inscrutable sphinx; blood-craving Moloch; the tyrannical Jehovah) and is elaborated through a well integrated pattern of images (chiefly isolation and blindness). Both the *Old Testament* references and the religious associations of litany are apposite in that they suggest modern man's idolatrous machine worship which confers charismatic sanction upon the power of the mechanized, militarist state. Even the final abandonment of the litany in favor of a series of loosely associated images can be justified on the grounds that the symbolic movement here makes madness the ultimate result of an ever increasing rationalization of life. To pretend, however, that Ginsberg's achievement has anything to do with the Beat cult of spontaneity is pure hokum. Quite the contrary. Discussing "Howl" with his disciples, Ginsberg speaks enthusiastically about bop prosody and trace-like rhythm, but in his rare moments of genuine accomplishment he employs techniques common to all good poetry since the time of Pindar: controlled figure, meaningful allusion and consistent rhetorical progression within a recognizable literary form. Like most of the Beat fraternity, though, Ginsberg is so suspicious of craft and design that he is not likely to write very well very often.

---

[11] "Notes Written on Finally Recording 'Howl,'" Parkinson, *Casebook*, p. 28.

Hence the eventual fate of the Beat movement: early or late it will fizzle out and be remembered only as a literary hotrod that blew its gaskets before completing the race. For the Beats have little to offer belles lettres. Confronted by the wholesale corruption of language, they have countered feebly with a poetic jargon which is as manneristic and jaded as the prose of Madison Avenue. Set upon by the encroachments of philistine technocracy, they have withdrawn into a spiritual nirvana of peyote, marijuana and mescaline. Challenged by the appalling possibilities of political and social crisis, they have cowered into super-select coteries and now peer furtively at the world through the begrimed windows of their Grant Street pads. In short, the Beats have played perfectly the role of the adolescent delinquent who, despite his elaborate pretensions to omniscience, knows only enough about the adult world to sustain a boastful but shallow cynicism. Lacking the catholicity of experience necessary to major literary achievement, most of the Beat writers are destined for a quick eclipse of fame.

True, not all that the Beats stand for is bad. If nothing else, they have at least reminded us, at a time when the public poet is lucky to squeeze a short lyric between two soap ads, of poetry's historical relatedness to forms of communal expression such as the ritual chant and the oral saga. They have also shown, in spite of their gloomy airs, that there can still be something exciting about the profession of letters. Sometimes, I think, we may even be impressed by the praiseworthy candor of the best Beat sentiment, as expressed, for example, by John Wieners,[12] whose "A Poem for Painters" confesses itself to be

> Only the score of a man's
> struggle to stay with
> what is his own, what
> lies within him to do.

---

[12] Like Gary Snyder, Wieners belongs only to the periphery of the Beat movement, but he is generally associated with the San Francisco group because *The Hotel Wentley Poems* have been published by one of the more important Beat outlets, the Auerhahn Press.

Without the consolations of romantic elegance or cosmic myth, the poet, as Wieners perceives, must now summon from his own mind and will resources sufficient to preserve the life of the emotions in a world increasingly more hostile to them. But though aware of these circumstances, the Beats have brought only the sensibility of an adolescent to bear upon a problem which requires the courage and mental stamina of a man. And they have failed pitifully.

That brings up the moral which I believe may be gleaned from having jostled elbows with the Beat generation, a moral germane to the predicament of the man of letters in contemporary America. Appropriately, the Beats have called attention to this predicament in their usual left-handed and negative way. Intellectually paralyzed by the burden the artist must carry, they have dramatically shown how great is the present inducement not to accept adulthood. And society, in its turn, has manifested a similar want of maturity by responding to the Beat revolt mostly with bewilderment and chagrin, rarely with tough-minded, responsible criticism. Reading most popular commentary, we can hardly escape the impression that if the Beats would just shave, wash and begin to compose Mother's Day verses everything would be all right. Really, the American public seems to wish only that the Beats would exchange the apocalyptic fury of Cassandra for the mellow piety of Polyanna. But these quite dissimilar young ladies are alike in one crucial respect: both share the viewpoint of the adolescent who sees either black or white, unaware of the manner in which a truly creative intelligence fuses assent and dissent, hopefulness and foreboding, into a dialectic of exploration and analysis.

This dialectic, fundamental to the health of society, is seriously lacking in America today, a fact which not only helps explain the Beat rebellion but also indicates why the dedicated artist, neither Beat nor Square, lives mostly in isolation. It indicates, for example, why the majority of today's American poets—poets with the refined sensuousness of Theodore Roethke and the searching social conscience of Randall Jarrell—have rejected the town for the gown.

For if, as Lionel Trilling asserts, "literature is the human activity that takes the fullest and most precise account of variousness, possibility, complexity, and difficulty,"[13] it follows that the literary man who would be true to his calling must cultivate the broadest possible contact with life. Ideally, then, the stimulus of his art should come from the whole community rather than from a specialized academic environment, whatever opportunities this environment affords. But when a society such as ours, eager to discourage the intellectual friction arising out of its pluralism, subtly represses its critical powers and transmutes much of its creative energy into idle gush over the adolescent, the artist feels compelled to retreat from the public world of thinking men's filters and filtered men's thoughts. Within the last generation, this withdrawal from the community has become a typical gesture on the part of the American poet, though his estrangement has drawn small notice from the general public. And now come the Beats, desperately preaching a new kind of alienation, absolute and unremitting. Perversely extravagant, they are much harder to ignore than the temperate, rational academician, so hard to ignore, in fact, that before passing into oblivion they may shock a few people beyond the universities into re-examining the American dream, or perhaps more accurately, the American somnolence. If so, the Beats may yet render some service to the intellectuals whom they despise. So long as this remains a possibility, we might do well to tolerate their beards and bongo drums.

PROBLEMS FOR WRITING AND DISCUSSION

1. To what does Scott attribute the artistic failure of the Beats? To what "popular mystique" in their societal context is the failure related?
2. Why does Scott reject the explanation that dismisses the Beats as merely youths who must have their fling?

---

[13] *The Liberal Imagination* (New York: Viking Press, 1950), p. xiii.

3. How does Scott support his generalization that adolescent "attitudes and beliefs now threaten to become normative for the whole adult population"? Can you offer your own concrete illustrations?

4. Why does Scott call the Beats' predicament as artists "tragicomic"?

5. What is the relevance of the television Westerns to Scott's discussion? Scott offers the movie version of *By Love Possessed* as an example of American "sentimentalizing of youthful folly." Cite other movies or television programs that do the same thing.

6. Morris (p. 560) says that we have a "faculty" or an "intuition" by which "we transform adult works of art, few as they are, into children's books. We transform them into books that are *safe*." Does Scott, like Morris, charge that Americans end where they begin, with abuses of the past? Explain.

7. What is paradoxical about the respect for home, school, and church that coexists with "the canonization of immaturity"? How do Rockwell's calendars and magazine covers, according to Morris, embody the same paradox?

8. Scott says that the "current surfeit of adolescent sentiment . . . deprives the adult world of all defenses against the Beats except aimless ridicule and ill formulated disgust." Compare this observation with the one Kristol (p. 529) makes of the plight of the educated man in evaluating pornography.

9. According to Scott, how would most Americans be content to see the Beats act and think? What, as Scott sees it, do Cassandra and Pollyanna have in common? How is it inimical to maturity in criticism and creativity?

10. Scott decries the lack of responsible criticism of the Beats. Does his own critique show that serious study of individual Beat artists is fruitful?

11. Kouwenhoven (p. 585) complains of the divorce between art and reality urged by I. A. Richards, and Scott complains of the isolation of the serious American artist or of his "retreat" to the ivory towers of academe. Riesman (p. 488), on the other hand, believes that the old distinction between town and gown is diminishing and that the concentration of intellectuals in colleges means simply that the great generative ideas no longer come from the outside. Do you find an irreparable split between academic life and "reality"? Explain.

12. Mead (p. 24) describes the eagerness of American young people to ape their elders in marriage and family life. Scott emphasizes "how great is the present inducement not to accept adulthood." How may the early marriages Mead describes and the escapism of the Beats (as well as the withdrawal of serious artists) be seen as instances of the same compulsion?

13. How would Scott's explanation of the Beats as a product of the American culture deal with the fact that England currently confronts her own version of a Beat generation?

14. Kronenberger (p. 573) condemns American humor not only for its immaturity but for its decadence. Are he and Scott interested in the same broad phenomenon?

15. Do any of the essays in the "Education" section of Part II suggest that American schools foster the "adolescent leaning of our culture" which Scott condemns? Explain.

16. What distinction does Scott make between Zen Buddhism and Beat Buddha? Do the words *liberty* and *equality* mean to the Beats something they have not previously meant in America?

17. Langer (p. 634) says that art is form expressive of human feeling. Kouwenhoven points to the urgency of the modern age to find "new forms." How is the Beat desire to be emancipated from "form" a kind of "nay-saying"?

18. Does Scott's conclusion that the Beat movement "will fizzle out" develop logically from assumptions made earlier in his essay? Find out what you can about the Dada movement in America and abroad. What features does it share with the Beat movement? Were Dadaists also convinced of "the Impossibility of the Existence of Anything"?

Nobility and the United States

OSCAR MANDEL

> Oscar Mandel (1926-   ) received his Ph.D. from The Ohio State University in 1951. Since 1955 he has taught comparative literature, drama, and creative writing at the University of Nebraska. He has contributed articles to several magazines, including Prairie Schooner *and* The American Scholar, *and has published* A Definition of Tragedy (1961).

Many American intellectuals live in a state of amiable schizophrenia: as liberals they refuse to believe that they are "any better than the next fellow," but as intellectuals they leave the populace alone, or they revile it while voting in its favor. If we except the few who are still trying to "elevate the masses," our true intellectuals live in a corner. They have ceased to exhort because they have lost their audience. Nobody wants them unless they can furnish an atomic bomb or a better television script. Just as under absolute monarchs the intellectuals conceal a part of themselves and are not in private quite what they seem in public, so in our democracy droves of the intelligent apply a lower faculty to the service of the masses, writing advertisements (for which they blush in private), composing scenarios and scripts (which they despise at cocktail parties), painting and drawing on salary (so they can earn enough money, they say, *really* to paint), inventing another toothpaste (while dreaming of research) or building a lavender ranch-type house (ridiculing their customers under their breaths). That which

---

Reprinted from The American Scholar, *Volume 27, Number 2, Spring 1958.* Copyright © *by the United Chapters of Phi Beta Kappa. Reprinted by permission of the publishers.*

is noble in them they despair of practicing, or else they practice it in seclusion, "after hours," when no one is looking. Thus, while they are called upon to do char-work with their lower faculties, that portion of them which ought to exhort and lead mankind, that which makes for aristocracy, is secreted out of sight. The worse part of society is fed, nursed, amused and cuddled (for reasonable wages) by the better part. Consequently the people are leaderless and content to be so. They even contrive to elect Presidents they will not have to revere. As for that section of mankind called Society, which used to set a few external rules making for aristocracy, it has altogether withdrawn into discreet conformity, and if it carouses, does so unnoticed. The rich have turned into chameleons on the tree of democracy.

Traditionally, the three sources of the feeling for aristocracy were the political aristocracy itself (in spite of its *actual* turpitude), the church with its saints or prophets (in spite of *its* actual turpitude) and the artists. The artists were either employees of the political aristocracy or independent but willing allies. No one, I think, will deny that with a few exceptions, serious art has been, up to our own time, an artistocratic pursuit, by which I understand that it was supported by the effective aristocracy (which, as in Athens, might go under another name), and that it had the feeling for aristocracy. The Greek drama is no exception, for though it addressed itself to the population, like Elizabethan drama it was supported and protected by the rich. We usually ignore the fact that even the characters of serious literature were members of the political aristocracy. We blink and say that this was a social concession or that nobility of rank is a symbol, et cetera, et cetera. But these are lies: part of the feeling for aristocracy consists in the equation between nobility of position and nobility of mind. A virtuous President of the United States is something finer than a kindly John Doe. Democratic though we may be, we still shudder more at the death of the great than at the everyday casualties reported in the newspaper. The feeling for aristocracy is the hope or, if you will, the vision of a fusion of every nobility, including that of rank and breeding no less than that of morals and intellect. That is why, furthermore, the traditional hero is not only socially noble but also intelligent. Our own literature does not pay much attention to the intelligent. Zola—perhaps Flaubert—inaugurated the epoch of dumb protagonists, which Faulkner, with his rich gallery of morons and idiots, has brought to its morbid perfection. Abandoning the hero as a fable, much of our contemporary literature has made its theme that mud can't help being mud, that it is unhappy or dirty or ought to be made comfortable; but I propose that none of these subjects is fit concern for a whole nation of serious writers. Their *ultimate* concern ought not to be *l'homme moyen sensuel,* photographed, for zoological or political reasons, in all his unedifying stances. Though the task, as Dostoevsky and Conrad and Silone knew, is not an easy one, a transfiguration must be performed. These three authors wrested heroism from the human muck by dint of an agony of effort, falling a thousand times on the way. Flaubert (the protovillain in our piece) merely became a zoologist; Hemingway said *nada*; and Mr. Ginsberg, looking for innocence, howls.

I have spoken of the minority who practice a kind of nobility in private. Because privacy still exists, the cultural climate has been favorable to the one form of art which can be noble and private at the same time: lyric poetry. Sappho entertained her friends at banquets by singing her poems and pinching her lyre. Her relations with mankind at large were not relevant to the quality of her art. And the immortal themes persist. If the lyric poets too have retreated from mankind, it has never been their function to conquer it. In fact, the lonely cage today has made them sing more exquisitely than did the public Victorians. Where form is the final test of greatness, the abandonment of mankind is no impediment.

With the spread of democracy, the upper classes began by losing their political influence and ended by losing their cultural ascendancy. In the United States, Adams is succeeded by Jackson; in England, the gentry is reduced to that empty role of "barbarians," as Matthew Arnold calls them; and in the twentieth century, demos inherits the realm. It would be foolish to deplore this as a mere calamity. But the glories of democracy have been sung too often to require another chorus. Enough to remark that the upper classes bled and deserved to bleed for their failure to realize the vision of aristocracy presented to them (and at their own instance!) by artists, philosophers and churchmen. Now they have withdrawn; some remnants live out their pathetic uselessness in dark areas of Boston or in English country houses open to the public for a fee. The rich now, to paraphrase Milton, are but the poor writ large. They do not form a different class. They too, like their employees, are leaderless and have lost the ability to look upward or to demand from others an upward glance. They are not interested in aristocracy. In the nineteenth century, instead of affording through their fortunes the chance of creating an American architecture (not to mention the other arts), they translated Loire chateaux in North Carolina. For all their money, they could not emerge from the proletariat and turn themselves into a true aristocracy. They did attempt lavishness; but the twentieth century is too serious for golden spittoons, and has neither lavishness nor aristocracy. The vision of moral heroism, intellectual perfection and good breeding has been supplanted by the vision, or rather the virtual accomplishment, of prosperity and social justice. True, I have read American protests against "American materialism" by the hundreds. We are blessed with an uncommon number of professional recriminators against material goods and upholders of "the finer things of life." But aristocracy embraces material prosperity; human dignity is not a concept of subsistence-level societies; even Diogenes and St. Simeon Stylites required rich societies as foils for their exertions. The real question is, "Who has the wealth, and what does he do with it?" Let Lorenzo the Magnificent and let Voltaire keep their money. But he who can only buy several pink Cadillacs with it, or travel over the world sporting a necktie adorned with large pineapples, unacquainted with his own language and replacing courtesy by heartiness—that man has money but not wealth, and the best answer to him is the federal tax.

When the leaders of society disappeared, the artist hung in the air with his great sermon in his hands. He had always worked for an elite and had never really lost his faith in his patrons; nowhere else could he find fit receptacles for the moral exhortation which is great art. Perhaps he actually hoped that some day they might acquire from him his own feeling for aristocracy. In the first enthusiastic years of democracy, many artists simply readdressed their message and sent it to the new public, so that for a while there were some considerable artists trying a vision of brotherhood on the masses: Hugo in France, Dickens in England, Tolstoy in Russia, Whitman in America.

But as an artistic goal, inspiring or converting the masses was soon forgotten. Long before educators began to doubt the efficacy of mass education, artists gave up hoping. The masses, they found, had more urgent business going than nobility. The great movement of mankind was speeding toward the consummation of pink Cadillacs, and, as I have said, even the vocabulary of hope—"nobility," "virtue," "heroism," "breeding," "ceremony"—became all but archaic. Facts always breed their apologetics: since there is no one left to exhort, our fashionable theories of art have conveniently substituted form for content and declare (not fearing the stares of Aeschylus, Dante and Milton) that art should not and does not exhort, that it has nothing to do with moral persuasion. From the days of moral art, one sad vestige remains—proletarian art—which convinces us that the rich are unjust, without satisfying us that their victims are admirable.

It is an instructive paradox that, whereas Greece, with its slaves, and medieval Europe, with its cruelly rigid class-divisions, produced an art in which all the people, high or low, rich or poor, could delight, in our democracies art has split in two, the larger part consisting of true confessions and quiz programs for the masses, and the smaller part of *Finnegans Wake* and the like for an aristocracy of practically nobody. To be sure, in all epochs there has been *some* division—e.g., a court literature of romances and a popular literature of fabliaux. But the division was less marked in these iniquitous societies (Chaucer wrote fabliaux, and Arthurian romances became popular property) and the best art, like Homer or religious sculpture, was held in common. But why does art tend to become unified in hierarchical societies and "dualized" in egalitarian ones? One answer may be that in hierarchical societies the masses have less power to demand art, and that, to the extent that they are not utterly crushed, they are in the habit of looking up to their betters and of trying to emulate them. That the merchants, artisans and yeomen did not enjoy quite the same aspects of a given work of art as those enjoyed by the upper or the educated class, we may safely suppose; yet, in general, circumstances induced them to share in the common idiom. This is why we rightly think of the masses of another day as having had better taste than mankind does today. With democracy, of course, the liberated populace became itself the buyer of art, and imposed its taste freely, without troubling to consult an elite. Hence the split in art: the caterers to mass taste on the one side, and the "true" artists without allegiance on the other.

In this connection, let me say a word about contemporary Russian art. I have seen a little of their statuary and their painting in reproductions, like everyone else, but I know their literature only by hearsay. Assuming that this literature is actually of the class which extols the manufacture of extra tractors as a sublime human achievement, I should say that we are wrong to blame this misery on the fact that Russia is ruled by dictators. Seeing two evils, we naturally conclude that they must be organically linked, and so we flatter ourselves with the figment that "there is no art where there is no freedom." In reality, some dictatorships do annihilate thought and creation ("I draw my pistol when I hear the word culture," someone says in that infamous Nazi play *Schlageter*), but others cultivate, honor and even finance them. To go no further than the obvious, Caesar Augustus and Louis XIV stand out as abolishers of freedom and patrons of culture. And in the days of the Greeks an intellectual could usually escape the persecutions of democracy by removing himself to the tyrannies of Sicily or

Macedonia. The real question is not that of freedom, but whether the intellectual can be genuinely loyal to the system—dogmatic, half-free or free—which prevails in his country. Medieval Catholicism did not allow substantial deviations, yet it commanded loyal support with the results in art and thought that we know. What ails Russian literature, therefore, is not so much a lack of freedom as a dedication to the ignoble by a dictatorship of proletarians over the proletariat.

With the disappearance of a political aristocracy, with the reduction of the church to a center of sociability and soothing homiletics, and with the quarantining of the artist and the theoretician, the leaderless plebeians (rich and poor alike) have dedicated themselves wholeheartedly to self-admiration. They do not seek models to imitate or a superior taste to emulate. True, we are not in a jungle. Occasionally we stumble on a modern house which is not shamed to dust by colonial architecture; occasionally the public patronizes a difficult and intelligent play. The trouble with the plebeians was never that they had low tastes or no morals, but that they jumbled good and bad together and could not distinguish. We know that they willingly clapperclawed Shakespeare's plays. They did as much for Lumpkin Ignoto's the next afternoon. The over-all effect of a landscape organized by the populace is unkemptness rather than uniform ugliness. The unkemptness is intellectual and moral as well as aesthetic. Much, for instance, could be said about the proliferation of bizarre Protestant sects—typical inventions of the unchecked popular imagination. Were and are not these sects *permitted* by the absence of a focus of leadership, everywhere respected even if not clearly understood? Superstition—all the ejaculations of vulgar prophets unaware of standards of thought—has given Christianity in the United States its uncouth diversity. Freed from the control of a superior caste, religion became intellectual bad taste.

The world does not live on correct taste, noble morality or even intellectual acuity, and I am not suggesting revolutions. This is merely an inquiry. If we ask an explanation for what ugliness we do discover in the life about us, we find it in the extinction of leadership, the loss of reverence, the muddling of hierarchy or, in short, the want of a feeling for aristocracy. Much has been written about our new suburbias, where flat boxes eye one another across barren hills stickled with telephone poles. Outside of the old residential centers, America is becoming a great slum equipped with social justice. Is cheap housing necessarily ugly? Not if popular taste is good. The residents of our slums think their houses beautiful. But these people are leaderless: no one with a feeling for aristocracy has been able to hold their attention and suggest models. They do not want, as the political aristocracy did, images of hope, images of a possible heroism, images of possible beauty shown to them. But if houses have been criticized, other blemishes have almost vanished from the consciousness of even the most atrabilious critics. Is it seemly that in a university the students should dress as though they were pausing between the digging of two ditches? In England they wear gowns; in many countries they still rise when their instructor enters the room. But when the populace becomes the country, there is no looking up. The word "snobbery" usually dismisses the subject. I recall the touching words Yeats wrote for his daughter:

> And may her bridegroom bring her to a house
> Where all's accustomed, ceremonious;
> .   .   .   .
> How but in custom and in ceremony
> Are innocence and beauty born?

The feeling for aristocracy, which this great man possessed so inveterately, unites appropriate dress and moral congruity, courtesy and heroism. An elegant Elizabethan lyric is understood only by an elegant mind. We teach it, in our folly, as though all the crowds at football games could stomach it.

With mass education the universities ceased to be centers of moral or aesthetic leadership. The tentative advance of a few scholars suddenly met a trampling army of plebeian students, and those poor few who entertained the idea of standards and hierarchies submitted without more ado to the stampede, like Don Quixote under the hogs. Today our universities, manned by tangential intellectuals, produce either more tangential intellectuals or additions to the populace or caterers to the populace. Our language has gone the same way: it keeps growing—but so does a cancer. "Eats," says the sign of the roadside diner. Wherever we look, wherever we listen, we find the depredations of a populace left without standards, and desiring none. Occasionally an affable dictatorship—like that of Parisian designers—creates an oasis of good taste. For the rest—automobiles with fins, geometry passing for interior decoration, neon signs on churches—fashions and customs meander from bad to bad. Moral excellence declines as well, for we are content as a nation to have the inducements and opportunities for doing evil removed from us ("Retro, Satana!" is the motto of every bureaucracy) and think ourselves lucky that occasions for moral and physical heroism have been reduced by machinery to nearly none at all. In the vast organizations of government, armed forces and business, decisions—the moral acts—are made by boards, committees or faceless and undiscoverable employees "somewhere along the line." Bureaucracy cannot be blamed, cajoled, exhorted or worshipped, as kings and even tyrants can. It is all mouth, no ears and nearly no brain, and it superannuates moral excellence, the virtue possible only to responsible individuals. In many business offices all employees contribute weekly to a "gift fund" which operates as an anonymous and automatic congratulator or condoler of the sick, the wedded and the parturient, so that even the minor exertions of generosity can be avoided. The instance is trifling but worth recording.

What shall we say of endeavors to "elevate the people"? This humane notion takes many forms. Mass education is one of them. Another is the multiplication of symphony concerts. Most of our cities have respectable museums and libraries. Ladies' groups sponsor a few chamber music recitals. Clubs discuss "great books." And what else? The whole nation is a vast and ghostly museum and a refuge for frightened or hungry Europeans. The good folk who are "elevating the people" are no doubt inheriting this office from the traditional occupation of conveying a feeling for aristocracy to the elite. Now their subjects are the whole people. And the people laugh at them, or else make a few pious motions. Then they return to the television sets and the basketball games which so offend the culture-dispensers. The people act from a right instinct. They have in a sense, watched TV programs since Adam begot them, and no one is going to disturb them now.

Where can the artist find a new elite willing to employ him? Where will he find an audience to revive in him the desire to show the life which might be? It would not matter if I knew, since these social movements are neither impelled nor directed by pamphleteers. But in any event, the alliance between the intellectuals and the proletariat is over. This alliance (if we can call such a one-sided affair an alliance) began about the time of the French and the Industrial Revolutions, and it was fed by an emotion which the eighteenth century practically invented: humanitarianism. The oppressed masses found their vocal cords in the educated and humane men and women who pitied them. Even those whose best solution consisted in the distribution of Bibles deserve our regard. In short, the victory of the lower classes owes much to the work of the intellectuals, but the intellectuals earned few thanks in return. What the thinking man earned was toleration: something less than apotheosis. It is no exaggeration to say that the new public cashiered him. Now that the work of pity is done, he cannot take his mind off the great betrayal. But he is still a left-winger, by and large, still a Democrat or a Socialist or what-have-you, out of a kind of habit perhaps, forgetting that the poor coal miner, to whom he had reached his hand in the evil days, is richer than he and has quite forgotten him.

I propose we let the matter rest there. The time has come to stop sulking; we must twitch our mantles and try new pastures.

The time has come to stop demanding "culture" of the masses and to stop reproving them for their "low tastes." Their tastes are normal. We resent them only because we expected too much: the more fools we. Horror or pity for the way of life of the majority, as expressed in novels and plays about human brutality, lust, greed and idiocy, is a product of disappointed idealism. If we could recall the artists of former ages, they would be astonished by the vehemence of our disgust. Even in Twain and Hardy we still find the common people as the natural subject of *humor* (though, indeed, we learn more truth about "plain folk" from *A Midsummer Night's Dream* and *Huckleberry Finn* than from a hundred solemn pieces of naturalism). To be sure, the serious approach to the masses was inevitable in the new civilization. The livelihood of the Renaissance artist did not, after all, depend on the masses, and one could be fond of a bumpkin who stayed more or less quietly in the place God had allotted him on earth. The Renaissance artist could afford his nonchalance. Yet, though time has changed us, this nonchalance is what we must regain. We need to forget our resentment, our sense of frustration over the uninspirable majority, and whatever sentimental expectations of a noble proletariat, viewing nothing but the classics on television sets, we may still be entertaining. The sooner we embrace once again the idea of hierarchy, the sooner we can send out emissaries toward a new elite fit to be addressed. Perhaps we can create this elite. Surely artists and all the "useless" thinkers are not condemned to write forever only to each other. We must find a deliverance from precious art on one side, and on the other side from those bitter and "depressing" novels which keep explaining, again and again, with never-ceasing and foolish despair, that the ignoble are ignoble. We must, above all, find *heroes* for our literature; we must return to the idealizing function of art.

We may wonder whether the vision of hope—that is to say, the feeling for aristocracy—is forever denied to the populace. Will there ever be a time when all men and women share in the same intellectual and emotional life—when a new Chrétien de Troyes, a new Spenser, a new Racine, a new Tolstoy reveal aspects of nobility to the commonest among men? Whatever we may think of the future, the time at any rate is not now. We have given the masses premature titles to maturity, and our punishment has been despair.

PROBLEMS FOR WRITING AND DISCUSSION

1. Would Lynes (p. 519) agree with Mandel that our "true intellectuals have lost their audience"? Would Mandel agree with Lynes that the mass of Americans are not barbarians? Explain.

2. What is the "amiable schizophrenia" of the American intellectual and the "dualization" of art in an egalitarian society? How does the "charwork" of intellectuals aid and abet the abhorrent features of mass taste? How is their "real" work divorced from a mass audience?

3. What has the artist's real work to do with "the vision of a fusion of every nobility, including that of rank and breeding no less than of morals and intellect"? Does Viereck (p. 324) assume an "equation between nobility of position and nobility of mind" for his aristocracy?

4. Why do the rich in America no longer provide either audience or inspiration for the artist? What in America has happened to the "political" aristocracy? To the religious? What American assumptions debilitate the leadership of all three of these groups?

5. Mandel (p. 616) says it is rare that a modern author can "transfigure" the common man into a hero, can wrest "heroism from the human muck." How is his detachment from the common man like Cooper's (p. 399), Lippmann's (p. 381), and Hand's (p. 388)?

6. Like Scott (p. 598), Mandel implies that privacy is the only sphere in which the American artist can honestly function. What dangers in the artist's withdrawal does each man see? Galbraith (p. 180) notes that members of the New Class combine their interests with their jobs and employ their leisure in intellectual and artistic pursuits. Would such a New Class provide the audience that Mandel hopes may be created?

7. Riesman (p. 488) calls upon college graduates to insist that the world outside of college meet their expectations. Does Mandel share Riesman's hope that education will breed a new aristocracy? Does Novak (p. 690)?

8. "Where form is the final test of greatness, the abandonment of mankind is no impediment," writes Mandel. If form is *not* the final test of the greatness of art, what, according to Mandel, is?

9. Examine Kennedy's inaugural address (p. 508). Does it use predominantly what Mandel calls the "vocabulary of hope" or does it promise "prosperity and social justice"? Explain.

10. Mandel says that "demos inherits the realm" in the twentieth century. Does he deplore the reign of the common man? Does he believe that materialism, prosperity, and social justice are enemies of the arts? What then is wrong with a "dictatorship of proletarians over the proletariat"?

11. What is ironic about the alliance of the artist with the proletariat? When did it reach its height in America and why? "We have given the masses premature titles to maturity," says Mandel. Would Kristol (p. 529) agree? Compare their solutions to the dilemma of American art with those of Kouwenhoven (p. 585) and Scott.

12. Mandel does not take up the question of whether "images of hope, images of a possible heroism, images of a possible beauty" are still conceivable. In an atmosphere in which "moral excellence" declines, in which prosperity and social justice are actualities rather than dreams, and in which bureaucracies rather than human beings make decisions, what images do you think are possible?

The American Finds His Country

HILTON KRAMER

> Hilton Kramer (1928-), art critic and lecturer, was graduated from Syracuse University (1950) and studied at Columbia, Harvard, and Indiana universities. He has written on art for various magazines and is contributing editor for Arts Magazine and Art in America. In 1962-63 he was a member of the art faculty at Bennington College.

"Let us look at this American artist first.... Why isn't he a European still, like his father before him?"—D. H. Lawrence.

The history of American painting in the twentieth century is a history of ambiguities, and at the heart of these ambiguities is the figure of the *pure American* as he was defined by Henry James when, in 1872, in a review of the European notebooks of Nathaniel Hawthorne, he remarked of his precursor: "We seem to see him strolling through churches and galleries as the last pure American—attesting by his shy responses to dark canvas and cold marble his loyalty to a simpler and less encumbered civilization." It was a shrewd observation, made by a writer who himself lacked anything but shyness in the presence of art, the writer who probably more than anyone else bequeathed to the American artist of the twentieth century that total commitment to art which has been his most marked characteristic and often his only solace. This figure of the *pure American*, with his shy response to artistic culture in the European sense, came over into the twentieth century somewhat changed, of course. He went underground. "Modern Art" was European art; the very conception of a modern American art implied a trans-Atlantic dialogue in which the aspiration for an ex-

Reprinted from The Nation, *April 21, 1962, by permission of the publisher.*

pression purely American was continuously announced and just as often defeated. Nevertheless, the *pure-American* element persisted. It was constantly invoked against the claims of European art, and very often submitted in the end to that peculiar synthesis of European and American elements that often characterizes our best achievements in the arts. Yet such a synthesis failed to satisfy the ideal of an art without foreign contingencies, and in the foreground of our national aesthetic consciousness there still remained the inviolate dream of a *pure-American* style that would somehow serve as a symbolic equivalent for that "simpler and less encumbered civilization" which had now been lost forever.

The American art of our century has suffered two definitive crises in the search for that style. Both generated a new impulse in our art, and both were reflections of painful historical moments. Moreover, they both came directly from Europe. The first was the Armory Show of 1913; the second, the emigration during the Second World War of the leaders of the European *avant-garde* (Léger, Miró, Breton, Lipchitz, Mondrian and others). In the history of American art, these events form the historical parentheses of our first modern period, marking it off from what came before and what followed. They were New York events. In the latter case, the political debacle of Europe removed the center of artistic gravity from Paris to New York; in the former, the sheer documentation of the European achievement was itself sufficient to cause a radical change.

The two events differed profoundly, however. The Armory Show of 1913 came at the beginning of a period, the emigration at the end of one. In both instances there was an effort to introduce into America the most vital impulses of the European *avant-garde,* but in the interim the *avant-garde* itself had been radically altered— if, indeed, it could any longer be said to exist in the old sense. In 1913 it was at the height of its powers; as communicated in the Armory Show, its effect was to shatter our assumptions about the nature of art and to stimulate again, with even greater self-consciousness, what had always been a principal anxiety in American art life: the assimilation of European achievements. The second crisis was entirely different. By the end of the thirties—and indeed, long before that—the Parisian *avant-garde* was fragmented and without a definitive direction. It had lost its inner conviction as an *avant-garde*. When political events forced its removal to New York, its validity had already been called into question. Modern art in Paris had become what it had always been in America: a personal predicament. One is tempted to observe that New York was the perfect burial place for a shattered and demoralized *avant-garde*. The equation of history and geography had a frightening appropriateness.

For the Americans, the art that came out of the Second World War and immediately after, was still an art of dialogue with the School of Paris. The principal formal capital was still provided by Picasso, Matisse, Miró, Klee, Kandinsky and Mondrian—above all, by Picasso—even though it was a capital spent drastically, rebelliously and utterly without regard for perpetuating the premises of its own existence. The recklessness of the spending was motivated perhaps by a desire on the part of these Americans to see what minimal aesthetic viability would remain once all this inherited capital had been spent. Their effort was all toward an undoing of European art, and therefore an undoing of their own premises. It became more and more an art constructed out of the ruins of the School of Paris. The irony is that so much that is now taken for vitality, new growth, and so on, was in reality an act of burial.

The ghost of Henry James's *pure American,* then, with his affinities for a "simpler and less encumbered civilization," was burying the European *avant-garde*. The nature of his ambiguous achievement reminds me of a judgment that R. P. Blackmur once made on the style of American ballet:

> We Americans have the technique to bring something to performance so well that the subject is left out. There is nothing we throw away so quickly as our *données;* for we would make always an independent and evangelical, rather than a contingent, creation. This is why other people in the world in part take us up and in part repudiate us; and it is

why they find us both abstract and hysterical: we throw away so much and make so much of the meagre remainder. We make a great beauty, which is devastated of everything but form and gait.

It was in precisely such a devastation that the "New York School" was born.

If one can speak of a New York School today, however, one means something else, for the compulsions that motivated the Abstract Expressionism of the forties and fifties already have the look of history. We now face a situation in which the variety of living artistic statement in New York will no longer submit to an easy, unified characterization. Artists in New York share a tone, a spirit, an atmosphere, a place, but those who look to the future rather than the past no longer seem intent upon proving themselves in the face of a dead *avant-garde*. They confront the culture of New York, with all its inhuman proportions and its raw taste, and they do so for the first time without the advantage of a European ideal to guide them. That is their historical uniqueness, and it is that which separates them from the artists who began doing their serious work fifteen or twenty years ago.

It is the habit of certain critics of the older generation to regard this variety of artistic statement—this effort on the part of artists to re-examine all the possibilities their elders closed the door on a generation ago—as a failure of nerve. They cannot themselves conceive of art except as a death struggle with the phantoms of the old *avant-garde*. Their inability to sympathize with a generation that no longer regards such a struggle as central to the artistic enterprise marks them, too, as being slightly historical.

There can be no question, of course, that the end of the European *avant-garde* was a critical loss for the American sensibility. Its energies and its ideals had always been a cushion against the raw experience of American life. This has been particularly true for the artist in New York, for nowhere else does this rawness impose itself so drastically on the artist's sensibility. The rhythm of life in New York is a destructive rhythm; the measure of human emotion counts for nothing. It is no wonder that Sartre, on his first visit to New York after the war, could ask: "Is it a city I am lost in, or is it Nature?"—so little did it seem to accommodate the human equation.

A European city is a repository of the past; at every turn one is reminded of an affinity with a history that still counts, that remains the irreducible *donnée* of the present. In America, as Mr. Blackmur remarks, the *donnée* is abandoned as so much baggage. The present is not felt to be contingent on the past; it exists as a pure, abstract possibility. In Europe it required a war to destroy a city, but New York destroys itself every day as an expression of its own prosperity.

What the artist in New York faces for the first time now is the necessity of confronting this experience, of actually *seeing* it, without the ghost of the dead *avant-garde* guiding his hand. Many artists today find themselves in a position that is roughly analogous to that of political radicals. For them those large, beautiful, all-embracing European systems of thought and feeling are simply not *there* any more. They do not account for enough of the particularity and complexity of American experience. Their categories seem not to be able to accommodate the shape of life as it is actually lived. And just as many radicals have had to abandon traditional Socialist ideology in order to reconstruct their radical stance from more empirical materials, so also I think many artists who a generation back would have been content to form themselves in the *avant-garde* mold, now find it impossible to think of their work in those terms.

But just as we have a false radicalism that still clings to the old concepts in the face of all the contradictions of experience, so we also have a false *avant-garde* that perpetuates the myth of aesthetic intransigence while enjoying the rewards of aesthetic conformity. And basic to this myth is the old notion of the *pure American* confronting European culture. A great deal that passes for *avant-garde* expression in New York makes its appeal directly to our yearning for a "simpler and less encumbered civilization"; it transforms our difficult, urban experience into a kind of pastoral, acting as if the culture of Times Square and Madison Avenue were somehow a reincarnation of the frontier. It is, of course, a gross form of sentimentality masking itself as audacity.

It is this idea of the *pure American* that must be exorcised from the art of the sixties if it is really to tell us the truth about our experience. To cling to it now is to see American experience through European eyes. A few years ago Lionel Abel wrote that "Most Europeans believe that their culture is dead. . . . Any doctrine which presents a plan for a new beginning, for initiating a movement forward, is bound to find sympathy among people who feel that their inherited stock of ideas and attitudes is no longer fecund." And clearly the notion of America as a "simpler and less encumbered civilization"—not the real America, of course, but America as it is represented by our art—does constitute a "new beginning" for many Europeans. It is consumed as part of the world-wide cult of America that has no interest in making distinctions between what is best and what is worst, between what is living and what is the enemy of life, in our culture.

One does well to recall that James spoke of Hawthorne as the "*last* pure American," for even in James's day it was difficult to go on believing in so mythical a figure and in our own it has become ludicrous. The idea dies hard because it has had, like the convention of the European *avant-garde,* the comforting effect of disguising and softening our experience. Without it we are naked in the face of events. But it is precisely in that nakedness that one looks for the authentic art of the moment.

PROBLEMS FOR WRITING AND DISCUSSION

1. What effects did the Armory Show of 1913 and the emigration in World War II of the European *avant-garde* have on American art?

2. Why does Kramer suggest that New York may have been "the perfect burial place for a shattered and demoralized *avant-garde*"? Is Kramer in general agreement with Kouwenhoven's thesis (p. 585)?

3. Does Kramer's essay satisfactorily answer for you D. H. Lawrence's question quoted at the beginning—why isn't the American artist "a European still, like his father before him?" Why or why not?

4. Explain the analogy Kramer makes between American painting and American ballet as Blackmur describes it.

5. Compare Blackmur's remark—"We Americans have the technique to bring something to performance so well that the subject is left out"—with Morris' comment on Norman Rockwell's style (p. 560).

6. Henry James's pure American (p. 82) is loyal "to a simpler and less encumbered civilization." Would the artist Grandma Moses fit this definition? Would Norman Rockwell? Kramer says that the "'simpler and less encumbered civilization' has now been lost forever." Morris says that we look backward to our lost innocence and happiness. Does Morris believe such a time ever existed?

7. What analogy does Kramer make between the artist today and the political radical? Might both be compared with the social scientist whom Riesman (p. 488) urges to seek new and as yet unimaginable patterns for the future? Does Kramer say what "truth about our experience" American artists and the now undiscriminating Europeans have been avoiding?

8. Kramer speaks of New York's "rawness," of its "destructive rhythm" in which the "measure of human emotions counts for nothing." What aspects of New York's "rawness" are more comparable to "Nature" than to a man-made city such as that to which Sartre was accustomed?

The Cultural Importance of Art

SUSANNE K. LANGER

Susanne K. Langer (1895-) attended a French school in New York and then Radcliffe College, where she received three degrees and where she taught philosophy for fifteen years. Professor of Philosophy at Connecticut College since 1954, she has also taught and lectured at many other universities, including Columbia, Northwestern, Ohio State, and Washington. Among her books are Philosophy in a New Key *(1942),* Feeling and Form *(1953), and* Philosophical Sketches *(1962).*

Every culture develops some kind of art as surely as it develops language. Some primitive cultures have no real mythology or religion, but all have some art—dance, song, design (sometimes only on tools or on the human body). Dance, above all, seems to be the oldest elaborated art.

The ancient ubiquitous character of art contrasts sharply with the prevalent idea that art is a luxury product of civilization, a cultural frill, a piece of social veneer.

It fits better with the conviction held by most artists, that art is the epitome of human life, the truest record of insight and feeling, and that the strongest military or economic society without art is poor in comparison with the most primitive tribe of savage painters, dancers, or idol carvers. Wherever a society has really achieved culture (in the ethnological sense, not the popular sense of "social form") it has begotten art, not late in its career, but at the very inception of it.

From Philosophical Sketches *by Susanne K. Langer. Copyright © 1962 by The Johns Hopkins Press; reprinted by permission of the publisher.*

Art is, indeed, the spearhead of human development, social and individual. The vulgarization of art is the surest symptom of ethnic decline. The growth of a new art or even a great and radically new style always bespeaks a young and vigorous mind, whether collective or single.

What sort of thing is art, that it should play such a leading role in human development? It is not an intellectual pursuit, but is necessary to intellectual life; it is not religion, but grows up with religion, serves it, and in large measure determines it.

We cannot enter here on a long discussion of what has been claimed as the essence of art, the true nature of art, or its defining function; in a single lecture dealing with one aspect of art, namely its cultural influence, I can only give you by way of preamble my own definition of art, with categorical brevity. This does not mean that I set up this definition in a categorical spirit, but only that we have no time to debate it; so you are asked to accept it as an assumption underlying these reflections.

Art, in the sense here intended—that is, the generic term subsuming painting, sculpture, architecture, music, dance, literature, drama, and film—may be defined as the practice of creating perceptible forms expressive of human feeling. I say "perceptible" rather than "sensuous" forms because some works of art are given to imagination rather than to the outward senses. A novel, for instance, usually is read silently with the eye, but is not made for vision, as a painting is; and though sound plays a vital part in poetry, words even in poetry are not essentially sonorous structures like music. Dance requires to be seen, but its appeal is to deeper centers of sensation. The difference between dance and mobile sculpture makes this immediately apparent. But all works of art are purely perceptible forms that seem to embody some sort of feeling.

"Feeling" as I am using it here covers much more than it does in the technical vocabulary of psychology, where it denotes only pleasure and displeasure, or even in the shifting limits of ordinary discourse, where it sometimes means sensation (as when one says a paralyzed limb has no feeling in it), sometimes sensibility (as we speak of hurting someone's feelings), sometimes emotion (e.g., as a situation is said to harrow your feelings, or to evoke tender feeling), or a directed emotional attitude (we say we feel strongly *about* something), or even our general mental or physical condition, feeling well or ill, blue, or a bit above ourselves. As I use the word, in defining art as the creation of perceptible forms expressive of human feeling, it takes in all those meanings; it applies to everything that may be felt.

Another word in the definition that might be questioned is "creation." I think it is justified, not pretentious, as perhaps it sounds, but that issue is slightly beside the point here; so let us shelve it. If anyone prefers to speak of the "making" or "construction" of expressive forms, that will do here just as well.

What does have to be understood is the meaning of "form," and more particularly "expressive form"; for that involves the very nature of art and therefore the question of its cultural importance.

The word "form" has several current uses; most of them have some relation to the sense in which I am using it here, though a few, such as "a form to be filled in for tax purposes" or "a mere matter of form," are fairly remote, being quite specialized. Since we are speaking of art, it might be good to point out that the meaning of stylistic pattern—"the sonata form," "the sonnet form"—is not the one I am assuming here.

I am using the word in a simpler sense, which it has when you say, on a foggy night, that you see dimly moving forms in the mist; one of them emerges clearly, and is the form of a man. The trees are gigantic forms; the rills of rain trace sinuous forms on the windowpane. The rills are not fixed things; they are forms of motion. When you watch gnats weaving in the air, or flocks of birds wheeling overhead, you see dynamic forms—forms made by motion.

It is in this sense of an apparition given to our perception that a work of art is a form. It may be a permanent form like a building or a vase or a picture, or a transient, dynamic form like a melody or a dance, or even a form given to imagination, like the passage of purely imaginary, apparent events that constitutes a literary work. But it is always a perceptible, self-identical whole; like a natural being, it has a character of organic unity, self-sufficiency, individual reality. And it is thus, as an appearance, that a work of art is good or bad or perhaps only rather poor—as an appearance, not as a comment on things beyond it in the world, or as a reminder of them.

This, then, is what I mean by "form"; but what is meant by calling such forms* "expressive of human feeling"? How do apparitions "express" anything—feeling or anything else? First of all, let us ask just what is meant here by "express," what sort of "expression" we are talking about.

The word "expression" has two principal meanings. In one sense it means self-expression—giving vent to our feelings. In this sense it refers to a symptom of what we feel. Self-expression is a spontaneous reaction to an actual, present situation, an event, the company we are in, things people say, or what the weather does to us; it bespeaks the physical and mental state we are in and the emotions that stir us.

In another sense, however, "expression" means the presentation of an idea, usually by the proper and apt use of words. But a device for presenting an idea is what we call a symbol, not a symptom. Thus a word is a symbol, and so is a meaningful combination of words.

A sentence, which is a special combination of words, expresses the idea of some state of affairs, real or imagined. Sentences are complicated symbols. Language will formulate new ideas as well as communicate old ones, so that all people know a lot of things that they have merely heard or read about. Symbolic expression, therefore, extends our knowledge beyond the scope of our actual experience.

If an idea is clearly conveyed by means of symbols we say it is well expressed. A person may work for a long time to give his statement the best possible form, to find the exact words for what he means to say, and to carry his account or his argument most directly from one point to another. But a discourse so worked out is certainly not a spontaneous reaction. Giving expression to an idea is obviously a different thing from giving expression to feelings. You do not say of a man in a rage that his anger is well expressed. The symptoms just are what they are; there is no critical standard for symptoms. If, on the other hand, the angry man tries to tell you what he is fuming about, he will have to collect himself, curtail his emotional expression, and find words to express his ideas. For to tell a story coherently involves "expression" in quite a different sense: this sort of expression is not "self-expression," but may be called "conceptual expression."

Language, of course, is our prime instrument of conceptual expression. The things we can say are in effect the things we can think. Words are the terms of our thinking as well as the terms in which we present our thoughts, because they present the objects of thought to the thinker himself. Before language communicates ideas, it gives them form, makes them clear, and in fact makes them what they are. Whatever has a name is an object for thought. Without words, sense experience is only a flow of impressions, as subjective as our feelings; words make it objective, and carve it up into *things* and *facts* that we can note, remember, and think about. Language gives outward experience its form, and makes it definite and clear.

There is, however, an important part of reality that is quite inaccessible to the formative influence of language: that is the realm of so-called "inner experience," the life of feeling and emotion. The reason why language is so powerless here is not, as many people suppose, that feeling and emotion are irrational; on the contrary, they seem irrational because language does not help to make them conceivable, and most people cannot conceive anything without the logical scaffolding of words. The unfitness of language to convey subjective experience is a somewhat technical subject, easier for logicians to understand than for artists; but the gist of it is that the form of language does not reflect the natural form of feeling, so that we cannot shape any extensive concepts of feeling with the help of ordinary, discursive language. Therefore the words whereby we refer to feeling only name very general kinds of inner experience—excitement, calm, joy, sorrow, love, hate, and so on. But there is no language to describe just how one joy differs, sometimes radically, from another. The real nature of feeling is something language as such—as discursive symbolism—cannot render.

For this reason, the phenomena of feeling and emotion are usually treated by philosophers as irrational. The only pattern discursive thought can find in them is the pattern of outward events that occasion them. There are different degrees of fear, but they are thought of as so many degrees of the same simple feeling.

But human feeling is a fabric, not a vague mass. It has an intricate dynamic pattern, possible combinations and new emergent phenomena. It is a pattern of organically interdependent and interdetermined tensions and resolutions, a pattern of almost infinitely complex activation and cadence. To it belongs the whole gamut of our sensibility—the sense of straining thought, all mental attitude and motor set. Those are the deeper reaches that underlie the surface waves of our emotion, and make human life a life of feeling instead of an unconscious metabolic existence interrupted by feelings.

It is, I think, this dynamic pattern that finds its formal expression in the arts. The expressiveness of art is like that of a symbol, not that of an emotional symptom; it is as a formulation of feeling for our conception that a work of art is properly said to be expressive. It may serve somebody's need of self-expression besides, but that is not what makes it good or bad art. In a special sense one may call a work of art a symbol of feeling, for, like a symbol, it formulates our ideas of inward experience, as discourse formulates our ideas of things and facts in the outside world. A work of art differs from a genuine symbol—that is, a symbol in the full and usual sense—in that it does not point beyond itself to something else. Its relation to feeling is a rather special one that we cannot undertake to analyze here; in effect, the feeling it expresses appears to be directly given with it—as the sense of a true metaphor, or the value of a religious myth—and is not separable from its expression.

We speak of the feeling *of,* or the feeling *in,* a work of art, not the feeling it means. And we speak truly; a work of art presents something like a direct vision of vitality, emotion, subjective reality.

The primary function of art is to objectify feeling so that we can contemplate and understand it. It is the formulation of so-called "inward experience," the "inner life," that is impossible to achieve by discursive thought, because its forms are incommensurable with the forms of language and all its derivatives (e.g., mathematics, symbolic logic). Art objectifies the sentience and desire, self-consciousness and world-consciousness, emotions and moods, that are generally regarded as irrational because words cannot give us clear ideas of them. But the premise tacitly assumed in such a judgment—namely, that anything language cannot express is formless and irrational—seems to me to be an error. I believe the life of feeling is not irrational; its logical forms are merely very different from the structures of discourse. But they are so much like the dynamic forms of art that art is their natural symbol. Through plastic works, music, fiction, dance, or dramatic forms we can conceive what vitality and emotion feel like.

This brings us, at last, to the question of the cultural importance of the arts. Why is art so apt to be the vanguard of cultural advance, as it was in Egypt, in Greece, in Christian Europe (think of Gregorian music and Gothic architecture), in Renaissance Italy—not to speculate about ancient cavemen, whose art is all that we know of them? One thinks of culture as economic increase, social organization, the gradual ascendancy of rational thinking and scientific control of nature over superstitious imagination and magical practices. But art is not practical; it is neither philosophy nor science; it is not religion, morality, or even social comment (as many drama critics take comedy to be). What does it contribute to culture that could be of major importance?

It merely presents forms—sometimes intangible forms—to imagination. Its direct appeal is to that faculty, or function, that Lord Bacon considered the chief stumbling block in the way of reason, and that enlightened writers like Stuart Chase never tire of condemning as the source of all nonsense and bizarre erroneous beliefs. And so it is; but it is also the source of all insight and true beliefs. Imagination is probably the oldest mental trait that is typically human—older than discursive reason; it is probably the common source of dream, reason, religion, and all true general observation. It is this primitive human power—imagination—that engenders the arts and is in turn directly affected by their products.

Somewhere at the animalian starting line of human evolution lie the beginnings of that supreme instrument of the mind—language. We think of it as a device for communication among the members of a society. But communication is only one, and perhaps not even the first, of its functions. The first thing it does is to break up what William James called the "blooming, buzzing confusion" of sense perception into units and groups, events and chains of events—things and relations, causes and effects. All these patterns are imposed on our experience by language. We think, as we speak, in terms of objects and their relations.

But the process of breaking up our sense experience in this way, making reality conceivable, memorable, sometimes even predictable, is a process of imagination. Primitive conception is imagination. Language and imagination grow up together in a reciprocal tutelage.

What discursive symbolism—language in its literal use—does for our awareness of things about us and our own relation to them, the arts do for our awareness of subjective reality, feeling and emotion; they give form to inward experiences and thus make them conceivable. The only way we can really envisage vital movement, the stirring and growth and passage of emotion, and ultimately the whole direct sense of human life, is in artistic terms. A musical person thinks of emotions musically. They cannot be discursively talked about above a very general level. But they may nonetheless be known—objectively set forth, publicly known—and there is nothing necessarily confused or formless about emotions.

As soon as the natural forms of subjective experience are abstracted to the point of symbolic presentation, we can use those forms to imagine feeling and understand its nature. Self-knowledge, insight into all phases of life and mind, springs from artistic imagination. That is the cognitive value of the arts.

But their influence on human life goes deeper than the intellectual level. As language actually gives form to our sense experience, grouping our impressions around those things which have names, and fitting sensations to the qualities that have adjectival names, and so on, the arts we live with—our picture books and stories and the music we hear—actually form our emotive experience. Every generation has its styles of feeling. One age shudders and blushes and faints, another swaggers, still another is godlike in a universal indifference. These styles in actual emotion are not insincere. They are largely unconscious—determined by many social causes, but *shaped* by artists, usually popular artists of the screen, the jukebox, the shop-window, and the picture magazine. (That, rather than incitement to crime, is my objection to the comics.) Irwin Edman remarks in one of his books that our emotions are largely Shakespeare's poetry.

This influence of art on life gives us an indication of why a period of efflorescence in the arts is apt to lead a cultural advance: it formulates a new way of feeling, and that is the beginning of a cultural age. It suggests another matter for reflection, too—that a wide neglect of artistic education is a neglect in the education of feeling. Most people are so imbued with the idea that feeling is a formless, total organic excitement in men as in animals that the idea of educating feeling, developing its scope and quality, seems odd to them, if not absurd. It is really, I think, at the very heart of personal education.

There is one other function of the arts that benefits not so much the advance of culture as its stabilization—an influence on individual lives. This function is the converse and complement of the objectification of feeling, the driving force of creation in art: it is the education of vision that we receive in seeing, hearing, reading works of art—the development of the artist's eye, that assimilates ordinary sights (or sounds, motions, or events) to inward vision, and lends expressiveness and emotional import to the world.

Wherever art takes a motif from actuality—a flowering branch, a bit of landscape, a historic event, or a personal memory, any model or theme from life—it transforms it into a piece of imagination, and imbues its image with artistic vitality. The result is an impregnation of ordinary reality with the significance of created form. This is the subjectification of nature that makes reality itself a symbol of life and feeling.

The arts objectify subjective reality, and subjectify outward experience of nature. Art education is the education of feeling, and a society that neglects it gives itself up to formless emotion. Bad art is corruption of feeling. This is a large factor in the irrationalism which dictators and demagogues exploit.

PROBLEMS FOR WRITING AND DISCUSSION

1. Explain the terms in Langer's definition of art as "the practice of creating perceptible forms expressive of human feeling."
2. In what sense is a novel or a painting an "apparition"? Langer says that it is "as an appearance, that a work of art is good or bad . . . not as a comment on things beyond it in the world, or as a reminder of them." Does her statement help you differentiate between a novel and a history, between a painting and a photograph?
3. What distinction does Langer make between symptoms of feeling and symbols of feeling? Why is discursive symbolism inadequate to the expression of feeling?
4. Why does Langer believe that the forms of feeling are not "irrational"?
5. If art is not "practical," what "cognitive value" does it have? What is its tutorial value? How does it not only contribute to a cultural whole but actually "spearhead" its development?
6. What is the most serious consequence Langer foresees in a "wide neglect of artistic education"? Do Kristol (p. 529) and Mandel (p. 614) object to the jukebox and comic books for the same reason that Langer does? Why or why not?
7. Explain Langer's ideas on the educative function of the arts. How do these ideas explain the fact that the common people in Europe, as Mandel

and others point out, have much "better taste" than do their counterparts in America?

8. Langer says that a society which neglects the education of feeling "gives itself up to formless emotion." What, according to Mandel, happens to a people without an "aristocracy of feeling"?

9. Explain Langer's conclusion: "The arts objectify subjective reality, and subjectify outward experience of nature." Why does she say that "a new art or even a great and radically new style always bespeaks a young and vigorous mind . . ."? Kramer (p. 627) sees that today for the first time American artists confront the "outward experience of nature" (the raw, as yet unformulated, New York) "without the ghost of the dead guiding their hand. . . . For them those large, beautiful, all-embracing European systems of thought and feeling are simply not *there*. . . ." In the light of what Langer says, may the success of these artists be the *avant-garde* of a cultural rebirth in America? Explain.

10. "Bad art is the corruption of feeling," according to Langer. Compare what she says with what Kronenberger says (p. 573) of the "decadence" of American humor.

11. How would Langer explain the mass culture that Kristol sees as a threat to the stability of democracy? The "vulgarization of art is the surest symptom of ethnic decline," Langer asserts. Why in particular does she fear "formless emotion"? Do you see in America symptoms of "formless emotion"? Explain.

3. Religion

Roger Williams

MOSES COIT TYLER

> Moses Coit Tyler (*1835-1900*) taught English at the University of Michigan (*1867-81*) and American history at Cornell University (*1881-1900*). Although he published several biographical studies of prominent Americans, including one of Patrick Henry (*1887*), today he is chiefly remembered for his History of American Literature, 1607-1765 (*2 vols., 1878*) and The Literary History of the American Revolution, 1763-1783 (*2 vols., 1897*). Both works represent some of the earliest attempts at the scholarly study of American literature.

Roger Williams, never in anything addicted to concealments, has put himself without reserve into his writings. There he still remains. There if anywhere we may get well acquainted with him. Searching for him along the two thousand printed pages upon which he has stamped his own portrait, we seem to see a very human and fallible man, with a large head, a warm heart, a healthy body, an eloquent and imprudent tongue; not a symmetrical person, poised, cool, accurate, circumspect; a man very anxious to be genuine and to get at the truth, but impatient of slow methods, trusting gallantly to his own intuitions, easily deluded by his own hopes; an imaginative, sympathetic, affluent, impulsive man; an optimist; his master-passion benevolence; his mind clarifying itself slowly; never quite settled on all subjects in the universe; at almost every moment on the watch for some new idea about that time expected to heave in sight; never able by the ordinary means of intellectual stagnation to win for himself in his life-time the bastard glory of doc-

From A History of American Literature, 1607-1765, Vol. I, Putnam, 1878.

trinal consistency; professing many things by turn and nothing long, until at last, even in mid-life, he reached the moral altitude of being able to call himself only a Seeker—in which not ignoble creed he continued for the remainder of his days on earth.

It must be confessed that there is even yet in the frame of Roger Williams a singular vitality. While living in this world, it was his fate to be much talked about, as well as to disturb much the serenity of many excellent people; and the rumor of him still agitates and divides men. There are, in fact, some signs that his fame is now about to take out a new lease, and to build for itself a larger habitation. At any rate, the world, having at last nearly caught up with him, seems ready to vote—though with a peculiarly respectable minority in opposition—that Roger Williams was after all a great man, one of the true heroes, seers, world-movers, of these latter ages.

Perhaps one explanation of the pleasure which we take in now looking upon him, as he looms up among his contemporaries in New England, may be that the eye of the observer, rather fatigued by the monotony of so vast a throng of sages and saints, all quite immaculate, all equally prim and stiff in their Puritan starch and uniform, all equally automatic and freezing, finds a relief in the easy swing of this man's gait, the limberness of his personal movement, his escape from the paste-board properties, his spontaneity, his impetuosity, his indiscretions, his frank acknowledgments that he really had a few things yet to learn. Somehow, too, though he sorely vexed the souls of the judicious in his time, and evoked from them words of dreadful reprehension, the best of them loved him; for indeed this headstrong, measureless man, with his flashes of Welsh fire, was in the grain of him a noble fellow; "a man," as Edward Winslow said, "lovely in his carriage." Evidently he was of a hearty and sociable turn, and had the gift of friendship. Some of the choicest spirits of that age were knit to him in a brotherly way, particularly the two Winthrops, John Milton, and Sir Henry Vane. Writing, in the winter of 1660, to the younger Winthrop, Roger Williams says: "Your loving lines in this cold, dead season were as a cup of your Connecticut cider, which we are glad to hear abounds with you, or of that western metheglin which you and I have drunk at Bristol together." Here, indeed, was an early New-Englander that one could still endure to have an hour with, particularly at Bristol; in truth, a clubable person; a man whose dignity would not have petrified us, nor his saintliness have given us a chill.

From his early manhood even down to his late old age, Roger Williams stands in New England a mighty and benignant form, always pleading for some magnanimous idea, some tender charity, the rectification of some wrong, the exercise of some sort of forbearance toward men's bodies or souls. It was one of his vexatious peculiarities, that he could do nothing by halves—even in logic. Having established his major and his minor premises, he utterly lacked the accommodating judgment which would have enabled him to stop there and go no further whenever it seemed that the concluding member of his syllogism was likely to annoy the brethren. To this frailty in his organization is due the fact that he often seemed to his contemporaries an impracticable person, presumptuous, turbulent, even seditious. This it was that tainted somewhat the pleasantness of his relations with the colony of Massachusetts during his residence in it. For example, he had taken orders in the established church of England, but had subsequently come to the conclusion that an established church was necessarily a corrupt organization. He acted logically. He went out of it. He would hold no fellowship with it, even remotely or by implication. He became an uncompromising Separatist. Furthermore, on arriving in New England, the same uncomfortable propensity was put into action, by the spectacle of the white men helping themselves freely to the lands of the red men, and doing so on pretence of certain titles derived from a white king on the other side of the Atlantic. He was unable to see that even so great a monarch as the king of England could give away what did not belong to him. To Roger Williams it appeared that these lands actually belonged to the red men who lived on them; hence, that the white men's titles to them ought to come from the red men, and to be the result of a genuine and fair bargain with the red men. Thus, he became an assailant of the validity, in that particular, of the New England charters. It happened, moreover, that his views in both these directions constituted offences, just then, for the colony of Massachusetts, extremely inopportune and inconvenient. But these were not his only offences. Roger Williams also held that it was a shocking thing—one of the abominations of the age—for men who did not even pretend to have religion in their hearts, to be muttering publicly the words of religion with their mouths; and that such persons ought not to be called on to perform any acts of worship, even the taking of an oath. Finally, he held another doctrine—at that time and in that place sadly eccentric and disgusting—that the power of the civil magistrate "extends only to the bodies and goods and outward state of men," and not at all to their inward state, their consciences, their opinions. For these four crimes, particularly mentioned by Governor Haynes in pronouncing sentence upon him, Massachusetts deemed it unsafe to permit such a nefarious being as Roger Williams to abide anywhere within her borders.

With respect to the sympathy of Roger Williams with the Indians, it concerns us, at present, to note that it did not exhaust itself in the invention of a legal opinion on their behalf: throughout his whole life, early and late, he put himself to much downright toil and self-denial for their benefit, both in body and in soul. He and John Eliot had come to New England in the same year, 1631; but at least a dozen years before John Eliot had entered upon his apostolic labors among the Indians, Roger Williams had lodged "with them in their filthy, smoky holes . . . to gain their tongue," and had preached to them in it. "My soul's desire," he said, "was to do the natives good." Later, he knew from his own experience, that it was possible for the English to live at peace with the Indians; when, however, that peace was broken, though he wished the English to acquit themselves manfully and successfully, he evermore stood between them and their vanquished foes, with words of compassion. In 1637, amid the exasperation caused by the Pequot war, the voice of Roger Williams was heard imploring the victors to spare. "I much rejoice," he writes to the governor of

Massachusetts, "that . . . some of the chiefs at Connecticut, . . . are almost adverse from killing women and children. Mercy outshines all the works and attributes of Him who is the Father of Mercies." In another letter he expresses the hope that all Christians who receive as slaves the surviving Pequots, may so treat them "as to make mercy eminent." In still another letter he invokes mercy upon the miserable Pequots, "since the Most High delights in mercy, and great revenge hath been already taken." This, to the end of his life, was his one cry in the midst of all storms of popular wrath and revenge.

And the benignity of Roger Williams was large enough to go out toward other people than the Indians. His letters, public and private, are a proof that the sight of any creature in trouble, was enough to stir his heart and his hand for quick relief. His best clients appear to have been those who had no other advocate, and who could pay no fees: poor people; sick ones; wanderers; "the dead, the widows, and the fatherless;" and, especially, all who had been turned adrift for the crime of having an independent thought. Nay, his generosity threw its arms not only around those who were then actually unfortunate, but even around those who might ever become so; and for them, too, he tried to make tender provision. In 1662, the people of Providence resolved to divide among themselves the lands that still remained common. When Roger Williams heard of this, he wrote a warm-hearted and moving appeal to them, as his "loving friends and neighbors," beseeching them that as he first gave to them all the lands, so they would permit some to remain unappropriated, as a possession in reserve for such homeless persons as, driven from any country for conscience' sake, might thereafter flee to them for refuge: "I earnestly pray the town to lay to heart, as ever they look for a blessing from God on the town, on your families, your corn and cattle, and your children after you, . . . that after you have got over the black brook of some soul-bondage yourselves, you tear not down the bridge after you, by leaving no small pittance for distressed souls that may come after you."

PROBLEMS FOR WRITING AND DISCUSSION

1. How does Tyler's use of irony in listing Roger Williams' "offenses" present the prevailing views of the Massachusetts colony simultaneously with those of Roger Williams?

2. What were the "offenses" and "crimes" of Roger Williams? What principle of personal or public integrity was at the root of each?

3. What divine principle in practical measures with the Indians did he invoke against the "storms of popular wrath and revenge"?

4. How did he try to provide in Providence for the distress of those who had been "turned adrift" for "conscience' sake"? How was his example prophetic of provisions in the Bill of Rights insuring freedom of speech and worship to all comers?

5. What, according to Mandel (p. 614), is the price a democracy pays for allowing freedom of conscience? From what you know of Roger Williams' experience with the Massachusetts colony and of the Salem trials of "witches," would you say the price is worth paying? What would Novak (p. 690) say?

6. What contemporary issues still depend upon the separatist principle on which Roger Williams acted?

Religion in Virginia

THOMAS JEFFERSON

[*For biographical material, see p. 309*]

The legitimate powers of government extend to such acts only as are injurious to others. But it does me no injury for my neighbor to say there are twenty gods, or no God. It neither picks my pocket nor breaks my leg. If it be said, his testimony in a court of justice cannot be relied on, reject it then, and be the stigma on him. Constraint may make him worse by making him a hypocrite, but it will never make him a truer man. It may fix him obstinately in his errors, but will not cure them. Reason and free inquiry are the only effectual agents against error. Give a loose to them, they will support the true religion by bringing every false one to their tribunal, to the test of their investigation. They are the natural enemies of error, and of error only. Had not the Roman government permitted free inquiry, Christianity could never have been introduced. Had not free inquiry been indulged at the era of the Reformation, the corruptions of Christianity could not have been purged away. If it be restrained now, the present corruptions will be protected, and new ones encouraged. Was the government to prescribe to us our medicine and diet, our bodies would be in such keeping as our souls are now. Thus in France the emetic was once forbidden as a medicine, the potato as an article of food. Government is just as infallible, too, when it fixes systems in physics. Galileo was sent to the Inquisition for affirming that the earth was a sphere; the government had declared it to be as flat as a trencher, and Galileo was obliged to abjure his error. This error, however, at length prevailed, the earth became a globe, and Descartes declared it was whirled

From Notes on Virginia *(1784).*

round its axis by a vortex. The government in which he lived was wise enough to see that this was no question of civil jurisdiction, or we should all have been involved by authority in vortices. In fact, the vortices have been exploded, and the Newtonian principle of gravitation is now more firmly established, on the basis of reason, than it would be were the government to step in, and to make it an article of necessary faith. Reason and experiment have been indulged, and error has fled before them. It is error alone which needs the support of government. Truth can stand by itself. Subject opinion to coercion: whom will you make your inquisitors? Fallible men; men governed by bad passions, by private as well as public reasons. And why subject it to coercion? To produce uniformity. But is uniformity of opinion desirable? No more than of face and stature. Introduce the bed of Procrustes then, and as there is danger that the large men may beat the small, make us all of a size, by lopping the former and stretching the latter. Difference of opinion is advantageous in religion. The several sects perform the office of a *censor morum* over such other. Is uniformity attainable? Millions of innocent men, women, and children, since the introduction of Christianity, have been burnt, tortured, fined, imprisoned; yet we have not advanced one inch towards uniformity. What has been the effect of coercion? To make one half the world fools, and the other half hypocrites. To support roguery and error all over the earth. Let us reflect that it is inhabited by a thousand millions of people. That these profess probably a thousand different systems of religion. That ours is but one of that thousand. That if there be but one right, and ours that one, we should wish to see the nine hundred and ninety-nine wandering sects gathered into the fold of truth. But against such a majority we cannot effect this by force. Reason and persuasion are the only practicable instruments. To make way for these, free inquiry must be indulged; and how can we wish others to indulge it while we refuse it ourselves. But every State, says an inquisitor, has established some religion. No two, say I, have established the same. Is this a proof of the infallibility of establishments? Our sister States of Pennsylvania and New York, however, have long subsisted without any establishment at all. The experiment was new and doubtful when they made it. It has answered beyond conception. They flourish infinitely. Religion is well supported; of various kinds, indeed, but all good enough; all sufficient to preserve peace and order; or if a sect arises, whose tenets would subvert morals, good sense has fair play, and reasons and laughs it out of doors, without suffering the State to be troubled with it. They do not hang more malefactors than we do. They are not more disturbed with religious dissensions. On the contrary, their harmony is unparalleled, and can be ascribed to nothing but their unbounded tolerance, because there is no other circumstance in which they differ from every nation on earth. They have made the happy discovery, that the way to silence religious disputes, is to take no notice of them. Let us too give this experiment fair play, and get rid, while we may, of those tyrannical laws. It is true, we are as yet secured against them by the spirit of the times. I doubt whether the people of this country would suffer an execution for heresy, or a three years' imprisonment for not comprehending the mysteries of the Trinity. But is the spirit of the people an infallible, a permanent reliance? Is it government? Is this the kind of protection we receive in return for the rights we give up? Besides, the spirit of the times may alter, will alter. Our rulers will become corrupt, our people careless. A single zealot may commence persecutor, and better men be his victims. It can never be too often repeated, that the time for fixing every essential right on a legal basis is while our rulers are honest, and ourselves united. From the conclusion of this war we shall be going down hill. It will not then be necessary to resort every moment to the people for support. They will be forgotten, therefore, and their rights disregarded. They will forget themselves, but in the sole faculty of making money, and will never think of uniting to effect a due respect for their rights. The shackles, therefore, which shall not be knocked off at the conclusion of this war, will remain on us long, will be made heavier and heavier, till our rights shall revive or expire in a convulsion.

PROBLEMS FOR WRITING AND DISCUSSION

1. What, according to Jefferson, are "the only effectual agents against error"? What are the only "legitimate powers of government"?

2. What does Jefferson see as the consequence of "constraint" and of suppression of free inquiry? Do Jefferson's principles and arguments persist today in controversies over the relation of church and state and over rights of minorities to hold and express ideologies at variance with the American ideology? Of what attempts to abridge these rights or to defame those holding "un-American" views do you know? What effects have these attempts had?

3. Jefferson argues for free inquiry in religious matters by analogy with the mergence of truth in science. In what way does irony contribute to the effectiveness of his argument? Compare his premises with those of Franklin (p. 257) and Oppenheimer (p. 264).

4. Jefferson sees that of a thousand different systems of religion "ours is but one." Is Jefferson, then, a relativist? Does he consider the truth of religion to be as absolute as the "natural law" of gravitation? Explain.

5. Compare Jefferson's assertion that "It is error alone which needs the support of government" with Kristol's assertion (p. 529) that the right to lie is the exclusive property of despotisms.

6. Although Jefferson declares, "Truth can stand by itself," what does he fear from fallible men "governed by bad passions"? Is his fear comparable to Cooper's (p. 399)? To Roger Williams' (p. 647)?

7. Defend or attack Jefferson's assumptions in the following: (1) "Difference of opinion is advantageous in religion"; (2) ". . . the way to silence religious disputes is to take no notice of them."

8. Jefferson asks his readers: "whom will you make your inquisitors?" Does he rely on the common man? On the majority? What does he foresee as the aftermath of the war? To what extent has his prophecy come true? What guarantee against the probabilities of the future does he desire? Would you call Jefferson an idealist or a practical politician? How would Kristol and E. B. White (p. 449) regard Jefferson's insistence that "every essential right" be fixed "on a legal basis"?

The Contemporary Upswing in Religion
WILL HERBERG

> *Will Herberg (1908-   ) has written numerous articles on religion in contemporary America. Formerly the educational director for the International Ladies Garment Workers Union, he is now Graduate Professor of Judaic Studies and Social Philosophy at Drew University. Protestant-Catholic-Jew, perhaps his best-known book, is now in its second edition (1955, 1960). Reinhold Niebuhr has said that "it throws as much light on American society as a whole as it does on the peculiarly religious aspects of American life."*

I

No one who attempts to see the contemporary religious situation in the United States in perspective can fail to be struck by the extraordinary pervasiveness of religious identification among present-day Americans. Almost everybody in the United States today locates himself in one or another of the three great religious communities. Asked to identify themselves in terms of religious "preference," 95 per cent of the American people, according to a recent public opinion survey, declared themselves to be either Protestants, Catholics, or Jews (68 per cent Protestants, 23 per cent Catholics, 4 per cent Jews); only 5 per cent admitted to no "preference." Some differences, one or two perhaps of real significance, are indicated when these figures are broken down according to race, age, sex, education, occupation, income, region, and degree of urbanization; but, by and

---

From "*The Contemporary Upswing in Religion*" from Protestant-Catholic-Jew: An Essay in American Religious Sociology *by Will Herberg. Copyright © 1955 by Will Herberg. Reprinted by permission of Doubleday & Company, Inc.*

large, the conclusion seems to be that virtually the entire body of the American people, in every part of the country and in every section of society, regard themselves as belonging to some religious community. The results of the survey are fully borne out by the reports of informed observers of the American scene.

Such information as that which this survey provides is unfortunately not available for earlier times, and so direct comparison is impossible. But it seems safe to assume that these figures, reflecting the situation in the early 1950s, represent an all-time high in religious identification. Through the nineteenth century and well into the twentieth America knew the militant secularist, the atheist or "free-thinker," as a familiar figure in cultural life, along with considerably larger numbers of "agnostics" who would have nothing to do with churches and refused to identify themselves religiously. These still exist, of course, but their ranks are dwindling and they are becoming more and more inconspicuous, taking the American people as a whole. The "village atheist" is a vanishing figure; Clarence Darrow and Brann the Iconoclast, who once commanded large and excited audiences, have left no successors. Indeed, their kind of anti-religion is virtually meaningless to most Americans today, who simply cannot understand how one can be "against religion" and for whom some sort of religious identification is more or less a matter of course. This was not always the case; that it is the case today there can be no reasonable doubt. The pervasiveness of religious identification may safely be put down as a significant feature of the America that has emerged in the past quarter of a century.

The figures for church membership tell the same story but in greater detail. Religious statistics in this country are notoriously inaccurate, but the trend is so well marked that it overrides all margins of error. In the quarter of a century between 1926 and 1950 the population of continental United States increased 28.6 per cent; membership of religious bodies increased 59.8 per cent: in other words, church membership grew more than twice as fast as population. Protestants increased 63.7 per cent, Catholics 53.9 per cent, Jews 22.5 per cent. Among Protestants, however, the increase varied considerably as between denominations: Baptist increase was well over 100 per cent, some "holiness" sects grew even more rapidly, while the figure for the Episcopal Church was only 36.7 per cent, for the Methodist Church 32.2 per cent, for the Northern Presbyterians 22.4 per cent, and for the Congregationalists 21.1 per cent. In general, it may be said that "practically all major types of American religion have staged what is vulgarly called a 'comeback'."

In 1950 total church membership was reckoned at 85,319,000, or about 57 per cent of the total population. In 1953 it was recorded as 94,842,000; the percentage now was 59.5, marking an all-time high in the nation's history. Indeed, all available information tends to show that the proportion of the American people religiously affiliated as church members has been consistently growing from the early days of the republic. . . .

II

That there has in recent years been an upswing of religion in the United States can hardly be doubted; the evidence is diverse, converging, and unequivocal beyond all possibilities of error. It is another matter, however, when we come to assess the factors that have made, and are making, for this notable shift in the social attitudes and cultural climate of our time. When we try to isolate these factors or reveal their mode of operation, we begin to sense the inadequacy of all sociological "explanation" of phenomena that in their very nature transcend the sociological. Nevertheless, it seems to me that certain significant things may be said about the present religious situation which might contribute to an understanding of the current turn to religion in America.

We may proceed with our analysis on various levels. Most generally and comprehensively, the rise in religious identification, membership, and attendance would seem to be closely related to the change in social structure of the American community we have described in earlier chapters. America, it was there pointed out, has changed from the "land of immigrants," with its thriving ethnic groups, to the "triple melting pot," in which people tend more and more to identify and locate themselves socially in terms of three great sub-communities—Protestant, Catholic, Jewish—defined in religious terms. To find a place in American society increasingly means to place oneself in one or another of these religious communities. And although this process of self-identification and social location is not in itself intrinsically religious, the mere fact that in order to be "something" one must be either a Protestant, a Catholic, or a Jew means that one begins to think of oneself as religiously identified and affiliated. *Naming* oneself a Protestant, a Catholic, or a Jew carries with it a distinctive attitude to "one's" church, an attitude that is definitely favorable. Since one "is" a Protestant, a Catholic, or a Jew, and recognizes oneself as such, one tends to think of oneself as somehow part of a church and involved in its activities and concerns. Whether one actually joins or not, the inclination is to think of oneself as a member: hence the significant fact that many more people report themselves as members of churches than are on church rolls. And increasingly one does actually become a member and join in the activities of the church; increasingly too the children are sent to church and church school—for many reasons, not least, however, because "the church supplies a place where children come to learn what they are." There does not seem to be any real question that the restructuring of American society that emerges with the third generation has been a major factor in the turn to religion so characteristic of our time.

Another factor of prime sociological importance has worked toward the same end, and that is the basic change in character structure that seems to be under way among certain sections of the American people. The reference here is to the shift from inner-direction to other-direction, which David Riesman has analyzed and documented so impressively. Riesman, it will be recalled, distinguishes three types of character structure—tradition-directed, inner-directed, and other-directed—which he finds predominating at different times in different societies yet also entering in different degrees into contemporary American life. Tradition-direction, in which each generation receives from its predecessor and internalizes for itself a fairly fixed pattern of folkways, is characteristic of primitive and stable peasant societies; it has never really been part of the ongoing life of a dynamic society such as ours, although the collapse of tradition-direction upon the peasant immigrant's first encounter with the New World has had repercussions into our own time. American society has hitherto been, and still is, predominantly inner-directed; each succeeding generation internalizes not a traditional pattern of folkways but a set of "goals" or "principles," to which the individual is kept true by a powerful inner drive. Borrowing a figure from Gardner Murphy, Riesman pictures the inner-directed man as operating with a kind of built-in gyroscope which holds him steadily, sometimes ruthlessly, to his course, driving ahead for the fulfillment of his purposes. The inner-directed man is work-conscious, intent upon achievement, not afraid to stand on his own feet and if necessary against the crowd, interested in "results" not in "personalities." It is the inner-directed man who has been characteristic of American life and achievement so far.

Lately, however, for reasons that are still obscure though we are beginning to get some inkling of them, there has been emerging on certain levels another character type, described as other-directed. Instead of possessing a built-in gyroscope to keep him true to his course, the other-directed man operates with a kind of built-in radar apparatus which is ceaselessly at work receiving signals from the person's "peer group" and adjusting him to the situation indicated by these signals. The other-directed man is a man who is concerned with adjustment rather than with achievement; he is personality-conscious rather than work-conscious, bland, tolerant, co-operative, "civilized"—but dreadfully afraid of being too "different," of getting too much out of line with his "peer group." Indeed, the greatest horror of the other-directed man, that which renders him so acutely uncomfortable, is to feel "unadjusted" and "unsociable" ("antisocial"); whereas the inner-directed man, as we have seen, is always ready to stand up against his environment and indeed seems to get a kind of grim satisfaction out of doing so. The "morality" of the inner-directed type becomes "morale" for the other-directed; "character" becomes "personality"; moral indignation and intolerance give way to a kind of all-embracing tolerance—tolerance of everything and everybody except the "unadjusted" and the "antisocial." The operative law of life of the other-directed man is conformity and adjustment; the built-in radar that characterizes other-direction sees to it that such adjustment to a fluctuating environment is generally achieved quite unconsciously and is therefore invested with the emotional power of unconscious motivation.

In America today, though inner-direction remains dominant, other-direction has already become prevalent in the new suburban middle-class society consisting of professionals and junior executives, and seems bound to spread upward and downward in the social hierarchy. The emergence of this type, and its growing prominence in the community, bring with it a number of far-reaching consequences for the social and cultural life of our time.

In particular, it is not difficult to see the current turn to religion and the church as, in part at least, a reflection of the growing other-directedness of our middle-class culture. The people in the suburbs want to feel psychologically secure, adjusted, at home in their environment; the very character structure that makes this so urgent a necessity for them also operates to meet the need. Being religious and joining a church is, under contemporary American conditions, a fundamental way of "adjusting" and "belonging"; through the built-in radar apparatus of other-direction it becomes almost automatic as an obvious social requirement, like entertaining or culture. The vogue of Van Gogh and Renoir reproductions in the suburban home and the rising church affiliation of the suburban community may not be totally unconnected; both may, without disparagement, be interpreted, in part at least, as the consequence of the craving for adjustment and conformity involved in other-direction. The right kind of art reproductions testify to one's being adjusted to the culture of one's "peer-group"; belonging to the church is experienced as the most satisfactory form of social "belonging." The trend toward religious identification and church affiliation may thus to an extent be a reflection of the growing need for conformity and sociability that the drift to other-direction brings with it.

The operations of other-direction fall in rather neatly with the over-all effects of the restructuring of American society in terms of religious community. To identify and locate oneself in the social context is a requirement under all conditions; it becomes particularly pressing and urgent under conditions of other-direction, since other-direction craves conformity and adjustment as a veritable necessity of life. On the other hand, the other-directed need for "belonging" finds its most direct and appropriate expression in present-day America in identifying oneself with a religious community and joining a church. Whether we approach it from one direction or the other the result seems to be the same: a marked trend toward religious identification and church affiliation.

These more obviously sociological factors ought not, however, to obscure other, perhaps less definable, forces operating at other levels of human life. The contemporary crisis of Western civilization, which has brought a sense of total insecurity to men everywhere, is surely one of the most significant of these. The utter predicament of human existence is no longer simply a philosophical or theological proposition; it is the most patent of everyday facts. The hydrogen bomb, on which our survival depends, yet which threatens us with destruction, is the sinister symbol of our plight. Confronted with the demonic threat of Communist totalitarianism, we are driven to look beyond the routine ideas and attitudes that may have served in easier times. On every side insecurity assails us, and yet security is becoming more and more the urgent need of our time.

In this situation of pervasive crisis and danger, religion appeals to many as "synonymous with peace," indeed as offering the "best hope of peace in the world today"—"peace of mind" for the individual amid the anxieties and confusions of contemporary existence, peace for the nation in the life-and-death struggle with Communism. Particularly in this latter conflict religion commends itself as our greatest resource and most powerful "secret weapon." In the week in which I write this three outstanding clerical leaders of the three religious communities of the nation made eloquent pleas for religion on this ground: one called religion the "shield of the nation"; the other proclaimed it as "more powerful than the H-bomb"; the third recommended it as "America's strongest weapon against atheistic Communism." Even erstwhile secularists are beginning to see things in a new light; the *Zeitgeist* has not been without effect among them, nor the urgencies of the present world situation. They are beginning to show a growing appreciation of the social utility of religion for Western culture, especially in fighting Communism. Quite a few old-time secularists are no longer so sure that religion is on its way out; nor for that matter are they so sure that they would be happy to see religion go, for when religion goes (many secularists now ruefully admit), it is only too often replaced not by "reason" and "enlightenment" but by one or another of the wild superstitions and demonic cults that the modern age has spawned. Religion has suddenly emerged as a major power in the "hundred years of Cold War" that appears to confront mankind.

On another, more personal, or rather more domestic, level, too, religion has been found to serve the need for security. On this level the turn to religion is to be linked, many think, with the sensational reversal of long-time population trends and the sudden rise of birth rates among college graduates and professional people in the United States. Since 1946 these rates have been increasing every year, and in 1954 married graduates of the class of 1944, ten years out of college, already averaged more children than the class of 1921 when it had been out twenty-five years in 1946, the year the study we are citing was initiated. This demographical fact would seem to confirm the impression many observers have had in recent years that, amid the mounting insecurities of our time, increasing numbers of younger people are turning to the security to be found in the enduring, elemental ways and institutions of mankind; in the family, they feel, they can find the permanence and stability, the meaning and value they crave amid a world falling into chaos. Religion, like the family, is one of the enduring, elemental institutions of mankind; indeed, the two have been closely linked from the very earliest times. The search for meaning and security in what is basic and unchanging, rather than in the fluctuating fortunes of social or political activity, is one of the major factors in the upswing of religion among the American people today.

It is perhaps not without significance that the Oak Ridge community in Tennessee, consisting largely of atomic scientists and technicians with their families, has shown little interest in the political status of the community but an intense concern for building religious institutions. Early in 1953 the Oak Ridgers, by a big majority, turned down a proposal for local autonomy and voted to let the AEC continue operation of their municipal services. But, as the report points out, that was not because they were apathetic or regarded themselves as transients at Oak Ridge; rather it was because they saw the "key" of their family and community development in the development of their churches. The first meeting to establish a church was held in 1943, within a few weeks after the launching of the Oak Ridge project; in 1953, ten years later, Oak Ridge, with a population of 31,000, had thirty-seven different congregations holding regular services and performing the multiform functions of the American church. Building activity was still going on, in many cases church members performing part of the work with their own hands. For Oak Ridge, though a prosperous community, had no rich people to endow churches or make huge contributions; everything had to be done by the people themselves. "While residents here feel that Oak Ridge still has some years to go before it can completely cut its municipal ties with the federal government," the report concludes, "most of them agree that in the religious growth here, the community's roots are very definitely showing." In the Oak Ridge scheme of priorities religion and the church obviously rank at the top, along with the home and the school. It is surely of considerable import that this age-old trinity of American life—the home, the church, and the school—should find so impressive a rebirth in this most modern of communities of the atomic age.

Personal need enters into the present religious situation in still another way. Confronted with the depersonalizing pressures of contemporary life, modern man experiences a profound exigency to preserve some remnant of personality and inwardness against the erosions of a mass culture. Increasingly, he turns to religion to provide him an inexpugnable citadel for the self in a world in which personal authenticity is threatened on every side; indeed, the quest for personal authenticity is itself substantially a religious quest. Reflecting, as it does, the crisis of our time, it also points to its deeper meaning. For ultimately, the crisis of our time is a crisis of faith. The secular faiths of our culture have ignominiously collapsed under the shattering impact of the events of our time. Many of the "truths" by which "modern-minded" men lived in earlier decades have revealed themselves to be little more than vain and fatuous illusions. We can no longer look to science, to "progress," to economics, or to politics for salvation; we recognize that these things have their value, but we also know that they are not gods bringing redemption from the confusions and perils of existence. An age intoxicated with utopian dreams about the boundless possibilities of "scientific progress" and "social reconstruction" has been succeeded by an age more sober, more realistic—some would say too much so. But one cannot live by sober, limited, pragmatic programs for restricted ends; these soon lose whatever meaning they have unless they are embedded in a transcendent, actuality-defying vision. Man needs faith, a total, all-embracing faith, for living. The faiths by which men live in a secular age "base the meaning of existence upon some assumed stability of human virtue or reason [or power], some pattern of history or societal security"; when these are swept away by the great upheavals of history, the way is opened for a better appreciation of the power and relevance of the historic faiths. How far turning to these faiths at a time of crisis represents "escapism" in the bad sense of the term, and how far it reflects a deeper searching for the realities of existence, no one can tell for another, perhaps not even for himself; we may safely assume that something of each is present, compounded with the other. But that it is not simply irresponsibility or a "failure of nerve," that it may indeed help to nerve one for greater endurance and unyielding resistance to evil and unreason, is surely sufficiently attested by the events of our time. At its deepest level the turn to religion we are witnessing owes much of its force to the search for a new and more viable "philosophy" of existence amid the spiritual chaos of our age.

PROBLEMS FOR WRITING AND DISCUSSION

1. Does Herberg take comfort from the percentages yielded by a statistical survey of religious congregations? Why or why not?

2. Is the desire to identify with a group a religious motive or an instance of what Novak (p. 690) calls the "secular faith"? To what extent may identification with religious groups reflect simply the response of men to questionaires for purposes of gaining employment, admission to college or to organizations, etc.—a quick way to gain "respectability"?

3. Herberg borrows Riesman's terms (p. 488) "inner-directed" and "other-directed." What do they mean and how do they help explain the "upswing in religion"? What other essays in this book contribute to an understanding of these terms and of the change they signify? What in your own experience shows the shift in concern from morality to morale, from character to personality, from rugged individualism to being well-adjusted?

4. Herberg says that an adjustment made by "built-in radar" is "invested with the emotional power of unconscious motivation," suggestive of the conditioned responses of animals—the "formless emotion" Langer (p. 634) calls "irrational"—the breeding ground of totalitarianism in the mass-man. Do you believe with the secularists to whom Herberg refers that when religion goes "it is only too often replaced not by 'reason' and 'enlightenment' but by one or another of the wild superstitious and demonic cults that the modern age has spawned"? *Is* religion the opiate of the masses? Does it seem significant that the largest percentage gains in church membership were made by the evangelical Protestant sects?

5. Herberg cites the threat of mass destruction as another reason for the increasing interest in religion. Compare his evaluation of this motive with that of Meserve (p. 669).

6. Is the supposed near-disappearance of the atheist and the agnostic from the American scene a good sign in the light of what Jefferson (p. 653) has to say about "freedom of inquiry"?

7. How do any of the essays in the Science Section (Part II) help explain why "in the Oak Ridge scheme of priorities religion and the church obviously rank at the top, along with the home and the school"? What would other writers on religion in this section make of the situation at Oak Ridge?

8. Herberg says "we can no longer look to science . . . for salvation." Would Stewart (p. 287) subscribe to this view? Would Oppenheimer (p. 264)?

9. Both Herberg and Riesman say that we have lost some of our utopianism. How do they differ in their evaluation of this loss?

10. Herberg insists that "many of the 'truths' by which 'modern-minded' men lived in earlier decades have revealed themselves to be little more than vain and fatuous illusions." What "truths" does he have in mind? Would Herberg—would you—include the ideals in the Declaration of Independence among those "vain and fatuous illusions"?

11. Are the recent religious changes Herberg sees in America reflected in the changes within the family that Mead (p. 24) describes? Herberg calls "the home, the church, and the school" the "age-old trinity of American life," implying by the term *trinity* that this tangible threesome has been an object of worship. Does this remark throw light on the paradoxical American veneration for "the parent, the teacher, and the clergyman" that Scott (p. 598) notes?

12. What hope does Herberg see for the future of religion in America? On what does he base his hope? Is religion the "best hope of peace in the world today"? What kind of "peace" does Niebuhr (p. 705) believe that religion will supply?

13. Herberg says that men turn to religion as a "citadel" when their "personal authenticity is threatened on every side." Does Novak regard religion as a "citadel" in a world that threatens "personal authenticity?" Does Meserve?

14. What writers in other Sections of this book have called, like Herberg, for a "transcendent, actuality-defying vision"? Which vision do you find the best restorative for the failure of nerve: the statesman's, the scientist's, the educator's, the artist's, or the theologian's?

The New Piety

HARRY C. MESERVE

Harry C. Meserve (1914-   ) is a Unitarian minister and Program Director for the Academy of Religion and Mental Health in New York. He has published articles in the Christian Register, The Atlantic Monthly, *and other periodicals. Many of his articles have been collected in* No Peace of Mind (1958).

I

Is there a revival of religion in America today? Many signs suggest it. Books dealing with frankly religious themes appear high on the best-seller lists. Movies on Biblical and religious subjects are popular box-office attractions. Gospel songs sung by crooners and swing quartets can frequently be heard on radio and television. Popular mass-circulation magazines seem to include articles on religion more frequently than they used to. Bishop Sheen, Billy Graham, and Norman Vincent Peale each number their adherents and admirers in the thousands if not the millions.

Church membership and attendance are definitely up in almost all churches. Skepticism is no longer smart. Faith is fashionable. Each Saturday night the newspapers announce that the President and Mrs. Eisenhower plan to attend church on Sunday. Each Monday morning the papers announce that they did in fact do so. The Assembly of the World Council of Churches at Evanston, Illinois, last summer received more extended publicity coverage than any other religious event in the history of our country. Even Jane Russell, not hitherto noted as a theologian, recently announced that she

From No Peace of Mind © *1955, 1958, by Harry C. Meserve. Reprinted by permission of Harcourt, Brace & World, Inc., and Constable & Company, Ltd.*

had found God to be "a livin' doll." Cabinet meetings open with prayer. We pledge allegiance to the flag as "one nation under God" where before we were merely "one nation indivisible." A new stamp issue proclaims what our coinage has traditionally proclaimed: "In God we trust." These and many other signs point toward some kind of stirring of renewed interest in religion.

All in all, it is certainly true that religion is receiving a better press today and far more general attention and respect than it has had in many years.

But there is a real question as to what kind of religion is being revived in the new piety. Is it a discovery of a deep ethical faith and of the resources of courage and strength which can enable us to meet the severe challenges of this time? Or is it a more or less superficial interest in certain outward signs and gestures without the deep inward changes of mind and spirit which always mark a revival of genuine religion?

The new piety takes various forms. One of them is the peace of mind, peace of soul variety. Anxiety is one of the major characteristics of our time. Millions of people have left behind the "faith of our fathers" and have found little or nothing to put in its place. These are the spiritually displaced persons of the modern world. They are aware of a deep anxiety about their own meaning as persons and about the meaning of life as a whole. They are aware of a great need for reassurance and for self-confidence.

There can be no doubt whatsoever that their anxiety is real and justified and that their need and hunger are sincere. But what does the new piety of peace of mind and soul offer them? It says in effect: "Everything is really all right. It is you who are out of tune with the Infinite. If you can just get right with God, cooperate with Him, get Him on your side, so to speak, then the things you want and have striven for so far with such disappointment can be yours. Your anxieties will be relieved. Your frustrations will be removed and you will be on the way to success and happiness."

In this form of the new piety, religion appears as a means to an end. It justifies itself because it is useful to us in getting the things that we want and adjusting ourselves to the world. It helps us to "stop worrying and start living" or to get that promotion or to smooth out that unpleasant situation in our personal relationships.

All these things are undoubtedly good and necessary. But the interpretation of religion as primarily a means to getting the things that we want belongs in the realm of magic. Primitive religions do make this emphasis. But the more mature and highly developed religions have insisted for centuries that the best and truest experiences of religion come when a person has given up asking "What do I require of God?" and learned to ask humbly "What does God require of me?"

Peace of mind, self-confidence, courage, strength, and faith are all precious spiritual gifts. All of us want and need more of them than we have. But if there is one consistent lesson of our historic religious tradition, both in Judaism and in Christianity, it is that these gifts come as by-products of our sincere and humble commitment to the task of doing justly, loving mercy, and walking humbly with our God.

It is a strange and persistent paradox of man's religious experience that his peace of mind and his courage and strength lie on the other side of his faithful commitment to purposes and ends larger and more durable than his personal destiny and so worthy of his loyalty that he is able to give himself to them come what may. Jesus stated this paradox in two arresting passages: "Come unto me all ye that labor and are heavy-laden, and I will give you rest. Take my yoke upon you, and learn of me." That is to say, take up something of my labors; and in them, mysteriously you will find the rest which you could not find elsewhere. Again, in even more familiar words: "Whoever will save his life shall lose it and whoever will lose his life, for my sake, shall find it."

The new piety of peace of mind and soul, in spite of the fact that it is helping many people to adjust themselves better to life and to the world as it is, must also come to terms with that aspect of religion which is concerned with man's efforts to transform himself and the world in the direction of what ought to be.

A gospel of smooth adjustment to the world as it is, with all its mediocrity and evil, leaves out that austere side of religious experience in which we see ourselves as pilgrims and pioneers, the creators of the colony of heaven in the wilderness of the world that is. The religious person at his best is never wholly content with himself and at peace with the world, for he knows how far he falls short of what he ought to be and can be. There is a positive and healthy tension between what is and what ought to be that forbids complacency and incites to action. We are admonished by St. Paul not to be conformed to this world, but to be transformed by the renewing of our minds that we may prove what is the good and acceptable and perfect will of God.

In so far as the new piety of peace of mind and soul permits us to forget or ignore the transforming task of religion, it is failing to offer a revival of individual conscience and ethical social concern. Remove these elements from religion and what is left is a palliative, a pain-killer, but not a healer and a restorer of courage and strength. The stern lesson of religion though the ages is: no peace of mind without adventurous thought and faith; no comfort without bold commitment to something better than the world that is; no abiding joy and security without loyalty to the best.

II

A second form of the new piety is the patriotic type. The intensity of the struggle with communism in recent years has led many to believe that since communism is dogmatically atheistic in its philosophy, those who are opposed to communism must be dogmatically theistic. From here it is not a long step to the point where we make belief in God a test of a proper hatred of communism. And from this point one proceeds quickly to the assumption that God is not the Father of all mankind but the peculiar protector of the chosen people against the rest of the world. By this process we reduce our idea of God to the level of the fierce tribal deity of the early Old Testament. We make Him into "an angry man, hating half the world." He becomes a sort of Big Brother upon whom we call for aid in our struggle. We assume His sanction and aid for whatever we propose to do since He is on our side.

Now there are many sound reasons for opposing communism, and the person who today can see no differences of ethical value between the ways of communism and the ways of democracy has certainly lost his power to discriminate between relative good and evil; but the tendency to think of God as the Big Brother destroys a higher and nobler vision of God which has been one of the best contributions of Judaeo-Christian faith. God is not the guarantor of any particular nation's destinies. As the prophets of Israel and Jesus after them insisted, God stands for that power of truth and justice and righteousness and love before which all men and all nations are judged. The very foundation of an ethical view of the world is the realization that "God is no respecter of persons, but in every nation he that feareth him and worketh righteousness is accepted with him." We may trust that in our struggles we are on God's side. But it is presumptuous and untrue to insist that God must back us up whatever we do.

We do not become a better or more religious people because the name of God is engraved on our stamps and coinage, or even by adding the words "under God" to the pledge of allegiance to the flag. We shall not survive as a nation by trusting that God will turn out to be our Big Brother in the conflict with our enemies. We become worthy to survive and to draw on the strength of God in the measure that our personal attitudes and our policies and actions as a nation genuinely reflect something of the divine justice, mercy, and love.

In so far as the new piety of patriotism permits us to forget this austere truth, it weakens our moral fiber as a people, degrades the idea of God, and points backward in time toward the primitive superstition and tribalism which the Hebrew prophets fought to overcome 2500 years ago. If we as a nation are truly under God, we will know ourselves as under the divine judgment, called to penitence and challenged to reveal in history a more universal justice, a wider compassion, and a more patient and long-suffering love than any nation has yet shown.

A third form of the new piety might be called the emotional shock treatment type. We live in anxious, desperate times and nobody can blame us if we are hungry for a sense of assurance and certainty which we cannot find. The temptation is always upon us to escape from the severe disciplines of reason, from the effort to think things through to some sort of sensible conclusion, from the tensions of doubt and questioning, from the challenges which make faith an adventure involving risk and the possibility of failure. Piety of the emotional shock treatment type offers a way out of all this. It calls on us to abandon thought, to ridicule reason, to acknowledge the complete helplessness and incompetence of our minds and by an act of desire and will to throw ourselves on the mercy of God and accept a scheme of supernatural salvation.

The prospect is in many ways alluring. No man who has attempted to think his way through the great problems of life can fail to regard with humility the vast gap between the reach of the human mind and the size of the mystery which surrounds and includes it. No one knows better than the thinker that reason is not enough, and that all human thought is at last defeated by the stubborn mysteries of life. But to the appeal of those who offer the emotional shock treatment, he can only reply that the abandonment of thought is not enough either. It would doubtless be a great relief to feel oneself "safe in the arms of Jesus." The vast crowds, the skillful modern techniques of presentation, the repetitive dogmatic assertions, are emotionally stirring and satisfying. But the thoughtful religious person cannot get out of his head the great command which says: "Thou shalt love the Lord thy God with all thy mind" —the heart and soul and strength along with, not instead of, the mind.

While the piety of emotional shock treatment may well induce a vigorous, positive response and even a deep desire to live a new life, it does not show much evidence as yet of aiding the growth of the whole person into an intelligent devotion to higher ethical and spiritual values, which is the only true revival of the religious spirit. In the midst of all the crowds, the floodlights, the techniques, the yelling and the general excitement, the earthquake, wind, and fire, a still, small voice whispers to the consciences of thoughtful men: "What doth the Lord require of thee but to do justly and to love mercy and to walk humbly with thy God?" And the words of Jesus set the standard of judgment: "By their fruits, ye shall know them."

It may be that a necessary part of a revival of genuine religion is to be found in the piety of emotional shock treatment, just as necessary parts are also found in the piety of peace of mind and of patriotism, but in themselves these three types of religious revival are not enough.

The piety of patriotism, now in danger of losing itself in the very nationalism which is threatening to plunge the world into total war, must grow up until it dares confront us with a vision of God who is the God of all mankind and a humanity made up of many peoples and nations all precious in His sight. Any smaller idea of God simply dooms us to the tribal conflicts and hatreds from which we have been trying to escape for centuries.

The piety of peace of mind and soul must grow up until its priests and adherents dare present it as something more than psychotherapy with a religious tinge and smooth adjustment to the world as it is. Somehow it must arouse in men not only the longing for comfort and peace but a vision of themselves as they long to be and of the cleaner world they can help to make. Something of the ancient prophetic and apostolic fire needs to be rekindled in the piety of peace of mind so that its adherents can move out of the vicious circle of their own neurotic fears and anxieties and seek their peace of mind in bold commitment to the effort to do something of God's will on earth.

The piety of emotional shock treatment will have to face the fact that religion is something more than emotional shock treatments, necessary and important as these may sometimes be. Religion is also the steady, sober search for intellectual and emotional integrity, for wholeness and harmony of mind and heart, and for the expression of this wholeness in patient, intelligent effort to realize, in the world as it is, the best possible ethical ideals and policies.

If these changes can take place in the prevailing popular pieties, there is at least a chance that our age may indeed witness an authentic revival of the religious spirit which could save us and our children from the prospect of continual frustration and anxiety and the ever-present dread of total destruction.

III

Meantime, there is another evidence of the possible existence of a religious revival which seems to me both more general and more important than any of the prevailing popular pieties. There has been a slow and subtle change in the mood of thought and feeling with which people approach religion. This has been due to the collapse of certain illusions by which many people lived until quite recently. There were in the 1930's hosts of people whose interest in religion centered in it as a means to social and political reform. Their real faith was that social and political reforms were ends in themselves and that religion could be a powerful aid in bringing about the necessary changes.

One meets this attitude today far less often than one used to. It is not that the concern for social change has decreased. Rather the problem is now seen by many in larger dimensions. The reformation of society, the idea of the kingdom of God on earth, is seen to be not merely a matter of laws, commissions, organizations, and programs. It is also a matter of man's spiritual orientation, his knowledge of himself, his faith in his own powers, his feeling of belonging not only to the human community but to some deeper and more enduring community of faith and meaning which was before he was and will be after he is gone. There has been an unmistakable revival of interest in what we used to call "personal religion" as distinguished from "social religion" or "the social gospel." This revival is healthy in that it recognizes the roots of faith and hope from which all significant action springs and is a sincere search for a better understanding of those roots as they exist and influence the lives of individuals.

A second evidence seems to me to exist in the widespread abandonment of what might be called the negative dogmatisms. One meets some people today who are frankly cynical and many who are skeptical as to religious faith. But there are few of these, who are happy about it or proud of it. The smugness has gone out of cynicism and the skeptics are asking the questions which will lead at length to affirmation of some kind. One meets few atheists, though many agnostics. But the agnosticism is humble and open rather than self-satisfied. Whereas the agnostic of yesterday appears to have enjoyed his condition, the agnostic of today would like to be convinced of some positive content in religion, if such a thing is possible. He knows that it is frivolous to confront the ultimate issues of life as if he were not really concerned with them. He does care about the meaning of life and he would like to know more.

Disillusioned with force, with politics, and with science as saviors, man today searches within himself for hints of those foundations of truth and justice and love on which his thought and action must be based if his power is to be put in the service of justice, his politics redeemed from triviality and corruption, his science devoted to the enrichment of life.

"Man," said Albert Schweitzer when he accepted the Nobel Prize for Peace, "has today become superman because of the power for good or evil which science has placed in his hands. But the superman suffers from a fatal imperfection in his spirit. He is not elevated to that level of superhuman reason which must correspond to the possession of superhuman force."

Perhaps the single greatest factor which makes for a genuine religious revival today is the fact that men everywhere are becoming aware of this terrible truth and are uneasy about it. It is in this uneasiness and restlessness that the search for higher values, the search for God, can begin. Insofar as the new pieties of peace of mind and soul, of patriotism, and of emotional shock treatment are deepened and enlarged enough to aid men in this search, they will be of help in bringing about a general revival of authentic religion. Certainly they should not be condemned out of hand, however distasteful they may be. But neither should they be blindly accepted and approved. For if they are, they may divert our attention from the most important need. That need is: the reorientation of the human spirit so that man sees himself as a child of the Universal God, conceived in dignity and in freedom, sharing a common humanity with all men the world over, answerable to abiding values of truth, justice, and love, in the service of which he finds himself and the things which belong to his peace.

PROBLEMS FOR WRITING AND DISCUSSION

1. Meserve, like Herberg (p. 657), begins by marshaling evidence for a revival of interest in religion. How do their differing attitudes toward the revival become clear through their choices of detail? How is the difference crystallized by Meserve's use of the word *piety*?

2. What three forms does Meserve say the "new piety" takes? Are the motives behind these forms motives that Herberg discusses? Which author examines the motives more critically? Explain your answer.

3. Just as Kronenberger (p. 573) says our humor is the "handle of our acquisitiveness," so Meserve says religion for some of us becomes "a means to an end." Why does Meserve say such an interpretation "belongs in the realm of magic"?

4. A maturely religious man, Meserve says, will ask not "What do I require of God?" but "what does God require of me?" Is this pair of questions reminiscent of the pair Kennedy (p. 508) juxtaposes for the consideration of Americans? Does Kennedy plead for an American "commitment to purposes and ends larger and more durable" than any single man's destiny?

5. Morris (p. 560) says that the Rockwell version of Don Quixote would omit the element of wonder that transforms a man from what he is to what he would be. Mandel (p. 614) complains that American writers have not transfigured *L'homme moyen sensuel* into a hero. What is Meserve's complaint against the "gospel of smooth adjustment"?

6. Does the "transforming task of religion" Meserve describes have anything in common with the original American dream of transforming a virgin wilderness into a humanized utopia? Anything in common with the transforming power of imagination that Langer (p. 634) says provides forms by which we conceive "what vitality and emotion feel like"? Explain.

7. Would Meserve's "pilgrims and pioneers" incited to action by the "healthy tension between what is and what ought to be" be inner-directed or other-directed?

8. Does Meserve think that making "belief in God a test of a proper hatred of communism" would render, as Jefferson says (p. 653), half the world fools and the rest hypocrites? Does Meserve, like Jefferson, ultimately repose his faith in man's rationality? Why or why not?

9. What is Meserve's strongest objection to the patriotic type of piety? For what, in Meserve's estimate, does God stand? Do Jefferson and Lincoln presuppose a tribunal of good and evil above all men from which laws and institutions of government derive their sanction? What other writers in this book in different connections have seen the necessity of rational discrimination between good and evil as the only basis for authority and stability in human affairs?

10. Compare Meserve's warning that we shall not survive simply by trusting that God is on our side to the sentence that concludes Kennedy's Inaugural Address. Did Roger Williams (see p. 647) assume that God's work on earth is man's work?

11. Like Meserve, Stevenson (p. 478), Judge Hand (p. 388), and Jefferson understood the temptation to abandon "the severe disciplines of reason," the "tensions of doubt and questioning," and the "adventure involving risk and the possibility of failure" that faith demands. What effects of this abandonment do these writers fear? What effects do Scott (p. 598) Mandel (p. 614) and Langer fear?

12. Meserve speaks of the "vast gap between the reach of the human mind and the size of the mystery which surrounds and includes it." Would Don Quixote (see Morris' article) be capable of comprehending this mystery? Has the gap become too vast for modern man, or has he simply lost the capacity to wonder and adventure? What does Meserve think? What evidence to support his opinion does he give?

13. Several other writers in this book speak of modern man's alienation from or disorientation within his community. How does Riesman (p. 488) suggest that a "feeling of belonging" be achieved? Do you think Meserve's suggestion is superior? What does he mean by a "community of faith and meaning which was before he [man] was and will be after he is gone"? Is there substance enough in the American dream to foster such a community of faith?

14. Did William James (p. 502) foresee the "terrible truth" that Meserve believes may inspire a "search for higher values"? Is it true, as Meserve says, that we are "disillusioned with force, with politics, and with science as saviors"? Support your answer by reference to specific authors in this book who write on these subjects.

15. Do you see the Communists as children "of the Universal God"? In the light of your answer, what way do you find "to do justly and to love mercy and to walk humbly with thy God"?

My Father Enters the Church

CLARENCE DAY

> Clarence Shepard Day (1874-1935), essayist, was graduated from Yale and then joined his father in the stock brokerage business. His career was interrupted by the Spanish-American War, and after it, severely crippled by arthritis, he turned primarily to writing. Although he published many books and articles, and for a time was on the staff of The New Republic, his reputation rests on his autobiographical work and particularly on Life With Father *(1935)* and Life With Mother *(1937)*. Both books are humorous accounts of the Victorian traditions of his moderately wealthy family. Each was successfully dramatized by Howard Lindsay and Russell Crouse.

The way it ended was simple. Mother's family had lived at one time in a pretty little two-storied house, called "The Cottage," in East Twenty-ninth Street; it had casement windows, set with diamond-shaped panes of leaded glass, and a grass plot in front. On the other side of the street, at Fifth Avenue, stood the church that is now known as the Little Church Around the Corner. The first Dr. Houghton was the rector in those times, and Mother was fond of him. One day Mother heard that a young relative of his, the Reverend Mr. Morley, had taken a far-away parish near what was then Audubon Park, a mile or two north of where in later years they erected Grant's Tomb. This part of the city was so

---

Reprinted from The Best of Clarence Day, by Clarence Day, by permission of Alfred A. Knopf, Inc. Copyright, *1931, 1932,* by Clarence Day. Copyright, *1948,* by Katherine B. Day.

thinly settled that it was like a remote country suburb. There were dirt roads and lanes instead of streets; and thick, quiet old woods. Mother suddenly got the idea that perhaps this would suit Father, since he seemed bent on "confessing God before men" only where no one was looking. Besides, Mother knew young Mr. Morley, and she felt that here was someone she could go to with her curious problem. She asked him to come down and see her. He was sympathetic. He agreed to make everything as easy for Father as possible.

I don't know just why it was, but somehow that was all there was to it. Father still got in a very bad humor whenever the subject was mentioned; but at least Mother wasn't, any longer, asking the impossible of him. It was thoroughly distasteful and he hated it, but he supposed he could go through it sometime. Perhaps he even got to the point of wishing to get the thing over with.

So the day came on which Father had agreed he would enter the church. The only person who had to be reminded of it was Father himself. I remember excitedly looking out of the window at breakfast, and seeing a hired brougham from Ryerson & Brown's in the street. The coachman had on a blue coat with a double row of bright buttons, and on his legs were faded green trousers from some other man's livery. He was looking up at our front door. His horse was as weather-beaten as the horse on the plains of Siberia, in the picture in my Geography; and he too seemed to be looking up at our house and wondering what would come out of it.

I stood out on our front stoop staring down at them, and listening to the sounds in our hallway. Father had come down to breakfast in a good temper that morning, and the bacon and eggs had suited him for once, and the coffee too had found favor. Mother gave a happy, tender look at this soul she was saving. The dining-room seemed full of sunshine, and the whole world light-hearted. But when Mother said it was nearly eight o'clock and the cab would soon be here, Father had demanded what cab. He listened to her answer in horror, and sprang up with a roar.

It was as though an elephant which had been tied up with infinite pains had trumpeted and burst every fetter, after the labor of months. It was all to do over again. Father not only had to be convinced that a day had been set, and that this was the day, but the whole question of baptism had to be reopened and proved. All the religious instruction that had been slowly inscribed on his mind had apparently utterly vanished—the slate was wiped clean. He was back at his original starting-point, that this thing was all folderol—it was nothing but a wild idea of Mother's with which he had no concern.

A woman of less determination would have given up, Father was so indignant. But Mother, though frightened and discouraged and tearful, was angry. She wasn't going to let Father off, after all she had done. At first I thought she surely had lost. He was completely intractable. She stood up to him, armed with God's word and the laws of the church, and also, as she despairingly reminded him, with his own "Sacred Promise," and again she learned that not a one of them was any good. But she had one other weapon: Ryerson & Brown's waiting cab.

There were some things that were unheard of in our family: they simply weren't done. One was wasting money on cabs. When we went to the length of ordering a cab, we did not keep it waiting. And the sight of this cab at the door seemed to hypnotize Father. It stood there like a link in some inevitable chain of events. At first he declared it could go to the devil, he didn't care if there were fifty cabs waiting. But he was by habit and instinct a methodical man. When he helped himself to a portion of anything at the table, for instance, he did his best to finish that portion, whether he liked it or not. He got all the more angry if it didn't taste right, but his code made him eat it. If he began a book he was bound to go on with it, no matter how much it bored him. He went through with any and every program to which he once felt committed. The fact that this cab had been ordered, and now stood at the door, prevailed in those depths of his spirit which God couldn't reach. Where I sat on the steps I could hear him upstairs in his room, banging doors and putting on his overcoat and cursing at fate.

Mother darted out and told the coachman where he was to take us; and then she got in, bonneted and cloaked, to wait for Father to come. The coachman looked puzzled when he found we were going to church. He could see we weren't dressed for a funeral, yet it was hardly a wedding. Perhaps he thought we were a very devout family, seeking for some extra worship.

Then Father came down the steps, blackly. He got in the cab. And the horse and the coachman both jumped as Father slammed the door shut.

The cab bumped along over the cobblestones, with its ironshod wheels. The steady-going rattle and jolting made me dreamy. It was soothing to see the landscape slide by, at five or six miles an hour. Milkmen, ladling milk out of tall cans. Chambermaids polishing door-bells. Ladies, with the tops of their sleeves built up high at each shoulder. Horses straining at street-cars. Flocks of sparrows hopping about, pecking at refuse and dung, and waiting until a horse almost stepped on them before flying off.

We drove up Madison Avenue to the Park, and out at West Seventy-second Street. Then under the Elevated, with its coal-dust sifting down and stray cinders, blackening the pools in the street; and its little locomotives chuff-chuffing along overhead. At the Boulevard, as upper Broadway was then named, we turned northward. Over toward the river were rocky wastelands, old shanties and goats. The skyline along the Boulevard was one of telegraph poles, along bare blocks and rail fences. I liked the looks of this ungraded district; it was all up-and-down and had ponds in it. And it ought to have comforted Father. No members of the club or the stock exchange could be sighted for miles; they probably never set foot in such regions. What more could Father ask?

But Father was glaring about, looking like a caged lion. Apparently he had confidently believed up to this very moment that Heaven would intervene somehow, and spare him this dose. He had never done Heaven any harm; why should it be malignant? His disappointment was increasingly bitter as he saw he was trapped.

Another sort of man would have opened the cab door and bolted. But Father was drinking his hemlock. He also was freely expressing his feelings about it. The hardships of marriage had never before impressed him so sharply. A woman's demands on her husband were simply beyond human reckoning. He felt, and he said plainly to Mother, as the cab rattled on, that if he did this thing for her, it must be understood that it was his supreme contribution. No diamond necklace. No other sacrifices of any kind. He must never be asked to do anything more all his life.

Mother tried to point out that he wasn't doing it for her but for God, but Father said: "Pshaw! I won't hear to it." He had never had any trouble with God till Mother appeared on the scene.

Mother quoted Dr. Garden again to him, but Father said "Pish!"

"Oh Clare, you mustn't," said Mother.

"Bah!" Father roared. "Bah! What do you suppose I care for that fellow!"

"But it's in the Bible."

"Pooh! Damn!"

Mother shuddered at this. Here was a man who defied even the Bible. She half-expected God to come bursting right out of the sky, and bang his fist down on the Ryerson & Brown cab and all in it.

"Damnation!" Father repeated, consumed by his wrongs.

Mother said, oh how could he talk so, on his way to the font! She drew away from him, and then looked back with awe at this being, whose sense of his powers was so great that he would stand up to Anyone.

We had now come in sight of the church. It stood halfway up a steep hill, which the horse climbed at a walk, although Father said if the cab didn't hurry he wouldn't have time to be baptized—he'd be late at the office.

"What is the name of this confounded place?" he said, as we got out, making a jab at the little House of God with his cane.

"Oh Clare dear! Please don't. It's the Church of the Epiphany, I told you."

"Epiphany! Humph," Father grunted. "More gibberish."

Inside it was cold and bare, and it smelled of varnish. The pews were of new yellow pine, and the stained-glass looked cheap. There was nobody present. The sexton had hurried away to fetch the minister, after letting us in.

Father glowered around like a bull in some Plaza del Toro, waiting to charge the reverend toreador and trample upon him. He stood there, boxed up in surroundings where he didn't belong, hurt and outraged and lonely. His whole private life had been pried into, even his babyhood. He had kept decently aloof from the depths of religion, as a gentleman should—he was no emotional tinker like that fellow, John Bunyan—yet here he was, dragged into this damned evangelist orgy, far from his own proper world, in the hands of his wife and a parson.

A footstep was heard.

"Oh, good morning, Mr. Morley," said Mother. "This is Mr. Day."

Mr. Morley was a young man, shy but friendly, with a new-looking beard. He approached our little group trustingly, to shake Father's hand, but he got such a look that he turned to me instead and patted me on the head several times. There was a rich smell of something about him. It wasn't bay-rum, such as Father sometimes used after shaving. It was far more delicious to me than any cologne or sachet scent. And besides, it had much more body to it; more satisfaction. But I couldn't identify it. I only knew that it was a magnificent fragrance, and seemed to come from his beard. He led us up to the front of the church and the service began.

It says in the prayer-book that when a person of riper years is to be baptized, he shall be exhorted to prepare himself, with prayers and with fasting. And if he shall be found fit, "then the Godfathers and Godmothers (the People being assembled upon the Sunday or Prayer Day appointed) shall be ready to present him at the font." I suppose that was why I was taken along, so that there would be enough people there for a congregation: Mother and the sexton and me. The sexton, who seemed a nervous man, was skulking in a rear pew; but Mother and I stood just behind Father, to bolster him up. It was a curious situation for a small boy to be in, as I look back on it.

Mr. Morley presently read an address to the three of us, as we stood there before him. (I condense this and the following quotations, from the service in my old prayer-book.) "Dearly beloved," he said to us, "forasmuch as all men are conceived and born in sin, and they who are in the flesh cannot please God, but live in sin; and our Saviour Christ saith, none can enter into the kingdom of God, except he be regenerate and born anew; I beseech you to call upon God that of his bounteous goodness he will grant to this person that which by nature he cannot have; that he may be baptized with Water and the Holy Ghost, and received into Christ's holy Church, and be made a lively member of the same."

Next came a prayer in which Mr. Morley went back to the ark, and spoke of how God saved Noah and his family from perishing by water; and of how God also led the children of Israel safely through the Red Sea; and of how Jesus was baptized in the Jordan. These three incidents were cited as proof that God had sanctified "the element of Water to the mystical washing away of sin."

"We beseech thee," Mr. Morley continued, "that thou wilt mercifully look upon this thy Servant; wash him and sanctify him with the Holy Ghost; that he, being delivered from thy wrath, may be received into the ark of Christ's Church; and being steadfast in faith, joyful through hope, and rooted in charity, may come to the land of everlasting life."

Father was getting restive by this time, but Mr. Morley kept on. He read us a part of the Gospel of John, and a long exhortation and prayer; and after this he bravely turned and spoke as follows to Father:

"Well-beloved, who are come hither desiring to receive holy Baptism, you have heard how the congregation hath prayed that our Lord Jesus Christ would release you of your sins, to give you the kingdom of Heaven, and everlasting life. You have heard also that our Lord hath promised to grant all those things that we have prayed for. Wherefore you must also faithfully, in the presence of these your Witnesses and this whole congregation, promise and answer to the following questions:

"Dost thou renounce the devil and all his works, the vain pomp and glory of the world, with all covetous desires of the same, and the sinful desires of the flesh?"

The answer to this was rather long, and Father of course had not learned it; but Mother whispered the words in his ear, and he repeated some of them impatiently, in a harsh, stony voice. He looked as though he might have been an annoyed Roman general, participating much against his will in a low and barbaric rite.

There were only three more questions, however, and the answers were short.

"O Merciful God," said Mr. Morley, when these were finished, "grant that the old Adam in this person may be so buried, that the new man may be raised up in him. Amen." He had to say this, because it was in the prayer-book; but Father's eyes were on fire, and there was a great deal of the old Adam in him, and it didn't look buried.

Four more little prayers followed, and then came the great moment, when Mr. Morley tried to pour water on Father. Owing to Father's being no longer an infant, the prayer-book didn't require Mr. Morley to take him into his arms for this purpose, and hold him over the font; but he did have to wet him a little. I don't know how he managed it. I remember how Father stood, grim and erect, in his tailed morning-coat; but when I saw Mr. Morley make a pass at Father's forehead, I am sorry to say I shut my eyes tightly at this frightful sacrilege, and whether he actually landed or not I never knew. But he did go on to say, "I baptize thee," and all the rest of it, to Father. "We receive this person into the congregation of Christ's flock," he added; "and do sign him with the sign of the Cross, in token that hereafter he shall not be ashamed to confess the faith of Christ crucified, and manfully to fight under his banner, against sin, the world, and the devil; and to continue Christ's faithful soldier and servant unto his life's end. Amen."

The baptism part was now over. Father started to leave, but we managed somehow to detain him while we knelt and gave thanks. And, to end with, Mr. Morley urged Father to "mortify all his evil affections," and exhorted Mother and me to remember that it was our part and duty to put Father in mind what a solemn vow he had now made, that so he might grow in grace and the knowledge of Christ, "and live godly, righteously, and soberly, in this present world."

We stood awkwardly still for a moment, but there was nothing else. Mr. Morley started in being chatty, in a more everyday voice. He stood next to me as he talked, and I remember how absorbed I was, again, by his mellow aroma. The odor was so grateful to my senses that it seemed almost nourishing. I sniffed and I sniffed—till all of a sudden I knew what it was. It was cocoa. We seldom had cocoa at our house. It made me feel hungry. I greedily inhaled the last bits of it while Mr. Morley talked on. He said he hoped we'd attend services in this new church of his, sometimes. He began to describe how the bishop had come there to consecrate it.

But Father broke in, saying abruptly, "I shall be late at the office," and strode down the aisle. Mother and I hurried after him. He was muttering such blasphemous things that I heard Mother whisper: "Oh, please, Clare, please; please don't. This poor little church! It'll have to be consecrated all over again."

As we drove off, Mother sank back into her corner of the cab, quite worn out. Father was still seething away, as though his very soul was boiling over. If he could only have known it, long quiet days were ahead, when he and God could go back in peace to their comfortable old ways together; for he was never confirmed, or troubled in any way again by religious demands. But all he could think of, for the moment, were his recent indignities.

He got out at the nearest Elevated station, to take a train for the office, with the air of a man who had thoroughly wasted the morning. He slammed the cab door on us, leaving us to drive home alone. But before he turned away to climb the stairs, he thrust his red face in the window, and with a burning look at Mother said, "I hope to God you are satisfied." Then this new son of the church took out his watch, gave a start, and Mother and I heard him shout "Hell!" as he raced up the steps.

PROBLEMS FOR WRITING AND DISCUSSION

1. How does Father, a prosperous American businessman, reflect the struggle between rugged individualism and conformity?

2. Meserve (p. 669) discusses shortcomings in the recent resurgence of religious activity in America. How might Meserve react to Father's pledge "manfully to fight" under Christ's banner "against sin, the world, and the devil"?

3. Presumably Father undergoes his "indignities" because Mother has discovered an oversight in his "babyhood." Which is Day more interested in: the triumph of Mother and Mr. Morley, or the "sacrilege" they commit upon Father's personal inviolability? Explain.

4. How does this selection point up Niebuhr's contention (p. 705) that in America prosperity and virtue are often considered concomitants of each other?

5. What does Day make the baptism itself? Does Day himself regard the ceremony as "gibberish" and "folderol"? Does he see anything wrong with the "comfortable old ways" to which Father and God would return?

God in the Colleges

MICHAEL NOVAK

> Michael Novak (1933-), born in Johnstown, Pennsylvania, holds a degree in theology from Gregorian University in Rome and is presently a candidate for the Ph.D. in philosophy at Harvard. He has published a novel, The Tiber Was Silver (1961), and many articles in The New Republic, The Nation, and Commonweal, as well as in philosophical and theological journals.

The professor looked into the faces of the freshmen in Philosophy I. "How many of you," he asked, "believe in the existence of God?"

He walked up and down a little. The class was intellectually alive and usually argued. No hands went up.

"Good. I'll give you Anselm's proof for the existence of God." In a few minutes of lecturing, the professor presented Anselm's proof. "Now," he paused. "How many of you see anything wrong in this proof?"

No hands went up.

"Well, then, some of you now believe in God. How many?"

Still no hands went up. When the professor told about it later, he shrugged. "What can you do when thinking doesn't seem to make any difference?"

The experience of this professor is not a solitary one. The fact that the life of personal conviction is separated from the life of academic intelligence is frequently remarked in university life. The phenomenon is not even confined to this country, for it is

From "God in the Colleges" by Michael Novak, Harper's Magazine, Vol. 223, October 1961. Reprinted by permission of Curtis Brown, Ltd.

well known in England. In *Lucky Jim*, Kingsley Amis makes fun of the noncommitment and the sham which he finds in middle-class education; Wilfrid Sheed's American-English novel, *A Middle Class Education*, extends the observations well beyond the classroom. In our day it is precisely this that education in England and America has become: middle-class. John K. Galbraith's *The Affluent Society* brought the emergence of the new and numerous educated class to our attention: it is there for anyone to see.

The present essay pretends to no special statistical wisdom; its material has been gathered from a long-time interest in religion and the university, from reading, from conversations at Harvard and other colleges. Undoubtedly, the essay has fuller relevance for the liberal-arts college: I have hardly broached the problem of religion in the scientific and technological schools. In the smaller colleges and the huge state colleges, the focus may be somewhat different.

How does God fare in a middle-class education? What happens to religion in a middle-class education?

First of all, we must remember that since medieval times the West has been becoming a middle-class civilization. The rise of the bourgeoisie has been concomitant with the rise of technology. And underneath the social and economic changes that made Europe capitalist and then industrialist, there was a change in world view. Even though the bourgeois classes might cling to the conventions and forms of an older tradition and an older faith, the impersonality of business and the objectivity of scientific method were molding their weekday spirits and their habitual attitudes. The very bourgeoisie that nourished the technological and scientific revolution, nourished within itself an intellectual avant-garde that strove to point out to it how very empty its forms had become. The avant-garde was usually increasingly irreligious: from Voltaïre and Hume, Comte and Zola, to Shaw and Russell, it has come to take its battle *vis-à-vis* religion as won. For its point has been that our culture is now *at base* irreligious, that the bourgeois businessman who pretends differently is either hypocritical or blind. Catholicism was long content with the status quo, and Protestantism for a long time praised the thrifty and the rugged and the strong. Thus the war on poverty which Marxism declared and which the democracies have taken up is (though it need not have been) a secular war, and the ideals which international civilization now pursues are secular ideals: the abolition of poverty and disease, of ignorance and indignity, of colonialism and tyranny. Giving itself to science and technology, our culture makes religion not central but optional, and the avant-garde has been trying to point out—and to form—the change.

Secondly, it is necessary to see that while Europe was torn nearly to its death by the ideological and physical contortions of recent revolutions and wars, America and England have tried earnestly to go on as before, as if nothing has happened. The war washed away the intellectual foundations of Europe's past, and intellectuals like Camus, Sartre, Marcel, Barth, and Guardini have fought desperately for intellectual starting points—whether they deny or affirm the possibility of religious faith. But in America and England, philosophy and art showed little such desperation; men tried to pick up where they had left off, a little more tired, a little more angry, worried about the bomb, but not fundamentally changed. Moreover, education in England and America has become financially cushioned as never before. The government, corporations, unions—all give grants for specialized research or simply for the maintenance of students and professors. A distinctly comfortable and entrenched kind of existence is growing up. The small, modestly optimistic world view which Europe shared before the wars is still almost possible. The radicalism of the American 'thirties has been fragmented by prosperity and by disillusion with ideology.

Although the colleges pride themselves on the awakening of young minds, on the asking of the Big Questions of life (who and what is man, whence has he come, where is he going, what is love, what is passion, what is reason, is there a God?), it is soon clear to college students that the Big Questions don't count—either in academic standing, or in later life, or in research grants.

In the first place, the standing assumption is that ultimate questions are in principle unanswerable, and hence not worth asking seriously. This assumption may not discourage freshmen, but over a four-year period it is pretty well driven home. In the second place, nobody is much interested in students' answers to such questions, or deems them worth putting in competition with anybody else's. Even among the professors it is assumed that ultimate questions are nonintellectual, personal, and if matters of supreme importance and self-commitment, nevertheless not matters for passionate academic dispute. The university, on principle, concentrates on statistics, historical facts, historical intellectual positions, logic modeled on the discourse of the physical sciences, and ample documentation. Even the literature courses, under the impact of the New Criticism, have the students noting the occurrences of words, running down allusions, and abstracting from the conditions of history. The Anglo-American university has committed itself to all that is "objective," countable, precise, publicly verifiable. Though this commitment suits the middle-class temper capitally, it stifles religion almost to death.

Not only religion is stifled. More fundamentally, it is possible— it is even common—for a student to go to class after class of sociology, economics, psychology, literature, philosophy, and the rest, and hardly become aware that he is dealing with issues of life and death, of love and solitude, of inner growth and pain. He may never fully grasp the fact that education is not so much information and technique as self-confrontation and change in his own conscious life. He may sit through lectures and write examinations—and the professors may *let* him do merely that—collecting verbal "answers," without really thinking through and deciding about any new aspect of his own life in any course. The dilemma of education has always been to combine merely mental skills with personal experiencing and growth. The educational currents in American colleges tend to oscillate from one pole to the other; and at present the attention in college to the formal and the public easily leaves the inner life of the student untouched.

It is true that in a place like Harvard, or among more serious students everywhere, the young collegian may experience beneficial crises of growth. He gets a taste of rebellion against his origins; he may become, for a while, "avant-garde." The folks at home find him restive, critical, hostile, in his approach to a world he had hitherto peacefully shared. He has learned to despise the organization man and the many patterns of conformity in mass culture; he has learned a certain contempt for suburbia and its values. Yet he likes the comforts of home. Worst of all, in college he has not really had to rebel (except perhaps against not having Latin on his diploma). The college gave him rebellious, critical books, but also gave him a cool grove to read them in. No commitment, no crusading, no heroism is asked of him. The college merely wants him to "have the facts," to show mental control of the concepts. Yet he, so everyone tells him, is not at all like the collegians of the 'thirties, or even of the 'forties. He is cautious, quiet, studious. And no wonder. So is the institution in which he is studying. The higher-powered institutions are committed to testable information and techniques; the patterns of conformity in lower-powered institutions do not far transcend the interests of the society that fosters them.

Middle-class Christianity—the bourgeois Christianity which Nietzsche, Kierkegaard, Péguy, Bloy, and others so hated—was always prudent, small-visioned, secure. It dared little, with its gaudy-colored plaster statues, or its devices to protect the little world of the entrepreneur. In the person of many university professors, middle-class secular humanism is not much more daring. It thinks of itself as humble in its agnosticism, and eschews the "mystic flights" of metaphysicians, theologians, and dreamers; it is cautious and remote in dealing with heightened and passionate experiences that are the stuff of much great literature and philosophy. It limits itself to this world and its concerns, concerns which fortunately turn out to be largely subject to precise formulation, and hence have a limited but comforting certainty. (It has a particularly comfortable ambiance if it works within the physical sciences, or mathematics, or the statistics of sociology and economics.) If we cannot control the great uncertain questions in the universe, nevertheless we can make a universe of little certainties we can control.

The agnosticism—atheism would be too strong a word—of the classroom is not militant. It is only, in principle, unconcerned. It is bourgeois Christianity all over again, to so great an extent that, in college, in spite of differences in belief, the behavior of agnostic and of religious man is pretty much the same.

The agnosticism of the classroom does not have to be militant. Once upon a time it was fighting for its life; now it is an accepted part of the college scene, in fact the predominating part. The old battles between positive science and religion which delighted, or angered, our grandfathers—about chance and design, monkeys and Adam—seldom resound now in academic halls. The distinction between empirical and theological activity seems pretty well recognized —each side preserves a certain calm and only occasionally do tempers flare. Perhaps psychologists more than others are given to writing off religion as illusion; anthropologists, in turn, are habituated to data on revelations and recurrent religious themes, and correspondingly casual about the traditions of Judaism and Christianity. One school of analysis in philosophy, of which Russell and Ayer among others are examples, believes that nothing that cannot be reduced to sense experience can have meaning, and most religious questions of course lie outside this restricted zone. Some partisans of another movement, linguistic analysis, following the later Wittgenstein, do not require the discourse of faith and theology to conform to other kinds of discourse, but study it in its own right; but religion does not lie in words.

Professional disciplines aside, a bland tolerance seems to be everybody's ideal. Say nothing that will offend. Say nothing that involves personal commitment. Stay close to the public facts. "You've got to teach these youngsters to forget the *shoulds* and *musts* they came here with," one new teaching fellow was recently admonished by his program director. "The students have to learn to be objective." And of course such a critique is excellent, since some *shoulds* and *musts* are what a man dies for. But there seems to be correspondingly little concern about which ones he will acquire and keep.

Professor Raphael Demos of Harvard was once quoted as saying, with perhaps his touch of irony, "*Veritas* means we are committed to nothing." It may be that the American consensus has forced a "commitment to nothing" upon our universities; we are a pluralist people, and it seems very difficult to discover a way to teach about those differences on ultimate questions that make us so. The colleges make a "commitment to noncommitment," have a "faith in non-faith." They demand perpetual re-examination and have nowhere to rest.

Thus the new middle-class tolerance of the colleges neither destroys—nor transforms—the religion of the incoming freshmen. Of one hundred students who marked themselves "atheistic or agnostic" on the poll of the Harvard *Crimson* in 1959, only ten felt "obliged . . . to enlighten others to abandon their faith." The new tolerance merely establishes, officially and in principle, that personal conviction be separated from teaching and learning. If a student wishes to commit himself to answers to ultimate questions (by commitment to some personal synthesis, or to traditional religion or ethics, or anything), he may do so—is even encouraged to do so—but not publicly, nor officially, not in his daily work. He will do well to keep his answers to himself. In term papers and on tests they will not be welcome; there he is obliged to prove rather that he knows facts and correlations, and can run, seeking, as well as anyone else. No one in *official* university life seems to care about his convictions.

There is good reason for the university's position. One of its tasks is to turn out professional men. Think of the difficulty there would be in correcting exams and term papers if each student were engaged in a highly personal way in working out a position important to himself. What if the student found that something of importance to him was of minor importance to the course—or outside its confines? The dilemma of professionalism versus full human experience is a pressing one, and cannot be solved by making light of it.

How relevant is this dilemma to the actual church affiliations of college students? A Catholic report published in *America* (April 8, 1961) quotes Bishop Robert E. Lucey as saying: "The dangers to faith and morals are at least as great in a downtown office as on a secular campus." The national survey of *Time* magazine (1952) is cited to the same effect. "No appreciable number of defections," say Newman Club chaplains at the University of Illinois and the University of Iowa; those which do occur "result rather from weak religious background prior to college than from campus living and experiences." The Harvard *Crimson* poll I referred to earlier records a high rate of defections—40 per cent among Protestants, 25 per cent among Catholics, 12 per cent among Jews—among the 310 students who answered. But in almost every case the defection had its roots in precollege days, especially in high-school experience.

Although it is not clear what constitutes religious "strength," it is clear that if the student's faith goes through a personal trial-by-fire, that is his affair. There are few courses in critical theology, few in modern critical Biblical theory, few in the theory and practice of organized religion, to help him explicitly and formally to mature his theological intelligence. In the view of some religious men, this is a good thing; religion, after all, is not something that can be formally taught. It is a living commitment to be enkindled from person to person, a life to be lived rather than lessons to be learned. Besides, formal theological studies imply a living content of religious experience; but it is precisely this living content which in our day most men no longer possess. If religion is to enter the university, it must enter first at the most elementary level: in experience, in awareness, in slow and gradual exploration. The traditional words are not relevant to the present religious development of most men. Our times are sub-, not only post-, religious. The institutionalized forms of religion did not originate in modern life, and modern science and technology have grown up outside them;

the two worlds of religion and modernity are strangers to each other. Were there to be merely formal courses in theology at the university, genuine religious life would fare hardly better than at present. As the New Criticism is to art, so is critical theology to religious awareness. Theology, like the New Criticism, has a role to play, but it is neither necessary nor sufficient for religious life.

If we admit that theologians would also contribute to the professionalism and formalism already thriving in the modern university, who might do better? The answer, I suggest, must be that the greatest contribution to the religious life of the university could come from teachers and scholars—formally religious or not— who could lead the student to the profound human experiences lying below the surface of the academic curriculum.

These experiences are often "prereligious"; they are barely starting points for full religious life. But they are the only foundation on which anything living can be built. I mean man's experience of his fragility, of his transitoriness, of his tininess; his consciousness of his uniqueness on the earth, of his endless and restless questioning; his personal choices whose motives and consequences he cannot fully know; his vast ability to be proud and to fail, to be isolated and to love, to be—and yet not to be—the master of his own destiny.

These experiences, and others like them, underlie the statistics of economics and of sociology, the laws and hypotheses of psychology, philosophy, and other disciplines; they are at the source of great poems and novels and histories now often taught as if they were technical puzzles.

Large and unsettling personal questions arise from these experiences. And it is by their answers, explicit or implicit, that men finally differ from one another: how they react to achievement, to pride, to love, to suffering, to feelings of life and energy, to death. Implicit in the actions of every man is his own particular bias and approach to economics, to social and political affairs, to all matters with which he deals. What are the biases and beliefs that make a student unique and color all his judgments even in his professional concerns? Instead of concentrating on this question, and hence helping the student toward self-discovery, the university takes the easier path: it tries to maintain an area of "objectivity" and "fact." But the truly crucial element in human knowing (I repeat: even in professional knowing) lies in the recesses of personal judgment. Our critical sciences, unlike our creative arts, have favored the "objective" over the "subjective." Our universities favor the one pole over the necessary two: notional-verbal competence, over the self-knowledge and self-commitment that also affect professional careers, and make up personal life.

If university teachers could right the balance, would religion begin to thrive? Those who have made faith central to their lives—who believe in the reality and relevance of God, and the interaction (in dark faith) of God and men—hold that it would. And if theology, as such, came to the campuses and became there embattled and truly controversial, this would be welcome; for the very fact that fundamental questions were posed would transform the experience of university life.

No one can know what the full consequences of such a transformation might be, but surely it would mean that university people would be far more closely engaged with the world outside than they are today. Religious men in colleges could follow the example of the clergymen who took part in the Freedom Rides, went to jail, went on a hunger strike in the name of justice and brotherly concern. Religion has played a large role in the commitment of the young Negroes to struggle for their rights. It must suggest *other* ways of acting when situations in our society call for justice and compassion and protest. Religious men must be "active." They are obliged to consider the forms a just society should take, and ways to achieve them. Again, in the silence, self-control, and patience required by the tactics of passive resistance, they find an excellent school in the "passive" strength of religion. The intellectual resources from which such a transformation might grow are now latent on our campuses. And they are quite carefully neglected.

Meanwhile, the student on the secular campus works out his religion for himself. Often his previous religious background will have been uncritical, informal, and unsophisticated; he may be the first member of his family pursuing a university education. His grasp of religious concepts like faith, hope, love may well be far less precise and intellectually defensible than it ought to be; his university career will offer him very little formal help in clarifying and criticizing them. It is possible that college life may be for him, then, a period of searing but private examination. For a time at least he may stop going to church or synagogue, and believe himself atheist or agnostic. But the chances are—in most schools and among most students—no such honest and fruitful personal critiques will occur, at least of any lasting depth. Where they do seem to occur, experienced religious men are pleased. "It's a more thoughtful kind of religion," seems to be the consensus of chaplains near Harvard. "It's better than merely going to church out of habit. They may be missing church services and undergoing changes now; but they'll be back when they return to their local communities and all the better for it."

But will they be? The fact seems to be that even among the more searching students, religion follows the pattern of their other personal convictions. The pattern of conformity they are taught in college, by which they systematically separate their inner convictions from the "objective" work of the classroom, will simply be continued in their business affairs, legal practice, or work of whatever kind in later life. A civilization pervaded by the laws and spirit of technology—on which profit and life itself are based—is a civilization prone to expediency and non-moral, nonpersonal considerations. The vice of academicians is to become intellectual technologists; this vice prevails. The consequent bourgeois life of the American university becomes with hardly a hitch the middle-class life of the organization man and the suburbanite. The pretense of nonconformity and intellectual liberty on campus is seldom tested by real and fundamental disagreement; for such disagreement is usually "subjective" and not amenable to the kind of debate the university tacitly approves. "Liberals" and "conservatives" in politics, for example, seldom touch the basic issues separating them; they both try to argue in terms of "facts"; but why they are committed, each in his separate way, to different ideals, and what precisely these ideals are and whence they are derived—this kind of discussion does not suit the pragmatic and "objective" temper of present intellectual life. It is too intangible, dialectical, personal, however lethal in its effect upon action.

One might have hoped that the religiously committed private schools in America might have made by now some major contribution to American intellectual life. In part, they have been too concerned with putting up buildings, with more or less ghetto-like defensiveness, and with hesitating between secular standards and their own long-ago tradition. In part, general American intellectual life rules out of professional discussion the very commitment which the religious schools primarily exist to foster. In any case, the potential strength of the religious school now goes almost for nought.

One might have hoped that religious men within the secular colleges might by their understanding and their leadership have restored to American universities a chance for a living and critical experience of religion. It is true that the Danforth Foundation, the National Council for Religion in Higher Education, and other groups are trying to favor the presence in our universities of talented religious men. But the strident tones of Fathers Feeney and Halton, and of William F. Buckley, Jr.'s essays and talks have sometimes soured the air. And for decades there have been too few men, at once intellectual and religious and wise, on the campuses. Vast empty spaces seem to surround the Niebuhrs and the Tillichs. The churches are filled with worshipers but intelligence has fled from the ranks of religion. Who or what can bring it back?

What, then, is the place of God in our colleges? The basic human experiences that remind man that he is not a machine, and not merely a temporary cog in a technological civilization, are not fostered within the university. God is as irrelevant in the universities as in business organizations; but so are love, death, personal destiny. Religion can thrive only in a personal universe; religious faith, hope, and love are personal responses to a personal God. But how can the immense question of a personal God even be posed and made relevant when fundamental questions about the meaning and limits of personal experience are evaded?

"God is dead. . . . What are these churches if they are not the tombs and sepulchers of God?" Nietzsche asked. But much of Western humanism is dead too. Men do not wander under the silent stars, listen to the wind, learn to know themselves, question, "Where am I going? Why am I here?" They leave aside the mysteries of contingency and transitoriness, for the certainties of research, production, consumption. So that it is nearly possible to say: "Man is dead. . . . What are these buildings, these tunnels, these roads, if they are not the tombs and sepulchers of man?"

God, if there is a God, is not dead. He will come back to the colleges, when man comes back.

PROBLEMS FOR WRITING AND DISCUSSION

1. What, according to Novak, "happens to religion in a middle-class education"? Does he exempt the "religiously committed private schools in America" from his condemnation? Why does he say that in American colleges the belief of the agnostic and of the religious man "is pretty much the same"?

2. What does Novak condemn in middle-class Christianity? What has it in common with "middle-class secular humanism"? What other writers in this section and in other sections have quarreled with what Novak calls a "bland tolerance" that is increasingly "everybody's ideal"?

3. Novak objects to a creed that "limits itself to this world and its concerns," yet he says a man dies for "some *shoulds* and *musts*." Where do questions of *"shoulds* and *musts"* arise? Does Novak, like Meserve (p. 669), call for commitment to a "community of faith" above the "human community"?

4. Novak maintains that college students soon discover that the "Big Questions don't count—either in academic standing, or in later life, or in research grants." Is he right? Are you "taught a pattern of conformity" in college? Is extracurricular activity in your college stimulated by controversy over the Big Questions? Is "subjective" response to these questions stifled in the classroom? Do your courses leave your "inner life . . . untouched"?

5. How does the anecdote that opens Novak's essay illustrate his observation that even "the more searching students" divorce personal convictions from the lives they will lead as professionals, lives guided by "expediency and nonmoral, nonpersonal considerations"? Compare this observation with Riesman's opinion (p. 488) that graduates abandon the expectations of life that college has fostered in them.

6. Novak complains that while college gives students "rebellious, critical books" to read, it gives them "a cool grove to read them in" and demands no "commitment, no crusading, no heroism." Why then do colleges give students such books? Where but in a "cool grove" does Novak suggest that one might properly read books and meditate?

7. Both Novak and Niebuhr (p. 705) see dangers in the attempt to make all knowledge objective and scientific. What are the dangers? To what extent is the noncommittal objectivity of the classroom based on the assumption "that ultimate questions are in principle unanswerable"? Do you think a four-year period is sufficient time in which to deal with "issues of life and death, of love and solitude, of inner growth and pain"? Does Novak suggest what "answers" to these issues theology would provide?

8. Novak at first protests the paucity of courses in theology and Biblical theory and then concludes that such courses would fail to stimulate "genuine religious life." Where then does he rest the weight of responsibility? Does he call for a new humanism to replace the old?

9. Novak ridicules the colleges for demanding "perpetual re-examination" and having "nowhere to rest." Is Novak himself against the freedom of inquiry Jefferson (p. 653) says is requisite to the emergence of truth? Meserve says that the search for God begins in "uneasiness and restlessness" and that the "religious person at his best is never wholly content with himself and at peace with the world." Are an "area of objectivity" and "perpetual re-examination" inimical to the search?

10. Is Herberg's approach (p. 657) to the "upswing in religion" characteristic of the commitment to what is "'objective,' countable, precise, publicly verifiable"? Is Meserve's? Would Meserve and Herberg agree with Novak that not only college students but Americans generally separate personal convictions from public life? Is Novak's statement that "the churches are filled with worshipers but intelligence has fled from the ranks of religion" a refutation of Herberg's thesis?

11. The headnote to this essay in *Harper's Magazine* reads in part: ". . . it seems doubtful if Michael Novak's critique of college faith will please many religious leaders anywhere." Who would be displeased by it? Which authors in this Section would it please?

12. "Religion can thrive," Novak says, "only in a personal universe." Is there an analogous relation, in America, between religion and art—

which certain writers in this Section say has little relation to "reality" or is conducted in private withdrawal or within academic walls? Do Novak and Langer (p. 634) agree about the importance of art in organizing a "personal universe"?

13. Compare Novak's charge that the "American consensus has forced a 'commitment to nothing' upon our universities" with Kristol's (p. 529) and Mandel's (p. 614) charges that Americans lack courageous leadership in establishing standards and goals. Does a "commitment to nothing" characterize the Beat writers Scott describes (p. 598)?

14. Novak asserts that the ideals of international civilization are "secular." Do you find an implicit morality in the specific "secular" ideals Novak names?

15. Novak says religious men must be "active." MacLeish (p. 439) says freedom is never accomplished but is attained only in repeated actions. Meserve, like Novak, calls for men to discover "ways of acting when situations . . . call for justice and compassion and protest." Is Novak then calling for uniquely religious goals? Is it possible that the ideals of religion have been totally absorbed by political and other secular creeds?

16. Is teaching, itself, an affirmative act? Is studying? Does either necessarily require less of a commitment to ideals than a "freedom ride"? Explain.

17. Novak writes that the "basic human experiences that remind man that he is not a machine, and not merely a temporary cog in a technological civilization, are not fostered within a university." How many writers in this book work on the assumption that man is merely a machine and should be nothing more?

18. "God, if there is a God, is not dead. He will come back to the colleges, when man comes back." How does Novak reveal, in this and the preceding paragraph, his own agnosticism and secularism?

Happiness, Prosperity and Virtue

REINHOLD NIEBUHR

Reinhold Niebuhr (1892-   ), was born in Wright City, Missouri. He attended Eden Theological Seminary in St. Louis and Yale Divinity School. After a pastorship in Detroit (1915-28), he went to the Union Theological Seminary, where he remained until he retired in 1960. He is presently a research associate with the Institute of War and Peace Studies at Columbia University. The more recent of his numerous books are The Irony of History *(1952),* Christian Realism and Political Problems *(1953), and* The Self and the Dramas of History *(1955). Arthur Schlesinger, Jr., has said of him: "No man has had as much influence as a preacher in this generation; no preacher has had as much influence in the secular world."*

The Declaration of Independence assures us that "the pursuit of happiness" is one of the "inalienable rights" of mankind. While the right to its pursuit is, of course, no guarantee of its attainment, yet the philosophy which informed the Declaration, was, on the whole, as hopeful that all men, at least all American men, could attain happiness as it was certain that they had the right to pursue it. America has been, in fact, both in its own esteem and in the imagination of a considerable portion of Europe, a proof of the validity of this modern hope which reached its zenith in the Enlightenment. The hope was that the earth could be transformed

"Happiness, Prosperity and Virtue" is reprinted with the permission of Charles Scribner's Sons and of James Nisbet and Company, Limited, from The Irony of American History *by Reinhold Niebuhr, pp. 43-64. Copyright 1952 Charles Scribner's Sons.*

from a place of misery to an abode of happiness and contentment. The philosophy which generated this hope was intent both upon eliminating the natural hazards to comfort, security and contentment; and upon reforming society so that the privileges of life would be shared equitably. The passion for justice, involved in this hope, was of a higher moral order than the ambition to overcome the natural hazards to man's comfort and security. It is obviously more noble to be concerned with the pains and sorrows which arise from human cruelties and injustices than to seek after physical comfort for oneself. Nevertheless it is one of the achievements of every civilization, and the particular achievement of modern technical civilization, that it limits the natural handicaps to human happiness progressively and gives human life as much comfort and security as is consistent with the fact that man must die in the end.

All the "this-worldly" emphases of modern culture, which culminated in the American experiment, were justified protests against the kind of Christian "other-worldliness" which the "Epistle of Clement," written in the Second Century, expressed in the words: "This age and the future are two enemies . . . we cannot therefore be friends of the two but must bid farewell to the one and hold companionship with the other."

Contrary to modern secular opinion this consistent depreciation of man's historic existence does not express the genius of Christianity. In contrast to Oriental faiths it laid the foundation for the historical dynamism of the western world precisely by its emphasis upon the goodness and significance of life in history. Ideally the Christian faith strives for a balance of "a sufficient other-worldliness without fanaticism and a sufficient this-worldliness without Philistinism." *

Whether it was this ideal balance or the defeatist distortion which was challenged in Renaissance and Enlightenment, inevitably the decay of traditional and unjust political institutions and the remarkable success of the scientific conquest of nature unloosed the

---

* Friedrich von Hügel, *Eternal Life*, p. 255.

hope that all impediments to human happiness would be progressively removed. In the words of Priestley, "Nature, including both its materials and its law, will be more at our command; men will make their situation in this world abundantly more easy and comfortable, they will prolong their existence in it and grow daily more happy. . . . Thus whatever the beginning of the world the end will be glorious and paradisiacal beyond that our imagination can now conceive."

These hopes of the past centuries have not all been disappointed. But the irony of an age of science producing global and atomic conflicts; and an age of reason culminating in a life-and-death struggle between two forms of "scientific" politics must be admitted. This general pattern of history concerns us particularly as it is exemplified in American life and gives our American contemporary experience a peculiarly ironic savor.

The prosperity of America is legendary. Our standards of living are beyond the dreams of avarice of most of the world. We are a kind of paradise of domestic security and wealth. But we face the ironic situation that the same technical efficiency which provided our comforts has also placed us at the center of the tragic developments in world events. There are evidently limits to the achievements of science; and there are irresolvable contradictions both between prosperity and virtue, and between happiness and the "good life" which had not been anticipated in our philosophy. The discovery of these contradictions threatens our culture with despair. We find it difficult to accept the threats to our "happiness" with a serenity which transcends happiness and sorrow. We are also offended by the contumely of allies as well as foes, who refuse to regard our prosperity as fruit and proof of our virtue but suggest that it may be the consequence of our vulgar Philistinism. We are therefore confronted for the first time in our life with the questions:—whether there is a simple coordination between virtue and prosperity; and whether the attainment of happiness, either through material prosperity or social peace is a simple possibility for man, whatever may be his scientific and social achievements.

I

It is difficult to isolate and do justice to the various factors which have contributed to the remarkable prosperity and the high standards of comfort of American civilization. It is even more difficult to make a true estimate of the effect of these standards upon the spiritual and cultural quality of our society. Both the Puritans and the Jeffersonians attributed the prosperity primarily to a divine providence which, as Jefferson observed, "led our forefathers, as Israel of old, out of their native land and planted them in a country flowing with all the necessaries and comforts of life." Among the many analogies which our forefathers saw between themselves and Israel was the hope that the "Promised Land" would flow with "milk and honey."

Despite the differences between the Calvinist and the Jeffersonian versions of the Christian faith, they arrived at remarkably similar conclusions, upon this as upon other issues of life. For Jefferson the favorable economic circumstances of the New Continent were the explicit purpose of the providential decree. It was from those circumstances that the virtues of the new community were to be derived. For the early Puritans the physical circumstances of life were not of basic importance. Prosperity was not, according to the Puritan creed, a primary proof or fruit of virtue. "When men do not see and own God," declared Urian Oakes (1631), "but attribute success to the sufficiency of instruments it is time for God to maintain His own right and to show that He gives and denies success according to His own good pleasure." But three elements in the situation, of which two were derived from the creed and the third from the environment, gradually changed the Puritan attitude toward the expanding opportunities of American life.

The third was the fact that, once the first hardships had been endured, it became obvious that the riches of the New Continent promised remarkably high standards of well-being. These were accepted as "uncovenanted mercies." As Thomas Shepard (1605-49) put it: "To have adventured here upon the wilderness, sorrows wee expected to have withall; though wee must confess that the Lord hath sweetened it beyond our thoughts and utmost expectations of prudent men." John Higginson, in a sermon preached to the General Court of the Massachusetts Colony in 1663 was able to assess this "sweetening" process across some successful decades. He expressed the early faith as follows: "When the Lord stirred up the spirits of so many of his people to come over into the wilderness it was not for worldly wealth or better livelihood for the outward man. The generality of the people that came over, professed the contrary. Nor had they any rational grounds to expect such things in such a wilderness. Thou God hath blessed His poor people and they have increased here from small beginnings to great estates. That the Lord may call His whole generation to witness. O generation see! Look upon your towns and fields, look upon your habitations shops and ships and behold your numerous posterity and great increase in blessings of land and see. Have I been a wilderness to you? We must need answer, no Lord thou hast been a gracious God, and exceeding good unto thy servants, even in these earthly blessings. We live in a more comfortable and plentiful manner than ever we did expect." This is a true confession of the lack of material motives among the first Puritans and a healthy expression of gratitude for the unexpected material favor of the new community. From that day to this it has remained one of the most difficult achievements for our nation to recognize the fortuitous and the providential element in our good fortune. If either moral pride or the spirit of rationalism tries to draw every element in an historic situation into rational coherence, and persuades us to establish a direct congruity between our good fortune and our virtue or our skill, we will inevitably claim more for our contribution to our prosperity than the facts warrant. This has remained a source of moral confusion in American life. For, from the later Puritans to the present day we have variously attributed American prosperity to our superior diligence, our greater skill or (more recently) to our more fervent devotion to the ideals of freedom. We thereby have complicated our spiritual problem for the days of adversity which we are bound to experience. We have forgotten to what degree the wealth of our natural resources and the fortuitous circumstance that we conquered a continent just when the advancement of technics made it possible to organize that continent into a single political and economic unit, lay at the foundation of our prosperity.

If it is not possible for modern man to hold by faith that there is a larger meaning in the intricate patterns of history than those which his own virtues or skills supply, he would do well to emphasize fortune and caprice in his calculations. On the other hand, a simple belief in providence also does not rescue us from these perils of a false estimate of our own contributions. Of this, the course of Puritanism in our history is proof.

There were two elements in the Calvinist creed, which transmuted it from a faith which would take prosperity and adversity in its stride to a religion which became preoccupied with the prosperity of the new community. The Puritans became as enamored with it as the Jeffersonians. The latter regarded "useful knowledge" as the only valuable knowledge and defined such knowledge (to use the words of the "American Philosophical Society for the Promotion of Useful Knowledge," a focus of Jeffersonian thought) as knowledge "applied to common purposes of life, by which trade is enlarged, agriculture improved, the arts of living made more easy and comfortable and the increase and happiness of mankind promoted."

The one element was the emphasis upon special providence. The other element was the belief that godliness is profitable to all things, including prosperity in this life. Any grateful acceptance of God's uncovenanted mercies is easily corrupted from gratitude to self-congratulation if it is believed that providence represents not the grace of a divine power, working without immediate regard for the virtues or defects of its recipients (as illustrated by the sun shining "upon the evil and the good and the rain descending upon the just and the unjust"); but rather that it represents particular divine acts directly correlated to particular human and historical situations. Inevitably this means that providence intervenes to punish vice and to reward virtue.

Such a theory of providence means that every natural favor or catastrophe has to be made meaningful in immediate moral terms. Thus an early Puritan, Michael Wigglesworth, saw the judgment of God upon New England in the great drought of 1662. In his "God's Controversy with New England" he warned:

> This O New England has thought got by riot
> By riot and excess
> This hast thou brought upon thyself
> By pride and wantonness
> Thus must thy worldliness be whipt.
> They that too much do crave
> Provoke the Lord to take away
> Such blessings as they have.

Naturally in a community so greatly favored as the New Colony there were bound to be more signs of favor than of judgment. The theory that a divine pleasure and displeasure expressed itself in these historical vicissitudes inevitably leads to the strong conviction that our conduct must have been very meritorious. Thus confidence in "special" providence supported the belief in the complete compatibility between virtue and prosperity which characterized later Calvinist thought. William Stoughton (1631-1703) expressed it as follows in "New England's True Interest": "If any people have been lifted up to advantages and privileges we are the people.... We have had the eye and hand of God working everywhere for our good. Our adversaries have had their rebukes and we have had our encouragements and a wall of fire round about us."

In Calvinist thought prosperity as a mark of divine favor is closely related to the idea that it must be sought as part of a godly discipline of life. "There is no question," declared Calvin, "that riches should be the portion of the godly rather than the wicked, for godliness hath the promise in this life as well as the life to come." We are long since familiar with Max Weber's thesis in *The Protestant Ethic and the Spirit of Capitalism* that the "intra-mundane asceticism" of Calvinism was responsible for creating the standards of diligence, honesty and thrift which lie at the foundation of our capitalistic culture. Actually Weber draws some of his most significant conclusions from American evidence. He finds it particularly interesting that "capitalism remained far less developed in some of the neighbouring colonies, the later Southern States of the U. S. A., in spite of the fact that these latter were founded by large capitalists for business motives, while the New England colonies were founded by preachers . . . for religious reasons." *

At any rate, the descent from Puritanism to Yankeeism in America was a fairly rapid one. Prosperity which had been sought in the service of God was now sought for its own sake. The Yankees were very appreciative of the promise in Deuteronomy: "And thou shalt do that which is right and good in the sight of the Lord: that it may be well with thee, and that thou mayest go in and possess the good land which the Lord sware unto thy fathers" (Deuteronomy 6, 18). A significant religious reservation about the relation of achievement to prosperity, which the Book of Deuteronomy also contains, was not heeded: "For the Lord thy God bringeth thee into a good land, a land of brooks of water, of fountains and depths. . . . When thou hast eaten and art full, . . . Beware that thou forget not the Lord thy God. . . . Lest when thou . . . hast built goodly houses, and dwelt therein; and when thy herds and thy flocks multiply, and thy silver and thy gold is multiplied . . . then thine heart be lifted up . . . and thou say in thine heart, My power and the might of mine hand hath gotten me this wealth" (Deuteronomy 8, 7-17).

Such religious awe before and gratitude for "unmerited" mercies was dissipated fairly early in American life. It remains the frame of our annual presidential thanksgiving proclamations, which have however contained for many years a contradictory substance within the frame. They have congratulated God on the virtues and ideals of the American people, which have so well merited the blessings of prosperity we enjoy.

---

* Max Weber, *The Protestant Ethic and the Spirit of Capitalism*, p. 55, Engl. transl.

In short, our American Puritanism contributed to our prosperity by only a slightly different emphasis than Jeffersonianism. According to the Jeffersonians, prosperity and well-being should be sought as the basis of virtue. They believed that if each citizen found contentment in a justly and richly rewarded toil he would not be disposed to take advantage of his neighbor. The Puritans regarded virtue as the basis of prosperity, rather than prosperity as the basis of virtue. But in any case the fusion of these two forces created a preoccupation with the material circumstances of life which expressed a more consistent bourgeois ethos than that of even the most advanced nations of Europe.

In 1835 De Toqueville recorded his impressions of this American "this-worldliness" as it had developed from the earliest Puritanism to the "American religion" of the nineteenth century. "Not only do Americans," declared De Toqueville, "follow religion from interest but they place in this world the interest which makes them follow it. In the middle ages the clergy spoke of nothing but the future state. They hardly cared to prove that Christians may be happy here below. But American preachers are constantly referring to the earth. . . . To touch their congregations they always show them how favorable religious opinion is to freedom and public tranquillity; and it is often difficult to ascertain from their discourses whether the principal object of religion is to obtain eternal felicity or prosperity in this world." *

Perhaps one of the difficulties of this problem is exhibited in De Toqueville's own contrast between "eternal felicity" and "prosperity in this world." The real choice does not lie between religions which promise future bliss at the expense of indifference toward the joys and sorrows of our present life; and those which are concerned with material security and comfort. The real question is whether a religion or a culture is capable of interpreting life in a dimension sufficiently profound to understand and anticipate the sorrows and pains which may result from a virtuous regard for our responsibilities; and to achieve a serenity within sorrow

---

* De Toqueville, *Democracy in America*, Vol. II, p. 127.

and pain which is something less but also something more than "happiness." Our difficulty as a nation is that we must now learn that prosperity is not simply coordinated to virtue, that virtue is not simply coordinated to historic destiny and that happiness is no simple possibility of human existence.

II

There is an ironic aspect in the communist indictment of a religious culture, particularly when applied to America. According to communism, religion is a consolation for weak hearts who have failed to master life's "extraneous forces." It will vanish away when man learns not only to "propose" but to "dispose" over "the extraneous forces which control men's daily lives." Actually all the healthy western nations who have managed to throw off the poison of communism have been prompted by both religious and secular motives to conquer nature and reform society in the interest of man's comfort and security. They have succeeded rather better than communism in bringing "abundance" to the people. They have erred not so much in despising the comforts of this life as in promising men more comfort in life than can be fulfilled, particularly since the same technics which provide the comfort also create the weapons by which the enmity between ourselves and our brothers is sharpened.

Consideration of the American cult of prosperity cannot be dismissed without viewing one additional facet of the phenomenon. If the alleged preoccupation of the American people with living standards is primarily derived from the breadth of opportunity on a new continent and from Calvinist and Jeffersonian conceptions of religion and virtue, it also has other, less observed, roots. It is Spengler's thesis that the extravert interests, related to the scientific, technical and social problems of a civilization, are released when the death of a culture has chilled the intravert interests, which create philosophical, religious and æsthetic disciplines. Thus American "go-getting" would be related to the flowering of Western

European civilization as Roman bridge and road building was related to the spring-and-summer-time of Græco-Roman culture. In each case it represents the winter of decay. De Toqueville suggests a similar thesis in his observations of American life, when he contrasts the extravert activities of our "democracy" with the purer culture of the more traditional world. "A democratic state of society," he declared, "keeps the greater part of man in a constant state of activity; and the habits of mind which are suited for the active life are not always suited for a contemplative one. ... The greater part of men who constitute these (the democratic) nations are extremely eager in the pursuit of actual and physical gratification. As they are always dissatisfied with the position which they occupy and are always free to leave it, they think of nothing but the means of changing their fortune or increasing it." *

In ascribing preoccupation with the material basis of life to democracy De Toqueville may not do justice to all aspects of the issue, but he does place his finger upon an unsolved problem of our democracy. For it is certainly the character of our particular democracy, founded on a vast continent, expanding as a culture with its expanding frontier and creating new frontiers of opportunity when the old geographic frontiers were ended, that every ethical and social problem of a just distribution of the privileges of life is solved by so enlarging the privileges that either an equitable distribution is made easier, or a lack of equity is rendered less noticeable. For in this abundance the least privileged members of the community are still privileged, compared with less favored communities. No democratic community has followed this technique of social adjustment more consistently than we. No other community had the resources to do so. It would be quite unjust to make a purely cynical estimate of this achievement. For the achievement includes recognition by American capitalists (what French capitalists, for instance, have not learned) that high wages for workers make mass production efficiency possible. Perhaps it ought to be added that this insight was not a purely rational achievement. It

---
* *Ibid.*, pp. 42-45.

was forced upon the industrialists by the pressure of organized labor; but they learned to accept the policy of high wages as not detrimental to their own interests somewhat in the same fashion as monarchists learned the value of constitutional monarchy, after historic pressures had destroyed the institution of monarchy in its old form.

Yet the price which American culture has paid for this amelioration of social tensions through constantly expanding production has been considerable. It has created moral illusions about the ease with which the adjustment of interests to interests can be made in human society. These have imparted a quality of sentimentality to both our religious and our secular, social and political theories. It has also created a culture which makes "living standards" the final norm of the good life and which regards the perfection of techniques as the guarantor of every cultural as well as of every social-moral value.

III

The progress of American culture toward hegemony in the world community as well as toward the ultimate in standards of living has brought us everywhere to limits where our ideals and norms are brought under ironic indictment. Our confidence in the simple compatibility between prosperity and virtue is challenged particularly in our relations with Asia; for the Asians, barely emerging from the desperate poverty of an agrarian economy, are inclined to regard our prosperity as evidence of our injustice. Our confidence in the compatibility between our technical efficiency and our culture is challenged, particularly in our relations with Europe. For the European nations, France especially, find our culture "vulgar," and pretend to be imperiled by the inroads of an American synthetic drink upon the popularity of their celebrated wines. The French protest against "Cocacolonialism" expresses this ironic conflict in a nutshell. Our confidence in happiness as the end of life, and in prosperity as the basis of happiness is challenged by every duty and sacrifice, every wound and anxiety which our world-wide responsibilities bring upon us.

The cultural aversion of France toward us expresses explicitly what most of Europe seems to feel. In its most pessimistic moods European neutralism charges, in the words of *Le Monde,* that we are a "technocracy" not too sharply distinguished from the Russian attempt to bring all of life under technical control. It is doubly ironic that this charge should be made against us by France. Europe accuses us of errors of which the whole of modern bourgeois society is guilty and which we merely developed more consistently than European nations; for the cult of technical efficiency was elaborated among us without the checks which the ethos of a traditional aristocratic culture provided in Europe. On the other hand, there is a measure of truth in the charge of similarity between our culture and that of the pure Marxists because both are offshoots of the ethos which had its rise, significantly, in the same France which is now our principal critic in Europe. Marxism transmutes every illusion of a technical society into an obvious corruption by giving a monopoly of power to an elite, who desires to remold life within terms of the simple limits which it has set for life's meaning. Against such corruptions our democratic society offers guarantees, and prevents the consistent application of standards of technical efficiency to all the ends and purposes of life.

But it cannot be denied that a bourgeois society is in the process of experiencing the law of diminishing returns in the relation of technics and efficiency to the cultural life. The pursuit of culture requires certain margins of physical security and comfort; but the extension of the margins does not guarantee the further development of cultural values. It may lead to a preoccupation with the margins and obsession with the creature comforts. The elaboration of technics is basic to the advancement of culture. The inventions of writing and printing represent two of the most important chapters in the history of culture. But the further elaboration of communications in the arts of mass communication have led to the vulgarization of culture as well as to the dissemination of its richest prizes among the general public. Television may represent a threat to our culture analogous to the threat of atomic weapons to our civilization. America is the home of Hollywood in the imagination of Europe; though Europe hardly makes a fair appraisal of the relative involvement of producer and consumer in the purveyance of vulgar or sentimental art, holding us responsible for the production of what its millions avidly consume. In this, as in other respects, we must discount some of the European criticisms. Europe's belief that a nation as fortunate as our own could not possibly also possess and appreciate the nobler values of life may sometimes hide frustrated desire.

Yet we cannot deny the indictment that we seek a solution for practically every problem of life in quantitative terms; and are not fully aware of the limits of this approach. The constant multiplication of our high school and college enrollments has not had the effect of making us the most "intelligent" nation, whether we measure intelligence in terms of social wisdom, æsthetic discrimination, spiritual serenity or any other basic human achievement. It may have made us technically the most proficient nation, thereby proving that technical efficiency is more easily achieved in purely quantitative terms than any other value of culture.

Our preoccupation with technics has had an obviously deleterious effect upon at least one specific sector of our classical cultural inheritance. No national culture has been as assiduous as our own in trying to press the wisdom of the social and political sciences, indeed of all the humanities, into the limits of the national sciences. The consequence of this effort must be analyzed more carefully in another context. It is worth noting here that, when political science is severed from its ancient rootage in the humanities and "enriched" by the wisdom of sociologists, psychologists and anthropologists, the result is frequently a preoccupation with minutiæ which obscures the grand and tragic outlines of contemporary history, and offers vapid solutions for profound problems. Who can deny the irony of the contrast between the careful study of human "aggressiveness" in our socio-psychological sciences, and our encounter with a form of aggressiveness in actual life which is informed by such manias, illusions, historic aberrations and confusions, as could not possibly come under the microscope of the scientific procedures used in some of these studies?

IV

Happiness is desired by all men; and moments of it are probably attained by most men. Only moments of it can be attained because happiness is the inner concomitant of neat harmonies of body, spirit and society; and these neat harmonies are bound to be infrequent. There is no simple harmony between our ambitions and achievements because all ambitions tend to outrun achievements. There is no neat harmony between the conscious ends of life and the physical instruments for its attainment; for the health of the body is frail and uncertain. "Brother Ass" always fails us at some time; and, in any event, he finally perishes. There is no neat harmony between personal desires and ambitions and the ends of human societies no matter how frantically we insist with the eighteenth century that communities are created only for the individual. Communities, cultures and civilizations are subject to perils which must be warded off by individuals who may lose their life in the process. There are many young American men in Korea today who have been promised the "pursuit of happiness" as an inalienable right. But the possession of the right brings them no simple happiness. Such happiness as they achieve is curiously mixed with pain, anxiety and sorrow. It is in fact not happiness at all. If it is anything, it may be what Lincoln called "the solemn joy that must be yours to have laid so costly a sacrifice upon the altar of freedom."

There is no simple congruity between the ideals of sensitive individuals and the moral mediocrity of even the best society. The liberal hope of a harmonious "adjustment" between the individual and the community is a more vapid and less dangerous hope than the communist confidence in a frictionless society in which all individual hopes and ideals are perfectly fulfilled. The simple fact is that an individual rises indeterminately above every community of which he is a part. The concept of "the value and dignity of the individual" of which our modern culture has made so much is finally meaningful only in a religious dimension. It is constantly threatened by the same culture which wants to guarantee it. It is threatened whenever it is assumed that individual desires, hopes and ideals can be fitted with frictionless harmony into the collective purposes of man. The individual is not discrete. He cannot find his fulfillment outside of the community; but he also cannot find fulfillment completely within society. In so far as he finds fulfillment within society he must abate his individual ambitions. He must "die to self" if he would truly live. In so far as he finds fulfillment beyond every historic community he lives his life in painful tension with even the best community, sometimes achieving standards of conduct which defy the standards of the community with a resolute "we must obey God rather than man." Sometimes he is involved vicariously in the guilt of the community when he would fain live a life of innocency. He will possibly man a bombing plane and suffer the conscience pricks of the damned that the community might survive.

There are no simple congruities in life or history. The cult of happiness erroneously assumes them. It is possible to soften the incongruities of life endlessly by the scientific conquest of nature's caprices, and the social and political triumph over historic injustice. But all such strategies cannot finally overcome the fragmentary character of human existence. The final wisdom of life requires, not the annulment of incongruity but the achievement of serenity within and above it.

Nothing that is worth doing can be achieved in our lifetime; therefore we must be saved by hope. Nothing which is true or beautiful or good makes complete sense in any immediate context of history; therefore we must be saved by faith. Nothing we do, however virtuous, can be accomplished alone; therefore we are saved by love. No virtuous act is quite as virtuous from the standpoint of our friend or foe as it is from our standpoint. Therefore we must be saved by the final form of love which is forgiveness.

The irony of America's quest for happiness lies in the fact that she succeeded more obviously than any other nation in making life "comfortable," only finally to run into larger incongruities of human destiny by the same achievements by which it escaped the smaller ones. Thus we tried too simply to make sense out of life, striving for harmonies between man and nature and man and society and man and his ultimate destiny, which have provisional but no ultimate validity. Our very success in this enterprise has hastened the exposure of its final limits. Over these exertions we discern by faith the ironical laughter of the divine source and end of all things. "He that sitteth in the heavens shall laugh" (Psalm 2, 4). He laughs because "the people imagine a vain thing." The scripture assures us that God's laughter is derisive, having the sting of judgment upon our vanities in it. But if the laughter is truly ironic it must symbolize mercy as well as judgment. For whenever judgment defines the limits of human striving it creates the possibility of an humble acceptance of those limits. Within that humility mercy and peace find a lodging place.

PROBLEMS FOR WRITING AND DISCUSSION

1. Niebuhr asserts that the "genius of Christianity . . . laid the foundation for the historical dynamism of the Western world precisely in its emphasis upon the goodness and significance of life in history." What limits to the dynamism does Niebuhr say we have reached? What irony, consequently, does America face today? What other writers in this book have noted the same irony?

2. What distinction does Niebuhr draw between Jeffersonianism and American Puritanism? Upon what conclusion, however, did they agree? What subtle shift in moral emphasis changed the early Calvinist indifference to worldly blessings into the Yankeeism Niebuhr describes? What basic moral confusion does Niebuhr say entered American thought once we overlooked the fortuitous nature of our prosperity? How might the "self-congratulation" of Americans well earn not only the hostility of other countries but the derisive laughter of God?

3. Do modern expressions of the American dream [Oppenheimer's (p.

264), MacLeish's (p. 439), and Kennedy's (p. 508), for example] see not only America but the world as a kind of "Promised Land" that, with scientific and social progress, will "flow with milk and honey"? Is there an awareness in these expressions of a divine providence from which all blessings flow?

4. Niebuhr shows that the early religious settlers believed that God had called them into a wilderness and blessed them. Do any of the writers of the selections you have read in this book understand America's destiny as a call to go forth into a new or different "wilderness"? Explain.

5. Niebuhr warns against equating "divine pleasure and displeasure" with "historical vicissitudes" and against believing there is a "special" providence for Americans and another for our adversaries. What philosophical support does Meserve (p. 657) give to this warning?

6. If the principal purpose of religion is not to obtain prosperity in this world, what, according to Niebuhr, is it? What lesson, then, does Niebuhr want Americans to learn? Compare his conception of the role of religion with that of Herberg (p. 657), of Meserve, and of Novak (p. 690).

7. What is ironical in the "communist indictment of a religious culture," particularly that of America? What, however, especially in the eyes of Europeans, does Niebuhr say the American technocracy has in common with the communistic? Does he himself distinguish between the two?

8. Are the terms in which Spengler described the death of a culture commensurable with the terms Riesman (see Herberg, p. 660) devised to describe the changes in basic American character? Do Lipset's terms (p. 348) "ends-oriented" and "means-oriented" describe the same phenomena? Explain.

9. By what means have Americans resolved "social tensions" and economic inequities? Does Niebuhr altogether approve of these means?

10. Is De Toqueville's observation on "the greater part of men" in America valid today? To what extent does Niebuhr see America's material development and present problems as Potter (p. 328) does?

11. Explain the workings of the "law of diminishing returns in the relation of technics and efficiency to the cultural life." Compare Niebuhr's comments with those made by other writers in this Section on "mass culture."

12. Would Novak agree with Niebuhr that "we seek a solution for practically every problem of life in quantitative terms"? What "deleterious effect" does Niebuhr see resulting from the arbitrary imposition upon the humanities of what Conant (p. 247) calls the "Tactics and Strategy" of science? Are Conant, Stewart (p. 287), and Oppenheimer aware of the incompatibility of the "limits" of the two disciplines? Do any of the writers in the Education Section of Part II see the dangers of the "preoccupation

with minutiae" that Niebuhr describes? Do Handlin (p. 368) and Riesman (p. 488)? What in the American experience of which Niebuhr writes explains our bias in favor of the "quantitative" and "scientific"?

13. In the light of Alan Levy's essay (p. 129), discuss Niebuhr's statement that a man sometimes "is involved vicariously in the guilt of the community when he would fain live a life of innocency."

14. Does Niebuhr's assertion that "an individual rises undeterminately above every community of which he is a part" have anything in common with Novak's belief in the tragic dignity of every man? What other writers in this book have emphasized the need for Americans to realize that "happiness" is "curiously mixed with pain, anxiety and sorrow"?

15. How does Niebuhr's conception of "happiness" lead him directly to the advocacy of faith, hope, and charity for our salvation? How are God's judgment and mercy, in Niebuhr's opinion, inextricable?

INDEX OF AUTHORS AND TITLES

INDEX OF AUTHORS AND TITLES

Abraham Lincoln (Francis Grierson), 115
Abundance, Mobility, and Status (David Potter), 328
Abuse of the Past—Norman Rockwell (Wright Morris), 560
Agar, Herbert, 405
Agee, James, 191
Allen, Frederick Lewis, 139
America Under Pressure (Adlai E. Stevenson), 478
American Family, The (Margaret Mead), 24
American Finds His Country, The (Hilton Kramer), 627
American Immigrant and Ideologies, The (Oscar Handlin), 368
American Sense of Humor, The (Louis Kronenberger), 573
Analysis of the American Character (Henry S. Commager), 14
Aristocratic Origin of American Freedom, The (Peter Viereck), 324
Arnold, Thurman, 162
Art in America (John A. Kouwenhoven), 585
Art of the Primary, The (Theodore H. White), 428

Beat Literature and the American Teen Cult (James F. Scott), 598
Berle, Adolf A., Jr., 170
Billy the Kid: Faust in America (Marshall Fishwick), 548
Boorstin, Daniel, 5

Bringing Up Children—French Way, Our Way (Lawrence Wylie), 204
Burlingame, Roger, 152

Camping (Bernard De Voto), 93
Catcher in the Rye Complex, The (Henry Ebel), 213
Commager, Henry S., 14
Conant, James B., 247
Contemporary Upswing in Religion, The (Will Herberg), 657
Contributions of the West to American Democracy (Frederick Jackson Turner), 315
Cooper, James Fenimore, 399
Corporate Capitalism and "The City of God" (Adolf A. Berle, Jr.), 170
Corrigan, Kevin, 122
Cultural Importance of Art, The (Susanne K. Langer), 634

Day, Clarence, 680
Declaration of Independence, The, 309
Democracy: Its Presumptions and Realities (Learned Hand), 388
Democratic Malady, The (Walter Lippmann), 381
De Voto, Bernard, 93

Ebel, Henry, 213
Education (James Agee), 191

727

Education and Some American Temptations (William Lee Miller), 225
Eggleston, Edward, 54
Eiseley, Loren, 299
Encouragement of Science, The (J. Robert Oppenheimer), 264
Equal or Better in America (Seymour Martin Lipset), 348

Fishwick, Marshall, 548
Ford, Henry, 143
Franklin, Benjamin, 257

Galbraith, John Kenneth, 180
George Washington (William Carlos Williams), 106
God in the Colleges (Michael Novak), 690
Grierson, Francis, 115

Hand, Learned, 388
Handlin, Oscar, 368
Happiness, Prosperity and Virtue (Reinhold Niebuhr), 705
Henry Ford (Roger Burlingame), 152
Herberg, Will, 657
High, Low, and Modern (Irving Kristol), 529
Hoffer, Eric, 175
Holiday Ramble, A (James Thurber), 34
Horatio Alger (Frederick Lewis Allen), 139
How Human Is Man? (Loren Eiseley), 299
How I Became President (Harry S. Truman), 417

Inaugural Address, 1961 (John F. Kennedy), 508

Jaffa, Harry V., 360
James, Henry, 82
James, William, 502
Jefferson, Thomas, 309, 653

Kazin, Alfred, 64
Kennan, George F., 233
Kennedy, John F., 508
Kitchen, The (Alfred Kazin), 64
Kouwenhoven, John A., 585
Kramer, Hilton, 627
Kristol, Irving, 529
Kronenberger, Louis, 573

Labor, Leisure, and the New Class (John Kenneth Galbraith), 180
Lang, Daniel, 275
Langer, Susanne K., 634
Last Full Measure, The (Kevin Corrigan), 122
Levy, Alan, 129
Lincoln and the Declaration (Harry V. Jaffa), 360
Lippmann, Walter, 381
Lipset, Seymour Martin, 348
Lynes, Russell, 519

MacLeish, Archibald, 439
Mandel, Oscar, 614
Matthews, T. S., 99
Mead, Margaret, 24
Meserve, Henry C., 669
Miller, Arthur, 59
Miller, William Lee, 225
Morris, Wright, 560

Index of Authors and Titles

Mumford, Lewis, 76
My Father Enters the Church (Clarence Day), 680
My Philosophy of Industry (Henry Ford), 143

National Purpose, The (Archibald MacLeish), 439
New Piety, The (Henry C. Meserve), 669
New Yorker, The, 113
Niebuhr, Reinhold, 705
Nobility and the United States (Oscar Mandel), 614
Notes and Comment (on the Death of Grandma Moses) (The New Yorker), 113
Novak, Michael, 690

Off Limits for Conscience (Alan Levy), 129
On the Publick (James Fenimore Cooper), 399
Oppenheimer, J. Robert, 264
Our National Talent for Offending People (D. H. Radler), 462

Personification of Corporation, The (Thurman Arnold), 162
Potter, David, 328
Price of Union, The (Herbert Agar), 405
Proof That We Are Not Barbarians (Russell Lynes), 519

Radler, D. H., 462
Religion in Virginia (Thomas Jefferson), 653

Remarks at the Peace Banquet (William James), 502
Riesman, David, 488
Roger Williams (Moses Coit Tyler), 647

Salem Village (Edward Eggleston), 54
Saratoga (Henry James), 82
Science (E. B. White), 262
Science and Social Change (Bruce Stewart), 287
Scientific Experiment, A (Benjamin Franklin), 257
Scott, James F., 598
Search for Challenge, The (David Riesman), 488
Sevareid, Eric, 45
Shape of the U.N., The (E. B. White), 449
Small Western Town, A (Eric Sevareid), 45
Stevenson, Adlai E., 478
Stewart, Bruce, 287
Suburban Way of Life, The (Lewis Mumford), 76

Thurber, James, 34
Training for Statesmanship (George F. Kennan), 233
Truman, Harry S., 417
Turner, Frederick Jackson, 315
Tyler, Moses Coit, 647

Understanding Science (James B. Conant), 247

Vapor Moving North-Northwest, A (Daniel Lang), 275

Viereck, Peter, 324
Visit to Salem, A (Arthur Miller), 59

We, the People, In Quest of Ourselves (Daniel Boorstin), 5
White, E. B., 262, 449
White, Theodore H., 428
Williams, William Carlos, 106
Workingman Looks at the Boss, The (Eric Hoffer), 175
Wylie, Lawrence, 204

"You French?" (T. S. Matthews), 99